THE COLLECTED POEMS OF HAFIZ

Translated by JOHN PAYNE

A Digireads.com Book
Digireads.com Publishing

The Collected Poems of Hafiz
By Hafiz
Translated by John Payne
ISBN 10: 1-4209-4069-4
ISBN 13: 978-1-4209-4069-5

Please visit *www.digireads.com*

THE POEMS OF SHEMSEDDIN MOHAMMED HAFIZ OF SHIRAZ

NOW FIRST COMPLETELY DONE INTO ENGLISH VERSE FROM THE PERSIAN, IN ACCORDANCE WITH THE ORIGINAL FORMS, WITH A BIOGRAPHICAL AND CRITICAL INTRODUCTION, BY JOHN PAYNE, AUTHOR OF "THE MASQUE OF SHADOWS AND OTHER POEMS," ETC., AND TRANSLATOR OF "THE POEMS OF FRANCOIS VILLON," "THE BOOK OF THE THOUSAND NIGHTS AND ONE NIGHT", "THE DECAMERON OF BOCCACCIO," "THE NOVELS OF BANDELLO" AND "THE QUATRAINS OF OMAR KHEYYAM." IN THREE VOLUMES. VOLUME THE FIRST.

TO
THE MEMORY OF
MY FRIEND
EDWARD BURNE JONES
I DEDICATE
THIS BOOK
WHICH OWED ITS COMPLETION
TO HIS
URGENT
INSTANCE.

CONTENTS

VOLUME 1

VOLUME 2

VOLUME 3

PRELUDE

Hither, hither, o ye weary, o ye sons of wail and woe,
Ye, who've proved the hollow shimmer of this world of fleeting show,
Ye, who've seen your hearts' hopes vanish, like the firstlings of the snow

Ye, who scorn the brutal bondage of this world of misbelief,
Ye, who bear the royal blazon of the heart afire with grief,
Hearken, hearken to my calling; for I proffer you relief.

I am he whom men call teller of the things that none may see,
Tongue of speech of the Unspoken, I am he that holds the key
Of the treasuries of vision and the mines of mystery.

I am he that knows the secrets of the lands beyond the goal,
I am he that solves the puzzles of the sorrow-smitten soul,
I am he that giveth gladness from the wine-enlightened bowl;

I am he that heals the wounded and the weary of their scars,
I am Hafiz, son of Shiraz, in the pleasant land of Fars,
Where I flung my flouting verses in the faces of the stars.

See, my hands are full of jewels from the worlds beyond the tomb:
Here be pearls of perfect passion from the middle dreamland's womb;
Here be amethysts of solace, for the purging of your gloom:

Here be rubies red and radiant, of the colour of the heart,
Here be topazes sun-golden, such as rend the dusk apart,
Here be sapphires steeped in heaven, for the salving of your smart.

If your souls are sick with sorrow, here is that which shall appease;
If your lips are pale with passion, here is that which hath the keys
To the sanctuaries of solace and the halidomes of ease.

Let the bigot tend his idols, let the trader buy and sell;
Ears are theirs that cannot hearken to the tale I have to tell,
Eyes that cannot sec the treasures that are open to my spell.

Where is he that's heavy-laden? Lo, my hand shall give him peace.
Where are they that dwell in darkness? I am he that can release.
Where is he that's world-bewildered? I will give his cares surcease.

Hither, hither with your burdens! I have that shall make them light.
I have salves shall purge the earth-mists from the fountains of your sight;
I have spells shall raise the morning in the middest of your night.

Come, o doubt-distracted brother! Come, o heavy-burthened one!
Come to me and I will teach you how the goal of rest is won;
Come and I will cleave your darkness with the splendours of the sun.

Leave your striving never-ending; let the weary world go by;
Let its bondmen hug their fetters, let its traders sell and buy;
With the roses in the garden we will sojourn, you and I.

Since the gladness and the sadness of the world alike are nought,
I will give you wine to drink of from the ancient wells of thought,
Where it's lain for ages rip'ning, whilst the traders sold and bought.

What is heav'n, that we should seek it? Wherefore question How or Why?
See, the roses are in blossom; see, the sun is in the sky;
See, the land is lit with summer; let us live before we die.

INTRODUCTION

I

There are many so-called lives of the greatest of Persian poets; but they are all, without exception, mere collections of pointless and irrelevant anecdotes, mostly bearing manifest signs of ex post facto fabrication and often treating of matters completely foreign to the nominal subject, [1] and carefully refrain from touching upon the essential points of Hafiz's history. For instance, in none of these insipid compilations are we vouchsafed any particulars as to his family and extraction, nor is even the date of his birth stated; and indeed the only real biographical information, such as it is, which is to be gleaned from their jejune and wearisome pages, is that the poet was born and lived all his life at Shiraz and that there he died at some date, towards the end of the fourteenth century of our era, variously stated as from A.D. 1384 to A.D. 1393. In this absence of official record, the only trustworthy data at our disposal, respecting the life and career of Hafiz, are those to be gathered from the study of his poems and from such painstaking and authoritative commentaries upon the latter as that of the Turkish seventeenth century writer Soudi. Pursuing this line of research, with the primary object of establishing some probable date as approximately that of our poet's birth, the earliest landmark which offers itself to us is the mention, as a prince contemporary with himself, of Sultan Shah Mesoud, (Emir Jelaleddin Mesoud Injou), Viceroy or Sultan of Fars, A.D. 1335—6, to whom he, in Ode DXCII, addresses a petition on the subject of his mule, which had apparently been stolen from him and hidden in the royal stables, and complains that all the substance, which he had, in three years' space, amassed by the munificence of the king and his minister, had been ravished from him by malignant Fortune. From this latter statement it is evident that Hafiz must have been established at the court of Shiraz, in high favour with the reigning prince and his ministers and probably in some official character, such as court-poet, at least as far back as A.D. 1333, which would bring us to the later years of the viceroyalty of Mesoud's father, Mehmoudshah Injou. It may fairly be supposed that, at this date (1333), the poet had at least reached man's estate, or he would hardly have attained the position which he seems to have held at Shiraz; and this supposition is corroborated by the fact that, as the commentators tell us, he had, in his youth, followed the regular collegiate course of education, necessary to fit the Muslim aspirant for any kind of public career, and had taken the theological degree of *Hafiz* (whence his sobriquet) [2] which after enabled him to fill the chair of Koranic exegesis founded for his benefit by a later patron. We are, therefore, entitled to assume that he must have been at least twenty years old in 1333, and this assumption would fix his birth as having occurred in 1313 at the latest, a postulate to which there seems to be no reasonable objection, as the latest estimate of the date of his death would not thus attribute to him an age of more than eighty years. Shiraz, the poet's birthplace and life-long residence, is a town of considerable size, pleasantly and picturesquely situated in a small but beautiful and fertile plain surrounded by a chain of lofty hills, in the heart of the great South-Western mountain-system of Coelo-Persia. It is the capital of the great province of Fars or Persia Proper and was, in Hafiz's time, a place of more than its present importance, being the seat of a Sultan and possessing, in all probability, at least double its present population. It is, however, still a thriving town of some forty or fifty thousand inhabitants and is (as in the Middle Ages) celebrated for the production of wine and rosewater, of which it exports considerable quantities to all parts of the East. In addition to the pleasance-place of Musella, in which Hafiz's grave is situated, some two miles without the walls, Shiraz possesses numerous beautiful pleasure-gardens and is famous for its orchards and rose-fields. The climate is, however, not altogether congenial, the cold being severe in winter, and the country is said to be malarious in the hot season. The province of Fars formed part of the vast dominions of the Khalifate; but, after the fall of Baghdad in 1258, it passed under the sway of the new dynasty founded by the Mongol conqueror Hulagou (or Holagou) upon the ruins of the Abbaside power, the seat of government of which continued to be the ancient capital of the Khalifs on the Tigris and which was styled the Ilkhani or Tribal dynasty, as being nominally subject to the suzerainty of the Khacans or Mongol emperors of China and Tartary. The last effectual ruler of Hulagou's house was Abou Said, the eighth Sultan in succession from the conqueror of Baghdad, upon whose death, in 1335, the Persian portion of the Ilkhani empire, although continuing to be nominally ruled, first, by a succession of puppet princes of the same family and later by the powerful Emirs of the Jelayir house, (who also assumed the title of Ilkhani, as claiming kinship with the original founder), was, until the irruption of Tamerlane (Timour-i-Leng) at the end of the century, divided among a number of petty princes, who, although professedly viceroys and vassals of the suzerain Sultans of Baghdad, were, in all but name, independent rulers. The principality of Fars, with its capital Shiraz, fell to the lot of Abou Said's former Grand Vizier, Mehmoudshah Injou before-mentioned, who appears to have, during the last years of that monarch's reign, acted as viceroy of the province and survived his master but a few months. He was succeeded by his son, Sultan Shah Mesoud, who died in 1336 and left the throne of Fars to his brother, Shah Sheikh Abou Ishac. Hafiz's position at the court of Shiraz was unaffected by the accession of Abou Ishac, with whom (probably owing to the fact that they had both been members, in youth, of the same Soufi order,) he remained in high favour during the whole of his reign, and the new prince's Grand Vizier, Hajji Kiwameddin Hassan, so often mentioned and eulogized by Hafiz, was the latter's constant friend and patron and appears to have befriended and supported him on every occasion until his own death, which occurred in 1353. It is he who is said to have founded, for the poet's benefit, a professorship of; Koranic exegesis, the duties of which (according to Soudi) Hafiz actually; performed, at all events, from time to time, during his benefactor's lifetime, signalizing his occupation of the chair by annotating the *Keshf-ul-Keshshaf*, Ez Zemekhsheri's famous Commentary on the Koran, and the *Miftah-ul-Uloum* (Key of the Sciences or Encyclopædia) of Sekkaki, copies of which; two works, with marginal glosses in the poet's handwriting, are stated by Soudi to have been still extant at Shiraz in his own time. Shah Sheikh Abou Ishac was, in 1353, ousted from Shiraz and afterwards, in 1357, from Ispahan, where he lost his life, by the robber prince, Mubarizeddin Muhemmed el Muzeffer, Sultan of Yezd and Kirman, and the Muzefferi dynasty replaced that of Injou on the throne of Fars and Persian Irac. Hafiz does not seem to have in any way suffered by the change of dynasty, being apparently confirmed in his official position by the new sovereign, whose Vizier, Khwajeh Kiwameddin-w'ed-daulet Sahib Eyar, [3] became his patron and continued to protect and befriend him until his own death, ten years later; and he appears to have enjoyed the consistent favour and protection of the succeeding princes of the house of Muzeffer (all of whom, with the exception of Zein-ul-abidin, 1384-7, are mentioned and eulogized by him,) until their final overthrow and expulsion by Timour in 1393. A well-known anecdote represents the Tartar conqueror as having, on his entry into Shiraz, summoned the famous Persian lyrist to his presence and reproached him, with grim jocularity, for the affront which he had put upon his (Timour's) two famous cities of Bokhara and Samarcand, in presuming to promise them as an equivalent for such a trifle as the mole or beauty-spot upon his mistress's cheek; to which Hafiz is said to have replied that it was the practice of such extravagant acts of generosity which had reduced him to his present state of indigence or (according to another version of the story) by asking how the gifts of the slave (himself) could impoverish the lord (Timour). The poet's ready reply is said to have at once established him in the favour of the rough soldier of fortune; but it is doubtful whether the interview in question ever took place, as there is no certain record of Timour having personally visited Shiraz during Hafiz's lifetime. It seems, at all events, certain that Hafiz was not molested by the Tartar invaders [4] and was allowed by them to end his days in peace at Shiraz, where, according to the *tarikh* or chronogram on his torn which is still extant at Musella aforesaid, he died in 1389. There is, however, as has already been remarked, no consensus of opinion as to the actual date of his death, some authorities holding that he died as early as 1384, whilst others prolong his life till 1393, the year of the definitive defeat and slaughter by Timour of Shah Mensour, the last Muzefferi Sultan of Fars. Nor is this last opinion without some basis of probability. Hafiz repeatedly mentions and eulogizes Shah Mensour as the regnant king and it is therefore evident that he survived till some time after that prince's accession in 1388 Indeed, to judge from the fact that the name of no other contemporary sovereign occurs with such frequency in his poems, [5] it is probable that he lived for several years at Shah Mensour's court, in the exercise of his function as poet-royal, and it is even possible that he may have survived till 1393 and so have come in contact with Timour, in accordance with the legend. However, had this been the case, it is difficult to account for the absence, in his poems, of any mention of the catastrophe which deprived him of so staunch a patron as the last Muzefferi Sultan of Fars and for the fact that no reference of any kind is made by him to the Tartar conqueror, although he [6] bestows an elaborate eulogy upon the latter's most troublesome and persistent antagonist, Sultan Ahmed, the last Jelayir sovereign of Baghdad, who was incessantly at war with Timour and his successors, now losing and now regaining his capital, from his accession in 1382 till his death in 1410. [7] Despite the continual complaints which he makes of the inappreciative and curmudgeonly character and behaviour of his fellow-countrymen and the chronic neglect and closefistedness which he attributes to the royal and noble patrons upon whom he depended for the means of subsistence, Hafiz appears, on the whole, (as he himself acknowledges in such poems as Odes CCCCVII and CCCCXLI) to have led a fairly comfortable life at Shiraz, under the protection of the various kings and viziers of his time. The continual intestine wars, which devastated the country, do not seem to have occasioned him any considerable inconvenience, as the various robber chieftains, who succeeded each other in the occupation of the province, appear not only to have respected his person and property, but to have treated him, as far as we can judge, with distinguished consideration and even munificence; and his situation, therefore, will compare not unfavourably with that of the other poets and scholars of his day. He seems, at any rate, to have been passionately attached to the land of his birth, and no promises or inducements, such as were, according to contemporary chronicle, not lacking on the part of the Sultans of Baghdad and the other princes of Persia and even India, appear to have availed to persuade him permanently to abandon those waters of Ruknabad and that earth and air of Musella of which he speaks with such fondness. Indeed, he is said by several of his biographers to have left Shiraz on but one occasion, that of the expedition, of whose ill results he speaks with such bitterness, to Yezd, in South-West Khorasan, then a town of some fifty or sixty thousand inhabitants and the seat of an independent Sultan, situate about 185 miles, as the crow flies, and 245 or 250 miles, by road, to the North-East of Shiraz. Nevertheless, it appears certain, on the evidence of his own poems, [8] that he made one or more journeys to Ispahan, the capital of Persian Irac, a town about 300 miles North-East of Shiraz, and even resided there awhile. It is also probable that he, at some time or other, (possibly in the reign of Sheikh Uweis or that of Sultan Ahmed, both patrons of his,) visited Baghdad, the seat of the suzerain power and the residence of his intimate friend and fellow-poet Selman Sewaji, and he seems, indeed, to have retained so favourable a memory of his stay there and of the local wine that he was apparently only prevented from returning thither by wand of means. [9] He appears, also, to have received at least two royal invitation to visit India, one (according to Ferishteh, the seventeenth century historian of the Mohammedan dynasties of the Peninsula) from Mehmoudshah Behmani I (A.D. 1378—97), King of the Deccan, and another from Ghiyatheddin Purbi, King of Bengal, to whom [10] he had addressed an eulogistic poem, which is not extant; and he is said to have actually travelled to Hurmouz or some other port on the Persian Gulf, with the intention of taking ship for India, but abandoned his purpose on being reminded, by the sight of the stormy sea, of the perils and hardships of the voyage. These scanty particulars represent all that can, with any certainty, be predicated as to the essential points of Hafiz's career: and the task of gleaning and winnowing these scattered grains of fact from the mass of his verse is much increased in difficulty and incertitude by the whimsical Oriental habit (already mentioned in the Introduction to my Translation of the Quatrains of Omar Kheyyam) of arranging the collected poems of an author, not in the order of their composition or according to the nature of their contents, or indeed in any other logical order, but after an arbitrary and unmeaning fashion, in the alphabetical sequence of the end-letters of their rhyme-words.

II

None of the Persian poets has been more strenuously and more persistently claimed as an affiliate and co-religionist by the mystical fraternity, known as the Soufis or Wool-wearers, than Hafiz; and none, to my mind, with less colour of reason. Of the followers of this curious religious sect (whose tenets are a sort of bastard offshoot of Vedantic pessimism, awkwardly grafted upon the alien stem of Semitic optimism, and who, for their insinuating persistence and their skill in adapting and fashioning to their own ends the most opposite of influences and currents of opinion and circumstance, may not inaptly be styled the Jesuits of the East,) and of their habit of claiming to interpret the writings of the most obviously unmystical and indeed anti-religious authors in a formal symbolical sense, in correspondence with their own theosophical doctrines, I have already spoken in the Introduction to my Translation of the Quatrains of Omar Kheyyam, where I have so fully stated the considerations, which seem to me to negative the theory of the Soufism of such poets as Kheyyam and Hafiz, that it is unnecessary to repeat them here. It need only be noted, in addition, that the anti-Soufi case is, in my judgment, much stronger with respect to Hafiz than to Kheyyam, as the later poet was certainly, in youth, a member of some Soufi community and tells us again and again, in his poems, that the insight, which his early connection with the sect had given him into the hypocrisy and insincerity with which the whole order was tainted and the scandalous system of falsehood and imposture, by which the Soufis and their like contrived to hoodwink the world and to exploit the credulity of the folk for their own mean purposes, had for ever disgusted him with the theosophists, and indeed with professional pietists and religionists generally, and had caused him to become a toper and an amorist, in the confidence that winebibbing and loverhood were venial sins, compared with the unpardonable crime of hypocrisy, which, with all its attendant and consequent vices, he is never tired; of ascribing to his former associates. Moreover, it is abundantly evident to those who have studied the history, literary and general, of the Mohammedan East, that the adoption by the pietists of the Epicurean poet of Shiraz as a symbolical writer, conveying abstract theosophical doctrines in poetical form and under the guise of sensuous exhortations to pleasure and gallantry, as well as the pretention to claim him as a secret affiliate of the Soufi order, whose dithyrambic effusions were to be construed, according to a set formula peculiar to that sect, as in reality hymning the praises of a personal God and inculcating the tenets of an anthromorphic cult, mystically sublimated after the regular theosophical recipe, was an afterthought, neither conceived nor acted upon until long after the poet's death and forced upon the adopters by irresistible stress of circumstance. Nothing, for instance, can be more obvious than the fact that Hafiz was, during his lifetime, generally regarded by the professors of religion as an enemy of the orthodox faith and that it was solely to the abiding favour in which his exquisite literary gift and the charm of his personality had established him with the easy-going monarchs and ministers, who ruled the land of his birth, that he owed his exemption from persecution and punishment at the hands of the pietists and zealots; whilst he himself continually tells us that the Soufis, in particular, were never weary of calumniating and backbiting him and endeavouring to compass his disgrace and ruin. Nor did their enmity cease with his life; no sooner had the breath left his body than the orthodox party with one voice denounced the dead man as a notorious unbeliever, evil liver and enemy of the Faith and protested against the concession to his remains of the customary rites of decent burial;

and it was not until his friends, by a happy stroke of luck or skill, extracted from his own works a *Sors* or oracular declaration, [11] in favour of his acceptance with the heavenly powers, that the superstitious deference of the Oriental to anything in the shape of a fatidical pronouncement from the Unseen World overrode the opposition of the poet's foes and he was suffered to be buried in peace. The pietists, silenced, but not convinced, soon recovered from their temporary defeat and continued to rail at the dead poet and to oppose, by all means in their power, the circulation of his poems, which were duly collected and made public, in Divan-form, by his friends and disciples and at once became popular throughout Persia, whence their reputation rapidly spread all over the Muslim East. In short, Hafiz quickly became the favourite poet of the Persian-speaking peoples of India and Asia generally, amongst whom he still holds much the same position as that of Shakspeare with ourselves; and in Turkey, in particular, the knowledge of his poems was so wide-spread and their popularity so great with all classes of the population as to raise to the highest pitch the alarm and indignation of the orthodox party, who, making a supreme effort to compass the defeat of the heretical influence, endeavoured to obtain a virtual decree of excommunication against the memory of the bard of Shiraz, in the shape of a canonical declaration that his poems were unfit, by reason of their immoral and unorthodox tendencies, for the perusal of the Faithful. Their machinations were, however, defeated by the common sense and impartiality of Abou Suoud, the Chief Mufti, or supreme authority on canonical jurisprudence, of the time, who, on the case being submitted to his decision, issued a *fetwa* or formal judicial pronouncement, to the effect that every one was at liberty to use his own judgment in the matter of the meaning to be assigned to Hafiz's poems and that, in fine, to the pure all things were pure. Thus baffled in their hopes of securing the help of the canonical authorities for the suppression of the obnoxious writings, the Soufis and other zealots of the orthodox camp executed a complete change of front and finding that they could not succeed in ousting the love and admiration of Hafiz from the popular intelligence, determined, with characteristic flexibility, to adopt him as one of themselves and so convert their deadliest foe into an actual auxiliary. To this end, they applied themselves to insist that the Shirazi poet was, in reality, although in secret, an affiliate of the Soufi order and that his apparent abuse of the Soufis was only to be held to apply to those false members of the brotherhood who perverted its forms and doctrines to hypocritical and egotistical uses; that his (apparently) dissolute and erotic verse was to be construed solely in a symbolic and mystical sense, according to a formula constructed to harmonize with the tenets of the sect; that, when he spoke of wine and intoxication, he was to be understood as meaning the love of God and the ecstasy of spiritual communion with the Deity; that the Beloved was only a symbolical name for the Supreme Being; that by the often-mentioned cupbearer and wineseller the *Murshid* or spiritual teacher and the *Pir* or Elder of the sect were in reality meant, and so on, in accordance with a regular vocabulary drawn up for the purpose; and this course they pursued with such consummate skill, persistence and success that the opinion of the Mohammedan world is still divided upon the point, the majority of men of culture, indeed, especially in India, inclining, to this day, (incredible, in view of the uncompromising thoroughness with which the poet contrives to dissemble any sneaking kindness he may have secretly cherished for the Soufis and their fashions and opinions, as it may seem to the European student of his works, who does not bear in mind the absorbing passion, well illustrated in such treatises as that of Gobineau on Oriental letter-magic and talismancy, [12] of the Eastern theologian and general reader for the extortion of an esoteric meaning from phrases and writings, the exoteric sense of which is obvious and sufficient,) to the belief that Hafiz's verse is only rightly to be understood, when paraphrased in the terminology of a cut-and-dried symbolical system of interpretation, which might, in the judgment of the unprejudiced critic, be applied with equal fitness and success to the Bab Ballads or L'Imitation de Notre Dame la Lune. [13]

III

It is evident to the impartial student of his poems that Hafiz was no mystic, except as every true poet is a mystic, in the sense that he sees life and the world through a haze of imaginative glamour, which invests them with a glory and a significance invisible and incomprehensible to the common herd. The unmistakable fragrance of personal goodness exhales from his verse; but otherwise there is nothing to show that he held any religious sentiments, in the ordinary meaning of the word, or that he professed any religious belief other than that of the poet, whose gospel is the worship of beauty, truth and righteousness and whose observance is to do justly and love mercy and to keep himself unspotted from the world. To his tenure of this creed his poems bear ample witness; but, beyond this, there is nothing to show that he in any way concerned himself with the forms and dogmas of technical religion. He appears, indeed, to have taken life and its problems altogether more lightly than his great predecessor, Kheyyam. Lacking the Indian and Greek culture of the latter, his attitude towards revealed religion was rather that of the tolerant man of the world than of the uncompromising philosopher who refuses to allow that the wise and the just should be deluded in a world such as ours. [14] If religion would leave him in peace, he was content to do likewise, to live and let live; and beyond the general insistance on the right of the poet to drink and make merry, to avail himself of such passing compensations as might offer for the toils and troubles of this sorry sublunary existence, and the bitter contempt with which he branded the sacrilegious pretenders to piety, we find little in his poems to account for the accusations of heresy and impiety with which he was pursued, both in his lifetime and after his death, by the orthodox party. The whole question, upon which the debate of religion turned, was manifestly without significance for his Olympian view and the matters in dispute were too trivial and too ill-defined for him to risk the spoliation of the rare sweet hours of life by the courting of unnecessary martyrdom for the sake of opinions which were, at bottom, indifferent to him. Hafiz was no Leopardi, no heaven-born "empêcheur de danser en rond", cast in the midst of the contemporary revel of inanity and impurity; no *desdichado de la vida*, divorced from all delight, like Heine; no eternal exile, like Lamennais, brow-branded with the Cain-mark of a divine despair, [15] whose stern soul refused to compromise with the brutalities and meannesses of life and who was incapable of solacing his Titanic miseries with its trivial pleasures. Though free from the coarseness of moral fibre and the ignoble weaknesses of the two French poets, he had this in common with Hugo and de Musset that "du pain, du vin et la première venue" sufficed for his satisfaction at those unirradiated hours when the angels forbore to warble to him from the battlements of heaven, reminding him of his celestial origin and of the obligations in which it involved him. There were two men in him; one the celestial poet, whose lips burned with the live coals of inspiration and whose soul was consumed with contempt for all that was not the "blauen Blumen" of the fields of heaven, whose eyes were blinded to the sights of this sublunary sphere by the visions of the viewless world and whose ears deafened to the sounds of life by the spheral harmonies of the Ideal; and another (the Div, to use his own language, who entered in, when the Angel departed from his soul,) the careless

Epicurean, for whom life was sweet and who was unconcerned to quarrel with a world in which wine and women, praise and pleasure, were to be purchased at the cost of a trifling song or a set of laudatory verses addressed to some king or man of wealth and liberality. His Epicureanism was that of the child of nature, who knows not, in his unclouded hours, of evil and is as incapable as Hawthorne's Donatello of forbearing to rejoice in the natural pleasures of unharassed existence, in the intoxication of the Spring's rebirth and the calmer, if fuller, joys of the Summer splendours, that of the poet rather than that of the voluptuary, and his needs and the satisfactions which he sought for them were rather moral than material. He was of the race of his own "Calenders of debauchery," the dreamers who, with "brick beneath the head for pillow and foot upon the Seven Stars," give and take away, at will, the diadems of kingship and the realms of night and day. It was little that he needed for the establishment of his own heaven here on earth; it was enough for him to sit at the willow-foot, to drink the bitter wine of Bihisht and listen to the chirp of the rebeck and the wail of the reed-pipe, by the marge of the rill, the silver lapse of whose waters recalled to him, with no unpleasing admonition, the fleeting character of those goods of life and the world which he was content to barter for the darling and less deceptive illusions of dreamland. Here, under the spell of the heart-kindling moonlight, the charm of the night-exhaled rose-breath and the music-making stress of the rivulet's ripple, he was fain to forget the sorrows and miseries, the gauds and glories of existence, and to dream away the hours in an Armida's garden of his own creation, for whose evocation there sufficed him a cup of wine and a handful of roses in blossom. The modest subsidies, upon which the man of letters, in a time when learning and literary and artistic ability of all kinds looked entirely to the patronage and too often the caprice of the rich and great for their reward, depended for the means of life and comfort, were often, it is true, hard to come by, capriciously or corruptly withheld or delayed; but, the necessary funds once forthcoming, the troubles of the time of straitness were quickly forgotten and the poet hastened to provide himself with the simple elements of mirth, "the gear of pleasance," as he calls it, roses and wine, a cupbearer and a minstrel and a fair-faced light of love to share and poetize the frugal debauch. These granted, life had yet sweet hours for Hafiz. When the rose-bride came once more to the festival of Spring, when the sweet bird had brought its dulcet pipe at Summer's sign and the tulips overran the April meadows with their red-raimented hosts, the loveling of youth's sweet season tarried not to return to the visions of the bard of Shiraz and he was content for awhile to dream the dreams of the lover and the poet in the banqueting-hall of the cornfields, overshaded by the canopy of the clouds. Who shall blame him? Who will not rather, in these our days of stress and storm, when the old naive remedies suffice us no longer against the culminating agonies of the Weltschmerz, look back with indulgence and sympathy upon the sweet singer of Fars and envy him his ableness to conjure from his path, by such simple spells, the troubles and wearinesses of life? Who would not wish that he could himself exorcise, at so cheap a rate, the giant phantoms that squeak and gibber in the streets of the city of our life, in this our eleventh hour of the night? Let us take Hafiz as he was; Epicurean and idealist, courtier (in the sense of Boccaccio and Baltasar Gracian) and poet; in his one shape, admirable and immortal, and in the other, surely not destitute of claim to our sympathy and our affection. We of these latter days, belated wayfarers wandering distractedly in the goblin-haunted mazes of our nightmare-dream of universal democracy, are apt to forget that Nature, in her eternal character of the most aristocratic of all institutions, still produces (as she has always produced and will forever continue to produce, until that supreme moment when this our distracted globe, "défonçant sa vieille et misérable écorce, Ira fertiliser de ses restes immondes Les sillons de l'espace où fermentent les mondes,") certain creatures of election, not alone distinguished above their fellows, but differing toto coelo from the rank and file of humanity, in that they are not to be appraised by the ordinary rules of criticism and that the laws of social conduct and the canons of everyday morality show, when applied to the appreciation of their actions and characteristics, but as the idlest of fables agreed upon. Exiled Sun-Gods, tending the Admetus-herds of an unappreciative contemporaneity, falcons-royal of the Empyrean, winged for the travel of the plains of heaven, they are among us, but not of us; their joys and sorrows are other than ours. The splendour of their celestial origin shines in their faces; the heavenly ichor that floods their veins is untroubled by the puzzles and perplexities that stir our sluggish blood. Unbound by our laws and unfettered by our prescriptions, above our approof and beyond our blame, such as Hafiz are not to be tried by our standards or condemned by our limitations; they have an inalienable title to the privilege which forms the foundation of our English judicial system; they can only be judged by their peers. Like Shakspeare, like Socrates, like Mendelssohn, Hafiz was of the children of the bridechamber, who mourn not, for the bridegroom is with them. Happy, thrice happy those rare elect ones among the servants of the Ideal, to whom it is given, through shower and sunshine and without default against their august vocation, to cull the rose of hilarity from the storm-swept meads of life, who are gifted to respire with impunity the intoxicating breath of the lilies and jessamines of love and joy, unconstrained by iron necessity to sate the burning longings of their souls with the hueless and scentless blossoms of the plant of Sad Content, that austere flowerage of renouncement which is the common portion of those who seek the things of the spirit, the one stern solace which the Gods vouchsafe to the majority of their servants! These are the Parthenogeniti of life; they need no purification, as do those who have come out of great tribulation and have made white their robes in the blood of the Lamb; intemerate and free were they born, as the flowers of the field, and pure and incontaminable Shall they abide for ever. Like Ben Jonson's lily of a day, they are the plants and flowers of light; they toil not neither do they spin; yet eternity is full of their glory.

[1] E. g. the lengthy account of Sultan Ahmed, the last Jelayir sovereign of Baghdad, and his struggles with Timour-i-Leng, which occupies a full quarter of Dauletshah's so-called Life of Hafiz.

[2] His own name was Shemseddin Mohammed. His family name is not known.

[3] In the note to Ode CLXVI, 1, the name "Hajji Kiwameddin Hassan" should read "Khwajeh Kiwameddin". The mistake is that of Soudi, who constantly confounds the two Kiwameddins with each other and with another Vizier of the Ilkhani Sultans bearing the same name. The second Kiwameddin, the Vizier of Mubarizeddin and of his son Shah Shejaa, is stated by some biographers to have been the patron who founded for Hafiz the chair of Koranic exegesis before-mentioned; but Soudi asserts Hajji Kiwameddin Hassan to have been the benefactor in question and (as the Orientals say) "God [alone] is most (i.e. all) knowing!" It may here also be conveniently explained (in replacement of an accidentally omitted note) that these and other Viziers are styled by Hafiz the "*Asefs* of the time" in a complimentary sense, as likening them to Solomon's famous but mythical Vizier, Asef ben Berkhiya, who is the Muslim type of good government.

[4] A fact which testifies to the comparatively high culture and esteem for poetry and

poets of the people of mediaeval Asia and one which it would be difficult to match in our ruder days. One cannot, for instance, imagine any special consideration being shown to Mr. Swinburne, as the greatest of living poets, by French, Russian or eve: Prussian invaders of London.

[5] See Odes CLXVII, CCLXXVI, CCLXXVII, CCCLXXX, CCCCXVIII, CCCCXXXVIII, CCCCLIII, CCCCLVI, DLXXVIII and Skinker-Rime, also Odes DXIII and DXXII, in which Mensour's Finance Minister, Imadeddin, is mentioned.

[6] Ode CCCCXCVII.

[7] Five years after that of Timour

[8] See Odes CCLIII, CCLXX, CCCXCI etc.

[9] See Odes CCXIV, CCCCXCVII, etc.

[10] See Ode CLVIII.

[11] According to the biographers, such of the (as yet uncollected) poems of Hafiz as were accessible were cut up into slips, each containing a single couplet, and thrown into an urn, from which a young child was deputed to draw a slip at random. The couplet drawn was the last of Ode LX, i. e. "Withhold not the foot from the funeral of Hafiz; For, though he be drowned in sin, he fareth to heaven"; which, of course, formed a victorious answer to the poet's traducers. The story is probably apocryphal; but the custom of using the Divan of Hafiz for bibliomantic purposes, after the fashion of the Sortes Coranicae, Virgilianae, Biblicae etc., has long been established in the East.

[12] See Traité des Écritures Cunéiformes par le Comte A. de Gobineau.

[13] In this connection it may be interesting to note a fact which has been overlooked by the translators and commentators of Hafiz, to wit, that Soufism, which is now (like Agnosticism with us) a mere abstract opinion, its place as an active religious force having been, to a great extent, taken by Bâbism, appears, on the evidence of his poems, to have been, in Hafiz's time, a regular *business*, the affiliates of the sect forming, it would seem, an ordinary mendicant order, like the Dervishes, Fakirs and Calenders of the present day, the members of which, like the latter, contrived, under colour of religious enthusiasm and on pretence of the practice of extreme asceticism, to fare royally at the expense of the credulous and wealthy of the day, putting in action by anticipation the doctrine of the Sage of Wapping; "Them as has plenty money and no brains is meant for them as has plenty brains and no money." It will be seen that Hafiz, in many passages of his poems, accuses the Soufis of his day of being, not only hypocrites and impostors, but thieves and "oppressors", i. e. reprobates and malefactors, of the deepest dye.

[14] Kheyyam, Q. 296.

[15] "Celui que Dieu a touché est toujours un être à part; il est, quoiqu'il fasse, déplacé parmi les hommes; on le reconnait à un signe. Il n'a point de compagnon parmi ceux de son age; pour lui les jeunes filles n'ont point de sourire".—*Renan.* "L'exile partout est seul". Paroles d'un Croyant.

ODES

I

1. Ho, there, skinker! Fill the wine-cup; Pour and pass to me as well!
First Love's way showed light; but after Lets and hindrances befell.

2. Waiting till the East wind loosen Fragrance from the Loved One's tress
And her musky curling browlocks, How the hearts with blood did swell!

3. Dye the prayer-carpet with liquor, If the Magian Elder [16] bid;
For the wayfarer the stages And the way alone can tell.

4. How were mine the lot to linger In the Loved One's dwelling place,
When, each breath, "Bind on your burdens!" Clamoureth the camel-bell? [17]

5. Dark the night and fears possess us Of the waves and whirlpools wild:
Of our case what know the lightly Laden on the shores that dwell?

6. For self-will'dness all my striving Unto ill repute is come. [18]
How shall that bide hid, whose secret's Grown the public parable?

7. Hafiz, an thou seek heart's easance, Be thou mindful of my saw:
When thou findest whom thou lovest, Leave the world and say "Farewell!"

[16] i. e. the tavern-keeper, adopted by the Persian free-thinking poets as their "Elder" and spiritual director, in mockery of the Soufis and other religious orders. Wine being prohibited by the Mohammedan law, the taverns appear to have been, on the installation of Islam as the state religion of Persia, clandestinely established in out-of-the-way places, such as ruins (hence the common name, *kherabat*, ruins, for tavern) of old buildings, and especially in the deserted temples of the Magians or Zoroastrian fire-worshippers (hence "Temple" or "Convent of the Magians" = winehouse); and the sectaries of the old religion, being unbound by the prohibitions of the new faith, seem to have commonly acted as vintners and wine sellers; hence the expressions "Cup of the Magians", "Wine of the Magians" etc.

[17] "Camel-bell"; i. e. the signal for departure of the caravan. The allusion is to the uncertainty of life.

[18] i. e. As a lover, I have fallen into disgrace, in the eyes of true lovers, by my "self-willedness", to wit, my selfish heedlessness in allowing, by my immoderate wailing and complaining and lack of true-loverly patience and constancy, the secret of my love to become known to the profane vulgar. Secrecy is one of the primary obligations of the Oriental lover and its breach one of the gravest of offences against the Beloved.

II

1. My fair, the moon of beauty takes Its light from that bright face of thine
And loveliness its glory on That dimpling chin doth base of thine.

2. I wonder when this wish of mine Shall be vouchsafed me, that my heart
May in composedness with yon Disordered tress enlace of thine!

3. Of its intent to look on thee, My life unto the lip is come. [19]
Say, shall it issue forth or turn Back to its room by grace of thine? [20]

4. Guard well thy skirt from dust and blood, Whenas thou passest by our way,
For many of thy victims lie Slain in that passage-place of thine. [21]

5. Warn her that layeth waste my heart; Yea, bid the charmer pity have
Friend, have a care; for, sooth to say, This case of mine is case of thine.

6 Since continence against thine eyes Availeth nought, of soberness
'Twere better not to boast before Those tipsy [22] castaways of thine.

7. Belike, our fortune slumber-steeped [23] Shall yet to wakefulness be stirred,
Since water [24] on its sleep-stained eye Cast that resplendent face of thine. [25]

8. Send us a handful from thy cheek Of roses, by the East wind's hand,
So from that garden-earth some whit Of fragrance we may trace of thine.

9. Thine be long life and wish achieved, O skinker of Jem's banquet-hall, [26]
Albeit never was my cup With wine fulfilled by grace of thine!

10. For us, o East wind, say to him Who dwelleth in the town of Yezd,
"The heads of the ungrateful be As balls beneath that mace of thine!" [27]

11. "Though distant in the flesh we be, Yet is our thought from thee unfar;
"Slaves of Yezd's King, indeed, we are And speakers of the praise of thine.

12. "O high-starred prince, o king of kings, Grant me this boon, for heaven's sake,
"That I may kiss, as 'twere the sphere, The pavement of that dais of thine!"

13. This Hafiz prayeth, (Hear and say "Amen!") to wit, "Our daily bread
"Be still that sugar-shedding lip And life-giving embrace of thine!" [28]

[19] i. e. My life (syn. soul) is on the brink, ready to depart; I am like to give up the ghost.
[20] i. e. It rests with thee to bid me die or live.
[21] i. e. Be not heedless of my case; for what hath happened to me may also happen to thee. Second line addressed to the Beloved.
[22] The Easterns call the drowsy, languishing appearance of a beautiful eye "tipsy".

[23] According to the Persians, an unlucky man's fortune is said to sleep and that of a fortunate one to wake.

[24] "Water"; syn. "lustre"; word used for sake of word-play.

[25] Rhyme-word of 1. I here repeated in original.

[26] Couplets 9 and 10 are a hit at the king of Yezd and his courtiers, who seem to have treated Hafiz somewhat scurvily. He made what is stated by some authorities to have been the only journey of his life (although there is evidence to show that he made others, notably to Ispahan and the sea-shore, of at least equal length) to the small state of Yezd, three days distant from Shiraz, on purpose to see and panegyrize the king, who took no notice of him and sent him away empty-handed; whilst the royal officers and the principal townsmen appear to have followed their master's example in neglecting the poet, who never forgave the affront and repeatedly refers to it in his poems.

[27] An allusion to the well-known Oriental game of mall, a kind of polo, repeatedly mentioned in the Thousand and One Nights.

[28] These last three couplets appear to be ironical.

III

1. Skinker, with light of wine Kindle our cup and fill!
Sing, minstrel, sing; for the course Of the world is come to our will!

2. Glassed in the goblet we see The face of the Friend. O thou
That know'st not the sweets of our draught, Hold it us not for ill!

3. The glance and the gait of the straight Shaped lovelings avail until
Our pine-waving cypress comes In glory, and then they're nil. [29]

4. He dieth never whose heart With love is vivified:
Our durance fast in the Book Of the World is stablished still.

5. I doubt me, the lawful bread Of the sheikh, on the Reckoning Day,
No vantage will have above The water forbid we swill. [30]

6. O wind, an thou chance to pass By the rose-garden of the Friend,
prithee, our greeting of love Lay on the earth of her sill.

7. Say, "Why hast thou put out our name From memory? Near is the time
"When of our name shall bide No memory, will or nill".

8. When, Bird of Fortune, tame Wilt thou to us become?
My soul, as the tulip it were, Shuts in the weather chill.

9. Excellent drunkenness is In the eyes of our heart-binding fair; [31]
To drunkenness hence have the Fates Given the reins of our will.

10. The boat of the crescent moon And the azure sea of the sky
Are drowned in the cup that the grace Of our Hajji Kiwám doth fill. [32]

22

11. The grain of the tears from thine eyes Strew, Hafiz; it may be the bird
Of union shall make for our snare And take our bait in his bill. [33]

[29] i. e. other fair ones are admired and regarded till our Beloved, who is as straight and
    slender and sways as gracefully in her walk as a cypress waving in the wind, makes
    her appearance, when they at once sink into insignificance and oblivion.
[30] i. e. I doubt whether the piety of the devotee, who lives upon mosque-funds and
    pious endowments (or, as we should say, eats the bread of charity) will find more
    favour in God's eyes, on the Day of Judgment, than the heedlessness of us topers,
    who drink the forbidden water, i.e. wine.
[31] i. e. languorous, drowsy expression, as before explained.
[32] A hyperbolical eulogy of the abounding munificence of the poet's patron, Hajji
    Kiwameddin Hassan, who was Grand Vizier to Shah Sheikh Abou Ishac, Viceroy of
    Shiraz, A. D. 1336-1353—This couplet is said to have been an impromptu,
    suggested by the accidental reflection of the blue sky and the boat-shaped crescent of
    the new moon in Hafiz's cup, whilst banqueting at the table of the Grand Vizier.
[33] i. e. my weeping may soften the heart of the Beloved and incline her to grant me her
    favours.

IV

1. Soufi, come see; For the glass of the cup is bright.
On the ruby sheen Of the wine come feast thy sight.

2. None maketh prize Of the Anca; [34] nay, gather the net;
For here is but wind To be gotten of any wight. [35]

3. Ease present ensue, [36] For, when Fortune's cistern ran dry,
E'en Adam from out The Garden of Peace [37] took flight.

4. At the banquet of Life Drain one or two cups and go:
Nay, look not to Time And Fate for enduring delight. [38]

5. Youth's gone and no rose From life hast thou culled, o heart!
For name and repute Come strive, now thy head is white. [39]

6. The winebibber ask Of the secret behind the veil;
For hid is this case From the haughty pietist's sight.

7. Many are our dues For service done at thy door.
'Fore heav'n, great sir, Have ruth on thy servant's plight!

I severed fore'er My hope from salvation what time
This' heart in the hand Of thy love placed the reins of my spright.

9. A scholar o' the cup [40] Is Hafiz; O East wind, go,
To the Elder of Jam [41] His service convey forthright!

[34] A fabulous bird, supposed to inhabit the inaccessible summits of the Caucasus.

[35] "To seek to make prey of the Anca" is an Oriental saying, meaning to seek the impossible.

[36] Carpe diem.

[37] Paradise.

[38] Be content with what cometh to thy hand and fret not for the impossible.

[39] Apparently ironical.

[40] *Jam* (cup), is also the name of a town in North Khorasan.

[41] i. e. Sheikh Ahmed Nemeki of that place, a celebrated doctor of the law, who however would seem to have died before Hafiz's time. Otherwise, the "great sir" of Couplet 7 is apparently addressed to him. Perhaps, however, we should read "Elder of the Cup", in which case the tavern-keeper would be meant.

V

1. Up, skinker, and give me In hand the bowl!
Cast dust on the costard of Fortune's dole!

2. A cup of wine set on my palm, so withal
This patchcoat of blue I may draw o'er my poll. [42]

3. Though't infamy be in the eyes of the wise,
Fair fame, ay, and honour Are none of our goal.

4. Give wine! How much dust by the wind of conceit
Hath been cast on the head of the good-for-nought-soul! [43]

5. The smoke of the sighs of my breast all a-fire
Hath burnt up these dull-witted dolts, [44] part and whole.

6. Man worthy my frenzied heart's secret to know,
Midst gentle and simple, I see not one sole.

7. With a heart-soothing charmer my soul is content,
From my heart at one stroke rest and easance who stole.

8. None, none who our silver-shanked cypress [45] had seen
Would look on the cypress of meadow and knoll.

9. Be patient, o Hafiz, in stress, night and day:
Thou yet shalt attain to thy heart-desired goal.

[42] i. e. that I may formally reject the fashions of the Soufis, whose distinctive wear was a much-patched gaberdine of blue wool, the colour being in token of piety, as that of heaven, and the material in token of humility and obedience, silk wear being forbidden to the strict Muslim. This garment was made all in one piece and was put on and off by an opening at the neck, like the Chilian poncho.

[43] i. e. how many fools have been brought to ruin and disgrace by conceit!

[44] According to Soudi, this obscure couplet (as well as the preceding one) is a hit the poet's dearest foes, the Soufis.

[45] i. e. His erect and slender mistress.

VI

1. From hand my heart goeth: help! help! Ye pious! By all that's Divine!
Alack, for it's like to wax known, This close-hidden secret of mine!

2. We're folk aboard ship, weather bound; O breeze of fair auspice arise!
Mayhap on the face of the Friend Once more we shall pasture our eyne.

3. This ten-day long favour of Fate Is nought but delusion and fraud:
Friend, seize opportunity friends To pleasure, or e'er it decline!

4. Sweet carolled the bulbul last night, In the circle of wine and of rose,
"Make ready the dawn-draught! [46] Awake! Come hither, ye topers of wine!"

5. Iskender his mirror, indeed, The cup is: to thee, if thou look,
The case of Darius's realm Discover it will, by this sign. [47]

6. O bountiful one, [48] of the case Of the famishing dervish, [49] one day,
Enquire, as an off'ring of thanks For safety from Fortune malign!

7. This precept, "Benevolence use With friends and dissembling with foes;"
The secret of both worlds' content These two little clauses enshrine.

8. The Fates have refused us access To the street of good name and repute;
If this thou approve not, then change The Lot and Appointment Divine. [50]

9. That bitter, [51] which Soufis, to wit, "The Mother of Lewdnesses" style,
More sweet and delectable is Than the kisses of maids in our eyne.

10. In season of straitness, thyself To pleasure and toping apply;
Th'elixir a Korah [52] that makes Of a beggar's the juice of the vine.

11. Stiffneckéd be not, lest the fair, In whose hand the hard rock is as wax,
Thy heart with estrangement consume, Like candles that waste in the shine.

12. Bestowers of life are the fair, That babble the sweet Persian speech:
To pietists, cupbearer, tell, O tell these glad tidings of thine!

13. The winebibbers' minstrel will bring The pietist elders to dance
And ecstasy, if he recite These sweet Persian couplets of mine.

14. Hold, hold thou poor Hafiz excused, O elder unsullied of skirt!
'Twas not of himself that he donned This patch coat bespattered with wine. [53]

[46] The moment of dawn is the favourite drinking-time of the Oriental toper.

[47] Iskender (Alexander the Great) is fabled by the Persians to have possessed a magical mirror, fabricated for him by Aristotle, which showed the possessor whatever was toward in the world and by which, in particular, he was kept aware of Darius's movements and intentions.

[48] The beloved.

[49] The wretched lover, so called because dervishes are under a vow of poverty and solitude.

[50] It behoveth not any to carp at what is the work of Foreordained Fate and cannot therefore be altered.

[51] Wine.

[52] The Korah of the Bible, so scurvily used by Moses, is the Muslim type of wealth.

[53] i. e. he was foreordained to toping by Destiny.

VII

1. The sheen of the season of youth Again on the garden glows;
The nightingale, dulcet of note, Hath heard the glad news of the rose.

2. O wind of the East, if thou reach The younglings of meadow and lea, [54]
At the foot of the cypress, the rose And the basil our homage depose.

3. The dust of the winehouse's door I'll sweep with mine eyelash, in thanks
For the amorous blandishing grace The maid of the Magians [55] shows.

4. Make, make me not passion-distraught, Who head a-whirl am, o thou fair,
The moon at the full in a mall Of ambergris who dost enclose! [56]

5. The railers that presently scoff At the dreg-draining crew when I note,
Religion, I fear, like to waste In the winehouse's traffic are those. [57]

6. The friend of the men of God be; For in Noah his ark, of old time,
Was a handful of dust that no drop Did reck of the Flood, as it rose. [58]

7. To him, whose last slumbering-stead Two handsful of earth is, say thou,
"What booteth thee raise to the skies Pavilions and porticoes?" [59]

8. "Go forth of the house of the Sphere And seek thou not bread at its hand;
"For yon black-hearted niggard, the world, Still slayeth its guests in the close."

9. Since thine, o my Canaanite moon, The kingship of Egypt's become,
The time for thee come is to bid Adieu to the prison of woes. [60]

10. Once more hast thou tangled, my fair, Those musk-shedding ringlets of thine:
What evil design in the head [61] Of thy tresses thou harbour'st, God knows!

11. No tittle shalt thou apprehend Of the secrets of Being, if dazed
Thou be of the whirl of the Sphere, As round without ceasing it goes. [62]

12. A treasure is Liberty's realm And the corner of quiet content,
Which heav'n, for himself with the sword To win, on no Sultan bestows.

13. Go, Hafiz, drink wine without stint; Make merry and be of good cheer;
But make not the Koran the snare Of imposture and fraud, as do those. [63]

[54] i. e. the freshly-blossomed flowers and newly-leaved trees.
[55] The taverner's girl.
[56] An allusion to the game of mall before mentioned. The full moon is the beloved's face, here also likened to the ball used in the game, and the mall or "polo-club" of ambergris is the curving tress of hair, so called on account of its shape, scent and colour.
[57] I adopt Soudi's reading of this obscure couplet, which he does not explain, but of which the meaning seems to be that the professors of piety, who blame topers, are likely in the end, being, like them, mere fallible mortals, to be drawn into the vortex of debauchery and make shipwreck of their boasted religion.
[58] i. e. consort with those who live the life of the spirit and whose company alone can safeguard thee against the delusions of Time and Fortune. "The handful of dust" is Noah himself.
[59] A warning of the vanity of worldly endeavour.
[60] A reference to the history of Joseph (here meaning the Beloved) who is the Oriental type of personal beauty, whether male or female. Soudi explains "the kingship of Egypt" as meaning the possession of the lover's heart; but this seems doubtful; the idea of the couplet appears rather to be simply that the end of grief and the time of union is come; ergo carpe diem.
[61] *Ser*, syn. "end, tip"; word used for sake of double meaning.
[62] He whose head is turned by the illusions of the world can have no insight into things spiritual.
[63] i. e. make not religion the means of hypocrisy and fraud, as do the Soufis and other professing sects.

VIII

1. So but that Turk [64] of Shiraz take My heart within her hand of snow,
Bokhara, ay, and Samarcand On her black mole will I bestow.

2. Give, cupbearer, the wine that's left; For thou'lt not find in Paradise
The banks of Ruknabád nor yet Musella's rosegarths all a-blow. [65]

3. Alack, these saucy sweet-sellers, These town-perturbing gipsy maids!
They ravish patience from the heart, As Turkmans plunder from the foe.

4. The beauty of the Friend of love Imperfect independent is;
What need of patch and pencilling And paint have lovely faces, trow?

5. The tale of wine and minstrel tell Nor after heaven's secrets seek;
For this enigma to resolve None ever knew nor yet shall know.

6. For that still-waxing loveliness That Joseph had, too well I knew
That Love would cause Zuleikha forth The veil of continence to go. [66]

7. Thou spak'st me ill; yet I'm content. God pardon thee! Thou spakest well;
For bitter answers well on lips Of sugar-dropping ruby show.

8. To admonition lend thine ear, O soul; for dearer than the soul
To happy youths the counsels are Which from wise elders' lips do flow.

9. Songs hast thou made and jewels strung. Come, Hafiz, and recite them well,
So heaven on thy string of pearls The clustered Pleiades may strow. [67]

[64] The inhabitants of Turkestan are famous for their beauty; hence the epithet "Turk" (or "Turcoman") which poets love to bestow on their mistresses, with a sly allusion to the Turcoman-like wantonness, cruelty and predaciousness of the latter.

[65] "Ruknabad" is the wellknown stream and "Musella" the famous pleasaunce in the neighbourhood of Shiraz.

[66] i. e. that the beauty of the beloved would drive the lover to frenzy and cause him reveal the secret of his love to the world. "Zuleikha" is the Persian name of Potiphar's wife.

[67] Allusion to the Oriental habit of strewing money and valuables as largesse upon musicians and poets. "To string pearls" is with the Persians a common figure for composing verses, jewels being in the East commonly bored and strung upon wire or silk, instead of being set, as with us. The poets compare the Pleiades to a necklace of pearls.

IX

1. Wind of the East, to yonder Graceful gazelle go say,
"Lo, to the waste and the mountain Castest thou us away!" [68]

2. Harkye, o sugar-seller! Why (May thy life be long!)
Askest thou not of the parrot, The chewer of sugar, aye? [69]

3. Whenas thou sitt'st with the Lov'd One And measurest out the wine,
Think of the luckless lovers Who measure the wind of the way. [70]

4. Haply, conceit of beauty Forbiddeth thee, o rose, [71]
To ask of the frenzied bulbul, [72] That pineth on the spray.

5. With fair and seemly fashions Are men of insight caught:
No bird of wit and knowledge With toils and snares take they. [73]

6. Wherefore faith's fashion is not In those of cypress-shape,
Black eyes and moonbright faces, I know not, welladay! [74]

7. Save in this much, thy beauty Is flawless, that the use
Of love and faith pertaineth Not to the fair-faced may.

8. In thanks for fortune's favours And friends' companionship,
Be mindful of the exiles In plain and waste that stray.

9. What wonder if in heaven Messiah's [75] self to dance
Be stirred by Zuhreh's [76] singing Of Hafiz' dulcet lay?

[68] i. e. makest us betake ourselves to the hills and deserts, like madmen and ecstatics.
[69] "Sugarseller", i. e. loveling, one of sweet fashions and qualities. "Sugar-chewing parrot", a curious Persian metaphor for a sweet-voiced poet or man of eloquence.
[70] i. e. the frenzied lovers, that wander hither and thither at hazard.
[71] Beloved.
[72] Lover.
[73] Cf. English saying, "One does not catch flies with vinegar".
[74] i. e. why fair ones are capricious and inconstant.
[75] Jesus is regarded by the Muslims as a prophet and is supposed to dwell in the fourth heaven, that of the sun.
[76] "Zuhreh", the Planet Venus, the patron of singers and dancers, hence fabled by the poets to be the minstrel of heaven.

X

1. From the mosque unto the winehouse Came our elder yesternight:
What's to do for us, o way-mates, With our guide in such a plight?

2. We disciples, towards the Kaabeh [77] How shall we our faces turn,
Since our elder to the dwelling Of the vintner's set his sight?

3. Fellow-lodgers in the tavern Of the Magians let us be,
For the Pen of Fate this fashion Did to us of old forewrite.

4. Knew the wise how blest the heart is In the bondage of her locks,
Ah would follow madly after These our fetters of delight.

5. Peace into the snare had fallen Of the falcon of our heart;
But thou shookest out thy tresses And our prize from hand took flight.

6. Thy fair face to us expoundeth Many a verse from Beauty's book;
Wherefore, in our Commentary, Grace and loveliness unite. [78]

7. This our nightly lamentation And our sighs that scatter fire,
On thy heart of stone, I wonder, Will they take effect one night?

8. Blew the wind upon thy tresses And the world on me grew black; [79]
Saving this, thy tress's traffic [80] Nothing profited our spright.

9. Lo, the arrows of our sighing Pass the Sphere; but "Peace!" quoth she;
"Hafiz, on thyself have mercy: 'Ware the shafts of our despite!" [81]

[77] "Kaabeh" (dissyllable); The Holy House at Mecca, the goal of prayer of the Muslim.
[78] i. e. the contemplation of thy beauty it is which lendeth such grace and loveliness to our verse.
[79] i. e. the wind loosed and dishevelled thy tresses, So that the whole world seemed to be turned black by their sable volume.
[80] *Sauda*, syn. "Blackness." This word, which also signifies (*a*) "desire, passion" and (*b*) "gain, profit", is used for the sake of the quadruple meaning.
[81] i. e. the Beloved said, "Weary us no more with thine immoderate complaining; bear thy sufferings with decent patience or look to be consumed by our displeasure".

XI

1. To the courtiers of the Sultan [82] Who will bear this prayer for me?
"In thankoffering for kingship, Drive the beggar not from thee!"
2. 'Gainst the rival, demon-natured, Refuge with my Lord I seek;
So belike vouchsafed may succour From that blazing meteor [83] be.

3. All the world's heart thou consumest, When thou blazonest thy cheek:
What by this, then, dost thou profit, That thou dost not courtesy?

4. What a resurrection-tumult In thy lovers' hearts thou wak'st
With thy cypress-shape heart-stealing And thy cheek moon-bright of blee!

5. In this hope all night I languish, That the breezes of the dawn
Will, with greeting from the loved ones, Stir the friend to jubilee.

6. If thy jetty lashes beckon For our blood, bethink thee, fair,
Nor misled be into error By their fraud and perfidy.

7. All a bleeding lo! our heart is For thy wizard eye's deceit:
Look and see how it hath slain us: Sweet my soul, ah, look and see!

8. To the dawn-arising lover Give a draught, for Heaven's sake!
Be the morning prayer effective, [84] Cause thee harken to my plea!

9. Oh, the anguished heart of Hafiz, All for severance ableed,
How were it if unto union With the Friend one day won he!

[82] i. e. the Beloved.
[83] i. e. the Beloved; an allusion to the shooting-stars wherewith the angels are supposed to drive off the demons who approach heaven too closely.

[84] Prayers offered in the early morning are supposed by the Muslims to have peculiar efficacy. See my "Book of the Thousand Nights and One Night", Vol. IX, p. 168, for a curious instance of this.

XII

1. Where is it, righteousness, And I, poor sot, ah where? [85]
Where is the path that joins This and that lot, ah where?

2. What hath devoutness to do And virtue with winebibbing?
Where is the preacher's drone And the wail of the rote, ah where? [86]

3. My heart from the cloister-cell And hypocrisy's patch-coat [87] turns:
Where is the wine unmixed And the Magians' grot, ah where?

4. Gone are the days of delight: Fair may their memory be!
Where is the languishing glance And the chiding, love-fraught, ah where?

5. What doth it profit the foe To look on the face of the Friend?
Where is the douted lamp And the sunlight hot, ah where? [86]

6. Since that the salve of our eyes The dust of thy doorsill is,
Where, wellaway! shall we go, Say, from this spot, ah where?

7. View not the peach of the chin [88]; For see, in the way is the pit [89].
Where in haste goest, heart, Prudence forgot, ah where?

8. Patience and fortitude Seek not from Hafiz, friend!
Fortitude, patience, sleep, Where are they, what? ah where?

[85] i. e. what affinity is there between this and that? What has one to do with the other?
[86] Same as footnote 85.
[87] "Patchcoat". The distinctive garment of the dervish or religious mendicant, the more valued the more it is patched and handed down from one to another, hi! it drops in pieces.
[88] The Persians call the round part of the chin the peach or apple.
[89] i.e. the dimple of the chin, in which it is a favourite device of the Poets to represent lovers as being taken, as in a pit-fall, and prisoned.

XIII

1. We're gone, thou knowest and my heart [90], That's eaten up with care;
Ah, whitherward our watering-place Shall sorry fortune bear?

2. With our eye's strewage, like thy tress [91], Will we in pearls enchase
His feet who salutation brings To us from thee, my fair.

3. In prayer am I; do thou, too, lift The hand in prayer! Be *mine*
"Fidelity with thee abide!" And "God us aid!" *thy* prayer!

4. If all the world, on thine account, Smote swords upon my head,
They might not win to do away The love of thee from there.

5. The heav'n of our soul-fostering love Is jealous grown and so
It, as thou knowest, maketh me A wand'rer everywhere.

6. Though all the world on thee and me Oppression wreak, our Lord
Will justify us of unright On all folk, far and near.

7. Since of that lovely cheek of thine The praises we have sung,
Put by the leaves of this our book To shame the rose-leaves were.

8. "O sweet the day when he to us Shall turn with "Peace on thee!"
"Soon be the time that him to us In safety back shall bear!" [92]

9. To whoso saith, "'Fore heaven, where Is Hafiz gone?" say thou,
"Unwillingly our side he left And did a-travel fare". [93]

[90] i. e. Thou (his mistress) and my heart alone know that I have departed.
[91] The long tress, being allowed to trail on the ground, would seem to envelop the feet.
[92] This couplet appears to be spoken by the beloved.
[93] This ode was apparently written at the time of the poet's taking leave of his mistress,
   on the occasion of his undertaking a journey.

XV [94]

1. Lovers all to thine enjoyment Since thy beauty did invite,
For thy tress and mole, in ruin Fallen are they, heart and spright.

2. That which at the hand of sev'rance From thy presence lovers feel,
Saving Kérbela's athirst ones [95], Never suffered mortal wight.

3. If to winebibbing and toping Turn my fair one, o my soul,
Piety and sober living 'Twill behove thee leave forthright.

4. Springtide 'tis and pleasure's season And the time of drinking wine:
Seize the five days' fryst of Fortune, ere for ever it take flight.

5. Hafiz, if it be vouchsafed thee Her thy sov'reign's foot to kiss,
Both in *this* world and the other Find'st thou glory, rank and might.

[94] Ode XIV is omitted as undoubtedly spurious. Soudi attributes it to a namesake of the
   poet, Hafiz Shaneh the Combmaker of Tebriz. It is a weak and insipid production.
[95] "The thirsty ones of Kerbela" are the seventy adherents of Husein, son of the Khalif

Ali, who were slain in his company at that place, on the occasion of the battle which transferred the Khalifate from the Alide to the Ommeyade dynasty. They are looked upon as martyrs by the Shiah sect, to which the modern Persians belong, and are called "the thirsty ones" because, in the course of the fight, they were cut off from the Euphrates by the opposing host.

XVI

1. "Pity, monarch of the lovely", Quoth I, "to this stranger [96] show!"
"If," said she, "the heart they follow, Wretched strangers straying go".

2. "Stay awhile", quoth I; but "Prithee, Hold me" answered she "excused.
"How shall one house-reared and nurtured Bear so many a stranger's woe?"

3. What reck tenderlings, who couch them On imperial minever,
If the stranger's bed and pillow Thorns and pebbles be or no?

4. Thou, in whose tress-fetters captive Is so many a lover's soul,
Wonder-fair the black mole showeth On thy face's rosy snow!

5. Passing strange appear the ant-like Characters about thy cheek, [97]
Though musk-strokes in China's pictures Are familiar enow. [98]

6. Wonder-goodly on thy moonface Shows the mirrored flush of wine,
Like the blossom of the Redbud [99] On the eglantine in blow.

7. "Thou," quoth I, "whose night-hued browlocks Are the strangers' eventide,
"Have a care lest I bewail me 'Gainst thee in the foredawn glow." [100]

8. "Moon of me", again I pleaded, "Cover not that rosehued cheek,
"An thou wouldst not make us strangers Weariful and full of woe."

9. "Hafiz", said she, "those who know me In amazement's stead abide.
"Where's the wonder, then, if strangers Woeful and distracted grow?"

[96] syn. "exile".
[97] i. e. the down, commonly compared by poets to writing and to ants creeping over the cheek.
[98] Chinese pictures are outlined in Indian ink, which smells strongly of musk; hence the comparison. The type of beauty pourtrayed in them is specially pleasing to the Persians, who like a "full-moon" cheek.
[99] "The Redbud" (*Cercis Siliquastrum*) or Judas-tree, which covers itself with bright red blossoms, before putting forth leaf.
[100] When prayers are answered. He warns the Beloved to have pity on her lovers, lest their prayers and complaints call down heaven's wrath on her head. "Stranger" or "exile" in this ode means "rejected" or "ill-used lover".

XVII

1. Day breaketh and donneth the cloud-veil white. [101]
The dawn-draught, companions! The dawndraught forthright!

2. On the cheek of the tulip there trickles the dew;
Wine, friends! let us drink to the new-blossomed light!

3. The breezes of Paradise blow from the meads;
Drink, drink of sheer wine without cease, day and night!

4. On the sward hath the rose spread her emerald throne;
Go, get thee of wine, like to rubies fire-bright!

5. The door of the winehouse once more have they shut; [102]
O open, Thou Op'ner of Doors, [103] of Thy might!

6. Strange, the winehouse's door at a season like this [104]
They should hasten to shut, in the topers' despite!

7. An the trace thou ensue of the water of life,
To the viol's sweet sound pour the wine of delight!

8. O Hafiz, mourn not, for the bride of good luck
Her face in the end will unveil to thy sight.

[101] A day, when the clouds are high and it is not likely to rain, is considered by the Persians and Arabs especially favourable for wine-drinking. Cf. Heriri, M. XXIV; "A day whose mist had risen, whose beauty was waxing and whose light cloud bade to the morning draught."
[102] Apparently on the occasion of one of the many temporary prohibitions of wine.
[103] God is called (Koran, XXIV, 25) *El Fettah*, The Opener *par excellence*", interpreted by Ibn Athir to mean "The Opener of the doors of subsistence to His creatures"; which reading is generally accepted.
[104] i. e. in Spring, when everything calls to mirth and merrymaking

XVIII

1. The morning of Fortune hath dawned: Where is the cup like the sun?
When were a moment more apt? Give me the winecup, my son!

2. House quiet and skinker the friend And minstrel sweet-spoken;—the time
Of joyance, the season of youth And the round of the cup is begun.

3. For the sake of rejoicing the soul And adding adornment to mirth,
Gold goblet with rubies in flow To marry, God wot, were well done!

4. See, sweetheart and minstrel clap hands And tipsy ones dance to the sound,
Sleep reft by the cupbearer's glance From th' eyes of each winebibbing one.

5. Seclusion untroubled and sure And quiet communion with friends,
Whoever such pleasance may find An hundredfold vict'ries hath won.

6. Shrewd tirewoman Nature, in view Of the pleasance of wine, in the heart
Of the roseleaf hath rosewater hid And bringeth forth wine by the tun. [105]

7. Since that moon-faced one Hafiz's pearls With her soul bought, in Venus's ears,
The sound of the viol still is, From rising to setting of sun. [106]

[105] i. e. Nature, seeing that wine is more apt to rejoice the heart of mankind than
rosewater, produces the former in profusion and hides the latter in the heart of the
rose, whence it is only to be extracted in small quantities and with difficulty.
[106] i.e. since the Beloved has set the stamp of her approval on Hafiz's songs, they are
sung in every assembly, so that the sound of the musical instruments, to which they
are chanted, continually rises up to the heavens.

XIX

1. From thine enjoyment Paradise Doth lustre take and e'en
Hell from the sharpness of thy loss Doth heat and torment glean.

2. Unto the beauty of thy cheek And thy shape's elegance
Heav'n doth for greater grace resort And Touba's Tree of Treen. [107]

3. Yea, of the streams of Paradise, As of mine eye, all night
Thy languorous narcissus eye In visions still is seen.

4. Spring, in each chapter of its book, Thy beauty doth comment;
Thy glorious name on every gate Is writ of heav'n's demesne.

5. Burnt is my heart nor hath my soul Achieved my heart's desire;
Else would it not with tears of blood Mine eyes incarnadine.

6. O'er wounded hearts and burning breasts, Alack, how many rights
Unto thy lip and mouth pertain Of salt [108] and suff'rance keen!

7. Deem not that lovers only are Made drunken by thy cup:
Hast thou not heard of pietists O'ercome with love's chagrin?

8. The vision of thy lip and face Hath made it clear to me
How from the world-enlight'ning sun The ruby hath its sheen. [109]

9. Draw back the face-veil: why affect Thus to seclude thyself?
Except seclusion, what hast thou Of vantage from this screen?

10. The rose thy face saw and became A-fire for jealousy;
Thy scent it smelt and rosewater Became for shame and spleen. [110]

11. Hafiz, for love of thee, is like To drown in passion's sea:
Behold, alack! he perisheth! Ah, save him thou, my queen!

12. Hafiz, why lettest thou the days Thus without profit go?
Bestir and suffer not dear life To pass in waste and teen.

[107] *Touba*, a fabulous tree in the Seventh Heaven, really an imaginary name for the *Sidret-el-Munteha*, the Lote-tree of the Limit, (supposed to be the abiding place of the Angel Gabriel) derived from an absurd misconception of the Koranic passage (K. XIII, 28) "*Touba* (properly *Tiba*, a grammatical mistake of Mohammed's) le-him!" i. e. "Felicity to them!" According to Shakspear, *Touba* is the name of a tree in Indra's heaven, which gave every thing that was desired of it.

[108] "Rights... of salt," a double allusion to (*a*) the use in Oriental surgery of salt for keeping open wounds and so preventing internal suppuration, the application, of course, having at once an irritative and a sanative effect and (*b*) the mutual rights and obligations contracted by persons who have eaten "bread and salt", as typifying food in general, together, called by poets the "right of salt." The meaning is that the Beloved's lip, whose kisses, like salt strewn upon an open wound, at once solace and irritate the lover's wounded heart, has, by the imaginary consumption of salt between it and the heart, acquired the rights over the latter which arise from the relation of host and guest in the exercise and receipt of hospitality, a relation peculiarly sacred to the Oriental mind. The "salt-right" figured by the poets to have been acquired by the Beloved's lip over the lover's heart may perhaps also be taken to involve the consequent obligation to heal the latter of the irritation which it has caused.

[109] The Persians suppose the ruby to come forth of the mine colourless and to become red only after having been exposed for some time to the rays of the sun, for which purpose it is placed on a piece of fresh liver.

[110] i. e. the rose was so confounded and mortified at the sight of thy peerless beauty that it became drowned in sweat. The sweat of the rose is rosewater.

XX

1. By the Vizier's soul and the ancient right And the covenant firm I swear,
My wont in the dawn for thy happiness Is still to offer prayer!

2. My tears, that Noah his flood surpass, From the tablet of my heart
Avail not to wash the script of love For thee that's graven there.

3. Come, traffic with me and buy this heart; For, broken though it be,
An hundred thousand hearts 'tis worth, Unworn of love and care.

4. Blame thou me not for debauchery; For Love, the Pilgrim's guide,
The tavern, upon Creation day, Appointed me to share.

5. For truth endeavour, that from thy soul The sun may still be born:
The first of the dawn, for truthlessness, A blackened face must wear. [111]

6. I rede thee, o heart, despair thou not Of the boundless grace of the Friend.
An thou boast thee of lovership, quick, come stake Thy head for the love of the fair. [112]

7. A madman of mountain and waste am I, On thine account, become;
Yet loosest thou not the girdle-chain That I for thee must bear.

8. The tongue of the ant was loosed in blame 'Gainst Asef; and meet it was;
For Solomon's signet-ring he lost And sought it not whilere. [113]

9. Nay, fret not, Hafiz, nor constancy Seek from heart-ravishers:
What fault of the garden is it, trow, If this herb [114] spring not there?

[111] The first dawn is a false dawn or *Vorschein*, which appears an hour or two before the true and is again succeeded by darkness; hence the "blackened face", a figurative expression for being put to shame.
[112] The first condition of true love is self-surrender.
[113] According to Muslim legend, it was Solomon's vizier Asef ben Berkhiya, a mythical personage, who (not by losing, but by neglecting to seek the famous signet-ring which gave the King his power over the spirit world and animals and which he himself had foolishly entrusted to one of his wives, who lost it,) brought about the catastrophe of the temporary usurpation of the throne by a Demon in Solomon's shape and was rebuked for his neglect by the ant.
[114] i. e. constancy.

XXI

1. The apple of mine eye, my fair, Thy place of session grown is;
Show favour, then, and light thee down; For lo! the house thine own is.

2. By dint of grace of down and mole, The sages' hearts thou stealest;
Many a rare charm beneath thy snare And grain [115] for bait there sown is.

3. Glad in th'enjoyment of the rose Thy heart be, bird of morning! [116]
For all the amorous descant Thine in the meads alone is.

4. Our sick heart's tending to thy lip Commit thou; for that ruby
Exhilarant [117] no otherwhere Than in thy treasure known is.

5. On thee in person though to wait Is happiness denied me,
My soul's quintessence as the dust Upon thy threshold strown is.

6. Not one am I that give the heart's Fine gold to every wanton:
Sealed with the seal the treasure-door Upon thy signet-stone is.

7. How skilled a cavalier thou art, O fair one; since of Fortune
(That unbroke colt) obedience, Beneath thy whip-lash, shown is! [118]

8. What can I do against thy craft, Since even juggler Fortune
By what thy budget of pretence [119] Holdeth of tricks o'erthrown is?

9. The music of thy banquetings The heav'ns to dancing moveth,
Now Hafiz' dulcet verse combined With thy sweet voice's tone is.

[115] "Snare and bait", i. e. the beloved's down and mole.
[116] "Bird of morning", nightingale.
[117] "Ruby Exhilarant", a kind of electuary compounded with rubies, in great favour
    with Persian physicians and supposed to have an exhilarating effect. The beloved's
    lip is of course meant.
[118] i. e. thou hast even brought skittish Fortune under thy control.
[119] "Budget of pretence", a juggler's bag of tricks.

XXII

1. Of the love of her my heart the holy place is;
Mirror-holder this mine eye unto her face is.

2. I that bow not down to this world nor the other,
See, my neck beneath the burden of her grace is.

3. Thou the Touba, I the shape of the Beloved; [120]
Each man's way of thought according to his case is.

4. In that sanctuary what am I, where the zephyr
Curtain-holder of her honour's altar-space is? [121]

5. Skirt-polluted [122] an I be, what matter? Witness
To *her* purity the whole world, good and base, is.

6. Past and gone is Mejnoun's [123] time and now our turn 'tis:
Every mortal's turn in this our world five days is.

7. Love's dominion, mirth its treasure, all I joy in,
In her happy fortune's auspice hath its basis.

8. Nay, what matter if my heart and I should perish?
Since her weal the only object of our chase is.

9. Never empty may mine eye be of her image,
For its apple her especial privy place is!

10. Every newborn rose, the meadows that adorneth,
Of the Loved One's scent and colour but the trace is.

11. Heed his seeming poortith not, for Hafiz' bosom
All the treasure of the love of her embraces.

[120] i. e. do thou, o pietist, set thy hopes on the Touba-tree (met. Paradise); I, for my
   part, yearn for the beloved's shape.
[121] Her dwelling is so sacred that even the breeze cannot enter there, but abides
   without at the door; hence it is called "curtain-holder", i. e. door-keeper.
[122] "Skirt-pollution" is a Persian idiom for sinfulness, blameworthiness, even as "Skirt-
   pureness" for the contrary.
[123] Mejnoun ("Mad-man") the well-known lover of Leila and one of the favourite Arab
   types of true-loverhood.

XXIII

1 The head of our purpose cleaves To the Loved One's threshold-sill,
For all that o'er us doth pass Betideth but of her will.

2. The like of the loveliness Of the Friend I've never seen,
Albeit with moon and sun Her cheek I mirror still.

3. How shall the East wind loosen The stress of our straitened heart,
That, fold upon fold, like the rosebud, Is twisted up with ill?

4. I'm not the only swillpot In this sot-burning [124] world:
How many a head in this workshop Is pot-clay for wine to fill!

5. 'Twould seem that thou passest the comb Through thine ambergris-shedding locks,
For the wind wafteth nard and the dust Doth ambergris distil.

6. The strewage be of thy face Each roseleaf that is in the meads!
The sacrifice be of thy shape Each cypress that stands by the rill!

7. Since mute is the tongue of speech In the tale of desire for her,
Where, where is the place of the split Tongued, idle-spoken quill? [125]

8. Thy cheek to my thought hath come: My will I shall sure attain,
Because that on auspice good Fair fortune followeth still. [126]

9. Afire for desire not now For the first time is Hafiz's heart;
Heartbranded was he from the Prime, [127] Like the tulip that groweth at will. [128]

[124] i. e. lover-tormenting.
[125] If speech fail to tell the tale of my love for the Beloved, how shall the pen avail to
   do so?
[126] The occurrence of the Beloved's face to the lover's thought (in dreams?) looked
   upon as an omen of good to come.
[127] i. e. the Day of Creation; from Time Everlasting, "Eternity without beginning", as

the Persians say.

[128] The wild (Persian, "self growing") tulip, which grows plentifully about Shiraz.

XXIV

1. Yonder swart-skinned fair, all sweetness That the world can show with her is;
Laughing lip and eye wine-coloured, Head with mirth aglow, with her is.

2. If the sweet-lipped ones be princes, She the Solomon of all is,
Ruler of the time, by reason That the signet [129] lo! with her is.

3. See the musky mole that nestleth On her wheat-hued cheek! The secret
Of that grain of wheat, which Adam Did of old o'erthrow, [130] with her is.

4. My heart-ravisher departure Meditateth: help, o comrades!
With my wounded heart what do I? For the salve, heigho! with her is.

5. Fair of face, of skirt unsullied [131] And in worth she is accomplished;
Hence th' approof of both worlds' pure ones, There and here below, with her is.

6. This enigma of whom other Can one speak, "Yon stone-heart slayeth
"Us, yet Jesus son of Mary's Healing breath [132] e'enso with her is."

7. Hafiz of the true-believers Is: in honour look ye hold him,
For the sympathy of many Blessed spirits, know, with him [133] is.

[129] "The signet" here is the Beloved's mouth, constantly likened by Persian poets to a ring, on account of its roundness and smallness.
[130] The Muslim legends of Adam substitute a grain of wheat for the apple, which was the cause of his expulsion from Paradise.
[131] See former note on "Skirt-pollution."
[132] Jesus is called by the Muslims "The Breath of God" and is credited with the power of reviving the dead by breathing on them.
[133] The Persian pronoun "*au*" or "*o*", here the penultimate syllable of the rere-word (*ba-o-'st*, "with him, her or it is"), serves for all three genders.

XXV

1. Of the august Friend's pardon Hopeful, indeed, am I;
Sinned though I have, in her kindness, Natheless, my hope doth lie.

2. Yea, my default, I know it, Will she o'erpass; for, though
Fay-like, she hath the nature Of angels from on high.

3. So have we wept for sorrow That, when our streaming tear
See they, "Lo, what is this river?" Say all who pass us by.

4. Our head, like the ball in the horse-course, We play at the end of thy street; [134]
But none is aware what that street is Nor what is the ball we ply. [135]

5. Thy tress, without word of gainsayal, All hearts to itself doth draw:
For who with thy heart-drawing ringlets Conclusions dareth try?

6. A life-time it is since I scented The perfume of that thy tress;
Yet still in my spirit's nostrils The traces thereof aby:

7. A hair is thy waist; I know not What manner of hair it is;
And as for thy mouth, 'tis nothing; No sign of it I descry. [136]

8. Indeed, at thine image I marvel, That, though, without cease, my tears
Still flood it and wash and scour it, It goeth not from mine eye!

9. Nay, ill is thy plight, o Hafiz, Distracted as thou art;
But yet in the scent of her tresses Fair hope for thee is nigh.

[134] i. e. we stake our lives for thy love.
[135] Yet we keep our love hidden from all. It is a capital duty of the lover to keep the
secret of his love from the profane; if, by his impatience and want of constancy, he
suffer it to become known, he is disgraced in the eyes of true lovers.
[136] It is a favourite conceit of the Persian poets to liken the slender waist of the beloved
to a hair and to style it and the mouth "nothing" and "invisible", on account of small-
ness. Slenderness is a sine quâ non of beauty with the Persians and Arabs; it is only
the negroïd races, such as those of North Africa, that admire fat women.

XXVI

1. That great night, [137] whereof the people Of seclusion speak, to night is:
Lord, I wonder from what planet This vouchsafement of delight is!

2. In a circle, dervish-fashion, Orisons each heart a-chanting,
That thy locks may not be sullied By the hand of worthless wight, is.

3. I'm a victim of the dimple Of thy chin; from every quarter
Many a soul-neck ringed and prisoned Underneath its rondure white is.

4. She, my queen, the mirror-holder Of whose countenance the moon is,
She, beneath whose courser's hoof-marks, Dust the glorious sun at height is.

5. On her cheek the sweat see glitter, For whose sake, as night, for longing,
Day, unto the sun swift-faring, Still, until it come to light, is. [138]

6. Ne'er will I renounce the Loved One's Lip of ruby nor the winecup;
Pietists, excuséd hold me: This my canon, wrong or right, is.

7. In that squadron, where the saddle On the East Wind's back they fasten,
How with Solomon may pace it I, whose steed an emmet slight is? [139]

8. God be praised! Of what a lofty Quality is this my crowquill!
Yea, from out its fluent nibble, See, Life's water still a-flight is!

9. She, that with her covert glances Arrows at my bosom launcheth,
In her lip, with laughter litten, Lo! the food of Hafiz' spright is.

[137] "That great night". *Sheb-i-Ckedr*, the Night of Foreordinance or Foreappointment,
commonly, but erroneously, called the Night of Power. On this night (the exact date
of which is not known, although it is conjectured, on the authority of one of
Mohammed's obiter dicta, to fall on the 20th, 22nd, 24th or 28th of the month
Ramazan,) the Koran is fabled to have been sent down from heaven and it is
accordingly considered the most sacred of the Muslim year. During it, all living
creatures (e. g. the cattle in the stall) speak aloud and praise God and all wishes
conceived are granted. See my "Book of the Thousand Nights and One Night", "The
Man who saw the Night of Power", V, 314.
[138] i. e. day is night to the sun himself, until her radiant cheek appears and illumines
the world; a fair specimen of the extravagant hyperboles affected by the Persian
poets.
[139] Solomon is fabled by the Muslims to have had power to compel the wind to carry
him hither and thither. The ant and Solomon are constantly cited by Oriental writers
as types of the infinitely great and the infinitely little respectively, as in this couplet.

XXVII

1. Virtue, piety, observance, Seek from drunken me not. Nay,
For to winebibbing predestined Was I on Creation's Day.

2. I, that moment when ablution In the Fount of Love I made,
At one blow the funeral service Over all things else did say. [140]

3. Give me wine, that I may give thee Knowledge of Fate's mystery,
Of whose face I am enamoured, With whose scent I'm drunken aye.

4. O wine-worshipper, despair not Of the door of clemency!
For the mountain's loins are weaker Than the emmet's in Love's way.

5. Save yon languishing narcissus, [141] (Far therefrom the Evil Eye!),
Underneath this dome of turquoise, [142] None abideth blithe and gay.

6. Be my spirit thy mouth's ransom! In the garden of the sight,
Nothing fairer than this rosebud [143] Did the World-maker array.

42

7. By the love of thee is Hafiz Solomon become; to wit,
He in hand, of thine enjoyment, Nought but wind [144] hath, wellaway!

[140] i. e. forswore all else but love.
[141] *Lit.* "Tipsy narcissus", the favourite Oriental simile for a large, languishing eye. The flower in question, the *Narcissus Poeticus*, is an apt object of comparison, owing to its pensile habit and its large white corolla, with the dark corona in the middle, like the iris of the eye, surrounded by the sclerotic.
[142] The heavens.
[143] "Rosebud", the beloved's mouth.
[144] A punning allusion to the legend, before mentioned, of Solomon's command over the wind. "Wind in hand" is a Persian idiom expressing disappointment, want of success.

XXVIII

1. In the bigot seeming-holy Knowledge of our state is not;
Whatsoe'er of us he speaketh, Cause for spite or hate is not. [145]

2. All the wayfarer betideth In the Way is for his weal;
Road-lost whosoever fareth In the pathway straight is not.

3. What, I wonder, will her cheek [146] play? Lo, a pawn I will advance. [147]
For the toper, on Love's chessboard, "Check" to say or "Mate" is not. [148]

4. What is yonder roof high-vaulted, Many-figured? [149] Here below,
This enigma known to any, Howso wise or great, is not.

5. What, o God, is this strange puissance Of disdain, whereby there be
Hidden wounds galore, but licence To complain of Fate is not? [150]

6. Sure our Vizier hath forgotten God's account; for, sooth to say,
With "For God's Account!" his mandate Signed above the date is not! [151]

7. "Whoso willeth", say, "Come hither!" What he willeth let him speak:
Pride of chamberlain or porter's Bluster at this gate [152] is not.

8. Whatso faileth to Thy favour Of our own shortcoming is:
Else, for any one the garment Of Thy bounty strait is not. [153]

9. Tavern-door-ward to betake them Is the part of single-hearts;
Entrance in that way for vauntards Self-infatuate is not.

10. I'm the Magian Elder's [154] servant, For his favour constant is,
Not like that of Sheikh and zealot, Which now is and straight is not.

11. In high place if Hafiz sit not, 'Tis of his high mind: the true
Lover in the bond of riches And of high estate is not. [155]

[145] i. e. whatever he saith or doth is unworth notice, he being an addle-pated ignoramus.

[146] *Rukh*, cheek, *syn.* castle (at chess); hence our "rook".

[147] i. e. I will be humble and patient.

[148] i. e. it pertaineth not to a lover to be audacious and "forthputting"; his only weapons are patience and self-abasement.

[149] The heavens.

[150] This couplet may be read as a complaint either of the beloved or of Fate, both whereof are alike in this particular, that they lend no ear to any complaints of their oppressions.

[151] Alluding to the formula or rescript with which Persian official mandates and state documents are countersigned (headed) and without which they are not executory. The couplet, however, appears to play upon the secondary meaning of the formula, "Reckoning is God's", i. e. it rests with God to reward and punish, and to mean, "The beloved", here called "our Vizier" for the sake of keeping up the metaphor, "forgetteth that God will reckon with all men for their deeds at the Last Day; else she would not use us with such faithlessness and inhumanity".

[152] i. e. at the door of the Divine Court of Appeal.

[153] "Thy", i. e. God's. All commentators, including Soudi, have made a hopeless hash of these three couplets, talking all manner of *Kram* (to borrow an expressive German word) about First and Second Viziers etc.

[154] i. e. the tavern-keeper, as before explained.

[155] i. e., the winebibbing lover is independent of rank and riches and recks nothing of the goods of the world.

XXIX

1. The messenger, letter-fraught, Who came from the land of the Friend
And th' amulet brought of the soul, Musk-writ by the hand of the Friend, [156]

2. That giveth us token full fair Of her beauty and loveliness,
That telleth a goodly tale Of the glory so grand of the Friend;

3. My heart, as a gift for good news, I gave him, albeit ashamed
Largesse thus to do for the sake, With coin below brand, [157] of the Friend.

4. To God be the thanks! With the aid Of Fortune consenting and fair,
Accomplished is all to the wish That's wroughten and planned of the Friend.

5. In the course of the sphere and the moon's Revolution what freewill is there?
They both in obedience turn To the will and command of the Friend.

6. Though the wind of calamity dash The two worlds together, the lamp
Of our eyes in expectancy still Should turn to the strand of the Friend.

7. O wind of the morning, anoint Mine eyes with collyrium of pearls [158]
From the dust of that fortunate earth, By the feet that is spanned of the Friend.

8. The head of our suppliance ne'er The dust of her door shall forsake:
I wonder who slumbereth sweet In the bosom and hand of the Friend!

9. 'Gainst Hafiz what mattereth it If enemies clamour and rail?
So (praiséd be Allah!) he be Unshamed and unbanned of the Friend?

[156] i. e. a letter from the beloved, written with musk-scented ink.
[157] The regular poetic depreciation of the value of the lover's heart; in connection with
which it may be noted that the Arabic word for "heart", *ckelb*, means also "base
coin".
[158] "Collyrium of pearls", the finest kind of eye-powder, one ingredient of which is
ground seed-pearl.

XXX

1. Welcome, messenger of gladness! Prithee, tidings tell of the Friend,
So my soul I may for ransom Of the mention sell of the Friend.

2. Like the bulbul caged, love-frenzied, Pines the parrot of my soul
For the sugar and the almond (Lip and eye as well [159]) of the Friend.

3. Lo, the snare the Loved One's tress is And her mole the bait thereof;
Of my hope the bait to come at, In the snare I fell of the Friend.

4. Not until the Judgment Morning Shall he wake from drunkenness
Who, like me, a draught hath drunken Of the passion-spell of the Friend.

5. No whit more in exposition Of my longing will I say,
Lest my fashery to aching Should the head compel of the Friend.

6. My inclining was to union, But to sev'rance her intent;
Wherefore I renounced my wishes, So the wish befell of the Friend.

7. These mine eyes, were't but vouchsafed me, As with tutty, would I salve
With the highway's dust, ennobled By the travel of the Friend.

8. Patience, Hafiz! Burn and suffer For her sake nor solace seek;
For no salve can the unresting Pain of love dispel of the Friend.

[159] The words in brackets are those given by Soudi in explanation of "sugar" and
"almond".

XXXI

1. Bring, wind of the East, an thou chance By the country to fare of the Friend,
A waft from the ambergris tress And the musk-scented hair of the Friend!

2. By her life, I will pour out my soul As off'ring of thanks for the boon,
An somewhat of news from the land To-me-ward thou bear of the Friend!

3. And if it should chance that accéss To her presence to thee be denied,
Bring a handful of dust for mine eyes From the threshold and stair of the Friend!

4. Far be it from beggars like me To ask her enjoyment! Enough
If in slumber the semblant I see Of the visage so fair of the Friend!

5. My pinecone-shaped heart [160] for desire, Like the aspen, still trembles and quakes
For regret of the pinetree-like shape And the cypress-like air of the Friend.

6. Albeit the Loved One no jot Of store by us setteth, withal,
Not a hair, though the world were its price, From the head would we spare of the Friend!

7. What profiteth it if his heart From the bondage of sorrow be free,
Since Hafiz, poor wretch, is the slave And the bondman fore'er of the Friend?

[160] The heart described as pinecone-shaped, merely for the sake of paronomasia. N.B.
When there is occasion to note this device in the following pages, the contraction, p.
g., (*paronomasia gratiâ*, "for the sake of paronomasia or word-play",) will be used,
for brevity's sake.

XXXII

1. Come, for Hope's fortress-base Unstable as the sea is
Bring wine, for rooted but Upon the wind life's tree is.

2. Slave of his spright am I, Who, 'neath yon dome of azure,
From whatsoe'er the taint Hath of dependence [161] free is.

3. How tell thee what glad news I' the winehouse, from the angel
Of the Unseen, last night, Come unto drunken me is?

4. Saying, "O falcon royal, High-looking, Sidreh-sitting, [162]
"This corner full of woes [163] No resting-place for thee is!"

5. "From heaven's battlements They warble to thee, saying,
"I know not how thy lot Fallen in this snare [164] to be is!"

6. This rede I give thee: look Thou practise it. (I mind me
From whom I hearkened it: Sheikh of the Pathway *he* is.)

7. "From yonder hair-brained hag, The world, good faith and honour
"Seek not, for lo! the bride Of thousand bridegooms she is."

8. Eat not the world's chagrin And this my rede forget not;
For from a wayfarer [165] This love-saw come to me is.

9. "Submit to fate and smoothe The wrinkles from thy forehead;
"The door of freewill shut, Indeed, to such as we is."

10. No sign of constancy Found in the rose's smile is:
Wail, bulbul-lover, wail! For cause for wail, perdie, is.

11. Why envy Hafiz, thou Of feeble verse? Acceptance [166]
Of nature and sweet speech The gift of God's decree is.

[161] Or "attachment"; i.e. I am the humble servant of the man who is free from the bonds of the world.
[162] i. e. whose proper place is the Lote-tree of the Limit in Paradise, the place of session of Gabriel.
[163] i. e. this weary world.
[164] i. e. the trammels of the base world.
[165] i. e. a man of experience in spiritual things. "Sheikh of the Pathway", in couplet 6, means a man of authority over, a leader of such "wayfarers".
[166] i. e. acceptability, the gift of finding acceptance with the folk.

XXXIII

1. Since into the hand of the breeze the end Of thy tress again hath fallen,
The heart of the passion-stricken one For grief in twain hath fallen. [167]

2. Thy sorcerer eye's the first compend And draft of th'art of magic; [168]
Yet such is this copy, in default That it, 'tis plain, hath fallen. [169]

3. In the curve of thy ringlet, knowest thou, What yonder swarthy mole is?
An inkspot, that into the round of a J, Like a musky grain, hath fallen. [170]

4. Thy musky tress, in the rosegarden Of the Paradise of thy visage,
What is it? A peacock, that in the meads Of Heav'n's domain hath fallen.

5. My heart, for desire of thy scent, indeed, O Solacer of spirits,
A dust-grain is, that at foot of the breeze, From highway ta'en, hath fallen. [171]

6. Alack that this earthy body mine Cannot, like dust, rise upward
From th'end of thy quarter; forasmuch It hard amain hath fallen!

7. The shade of thy cypress-shape on me, O thou, the Jesus-breathed one,
As Spirit of God on rotten bones Of dead and slain, hath fallen.

8. I've seen, whom nought but the Kaabeh erst Might serve for place of session,
When prone at the winehouse-door, in thought Of thy lip, he fain hath fallen. [172]

9. For thee, on the Day of the Primal Pact, [173] O dear and precious spirit,
Union 'twixt Hafiz the love-distraught And grief and pain hath fallen.

[167] The wind, dishevelling the beloved's hair and displaying it in its full richness, causes the lover's heart to be cleft in twain with love and longing.

[168] i.e. it is the original exponent of the art of magic, from which all magicians have learned its practice.

[169] *Seckim*, syn. sick, languorous, word used p. g. in allusion to the languishing (or, as it is often called, sickly, ailing) expression of the beloved's eye.

[170] The Arabic letter *Jim* is much like an old-fashioned Court-hand ح, with a dot in the centre of the curve, which distinguishes it from the letter *Hha*. The tress is here likened to the curve of the *Jim* and the mole to the diacritical point. The epithet "musky" refers to the blackness, as well as to the scent, of musk and also of Indian ink, which is scented with it.

[171] i. e. for desire of thee, my heart is restless as a grain of dust tossed about by the breeze.

[172] i. e. I have seen the pietist, who made his constant sojourn in the mosques and prayer-places, brought to become a winebibber by the love of thee, "wine", adds Soudi, "reminding him of the colour of thy lip."

[173] "The Primal Pact", i. e. the covenant assumed to have been made between the Deity and mankind on what the Muslims call "the Day of *A-lest*", a proverbial synonym of *Azel*, "Eternity-without-Beginning"; because God is fabled (see Koran, VII, 171) to have said, on the Primal Day (or Eve of Creation), to the as yet unincarnated souls, "Am I not your Lord?" (*A-lestu-bi-rebbi-kum?*) to which they answered, "Yes, (*bela*), thus incidentally, according to the fanciful interpretation of the commentators, binding themselves to a life of calamity and misery, "*bela*" having the secondary meaning of "calamity." This, by the way, is a fair specimen of the solemn puns which the Orientals introduce into the most serious compositions and which they, indeed, consider one of the most desirable ornaments of imaginative composition. The Persians use this device to excess, far more so than do the Arabs; indeed its outrageous abuse, whilst barely tolerable in their poetry, renders their prose compositions almost unreadable and makes the European reader sympathize with the Arab savant (cited by Ibn Khaldoun) who desired to see the exponents of the so-called "flowery" style well flogged in public, whilst a crier proclaimed aloud their misdeeds for the edification and admonition of the literary class. What would the old Arab have said to our "New Journalism" and "New Criticism"?

XXXIV

1. Roses in bosom, wine in hand And she I love submiss is;
The Sultan of the world my slave On such a day as this is.

2. Bring ye no candles; for, to night, In this our congregation,
The moon of the Friend's cheek's at full And other light dismisses.

3. Wine in our order lawful is; But, in thy face's absence,
O cypress-statured rose, the cup Forbidden and amiss is.

4. No perfumes for our banquet mix; For, from thy tress, each moment,
Borne to the nostrils of our soul The scent of ambergris is.

5. Mine ear is all ta'en up with wail Of reed and clang of harpstrings;
Mine eye all on thy ruby lip And circling cup of bliss is.

6. Bespeak me not of sugar's taste Nor that of sugar-candy;
By reason that my one desire Thy dulcet lip to kiss is.

7. Since that grief's treasure for thy sake My heart's waste places holdeth,
The tavern-corner still for me Sole dwelling-place, ywis, is.

8. What pratest thou of shame? My shame In good repute consisteth.
What askest of repute? For me, Repute repute to miss is. [174]

9. Winebibber, wencher, giddypate, Toper, I am, I own it;
And where is he who not as I, In such a town as this, [175] is?

10. Me to the Mohtesib [176] to blame 'Twere idle; for he also,
Like us, in quest of wine-bibbing, [177] Forever unremiss is.

11. Without beloved one and wine, Sit not a moment, Hafiz;
The Feast-tide [178] 'tis and come the time Of jasmine, rose and lys is.

[174] The true self-surrendering lover glories in passing for a reprobate in the eyes of the profane.
[175] App. Shiraz, which was full of Tartar settlers (the descendants of those of Holagou's soldiers who had taken up their abode there) and gipsies and whose population accordingly bore a bad name for debauchery and turbulence.
[176] The Mohtesib, (*Muhhtesib*) an officer who, as his name indicates, was originally a mere inspector of weights and measures, but seems, in course of time, to have become a sort of Censor Morum, charged with the suppression and punishment of offences against morals, such as gambling, drinking and "chambering and wantonness" generally. He was the especial bugbear of freethinking poets, such as Hafiz and Omar Kheyyam, who lose no opportunity of girding at him.
[177] *Shurb, syn.* "drinkers"; so that this line may be read in a double sense, (*a*) it is no

use denouncing us to the Mohtesib, for he is himself a tippler; or (*b*) he is always in pursuit of winebibbers. The *double entente* is intentional.

[178] The Festival of Shewwal, immediately succeeding the conclusion of the terrible month-long fast of Ramazan, obligatory on all Muslims.

XXXV

1. Our garden in no need Of cypress and of pine is;
For less than none of worth Yon shade-reared box [179] of mine is?

2. O loveling fair, what faith Hast taken, by whose canons
Our blood than mother's milk More lawful in thine eyne is? [180]

3. Whenas chagrin thou seest Loom afar off, for wine call:
Proof have we made and sure The cure for all repine is.

4. Why should I lift my head From off the Magians' threshold, [181]
Since of felicity And ease this door the shrine is?

5. Nought but the broken heart In this our Path they purchase;
The self-sellers' bazaar In quite another line is. [182]

6. Yesterday, wine in head, She promised me enjoyment.
What will she say to day, When in her head no wine is?

7. The tale of Love's chagrin All one is; yet, o wonder!
Repeated by no man I've heard The thing, in fine, is. [183]

8. Come, for, in severance, Even as the faster's hearing
On "Allah Akber!", bent This hopeful eye of mine is. [184]

9. Rail not at Shiraz town, Its pleasant streams and breezes,
For on the sev'n climes' [185] cheek This country as the shine is.

10. 'Twixt Khizr's fount, that wells In darkness, [186] great's the diffrence
And ours, whose source the hill, That bears the Name Divine, is. [187]

11. We will not cast away Content and poortith's lustre:
Provision (tell the king) Forewrit of Fate benign is. [188]

12. Since sweeter are its fruits Than honey and than sugar,
What a rare sugarcane, Hafiz, this reed [189] of thine is!

[179] "Box"; i. e. the Beloved. The box in the East grows to a great height and is a tall, slender tree, to which it is common to liken a beautiful woman's shape.
[180] To what religion dost thou belong, that thou drinkest (i. e. sheddest) lovers' blood with no more scruple than if it were thy mother's milk? "Mother's milk" introduced in token of the Beloved's tender youth.

[181] Here, in Love's mart, only humility and self-abasement are regarded; there is no market here for self-conceit and self-willedness.

[182] "Self-sellers", *id.* = self-vaunters.

[183] i. e. though the circumstances of love are the same with all, every one tells a separate tale of his own sufferings, regarding his experiences as something unique, which has happened to himself alone.

[184] "Allah Akber!" "God [is] Most Great!" the commencement of the Muezzin's cry, announcing the end of the fast of Ramazan, also the name of a hill to the north of Shiraz, from whose foot the Rukna (or Ruknabad) issues and from whose summit the traveller, coming through the mountain passes from the direction of Hemedan, first perceives the city of Shiraz spread out at his feet and exclaims "Allah Akber!" in admiration of the spectacle; hence the name. The poet's Beloved had probably gone on a journey and was expected to return by the hill-pass aforesaid.

[185] The Persians divide the world into seven climes or zones.

[186] "Khizr", (*Khidsr*) a fabulous Muslim saint, apparently confounded with Elias by one of those ignorant misconceptions which abound in the work of the "Illiterate" Prophet; he is said to have been a general of Alexander the Great and to have accompanied that conqueror on his invasion of India, which has been converted by Oriental romancers into an expedition to the Regio Tenebrarum (a mythical region supposed to be involved in perpetual darkness,) in quest of the Water of Life. The King failed in his emprise; but his follower succeeded in finding the miraculous spring and having drunken of it, became immortal and was made by Divine appointment guardian of the fount.

[187] The hill *Allah Akber* above mentioned.

[188] i. e. we will not barter the jewel of contented poverty for the mean goods of the world, but will trust in God to provide us with our daily bread.

[189] "Reed", i. e. pen.

XXXVI

1. The Garden of Eternity's [190] The privy cell of Dervishes;
The source of honour doth from out The service well of Dervishes.

2. Seclusion's treasury, wherein Are many wondrous talismans,
The key thereof is in the look And favouring spell of Dervishes.

3. The very sun his crown of pride Lays down before the venerance
And majesty, in humbleness Perceptible, of Dervishes.

4. The palaces of Paradise, Whose portal-keeper Rizwan is,
Are but ensamples of the meads Delectable of Dervishes.

5. The alchemies, whereby the heart's Base metal gold becometh, all
In the familiarity And friendship dwell of Dervishes.

6. Oppression's hosts from pole to pole Stretch; but from Time's beginning-day
Unto its end, the victories Men chronicle of Dervishes.

7. A fortune, quit of all concern Of trouble and cessation is
The fortune (without ambages The truth to tell) of Dervishes.

8. Kings are the mark of prayer and praise; Yet this to them ensueth but
Because they serve the majesty Unspeakable of Dervishes.

9. Vaunt not thyself, o man of might; For lo! thy life and riches all
Are in the keeping of the prayers Acceptable of Dervishes.

10. The fall of Korah and his wealth, That underneath the earth lies hid,
Thou wilt have read how of the wrath The thing befell of Dervishes. [191]

11. The radiance of the heart's desire, Whereafter monarchs strive with prayer,
Bright-mirrored, in the countenance Is visible of Dervishes.

12. Slave of the Asef of the age [192] Am I, for that the utterward
Of lordship and the innerward He hath, as well, of Dervishes.

13. Hafiz, if thou the water seek Of Everlasting Life to find,
Its source is in the threshold-earth Before the cell of Dervishes.

14. Bear thyself humbly at this door, Hafiz; for might and sovranty
All from the service of the power And puissance well of Dervishes. [193]

[190] "The Garden of Eternity", one of the eight Mohammedan Paradises
[191] The poet here makes Moses and Aaron dervishes.
[192] The Grand Vizier.
[193] This curious eulogy of the mendicant orders was probably written in Hafiz's youth,
    when he was a Soufi or a member of some similar religious sect. He afterwards
    became disgusted with the cant, hypocrisy and rapacity of the mendicant orders and
    not only severed all connection with them, becoming a freethinker of an Epicurean
    cast, but lost no opportunity, in after life, of exposing their pious juggleries and
    fraudulent practices and inveighing against their habits of deceit and dissimulation.

XXXVII

1. Into the tavern came, cup in hand, Yon sweetheart of mine,
Drunken with wine and the topers drunk With her tipsy eyne.

2. The hoofs of her steed the fashion show Of the crescent moon
And lowly, beside her stately shape, 's The height of the pine.

3. Of what shall I say "It is," of self When I have no wit?
Of what shall I say "'Tis not", by her When I see, in fine? [194]

4. The lamp of the comrades' hearts sinks down, When she riseth up;
She sitteth and lovers uplift the voice For love-repine. [195]

5. If civet smell sweet, it is because It clung to thy locks;
If woad's bow-drawing, [196] it is that it clave To those brows of thine.

6. My life, like the candle, from night till morn, Consumeth away;
It knoweth no moment of rest, like the moth, Till morning shine.

7. Return, that Hafiz's life forspent May eke return,
Albeit the arrow returneth not, Once sped from the twine.

[194] i.e. the lover is all absorbed in the Beloved and knows and sees only by and
    through her.
[195] i. e. the lovers' hearts sink within them, when the Beloved riseth up to leave the
    assembly; and when she sitteth down to remain, they cry aloud for love and longing.
[196] Woad is used by Oriental ladies for pencilling their eyebrows; hence it is called by
    the poet "bow-drawing", i. e. skilled in archery. The word-play is evident, the brows
    being commonly likened to bows, by means whereof the fair launch the arrows of
    their looks at lovers' hearts.

XXXVIII

1. The sleep of that seductive eye Of thine is not for nought;
That tress's curl, thus blown awry, Of thine is not for nought. [197]

2. Yet from thy lip the mother's milk Ran, when, "This sugar, strewn
About that salt-box mouth," quoth I, "Of thine is not for nought." [198]

3. Source of life's water is thy mouth; But on the brink thereof
The pit, [199] that in that chin doth lie Of thine, is not for nought." [200]

4. Long mayst thou live, although too well I know the eyelash-shaft,
That lurks within that eyebrow-bow Of thine, is not for nought. [201]

5. With parting's grief and misery And pain thou stricken art,
O heart; this wail and moan and sigh Of thine is not for nought. [202]

6. A wind from out her street last night Passed o'er the rosegarden.
O rose, that collar, rent in twy, Of thine is not for nought. [203]

7. Hafiz, although the heart the pangs Of love from the folk's sight
Hold hidden, yet this weeping eye Of thine is not for nought. [204]

[197] i. e. these are tricks to take hearts withal.
[198] i. e. it is a bait to catch lovers. The poets liken the Beloved's mouth to a salt-box,
    because it is said to strew salt upon wounded hearts: see former note on this subject.
[199] i. e. dimple.
[200] i. e. it is a pitfall for lovers.
[201] i. e. it is designed to shoot at lovers' hearts.
[202] i. e. thou hast good cause for lament.

[203] i. e., o rose, the scent of the beloved, brought to thee by the wind, hath so stirred thee to love and longing that thou hast rent thy collar for passion, like a frenzied lover; i. e. thou hast burst into blossom.

[204] i. e. thy tears divulge the secret of thy love.

XXXIX

1. Go thy ways, preacher! In vain This all thy clamour and prate is:
Irketh it thee, if my heart Fall'n from the pathway straight is?

2. The waist of my fair, which God Created whilere out of nothing,
A subtlety is, that solved Of never a soul create is. [205]

3. Free of this world and of that Thy bondman is; yea, independent
The mendicant one of thy street Of all of the heavens eight is. [206]

4. What if the liquor of Love Have rendered me drunk and ruined? [207]
Indeed, on that ruin based Existence's fair estate is.

5. Rail not, o heart, at the Friend's Injustice and barbarous dealing;
All that she doth with thee just And foreappointed of Fate is.

6. What season her lips to my wish Further me not, like the reed-pipe, [208]
The whole world's admonishment nought But wind in mine ear, anygate, is.

7. "Hafiz, go; chant thou no charms And mutter no spells!" quoth the Loved One;
"For full of such charms and such spells My memory early and late is." [209]

[205] Waist likened, for smallness, to "nothing" and called "a subtlety".
[206] He who is possessed of the love of thee has no thought to spare for this world or that, heaven or hell.
[207] "Drunk and ruined" is the Persian equivalent of our "dead-drunk".
[208] i. e. until she caress me with her lips, as a flute-player does a flute.
[209] i. e. I am sated with lovers' vows and imprecations.

XL

1. Dewy-fresh, blood-thirsty rubies That her lip, yon fair of mine, is;
For their sight my soul to render Sole concern fore'er of mine is. [210]

2. Shamed be he by those long lashes And that eye of black who seëth
Her heart-ravishing and blamer Yet of this despair of mine is!

3. Forth the town-gate, camel-driver, Bear my gear not: see, this street-end
Is the King's highroad, for yonder Charmer's dwelling there of mine is.

4. I'm the thrall of my ill fortune, Since, in this faith-lacking epoch,
Love of yonder tipsy gipsy Lord of this affair of mine is.

5. Lo! the rose's amber-shedding Cup and calyx but a scantling
Of the overflow of fragrance From yon Scent-the-air of mine is.

6. From thy door, o gard'ner, breeze-like, Drive me not, for that thy rose-field
Watered by these tears, pomegranate-Flowerlike, [211] red and rare, of mine is.

7. Draughts of rosewater and sugar From her lip her eye prescribeth,
That physician of this bosom, Sick with love and care, of mine is.

8. Hafiz' teacher, in th' adorning Of his verse who taught him deftness,
None but yonder subtle-spoken, Sweet-voiced Friend and Fair of mine is.

[210] i. e. I have no other occupation than to seek to gain the sight of the Beloved's ruby
    lips, though it cost me my life and soul.
[211] i.e. bloody.

XLI

1. From of old the love of fair ones Only wont and goal of mine is
And the care thereof the solace Of this heart in dole of mine is.

2. To discern thy mouth of ruby Eyes soul-seeing there behoveth.
What room for this eye, that seeth Body, but not soul, of mine is? [212]

3. Be my friend; for the adornment Of the world-all from thy moonface
And the tears that, like the Pleïads, From these eyes do roll of mine, is. [213]

4 Since the love of thee in speechcraft Lessoned me whilere, the practice
Of all people's tongues these praises Ever to extol of mine is.

5. Poverty, o Lord, vouchsafe me; For the very cause its blessing
Of this puissance and this glory, Spread from pole to pole, of mine is. [214]

6. Vaunt thyself not thus, o preacher, That thou knowest men of worship;
Lo, the dwelling of the Sultan This sad heart and sole of mine is. [215]

7. Lord, whose pleasaunce is that Mecca Of the heart's desire [216], each thornbush
Of whose way than rose and wild rose Sweeter to this soul of mine is?

8. Who to steer it o'er the ocean [217] Taught thine image? Nay, its guider,
Sure, the tears, that, like the Pleïads, From these eyeballs roll of mine, is. [218]

9. Tell me no more tales, o Hafiz, Of the might of Khusrau Perwiz: [219]
Dreg-drainer [220] his lip of yonder Shirin Khusrau's bowl of mine is. [221]

[212] The poet likens the beloved's mouth, on account of its extreme smartness, to the
    soul, which is invisible.

[213] i. e. we both contribute to the adornment of the world, which should be a bond of affinity between us.

[214] Poverty, i. e. voluntary detachment from the goods of the world, is the cause of my renown as a poet.

[215] "Sultan", says Soudi, here means God Almighty; but I should rather suppose the reference to be, as usual, to the Beloved.

[216] i. e. the Beloved's dwelling.

[217] i. e. the ocean of my weeping eye.

[218] Rhyme-word of couplet 3 repeated in original.

[219] Khusrau Perwiz, the celebrated king, whose mistress was Shirin of poetic fame.

[220] "Dreg-drainer", i. e. parasite.

[221] *Lit.* "Sweet Monarch", i. e. the Beloved.

XLII

1. Such am I that the tavern-nook A hermitage for me is;
The dawntide exercise to greet The Ancient Mage for me is. [222]

2. If not for me the morning harp Be smitten sweet, what matter?
My own contrite lament at dawn Fit minstrelage for me is.

3. Of King and beggar am I quit, [223] Thanks be to God! The beggar
Of the Beloved's threshold-dust King of the age for me is.

4. What I from mosque and tavern seek Reunion with thee [224] is;
No other aim or thought than this, God be my gage! for me is.

5. Better thy beggar be than king! True honour and true glory
The meek endurance of thy bonds And vassalage for me is.

6. Yea, since the time I laid my face Upon thy noble threshold,
Above the throne-place of the sun A harbourage for me is. [225]

7. Except the sword of Death uproot The tent of my existence,
From this thy happy-fortuned door No pilgrimage for me is.

8. Good breeding, Hafiz, use and say, "Mine is the fault," [226] albeit
No choice in this affair t'engage Or not engage for me is.

[222] i. e. to greet the tavern keeper stands me in stead of morning-prayers.

[223] i. e. I am independent of all, great and small.

[224] "Thee", possibly here God, the Undifferenced Self.

[225] i. e. the devotion of myself to thy service hath uplifted me to the fourth heaven.

[226] i. e. show the generosity which marks the true lover and say, "It is my fault that I fell in love with a faithless fair one and so brought on myself all these sufferings", albeit, in very fact, I had no choice in the matter, the Beloved's beauty compelling me to love, willy nilly.

XLIII

1. Full blown the red rose is and drunken Become is the nightingale.
They call us to drink and make merry; Wine-worshipping Soufis, all hail!

2. The basis, behold, of repentance, In strength as the rock that appeared,
On marvellous fashion hath shattered A goblet of crystal frail! [227]

3. Bring wine, for, indeed, in her presence, That stead of unwishful disdain,
What, marry, may Sultan or shepherd, What sober or drunken avail? [228]

4. Since needs we this double-doored hostel [229] At last must depart, if the roof
And the arch of our life-stead be lofty Or lowly, nay, what doth it ail?

5. To no one vouchsafed is abiding On life without dole and annoy;
The Pact of the Prime on condition They stablished of sorrow and bale. [230]

6. With "Is" and with "Is not" [231] thy spirit Concern not; but be of good cheer;
Whatever betide of perfection, Still Death is the end of the tale.

7. To wind went all Solomon's glory And nothing it profited him
That giv'n him to know was the bird-speech And ride on the steed of the gale.

8. With pinion and wing from the pathway Swerve not, for the arrow of flight,
Though it keepeth the air for a season, Syne falleth to earth without fail. [232]

9. The tongue of thy pen, to God, Hafiz, What thanks shall it render for this,
That the words which it's gifted to utter From hand unto hand they retail?

[227] i. e. the wine-cup.
[228] All are alike before the equalizing majesty of Love.
[229] i. e. the world, likened to an inn with two doors, Birth and Death.
[230] See note 7 to Ode 33.
[231] i.e. with the Problems of existence and non-existence.
[232] Be not diverted from the path of right by the temptations of worldly wealth and worship; for, however high thou mayst rise in the world, thou must needs at last vail thy pinions at the bidding of Death.

XLIV

1. Flask in hand and verse-reciting, Warm with wine and laughing-eyed,
All a-sweat, with hair dishevelled, Raiment rent and shift awried;

2. Her narcissus-eye strife seeking And her lip a-frolicking,
Yestermidnight to my pillow Came and sat she by my side.

3. To my ear her head she bended And with soft, complaining voice,
"Sleepest thou, o ancient lover Mine, or dost thou wake?" she sighed.

4.What she poured into our goblet, That we quaffed, unheeding if
With the topers' wine she served us Or with Heaven's nectar plied.

5. If unto a sage a night-draught Such as this the Fates vouchsafe,
Infidel to Love the man were Who to worship wine denied!

6. Go o pietist, and rail not At us wine-bibbers; for They [233]
But this boon [234] to us allotted In Creation's morning-tide.

7. O how many a repentance, Like to Hafiz's, the laugh
Of the winecup and the loveling's Knotted locks have nullified!

[233] Fate-and-Fortune-foreordained, the Fates.
[234] i. e. that of wine.

XLV

1. A thousand hearts her tresses Bind with a single hair
And block the way on thousands Who succour fain would bear.

2. So all the soul may render, In hope of her sweet scent,
Musk-pods she op'neth, shutting Hope's door, when they draw near [235]

3. I am become distracted, Because her new-moon brows
And beauty now discovers, Now veils her face my fair.

4. The skinker in the goblet Pours many-coloured wine:
See, in the gourd he formeth How many pictures rare!

5. What fault, Lord, hath the flagon Done that the grapeblood fast
Sticketh, for all its gurgling, Within its gullet e'er? [236]

6. What measure plays the minstrel That, in mid dance, upon
Th'ecstatics shuts the portal Of speech with its sweet air? [237]

7. The sage who'th seen the juggle Of yonder trickster-sphere,
Foldeth his rug and shutteth The door on the affair. [238]

8. He who, Love's rites unpractised, Doth, Hafiz, union seek
Would the heart's pilgrim-garment, Without ablution, wear. [239]

[235] i. e. she tantalizes lovers by shaking out perfume from her dishevelled locks, whilst
    debarring them from drawing near to her.
[236] Surely, the wine-flask must have committed some sin, that the blood of the grape

sticketh thus fast in its throat and it can, for all its efforts, say nothing but "Gurgle, gurgle".

[237] i. e. so transports the dancing dervishes that they are stricken dumb, they whose wont it is to howl and yell out "Ha! and "Hou!", whilst whirling in the religious dance.

[238] The wise man, when once he has proved the illusiveness and faithlessness of fortune, withdraws from all concern of the world and declines debate of its affairs.

[239] The pilgrimage to Mecca involves the wearing by the pilgrim of a peculiar dress called the *Ihram*, made of two new cotton cloths, which are wrapped about the body in a prescribed manner. The *Ihram* is donned by the pilgrim, at the moment of sighting the Holy City, and is worn, to the exclusion of all other clothing, during his sojourn in the sacred territory. Before assuming it, he must rigidly observe the canonical rites prescribed for the occasion, chief among which are ceremonial ablutions of the strictest character and without which the whole pilgrimage is invalid and without merit. Hafiz aptly compares the lover, who should seek the enjoyment of the Beloved, without having complied with the obligations and conditions precedent of love, such as self-surrender etc., to the pilgrim who neglects to observe the canonical rites of the pilgrimage.

XLVI

1. When the Maker the fashion and form Of thy heart-easing eyebrows pourtrayed,
The solving of this mine affair By thy glances, He willed, should be swayed. [240]

2. Repose from my heart and the heart Of the bird of the morning He took,
When *this* one and *that* one lament For thee in the dawn tides He bade.

3. When Fortune the broidery wrought Of thy robe of narcissus-like hue,
Myself in the road-dust it set, With the cypress of meadow and glade.

4. An hundredfold knots from my case And the heart of the rosebud it loosed,
When the breeze of the dawning its heart To the love and pursuit of thee laid. [241]

5. The sphere's revolution content Hath made me thy bondman to be;
What profit, since in thine approof It stablished the end of the braid? [242]

6. Knots, prithee, on this my poor heart Bind not, as a muskpod it were;
For a pact of alliance my heart With thy knot-loosing ringlets hath made.

7. Mayhap, like the rosebud, whoe'er His heart to the love of thee sets
Shall find all his troubles one day By the breeze of thy fragrance allayed.

8. O zephyr of union, the life Of another thou wast. See the fault
That I made, when my heart set its hopes On the faith of a fair fickle maid!

9. Quoth I, "From the town, on account Of thy cruelty, will I depart."
She laughed and "Go, Hafiz! Thy feet Who is it that bindeth?" she said.

[240] i. e. that my heart's case should depend on thy kind looks.
[241] And consequently, frequenting thy quarter, solaced our hearts by bringing us thy scent.
[242] What booteth it that heaven predestined us to be thy servants, if thou wilt not accept of our service?

XLVII

1. Since in this age, companion Nor comrade, that fault-free is,
Except th' unmingled winecup And book of songs, to see is,

2. Fare thou alone, for narrow's The pathway of salvation;
Drink wine, for no returning Of precious life for thee is.

3. Not I in this world only For lack of works am troubled;
For knowledge without practice, Heart-sick the devotee is.

4. In this highroad of trouble, Unto the eye of reason,
The world, with all its business, Unstable vanity is.

5. My heart much hoped for union With thee; but in Life's pathway
The Term [243] the highway-robber Of hope from all that be is.

6. The face of those predestined To fortune black, for scouring
Nor scrubbing, waxeth whitened: A proverb this, perdie, is.

7. Toy with a moon-cheek's ringlets Nor cite the old wives' fable
That weal and bale from Saturn's Or Venus's decree is.

8. Each edifice thou seest Is subject to mutation,
Save that of Love, which only From alteration free is.

9. Never, whatever happen, They'll find our Hafiz sober,
For with wine Fore-eternal Intoxicated he is.

[243] i. e. the foreappointed end of life, Death.

XLVIII

1. Since that thine image we have, Of liquor for us what need is?
Say to the winejar "Be stopped;" For the winehouse's ruin decreed is. [244]

2. Though heaven's own nectar it be, Spill, spill it, for, lacking the Loved One,
Each draught that thou giv'st me of sweet The essence of torment, indeed, is.

3. Alack for the Charmer is gone And now on mine eye full of weeping
The image we grave of her down As writing on water to read is.

4. Be wakeful, o eye; for, God wot, From the torrents [245] that flow without ceasing,
In the place of abidal of dreams, [246] Assurance for none without heed is.

5 By thee, face to face and unveiled, To pass the Beloved still useth;
But strangers she spied and so bound Her head with the face-veiling wede is.

6. The rose, since the grace of the sweat On thy rose-cheek it saw, for heart-sickness,
To rosewater all to-dissolved, On the furnace of envy and greed, is. [247]

7. In the corners and nooks of my brain Go seek not a place for good counsel;
This closet all full of the hum Of viol and ghittern and reed is.

8. The way of thy love, what a way It is! For, compared with its vastness,
The world-rounding sea of the sky, God wot, a mere bubble and bead is!

9. See, verdant are valley and plain! Come, let us beware of withholding
The hand from the wellspring of mirth; [248] For the world-all a mirage, indeed, is.

10. In the halls of the heart, from thy face Are hundreds of tapers enkindled
And that, strange to say, whilst thy cheek From its hundredfold veils yet unfreed is!

11. Without thy soul-solacing face, O candle, the heart that illumest,
My heart, like roast meat on the fire, [249] With dole and chagrin all ableed is

12. If Hafiz a winebibber be, A lover and wencher, what matter?
Full many an usance right strange To youth appertaining of need is.

[244] The contemplation of the Beloved's image is sufficient intoxication for the lover; shut the wine-houses; we need them not.
[245] "torrents" of tears.
[246] The eye.
[247] The rose is all dissolved in sweat for envy and greed of thy beauty. Rosewater is obtained by exposing the rose-petals to heat in a cistern over a furnace, when the volatile oil rises and forms on the surface of the water.
[248] "The wellspring of mirth", according to Soudi, is the wine-cask.
[249] "Roast meat on the fire". This singular metaphor is a favourite one with the Persians and is constantly used in all seriousness by their poets; it reminds us of the lover in Dibdin's musical farce, "The Waterman", who likens his heart to "a mutton-chop upon a gridiron".

XLIX

1. Now that the hand of the rose The wine cup clear upraises, [250]
With an hundred thousand tongues The bulbul chants her praises.

2. Call for the book of songs And take the way of the desert. [251]
Is it a time for the schools Or the chewing of schoolmen's phrases? [252]

3. Sever thyself from the folk And pattern take by the Anca; [253]
The name of the sitters-alone From pole unto pole Fame blazes.

4. The Sheikh of the mosque last night Was drunken and gave pronouncement
That better on wine forbid To live than by almous ways is. [254]

5. No option is thine of clear Or troubled; [255] drink and be silent;
For goodness itself whate'er Our Cupbearer [256] us purveys is.

6. As the tale of the worker in gold And the weaver of mats, the pretender's
Conceit and the clamour of those Who think to rival my lays is. [257]

7. Peace, Hafiz, and these thy traits, Like thrice-refined gold, watch over;
The city's forger of coin The mint-master grown nowadays is. [258]

[250] The Persian poets liken the red rose in full bloom to a hand holding aloft a cup full
of wine.
[251] i. e. the open country. A song of Spring.
[252] *Lit.* "the discussion of the *Keshf-el-Keshshaf*", the well-known commentary of Ez
Zemekhsheri on the Koran.
[253] "Anca". The mythical bird, before mentioned, said to be unique of its kind and to
live alone in the inaccessible solitudes of the Caucasus.
[254] i. e. better be an honest toper than live on the charity of the Faithful, as do the
hypocritical pietists.
[255] i. e. thou canst not control the course of Fate nor choose whether thy life shall be
serene or troubled.
[256] "Our Cupbearer"; according to Soudi, God.
[257] A rush-mat weaver once, says Soudi, went to the market of the gold-embroiderers
and said, "You and I are both of one trade and fellow-crafts-men; because we are
both owners of workshops and both our crafts are wrought with tools". Proverbially
said of an impudent pretender; here apparently referring to some worthless rival of
Hafiz.
[258] i. e. the humbugger and intriguer is become the judge, the dispenser of praise and
blame. Hafiz must have had a prophetic foreknowledge of the "Log-rollers" and
"Press-nobblers" of our own day, who are (like Rabelais' monks) "banded together to
deceive and hoodwink the world".

L

1. If thou with kindness call us, Pure grace it on thy part is;
And if thy wrath reject us, Untroubled still our heart is. [259]

2. In writing to describe thee The possible o'erpasseth;
Beyond description's puissance Thy graces to impart is.

3. The face of the Beloved The eye of love discerneth;
The light of the fair's aspect, From pole to pole a star 'tis. [260]

4. Read from her face's Koran A verse; for the solution
Of all the knotty sayings, In the Keshsháf [261] that are, 'tis.

5. Unbending as the cypress Art thou with us, Beloved;
How many an eye, from allwhere, Fixed on thy face, flint-heart, is?

6. O thou, whose food Heav'n's manna And equal's none, no likeness
For thee, save in the ramparts, That Heav'n and Hell dispart, is. [262]

7. The likeness of the swallow, That boasts himself a Huma, [263]
The foe that envies Hafiz His rare poetic art is.

[259] i. e. everything that the Beloved doth is acceptable to the true lover.
[260] The light of the Beloved's countenance is world-illumining: but only the eye of love can discern it. "The world is the mirror of the beauty of our Beloved; For the face of the Beloved is in every atom"; says the Soufi poet Jami.
[261] i. e. Ez Zemekhsheri's Commentary, before mentioned, on the Koran, which is considered, as is the right of a Commentary, to overpass the original in obscurity.
[262] *El Aaraf*, the partition, thinner than a sword-blade, which separates heaven from hell. The commentators give no satisfactory explanation of this couplet; but the only apparent reason for the choice of such an object of comparison for the Beloved would seem to be its *uniqueness*.
[263] "Huma"; a mythical bird, that has no feet and therefore never alights on the earth. It hurts no living thing and its shadow, falling on any one, n augury of good fortune and (some say), of sovereignty.

LI

1. For him who hath solitude chosen, Of pleasance and gain what need is?
For who hath the street of the Loved One, Of meadow and plain what need is?

2. O soul, [264] by the need which thou feelest Of God the most High, I conjure thee,
Bethink thee a moment and question, For us, the love-slain, what need is.

3. Sore, sore is our need; but, for asking Of favours, no tongue can we muster:
Indeed, in the Bountiful's presence, For asking in vain what need is?

4. No need is of talk or pretention, If 'tis at our life that thou aimest;
Of plunder and pillage, when chattels Are thine and domain, what need is?

5. The luminous heart of the Friend is The world-showing cup of the legend; [265]
What need, then, one's need of expounding? I say it again, what need is?

6. Time was when I wont to put up with The chiding and flouts of the sailors;
But now that the pearls have been gotten, For sailing the main what need is? [266]

7. The life-giving lip of the Loved One Thy fated allowance foreknoweth;
For wearisome asking and craving, O beggarly swain, what need is?

8. We're burning, o monarch of beauty! At least, for God's sake, we implore thee
Thou ask, for the beggar, who pineth In passion and pain, what need is?

9. A vaunt and begone, o pretender! With thee I have nothing in common:
When loved ones are present, of foemen, Affection who feign, what need is?

10. Come, Hafiz; a truce to this prating! For worth of itself is apparent:
Indeed, of dispute and contention With rivals profane what need is?

[264] Addressed to the Beloved.
[265] The Beloved's heart is like the fabulous cup o the prehistoric King Jemshid, which
is said to have shown him all things, past, present and future. The reader may be
reminded that the Persians consider the heart the seat of reason, the liver being the
seat of love.
[266] Love likened to a sea-voyage in quest of pearls.

LII

1. Joy-bestowing is the garden And friends' company is pleasant;
Fair befall the time of roses! Topers then to be is pleasant.

2. By the East wind every moment Scented are our souls: the fragrance
Of the breath of the desireful Lover, [267] verily, is pleasant.

3. See, the rose, her veil unlifted, Maketh ready for departure!
Bulbul, moan; for heartsick lovers' Sad complaining plea is pleasant.

4. To the Bird of Night [268] be guerdon For good news, in that "The wailing
"Of the wakeful in the night-time To the Friend" quoth she "is pleasant."

5. From the tongue of the free lily [269] Came this saying to our hearing;
"In this world of ours, the portion Of the burden-free is pleasant."

6. Though there be in this world's market But the name of heart-contentment,
Yet the usance of the vagrant And the debauchee is pleasant.

7. Trust me, Hafiz, world-renouncement Is the way of heart-contentment;
Never deem that world-possessors' Case (I counsel thee) is pleasant!

[267] i. e. the wind, which is fabled by poets to be enamoured of the rose. *Hawadar*, desireful, means also breath-, air-, waft-having: note the word-play.

[268] The nightingale.

[269] The white lily (*Lilium Candidum*) is called by the Persians "free", probably on account of its pure whiteness and stately and upright bearing. Soudi says that it is because it is at all seasons fresh and green and free from the winter s scathe and that, bearing no fruit, it is neither shaken nor stoned, like fructiferous plants; but this is an evident error, arising, in all probability, from the fact that the Persian name, *sousen*, of the lily is also that of the fir-tree, which latter really answers the above description, whilst the lily does not.

LIII

1. Whose dwelling, Lord, by yonder heart-Enkindling taper's [270] lit?
Our soul's afire! For God's sake, ask Whose soul's delight is it.

2 I wonder in whose arms she lies And who her housemates be,
She who the edifice o'erthrown Hath of my faith and wit!

3. Whose soul's delight is yonder wine Of rubies of her lip?
Unto whose cup for cupgiver Did Fortune her commit?

4. Each at her casteth spells of love; But to whose sorceries
Her dainty heart inclining is, None knoweth anywhit.

5. O Lord, yon queenlike, mooncheeked maid, Yon Venus-fronted fair,
Whose peerless pearl is she, whose gem Past value exquisite?

6. That fair whose ruby wine, undrunk, [271] Hath made me drunk and mad,
For whom doth she the goblet fill? In whose assembly sit?

7. Ask ye, 'fore God, to whom the bliss Of the companionship
Of yonder candle of delight Hath Destiny forewrit?

8. "Alack, for Hafiz' heart distraught," Quoth I, "withouten thee!"
She answered, with a covert smile, "For whom distraught is it?" [272]

[270] Apparently some girl with whom the poet had fallen in love at first sight, without knowing who she was or where she lived.

[271] i. e. The sight and thought of her ruby lip, though untasted, have intoxicated me.

[272] i. e. as who should say, I am not responsible for its distraction; 1 have nothing to do with it".

LIV

1. Though of deserving, indeed, to vaunt me Unto the Friend unfit is,
Dumb if the tongue be, of Arab learning Brimful the mouth and wit is.

2. Peri cheek-hidden is she, yet demons Lurk in her roguish glances:
Lo, for amazement reason consumeth! Yea, what a marvel *it* is! [273]

3. Nay, of the reason ask not why Fortune Ever the worthless fosters;
Sure, for her favour absence of reason Reason enough, to wit, is.

4. In this world-meadow none ever plucketh Rose without thornprick; never
Even the heav'n-lit lamp of Mohammed Of Boulehéb's sparks quit is. [274]

5. Hassan from Basreh, Suheib from Syria, Bilal from Abyssinia,
And Abou Jehl from the land of Mecca; Stranger than this what writ is? [275]

6. Not at a wheatcorn college and hospice Set I; the bench of the tavern
Is my saloon and the foot of the wine jar The summering-stead [276] where I sit is.

7. E'en as the lustre and light of our eyes is The maid of the grape-vine's beauty;
Now in the grape-veil, Now in the flagon's Face-veil of glass [277] it lit is.

8. Yea from yon ruby giver of gladness [278] Seek thou the salve of thy suffrance,
That in Aleppo's flagons and China's Fair alike seen and fit is.

9. Parts by the thousand of wit and breeding Had I; and now I'm drunken,
Whatso unmannerly from me proceedeth Blazon of lack of wit is. [279]

10. Hither the goblet! A constant helper Wine unto me, like Hafiz,
In the dawn-weeping and midnight calling On heaven to sins remit, is.

[273] i. e. The reason is astounded to see Peri and Div (demon) combined in the same person.

[274] "Bouleheb", properly Abou Leheb, Father (i. e. He) of the Blaze, to wit, Man of Hell; a nickname given by Mohammed to his uncle Abd-ul-Uzza, who refused to accept his revelation and opposed his mission by every means in his power. The word (*sherar*) here used for "sparks" means also "wickedness, malice".

[275] Hassan of Basreh, Suheib of Damascus and Bilal the Abyssinian (the latter the Prophet's famous negro crier) were three of Mohammed's most zealous adherents and were all foreigners, whilst Abou Jehl ("Father of ignorance or folly", a nickname bestowed by Mohammed on Amr ibn Hisham, one of his bitterest opponents,) was a compatriot and a native of the sacrosanct territory of Mecca.

[276] *Dtembi*, an open-fronted sitting-room for fine weather.

[277] "Grape-veil", the choroid membrane of the eye, so called by the Arabs. "Face-veil of glass", the vitreous humour of the eye. The word-play is patent.

[278] Wine.

[279] i. e. If I behave not according to good breeding, it is not that I am not naturally a man of sense and conduct, but that love has intoxicated me and bereft me of reason.

LV

1. More goodly than pleasance and mirth In garden and Spring what is?
Where is the skinker? The cause Of his tarrying what is?

2. Each moment of gladness of Fate Vouchsafed to thee, reckon it gain;
For to none is it given to know The end of the thing what is.

3. The bond of our life with a hair Is bounden: be wise, then, and care
For thyself; for the use of concern For Time on the wing what is?

4. The meaning of "Water of Life" And "Garden of Irem," [280] indeed,
Save wine that is eath to digest And margent of spring, what is?

5. Since sober and drunk of one tribe Alike are, to whether's allure
The heart shall we render? The choice, For our imitating, what is?

6. What knowledge hath heaven itself Of the secret behind the screen?
Peace, prater! Advantage hard words At the porter [281] to fling what is?

7. In God if allowance be not For the errors and faults of the slave,
The meaning of "Pardon and grace Of the Merciful King" what is?

8. The pietist Kauther [282] desires And Hafiz the winecup. The will
Of the Maker, I wonder, indeed, 'Twixt this and that thing, what is? [283]

[280] Irem", the fabulous Paradise of Sheddad ibn Aad, supposed to be still in existence in the wilds of Arabia. See my "Book of the Thousand Nights and One Night", "The City of Irem", III, 334.
[281] i. e. Heaven, treated as the mere doorkeeper of the Unseen, the blind servant of fatality.
[282] "Kauther", a stream or reservoir of nectar in Paradise.
[283] i. e. I wonder what is the real will of God in these matters and what is foul and fair in His sight. As we have no means of ascertaining the real nature of the Divine Will, better stick to the winecup and eschew hypocrisy.

LVI

1. My moon this week the city left; And in mine eyes a year 'tis;
What wottest thou of severance, How hard a case and drear 'tis?

2. The apple of mine eye in her Bright cheek its own reflection
Espieth, as a musky mole It were, so smooth and clear 'tis.

3. From yonder sugared lip of hers The milk yet drips, albeit
"A lover-murd'rer," one may say Of each her eyelash-spear, "'tis."

4. Thou, who'rt the byword of the town For bounteousness, a marvel,
That unto strangers [284] thou so cold Shouldst be and so austere, 'tis.

5. The Atom Indivisible [285] Nowise henceforth I doubt of:
Thy mouth best proof of what the wise Upon this point assert is. [286]

6. They give me the glad news that thou To pass by us intendest:
Change not thy purpose; for, in sooth, An omen of good cheer 'tis.

7. The mountain-burden of thy loss How should poor Hafiz' body
Support? For fragile as a rush, For love and sorrow sheer, 'tis.

[284] i. e. wretched, rejected lovers.
[285] One of the many chimerical objects of research of mediaeval savants, before the
modern recognition of the infinite divisibility matter.
[286] i. e. thy mouth is so small, that it may be taken as a proof of the existence of an
atom too small to be further divided.

LVII

1. Though fraught is the breeze with the scent of the rose And the season of joyance here
is,
Beware lest thou drink to the clang of the harp, For the Mohtesib severe is.

2. But if of heaven to thee vouchsafed Be flagon and Friend, with reason
And circumspection I rede thee drink; For Fortune a trouble-cheer is.

3. The beaker of wine look thou conceal In the hanging sleeve of the patchcoat
For, like to the eye [287] of the flask, the time A shedder of blood, I fear, is. [288]

4. With the tears of the eye from our gaberdine Let's wash the stains of the grapejuice
For lo! this the season of soberness And abstinence austere is.

5. Yon high-reared vault of the firmament Is but a sieve blood-scatt'ring;
Perwíz's heart and Cyrus' crown The dropping of the Sphere is.

6. Look not for pleasance of life from that Inverted bowl's [289] revolving,
For mixed with the dregs of yonder vat Its every whit of clear is. [290]

7. Irác and Fars with thy sweet verse Thou'st captivated, Hafiz:
Come, for the turn now of Tebríz And time of Baghdad here is.

[287] The eye of the flask, i. e. its mouth, which drips with the blood of the grape.
[288] i. e. it is a cruel and oppressive time. This ghazel was apparently written during one
    of the periodical prohibitions of wine and persecutions of wine drinkers from time to
    time forced upon the government by the orthodox party.
[289] The Persians liken the vault of heaven to a bowl or basin inverted over the Earth.
[290] i. e. Fortune allows no mortal to enjoy untroubled felicity. "Surgit amari aliquid . .
    .".

LVIII

1. Wail, bulbul, if with me Thy heart to friendship fain is:
Afflicted lovers both, Our business to complain is.

2. Whereas the fragrant breeze From the Friend's browlock wafteth,
Of pods of Tartar musk Mention to make in vain is.

3. Bring wine, that we may dye Hypocrisy's patched garment;
For sober though our name, Drunk with conceit our brain is. [291]

4. The door of penitence They've shut not. Up! Repentance
From loverhood, in time Of roses, sure, insane is.

5 The bondage of her tress To bear's no dullard's business;
The knowing sharper's wont To fare beneath the chain is. [292]

6. A hidden charm it is Whence Love, indeed, ariseth,
Whose name nor ruby lip Nor tresses' silken skein is.

7. True beauty's not in eye Or cheek or mole or ringlet;
To charmerhood great store Of subtleties germane is.

8. Unto the devotee Of Truth the satin raiment
Of those who're void of worth Not worth one half-a-grain is.

9. Thy threshold to attain Uneath is; to the heaven
Of lordship the ascent In hardship and in pain is.

10. I saw in sleep, at dawn, A glimpse of her enjoyment.
O noble dream, than wake Which goodlier amain is!

11. The Friend's oppression's come To the extreme: I fear me,
Oppression's end the first Of anger and disdain is.

12. Hafiz, oppress thou not Her heart with thy complaining;
For from oppression peace Eternal to abstain is. [293]

[291] A hit at the Soufis, whose name (signifying "wool-wearer") is a token of humility.
[292] Alluding to the Oriental custom of allowing convicted malefactors to go about in
    chains during the day-time, returning to prison at nightfall.
[293] i. e. if thou desire peace, oppress not (i. e. vex not) any, especially the Beloved.

LIX

1. Rail not at the topers, zealot Clean-created, rind and core: [294]
Well I wot, the sins of others Not against thee will They score.

2. Be I good or be I evil, Go, concern thee for thyself!
For, in fine, what each man soweth, That he reapeth and no more.

3. Seek thou not to make me hopeless Of His wrath-forestalling grace! [295]
How know'st thou what foul, what fair is, Once behind yon shrouded door?

4. Be they sober, be they drunken, All are seekers of the Friend;
Every place the abode of Love is, Mosque or temple, sea or shore.

5. From the sanctuary of virtue Fallen not alone am I;
From his hand my father Adam Paradise let go of yore.

6. Still the head of our submission To the tavern dust shall cleave.
If thou take my sense not, prater, Beat thy head against the floor.

7. Fair are Paradise's gardens; Yet beware that by the shade
Of the willow and the marges Of the meads thou set no store. [296]

8. Lean thou not upon endeavour; On the Primeternal Day,
Know'st thou what the Pen Creative 'Gainst thy name wrote heretofore?

9. If in hand a cup, o Hafiz, In the hour of death, thou hold,
straight to Heaven, from the quarter Of the winehouse, shalt thou soar.

[294] Ironical.
[295] Alluding to the saying of God, as stated in the Traditions of the Prophet to have
    been transmitted by Gabriel to Mohammed, "Verily, I [am] God; My mercy hath
    precedence over (or forestalleth) My wrath".
[296] Carpe diem; neglect not present pleasure, in reliance upon felicity to come.

LX

1. Now from the garden there breathe The breezes of Paradise,
My portion be joy-giving wine And Friend with the Houris' eyes!

2. Why boasts not the beggar to day Of kingship, whose banqueting hall
Is the marge of the field and whose tent The shade of the clouds of the skies?

3. The meadows are telling aloud The story of April and Spring:
The man who buys payment to come And scorns present cash is unwise. [297]

4. With wine, then, come build up thy heart; For the course of this ruinous world
To nought, except bricks of our clay To make, its endeavour applies.

5. Good faith from the foe [298] seek thou not; For never a twinkle he gets,
The torch of the cloister to light At the lamp of the temple who tries.

6. If black be the book of my deeds, Ne'er blame me, poor sot that I am:
Who knows in the lines of his skull What written of Destiny lies? [299]

7. I rede thee, withhold not thy feet From Hafiz's funeral train;
For, though he be sunken in sin, He fareth to Paradise.

[297] i. e. who renounces present ease in the hope of Paradise to come.
[298] The world of Fortune.
[299] The Orientals believe that every man's destiny is written (if we could but read the charactery) in the sutures of his skull.

LXI

1. Go, o zealot! Never bid me Unto Heaven; sooth to say,
God of Paradise's people Made me not the Primal Day.

2. Not a wheatcorn from the harvest Of existence shall he reap
Who, in this abode of frailty, Hath not sown in Truth's highway.

3. Thine be rosary and prayer-place, Pious works and use austere,
Tavern mine and going [300] and convent, Magian wine and Christian lay! [301]

4. Nay, forbid us not from drinking, Soilless [302] Soufi; for the Lord
With sheer wine, in the Beginning, Mixed and kneaded this our clay.

5. No true Soufi, fit for heaven,'s He who hath not, like to me,
Left his patchcoat in the tavern Pawned, his scot for wine to pay.

6. Ease of Houri's lips and Heaven's Pleasaunces is not for him
Who the skirt of the Beloved Letteth from his hand away.

7. Hafiz, so God's grace and favour Overwatch and succor thee,
Be thou quit of Hell's concernment And assured from Heaven aye. [303]

[300] "Gong", the *Nacous* used by the Christians in the East, in lieu of bells.
[301] The Oriental debauchee of the Middle Ages appears to have had a great liking for
the company of the young inmates of the Christian monasteries, male and female.
For instances see my "Book of the Thousand Nights and One Night", *passim.*
[302] Ironical.
[303] The lover of the truth neither fears Hell nor desires Heaven; both for him are
illusions of the World-Fiction (*Maya*).

LXII

1. Breeze of the dawning, where's the Friend's Abiding-place, ah where?
Where dwells that roguish lover's bane, That moon of grace, ah where?

2. Dark is the night and far in front The Vale of Safety lies:
Where's Sina's fire? The vision where Of Allah's face, ah where? [304]

3. Whoever comes into the world Th'impress of ruin bears;
Ask in the tavern where's the man Of sober case, ah where? [305]

4. Glad-news-bringer is he who knows The sign: much mysteries
There be; but where's th'adépt who can Their meaning trace, ah where?

5. Each hair of me to thee is bound By many a thousand ties;
But where are we and where the dull Revilers base, ah where? [306]

6. The wit's distraught: where is that chain Of musk? [307] The heart hath ta'en
The corner [308] : where's her brow, the heart's Withdrawing-place, ah where?

7. Roses and wine and minstrel all Are ready to our hand;
But where's life's pleasantness, without The Friend's embrace, ah where?

8. I'm sick of mosque and dervish-cell: Where is the vintner's house?
Where is the Friend, the lovely maid Of Christian race [309], ah where?

9. Hafiz, fret not if Autumn's wind Ravage the meads of life;
Where is the rose without a thorn Upon earth's face, ah where?

[304] Alluding to the Muslim story of God's appearance to Moses in the Wadi Eimen
(Coranicé, *Tuwa*). Whilst the Hebrew prophet, having married Jethro's daughter, was
returning to Egypt with his wife, the latter was taken with the pangs of labour in the
desert of Sinai. The night was cold and they needed fire. Moses, looking towards the
holy mountain, saw the light of the manifestation of God and accounting it a fire,
bade his wife tarry, whilst he repaired thither and fetched kindling-stuff. (v. Koran
XX, 8 &c.)

[305] i. e. in this world the winebibber is the only really sober and reasonable man

[306] i. e. what affinity is there between us and them?

[307] i. e. the beloved's tress to bind out wit, which has gone mad, it is being the custom to chain up madmen.

[308] i. e. gone into retirement. *Gausheh*, corner, *syn.* angle; word used p. g., in allusion to form of eyebrow.

[309] See note 2 to Ode 61.

LXIII

1. The curve, thy roguish brows, bow-wise, On Thy fore-head did cast,
They in that shape, my hapless blood That they might shed, did cast.

2. When, warm with wine and all a-sweat, Thou wentest in the meads,
Thy face's lustre [310] fire into The Ergh'wan red [311] did cast.

3. For one glance the narcissus cast In boastfulness, thine eye
Into the world an hundred kinds Of strife and dread did cast. [312]

4. The jessamine, for shame that folk Compared her to thy face,
Dust, by the hand of the East wind, Upon her head did cast. [313]

5. The rosebud me, last night, in doubt Of that thy rosy mouth,
As by the meadows' banquet hall, Drunken, I sped, did cast. [314]

6. The violet its twisted locks was knotting up, when lo!
The breeze the story of thy tress In the mid-bed did cast.

7. Me, for austereness ne'er who looked On minstrel or on wine,
Now into both desire of fair Ones tavern-bred did cast.

8 The patchcoat now with ruby wine I wash; for never man
Off the primæval lot, to him Of Fate foresaid, did cast.

9. Or ever yet the two worlds were, The use of friendship [315] was;
'Tis not of late that Heaven Love's Foundation-stead did cast.

10. Drunk with thy downy cheek I am: Glory to God, what pen
Thereon that charact'ry, that takes Both heart and head, did cast?

11. The world is grown to my desire, Since in the servitude
Of the world's lord and master [316] me Time's circling tread did cast.

12. Belike good luck for Hafiz is In this calamity
That Fate his lot with those that quaff The vinejuice red did cast.

[310] *Lit.* "Water of thy face". "Water-of-the-face", as before remarked, is a Persian idiom for "lustre, honour". Word used p. g. with "fire".

[311] "To cast fire into anything" is to trouble, worry, disturb it. "Ergh'wan", i. e. Redbud.

[312] i. e. in wrath at the insolence of the narcissus in presuming to vie with it.

[313] In sign of repentance and self-abasement.

[314] i. e. (according to Soudi) Seeing the rosebud, I said to myself, "I wonder, doth it resemble the beloved's mouth?"

[315] *Sic*; but "Love" is meant.

[316] According to Soudi, the Grand Vizier, Hafiz's patron, is here referred to.

LXIV

1. Each pathway-farer, who unto The winehouse street his way knows,
To knock at any other door, Indeed, a vain essay knows.

2. Yea, from the winecup's overflow The secrets of the cloister
Each man, unto the tavern-door Whose feet have learned to stray, knows

3. The crown of true debauchery Time giveth to him only
Who in the Tartar-cap-shaped cup [317] The world-all to survey knows.

4. Seek not obedience from the mad, Like us; for sense and reason
The Elder of our sect to be Transgression, sooth to say, knows.

5. Whoever from the skinker's down [318] Has read the two worlds' secret
The myst'ries of Jem's cup from out The dust-marks of Love's Way knows.

6. My heart no quarter for its life From the Friend's eye desireth,
For it the usances of that Blackhearted [319] bird of prey knows.

7. For the oppression of my star Of birth, mine eyes, of dawntides,
So weep that e'en the moon's self sees And Venus far away knows.

8. Happy his vision that in lip Of cup and skinker's visage
The one night's crescent and the full Moon of the fourteenth day knows! [320]

9. The case of Hafiz and the cup He plies by stealth, not only
Police and Mohtesib, but eke The King, whom all obey, knows;

10. A King august of majesty, Who the nine vaults of heaven
But as a model of the vault Of that his hall of sway knows.

[317] The tall slender cup likened to the Tartar cap, which is the form of the Persian royal head-dress.

[318] *Khedt*, syn. writing. "To him, whom Love hath initiated into the mysteries of life and death, those of the cup of Jemshid are a trifling matter, to be apprehended from the dust of the way".—*Soudi*. This does not seem a very satisfactory explanation of this obscure couplet; but it is not easy to suggest a better.

[319] Eye called "black-hearted", because of the black pupil.

[320] Cup-lip likened to crescent and skinker's face to full moon.

LXV

1. In the heart's fire my breast for love Of yonder fair consumeth;
Such fire is in this room the house All everywhere consumeth. [321]

2. My body, for its severance From yonder charmer, melteth;
My soul, at that her cheek's sun-heat, For love-despair consumeth.

3. Whoever on the ringlet-chains Hath looked of Peri-faces,
His stricken heart for me, distraught With love and care, consumeth. [322]

4. See my heart's burning! At the fire Of these my tears, for pity
And love of me, the candle's heart, Moth-like, o rare! consumeth.

5. Unstrange it is, indeed, that friends For me should heart-a-fire be;
For, since I'm grown distraught, The heart in strangers there consumeth.

6. My gaberdine of piety The tavern-flood hath taken;
My house of understanding, eke, The cellar's flare [323] consumeth.

7. My heart is broken, like the flask, Because I've made renouncement;
My liver, without wine and inn, Must-like, fore'er consumeth. [324]

8. The past forget thou and return; For see, mine eye [325] the patchcoat
Hath doffed and in thankoffering For granted prayer, consumeth.

9. Hafiz, leave idle talk and drink Awhile; for lo! we sleep not
Anights, what while the candle all In empty air consumeth.

[321] The heart (says Soudi) is the room and the bosom the house.
[322] Whoso hath known love knoweth what I suffer and pitieth me.
[323] Wine.
[324] i.e. my heart and liver are a-fire for regret at having vowed to renounce wine. "Consumeth" in last line = "fermenteth like must or new wine."
[325] "Mine eye" is here (says Soudi) equivalent to "I myself"; "i. e. in thank offering for reconciliation with thee, I have (or rather, will) put off the patchcoat and have burned (or will burn) it in token of renouncement of pietism and return to winebibbing.

LXVI

1. The hidden secret of things The wise from the wine-cup's ray know;
The jewel [326] of each man's soul By means of this ruby they know.

2. The worth of the book of the rose None knows but the bird of the morning; [327]
Not all men who look on a leaf The meaning it would convey know.

3. The case of this world and of that To the world-knowing heart I propounded:
And it, save the love of thee, all Did subject to passing away know.

4. By the spells of their looks those, who know The worth of the breath of the breezes
Of Araby, [328] rubies of stones To make and cornelians of clay know. [329]

5. Past, past is the time when I recked Of the prate of the sons of the people; [330]
And this for the secret of ease The Mohtesibs, even, they say, know.

6. O thou who the Lesson of Love Wouldst learn from the Record of Reason,
I fear me this subtlety rare Thou canst not by thought-taking aye know.

7. Bring wine, for they vaunt themselves not Of the roses of this our world's garden
Who the wind of the Autumn's despite And the ravage of death and decay know.

8. Unmeet the heart-ravisher [331] deems Repose for the nonce to vouchsafe us,
Albeit too surely doth she Our sickness of heart for delay know.

9. These fair-ordered pearls, from his soul Which Hafiz hath wrought, for the produce
He doth of the fostering care Of the Asef and Sage of the Day know. [332]

[326] *syn.* essence. In vino Veritas.
[327] The Nightingale.
[328] An allusion to the traditional saying of Mohammed, "Verily, I perceive the perfume of [God] the Compassionate from the direction of Yemen", explained by the commentators to refer to the Sherif Uweis el Kerani, who however was not a contemporary of the Prophet. He was one of the *Tabis* or Followers (i. e. those who had known and spoken with the Companions of Mohammed) and founded the first and strictest great order of Fakirs or religious ascetes. He was killed, fighting on the side of the Khalif Ali, at the battle of Siffin, in A. D. 657; and on account of his austere piety and devout practice of the tenets of Islam, it is pretended by the commentators that Mohammed meant to foretell his appearance in the Tradition above cited.
[329] The meaning of this couplet is that he who is cognizant of the mysteries of the invisible world, the initiated servant of the ideal, is able to work wonders by the mere act of his will; practically the same claim as that made by the Indian theosophists, expressed in orthodox theological phrase for obvious reason of expediency.
[330] "Sons of the people", i. e. the profane vulgar.
[331] The Beloved.

[332] The poet declares that he owes the beauty of his verse to the fostering care of his patron the Grand Vizier.

LXVII

1. Thy beauty, in accord with grace, The world hath wholly taken;
Yea, for by union and accord, The world may still be taken.

2. The envious taper would divulge The solitaries' secret;
Thank God, the secret of its heart Hath on its tongue, see, taken. [333]

3. The rose of the Friend's scent and hue Would fain herself have vaunted;
But in her mouth the East the breath Hath, jealous for thee, taken.

4. Of this consuming fire of love, That in my bosom lurketh,
The sun is but a spark that hath On heaven's roof-tree taken.

5. At peace upon the bank I was, Like to the compass-circle;
Until Time's vortex in the midst Hath, like the point, me taken.

6. Love of the bowl that day consumed The harvest of my being
When, mirrored from the Skinker's cheek, Fire hath its ruby taken. [334]

7. Sleeve-shaking, [335] will I get me gone Unto the Magians' quarter,
From all those ills that on Time's skirt Their hold have lately taken.

8. Drink, for the end of the world's case Who seëth, care off-shaking,
Lightly in hand the heavy cup, Full measure, hath he taken. [336]

9. They [337] with the Redbud's life-blood have Upon the roseleaf written,
"All ripe of wit have wine in hand, Like th'anemone, [338] taken."

10. Give wine in cup of gold, for lo! The dawn-draught of the topers,
King-like, with golden glittering sword, Hath all the world y-taken. [339]

11. Th' occasion use; for, since upon The world hath trouble fallen,
The sage, to 'scape from care, himself Hath to the cup betaken.

12. Hafiz, since water of delight Still trickleth from thy verses,
How can exception thereunto By enviers be taken?

[333] The fire of the candle's heart hath taken hold upon its tongue, i. e. wick, and so prevented it from speaking and revealing the secret of the recluses.
[334] i. e. was love made me a toper.
[335] "Sleeve-shaking", i. e. dancing. It is well known that the people of the East dance with their arms and bodies, more than with their legs and feet.
[336] The sage, who hath become aware of the worthlessness and instability of the world, still consoleth himself with the winecup.

[337] Fate and Fortune Foreordained.

[338] The anemone of the Persian and Arab poets is the *Shecaïc en Numan*, i. e. the anemone of the old Arab King En Numan or the blood-red anemone; hence the use of the flower as an object of comparison for Wine.

[339] *Tigh*, "sword", *syn.* "brightness"; hence, "the wine of the dawn-draught hath illuminated the world with its radiance."

LXVIII

1. Cupbearer, come, for the Friend From her visage the veil hath taken;
New light the recluses' lamp, That like was to fail, hath taken.

2. Yon taper, whose light was grown dim, Its visage anew hath kindled; [340]
This year-stricken elder [341] new life And youthfulness hale hath taken.

3. Such blandishments practised the Friend, That piety swerved from the pathway;
Such favour she showed, that affright The rivals who rail hath taken.

4. Nay, prithee, a truce to this sweet, Heart-ravishing speech! One would say
Thy pistachio in sugar its speech, To compass our bale, hath taken. [342]

5. Our weariful hearts were oppressed With a burden of care and affliction:
A Jesus-breathed one [343] hath God sent Who away all our ail hath taken.

6. Each cypress-shaped fair, that whilere Of beauty o'er sun and moon boasted,
To pursuit of another affair, Since thou ent'redst our pale, hath taken. [344]

7. Heav'ns cupolas seven are full Of the echoing sound of love's story;
And shame on the short-sighted man, Scant heed of the tale hath taken!

8. O Hafiz, whence learn'dst thou this spell, That, in jewels and gold thy verse chasing,
The Friend as an amulet it 'Gainst sorrow and wail hath taken?

[340] i. e. has become radiant.
[341] app. himself.
[342] i. e. Thy mouth, likened, by a common figure of speech, to a pistachio-nut, (hence the "candied" metaphor) hath spoken on dulcet, blandishing wise, with intent to beguile us to our destruction.
[343] i. e. one gifted with Jesus's power of restoring the dead to life; the Beloved.
[344] This couplet calls to mind the hero of the pleasing poet of the Bab Ballads, him I mean who "suddenly remembered He'd business at the Bank".

LXIX

1. 'Twas a bulbul did a roseleaf, Sweet of hue and scent, hold
In his bill and o'er that treasure Bitter-sweet lament hold.

2. "In the midst", quoth I, "Of union, Wherefore this complaining?"
"Me," said he, "doth my love's beauty In this languishment hold."

3. If the Friend with us abide not, Cause there's none for cavil.
For in scorn doth she, the sovran, Beggars indigent hold. [345]

4. Happy he who with the fair ones Favour hath! From-us-ward,
On the Loved One's beauty taketh Prayer nor blandishment hold.

5. Strew we on that Painter's pencil Heart and soul, [346] who moulded
All these wonders that the rondures Of the firmament hold!

6. Ill repute, if Love thou follow, Heed not: in the winehouse
Sheikh Senáan [347] in pledge his patchcoat Let for liquor lent hold.

7. Fair befall that sweet Calénder, [348] who, in exile's stresses,
Girdle-girt, did to the calling On th' Omnipotent hold!" [349]

8. Hafiz' eye, beneath yon Houri's Terrace, doth the usance
Of the rivers Paradisal, Under gardens pent, hold. [350]

[345] i. e. She being a queen, it is but natural and right that she should scorn beggars like myself.

[346] In token of honour and admiration.

[347] Sheikh Aboubekr Abdurrezzac es Senaani (*Szen'aani*) was a native of Senaa (*Szen'aa*) in Yemen, A. D. 743—827. The celebrated Persian poet Ferideddin Attar devotes more than four hundred couplets of his didactic poem Mentic-et-Teir (The Speech of Birds) to telling his story or rather legend in the most high-flown style, for which (to borrow a favourite phrase of Soudi's) may God forgive him! See Mentic-et-Teir, couplets 1159—1564; "Sheikh Senaan was the Elder (sage) of his time; In accomplishments, as to whatsoever I (can) say, he was foremost. He was Sheikh (teacher of the Law) in the Harem (Temple) of Mecca fifty years, With a discipleship of 400 (i.e. four hundred pupils), endowed with (all) perfection". The poet goes on to tell how the Sheikh fell in love with a Christian girl of Cæsarea and apostatizing for her sake, pawned his gaberdine for liquor and kept swine. He was finally reconverted to Islam by the miraculous intervention of Mohammed himself, whose appearance is described by the mystic poet in the most approved "erotic" fashion, not forgetting the musky tress and the swimming gait.

[348] *Calénder*, a member of a dervish sect professing great things in the way of piety and austerity, but generally considered *canaille* of the lowest order; the name is here used to signify an enthusiastic devotee.

[349] i. e. Sheikh Senaan himself, who is said, even whilst wearing the girdle or zone, the

sign of the Christian in the East, (i. e. the ropegirdle of the Franciscan monks or perhaps a reminiscence of the Sacred Thread of the Brahmins), to have never omitted the daily recital of the Muslim rosary, i. e. the Ninety-Nine names of God, and to have thus kept in touch with Islam.

[350] An allusion to a phrase in the Koranic description of Paradise, "Gardens, under them run rivers", K. II, 23. It may be remarked, in conclusion, that all sorts of mystic and pietistic meanings have been read by the commentators into Hafiz's mention of Sheikh Senaan; but, to the unprejudiced reader, it only amounts to the fact that Hani found it convenient, for obvious poetical reasons, to adopt the erring doctor as a saint of the topers' order.

LXX

1. Intent, save of oppression, Thou seest, the fair hath not;
The pact she broke and pity On our despair hath not.

2. Lord, chide her not, albeit My heart, dove-like, she slew
And of the Temple-pigeons Respect or care hath not. [351]

3. 'Twas Fate, not she, injustice That did me; else the Friend,
Save in the way of kindness, Intent to fare hath not.

4. Withal, whoe'er abasement From her hath not endured
Regard from any person Or any where hath not.

5. Bring thou of wine, cupbearer, And to the censor say,
"Rail not, for such a goblet Jemshid, I swear, hath not".

6. The wretch who hath not compassed Her threshold's sanctuary
The desert passed, but entered In Mecca's air hath not.

7. Fair fall the tipsy toper Who *this* world and the next
Giveth from hand and sorrow For whatsoe'er hath not!

8 Hafiz, the palm of versecraft Bear thou; for yonder foe
Merit, or even knowledge Of what it were, hath not.

[351] The poet likens his heart to the pigeons of the Temple precincts at Mecca, which it is forbidden to molest.

LXXI

1. No day for me, without Thy cheek sunbright, abideth;
And nought of life for me, Save darkling night, abideth.

2. For my much weeping, when We parted, in mine eyeballs
(Far be it from thy cheek!) No whit of light abideth.

3. Thine image hath mine eye Departed, saying, "Pity
"That such a nook as this Ruined outright abideth!"

4. Thine union from my head Held far the term appointed, [352]
Which now, for lack of thee, Unfar from sight abideth.

5. Near (From thy door be far!) The hour when saith the watcher,
"No whit of yon forlorn, Forsaken wight abideth."

6. What booteth that the Friend Should turn her steps to-me-ward,
When in my body worn Nor life nor spright abideth.

7. If, for thy loss, mine eyes Of water lack, then bid them
Heart's blood weep; for, save this, Nor shift nor sleight abideth.

8. Patience my med'cine were, I know it, for thy sev'rance;
But who shall patience use, In whom no might abideth?

9. Hafiz, for grief and tears, No dealing hath with laughter;
To those that mourn, for mirth No appetite abideth.

[352] i. e. the appointed time of death.

LXXII

1. For weeping, all immersed in blood The apple of mine eye is;
See, now, I prithee, how the case With those for thee that sigh is.

2. In memory of thy ruby lip And drunken eye, wine-coloured,
Heart's blood the ruby-coloured wine, From sorrow's cup I ply, is.

3. If from thy quarter's East the sun Of thy bright aspect riseth,
The aspect of my fortune's star Auspicious made thereby is!

4. The story of Shirín's sweet lip The utt'rance of Ferhád [353] is;
The curl of Leila's locks the place Where Mejnoun's heart doth lie is. [354]

5. Cheer thou my heart; for heartis cheer Is that thy cypress-stature;
Speak, for delightsome thine address And music thy reply is.

6. Cupbearer, easance to my soul Bring with thy circling goblet;
For my heart troubled for despite Of yon revolving sky [355] is.

7. From that sad hour when from my sight That lovely one departed,
The rondure of my skirt for tears Like Oxus torrent-high is.

8. How should my woeful heart, forsooth, At will again be gladsome,
Since it of those, to whom the Fates Freedom of will deny, is?

9. Hafiz, that, all beside himself, After the Friend pursueth,
Like to a bankrupt wretch, who doth For Korah's treasures sigh, is.

[353] The well-known lover of Shirin, the beautiful concubine of Khusrau Perwiz, who
    promised her to him, if he would cut a passage for a certain stream through a hill,
    but, by treacherously conveying to him false information of the death of his beloved,
    caused him commit suicide in despair, just as he had completed his task.
[354] Leila and Mejnoun, the well known lovers of the legend.
[355] i. e. of froward Fortune.

LXXIII

1. The apple of mine eye of nought Regardful but thy face is;
My frenzied heart of nothing else Is mindful but thy graces.

2. Mine eye hath donned the pilgrim-wede, Thy sanctuary to compass; [356]
Though of the wounded heart's blood it No moment pure of trace is. [357]

3. Blame not the bankrupt lover, who No current coin possesseth,
If what he streweth at thy feet His heart's mere metal base is.

4. His hand and his alone shall win To that thy lofty cypress, [358]
Whose magnanimity, in fine, Sufficient for the chase is.

5. Of Jesus's life-giving might To thee no word I'll utter,
Since he in soul-augmenting was Less skilled than thine embrace is.

6. I that in passion's fire for thee Heave not a sigh, can any
Say that my heart unpatient, 'neath The brand of Time's disgrace, is?

7. Wild-fowl like, prisoned in a cage The Bird of Heaven's Lote-tree [359]
Be, if he fly not down, in quest Of thee, from Heav'n's high places!

8. Quoth I, what time I, at the first, Espied thy mazy tresses,
"No end to their entanglement, Whose hearts these chains enlace, is!"

9. The longing for thy bonds is not To Hafiz' heart peculiar:
Where is the heart of man alive, Indeed, but in like case is?

[356] The circuiting or compassing of the Kaabeh is the culminating rite of the Pilgrimage.

[357] Among the chief conditions of the donning of the pilgrim dress (*Ihram*, see previous note) is perfect purity, which would be nullified by a speck of blood.

[358] The beloved's shape; here (*met.*) herself.

[359] i. e. The Angel Gabriel.

LXXIV

1. The sea of Love a sea is, Whereunto shore is not;
There, saving soul-surrender, Resource in store is not.

2. Affright us not with Reason's Forbidments, but bring wine:
With us in credit yonder Apparitor [360] is not.

3. Each moment that thou givest The heart to Love is good;
Need, in good works, of praying, Direction for, is not.

4. Ask thou thine eye who slew us. O soul of mine, the blame
for this to lay at Heaven's Or Fortune's door is not. [361]

5. Thy face with pure eyes only, New-moon like, can one see:
That full moon cheek's unveiling Each eye before is not.

6. Hold thou the way of toping For gain; for, like the track
Of hidden treasure, patent To all this lore is not.

7. Unmoved of Hafiz' weeping Art thou: at that thy heart
I marvel, which than granite Less hard of core is not.

[360] i. e. Reason.
[361] i. e. the blame is thine eye's.

LXXV

1. Blest may the coming of the Feast, [362] Cupbearer, be for thee
And may thy promises go not From memory for thee! [363]

2. Greet ye the daughter of the vine And say, "Come forth! For lo!
"Our favour from duresse hath wrought This setting-free for thee. [364]

3. "That thou thy heart, in all these days Of severance, from friends
"Withheldst and that it suffered this, It wond'reth me for thee!

4. "Thank God that from this autumn wind [365] Unto thy garth of rose,
"Jasmine and marjoram befell No injury for thee!

5. "Far be from thee the evil eye! Thy star renowned and luck
"Inborn from that thine exile did Return decree for thee!

6. "The coming of thy blessed feet Th' assembly's gladness is;
"Be every heart the stead of woe That wills not glee for thee!"

7. Hafiz, this Noah's ark (the cup) Look thou from hand set not:
Else will Time's deluge by the roots Pluck up Life's tree for thee. [366]

[362] i. e. The Festival of Shewwal.
[363] Apparently she had promised to visit the poet after the Fast-tide.
[364] i. e. the endeavours of the topers have resulted in the withdrawal of the interdict
    laid on wine-drinking.
[365] i. e. the oppression of the interdict.
[366] This ode was apparently written in celebration of some relaxation of the edicts
    against wine.

LXXVI

1. A goodly saying have I heard, Of Canaan's patriarch grey [367] bespoken;
"The pains which loss of friends entails Are not of those which may be spoken."

2. The tale of terrors of the Day Of Judgment, which the preacher telleth,
Is but a figure, of the woes Of lovers' parting-day bespoken.

3. Whom shall I question of the Friend Departed? For whatever tidings
The couriers of the East may bring All on distraction's way [368] be spoken.

4. "The ancient grief with year-old wine Repel; for this of heart's contentment
The seed is." Of th' old Villager [369] 'Twas on this wise, they say, bespoken.

5. Alack, that loveless moon, that friend And enemy, "From friends and comrades",
How lightly were these words of her, "Let us begone away", bespoken!

6. Henceforth, submission is my part; For lo! my heart, to pain grown wonted
For thee, renouncement hath from hope Of remedy for aye bespoken.

7. "Bind thou not knots upon the wind, [370] Albeit to thy wish it bloweth!"
Of the wind's self to Solomon Was this proverbial trait bespoken.

8. Go not, for Fortune's blandishments, From the right path, nor trust the story
That this old hag her craft's forsworn, Of whomsoe'er it may be spoken.

9. Come and drink wine, for, yesternight, Of the old keeper of the winehouse,
Was much of God's forgivingness To those who disobey bespoken.

10. Make thou no words of How or Why; With his whole soul the loyal servant
Each word the Sultan says accepts, Without or yea or nay bespoken.

11. If any say that from the thought And love of thee returned hath Hafiz,
Believe it not; for nought but lies And calumny have they bespoken.

[367] The Patriarch Jacob.
[368] i. e. confusedly, at random.
[369] Not explained by commentators; but *pir-i-dihcan*, the elder of the village or old
villager, is an idiomatic expression for "old wine".
[370] A proverbial phrase, meaning, "Rely not upon the fleeting world and faithless
fortune".

LXXVII

1. To the new blown rose the bulbul Spake this word at break of day,
"Leave disdain, for, like thee, many Here have bloomed and passed away."

2. Laughingly the rose made answer, "Vexed we are not by the truth;
"But hard words to the Beloved Never should the lover say."

3. Never was Love's fragrance wafted To his palate who his cheek
On the threshold of the winehouse Never in the dust did lay.

4. Those who covet wine of rubies From the jewelled cup of Love,
Many a pearl and many a jacinth With the eyelash pierce must they. [371]

5. In the rose-garden of Irem, Yesternight, in the soft air,
When the spikenard's tress was ruffled By the breeze of coming day,

6. "Throne of Jem", I asked the greensward, [372] "Where's thy world-revealing cup?"
[373]
"Fortune slept, alack!" it answered, "And the rosetime might not stay."

7. Not the word of love, indeed, is That which cometh to the tongue: [374]
Cupbearer, bring wine and grant us Truce from speech and answer, pray.

8. Hafiz' tears have cast discretion, Ay, and patience to the waves;
What is he to do, who cannot Hide the fire of Love's dismay?

[371] i. e. must weep tears, both plain and bloody.
[372] Greensward styled "throne of Jem" as being the seat of the rose, which is the
Jemshid or monarch of flowers.
[373] i. e. the full-blown rose itself. It will already have become abundantly evident to the
reader that the Persian poets have not the English (Anglo-Norman) horror of mixed
metaphors. Indeed, on the contrary, the latter and the kindred figure of enallage, in
their wildest developments, appear to be often deliberately employed by them, as a

desirable ornament.
[374] i.e. Deeds, not words, are the fitting speech of love.

LXXVIII

1. Gone my heart and faith are and the charmer, Her despite 'gainst me to show, ariseth:
"Sit thou not by us," quoth she; "for safety Even now from thee to go ariseth."

2. Marry hast thou ever heard of mortal Who a moment happy at this banquet
Sitteth but, at end of the assembly, In regret therefrom and woe ariseth?

3. See the taper, if itself of likeness To that laughing cheek of thine it boasteth,
Many a night and oft, before thy lovers, In atonement, Heart aglow, ariseth.

4. In the meadows, lo! the breeze of Springtime, From the soft embrace of rose and cypress,
Of its longing for thy cheek and stature, Tow'rds thy neighbourhood to blow, ariseth.

5. Flushed with wine, upon thy way thou passest And from all th'angelic world's recluses,
Hark, the clamour of the Resurrection, At thy sight, from high and low, ariseth.

6. Lo, with shame before thy gait confounded, With its foot unto the earth fast rooted,
Where the haughty, headstrong cypress standeth, That in pride of shape and show ariseth!

7. Harkye, Hafiz, cast away the patchcoat, An thou'dst save thy soul alive; for, certes,
Fire from out the cassock of dissembling And hypocrisy, we know, ariseth. [375]

[375] Hypocrisy is for the Muslims the deadliest of sins, after the unspeakable crime of attributing partners to God. According to the Mohammedan casuists, pious humbugs are destined to Hawiyeh, the Seventh Hell or Bottomless Pit of Fire. Dante, it will be remembered, treats hypocrites with equal severity.

LXXIX

1. No man hath seen thy visage, Though many an one thy spy is: [376]
For thee full many a bulbul, Though yet in bud, [377] a-sigh is.

2. If I unto thy quarter Repair, 'tis no such wonder;
In this thy land full many A stranger, [378] such as I, is.

3. Though I from thee am distant, (Be none from thee removéd!)
The hope of thine attainment Still to my thought anigh is.

4. In Love there is no diff'rence 'Twixt cloister-cell and tavern;
The light of the Friend's visage In all parts, low and high, is.

5. Wherever they make goodly The practice of the convent,
The Cross's name of glory And the monk's gong thereby is. [379]

86

6. Was ever lover's suff'rance Unnoted of the Loved One?
O sir, without physician No pain beneath the sky is. [380]

7. Nay, all this lamentation Of Hafiz not for nought is;
Rare cause and parlous reason, God wot, for his outcry is.

[376] Thou art the cynosure of all eyes.
[377] Beloved's veiled face likened to a rose yet shrouded in the bud.
[378] i. e. a forlorn, exiled lover.
[379] i. e. religion is a matter of practices, not of names. Wherever Christianity is
    practised on true and goodly wise, there (and not otherwise) is the Christian church;
    and so, by implication, with Islam and other religions.
[380] Every disease hath its appointed remedy.

LXXX

1. Lo in thy tress ensnared my heart A-bleed, of its own self, is; [381]
Come slay it with a glance; for that The meed of its own self is. [382]

2. If at thy hand our soul its wish Shall compass, give it quickly;
For kindness still in place, when done, With speed, of its own self, is.

3. Nay, by thy soul, sweet idol mine, My soul's wish (like the taper
In the dark nights) effacement sheer, Indeed, of its own self is.

4. When first thou thought'st to love, I bade Thee do it not, o bulbul;
For yonder rose grown up from out The seed of its own self is. [383]

5. The rose's fragrance needeth not The musk of Ind and China;
For musk-pod holding in each fold Its wede, of its own self, is.

6. To the ungenerous of the age Repair thou not for succour;
Thy soul's salvation in the nook Decreed of its own self is. [384]

7. Though Hafiz burn, yet, in the law Of Love and self-surrender,
His soul still faithful to the pact And creed, of its own self, is.

[381] i. e. my heart hath of its own proper motion cast itself into the snare of thy tress.
[382] *Sic*, i. e. ipsum est meritum.
[383] i. e. the beloved is self-willed and capricious, like the wild rose, that groweth at
    random.
[384] Lay not thyself under obligation to the mean, but seek thine own salvation in
    thyself.

LXXXI

1. My heart's sad case to thee To say my soul's desire is;
News of the heart that's gone Astray my soul's desire is.

2. Lo, now, the idle wish! To hide from spies and watchers
That which the winds to all Bewray my soul's desire is.

3. A holy night and dear As that of Fore-appointment [385]
With thee, my fair, to lie Till day my soul's desire is.

4. Alack, that pearl unique, So dainty and so lovesome,
In the dark night to cleave In tway [386] my soul's desire is!

5. Lend me thine aid, o East, [387] To night, for in the dawntide,
To blossom forth, like rose On spray, my soul's desire is.

6. So honour I thereby May gain, with mine eyelashes
The dust to sweep upon Thy way my soul's desire is.

7. Like Hafiz, [388] scurril songs To make, how much soever
My censors thereagainst Inveigh, my soul's desire is. [389]

[385] i. e. that commonly (in error) called the Night of Power.
[386] i. e. *Vaginam amicae forare gestio.*
[387] According to Soudi, "the East [Wind]"here means the Grace of God, Divine Favour.
[388] "Like Hafiz", a phrase constantly occurring in the last couplets of the Odes; it means, "as is the usance or wont of Hafiz, i.e. as is my wont". "Hafiz" here substituted for "myself, on account of the rule which prescribes the insertion of the poet's name in the last couplet of a ghazel.
[389] It will hardly be believed that the commentators insist upon interpreting even this unmistakably "scurril" song mystically. "May God forgive them"'.

LXXXII

1. O hoopoe of the East, [390] To Sheba's air [391] I send thee;
Consider thou and look From whence to where I send thee.

2 Pity a bird like thee Should roost on sorrow's dust-heap!
Hence to Faith's nesting place And Honour's lair [392] I send thee.

3. No stage in Love's way is Of nearness or of farness; [393]
I see thee face to face And greeting fair I send thee. [394]

4. Morning and evening, by The North wind and the East wind,
The wish's caravan, "Well mayst thou fare!" I send thee.

5. O absent from my sight, That in my heart abidest,
I greet thee from afar And praise and prayer I send thee.

6. So that the hosts of grief Thy heart's dominions waste not,
My soul, for provender 'Gainst cark and care, I send thee.

7. So that the minstrels known May make to thee my longing,
Verses and ditties, set To many an air, I send thee.

8. Skinker, a voice from heav'n Gave me glad tidings, saying,
"Be patient under pain: For solace rare I send thee."

9. In thine own countenance God's handiwork consider;
A God-revealing glass, [395]—My heart laid bare—, I send thee.

10. Hafiz, the praise of thee Is our assembly's burden;
Hasten, for horse to ride And wede to wear I send thee. [396]

[390] The East Wind likened to the hoopoe, which was the go-between Solomon and the
    Queen of Sheba.
[391] The abode of the Beloved.
[392] The abode of the Beloved.
[393] There is no distance for the lover's imagination.
[394] Addressed to the absent Beloved.
[395] Thy countenance, in which God reveals Himself by His handiwork, thou mayst see
    reflected in the mirror of my heart, which contains nothing but thine image; hence
    the lover's heart called a God-revealing mirror.
[396] Apparently spoken by one of the poet's patrons.

LXXXIII

1. O gone from sight, to God The keeping I commend of thee;
My soul thou rack'st; yet dear To me's the thought, o friend, of thee.

2. What while the gravecloth's skirt I trail not underneath the dust,
Believe me, from the skirt My hand shall never wend of thee.

3. The prayer-niche of thy brows Display, that in the dawn the hand
Of prayer I may uplift [397] And to the neck append of thee.

4. Though to Haróut it should In Babylon [398] behove me go,
I'd work an hundred spells, To me the heart to bend of thee.

5. Nay, suffer, of thy grace, That, of the burning of my heart,
Pearls from mine eyes I still Upon the feet may spend of thee.

6. About me, with my tears, An hundred rivers have I made,
In hope the seed of love The stony heart may rend of thee.

7. It [399] shed my blood and thus From parting's pangs delivered me;
So to the sworder-glance My thanks therefor I send of thee.

8 Before thy face I fain Would die. O faithless leach, at least,
Of the sick man enquire; For still this hope I tend of thee.

9. Wine, wench and wantonness, Hafiz, are none of thine affair:
Egad, I wash my hands (Excepting thou amend) of thee.

[397] As an amulet. As is well known, an outstretched hand is one of the most common
forms of amulet against the evil eye.
[398] Harout and Marout were two angels, who, being sent down to earth on a mission,
yielded to the seductions of a beautiful woman and fell into mortal transgression; for
which they were imprisoned by God, head downward and in chains, in a well at
Babylon, where they are fabled to instruct mortals in magic. Hence Babylon is for
the Muslims the metropolis of sorcery.
[399] i. e. the beloved's glance.

LXXXIV

1. Lord, of thy favour, cause That my Loved One safe and hale
Return and deliver me From the clutches of blame and bale.

2. Bring, bring of the dust of the way Of the Friend departed hence,
So heal that I may withal My world-wearied eye of its ail.

3. That mole and that down and that tress, That cheek and that face and that shape,
From all the six quarters at once, The path of my heart assail.

4. To day, whilst I'm yet in thy hand, Some little compassion display!
To morrow, when I shall be dust, Will tears or repentance avail?

5. O thou, that so learnedly prat'st Of Love, with expounding and proof,
With thee we have nothing to do: Begone thou in peace with thy tale!

6. O dervish, lament nor complaint Of lovelings' oppression make thou;
For these be a sort that are wont To take of their victims blood-mail.

7. Fire, fire, to the patchcoat come set; For the curve of the cupbearer's brow
O'er prayer-niche and portico-arch Of mosque and Imám doth prevail. [400]

8. Since lovelings' injustices all Sheer favour and pleasantness are,
Far be it from me, then, that I Thy cruelty e'er should bewail!

9. Nay, never is Hafiz at end With the tale of the chain of thy tress;
For this, though prolonged till the Day Of the Rising, would nevermore fail.

[400] i. e. Let us forswear pietism and hypocrisy; for the curve of the beloved s eye hath drawn all men to worship thereat and caused the regular places of worship to be deserted. *Imám*, the *foreman* or leader of a Muslim congregation at prayer, who acts as fugleman to the believers in the minute and complicated ritual of Muslim public worship.

LXXXV

1. To yonder Friend heart-soothing Thanks with complaint I mell;
If love's finesse thou wottest, List to the tale I tell.

2. All that I wrought of service Thank-and-reward-less passed;
God, be none else allotted Lord so implacable!

3. To topers athirst none giveth A drop of water to drink;
'Twould seem that the lovers of merit Have bidden the realm farewell!

4. O heart, of the snare of her tresses Beware; for therein to be seen
Are heads, for no fault dissevered, Of lovers uncountable.

5. Thine eye with its glances drinketh Our blood and thou sufferest it.
O soul, 'tis not lawful to further The bloodshedder fierce and fell!

6. Amidward this night of blackness, Lost, lost, is the way of my wish:
Arise, o thou star of guidance, And shine from thy secret cell!

7. Wherever I turn, there's nothing Increaseth on me save fear;
Oh, out on this way unending, This desert unsearchable!

8. No end unto this Love's highway May be conceived; for lo!
An hundred thousand stages, E'en in its first, befell.

9. My heart, o thou sun of the lovely, A-boil is. Suffer me,
Though but for a breath, in the shadow Of thy protection dwell!

10. Mine honour though thou hast ravished, Thy door I'll not forsake.
Friend's harshness than enemies' favour Is more acceptable.

11. Love to thine outcry only Cometh, though thou by heart
The Koran in all the versions, Like Hafiz, know full well. [401]

[401] i. e. Love is the only remedy for thy woes; learning and piety will avail thee nothing. The seven authoritative Versions or Readings of the Koran are those of Abou Umr, Nafi, Ibn Kethir, Hemzeh, Ibn Aamir, Aasim and Kisai; and there are two Traditions as to the method of reading each, the whole being known as "the

Fourteen Relations".

LXXXVI

1. I'm drunken still with yonder Curled browlock's fragrant air of thine;
Confounded with the witchery Of that false eye I fare of thine.

2. Shall we a night, I wonder, After such patience, see, wherein
We may the vision's candle Light in that niche of prayer of thine?

3. The eyeball's middle blackness For this unto my heart is dear
That it for me the likeness Of yon swart mole doth wear of thine.

4. If thou the world be minded At once for ever to adorn,
The East wind bid a moment The veil from that face tear of thine;

5. And if the use of transience From out the world thou'dst cast, thy head
But shake, so souls by thousands May rain from every hair of thine.

6. Two helpless, errant wretches, The East wind and myself, we are;
I drunk with thine eye's sorcery, It with that browlock's air of thine. [402]

7. Hail, Hafiz's lofty spirit! Since of this world and that his eyes
Hold nought, the dust excepted Of yonder street, my fair, of thine! [403]

[402] Rhyme word of line I here repeated in original.
[403] i. e. Bravo for Hafiz's magnanimity (high-mindedness), in that, of all the goods of
this world and the next, he regardeth nothing but the dust of the Beloved's street!

LXXXVII

1. Now praiséd be God That open the winehouse's door is,
for thereto addressed The face of our wish evermore is!

2. All drunken with glee, In clamour and ferment the jars are;
The liquor therein Reality, not metaphor, is.

3. In *her*, [404] sooth to say, All drunkenness, swagger and pride is;
All weakness in *us*, Imploring and sufferance sore is.

4. A secret, that ne'er I've told nor will tell to the vulgar,
I'll tell to the Friend; For skilled she in mystery's lore is.

5. Her tress, curl on curl, T' unfold, in the way of abridgment,
Impossible 'tis, For this is the longest of stories.

6. The cheek of Mehmóud With Ayaz's foot and the browlock
Of Leila still linked With the burden of Mejnoun's heart's core is. [405]

7. Mine eye from the sight Of the world I have seeled, like the falcon,
Since open it on The cheek of the maid I adore is.

8. Whoever himself To thy village's Kaabeh betaketh,
For th'arch of thy brows, In the eye-point of prayer at thy door is. [406]

9. Companions, the case Of the fire in the heart of poor Hafiz
Of the candle enquire, That melting and burning e'ermore is.

[404] The Beloved.
[405] i. e. Love's pains and burdens are inseparable from its pleasures. Ayaz was the
favourite slave of Sultan Mehmoud of Ghezni, the famous conqueror of India.
[406] The Beloved's abiding-place likened to the Holy House at Mecca, which is the
"eye" or centre of the Kibleh or point of direction of Muslim prayer.

LXXXVIII

1. Sum and produce of this Workshop Of the Sphere, all this is nought;
Wine come bring; for the world's business, Goods and gear, all this is nought.

2. Heart and soul ensue the honour Of the Loved One's company;
That is every thing; without it, Life and cheer, all this is nought.

3. What, without heart's bloodshed, cometh To the hand good fortune is;
Heaven won with toil and striving Were too dear; all this is nought.

4. Be not thou for shade beholden To the Touba or the Lote;
Look but well, o cypress-shaped one; 'Twill appear, all this is nought.

5. Take and use the five days' respite In this inn to thee vouchsafed;
Rest in peace, for time and season, Day and year, all this is nought.

6. Skinker, on the brink we tarry Of the sea of transience;
Seize th' occasion, lip-to-mouth like, While it's here; all this is nought.

7. Of discredit reck thou nothing And be gladsome as the rose;
For the fleeting world-all's puissance, Joy and fear, all this is nought.

8. Rest thou not assured, o zealot, 'Gainst the wiles of zeal: [407] beware!
For from cell to Magians' convent, Far or near, all this is nought. [408]

9. Need of proving and expounding What I suffer, I the lean
Sorrow-stricken man, there is not; Nay, 'tis clear; all this is nought.

10. Hafiz' name the seal of honour Hath received; but loss and gain,
Blame and honour, in the toper's Eye and ear, all this is nought. [409]

[407] Be not deluded into false security by zeal.

[408] Difference of forms in religion is nothing, the intent is everything. A good Guebre or Christian is better than a hypocritical Muslim.

[409] i. e. in the sight of the servants of the ideal, the censure and approval of the profane are as the other goods and ills of the world, i. e. nought.

LXXXIX

1. What kindness 'twas that, all at once, The droppings of thy quill
Our dues of service have recalled Unto thy gracious will!

2. Greeting to me with the pen's point Thou sendest: may thy writ
This workshop of vicissitudes (God grant!) for ever fill! [410]

3. I say not, 'twas in error thou Rememb'redst heart-lorn me;
For error, reason reckoneth, There is not in thy quill. [411]

4. Scorn thou me not, if but in thanks For this especial grace,
That constant Fortune holdeth thee In fame and honour still.

5. Come, with thy tress-tip so I may A compact make, that ne'er,
Although it perish, from thy feet My head uplift I will.

6. Thy heart will only then become Aware of this our case,
When tulips blossom from then dust Whom grief for thee did kill.

7. To every rose the East wind tells The story of thy tress:
How won the talebearer to thee, Despite the warder's skill?

8. Vouchsafe to succour with a draught Thy lovers' thirsting souls
Since They [412] the cup of Jem for thee Brim up with Khizr's rill. [413]

9. My heart abideth at thy door: I prithee, hold it dear,
Seeing that God hath holden thee Secure from pain and ill.

10. The world's a place of snares and yet Thou farest fast: have heed
Lest in the road of nothingness The Fates thy dust should spill.

11. Fair fall thy days, o Jesus-breathed East wind; for with new life
Poor Hafiz' sorrow-smitten soul Thy fragrant breathings thrill.

[410] i. e. Mayst thou live for ever!
[411] Rhyme of line 1 repeated here in original.
[412] "They", i. e. Fate and Fortune Foreordained.
[413] i. e. the water of life.

XC

1. Who, o celestial loveling, Thy face-veil's knot unties?
Who gives thee seed and water, O Bird of Paradise?

2. For this thought heart-consuming, Whose bosom is the place
And homestead of thy slumber, Sleep hath forsworn mine eyes.

3. All suddenly thou wentest From me, heart-wounded one:
I wonder, in what quarter Thy place of slumber lies!

4. 'Tis plain, o fair, that lofty Thy dignity is grown,
Since not a jot thou heark'nest To my complaining sighs.

5. Thou ask'st not of the wretched: I fear me, no concern
Of pardon or requital Thy spirit occupies. [414]

6. O palace, heart-enkindling, That art my love's abode,
God grant thou be not ruined Of Time's calamities!

7. Far, in this waste, 's the well-spring; Beware! thy mazéd sight
Lest, with the mocking mirage, The desert-ghoul surprise.

8. The shaft, that at my bosom Thou launched'st, went astray;
I wonder what thy malice will after this devise!

9. I wonder how the pathway Of eld thou'lt fare, o heart!
God knoweth that youth's season Thou'st spent on idle wise.

10. Thine eye wine-selling [415] stoppeth The way on lovers' hearts;
Forsooth, 'tis mortal poison, The wine which it supplies.

11. Hafiz no slave that fleeth His lord is: show thou grace;
Come back, or e'er, of grieving For thy despite, he dies.

[414] i. e. thou reckest not of the final reckoning, when God shall requite all according to
their deeds.
[415] Beloved's eye called "wine-selling", because of its intoxicating glances.

XCI

1. That fay-faced Turk, from-us-ward That yesternight away went,
What fault saw she, I wonder, That she towards Cathay went?

2. When that eye world-displaying From this our sight departed
Such things from out our vision, As speech can not convey, went.

3. Such smoke last night no candle From its heart's fire emitted
As from our bosom's burning, For grief without allay, went.

4. Since from her cheek I parted, From mine eye's fount each moment
A flood of tears, a deluge Of anguish and dismay, went.

5. To earth, when parting's sorrow Came, fell we and in anguish
We linger, since the med'cine, That was our only stay, went.

6. "Yet", quoth the heart, "her union By prayer may be re-gotten".
Long is it since my life-time In other than prayer's way went!

7. Why don the pilgrim-garment, Since Mecca is no longer?
Why weary in "the Running", Since Sefa from Merwéh went? [416]

8. For pity, when he saw me, "Alack, that this thine ailment
"Beyond the reach of healing," The leach last night did say, "went!"

9. Bestir thee of poor Hafiz To ask, ere "Yestereven",
They say, "He forth this hostel Of ruin and decay went." [417]

[416] i. e. why should I set out to visit the Loved One's quarter, since radiance easance
(*Szefa*) from the village (*Merweh*) departed, i. e. since she hath depart thence? Sefa
(*Szefa*) and Merweh are two hills near Mecca, the running backward and forward
seven times between which is one of the ceremonies of the Pilgrimage, intended to
commemorate the wanderings of Hagar.
[417] i. e. he hath departed this life.

XCII

1. Place, save thy sill, for me beneath The firmament is not;
Except this doorway, for my head Shelter or tent is not.

2. If the foe [418] draw the sword on us, The shield away we cast,
Since weapon in our hand, except Sighs and lament, is not.

3 Why from the vintner's quarter turn My face, since better path
Or way in all the world than this, For my intent, is not?

4. Into the harvest of my life If Time cast fire, say "Burn;"
For in mine eyes the whole thereof Worth one grass-bent is not.

5. Thrall to yon wanton straight-shaped maid's Narcissus-eye am I,
Wherein regard for man, for wine Of self-content, is not. [419]

6. Since snares and toils, on every side, Spread in the path I see,
Save by thy tress's shade, to me Asylum lent is not.

7. Go with drawn bridle-rein, [420] o queen Of beauty's realm; for end
Of road there's not where one who cries For solacement is not. [421]

8. Ensue not after cruelty And do what else thou wilt;
For otherwhat than this by sin In our Law [422] meant is not.

9. The eagle of oppression's spread His wings o'er all the land;
Therein recluse's bow or shaft Of his lament is not. [423]

10. The treasure of poor Hafiz' heart Give not to tress or mole;
For every blackmoor for such trust, Sure, competent is not.

[418] i. e. the Beloved.
[419] The Beloved's eye (commonly styled "drunken" by the poets) is so intoxicated with
the wine of self-conceit that it hath no regard for any.
[420] i. e. slowly, to pay attention to thy lovers.
[421] i. e. Every street-end and corner is thronged with thy victims.
[422] The Law of Love.
[423] "The recluse's bow" is his body bowed in the act of prayer and the "arrow" his
sighs; i. e. there are no pious folk in the land, whose prayers might avert the calamity
of the time.

XCIII

1. Skinker, bring wine, for the month Of fasting and prayer hath past;
Give me the bowl, for the time Of worship and care hath past.

2. To waste went the precious time. Come, quick let us pay the arrears
Of an age, that sans flagon and cup And minstrel and fair hath past.

3. On fire of repentance how long, Thus, aloes-wood like, shall we burn?
Give wine, for our life over long In idle despair hath past.

4. Come, make thou me drunk on such wise That for ecstacy I may ignore
Who fareth the plain of the thought, Who whence and who where hath

5. On the stone bench of prayer for thy weal, Each morn and each eve of our life
In the hope that a draught from thy cup May fall to our share, hath past.

6. To the heart of the soul, that was dead, Lo! life hath been added anew,
Since a waft o'er its palate of smell From the scent of thy hair hath past.

7. The bigots misled by conceit, The road of salvation fare not;
But the sot to the Garden of Peace, [424] By the pathway of prayer, hath past.

8. What heart's ready money I had On wine have I spent; 'twas base coin
And therefore to uses unfit And fashions unfair hath past.

9. Admonish ye Hafiz no more: For never a lostling yet found
The way of salvation, adown Whose gullet wine e'er hath past.

[424] i. e. Paradise

XCIV

1. Since in my heart for her Abode concern hath taken,
Like to her tress, my soul Blackness nocturn hath taken.

2. Life's water is her lip Like fire; and from its water
There sprang a fire that on Our heart, in turn, hath taken.

3. The Huma [425] of my wish Long since for the enjoyment
Of that thy shape with all Its heart to yearn hath taken.

4. Enamoured of her form And height august I'm fallen,
For that the lover's need The height etern hath taken.

5. Since in her favour's shade Content we were, why is it
That she her, shade from us, I fain would learn, hath taken?

6. The morning breeze to day With ambergris is scented;
Belike my friend the way Of mead and burn hath taken.

7. In chains of shining pearls The ocean of my weeping
The vessel of the world, From stem to stern, hath taken.

8. The speech of Hafiz, since, O cypress jasmine-bosomed,
Thy shape it hath described, The earth to spurn hath taken.

[425] Huma; see previous note

XCV

1. Queen of mine, thou go'st so goodly That for thee outright I die;
Turk of mine, thou swayest sweetly; For thy shape and height I die.

2. "When," sayst thou, "wilt die before me?" O my soul, what need of haste?
Lo, thou ask'st and ere thine asking Ended is, forthright I die.

3. I'm a drunken, exiled lover: Where's the idol-cupbearer?
Sway thy graceful stature hither, Till before thy sight I die.

4. Bid ye her, for whose estrangement 'Tis a lifetime that I'm sick,
"Give a look, so of thy glances, Darkling as the night, I die."

5. "Pain," sayst thou, "my lip of ruby Giveth, ay, and medicine."
Of thy pain and of thy med'cine, Turn by turn, poor wight, I die.

6. Gracefully thou goest swaying, Far from thee the evil eye!
At thy feet may (this one fancy Have I in my spright) I die!

7. Though no room there be for Hafiz In thy favour's sanctuary,
For thine every place, whose every Place is good and right, I die. [426]

[426] i. e. I will be content with the humblest place in thy favour, if thou wilt deign to
    look upon me with kindness.

XCVI

1. Long for her the fire of passion Burneth in this soul of ours,
Through the yearnings that this wasted Heart do still control of ours.

2. In blood-water of the liver Mine eye-apple have they drowned;
Hence the sun-fount of her cheek is In this breast in dole of ours. [427]

3. Khizr's water [428] but a trickle From that sugared ruby lip,
And a reflex, from that moon-face, Is the round sun's bowl, of ours.

4. Since the verse "I breathed thereinto Of my breath" [429] I heard, 'tis plain
To my mind that we of hers are And she part and whole of ours.

5. Apprehension of Love's myst'ries Is not giv'n to every heart;
Nay, that high and subtle secret's Known but to this soul of ours. [430]

6. Prate no longer, o expounder Of the Faith; for lo! our faith
In both worlds is the enjoyment Of that Loved One sole of ours. [431]

7. Hafiz, give God thanks for ever That, from the First Day, ordained
Was yon fair this soul to mate with, Comfort and console of ours.

[427] Pupil of the eye likened to the ruby, which (as before explained) the Persians
believe to become red by exposure, on fresh liver, to the sun-rays. Hence, the poet
says, "My eye-apple, being drowned in the blood of my liver", which, it must be
remembered, is, for the Persians, the seat of love, "is rubified by the sun-fount (i. e.
source of light) of thy radiant cheek, whose image is ever abiding in my bosom".
[428] "Khizr's water", i. e. the water of life.
[429] [Said the Lord] "I shaped it (the human form) and breathed thereinto of My breath
(spirit)", Koran XV, 29. The poet means that, as all souls are made of the breath of
God, his soul and that of the Beloved are necessarily one and the same.
[430] Rhyme-word of 1. I here repeated in original.
[431] i. e. The love of the Beloved's our whole religion.

XCVII

1. The image of thy face to us In every road way-mate is;
The bond of this our soul attent [432] The scent of thy tress-plait is.

2. In answer to the cavillers, Who Love forbid, the beauty
Of thy fair face an argument, That suff'reth no debate, is.

3. Hark, how the apple of her chin Declareth, "Many a Joseph
"Of Egypt fallen in our pit, Attracted by our bait, is."

4. If thy long tresses to attain To us be unvouchsaféd,
The fault but that of our short hand [433] And of our sorry fate is.

5. Say unto him who keeps the door Of that thy privy-chamber,
"Lo, such an one [434] of those that haunt The threshold of our gate is:

6. "Though in appearance from the sight Of us he be excluded,
"He ever present to the eye Of this our mind sedate is.

7. "If Hafiz at the portal knock On beggar-fashion, open;
"For on our moonface, many a year, He longingly await is."

[432] *Agah*, conscious, attent, wary. The meaning of this epithet is not obvious.
[433] "Short hand", Persian idiom for "lack of power".
[434] i. e. the poet himself.

XCVIII

1 If default from out thy musky Tress's hair hath past, 'tis past;
If from thy swart mole oppression To our share hath past, 'tis past.

2. If Love's levin burn the harvest Of the wool-wearer, 'tis burned;
If unright from King to beggar Poor and bare hath past, 'tis past.

3. If a heart must bear a burden From the charmer's glance, 'tis borne;
'Twixt the soul and the Beloved Whatsoe'er hath past, 'tis past.

4. Thanks to talebearers and sland'rers, Still reproach and blame arise;
But 'twixt friends if aught unseemly, Aught unfair, hath past, 'tis past.

5. In love's way forbid vexation Is of spirit. Bring thou wine;
Every trouble, like all gladness That whilere hath past, 'tis past.

6. To the game of Love long-suff'ring Appertaineth: heart, stand fast;
If chagrin or if oppression O'er thee there hath past, 'tis past.

7. Blame not Hafiz that the cloister He forsook. The freeman's foot
Bind how wilt thou? If it unto Anywhere hath past, 'tis past.

XCIX

1. Each man of happy sight, who would The way of heart's content fare,
Doth to the tavern-nook, the house Of will and free intent, fare.

2. The pilgrim, with the half-maund cup, All mysteries resolveth
Of the Unseen, that in the world, To vision evident, fare. [435]

3. Come and hear wisdom from my lips; For thence do words, still pregnant
With profitable subtleties, By Gabriel's favour lent, fare.

4. Nought but debauchery seek ye From me; for this same usance
Doth with the star that ruled my birth Forever in consent fare. [436]

5. On the wrong hand thou rosest up [437] This morning: peradventure
Did last night's tale of wine beyond Thy fitting complement fare. [438]

6. Except that leach, the Jesus-breathed, A miracle accomplish,
Long since past visits did my case And past medicament fare.

7. A thousand thanks that Hafiz from The winehouse nook, yest'reven,
Did to the coign of piety And faith obedient fare!

[435] i. e. the spiritual mysteries that exist in the Visible World.

[436] i. e. I w predestined to be a toper.
[437] *Sic.* The meaning is the same as our similar phrase.
[438] Addressed to a caviller.

C

1. Never once her lip of ruby Did we pree; and she is gone;
Ne'er our fill her moon-like visage Did we see;—and she is gone.

2. 'Twas as weariness possessed her Of our company; for she
Bound her burdens on, departed Hastily,—and she is gone.

3. Fátihéh [439] and Charm of Yemen [440] Oft recited we and blew, [441]
After we had said the chapter "Unity"; [442]—and she is gone.

4. "Never from thy wish's quarter," Coaxing, said she, "will I go."
How we bought her false caresses Seen have ye;—and she is gone.

5. "Whoso seeketh mine enjoyment From himself," quoth she, "must part."
Self from self, in hope of union, Did we free;—and she is gone.

6. In the meads of grace and beauty Went she proudly; but alack!
In the rose-garth of her favours Walked not we;—and she is gone.

7. All night long, as Hafiz' wont is, I bewail me that to take
Leave of her it was not granted Unto me;—and she is gone.

[439] First chapter of the Koran.
[440] A prayer of Mohammed's.
[441] As a charm. Blowing is a part of the machinery of Eastern sorcery; the Koran
    speaks of witches as "blowers upon knots".
[442] The 112th Chapter of the Koran, used as a charm.

CI

1. Alack, for the Loved One left us In sorrow and pain and went;
Like smoke on the top of the furnace She caused us remain and went.

2. She gave not a cup to the cropsick Of Love's mirth-kindling wine,
But caused us to taste of the bitter Of sev'rance's bane and went.

3. When once I was fallen her booty, Me wounded and sick at heart
In the sea of chagrin she abandoned, Her steed gave the rein and went.

4. "By practice", quoth I, "I may bring her In bonds." But at me she took fright,
Affrighted the steed of my fortune And broke through the chain and went.

5. When the blood of my heart in my bosom The place on it straitened found,
By the road of the eye, Gulgóun-like, [443] It fled to the plain and went.

6. Since fortune of service accepted Was not to the slave vouchsafed,
The threshold to kiss and obeisance To make he was fain and went.

7. The rose in the veil's secluded; The bird of the morning-tide
Came late into Hafiz's garden And made his complain and went.

[443] *Gulgoun*, "Rose-colour", was the name of Khusrau Perwiz's horse. For a study of the curious colours which horses assume (by reason of close shaving of the hair and climatic influences) in the East, see Fromentin, "Un Été dans le Sahara". The lover's bloody tears are likened to Gulgoun for obvious reasons.

CII

1. There's none who fallen victim Unto thy tress is not;
Who is there in whose pathway Snare of duresse is not?

2. 'Tis as thy face a mirror Were of the Light Divine;
Ay is't; and in this saying Two-facédness is not. [444]

3. The zealot bids me turn from Thy face: O rare! In him,
Before thy face and heaven, Lo! shamefastness is not!

4. Weep, candle of the morning, For my case and thine own;
For thine or mine this hidden Fire of distress is not. [445]

5. God witness is (and witness Sufficient God is) that
My tear than the blood-shedding Of martyrs less is not. [446]

6. Thine eye would the narcissus Fain ape; but in its head
And eye, poor wretch, or knowledge Or lightsomeness is not.

7. Busk not thy locks, 'fore heaven; For ours a night, when we
Not with the East wind battle For that thy tress, is not.

8. I, when she went, "Thy promise Keep, idol", said; and she
"Thou dot'st; such thing, at present, [447] As faithfulness is not".

9. Since from the corner-sitters [448] Thine eye the heart doth steal,
Sure, in thy train to follow For us excess is not.

10. Come back, for in the banquet Of friends, without thy face,
O heart-enkindling candle, Light or liesse is not.

11. What if the Magian Elder My teacher be? There's ne'er
A head where some God's secret, For more or less, is not.

12. To say, in the sun's presence, "I am the fount of light",
For little stars befitting, The wise confess, is not.

13. Fair fame by stranger-tending Is gotten: soul, 'twould seem
The usance in thy city Of gentilesse is not. [449]

14. Needs must the lover suffer The shafts of censure: shield
For champion 'gainst the arrows Of Fate and stress is not.

15. Lo, in the zealot's cloister, As in the Soufi's cell,
Except thine eyebrows' angle, A prayer-recess is not.

16. O thou, whose hand in Hafiz' Heart's blood is dipped, in thee,
'Twould seem, against God's Koran Fear to trangress is not.

[444] i. e. this is sincerely said; there is no doubt about it; the word "*roui*" "two-facedness" also = "face", simply; it is here used with a secondary meaning of "There is no dissembling in that (the Beloved's) face".
[445] i. e. "It is not only thy lot or my lot to burn; it is common to both of us".
[446] i. e. It is as great a sin to shed my tears as to shed the blood of martyrs.
[447] syn. "In this age"; used p. g.
[448] i. e. The pious recluses
[449] Addressed to the Beloved.

CIII

1. Eye there is not from thy face's Radiance full of light that is not;
To thy threshold's dust beholden, Yea, there is no sight that is not. [450]

2. Lookers on thy face all mortals Are that are possessed of vision;
There's no head fulfilled with longing For thy browlocks bright that is not.

3. If, of sorrow for thee, crimson Forth my tears come, 'tis no wonder:
There's no talebearer confounded At his own unright that is not. [451]

4. Nay, mine eyes, that are beholden To thy threshold's dust for tutty,
There's no doorway-dust beholden To them day and night that is not. [452]

5. So no grain of dust may settle From the breeze upon thy raiment,
There's no passage-way a torrent With my tears at height that is not!

6. To the tenderlings forbidden Is Love's travel; yea, forbidden;
In that way's least step no peril Is to left and right that is not.

7. So of thy locks' scent they prate not Every where, there's not a morning
There, betwixt me and the breezes, Wrangling and despite that is not.

8 'Tis not meet that secrets issue Forth the veil; although there's nothing
In th' assembly of the topers Proved and known outright that is not.

9. Of my luckless star I plain me, Since, myself excepted, sharer
In the blessings from thy quarter Flowing there's no wight that is not.

10. Of its shame before the sweetness Of thy lip, o fount of honey,
There's no sugar into syrup Melted at thy sight that is not.

11. Not I only, heart-bereft one, For thy sake am bloody-livered;
There's no heart, for thy sweet sorrow, Marry, in like plight that is not.

12. Nay, the lion, in the desert Of thy love, a fox becometh;
Out upon this way, where peril Is there nor affright that is not!

13. This much trace of my existence Still is mine, that it existeth;
Else therein no sign of sickness Is nor lack of might that is not.

14. Save this only point that Hafiz Still with thee is discontented,
In thy person, there's no merit, Ay, and no delight, that is not.

[450] i. e. for collyrium. The threshold-dust of the Beloved is the salve of the lover's eye.
[451] The tears disclose our love and blush (i. e. are dyed with blood) for consciousness
of their own ill-doing.
[452] i. e. for watering with their tears.

CIV

1. In the Magian Elder's favour Life and joyance without spare is;
In the winehouse-garden water, Yea, and wonder-goodly air is. [453]

2. It behoveth all the gen'rous At his feet to lay their foreheads;
Further comment on this subject, Of good breeding, to forbear is.

3. All the tale of Heaven's splendour And the High-built House [454] a figure
For the glory of the dwelling Of the grape-vine's daughter rare is.

4. After ruby wine our gen'rous Spirit seeketh, whilst the miser,
Striving after gold and silver, In the quest of wealth fore'er is.

5. In the Prime, o'er each man's forehead Passed the Pen of Fate in silence;
This the cause of mosque and josshouse, Hell the foul and Heav'n the fair, is.

6. Unvouchsafed, without the serpent, Is the treasure. [455] Leave thy prating;
Bouléhéb's despite with Ahmed's [456] Luck foreordered still to pair is.

7. True, a pure and perfect jewel Honour is; but thou, endeavour
For good works; for in high lineage And descent no honour there is.

8. In the quest of love and passion Day and night, for ever striving,
Hafiz' heart, by heaven's favour, In this self-same way [457] a-fare is.

[453] "Water-and-air" id. = climate. "Water" here may also mean "Wine" and "air "desire, love".

[454] According to Muslim legend, there once stood, on the site of Mecca, a temple of red cornelian. At the time of the Deluge, it was uplifted to the Seventh Heaven, where it now hangs, under the style of the Inhabited (or High-built) House, immediately over Mecca. Abraham is said to have built the Kaabeh in its likeness.

[455] i. e. There is no good without its drawbacks. Serpents, as well as treasures, are found in ruined places.

[456] "Ahmed", a form of "Mohammed see previous note as to *Bouleheb*.

[457] i. e. in the way of good works mentioned in Couplet 7.

CV

1 The curve of thy tress Of faith and unfaith the snare is;
And this but a jot Of the wildering craft of thy hair is.

2. Thy loveliness, sure, The miracle is of all beauty;
The tale of thy glance Sheer magic and sorcery bare is.

3. Thy lips still renew The miracles wroughten of Jesus;
The tale of thy locks The Rope of the Steadfast, [458] I swear, is.

4. On yonder black eye Be blessings an hundred! In slaying
Of lovers for it A sorcerer passing compare is.

5. This star-lore of Love, Wherein is the uppermost heaven
As nethermost earth, [459] A marvellous lore and a rare is!

6. Think not that by death The speaker of ill [460] his soul saveth;
With "Two August Scribes" [461] His account in the end of th' affair is.

7. The soul from thine eye, The wanton, can any deliver,
That ambushed in wait, With the bow of the eyebrow, fore'er is?

8. From the craft of her tress, O Hafiz, sit not in assurance;
Thy heart it hath ta'en And thy faith now intent to ensnare is.

9. In Time unbegun, A draught from Love's goblet drank Hafiz;
His drunkenness all And his toping unending from there is.

10. With constancy, heart, Like Hafiz, bear thou her caprices;
The lovelings 'caprice, Like themselves, ever lovesome and fair is.

[458] "The Rope of the Steadfast". "The Steadfast" is one of the names of God.
Mohammed (Koran III, 98) exhorts mankind to take fast hold of God's rope, (i. e.
His revelation through himself), whereby He may hoist them up to heaven; so
Beloved's tress compared to God's rope, as able to lift lovers to Paradise.
[459] i. e. the highest is as the lowest.
[460] i. e. the slanderer.
[461] i. e. The Recording Angels, of whom two are appointed to chronicle every man's
actions.

CVI

1. Gone the Fast and come the Feast is And all hearts to joy awake;
In the vat the wine astir is: Cup in hand behoveth take.

2. Past the time is of the dull-wit Traffickers in piety,
Come the season for the topers To rejoice and merrimake.

3. Howsoe'er the zealot censure Him like me who drinketh wine,
This no sin and no default is For the toper and the rake.

4. Better winebibbers, unsullied With dissembling and deceit,
Be than hypocrites professing Piety for profit's sake.

5. No dissembling mates, no topers Hypocritical are we;
Him who knoweth hearts to witness Of this case of ours we take.

6. God's commandments we accomplish And to no one ill we do;
And of what they say's unlawful, "It is lawful", ne'er we spake.

7. Wine the life-blood of the grape is, Not *your* blood. What matter, then,
With a cup or two if haply Thou and I our thirst should slake?

8. No such sin is this that any May thereby be damnified:
Fault if't be, a faultless mortal When did the Creator make?

9. Leave the prate of "How and Wherefore", Hafiz; drink a draught of wine:
What availeth "How and Wherefore" God's Foreordinance to break?

CVII

1. My heart of the world is weary And all that is therein;
There's nought in my mind save the Loved One, Of all the things that bin.

2. To me if a waft from the rosebed Of union with thee arrive,
My heart, like the bud, for joyance, Abideth not in its skin. [462]

3. Th'exhorting of me, the madman, Distraught in the way of Love,
Were nigh to the tale of the idiot And pitcher and stone akin. [463]

4. Go say to the bigot, sitting In solitude, "Blame us not
"If we've for our prayer-niche taken The curve of that eyebrow thin"

5. 'Twixt Kaabeh and Idol-temple No difference is: the Friend
Is present in every quarter, wherever the sight may win.

6. Caléndership's not in shaving Of eyebrows and beard and hair;
In hair-by-hair doing of duty It is and avoidance of sin.

7. Like Hafiz, the true Calénder Is he who renounceth self;
A trifle it is to part with The hair of the head and chin. [464]

[462] *Sic.*
[463] The Cadi Hemideddin Omar of Belkh (author of the *Mecamat* or Sessions, a
Persian commentary on the Koran) sent Anweri the poet a pitcher of grape-syrup, by
a halfwitted man, and gave the latter a letter to take with it. The messenger, by the
way, let the pitcher strike against a stone and broke it; then, continuing his journey,
he delivered the letter to Anweri, together with the neck and handle of the pitcher.
Anweri read the letter and asked for the grape-syrup; where-upon said the natural, "A
stone took it from me". "Then, why", "enquired Anweri, hast thou brought me
these?" pointing to the neck and handle of the pitcher. "To bear witness to the truth
of my story", replied the other. The application of the story to the poet's case is not
clear.
[464] The Calenders (see previous note) distinguish themselves from other mendicant
orders by shaving their heads and faces, eyebrows included.

CVIII

1. In view of the shape of the Friend, Of the cypress to speak were ill;
For the cypress erect from her shape Its loftiness borroweth still.

2. I picture me not her shape As that of the cypress, since
The cypress, though lofty it be, Grows wild in the meads at its will. [465]

3. The image still dwells in mine eye Of her cypress-like shape, because
The place of the cypress straight Was aye on the marge of the rill. [466]

4. The East of her tress and her down And her mole tells many a tale
To musk; whence comes it that musk Sweet savours doth so distil.

5. A line on her radiant face There is; but the new-risen moon
Or the curve of her brow if it be, To tell overpasseth our skill.

6. That man to the crook of the mall Of her tresses his head, like the ball,
Who giveth, a thousand dear lives, In ransom for him, would I spill!

7. The wish of the heart an thou seek, Thy need of her mouth do thou ask;
Ensue not, like Hafiz, her eye, That seeks but to trouble and kill.

[465] Whilst the Beloved, on the contrary, has been tenderly and carefully nurtured in the
house.
[466] Lover's tearful eye likened to a rill.

CIX

1. Say not, when the word of the wise Thou hearest, "The saying unfit is":
My fair, thou'rt no kenner of speech; The fault in thine own lack of wit is.

2. The head of me boweth not down To *this* world nor yet to the other;
No, (blessed be Heaven!) for all The tumult and coil that in it is.

3. Meknoweth not who is within This bosom of mine, the heart-wounded;
For I, I am silent and it In clamour and cry infinite is.

4. My heart is come forth of the veil Of patience: ho! where is the minstrel?
Come, sing to me quick, for my case Is lightened and eased by thy ditties.

5. I never had heed to the goods Of this weariful world; for its fairness
From that thy bright cheek, in mine eyes, All borrowed and drawn every whit is.

6. These hundred nights past I've not slept, For an image that haunteth my fancy;
Cropsick am I: where is the house Where the remedy,—wine, to wit—is?

7. Since thus with the blood of my heart Berayed are the cell and the cloister
With wine if ye wash me, the right In your hand (who can else but admit?) is.

8. In the Magians' convent, God wot, They hold me in honour and worship
For this, that a fire in my heart, That dieth not ever, alit is.

9. What instrument was it, indeed, That yesternight sounded the minstrel,
So life from me lapsed and my brain Still full of the sound of the fytte is?

10. Of the love of thee unto mine ear They yesternight made proclamation;
The plain of my heart, for desire, Of the sound of the cry yet unquit is.

11. Since first unto Hafiz there came The sound of the voice of the Loved One,
For yearning, the mount of his heart Yet full of the echo of it is.

CX

1. For our pain no cure, ywis, is. Help! Oh help!
For our woes no end in bliss is. Help! Oh help!

2. Faith and heart they've ta'en and threaten Now the soul:
'Gainst these cruel cockatrices, Help! Oh help!

3. Help, against the heart-enslavers Pitiless,
Souls who seek in price of kisses! Help! Oh help!

4. See, our blood they drink, these stony-Hearted trulls!
Muslims, say, what cure for this is? Help! Oh help!

5. Help the wretched, day of union! Save them from
Parting's long dark night's abysses! Help! Oh help!

6. Every time and tide betideth Some new pain
From that heartless fair's caprices. Help! Oh help!

7. Day and night, I fare distracted, Weep and burn,
As the wont of me, Hafiz, is. Help! Oh help!

CXI

1. Behoving 'tis that charmers all To thee should homage pay,
Crown-like, o'er all the lovelings' heads Of earth that holdest sway.

2. Thy tipsy eyes a trouble are Unto all Turkestán;
Yea, tribute to thy tresses' plaits Give India and Cathay.

3. The blackness of thy dusky tress Than midnight blacker is;
The whiteness of thy face more bright Than is the cheek of day.

4. For this my sickness, whence, indeed, Whence shall I healing find,
Except the anguish of my heart Enforce from thee allay?

5. To Khizr's water thy strait mouth Continuance gives; thy lip,
Like sugar candy, bears the vogue From Egypt's sweets [467] away.

6. Why breakest thou, o soul of mine, For stony-heartedness,
This heart of ours, that's frail as glass For weakness and dismay?

7. Thy shape's a cypress, waist a hair And bosom ivory;
Thy down is Khizr and thy lip Life's water doth purvey.

8. Strange that in Hafiz' head hath fall'n Love for a queen like thee!
Oh would that in thy threshold's dust A menial slave he lay!

[467] Egypt appears to have been celebrated for its refined sugar and sweetmeats.

CXII

1. If in thy canon the shedding The blood of the lover is right,
Good to us also seemeth That which is good in thy sight.

2. The black of thy tress declareth Of Him who appointed the dark [468]
And He who hath sundered the morning [469] Is shown of thy face's white.

3. From mine eyes to my lap a river Of tears, so deep that there
No sailor to swim availeth, Is running fore'er at height.

4. Thy lips, like the water of Khizr, The food of the soul contain
And in them the savour of wine is For earthly appetite.

5. From the grip of the noose of thy tresses Deliverance findeth none;
None 'scapeth the bow of thine eyebrow And shaft of thine eye of light.

6. Seek not at our hand repentance And grace and good works. Who looks
O lovers and sots and madmen For virtue and life contrite?

7. For an hundred of lovers' devices, Thy ruby lip giveth no kiss;
"or its wish can my heart of it compass, A thousand implorings despite.

8. Be ever the prayer for thy welfare The usance of Hafiz's tongue,
What while, in succession, there follow Each other the day and the night!

[468] "And He (God) appointed the darknesses and the light"; Koran, VI, I.
[469] [God] the Sunderer (or Cleaver open) of the Morning"; Koran, VI, 96.

CXIII

1. Behold the new moon of Muhérrem! [470] Quick, call for the goblet of wine.
Tis the month of assurance and safety, The first of the year benign.

2. Anent this base world and its fortunes, Go, let not the beggar strive:
The ball of success to the Sultan, O light of mine eyes, resign!

3. Behoveth the time of enjoyment To cherish; for swift of flight
It is, like the Day of the Handsel [471] And Night of Appointment Divine. [472]

4. Bring wine; for his day (and his only) In pleasance and good will pass
Who maketh the Cup of the Morning The lamp of the day in his eyne.

5. What fitting devotion can ever From me fuddle-headed proceed,
Who know not the Cry of the Even From "Cleaver of Morn," in fine? [473]

6. Of thine affair, heart, thou art heedless; And since thou hast lost the key,
I fear me that none, at thy calling, Will open the door of Love's shrine [474]

7. A night to day waken, like Hafiz, In hope of attainment; belike
The rose of thy fortune shall blossom, By th' Opener's [475] favour, and shine.

8. 'Tis Shah Shejáa's time [476] and the season Of wisdom and equity;
Be easance of heart and spirit, Both morning and evening, thine!

[470] Muherrem is the first month of the Muslim year and in it war is unlawful.
[471] Day of the Handsel", 20th Ramazan, date of surrender of Mecca to Mohammed.
[472] i. e. "Night of Power".
[473] i. e. who know not the difference between the calls to evening and to morning prayer.
[474] The key to Love's shrine is the due service of the beloved.
[475] i. e. God's.
[476] Shah Shejaa, Sultan of Fars, (A. D. 1359—1384) was a bon vivant and a debonair prince, who favoured poets and singers and allowed the drinking of wine. The name "Shĕjāa" is an iambic dissyllable and is also written "*Shujaa*". I have adopted Brockhaus's vocalization.

CXIV

1. My heart, for desire of the visage so fair Of Ferrúkh, [477]
Is tangled and mazed like the mazy hair Of Ferrukh.

2. There's no one excepting the Indian it be of her tress, [478]
Who's blest with the sight of the beauty so rare Of Ferrukh.

3. O happy that fair-fortuned blackmoor, for that it
The waymate and housemate is fore'er Of Ferrukh!

4. The proud garden cypress a-quake like the willow becomes,
At sight of the heart-luring stature and air Of Ferrukh.

5. Give, cupbearer, wine of the Redbud's hue, so we
A toast to the witching narcissus may bear Of Ferrukh.

6. My shape, for chagrin, is bended in twain like the bow,
Is bowed like the brows, for sorrow and care, Of Ferrukh.

7. The fragrance of Tartary musk is put to shame
By the waft of the ambergris-scented hair Of Ferrukh.

8. Yea, whithersoever men's hearts incline and tend,
My heart in the traces still doth fare Of Ferrukh.

9. The servant am I of his magnanimity,
Like Hafiz, who's bound in the tresses' snare Of Ferrukh.

[477] Apparently the name of the poet's mistress, although Soudi seems (from his referring to the object of this ode as Ferrukh Ago) to think the person eulogized an eunuch. He however gives no manner of reason for this supposition.
[478] Tress called "Indian" because of its blackness.

CXV

1. Sawest thou, o heart, the havoc That Love's pain hath wrought?
What, departing, she with lovers, True in vain, hath wrought?

2. That ensorcelling narcissus, [479] What a game't hath played!
And that tipsy one [479] to sober Folk what bane hath wrought!

3. As the afterglow [480] my tears are For her lovelessness.
See, what devastation Fortune Inhumane hath wrought!

4. Flashed from Leila's camp a levin In the dawn: alack
For what it with Mejnoun's harvest, Sorrow-slain, hath wrought!

5. Wine! None knoweth what the Limner Of th' Invisible,
In the compass of the ages' Wax and wane, hath wrought.

6. Nay, this mystery none knoweth, What behind the screen
He, who limned and fashioned yonder Azure plain, [481] hath wrought.

7. Thought of love the fire of sorrow Lit in Hafiz' heart:
See with comrade what old comrade [482] Once again hath wrought!

[479] The beloved's eye.
[480] i. e. ruddy (with blood).
[481] The heavens.
[482] The "old comrade" here referred to is Love, which long been the poet's familiar.

CXVI

1. The bulbul at dawn To the wind of the East his lament made
Of the havoc with him That the face of the rose and her scent made.

2. My heart all a-bleed With the bloom of that face Love hath rendered
And this my sad breast With the thorn of that rosebed all rent made.

3. The servant am I Of that lovesome one's soul, who good actions
Her practice, without Dissembling or fraud or ostent, made.

4. O sweet to her be That breeze of the dawn-tides, which ever
Hath solace for those, Who waken till night is forspent, made!

5. Of strangers no more I'll plain; for,—however they caused me
Annoy,—on like wise That Friend me to rue, of intent, made.

6. If aught of the king I hoped, 'twas a fault; from the charmer
The faith which I sought Oppression in her the event made.

7. On every side aye Have bulbuls enamoured lamented,
Whilst merry at will The wind of the East thereanent made;

8. Still drew back the veil Of the rose and the vest of the rosebud
Unbuttoned and loosed And the hyacinth's tresses y-sprent made.

9. Go bear the glad news To the winesellers' quarter that Hafiz
Of abstinence vain And fraud hath resolve to repent made.

CXVII [483]

1. 'Twas a bulbul drank his heart's blood And a rose his own made;
Jealous fortune's blast with hundred Thorns his heart to groan made.

2. Sugar hoping, joyed a parrot: but perdition's torrent
Hope's charáctery, effacing, As't had ne'er been known made.

3. Still remembered be that solace Of mine eyes, my heart's fruit!
Easy fled he and uneasy This my lot, when flown, made.

4. Cameleer, my load is fallen: Help me! For the journey
With this litter, I, relying On thy grace alone, made.

5. Scorn my dropping eyes and dusty Face not; for its pleasaunce
Of this straw-and-mud hath yonder Heaven's azure zone made. [484]

114

6. Woe that, for the eye invidious Of the moon of heaven,
Hath my bow-browed moon his dwelling 'Neath the graveyard stone made!

7. Hafiz, thou forgot'st to castle [485] And th'occasion past is.
Yet what help? Me Fortune's juggle Heedless of mine own made. [486]

[483] According to Soudi, this ode was written on the death of the poet's only son.
[484] Heaven, says Soudi, here = God; i. e. God delights in our frail human body, vile
mortal clay though it be.
[485] Figure taken from game of chess; i. e. (according to Soudi) thou neglectedst to
marry thy son, so that thou mightest have had grandchildren to console thyself withal
for his loss.
[486] i. e. Malignant Fortune's delusion made me overlook my own interest in this.

CXVIII

1. Come, for Heav'n's Turk a raid upon The Fast-tide's tray hath made; [487]
The Feast's new moon the sign to pass The wine-cup gay hath made.

2. Guerdon for fast and pilgrimage He only garnereth
Who visitation oft unto Love's winehouse-clay hath made.

3. Our true, our native dwelling place The tavern-corner is;
God guerdon him with good who this Abode (I pray) hath made!

4. Fair fall his prayers and suppliance, Who, thorough grief and pain,
With the eye's water and heart's blood, His soil away hath made! [488]

5. Look in the Friend's face: to this eye Be grateful; for what use
Of sight it maketh, it with true Discernment aye hath made.

6. What is the price of ruby wine? The jewel of the wit.
Drink, for he gaineth by this trade Who the essay hath made.

7. Out on the city elder, whose Askance narcissus-eye
Of those who drain the goblet's dregs Its mock to day hath made!

8 Prayer in the prayer-niche of thy brows He only offereth
Who with blood-water of the heart His soil away hath made. [489]

9. If the assembly of th' Imám Should question, "Shift to day
"For fulling [of his clothes] with wine The Soufi", say, "hath made." [490]

10. The tale of love from Hafiz hear, Not from the 'monisher,
For all th' expounding art whereof The wight display hath made.

[487] An allusion to the old custom of setting out, on certain days, a tray (i. e. table) of

food, for the Turkish body-guard of the Sultans of Baghdad to fall upon and scramble for, as a reminder and symbol of their origin and ancient custom of making their livelihood by pillage.

[488] i. e. weeping and contrition are the best ablution before prayer.

[489] A variant, with the same rhyme-word, of Couplet 4.

[490] The commentators give no explanation of this curious couplet, but the meaning appears to be that, if the orthodox and zelators ask what is become of Hafiz, they are to be boldly told that he hath set apart to-day for the cleansing of himself, by means of winebibbing, from the stains of hypocrisy and fraud, with which he had became polluted during his membership of the Soufi order.

CXIX

1. The sage with the shining water of wine His purification maketh,
What while of the winehouse, at break of day, He visitation maketh.

2. When hidden becometh the golden bowl Of the sun, the skinker's eyebrow,
That moon of the Festival, sign for the cup's Free circulation maketh. [491]

3. My heart from the curl of her tress, at the cost Of the soul, confusion buyeth:
I know not what profit it seeth, that it This speculation maketh.

4. Lo, even his rev'rence the Lord Imám, Him of long prayers who vaunteth,
God wot, of his gown, in the blood of the maid Of the vine, lustration maketh. [492]

5. Nay, come to the winehouse and see how near My station there to the throne is,
Albe us the zealot a butt for scorn And vilification maketh. [493]

6. The sign of the covenant of love From Hafiz' soul seek ever, [494]
Though sorrow for thee [495] of the house of the heart Sore spoliation maketh.

[491] The skinker's eyebrow likened to the new moon of Shewwal, the appearance of which is the signal for the ending of the Ramazan Fast and the beginning of the succeeding Festival.

[492] The usual quip at the pietists, accusing them of secret winedrinking.

[493] i. e., we are held in honour among topers and true lovers, though the pietists scoff at us.

[494] i. e. Hafiz may always be relied upon to keep his trothplight, how much soever he may suffer at the Beloved's hands.

[495] "Thee", i. e. the Beloved.

CXX

1. My way, like the breeze, To the Loved One's abode I will make;
My soul musky-breathed With the dust of her road I will make.

2. All honour and fame, That by learning and faith I have won,
As dust in the path Of that lovely one strowed I will make.

3. To waste, without wine And beloved, life lapseth amain;
Henceforward away With idleness' load I will make.

4. Where's the wind of the East? For my soul, blood-besteeped like the rose,
On the scent of her locks, As strewage, bestowed I will make. [496]

5. As the lamp of the morn [497] It is manifest grown unto me
That away with my life For her love, on this mode, I will make.

6. For the sake of thine eye, My self I'll lay waste and the base
Of the covenant old Withal firm and broad I will make.

7. Dissembling and fraud Give, Hafiz, not gladness of heart:
The pathway of Love And toping my road I will make.

[496] i. e. If the East wind (the messenger of the desireful lover) will bring me the scent
of her locks, I will give it my soul in exchange.
[497] i. e. the sun.

CXXI

1. Now that the rose in the meads To life is returned from the dead,
The violet prone at her feet Layeth in homage its head. [498]

2. The cup of the morning quaff To the clamour of tabret and harp;
Yea, kiss thou the cup-bearer's chin, To the warble of rebeck and reed.

3. Sit never in rose-time without Beloved and ghittern and wine,
For a week, like the season of life, Is the time of the roses red.

4. The earth, with the zodiac-signs Of the flow'rets, is grown as bright,
By the happy auspice of Spring, As the firmament overhead.

5. Arise; in the garden renew The rites of the Magians' creed,
Now Nimrod his fire once more Hath lit in the tulip-bed. [499]

6. At the hand of a lovely maid, A soft-cheeked one, Jesus-breathed,
Drink wine and of Aad and Themóud Be never a word more said! [500]

7. As the Garden Etern [501] is the world In the season of lily and rose:
But alack! what availeth? Therein [502] Was never abiding-stead.

8. Since, Solomon-like, on the air A rider the rose is grown, [503]
At dawn, from the throat of the bird When David's ditties are sped, [504]

9. Brim, brim thou the cup! To the health Of the Asef of this our age,
The Vizier Imádeddím, The blood of the grape be shed!

10. Come, Hafiz, from life in his time [505] Eternal felicity seek.
The shade of his grace o'er us For ever and aye be spread!

11. Bring wine; for Hafiz's trust On the mercy of God most High,
Forgiver of sins, is still And will be establishéd.

[498] The violet, which has of course a pensile habit, mostly (says Soudi) grows about
the skirts of the rose.
[499] i. e. Now that the tulip-bed is all aglow with fire-red blossom (likened to the fire
into which Nimrod is fabled by the Muslims to have cast Abraham and which
became a rosegarden under the latter's feet, it is time to renew the rites of Zoroaster
and to drink wine, that liquid fire.
[500] "Aad and Themoud", two tribes mentioned in the Koran (VII, 63); i. e. carpe diem;
concern yourselves not with the past.
[501] "The Garden Etern", one of the Eight Paradises.
[502] "Therein", i. e. in the world.
[503] The rose, as it sways to and fro in the breeze, likened to Solomon, as he rode upon
the wind.
[504] David is for the Mohammedans the type of the musician, as Joseph that of manly
beauty. Says the historian Tabari, "God sent David the Psalms and gave him a
goodly voice, so that he sang them to such fine airs and on such fair wise that none
ever heard the like; and when he went about to chant the praises of the Most High,
the birds of heaven came and settling about his head, hearkened to him. Moreover,
the mountains joined their voices to his, as is said in the Koran, 'We enforced the
mountains to celebrate Our praises with him night and morning,' (Koran XXXVIII,
17)." The whole story is, of course a fanciful enlargement upon the fact that David
was the responsible editor of a number of "Hymns Ancient and Modern" by various
writers, (many of which belonged to the ritual of other and older religions,)
published under his name.
[505] "His time", i. e. that of the aforesaid Vizier.

CXXII

1. The Soufi his snare set and open His trick-box anew hath made;
Ay, ready to bubble the heavens, That juggler of blue, hath made.

2. But the cup-and-ball player of Fortune Will e'en break the egg in his cap, [506]
Who bold sleight of hand with the folk Of the secret [507] to do hath made.

3. Come, cupbearer, prithee give wine; The Soufis' fair loveling is come
And of beauty and grace, the coquette, Display in our view hath made.

4. O whence is this minstrel, himself Who addressed to the mode of Irác
And then by the road of Hijaz [508] His home return who hath made? [509]

5. Come quick, o my heart! Let us go: Let us flee to the refuge of God
From the mischief which he of short sleeves And long hand thereto [510] hath made!

6. Dissembling use not; for the game Of Love if one play not aright,
In the face of his heart Love the door Of meaning shut-to hath made.

7. That day when the forefront of Truth Shall manifest be, put to shame
Shall he be who his feet in the path Of pretence to ensue hath made.

8. Where goest thou, partridge [511] so fair? Stay; be not deluded, because
The hypocrite-cat a pretence Of devoutness untrue hath made. [512]

9. Nay, Hafiz, the topers blame not; For God in Eternity's prime
Of pious hypocrisy quit The winebibbing crew hath made.

[506] i. e. flout him and put him to shame; alluding to a trick commonly played by jugglers on simple fellows, on whose head they set an egg, then, putting on the cap and giving it a smart blow, break the egg and make the yolk run down the victim's face, for the sake of raising a laugh among the spectators.
[507] i. e. Men of insight and knowledge.
[508] The mode of Irac is a cheerful and that of Hijaz a plaintive one. *Rah*, mode, measure, syn. "road".
[509] i. e. who began in one mode and after modulated into another.
[510] i. e. the Soufi, whom Hafiz constantly represents as a hypocritical oppressor and evil-doer, masking his villainies under a show of extreme piety.
[511] It is common with Persian poets to liken the Beloved's gait to that of the partridge
[512] Alluding to the popular fable of the cat, which, by feigning piety and absorption in devout exercises, lured a partridge into her snare and devoured it. In this couplet the poet means to warn young people against the tricks of the cunning and lascivious Soufis.

CXXIII

1. For Jem's cup our heart requirement Of us many a year made
And for what itself possesseth Suit to strangers sheer made;

2. For a pearl that in no oyster Is of Place-and-Being,
Of the lostlings of the seaboard Quest from far and near made.

3. Yesternight, my crux I carried To the Magian Elder,
Who by insight the solution Of th' enigma clear made.

4. Smiling-faced and blithe I found him, In his hand the winecup,
Wherein he an hundred visions Mirrored to appear made.

5. "When gave God this cup world-showing Unto thee?" I asked him.
"That same day whereon", he answered, "He the azure sphere made.

6. "Yonder friend, who made the gibbet Glorious, his crime was
"That he patent heaven's secrets To the general ear made. [513]

7. "Heart-bereft one, in all cases, God was ever with him;
"But he saw Him not and distant Him, when he was here, made.

8. "All that juggling show, that Reason Here against Love maketh,
"Erst, before the hand of Moses And his staff, Samír made. [514]

9. "If the Holy Spirit's favour Once more deigned assistance,
"Others yet would make the marvels Jesu's self whileare made."

10. "For what purpose are the idol's Chain-like locks?" I asked him.
"Hafiz' frenzied heart to fetter Were they," quoth the seer, "made."

[513] According to the commentators, the person here referred to was Sheikh Abou Mugheith El Husein Ibn Mensour, an ascetic, who was put to death (A. D. 919) by the Khalif Muctedir, on account of his practice of crying aloud, in the streets of Baghdad, "I am the Truth", i. e. "I am God". (This, at least, is the Soufi account; but the more probable explanation is that the person in question suffered for some political offence, the East and (*pace* the Bean-bag party) especially the Muslim East, being the land of religious toleration, where the most outrageous sectarian extravagations are winked at, as long as they are not used (as with the Bâbis and the modern so-called Eastern Christian) as a cover for intrigues á la Russe against the reigning power.) He appears to have been known as El Hellaj, the cotton dresser, probably from the name of his trade, and was regarded by the Soufis as almost divine, although they declare that he was allowed by God to suffer death, because he revealed the Divine secret of the unity of the devotee with the Deity. His disciples expected him to live again after forty days and Hafiz, adopting the Soufi opinion in this particular, alleges the very gibbet on which he suffered to have been glorified by

his touch. The expression "I am the Truth", (*Ana el Hhecc*), his use of which is asserted to have been punished by the Muslim bigots, as a blasphemous pretention to Divinity, is purely Soufistic and signifies that he felt himself, as a consequence of long practice of mystic contemplation and asceticism (Indian *Yoga*) absorbed into the Divine Unity. As says another Soufi, "I am God and God is I". Cf. Angelus Silesius ("Without me, God could not exist for a moment") and other European mystics, such as Böhme, Eckhard, Ruysbroek, etc. The three following couplets of the taverner's speech do not seem to apply to El Hellaj and I am therefore inclined to doubt whether the commentators are correct in supposing him to be the person referred to; but there is no indication in the original which warrants me in suggesting any more definite explanation.

[514] *Samir* or *Samiri*, a *Samaritan* juggler, who vied with Moses as a conjurer and to whom the Muslims attribute the making of the Golden Calf. As a matter of fact, he was a purely mythical personage, a creature of Mohammed's imagination.

CXXIV [515]

1. Renouncement, o friend, of seclusion The maid of the vine hath made;
With the Mohtesib's leave, her traffic She lawful, in fine, hath made.

2. From curtain [516] to banquet she cometh. Come, wipe ye her sweat off, that she
May tell us why she with this absence The comrades to pine hath made.

3. Behoveth with union's fetters To prison the tipsy fair,
Who all this long show of estrangement And coyness malign hath made.

4. The gift for glad news give! Love's minstrel Once more, heart, the winebibbers' lilt
Hath sounded and eke for cropsickness The remedy,—wine,—hath made.

5. No wonder the rose of my nature Bloomed out at her waft: the bird
Of night o'er the damask rose-leaves Right merry long syne hath made.

6. Seven waters and fires by the hundred Avail not to do out the stain
Which on the patchcoat of the Soufi The blood of the vine hath made.

7. O Hafiz, leave humbleness never; For th' envier offering still
Of honour, wealth, heart, religion At vainglory's shrine hath made.

[515] Apparently written on occasion of some relaxation of the laws against wine-drinking.
[516] i. e. from behind the curtain of seclusion.

CXXV

1. Thyself with the secret of Jemshid's cup Acquainted ill thou canst make,
The salve of thine eye with the threshold dust Of the tavern until thou canst make.

2. Sit not without winecup and song; for 'neath The vault of the sky, away
With grief from the heart, with the gurgle of wine And the minstrel's trill, thou canst
    make.

3. The rose of thy wish shall put aside Her face-veil and bloom, what time
Thyself, like the zephyr of dawn, attent On her service still thou canst make.

4. Be ever alert in the way of love: Press forward, stage by stage.
Great gain shall be thine if the journey to end, Betide there what will, thou canst make.

5. Nay, come, for possessed of delight and ease And life well-ordered thyself,
By the blessings and bounties, that from the folk Of vision distil, thou canst make.

6. Nor face-veil nor screen hath the loveliness Of the Friend: if the dust of the way
Thou lay with thy tears, then blest with her sight Thine eyes, to thy fill, thou canst make.

7. O thou, that withoutside the house of the flesh Ne'er settest thy foot to depart,
How deemst thou, thy way to the stead of the truth, O'er desert and hill, thou canst make?

8. In mendicanthood at the winehouse's door A marvellous alchemy is:
This craft an thou practise, to very gold The dust of its sill thou canst make.

9. O heart, if cognition thou once attain Of the light of austerity,
Lo, laughing, renouncement of head and life, Like candle and quill, thou canst make.

10. But, whilst thou ensuest the cup of wine And the ruby lips of the fair,
Deem, deem not withal that shift aught else To do that may skill thou canst make.

11. If, Hafiz, thou hearken and lend thine ear To this my royal rede,
The king's highroad of the way of Love Thy footpath still thou canst make.

CXXVI

1. Hand from skirt no more I'll sever Of yon cypress tall and straight, [517]
Root and stem, that hath up-torn me With her proudly swaying gait.

2. There's no need of wine and minstrel. Lift thy face-veil, so the fire
Of thy cheek to dancing bring me, Rue-seed like on chafing-plate. [518]

3. Save their faces, on the horsehoofs Of my fair who rub their cheeks,
None is meet to be the mirror Of the face of happy Fate.

4. Come what may, I've told the secret Of my sorrow for thy sake.
What's to do? I'm out of patience. How much longer shall I wait?

5. Slay not that my musk-deer fawnling, Hunter! Prithee, have thou shame
Of her night-black eye nor bind her With thy lasso long and strait.

6. I, a grain of dust, that cannot Lift my head from off this sill,
How shall I avail for kissing Yonder lofty palace-gate.

7. Hafiz' fresh and heart-alluring Songs when in Khujénd they hear,
Though Kemal's [519] it were, none other Worth the utterance they rate.

8. From those musky ringlets, Hafiz, Take thou not thy heart; God wot,
For a madman, to be fettered Ever was the better state.

9. Hafiz' heart hath no inclining, Save unto that tress of thine.
Out upon it! Bonds an hundred Have not made it more sedate.

[517] The beloved.
[518] Wild rue-seed is used for fumigation against the evil eye and when strewn upon a
     hot plate, would shrivel and crack and seem to dance; hence the comparison.
[519] Kemal-ed-din Khujendi, a celebrated contemporary poet and a native of Khujend
     (Khiva).

CXXVII

1. Set the hand within that loveling's Tress of double ply one cannot;
On thy promise and the wind-wafts Of the East rely one cannot.

2. What endeavour is and effort I in quest of thee have shown thee;
This much is, that Fate and Fortune Foreordained awry one cannot.

3. Loose the Loved One's skirt,—that, boughten With an hundred hearts' blood, fallen
In our hand is,—'spite the railers' Cavil and outcry,—one cannot.

4. Since with aught that's head-and-foot less The Beloved hath no kinship,
That her cheek compare and liken To the moon on high one cannot.

5. When my cypress-statured loveling Comes to dancing, where's the value
Of the soul's wede, since before her Rend and cast it by one cannot? [520]

6. Nay, what say I? For thy nature Is so dainty and so subtle
That to thee prefer the humblest Prayer or softest sigh one cannot.

7. Only to the pure of vision Visible the Loved One's cheek is;
For, if pure be not the mirror, Aught therein descry one cannot.

8. Slain am I with jealous rancour For that all the world doth love thee:
Yet with all God's creatures battle Day and night aby one cannot.

9. Love's enigmas are not holden In the bounds of mortal knowledge;
Nay, its tangles with this errant Brain and thought untie one cannot.

10. Marry, for the heart of Hafiz, There's no prayer-niche but thine eyebrow;
Save it be to thee, devotion, In our order, ply one cannot.

[520] Alluding to the habit, in vogue among the excitable Orientals, of rending the
garments, as a token of ecstasy or admiration.

CXXVIII

1. She bore away my heart And hid from me her face made:
Was e'er such sport with man, In any time or place, made?

2. When loneliness, at dawn, Threatened my life, her image
Me whole, with kindnesses Past count and many a grace, made.

3. Why, like the tulip, should I not be bleeding-hearted,
Since her narcissus-eye Hath us in rueful case made?

4. If remedy thou have, East wind, now is its season;
For love and pain resolve My life have to efface made.

5. On such wise have they burned Me, taper-like, that o'er me
The cup wept and the lyre Lament for my misgrace made.

6. What shall I say? With this Mine anguish life-consuming,
My leach design upon My sorry soul and base made.

7. How shall it unto friends Be told that the Beloved
Did this or that amiss And this speech out of place made! [521]

8. No foe with Hafiz' soul Might ever make such havoc
As have yon bow-browed fair's Bright eye and beauteous face made.

[521] The laws of Love forbid complaint to others of the Beloved's cruelty.

124

CXXIX

1. Be she mem'ried, who at parting Sign for us of mem'ry made not,
Though our hearts grief-laden lighter With a farewell word she made not!

2. Yonder child of youthful [522] Fortune, Other slaves when she enfranchised, [523]
Why, I know not, she this bondman Old (myself, to wit,) free made not.

3. Come, in tears of blood the paper Garment [524] let us wash, since heaven
To the standard-foot of justice [525] Able to attain me made not.

4. In the hope there may some echo Reach thy hearing, such a clamour
In this mountain my heart maketh As Ferhád's [526] self surely made not. [527]

5. Nay, the courier of the East wind From thy gait might learn his business:
Wind itself a nimbler ever Than this motion of thee made not.

6. Since thy shadow thou withdrewest From the meads, the meadow-warbler
Hath its nest within the curling Tresses of the box-tree made not.

7. Ne'er th' achievement of his wishes Hath Fate's pen to him forewritten
Who confession of thy beauty Giv'n of God Almighty made not.

8. Minstrel, change the mode; the measure Of Irác strike up, for thither
Went the Loved One and remembrance Of her lovers lorn she made not.

9. As the verses of Iráki [528] Are the melodies of Hafiz;
Who e'er heard these heart-enkindling Ditties and lament he made not?

[522] Youthful (i. e. favouring) Fortune. Cf. "Fortune favours the young."—Napoleon I.
[523] It was the custom, among the old Persians, to enfranchise a slave or do some other (canonically) acceptable good work, before starting on a journey or undertaking any considerable business, and thus secure the Divine blessing upon the enterprise.
[524] The ancient Persians, when they wished to complain of oppression, used to don a garment of paper and to burn the latter in the presence of the king or other man in authority, in token of appeal against injustice.
[525] The Kings of the East of old gave audience and rendered justice at the foot of a standard planted behind the throne.
[526] "Ferhad", the luckless lover of Shirin, see previous note.
[527] i. e. when he heard the false announcement of his mistress's death.
[528] "Iraki"; Fekhreddin Ibrahim ibn Shehriyar, a famous erotic poet of Hemdan in Irac, whence his ekename "Iraki", "Native of Irac". He died in A. D. 1289, a hundred years before Hafiz, and although a famous theologian and one of the chief lights of the Soufi order, was (says Soudi) an extremely debauched and dissipated man, with an especial inclination to boys. "His erotic nature (says Soudi) he showed freely in his verse; hence its heart-enkindling and passionate character".

CXXX

1. She went and aware of her going Her lovers distraught made not
And sign, that of city-companions Or way mates she thought, made not.

2. 'Twas either my sorry fortune, That swerved from the path of Love,
Or she by the road of usance Her way, as she ought, made not.

3. I was standing await, like the taper, To pour out my soul at her feet;
But the Loved One, withal, by us passage, Like breezes dawn-brought, made not.

4. Quoth I, "Peradventure with weeping Her heart I may melt;" but my tears
On her, like to raindrops on marble, Impression in aught made not.

5. My heart, wing and pinion, is broken With grief: yet the smart of my pain
Away from my head with love's passion, Though idle and naught, made not.

6. Whoever hath looked on thy visage Still kisseth mine eye in approof,
Because it its choice without insight, In that which it wrought, made not.

7. This tongue-slitten reed-pen of Hafiz, Until it had lost its head,
Thy mystery known in th'assembly, Whoever besought, made not.

CXXXI

1. My face in her way I laid, Who passage thereby made not;
Much favour I hoped; but me glad A glance of her eye made not.

2. O Lord, do thou have in Thy guard That reckless young leveling; since she
Provision to ward off the shaft Of th' anchorite's sigh made not.

3. The flood of our tears from her heart Hath rancour and malice not borne:
Impression upon the hard rock The rains of the sky made not.

4. I purposed to die at her feet, Like the taper; but she, like the breeze
Of the dawning, her passage, whereas In dust we did lie, made not.

5. Who ever, though hardest of heart And witless, o soul, [529] himself
A target and butt, for the shafts Of thy glances to ply, made not?

6. Fish and bird, yesternight, for the noise Of my groaning and wailing, slept not;
But a sign of uprising from sleep Yon wanton of eye made not. [530]

7. None, Hafiz, thy honey-sweet speech Yet heard, so bewitching it is,
That shift to commit it to heart, Or ever it fly, made not?

[529] Addressed to the Beloved.

[530] i.e. all living things were stirred to pity by my lament, except the Beloved, who slept through it all, unheeding.

CXXXII

1. Preachers, who in niche and pulpit All this great display do practise,
In seclusion other business And on other way do practise.

2. Yea, my soul is all amazement At these brazenfaced exhorters
To repentance, who so little What themselves they say do practise.

3. I've a difficulty; put it To the sage of the assembly;
Why these urgers to repentance No repentance aye do practise?

4. Thou would'st say that they believe not In the dreadful Day of Judgment,
Since this fraud and this deception In God's business they do practise.

5. Back, Lord, in their proper stable Set these upstarts, who, by reason
Of some bough ten Turk muledriver, All these airs to-day do practise. [531]

6. At the portal of Love's winehouse, Angels, say, "To God be glory!"
For that therewithin the leav'ning They of Adam's clay do practise. [532]

7. Often as her boundless beauty Lovers slayeth, other legions,
From th' Invisible, head-raising Unto Love straightway do practise.

8. I'm the servant of the Elder Of the tavern, whose disciples,
For sheer wishlessness, contemning Of the world's array do practise.

9. Ho, thou beggar of the cloister, Up! For, in the Magians' convent,
With a water [533] they the making Hearts both rich and gay do practise.

10. Make thou clear the house of idols For the abode of the Beloved;
For with heart and soul these harpies [534] Havoc and affray do practise.

11. Came a clamour in the dawning From the topmost heav'n. Quoth reason,
"Angels 'tis that getting Hafiz' Verse by heart, thou'dst say, do practise."

[531] i. e. who glory in having a *white* groom; as white slaves are only possessed by the rich and great, most people contenting themselves with black ones, such as Abyssinians, Nubians &c. The "upstarts" referred to may be either the preachers aforesaid or certain vulgar *nouveaux riches*, who had made themselves obnoxious to the poet. By praying for their return to their stables, he suggests that they are brute beasts, not fit to commerce with human beings.
[532] According to Soudi, this couplet alludes to [a Tradition of the Prophet], "[Quoth God the most High,] I leavened", syn. fermented, imbibed with wine, "the clay of Adam forty mornings" (cf. "I created man of clay", Koran XXXVIII, 71). "They", i.e.; "Fate and Fortune Foreordained".

[533] i. e. wine.
[534] "These harpies"; i. e. the preachers aforesaid or the idols mentioned in the preceding line.

CXXXIII [535]

1. Hark to the harp and the ghittern, What notification they make;
"In secret drink wine, lest in public Of thee reprobation they make."

2. The honour of Love and the glory Of lovers they ravish away;
Youth sorry with chiding and manhood With vilification they make.

3. Quoth they, "Speak ye not of Love's myst'ries Nor hearken to speech thereof."
Nay, marry, it is a hard saying, Whereof promulgation they make!

4. Withoutside the door of the Loved One, We're gulled with an hundred deceits:
I wonder, behind the dark curtain, What rare machination They make!

5. They harass the Magian Elder, These pestilent devotees:
Of the life of the Sage of the tavern Lo! what tribulation they make!

6. An hundredfold fashions of honour With half of a glance may be bought;
But alack for the fair! To this traffic But small application they make.

7. Some folk, for the Loved One's attainment, In stress and endeavour confide;
For others, their hope and reliance On Foreordination they make.

8. I rede thee, no trust in th' endurance Of Fortune unstable put thou;
For Time and the world are the workshops Where change and mutation They make.

9. There's nought here to get but base coinage, And yet fools conceit them that still
The philosopher's stone in this hostel Of woe and vexation They make!

10. Drink wine, then; for, Elder and Hafiz [536] And Mufti and Mohtesib all,
If thou look at it closely, a practice Of falsification they make. [537]

[535] Apparently composed in a time of persecution of winedrinkers.
[536] "Hafiz" here has its technical meaning of a student of the Koran, one who knows it by heart; the title is given to theological students who have passed certain standards of the collegiate course.
[537] "They", in Couplets I, 2, 3 and 5, refers to the railing pietists and in Couplets 4, 8 and 9, to the Fates.

CXXXIV

1. Those with the glance Who gold of the dust they espy make, [538]
Ah, might they us blest With a look from the tail of the eye make!

2. From leaches self-styled my pain better hide: They shall haply
With balm from the stores Of the Viewless me whole by and by make.

3. Since welfare etern In debauchery's not nor devotion,
'Twere best our affair That we over to God the most High make.

4. Since never the veil From cheek the Beloved One draweth,
A diff'rent conceit, Each man for himself, thereof why make? [539]

5. To day, in the veil [540], Much knav'ry betideth. I wonder
What excuse will the folk, What time the veil's rended in twy, [541] make?

6. Marvel not if the tale Of the heart, on fair fashion expounded
By people of heart, Very stones to lament and to cry make.

7. Be not without heed; God wot, in Love's auction-mart, sages
Their usance with none But known ones to sell and to buy make.

8. Drink wine, for defaults An hundred from sight hid are better
Than one act of faith, Which folk with dissembling a lie make. [542]

9. A shirt, whence there came The fragrance of Joseph to-me-ward,
His brethren's despite A surcoat thereof will, fear I, make. [543]

10. The winehouse toward Fare thou, so the host of thy lovers
Their prayers for thy weal May, whenas thou passest therenigh, make.

11. To enviers unknown, Call me to thyself; for the gen'rous
Their kindnesses oft A secret from all but the sky make.

12. Ne'er, Hafiz, to man Vouchsafed was abidal of union:
Kings little account Of beggars before them that lie make. [544]

[538] i. e. Sages, men of insight, initiates into the Divine mysteries.
[539] "The Beloved" here apparently = God. The couplet means, "Since it is impossible
to know God, why fret oneself with vain conjecture?"
[540] i. e., in this darkling world.
[541] i. e., in the next world, when all things are brought to light.
[542] Winedrinking and the like are venial sins, to be atoned in this world by repentance;
but hypocrisy is a mortal sin, which will be punished in the next world.
[543] i. e., will rend it from top to bottom. "Joseph" = Beloved. The commentators give
no explanation of this couplet; but the meaning appears to be that the poet's rivals

and ill-wishers and his mistress's watchers and spies had frustrated him of the enjoyment of her favours.

[544] The first part of this ode appears to be genuinely mystic; whilst the remainder is in the poet's usual erotic vein.

CXXXV

1. Fair ones, thus if use of charming Still they make,
Breaches in the faith of zealots Will they make.

2. Whereso that narcissus bloometh, Rose-cheeked ones
Eyes narcissus-holders, will they, Nill they, make. [545]

3. When the angels hear my loveling Fall to song,
Answer, clapping hands, from Heaven's Hill they make.

4. Fortune's sun its face will show thee, If thy heart's
Mirror shining as the morning's Sill They make. [546]

5. Over their own selves have lovers No command;
Whatsoe'er thou biddest, that their Will they make.

6. See, all blood-besmeared's the apple Of mine eye:
Where is it of man this usance Ill they make?

7. Strike, o cypress-statured youngling, Strike a ball,
Ere thy stature as the mall-stick's Bill They make. [547]

8. With mine eye's tear-torrent likened, But a drop
Were the tales that of the Deluge Still they make.

9. Show thy festal cheek to lovers And of life
Off'ring shall (and thus their pledges Fill) they make. [548]

10. Like th' initiates, heart, in anguish Blithesome be:
Merry, even on estrangement's Grill, they make. [549]

11. Midnight lamentation, Hafiz, Leave thou not,
Difficulties to thee easy Till They make.

[545] The Beloved's *person* here likened to the narcissus-plant. "Other fair ones, when they see our charmer, will make her narcissus-like person the cynosure of their eyes".

[546] i. e. if the Fates make thy heart pure and clear, fit for the reflection of the sun of fortune.

[547] i. e. before thy back become bowed with age, like the crook of the mall, strive for the attainment of happiness; seize the time of opportunity. Carpe diem.

[548] An appeal to the Beloved to make lovers' lives a festival with the radiance of her

unveiled cheek.

[549] i.e. the wise are not disheartened by ill fortune, because they know that neither ill nor good is abiding.

CXXXVI

1. "Thy mouth and thy lip", I asked her, "Me blest when will they make?"
"Thy bidding in all," she answered, "Shift to fulfil they make."

2. "Thy lips for a kiss the tribute Of Egypt seek," said I.
Quoth she, "At that rate who purchase, No bargain ill they make."

3. "To the point of thy mouth [550] who findeth The way?" quoth I; and she,
"That known to the subtlety-kenners, Not those lack-skill, They make."

4. Quoth I, "Be no server of idols; Abide thou with God", [551] and she,
"Their wont this and that in Love's quarter, The good and the ill, they make."

5. Quoth I, "Lo, the air of the winehouse Doth grief from the heart away;"
And she, "Happy folk, [552] if one bosom With gladness to thrill they make!"

6. Quoth I, "Wine and patchcoat [553] the canon Allows not"; and she, "In the sect
"Of the Magians, of one and the other Their habitude still they make."

7. Quoth I, "From the sweet-lipped ones' ruby What profit the old?" And she,
"The old young again with the sugar Their kisses distil they make."

8. Quoth I, "To the nuptial chamber When cometh the lord?" And she,
"'Twill not be, the Moon in conjunction With Jupiter till They make." [554]

9. Quoth I, "It is Hafiz's practice To pray for thy weal." And she,
"This prayer, mid the angels that people Heav'n's sevenfold hill, they make." [555]

[550] Beloved's mouth likened, for minuteness, to the imaginary point.
[551] i. e. fear God and oppress not the faithful.
[552] i. e. the wine-sellers.
[553] i. e. the combination of devotion and winebibbing.
[554] According to Soudi, the marriage of the Vizier Kiwameddin is here alluded to, the bride being likened to the moon and himself to Jupiter. But I incline rather to believe that by "Lord" the Beloved is meant and that Hafiz means to enquire when she will grant him her favours; to which she replies, in the next couplet, that it will not be till Fortune is especially friendly to him, i. e. till the conjunction of Jupiter and the moon, which (the latter being in Orion) is considered a very auspicious aspect.
[555] i. e. "the angels in heaven also make a practice of offering up prayers for my well-being; argal, (by implication) I have no need of thy prayers".

CXXXVII

1. Crowned kings the bondmen of thy drowsed Narcissus-eyne are still;
The sober drunken with thy lip Of ruby's wine are still.

2. Pass, like the East wind, by the beds Of violets and see
How, for thy tress's tyranny, All in repine are still.

3. Of thee the East wind and of me The tears are talebearers;
Else lover and beloved both Secret, in fine, are still.

4. Not only I to that rose-cheek Sing songs; on every side
Thousands of bulbuls praisers of Those charms of thine are still.

5. Look, from beneath thy double tress, Whenas thou passest by,
What restless ones, to right and left, Line upon line, are still.

6. Our lot foredoomed is Paradise; Begone, self-righteous one! [556]
Sinners deserving of God's grace And ruth Divine are still.

7. Go to the tavern; dye thy face With Redbud-coloured wine;
Not to the cloister, for those there Of heart malign are still.

8. O Khizr of auspicious foot, Take thou my hand; for I
Afoot go and a-horseback all Yon way-mates mine are still. [557]

9. Never from yonder shining tress Be Hafiz freed! For free
Those only are who bounden in Thy ringlet's twine are still.

10. Lo, from the writing on the face Of Hafiz may be known
That those who dwell at the Friend's door Mad, [558] by this sign, are still.

[556] Lit. "God-knower", i. e. one who claims to be in Heaven's confidence, like ex-President Krüger, the late Mrs. Plimsoll and a certain contemporary prince.
[557] O Beloved, succour me; for I am poor and helpless, whilst the rest of thy lovers have wealth and power.
[558] Lit. "Dust-dwellers", a term applied to the idiots and ecstatics who couch on the dustheaps without the city-walls. The word is used as a trope for madmen and is here applied (p. g.) to frenzied lovers who grovel (metaphorically) in the dust of the Beloved's door.

CXXXVIII

1. When jasmine-breathed ones lay them down To rest, they lay the dust of grieving;
When Peri-visaged ones wage war, For lovers' hearts they're peace-bereaving.

2. Hearts with oppression's saddle-girth [559] They bind, when up they bind their tresses;
Souls from their amber-scented locks They shake abroad in the unweaving.

3. When in a life-time they a breath With us have sat, they must be going;
Yea, they rise up and go, the seeds Of yearning in the spirit leaving.

4. Tears ruby-red, whenas they laugh, They cause from out mine eye to showér;
The hidden secret of my love By this my pallid face perceiving.

5. The cheek they turn not from their love Who wake a-nights, whenas they know it,
The sorrows of the anchorites, An if they wot thereof, relieving.

6. He, who conceiveth med'cining Of lovers' pains an easy matter
Is, for the folk who know the case, An ignoramus past conceiving.

7. They get their wish who like Mensóur, [560] On gibbet die; for those who're bounden
In bonds of healing of Love's pain [561] Fall ever short of its achieving.

8. When to this presence longing ones Make supplication, they disdain them:
When to this door they Hafiz call, They drive him forth, to die of grieving.

[559] Saddle-strap used in war and the chase for binding captives and game.
[560] i. e. El Hellaj, see note 1 to Ode 123.
[561] i. e. they who are hampered in Love's quest by the desire of obtaining relief from its
pains, those lovers who are not self-forgetting.

CXXXIX

1. Wine without mixture and skinker gent The twin snares of the Way are,
To the springes whereof the wise of the world Delivered for a prey are.

2. Though lover and drunkard and debauchee And black of book [562] myself am,
Thank God that our friends of the city free From sin (or so they say) are!

3. Thy foot in the tavern set not thou, Except in the way of breeding,
For the folk of its doorway confidants Of the king whom all obey [563] are.

4. No fashion fit for wayfarer Or dervish is oppression;
Bring wine, for no Sons of the Path, in truth, The zealots of the day are.

5. Do no oppression, for shattered is The glory of heart-bewitchers,
When bondmen flee from before their face And servants gone astray are.

6. View not the beggars of Love with scorn; For know thou that these people
Monarchs uncrowned and kings without Girdle and bright array are.

7. Beware of the wind of pride; for, when It blows, the fair unminded,
For crops of devotion a thousand, half A barley corn to pay are.

8. The slave of the high intent am I Of topers of one colour
And not of the crew who blue of gown And black of heart and way [564] are.

9. August is the majesty of Love: Pluck up a spirit, Hafiz;
For lovers to them but those admit Who pure of all affray are.

[562] "Black of book", said of a great sinner, the chronicle of whose misdeeds is
supposed to blacken the record kept in heaven of his actions.
[563] i. e. (according to Soudi) the Beloved; but rather (*me judice*) Love itself.
[564] i. e. Soufis. Blue is the favourite colour of the Muslim devotee, as recalling that of
the heavens. "Topers of one colour" are sincere, undissembling men, those whose
words are not of one colour (syn. "kind, sort",) and their actions of another.

CXL

1. What is it that this drunkenness On me of mine hath brought?
Who was the skinker and whence is't That he this wine hath brought?

2. What mode was it the minstrel, skilled In music, played, wherein
He to mine ear, midmost the song, That voice of thine hath brought?

3. The Hoopoe of King Solomon For us the East wind is,
That news from Sheba's rosegardens, To us that pine, hath brought.

4. Take thou the winecup in thy hand And seek the open fields;
For the sweet bird its dulcet pipe, At Summer's sign, hath brought.

5. Welcome the coming of the rose And jasmine! Come's the glad
Sweet violet; and happy cheer The eglantine hath brought.

6. Heart, like the rosebud, moan thou not Of straitened case; for, see,
Its heart-dilating airs the breeze Of morn benign hath brought.

7. The skinker's glance the remedy Is of our heart's unease:
Lift up thy head; the leach is come And medicine hath brought.

8. The Magian Elder's slave am I: Rail not at me, o Sheikh;
For that, which thou didst promise, he To pass, in fine, hath brought. [565]

9. The sacrifice, indeed, am I Of that rapacity,
Which to lay hands on abject me Yon Turk of mine [566] hath brought.

10. The heav'ns obedient service do To Hafiz, now that Fate
Him to the shelter of thy door, That Fortune's shrine, hath brought.

[565] *Thou* dost but promise us heaven in the world to come; *he* giveth us present
    Paradise.
[566] The Beloved.

CXLI

1. No account of thee thou writest, Past although is many a day:
Where's a trusty one who tidings Shall of us to thee convey?

2. To the lofty goal we aim at Nevermore may we attain,
Save thy favouring kindness meet us Many paces on the way.

3. Now the wine is in the flagon And the rose hath cast its veil,
Seize the moment of enjoyment, Drain the winecup, whilst ye may.

4. Sugar-candy, blent with roses, Is no balsam for our heart;
Give us kisses mixed with chiding; Bitter still with sweet allay.

5. Go from us in peace, o zealot, Lest, forsooth, the company
Of so many scurril topers Lead thee from the path astray.

6. Long enough at wine thou'st chidden; Of its virtues also tell:
Cast thou not the words of wisdom Off, for aught the dullards say.

7. Ho, ye beggars of the wineshop, Have a care ye rest no hope
On yon dunderheaded cattle; God's your only friend and stay.

8. Oh, how well the Magian Elder To his topers said, "The case
"Of the heart consumed with passion To the raw ones ne'er bewray!"

9. For thy sun-bright cheek with longing Hafiz burns. O happy fair,
Cast a glance on those who languish In the deserts of dismay!

CXLII

1. The universe from end to end, One moment's care unworth it is;
Our patchcoat sell for wine; for, sure, Better to fare unworth it is.

2. The Loved One's quarter bindeth us: But otherwise what booteth Fars?
For lo! the whole wide world, this stress We suffer there unworth it is. [567]

3. Since in the vintner's street will none Accept it for a cup of wine,
A fine prayer-rug, if one poor cup Of wine soe'er unworth it is!

4. The watchers chide me, saying, "Turn Thy face away from yonder door."
What ails my head, that of the door-Dust of the fair unworth it is?

5. This cassock wash of covetise; For in the single-hearts' bazaar,
Whate'er the patchcoat be, one cup Of red wine rare unworth it is.

6. Light, at the first, in hope of gain, Meseemed the stresses of the sea.
I erred; for, for a hundred pearls This flood to dare, unworth it is.

7. The splendour of the royal crown, Wherein life's danger is involved,
Heart-luring is; but it, at risk Of life, to wear, unworth it is.

8. Thy face 'twere better that thou hide From longing lovers, for, despite
The joys of conquering the world, The army's care unworth it is.

9. Like Hafiz, seek content and turn From this vile world; for one sole grain
Of obligation to the base, All gold whate'er unworth it is.

[567] i. e. "the presence of the Loved One binds me to Fars; otherwise the whole world
would not repay me for the slights and sufferings I endure at the hands of its people",
a complaint of his fellow-countrymen of Shiraz frequently repeated by the poet.

CXLIII

1. Except the love of moonfaced maids, This heart of mine a way takes not;
I counsel this and that; but it Advice, say what I may, takes not.

2. For Heaven's sake, admonisher, Bespeak me of the skinker's down;
For goodlier effect on me Whatever thou canst say takes not.

3. The wineflask hid with me I bear And folk suppose it is the Book: [568]
Strange if the fire of this my fraud [569] The Book itself some day takes not!

4. This particoloured gaberdine Some day I sure shall burn; since it
The Elder of the Winesellers For one poor cup in pay takes not.

5. Yon toper-monisher, who wars With God's foreordinance [570], I see
His heart sore straitened; 'Tis, belike, That he the goblet gay takes not.

6. 'Tis for this cause the pure of heart In ruby wine delight, that aught,
Except the truth, impress upon This gem of purest ray takes not. [571]

7. Midmost my tears I smile, for that My tongue in this assembly is
Afire, the candle like, and yet On others, wellaway, takes not. [572]

8. Thou bidst me from her face avert Mine eyes, for all its goodliness;
Go, for thine idle prate effect On me, for yea or nay, takes not.

9. The question is of this our need And of the Friend's disdain: what good
In incantation, [573] friend, effect Which on the charmer aye takes not?

10. I glory in thy tipsy eye: How happily my heart it took!
Wild birds on goodlier than this wise Fowler or bird of prey takes not.

11. Pity, 'fore God, o lovely one! Behold, the dervish [574] of thy street
Knows not another door than thine And other than thy way takes not.

12. Kindnesses, many an one, have I Had of the Magian Elder, who
The usance of hypocrisy For one sole cup in pay takes not.

13. For this one day, Sikender-like, This mirror [575] will I take in hand,
Whether its fire upon me takes Or (be that as it may) takes not.

14. For these his verses fresh and sweet, I wonder that the king of kings
Hafiz, from head to foot, in chains Of gold without allay takes not. [576]

[568] i. e. The Koran.
[569] Fire always connected with hypocrisy by Muslims, that meant being hell-fire, to
    which the hypocrite is infallibly doomed.
[570] i. e. who rails at our toping, which was fore-ordained to us by God.
[571] i. e. in vino veritas.
[572] i. e. my speech takes no effect on the Beloved.
[573] Hafiz jocularly assumes the grumblings and mutterings of the zealot to be charms
    and incantations and asks what is the use of these, the Beloved being herself too
    great a sorcerer to be affected by such devices.
[574] i. e. the forlorn lover, Hafiz himself.
[575] i. e. the wine-cup; allusion to Alexander's magic mirror; see previous note.
[576] Apparently a complaint of the royal neglect.

CXLIV

1. A fair I have, who round the rose A screen of hyacinths [577] arow hath;
A warrant for the Redbud's blood The Springtide, in her cheek a-blow, hath.

2. See, by the dust of that her down The sun-spring of her cheek is shadowed:
Lord, grant her life etern; for she Eternal loveliness, I trow, hath.

3. From whatsoever side I look, There from her eye is no escaping;
For from its coign it lieth wait And arrow evermore in bow hath.

4. 'Fore Heaven, ruler of the feast, Do justice thou for me upon her;
For wine with others hath she drunk And headache now with me, heigho! hath.

5. When first a lover I became, I said, "I've won the pearl desiréd."
Alack, what fell, blood-shedding waves This sea of Love, I did not know, hath!

6. Assure thou me against the fear Of sev'rance, if thou hope that heaven
Will save thee harmless from the eye Of whoso will to work thee woe hath.

7. Bereave mine eye not of the sight Of that thy shape's heart-taking cypress;
Nay, plant it by this fountain-head, [578] Which running water still a-flow hath.

8. If with thy girth thou wilt me bind, For God's sake, take me quick; for surely
Delay hath perils, ay, and harm For the pursuer, evenso, hath.

9. When the rose smileth in thy face, Into her snare fall not, o bulbul;
There's no relying on the rose, Though the world's beauty she to show hath.

10. Pour thou a draught upon the dust And note the story of the mighty;
For many a tale the earth to tell Of Keikobád and Keikhusró hath.

11. When from her tresses' snare she shook The dust of hearts and souls of lovers,
The blabbing East wind she enjoined Her secret keep from friend and foe hath.

12. What hath befallen in this way, That every man of wit and insight
Here in this doorway, as I see, His head upon the sill bowed low hath?

13. How for my case can I account, That yonder city-troubling sharper [579]
With bitterness hath Hafiz slain, Yet sugar in her mouth e'ermo' hath?

[577] i. e. The hyacinthine locks.
[578] i. e. His own tear-brimmed eye.
[579] i. e. the beloved.

CXLV [580]

1. A heart, that is secret-discovering And Jemshid's cup of might hath,
No great concern for a signet-ring, A moment lost from sight, [581] hath.

2. To Solomon's sealring give thou news Of glad and happy issue,
For the great Name [582] cut off therefrom The hand of Satan's spite hath. [581]

3. On down and mole of beggars base Bestow not the heart's treasure;
Nay, give it in hand to a kinglike one, That it in honour right hath.

4. Not every tree endureth 'gainst The tyranny of winter;
The slave of the cypress stout am I, That stableness of spright hath.

5. My heart, that of independence erst Boasted, an hundred traffics
Now, for thy tress-scent, with the winds That blow at morning-light, hath.

6. The season of mirth is come, when each, Like to the drowsed narcissus,
Six testers layeth at foot of the cup, [583] If so much coin the wight hath.

7. From whom shall I seek the heart's desire? Since there's no charmer living
That usance of generosity And vision clear and bright hath.

8. Gold, like the rose, from the price of wine Withhold not now, or ever
The sense of the general thee in doubt Of many a foul unright hath. [584]

9. Nay, fable not of the World Unseen; There's none its secret knoweth.
What sage access to this sanctuary, That's sealed from mortal sight, hath?

10. From Hafiz' monkish gaberdine What profit may be gotten?
We the Eternal seek and he In idols his delight hath. [585]

[580] According to Soudi, the two first couplets of this o' allude to the case of Shah
Mensour (ob. A. D. 1393), who was expelled by the Turcomans from Shiraz, but
afterwards levied an army and overcoming the enemy, reseated himself on the throne
of Fars.
[581] Alluding to the well-known story of the Div who stole Solomon's seal-ring and
became for a while King in his stead. Shah Mensour likened to Solomon and the
Turcomans to the Div.
[582] The secret name of God, which whoever knows hath command over all creation;
said to have been graven on Solomon's ring.
[583] The petals of the narcissus, surrounding the corona, likened to silver coins. "To lay
money at the foot of the cup" is to devote one's substance to buying wine and mirth.
[584] The red rose, on account of its gold-coloured stamens, is said to have gold in its
mouth and to bear the wine cup in hand, when it opens out into full blossom; hence
says the poet, "Like the rose, be not chary of spending thy substance on wine in the
rose-time, lest the people suspect thee of all manner hidden vices".
[585] "Hafiz" must apparently be taken here in its technical sense of "he who knows the
Koran by heart", i. e. the professional theologian. Gloss of couplet, "we lovers and
topers seek the Eternal God; but he (the theologian) delighteth only in idols, i. e. in
false doctrine and hypocrisy".

CXLVI

1. Whoever observance and faith With the people of faith keepeth,
Him God the most High, at all times, From sorrow and scaith keepeth.

2. Wilt have not the Loved One break Love's compact, the end of the twine
Keep thou and she also her end, 'Gainst whatso affray'th, keepeth.

3. I tell not the case of the Friend, Except to her worshipful self;
The comrade still secret the tale Of what his mate saith keepeth.

4. When "Keep thou in safety my heart From mischief", I bid her, quoth she,
"Nay, what can the slave? 'Tis God (Not whoso obey'th) keepeth." [586]

5. My heart and my life and my good The sacrifice be of the fair
Who the due and observance of love And friendship and faith keepeth! [587]

6. My heart in her tress an thou see, O wind of the East, prithee bid
It bide in contentment, whilst it The place where it stay'th keepeth.

7. O heart, [588] live thou still on such wise That if thy foot falter, thee aye
An angel, with both hands upreared, As he doth who pray'th, keepeth.

8. O warriors and champions, have heed And keep ye good watch o'er the lord [589]
Who you as his own proper soul, In whatso he may'th, keepeth.

9. Lo, where is the dust of thy way, Which Hafiz, in token and sign
Of the fragrance to him which the breath Of the East wind convey'th, keepeth?

[586] i. e. "do not ask that of me, but of God; I am but a slave commanded, who doth as
    God willeth".
[587] Rhyme-word of 1. 1 repeated.
[588] Addressed to the Beloved.
[589] "Lord", i. e., the Grand Vizier.

CXLVII

1. No true loveling's she who only Waist and hair possesseth:
Be her slave alone who "Thatness" To her share possesseth. [590]

2. Lovesome though the Houris' usance And the Peris' fashion,
That alone is grace and beauty Which my fair possesseth.

3. Prithee, smiling rose, the wellspring Of mine eye come visit,
Which, in hope of thee, fresh water Running e'er possesseth.

4. Lo, the curve of that thine eyebrow, In the bowman's practice,
Greater skill than any archer Whatsoe'er possesseth. [591]

5. Heart-impressing grown my verse is, Since thou didst accept it:
Yea, love's speech a power of impress Passing rare possesseth.

6. None for sure Love's secret knoweth; Yet each man, according
To his insight, some conception Of th' affair possesseth. [592]

7. Look of miracles thou prate not To the tavern-haunters;
Every word its place and season, When and where, possesseth. [593]

8. No wise bird will ever carol In a Springtide's meadows
Which in rear thereof an Autumn Of despair possesseth.

9. Who shall bear the ball of beauty Off from thee? Not even
The sun's self the will and spirit This to dare possesseth.

10. Bid pretenders quips and quillets Riddle not with Hafiz:
Our quill also tongue and speechcraft, Be ye ware, possesseth. [594]

[590] Beauty consists not in one or two bodily attributes, but in general charm and
    individuality. The Turkish poet Nejati says: "That which is desired in the charmer is
    Thatness (charm), not the body; Exhilaration is the aim in wine, not the cup".
[591] Cf. Old English ballad; "Come, Robin, lend to me thy bow".
[592] None is really initiate into Love's mysteries; but none will confess ignorance
    thereof.
[593] i. c. talk not theology to debauchees.
[594] i. e. let them not prate to Hafiz of matters which he understands far better than they.

CXLVIII

1. The blood of the heart from the eye All over our face passeth;
Beholdest thou not from the eye Thereo'er what ill case passeth? [595]

2. A wish and a longing we hold Concealed in our innermost heart;
Because of which longing, our heart On the wind-blasts of space passeth. [596]

3. In the dust of the path of the Friend Our face have we laid: and indeed,
'Tis fitting if over our cheeks She swimming apace passeth.

4. A torrent's the tears of mine eye: O'er what man soever they pass,
Albeit his heart were of stone, His heart from its place passeth. [597]

5. Contention I have day and night With the water that floodeth mine eyes,
That still tow'rd the end of her street, Ensuing her trace, passeth.

6. The sun of the Orient himself For jealousy rendeth his wede,
When that love-fost'ring moonface of mine In her garment of grace passeth.

7. Hafiz still in the winehouse's street, In candour and oneness of heart,
From sense, like the Soufis wool-clad And the cell-keeping race, passeth. [598]

[595] The eye, in this second line, according to Soudi, is "the evil eye".
[596] i. e. goeth to destruction, perdition.
[597] i. e. Whoever seeth my weeping Is moved to pity of me; his heart is carried away
    thereby.
[598] i. e. Hafiz taketh leave of his senses for ecstasy, as the Soufis and other religious
    orders (such as the dancing dervishes) feign to do in the mystic dance etc.

CXLIX

1. When hand to her tress I clap, away She in heat goeth;
And if concord I seek, in chiding's way Her conceit goeth.

2. With the curve of her crescent-moon-like brow, She cutteth the way
On the helpless onlookers and into the veil Of retreat goeth. [599]

3. O' winedrinking nights, she ruineth me With wakefulness;
And by day, if my story I tell, to sleep The cheat goeth. [600]

4. Full, full is the pathway of Love, o heart, Of trouble and strife;
Yea, still shall he tremble who in this way O'erfleet goeth.

5. When the wind of conceit in the bubble's head Befalleth, alack!
Its lordship [601] forthright, for desire of wine, To defeat goeth.

6. Boast beauty and lovesomeness not, o heart, When old thou'rt grown;
For this same traffic [602] except with youth Unmeet goeth.

7. When the scroll of the sable hair for once Is folded up,
The white ne'er, out though an hundred times Plucked be't, goeth. [603]

8. Sell not for the kingship thy beggarhood At the Loved One's door.
Who forth of this door-shade into the sun's Full heat goeth?

9. Thou callest me, "Covenant-breaker;" yet, Thyself, I fear,
On the Day of Uprising, the same address To greet goeth. [604]

10. Thy hindrance thyself in the way of Love Thou art, Hafiz;
O happy whoso in this way, sans let For his feet, goeth!

[599] i. e. she confoundeth lovers by raising her veil, so as to allow them a glimpse of her eyebrows, and immediately re-veileth herself.
[600] Brief, she doth all by contraries.
[601] as if, riding upon wine, it lorded over it.
[602] i. e. usage of boasting.
[603] i.e. when once the hair begins to lose its blackness, no plucking out of white hairs will restore the original colour.
[604] i. e. on the Day of Resurrection, when They summon every one by his name and quality, I fear me They will call upon thee by the name of "Covenant-breaker".

CL

1. Once on a time, a heart, o Muslims, mine was,
Wherewith I spoke, if trouble or repine was.

2. A feeling heart and helpful friend, that ever
For men of heart a shelter and a shrine was.

3. A mate expert and skilled, in every trouble,
It unto me, distraught of Fate malign, was.

4. When, for the Eye [605], I fell into a whirlpool,
Hope, by its aid, of winning forth the brine was.

5. 'Twas in thy street I lost it, o Beloved!
What a skirt-seizing [606] place that street of thine was!

6. Tears in its quest, like pearls, I spent; but fruitless
To get it back my effort all, in fine, was.

7. Never was worth untainted of rejection.
What beggar's case more abject aye than mine was?

8. Have pity on a wretch, who sage and honoured
Whilom, or e'er he drank of passion's wine, was.

9. My verses are the joy of all assemblies,
Since in sweet speech my teacher Love benign was.

10. Say no more, "Hafiz is a man of judgment".
He still a dunce (we've seen it with our eyne) was.

[605] i. e. the Evil Eye.
[606] i. e. ensnaring.

CLI

1. When my Beloved the cup in hand taketh,
The market of lovely ones slack demand taketh. [607]

2. I, like a fish, in the ocean am fallen,
Till me with the hook yonder Friend to land taketh. [608]

3. Every one saith, who her tipsy eye seëth,
"Where is a shrieve, that this fair firebrand taketh?"

4. Lo, at her feet in lament am I fallen,
Till the Beloved me by the hand taketh.

5. Happy his heart who, like Hafiz, a goblet
Of wine of the Prime Fore-eternal's brand taketh! [609]

[607] i. e. She throweth all other fair ones into disrepute.
[608] i. e. I am drowned in the sea of my tears, till she draw me to land with the hook of
her tress.
[609] i. e. who hath drunken of the wine of Infinity, who is a predestined servant of the
Ideal.

CLII

1. In whatso love-questing, wherein, Excepting fireflaught, there is not,
For amaze, if a harvest consume, Sure reason in aught there is not. [610]

2. A bird, to whose heart it ne'er fell With sorrow to make acquaintance,
A branch on the tree of his life, With leaves of mirth fraught, there is not.

3. No help in Love's workshop there is For infidelity's presence: [611]
What fuel is there for Hell-fire, If Boulehéb [612] naught there is not?

4. In the soul-sellers' canon good works In toping consist and good breeding;
There lineage is not esteemed And reckoning sought there is not.

5. In a company, whereas the sun Is reckoned no more than an atom,
To greaten one self by the Law Of courtesy taught there is not.

6. Drink wine; for if life without end To find in this perishing world is,
A means, save the wine of Bihísht, [613] Whereby it is wrought, there is not.

7. The Loved One's possession, for one Strait-handed [614] as thou art, my Hafiz,
Shall only betide when a day, To night which is brought, there is not. [615]

[610] i. e. when in love there is nothing but lightning, i. e. a transitory and idle fire of
lust, it is no wonder if the quest end in disappointment and disaster.
[611] i. e. all things entail their contraries.
[612] See previous note.
[613] *Bihisht*, (syn. heaven), a village near Shiraz, where a particularly strong and heady
wine is grown.
[614] i. e. poor.
[615] When a day comes which is unsucceeded by night, i. e. at the Greek Calends,
never.

CLIII

1. When the skinker wine in winecup With this air y-casteth,
Sages all into wine-drinking's Open snare he casteth.

2. When the mole-bait 'neath her tress-hook Thus the loveling streweth,
In the net she many a prudent Bird and wary casteth.

3. Goodly is that drunkard's portion, Who ignoreth whether
Head or turban in the pathway Of the fair he casteth.

4. Yonder zealot, rawness-seeking, In denial biding,
Waxeth cooked, on raw wine glances Whensoe'er he casteth. [616]

5. Skill [617] by day seek; for, who drinketh Wine by day, the mirror
Of the heart in rust of darkness And despair he casteth.

6. Dawn-bright wine to drink the season Is it when the night-tide
Evening's veil about the heavens' Sanctuary casteth.

7. Drink not with the city-censor; For thy wine he drinketh,
Ay, and stones into the winecup Then and there he casteth. [618]

8. Lift thy head from the sun's crownal, If thy lot, o Hafiz,
On that moon-faced one thy fortune Tutelary casteth.

[616] A couplet turning on the various meanings of *kham*, raw; i. e. "The pietist, who
followeth after vanity and still denieth love and blameth lovers and topers, becometh
matured (i. e. cured of his rawness, doltish ignorance) as soon as he taketh to
drinking raw (i. e. unalloyed) wine".
[617] "Skill", here (according to Soudi) = knowledge, wisdom; i. e. occupy thyself by day
with the acquisition of knowledge and wisdom and drink not.
[618] i. e. "for he will drink at thine expense and after break thy drinking gear and thine
instruments of mirth and music and enforce upon thee the penalties of the law
against winebibbing".—*Soudi*.

CLIV

1. Good news, o my heart, for once more The zephyr of Spring hath returned!
The hoopoe from Sheba's domain, glad tidings to bring, hath returned!

2. Forth, forth, o thou bird of the dawn, With the ditties of David of old,
For the Solomon-rose to the meads, On the breezes a-wing, hath returned. [619]

3. The tulip hath scented the waft Of wine from the breath of the morn;
Heart-wounded she was [620], but, in hope Of medicining, hath returned.

4. O where is a sage that is ware Of the tongue of the lily, that he
May ask why it went and again To the bank of the spring hath returned.

5. Mine eyes in that caravan's track Shed tears without ceasing, until
To the ear of my heart the sweet sound Of its camel-bells' ring hath returned. [621]

6. Yea, Fortune God-given with us Hath bounteously dealt; since to us
Yon stone-hearted fair, for the love Of the Merciful King, hath returned.

7. Though Hafiz first opened the door Of offence and his covenant broke,
See her bounty, who now to our door With a peace-offering, hath returned.

[619] The rose, which seems to be borne on the Spring breezes, likened to Solomon, who
    rode on the wind.
[620] The tulip is styled by the poets "heart-scarred, wounded or branded", on account of
    the black streaks in its cup.
[621] i. e. I wept from the time of the Beloved's departure till I heard the sound of the
    caravan-bells which announced her return.

CLV

1. The rose, sans the cheek of the Friend, is not goodly;
Sans wine, the Spring season to spend is not goodly.

2. Without yonder tulip-cheeked loveling, the air
Of the garden or eke the field-end is not goodly.

3. The sugar-lipped, rose-limbed Beloved, without
Or kiss or embracement, to tend is not goodly.

4. Rose-rapture or cypress's dancing, [622]—except
The nightingale's note with them blend,—is not goodly.

5. Excepting the semblant it be of the fair,
Each [623] figure that Reason hath penned is not goodly.

6. Sweet wine is and garden and rose; and yet each,
Withouten the face of the Friend, is not goodly. [624]

7. O Hafiz, that base-metal coinage, thy soul,
As strewage on her to expend is not goodly.

[622] "Cypress's dancing", i. e. the swaying motion of the cypress's boughs in the breeze.
[623] Rhyme-word of C. I here repeated in original.
[624] The lack in English of an equivalent of the Scotch (Old North English) ae, "any",
    opposite of "none", is badly felt in passages such as this.

CLVI

1. Yest'reven, the wind brought news Of the Loved One from oversea:
I also, I gave my heart To the breeze; [625] let what will be!

2. My case to such straits is come That the gleaming lightning's flash
A confidant is each night And each morrow the wind for me.

3. My faithless heart, in the plait Of thy browlocks caged, saith ne'er,
"The old accustomed abode Be holden in memory!"

4. The worth of the counsel of friends And dear ones [626] I know to day.
O Lord, may our counsellors' hearts Be gladdened, I pray, of Thee!

5. My heart with remembrance of thee A-bleed is, whene'er in the meads
The fold of the rosebud's vest Undone of the wind I see.

6. The peak of thy royal cap Comes still to my mind, when the wind
The crown on the daffodil's head Doth set, as the bride of the lea. [627]

7. My weakling existence from hand Was gone; but the wind new life
Brought back to my soul in the dawn With thy tresses' fragrancy.

8. O Hafiz, thy constant soul Shall bring thee to thy desire:
All souls be the sacrifice Of the man of constancy!

[625] i. e. as a gift for good tidings.
[626] i. e. who counselled me to avoid love, for fear of the consequences.
[627] Eastern brides are crowned.

CLVII

1. O monarch, a ball in the crook of thy mall The firmament round for thee be!
The compass of being and time and space An exercise-ground for thee be!

2. All quarters holdeth thy good report; All climes of the world hath conquered
The fame of thy goodness: a guardian true For ever its sound for thee be!

3. The tress of the Lady of Victory still To thy horsetail ensigns cleaveth;
The eye of success [628] to all thy steps A lover bound for thee be!

4. O thou, the praise of whose pomp it is That Mercury [629] still enditeth,
The slave of the royal privy seal All-wit profound for thee be!

5. Thy shape like the cypress put to shame The glory of the Touba! [630]
The envy of heaven the courts, that ring Thy palace round, for thee be!

6. May beasts not only and plants and stones To thee obeisance proffer!
Nay, still at command in the world of command [631] Whatso is found for thee be!

7. Sick Hafiz, in all sincerity, Thine eulogist become is;
Thy favour the leach of him, whose voice Doth praise resound for thee, be! [632]

[628] *Syn.* "success itself", "the essence of success".
[629] Mercury, for the Muslims, is the scribe of heaven.
[630] See previous note.
[631] i. e. the created world, the world to which God said, "Be!"—and it was.
[632] A broad hint at largesse.

CLVIII

1. The tale of cypress, tulip, rose By mead and rill betideth,
Skinker; and with the washers three [633], this story still betideth. [634]

2. Drink wine, for lo! The meads' new bride [635] Hath reached the bounds of beauty;
No need the business of the time Of tirer's skill betideth. [636]

3. See, sugar-chewers now become The parrots all of Hind are,
Since Farsi sugar in Bengal From Hafiz' quill betideth. [637]

4. This one night's child [638] a twelvemonth's road Hath gone [639]; see how, in travel
Of verse, the rolling up of Time And Space to nil betideth.

5. See yonder eye ensorcelling, The devotee-beguiler;
The caravan of magic from Its window-sill betideth. [640]

6 Asweat she [641] goes with swaying gait, And on the jasmine's visage,
For shame before her face, such sweat As dews distil betideth.

7. Astray, for the world's blandishments, Go not; for from this beldam,
Whether she sit or go, there's nought But fraud and ill betideth.

8. Samíri like [642], who, spying gold, [643] Left Moses of his folly
And followed after calves, be not, Or evil still betideth. [644]

9. From the king's rosegardens the breeze Of the Spring season wafteth
And on the tulip wine of dews, Its cup to fill, betideth.

10. Of longing for Ghiyātheddín His court, Keep thou not silence,
Hafiz; for, by complaint, to thee Thy need and will betideth. [645]

[633] "The washers three"; three cups of wine drunk immediately after food and held by
    Eastern doctors a sovereign remedy against indigestion and ill humours, as *washing*
    away impurities.
[634] The meaning here is that Spring is the season of wine-bibbing.

[635] i. e. the new flowerage and leafage, Spring vegetation generally.

[636] i. e. the beauty of the time of Spring is self-sufficient and needeth no tiring, busking and painting, as with other brides.

[637] i.e. all the poets of India produce dulcet Persian verses, in imitation of the sweet songs of Hafiz, since the latter have made their way to Bengal.

[638] i. e. "This one night's child", i. e. poem produced in one night.

[639] "A twelvemonth's road", i. e. to Bengal. Hafiz sent an eulogistic poem to Ghiyatheddin Purbi, (A.D. 1367—1373) King of Bengal, who in return invited him to visit his court and promised him a pension. The poet is said to have accordingly set out for Bengal, but, on arriving at the nearest sea-port, was so alarmed at the idea of the sea-voyage before him that he abandoned his intention and returned home.

[640] The Beloved's eye declared to be the source and starting-point of all magic.

[641] "She", i. e. the beloved.

[642] "Samiri"; the Samaritan enchanter and rival of Moses, to whom Mohammedan fable attributes the making of the Golden Calf.

[643] "He looked upon (i. e. was tempted by) gold" Koran, XX, 87.

[644] i. e. be not like Samiri, who forsook the road of righteousness, i. e. the service of the Ideal, and followed after the goods of the transitory world.

[645] i. e. by the exercise of thy poetical faculty in expressing thy needs to the King of Bengal, thou wilt obtain from him the accomplishment of thy desires.

CLIX

1. A purpose I have, By which, if aright cometh
The thing I design, The end of despite cometh.

2. The stage of the heart No meeting-place is of opponents:
When Div goeth forth, Then angel sun-bright cometh. [646]

3. The commerce of kings Is the gloom of the long nights of winter;
Ask light of the sun [647]; May be it (the light) cometh.

4. At the door of the great Of the world, lacking kindness and bounty,
How long wilt thou wait Till yon man of might cometh?

5. Leave beggarship not Nor quest, till the treasure thou find
Of a wayfarer's grace, Who belike in thy sight cometh. [648]

6. The good and the bad Each showeth his ware: who, I wonder,
To favour and who To shame and to slight cometh? [649]

7. O bulbul love-lorn, Despair not of life; for the garden
Once more waxeth green, The rose bloom-bedight cometh. [650]

8. In this our mean world Small wonder if Hafiz be heedless;
An inn 'tis, wherefrom, Sense-ravished, each wight cometh. [651]

[646] i. e. Opposites cannot coexist in the heart; before the angel of love and

righteousness can enter, it must be purged of the Div of selfishness and impurity.

[647] i.e. seek cheer from the sun of the wine-cup.

[648] i. e. suffer thyself not to be lured by the delusions of the world from the quest of the true Beloved (the service of the ideal), which is only to be achieved in poverty and solitude, detachment from matters mundane. The "wayfarer" may here be either the Beloved or some experienced man who will guide the seeker to his desire.

[649] i. e. Devotee and toper, each claims to be in the right way; I wonder which of them will find acceptance and which rejection in the sight of God.

[650] i. e. Spring will yet return.

[651] The World likened to a tavern, where every one is bemused with the wine of its illusions.

CLX

1. Thy loveliness the sun of every eye be!
Fairer thy face than beauty's self to spy be!

2. Under that falcon-feathered Huma's pinions,
Thy tress, may all kings' hearts beneath the sky be

3. May he, who is not captive of thy tresses,
Like them, embroiled and tangled all awry be!

4. His heart, who is not of thy face enamoured,
Drowned in his liver's blood still doomed to lie be!

5. O idol, when thy glances scatter arrows,
Their target may my wounded heart and I be!

6. And when thy honeyed ruby giveth kisses,
The palate of my soul made sweet thereby be!

7. Each breath new love for thee in me awaketh:
New beauties thine with all the hours that hie be!

8. Thy sight with all his soul desireth Hafiz:
Bent on the longing lovers' case thine eye be!

CLXI

1. May thy beauty on the wax for aye be!
Tulip-hued that cheek of thine alway be!

2. May the image of thy love, that harb'reth
In my head, increasing day by day be!

3. May the stature of Creation's charmers
Bent in homage to *thy* stature's sway be! [652]

4. Every cypress, in the meads that springeth,
Bowed before thy shape erect as A [653] be!

5. May the eye that's not by thee distracted
Still to seas of tears and blood a prey be!

6. Skilled thine eye in every sort of witch'ry,
That may serve for leading hearts astray, be!

7. Wheresoe'er a heart for thee is troubled,
May it without patience, ease or stay be!

8. O that far thy lip, which Hafiz' soul is,
From the lip of the unworthy may be!

[652] *Lit.*, "be as [the letter] *noun*", which is a semicircle, enclosing a diacritical point
[653] i. e. *elif*, which is a perpendicular stroke.

CLXII

1. Thy body of the leaches' care For aye in need be not!
Thy tender being ever harmed Of Fate's misdeed be not!

2. Upon thy weal dependeth that Of all this world of ours;
God grant that sufferance to thee Of chance decreed be not!

3. Beauty of form and soul ensue The blessing of thy health:
Thine inward sad and grief-obscured Thine outward wede be not!

4. When Autumn cometh to despoil Life's fields, God grant its scathe
Wreaked on that lofty cypress-tree, Queen of the mead, be not!

5. Whereas thy beauty flowereth In splendour, possible
For hate or spite to enter in, With word or deed, be not!

6. May all, upon thy moonlike face Who look with evil eye,
Upon the fire of sorrow aught But wild rue-seed be not! [654]

7. Of Hafiz' sugar-scatt'ring speech Seek healing for thine ill,
So that of rosewater for cure Or syrups need be not!

[654] i. e. may all thine ill-willers writhe ever (like rue-seed on the chafing-plate) upon
the fire of sorrow!

CLXIII

1. The winecup in hand whoso doth hold,
The emp'ry of Jem e'ermo' doth hold.

2. In the winehouse the fountain of Khizr [655] seek;
Its water the winecup a-flow doth hold.

3. The end of life's thread to the cup make fast;
For ordinance life therefro' doth hold. [656]

4. Zealots and piety; we and wine:
For whether the Friend, I'd know, doth hold?

5. Skinker, excepting thy lip, there's nought
Of worth that this world below doth hold.

6. The drowsed narcissus from thy fair eye
Its borrowed graces and show doth hold.

7. The praise of thy cheek and thy tress my heart
At dawn-white and evenglow doth hold.

8. Full salt-rights over the wounded breast
Thy lip of ruby, heigho! doth hold. [657]

9. O soul, in the chin-pit, thy beauty slaves,
Like Hafiz, hundreds arow doth hold.

[655] i. e. the fountain of eternal life.
[656] i. e. life is ordered and made fair by wine.
[657] For an explanation of "salt-rights" see previous note.

CLXIV

1. Whoe'er the beauty of the down On the Friend's cheek in sight hath
The goal of vision and of wit, Certes, attained the wight hath.

2. Pen-like, upon her royal writ [658] The head of our obeisance
We've laid, albeit she with sword To take it off the right hath. [659]

3. To thine enjoyment he alone Findeth accéss, each moment
Who, candle-like, another head, For that thy sword to smite, hath.

4. Unto the kissing of thy foot That man alone attaineth
Who, like the threshold, at thy door His head still day and night hath.

5. One day thy watcher at my breast Hath launched an arrow, seeing
The might of grief for thee my heart Defenceless made outright hath.

6. Of barren pietism sick Am I: bring wine unmingled;
For lo! its scent the power to hold My brain still fresh and bright hath.

7. If nought but this [660] wine profit thee, Is't not enough, a moment,
That it from reason's fasheries To set thee free the might hath?

8. He, who ne'er yet without the door Of piety foot planted,
Now, to the winehouse-quarter bound, Himself for travel dight hath.

9. The brand of passion to the dust Will bear heart-broken Hafiz,
Which on his liver, wellaway! Wild tulip-like, [661] the wight hath.

[658] *Perwaneh*, mandate, patent of admission (to the Beloved's presence), syn. "moth",
hence used p. g. An allusion is also intended to the Beloved's down, the name of
which (*khedt*) means also "writing".
[659] The simile of the reed-pen is carried throughout; i. e. the Beloved hath the right and
power to cut off the lover's head, as one decapitates a reed for the purpose of making
it into a pen.
[660] "This," i. e. deliverance from the annoy of reason.
[661] The black marks in the tulip's cup likened to brand or cautery-marks on its heart.

CLXV

1. She, whose hyacinthine ringlet Civet in despite still holdeth, [662]
Coquetry with heart-bereft ones, Ay, and sore unright still holdeth.

2. By the victims of her beauty, Like the wind, alack! she passeth;
What's to do? For she our life is And to haste of flight still holdeth. [663]

3. Since Life's water 'tis that welleth From the lip of the Beloved,
Khizr's fountain but a mirage, Plain it is to sight, still holdeth.

4. Her sun-seeming moon, that glitt'reth Through the curtain of her tresses,
Is a very sun, a cloud-screen That before its light still holdeth.

5. Lo, mine eye with tears a torrent From each coign hath set a-running,
Wherewithal thy mirrored cypress-Shape it fresh and bright still holdeth.

6. On unrighteous wise (the wantons!) Have thy glances shed my heart's blood:
Well and good! Their every motion What is just and right still holdeth.

7. Of my heart thine eye, that toper Warm with wine, my liver seeketh; [664]
Drunken Turk! Meseemeth longing For roast meat the wight still holdeth.

8. My sick soul of thee to question Dareth not. O happy lover
Who an answer from the Loved One, Ere he speak or write, still holdeth!

9. When a look at heart-lorn Hafiz Will thine eye vouchsafe, that toper
Which in every coign a victim, Ruined of its might, still holdeth?

[662] i. e., the scent of thy locks filleth civet with envious despite.
[663] i. e. the Beloved passeth by swiftly as life itself.
[664] i. e. seeketh my liver, (which is the seat of love,) to devour it.

CLXVI

1. The messenger with the glad news From Asef [665] last night is arrived,
That from Solomon's [666] presence the sign Of leave for delight is arrived. [667]

2. The dust of our being make thou Into clay with the tears of the eye;
For the season, the ruinous house Of the heart to redight, is arrived.

3. Come, cover thou up my reproach, O gaberdine liquor-berayed;
For to visit me yonder Belov'd, With skirt of pure white, is arrived.

4. The tales without end that folk tell Of the beauty and grace of the Friend
Of thousands one syllable are That to utt'rance outright is arrived!

5. The rank of each fair one to-day's Grown patent, since unto the place
Of honour yon moon, that illumes The feast with her light, is arrived. [668]

6. To Solomon's throne-top, whose crown Is the place of ascent of the sun,
Behold, with what courage an ant, Abjection despite, is arrived! [669]

7. Safe guard thy religion, o heart, From her wanton, ensorcelling eye;
For, on rapine and plunder intent, That bow-drawing wight is arrived.

8. O Hafiz, with poortith berayed Thou art: ask largesse of the King,
For that soul of largesse to make clean From poverty's blight is arrived. [670]

9. The Sultan's assembly's a sea Of grace; the occasion come seize;
Quick, loss-stricken one! For the hour Of traffic [671] in sight is arrived.

[665] "Asef, i. e. the Grand Vizier Hajji Kiwameddin Hassan.
[666] *Solomon*; Shah Shejaa.
[667] Shah Shejaa, on his accession, being a bon vivant and a lover of mirth and music, repealed the laws against wine and merrymaking.
[668] i. e. Other fair ones are relegated to their proper place in public estimation, when our beloved one showeth herself.
[669] Alluding to the story of the queen-ant, which is fabled to have climbed to the top of Solomon's throne and begged him to prevent his troops from trampling her subjects.

Beloved here likened to Solomon and lover to ant. "The place of ascent of the sun" is the Fourth Heaven, the abode of Jesus, and the whole couplet is meant as an incitement to resolution, according to Soudi, who quotes, in illustration, the two following Arabic proverbs; "Man flieth (or soareth) with his resolution [like as the bird with its wing]", (*Meidani* 2954) and "Man's resolution uprooteth mountains", (*Meidani* 3178).

[670] Shah Shejaa is said to have been a man of great liberality and a bountiful patron of poets and learned men. He showed Hafiz especial favour and his vizier was the poet's consistent friend and disciple.

[671] i. e. Now is the time to exert thyself and profit by the opportunity.

CLXVII

1. To me the East wind yesternight The tidings rare hath brought
That tow'rd an end its face the day Of grief and care hath brought.

2. Unto the minstrels of the draught Of dawn our raiment torn
We'll give as gift for the glad news The morning-air hath brought.

3. Come, come; for thee into the world, Houri of Paradise, [672]
For the sheer sake of thy slave's heart, Rizwan [673] from there hath brought.

4. The wind-waft of thy tress is grown My Khizr [674] in Love's way;
O what a way-mate unto me My fortune fair hath brought!

5. How many a moan my heart hath sent Up to the tented moon,
When it that moon-cheek to my thought, Haloed with hair, hath brought!

6. Strive ye the heart of dervishes To win; for this felt cap,
Many's the breach on kingly crowns That it whilere hath brought! [675]

7. Mensóur's [676] insignia to the sky Hath Hafiz raised, since Fate
Unto the King of Kings' high court Him to repair hath brought.

[672] To the Beloved.
[673] "Rizwan"; the gatekeeper of Paradise.
[674] Khizr was fabled to befriend and guide strayed wayfarers.
[675] i. e. conciliate men of piety and learning; for their prayers are effectual, both for blessing and banning. "Felt cap" here a figure for the dervish order, the members of which wear a high pointed cap of felt. "Dervishes" here probably = men of learning and poets, servants of the Ideal, such as Hafiz himself, who gives an instance of their power in the following couplet.
[676] Shah Mensour, the fifth Muzefferi prince of Fars. The mention of this king, who did not accede to the throne till A.I). 1388, shows that Hafiz survived till after that date.

CLXVIII

1. He who did of rose and wild rose On thy cheek the hue bestow,
Ease and patience, an He will it, Can on me, that rue, bestow;

2. And His bounty, who the usance Of oppression taught thy locks,
Can on me, the sorrow-stricken, Justice for my due bestow.

3. From Ferhád my hope I severed From the time when on Shirín's
Lip the bridle of his frenzied Heart he did, I knew, bestow. [677]

4. If the golden treasure fail us, We've the corner of content;
He, who gave kings *that*, on beggars Did this latter, too, bestow.

5. Yea, a goodly bride the world is In appearance; but their lives
Must on her, to wedding-dower, Those her smiles that woo bestow.

6. Hence my heart to skirt of cypress And to marge of rill shall cleave,
More by sign the East glad tidings Doth of Springtide new bestow.

7. In the grip of Time's affliction Hafiz' heart is all a-bleed:
Great Kiwam-ed-dín, requital For the lack of you bestow! [678]

[677] i. e. I renounced hope of Ferhad, when he became a lover.
[678] A complaint of the absence or estrangement of his patron, the Grand Vizier.

CLXIX

1. If after her I follow, On me she troubles reareth;
And if I sit from seeking, To rancour straight she veereth:

2. And if I for loveliking, Like highway-dust, a moment,
Fall at her feet, she fleeth Like wind and disappeareth.

3. If half a kiss I covet, With mockeries an hundred,
From out that sugared casket, Her mouth, at me she fleereth.

4. Love's desert, hill and valley, The snare-place of mischance is:
Where is the lion-hearted, Whom no mischance affeareth?

5. The guile in that narcissus [679] Of thine I see: O many's
The face's sheen its treason With highway-dust besmeareth!

6. When "Why", of her I question, "With so-and-so dost mingle?"
She doth so that mine eyeballs With bloody tears she bleareth.

7. Pray thou for life and patience; For Fortune's wheel, the juggler,
Tricks by the thousand, stranger Than this thou seest, upreareth. [680]

8. Come, lay thy forehead, Hafiz, Upon submission's threshold;
For, an thou wrangle, Fortune In wrangling persevereth. [681]

[679] "Narcissus", i. e. eye.
[680] *Sic.* = playeth.
[681] i. e. nothing is so calculated to disarm Fortune as submission.

CLXX

1. The soul to life inclining, Without the Loved One's grace, hath not:
Who hath not *this*, *that*, certes, In any time or place hath not.

2. A trace of yon heart-seizer In none alive have I beheld; [682]
'Tis or that I no insight Or else that she a trace hath not.

3. The station of contentment Unmeet it were from hand to give;
Light down, o camel-driver; For end this way of chase [683] hath not.

4. Each dewdrop on this highway's An hundred seas of fire. Alack
That answer or solution Th'enigma of Love's case hath not!

5. But little pleasance, certes, Hath life without the one belov'd;
Yea, living aught of savour, Without the Friend's embrace, hath not.

6. The usances of toping Learn from the Mohtesib, O heart:
He's drunken; but misdoubtance Of him the populace hath not. [684]

7. Though thy spy be the candle, Look thou from it thy secrets hide;
For on its tongue a bridle That head-lopped scant-o'-grace hath not.

8. He, whom thou callest "master," [685] An if thou look, a craftsman is
In very deed; but verses, [Like mine,] that flow apace, hath not.

9. The crook-back harp to joyance Inviteth thee: its bidding hark;
The elder's [686] rede save profit For those of human race hath not.

10. The tale of Korah's treasure, That Time gave to the wind, tell ye
The rosebud, so she hidden Her gold in hoarding base hath not. [687]

11. In this our world no mortal A servant such as Hafiz hath;
Since any one a monarch, So fair as Thou of face, hath not.

[682] i. e. I can see none like her.
[683] i. e. the way of the quest of love.

[684] i. e. None suspecteth him of winebibbing.
[685] i. e. Some contemporary poet, who had apparently been compared with Hafiz.
[686] Harp called "elder", because of its crooked back, as bowed with age.
[687] Bid the rosebud not hoard her beauties, but blossom and give them freely to the world; a hint to the Beloved. The rose's gold is the stamens in her corolla.

CLXXI

1. Lo, the shining moon thy face's Argent sheen hath not
And the rose, by thee, the grass's Lustre e'en hath not.

2. In the corner of thine eyebrow Is my soul's abode;
Goodlier dwelling than this corner King or queen hath not.

3. What will my heart's smoke, [688] I wonder, Do with that thy cheek?
Since the mirror power to suffer Sighs, I ween, hath not. [689]

4. Not I only the oppression Suffer of thy tress;
Who is't that of yonder blackmoor Branded been hath not?

5. Yonder eye of thine, my fairest, That black-hearted one,
Least regard for friend or comrade, That I've seen, hath not.

6. Quick, the heavy [690] pottle bring me, Youngling of the inn;
Here's a sheikh's good health, who cloister, Fat or lean, hath not! [691]

7. Drink thy blood, friend, and sit silent; For that tender heart
Strength to bear the justice-seeker's Wailing keen hath not.

8. See the face of the narcissus, Blooming in thy sight!
Nay, regard for breeding yonder Shameless quean [692] hath not.

9. With the blood of his own liver Bid him wash his sleeve
Who of access to this threshold Way or mean hath not.

10. Blame not Hafiz, if prostration He to thee perform;
For Love's infidel, o idol, Aught of sin hath not. [693]

[688] Sighs are called the heart's smoke.
[689] Girl's cheek likened to metal mirror, which would be rusted by sighs.
[690] Heavy, i. e. full of wine.
[691] Alluding (says Soudi) to Hafiz's old teacher Sheikh Mohammed Attar, who kept no cloister, but lived by his trade of a druggist or grocer (*Attar*); but the Sheikh (Elder) of the Magians, i. e. the tavern-keeper, I more probably meant.
[692] i. e. the narcissus, which has the impudence to flower in thy presence.
[693] A pun is here intended; Hafiz says, in effect, "the *Kafir* i.e. concealer (syn. "heretic, infidel") of love commits no sin; for to conceal love is praiseworthy".

CLXXII

1. Our Book, [694] for this many a year, In pawn for the vinejuice red is;
Yea, still from our lore and prayer The sheen of the winehouse shed is.

2. The Sheikh of the Magians' grace To us poor sots consider;
Whatever we do in the eye Of his favour goodlihead is.

3. With wine let us all to-wash The writ of the understanding;
For spite against those that know In heaven, I've seen, inbred is.

4. My heart, like the compasses, In all directions turneth;
And yet in that round the foot Of the dizzard fast in stead is. [695]

5. The minstrel such strains did sing Of passion and of anguish
That even the sage's eye With ruddy tears be-bled is.

6. In gladness I've blossomed out, Rose-like on the bank of the streamlet,
Because that her shade, that straight, Slim cypress, [696] o'er my head is.

7. THAT [697] from the fair, o heart, Seek, if thou know what's goodly;
For so said one in lore Of insight who well read is.

8. My elder, Sheikh Gulréng, [698] Anent yon blue-gowned gentry [699]
Misspeech and blame forbade; Else much there to be said is.

9. Hafiz's gilt base coin To him [700] is never proffered;
For 'ware of hidden faults The mate at board and bed is. [701]

[694] The Koran?
[695] Yet is it still centred fast in the love of the beloved.
[696] Because I am in the shadow of the Beloved's favour.
[697] i. e. the subtle inexpressible charm, the Spanish *Sal*, the French "je ne sais quoi".
[698] "Sheikh Gulreng", the title in religion of Hafiz's teacher, Sheikh Mohammed Attar,
     before named.
[699] i. e. the Soufis.
[700] i. e. Sheikh Gulreng.
[701] i. e. Those who have lived with a man know all his secret defects.

CLXXIII

1. All the talk with us yest'reven Of those ringlets rare of thine was;
Till the heart of night, the question Of that tangling hair of thine was.

2. Yea, the heart, though all a-bleeding For the arrows of thy lashes,
Once more longing for the bow-horns Of that eyebrow-pair of thine was.

3. God be gracious to the East wind, That of thee to us brought tidings!
Else, on none we lit who coming From that quarter there of thine was.

4. Ere thou wast, the world knew nothing Of Love's mischief and its stresses;
Nay, the world's first strife-exciter That bewitching air of thine was.

5. Of the people of salvation Even *I* was, the distracted,
Till I taken in that blackmoor Browlock's highway-snare of thine was.

6. Loose the fast'ning of thy tunic, So my heart may be expanded;
For whatso I've found of solace From that side, fore'er, of thine was.

7. By thy faith, I do adjure thee, Pass thou by the tomb of Hafiz,
Who the world hath left and longing For that face, my fair, of thine was.

CLXXIV

1. Be't remembered that my dwelling Erst thy door anigh was,
From thy threshold's dust that gotten Lustre for mine eye was.

2. What within thy heart was, truly, That my tongue did utter;
Like to rose and lys, for commerce With the pure, pure *I* was.

3. When the heart from Gaffer Reason Sayings hard reported,
Love expounded what uneasy For it to descry was.

4. In my heart, without the Loved One Ne'er to be, I purposed:
But to what avail? For idle All that I could try was.

5. Yesternight, in thought of comrades, Went I to the winehouse,
Saw the jar, that foot in clay set, Heart with blood [702] filled high, was. [703]

6. Far and wide I sought the reason Of the pain of sev'rance;
Reason's Mufti [704] to this question Pow'rless to reply was.

7. True it is Bou Ishac's [705] turquoise Seal-ring for a season
Glittered proudly; but his fortune Swift of passing by was.

160

8. 'Las, the evil and oppression In this place of ambush! [706]
'Las for all the ease and pleasance In that palace high [707] was!

9. Heardest thou the laughter, Hafiz, Of yon strutting partridge?
Heedless it of Fortune, hawk-like Swooping from the sky, was.

[702] i. e. red wine.
[703] Wine-jar the similitude of the lover of the Ideal, whose feet are fettered to earth and
whose heart is ableed with chagrin.
[704] *Mufti*, generally a professional assessor to the Cadi, here a lawyer who gives
decisions on cases of theological jurisprudence.
[705] Shah Sheikh Abou Ishac, Governor of Shiraz under the last (fainéant) Ilkhani
Sultans of Fars, from A. D. 1336 to A. D. 1353, when he was taken and put to death
by Mubariz-ed-din Mohammed Muzeffer, the founder of the Muzefferi dynasty of
Fars. He (Abou Ishac) was a Sheikh of the Soufi order and a great patron of the
learned and out of humility made the beazel of his seal-ring of turquoise, instead of
more costly jewels.
[706] i. e. The world.
[707] i. e. that of Abou Ishac.

CLXXV

1. What while there of wine and winehouse Name and trace shall still be,
Dust upon the Magian Elder's Path our face shall still be.

2. When thou passest by our grave-head, [In our name] ask blessing;
For the Mecca of the topers All the place shall still be.

3. From all time, the Magian Elder's Slave-ring in mine ear was;
As we were, we are and even Thus the case shall still be.

4. Go, proud zealot! For this myst'ry [708] From thine eye and mine is
Hid and hidden, while endureth Time-and-Space, shall still be.

5. Drunk, to-day my lover-slaying Turk [709] went forth. I wonder,
From what victim's eyes the heart's blood Shed apace shall still be?

6. Yea, the place of their prostration, For the folk of vision,
Wheresoever is the foot-mark Of thy pace, shall still be.

7. Till the Judgment-morn, that night-tide, [710] When for thee of longing
Died it, from mine eye Time pow'rless To efface shall still be.

8. If this fashion Hafiz' fortune Aid him, [711] the Beloved's
Tresses in the hand of others, More of grace, shall still be. [712]

[708] Soudi says, "the mystery of love"; but quaere?

[709] i. e. The Beloved.
[710] Apparently some night of union with the Beloved.
[711] Ironical.
[712] A complaint of his ill fortune, which severed him from the Beloved.

CLXXVI

1. Come the glad news is that the days Of woe will not abide for ever;
That (gladness) bided not and *this* Eenso will not abide for ever.

2. Though in the sight of the Belov'd Like dust, indeed, we are and abject,
The rival honoured on this wise, I trow, will not abide for ever.

3. Since with his falchion He the door That keepeth [713] smiteth all and several,
A mortal in this precinct, here Below, will not abide for ever.

4. Thy present union with the moth [714] Enjoy, o candle; for this commerce,
Thou hold'st till morning set the skies Aglow, will not abide for ever.

5. The angel of the Spirit-world Gave me this message of glad tidings,
That one afflicted in this world Of show will not abide for ever.

6. What room for thanks or plaint anent This fleeting show of good and evil,
Since on life's page the writ of Yea Or No will not abide for ever?

7. The song of Jemshid's banquetings Was (so they tell us) on this fashion,
"The wine-cup bring, for Jem himself, Heigho! will not abide for ever".

8. O man of might, bestir thyself To win the heart of this thy dervish;
For stores of silver, ay, or gold, We know, will not abide for ever.

9. On yonder sapphire dome of heav'n, Lo! "Aught", in words of gold they've written,
"Save kindly deeds, from generous hearts That flow, will not abide for ever".

10. To-day, at dawn, the ghittern's trill Gave me this message of glad tidings,
That any mortal in the bond Of woe will not abide for ever.

11. Despair not, Hafiz, of the Friend's Affection, for oppression's usance
And violence of angry Fate, The foe, will not abide for ever.

[713] i. e. Death, the keeper of the door of Life, frenzied lover.
[714]"The moth", emblem of the frenzied lover

CLXXVII

1. In the Friend's high places every Heart's initiate [715] abideth
And whoso this craft ignoreth Still a renegate abideth.

2. Blame my heart not, if it issue Forth the curtain of concealment;
God be thanked that it no longer In pride's prison-grate abideth! [716]

3. Lo, whilere I had a patchcoat And an hundred faults it covered;
Pledged for wine and song the rag was; But the girdle strait abideth.

4. Out of pawn for wine the Soufis Took their gaberdines; mine only
'Tis that in the vintner's keeping Early still and late abideth.

5. Goodlier object of remembrance Than Love's speech's sound I never
Knew of all that in this whirling Round of things create abideth.

6. Other patchcoateers have drunken Been of yore, and 'tis forgotten;
But *our* case at each street-corner Ever in debate abideth.

7. Save my heart that goeth loving Aye and evermore, I never
Heard of any one who constant Still to Love's estate abideth.

8. Every ruby draught I've taken From her crystal hand's grown water
Of regret and in mine eyelids, Raining pearls, await abideth. [717]

9. China's fair ones [718] all astonied Are for wonder at thy beauty;
So their case, in every quarter, Limned on wall and gate abideth. [719]

10. The narcissus sought by sickness Like thine eye to grow, but could not
Catch its glamour and so sickly And disconsolate abideth.

11. In thy tress's pleasaunce Hafiz' Heart one day itself adventured,
Thinking to return, but captive Ever in that plait abideth.

[715] i. e. Every one who is initiated into, hath apprehended the heart's mystery.
[716] This Ode seems to refer to the poet's rejection of Soufism, of which he had been, in early life, a follower. It appears to mean as follows: "If I threw off the screen of false doctrine, blame me not; rather, God be thanked that I cast off the veil of error and hypocritical conceit and self-delusion and became aware of the Truth".
[717] Apparently an allusion to the wine which used aforetime to be poured to him by the Beloved and the remembrance of which had now become for him "water of regret", i. e. tears of yearning.
[718] The female forms pictured in Chinese paintings are the Persian ideal of beauty.
[719] As if fixed there in motionless and speechless amaze.

CLXXVIII

1. In thy heart of yore, Beloved, More concern for lovers' care was;
Yea, with us thy loving-kindness Talk of people everywhere was.

2. Be that commerce of the night-time Aye remembered when of lovers'
Bond and circle and Love's myst'ries Talk among the sweet-lipped fair was!

3. Though those moonfaced lovelings' beauty Ravished heart and faith and reason,
Yet our love for pleasant nature, Grace and fashions debonair [720] was.

4. If the shade of the Beloved [721] On the lover fell, what wonder?
Her we needed and desirous She of us, to make the pair, was.

5. Ere yon dome and arch of azure They on high upreared, the Loved One's
Eyebrow for mine eye the archway Of its belvedere whilere was.

6. From the Prime without beginning To the night of Endless Ever
Was our love and on one fashion Will be still as it fore'er was.

7. On the Night of Power [722] a dawn-draught If I drank, nay, never blame me;
For with wine the Friend came merry And a cup on shelf-edge there was.

8. If the chaplet-string was broken, Prithee hold thou me excuséd;
For my hand upon the silver-Shanked cupbearer's fore-arm bare was.

9. On my case this pregnant saying At the King's door quoth a beggar,
"Still, at whatso table sat I, God purveyor of the fare was."

10. Lo, in Adam's time, in Eden, Hafiz' verse the decoration,
Wherewithal the roses' petals, White and red, bewritten were, was. [723]

[720] i. e. in preference to mere personal beauty.
[721] i. e. the shadow of her favour.
[722] See previous note. The night in question is, of course, considered a specially holy
one, on which it would be particularly disgraceful to drink wine.
[723] i. e. (*semble*) "Hafiz's verses are part of the writing in the Book of Nature, of which
the rose-petals etc. are the leaves".

CLXXIX

1. When thy face's mirrored semblance On the goblet's shine befalleth,
Longing vain the greatest sages From the laughing wine befalleth.

2. From one single revelation Of thy beauty in the mirror
All the many a kind of picture, That men's thoughts design, befalleth.

3. How shall mortal with the age's Course but turn, as doth the compass,
In the days' revolving circle Since his lot, in fine, befalleth?

4. Never more, o sir, thou'lt see me In the cloister! With the skinker's
Cheek and goblet's lip henceforward This affair of mine befalleth.

5. It behoveth for her victims 'Neath grief's sword to go a-dancing:
Whoso's slain of her a goodly Ending, by this sign, befalleth.

6. From the mosque unto the tavern, Not of my freewill, I've fallen;
Thus it me by fore-eternal Ordinance Divine befalleth.

7. Since Love's jealousy still muteth Every noble tongue, how is it
In the vulgar's mouth their secret, Who for her do pine, befalleth?

8. Some new favour she each moment On me heart-a-fire conferreth:
See how worship-worth this lowly Beggarman of thine befalleth!

9. From thy chin-pit my heart, reaching, To the curl clung of thy tresses
'Las, it, from the pit escaping, In the springe's twine befalleth!

10. Soufis one and all whoremongers Are and topers; but, among them,
Unto heart-sick Hafiz only Ill-repute for wine befalleth. [724]

[724] This couplet states, with uncompromising plainness of speech, the poet's opinion of
his former associates of the Soufi persuasion; the meaning appears to be that, whilst
they cover their secret transgressions with hypocrisy and dissembling, he, being
frank and undissembling, is generally blamed for his peccadilloes.

CLXXX

1. All the Soufi's coin not wholly Pure from tincture of allay is;
Marry, of the fire deserving Many a patchcoat, sooth to say, is!

2. This our Soufi, him who useth With the dawn-prayer to wax drunken, [725]
Note him in the evening-season, When with wine he blithe and gay is.

3. Well it were if into usance Came the touchstone of experience,
So that black-aviced should every One become in whom allay is. [726]

4. 'Tis not affluence's nursling To the Friend accéss that findeth;
Loverhood of none but topers, Tried with suffering, the way is.

5. Sorrow how long wilt thou suffer For this rascal world? Drink wine, man;
Pity that the heart of sages Should be troubled with affray is.

6. If the skinker's down this fashion Write upon her face's water, [727]
Many a cheek with bloody water [728] Overpainted night and day is.

7. Hafiz' prayer-rug and his patchcoat Off the wineseller shall carry,
If the wine his cup that filleth Skinked by yonder moonfaced may is!

[725] i. e. who feigneth to be cast into ecstasy or spiritual intoxication by the devotional
    exercises of dawntide.
[726] "Allay" here (Soudi) = fraud, hypocrisy. Rhyme-word repeated.
[727] The translucent smoothness of the skin of the cheek likened to water.
[728] "Bloody water", i. e. tears of blood.

CLXXXI

1. My soul cometh forth [729] and my wish, Belov'd, of thee cometh not forth; [730]
My fortune from slumber and sloth, Ah, woe is me! cometh not forth. [731]

2. The wind of the East in mine eye Cast a grain of the dust of her street,
So the water of life in my sight, Inapt to see, cometh not forth. [732]

3. So long as thy tall slender shape I clip not, my fair, in mine arms,
To fruitage the plant of my heart, My wishes' tree, cometh not forth.

4. My heart in thy tress made its home; For't saw it a populous place. [733]
Since, news from that exile, oppressed Of misery, cometh not forth.

5. Belike that heart-comforting face Our wish shall accomplish; but, else,
On othergates fashion our need To certainty cometh not forth.

6. From the bow of sincerity shafts Of prayer by the thousand I launch;
What booteth it? One to the mark, The heart of thee, cometh not forth.

7. The least obligation of Love's Surrender, o Hafiz, of life;
Begone, if its due from thy hand, To this degree, cometh not forth.

[729] i. e. I am nigh to give up the ghost.
[730] i. e. is not accomplished. The phrase "cometh forth" has a number of different
    meanings in Persian, several of which occur in this ode.
[731] i. e. my fortune ceaseth not to be drowsy, i. e. unfavourable.
[732] Meaning, apparently, that the dust of the Beloved's street, entering the lover's eye,
    prevents him, so potent is its action as an eye-salve, from heeding or seeking the

166

water of life.

[733] This curious and (to an English ear) unpleasantly suggestive expression means that the Beloved's tress is full of lovers' hearts, which have cloven thereto and abide captive there; a common figure with Persian poets.

CLXXXII

1. My heart from me's gone and fruition, My case to amend, cometh not;
Myself from myself have I severed, And natheless the Friend cometh not.

2. In this my conceit and delusion, The season of life passeth by,
And yet her long tress's oppression, Alack! to an end cometh not.

3. My heart hath great plenty of stories To tell to the breeze of the dawn;
But morn to the night of my fortune, The darkness to rend, cometh not.

4. The shafts of my dawn tide complainings Used never to fail of their aim:
How is it one sigh to the target, Of all that I spend, cometh not?

5. Our life (wellaway!) and our substance We sacrificed not for her sake: [734]
Alack, that for love our devotion Thus far to extend cometh not!

6. For the grievous despite and aversion It feeleth 'gainst all mankind,
Now Hafiz's heart from the ring of The Loved One's tress-bend cometh not.

[734] i. e. We are to blame for our own failure to achieve union, since we fell short of the first obligation of a lover, which is the sacrifice of life and substance for love.

CLXXXIII

1. O happy his heart is that after The lusts of the eye goeth not,
That unto each door where they bid him, Unwotting of why, goeth not!

2. For me, after that sweet ruby [735] That I should not hanker of hers,
Were better; but after sugar, Woe worth it! what fly goeth not?

3. O thou that art of the angels, God grant that forth of thy mind
The troth that to me thou plightedst, In seasons past by, goeth not!

4. The black of mine eye grief-smitten Oh wash not away with tears,
That so of thy mole the image Fore'er from mine eye [736] goeth not.

5. None see I whose book is blacker; [737] 'Twere strange if, as ink in pen,
The smoke to my head of the burning Of this my hearts' sigh goeth not.

6. Heart, be not like this a babbler And vagrant; for aught of good
Or profit, God wot, from-thee-ward, This craft an thou ply, goeth not.

7. From the Path with the crest of the hoopoe [738] Ne'er lure me; the falcon white,
For pride, after every sparrow, That it may espy, goeth not.

8. On me like the East, come lavish Thy fragrance; for unto me,
Withouten the scent of thy tresses, There's nought that awry goeth not.

9. The fault of me drunk with the skirt-hem Of clemency hide: for so slight
A matter, the sheen of the Canon Of God the Most High goeth not. [739]

10. I yearn for a cypress-shaped loveling, (I, beggar that am!), whose zone,
Excepting for gold and silver, The hand to untie goeth not. [740]

11. Bring wine and first give it to Hafiz In hand, on condition the talk
Thereof from our privy circle, For fear of the spy, goeth not.

[735] i. e. lip.
[736] Rhyme-word of 1. 1 of Couplet I here repeated.
[737] "Blackness of book" usually = "sinfulness"; in which case the phrase would mean
"I see none more polluted with sin than I"; but, taken in conjunction with the
remainder of the couplet, it would rather seem to indicate gloominess of thought, the
head being oppressed and the brain darkened by the smoke of the burning head. The
"ink in pen" similitude is used, because Oriental ink is made with lampblack, which
is of course the direct produce of "smoke".
[738] "Lure me not with the crest of the hoopoe", i. e. with small game; tempt me not
from the way of righteousness with the idle goods of the world.
[739] i. e. The sheen, (lustre, *syn.* "honour") of the Law of God will not suffer by the
condonation of so trifling a matter as my sin of winebibbing.
[740] i. e., who requires payment in hard cash for her favours.

CLXXXIV

1. My soul longed sore that my heart's need Should be fulfilled; and 'twas not.
In this vain yearning I consumed For that I willed: and 'twas not.

2. In questing for the talisman That ruled the wished-for treasure,
The world on me, for grief of her, Was all forspilled; and 'twas not.

3. Woe and alack that in pursuit Of present ease, the generous
I oftentimes besought, as do The begging guild, And 'twas not!

4. In jest, quoth she, "The chief, one night, I'll be of thine assembly."
I lived her bondman, on that hope Whilst I did build; and 'twas not.

5. She sent me news that she would sit With winebibbers and topers:
My name forthright for winebibbing The wide world filled; and 'twas not.

6. Well may the heart's dove in my breast Flutter; for lo, the twinings
And springes of her tresses' snare Its pathway filled; and 'twas not. [741]

7. Of my desire, for drunkenness, To kiss her lip of ruby,
How on my heart much blood, like wine In cup, distilled! And 'twas not.

8. Without a guide, adventure not Thy foot in Love's direction;
For many pains I used to gain The thing I willed; and 'twas not.

9. Hafiz a thousand shifts devised, By dint of thought and longing,
That he might make that wilding tame; [742] But nought it skilled and 'twas not.

[741] i. e. Well may the heart palpitate with regret that it escaped the snare of her tress
and was not taken therein!
[742] i. e. that he might bring the Beloved to consent to his wishes.

CLXXXV

1. The love of black-eyed maids, indeed, Forth of my pate will nowise go;
This is heav'n's ordinance and it On other gate will nowise go.

2. The spy stirred trouble up and strife And left no place for peace-making:
Sure, the dawn-risers' sighs unheard At heaven's gate will nowise go! [743]

3. Time Unbegun, no lot to me, But that of toping, They ordained:
Each earthly lot, save as that day Foreordinate, will nowise go.

4. A privy place and ruby wine, A loving friend to cupbearer;
It better, heart, for thee, than this Thy now estate, will nowise go.

5. Vouchsafe us, Mohtesib, the sound Of drum and pipe: the Law's rébeck
Sure, out of tune, for such a thing Of little rate, will nowise go. [744]

6. I can but love her secretly: Of clip and kiss how shall I speak?
Since these unto my wish, denied Of sorry Fate, will nowise go.

7. Wash not grief's charact'ry, o eye, From Hafiz' breast; the charmer's sword
Graved it, and stains of blood, though washed Early and late, will nowise go.

[743] i. e. Surely God will hearken to the prayers of lovers, who wake the night and rise
to pray at daybreak, (when prayers are certain of acceptance,) and punish the
malignant mischief-maker.
[744] i. e. See note 5 to Ode 183.

CLXXXVI

1. When Time Unbegun thy beauty's sheen In manifestation set,
Love patent became and fire forthright To all creation set.

2. The angels thy cheek's resplendence saw And loved not; whence sheer flame
'T incontinent grew and fire to man, For mortification, [745] set.

3. Reason its lamp at that flame would fain Have lit; but the levin-brand
Of jealousy flashed and all the world In conflagration set. [746]

4. The Foe [747] sought to win to the secret of Love; The hand of th' Invisible
There came and upon his breast the brand Of repudiation set.

5. All others the die of allotment did On pleasure and easance cast;
Our woe-stricken heart alone on grief The lot of vocation set. [748]

6. The lofty soul in the pit of thy chin For longing fell; and so
To the ring of thy tress's curl its hand It for salvation set.

7. The book of delight of the love of thee Will Hafiz close, when he
To all heart-gladdening doth the pen Of nullification set.

[745] i. e. being mortified at its failure to excite love in the angels.
[746] Reason and Love being incompatible.
[747] "The Foe"; i. e. Satan.—*Soudi.*
[748] On the Day of Creation, when their various lots were foreappointed to mankind, others chose (or were allotted) pleasure and ease; I alone chose the grief of loverhood.

CLXXXVII

1. O remember how in secret Erst with us thy grace was,
How the love of thee's sign-manual Patent on our face was!

2. Ay, remember how, with chiding When thine eye did slay me,
Jesu's leachcraft in thy sugared Lip and thine embrace was;

3. How, when we, in privy commerce, Plied the cup of morning,
Thou and I alone, yet, certes, God with us in place was;

4. How, when on my moon the fillet Bound, upon her stirrup
Still attendant yonder crescent Courier of space [749] was;

5. How I was a tavern haunter And how that which lacketh
In the mosque to-day vouchsafed me In the tavern base was.

6. Yea, bethink thee, when the jacinth Of the cup went laughing,
How between me and thy ruby Cómmuning apace was;

7. How thy cheek the taper kindled Of delight and joyance;
How this burning heart the heedless Moth about thy grace was!

8. How, indeed, in that assembly Of good sense and breeding,
Save the red wine's tipsy laughter, None in drunken case was!

9. How, (bethink thee), by thy judgment, Well and featly ordered
Was each unbored pearl that Hafiz Minded to enchase was! [750]

[749] i. e. the new moon.
[750] i. e. how Hafiz's verses were inspired and ordered by thy counsel.

CLXXXVIII

1. It may be, o heart, that the doors Of the winehouses they shall open,
That they of our straitened case The tangles one day shall open!

2. If them for the pietist's sake, Self-centred, They've shut, take courage;
Them haply they yet, in ruth On lovers' dismay, shall open.

3. For th' ease of the winebibbers' hearts, The morning-draught drinkers, o many
A door that is closed the key Of prayer in Love's way shall open!

4. The writ of the news of the death Of the vine-daughter write, so topers
The sources of blood in their eyes, Grief's tribute to pay, shall open.

5. For the death of sheer wine, cut the tress Of the ghittern! In token of mourning,
The plait of her twy-stranded tress Each cup-bearing may shall open. [751]

6. The door of the winehouse they've shut. The door of the house of dissembling
And fraud, suffer not, Lord, that they, To lead folk astray, shall open! [752]

7. To morrow, [753] o Hafiz, thou'lt see, From under this patchcoat thou wearest,
What girdles [754] to view They, perforce, On the Reckoning Day, shall open. [755]

[751] i. e. shall dishevel her hair, as do mourners.
[752] A prayer to God to prevent the hypocritical pietist from continuing to bubble the folk.
[753] "To-morrow", i. e. on the Judgment Day.
[754] "Girdles", emblem of Christianity and other non-Mohammedan confessions in the East; here = infidelities, hypocrisies generally.
[755] i. e. what corruption and rottenness will be brought to view from under the screen of pietistic dissimulation and sanctimonious ostentation. The poet speaks of himself, but the verse is aimed at the Soufis and religious orders generally.

CLXXXIX

1. Sweet is seclusion, if the Friend In company with me be,
But not if, whilst I burn, the light Of others' banquets she be.

2. That signet-ring of Solomon [756] At nought I set, if on it
The hand of Ahriman [757] to seize At any season free be.

3. Permit it not, o Lord, that in The sanctuary of union
The spy a confidant and I A castaway from Thee be.

4. Say to the Huma, [758] "Never cast Thy pinions' shade of honour
"Upon that land where greater kites Than parrots in degree be". [759]

5. There ne'er departeth from our head The longing for thy quarter;
Still with their native land the hearts Of exiles oversea be.

6. What need love's longing to expound, Since in the speech's ardour
The fires, that at the lover's heart Are burning, plain to see be?

7. Though, as the lily's fashion is, Ten-tongued, [760] indeed, were Hafiz,
Still in thy presence, rose-bud like, Seal upon mouth, would he be.

[756] Solomon's seal-ring likened to Beloved's mouth.
[757] "Ahriman", i. e. Sekhr, the Div who stole the signet aforesaid; also here = rival,
     adversary, losel generally.
[758] The Beloved.
[759] "Kites" are worthless pretenders and "parrots" poets and men of learning.
[760] The lily's tongues are its leaves.

CXC

1. Marry, what an idle story This of my renouncing wine is!
Sure, this much at least of reason And of understanding mine is.

2. I with drum and harp that nightly Stopped on piety the highway,
Turn me sudden to the Pathway! [761] What a fable this of thine is!

3. Even now to end I know not All the pathway of the winehouse;
So unto what end, I know not, Our abstaining, by this sign, is.

4. If the pietist the topers' Pathway fare not, 'tis excused him;
Love's a matter that dependent On the leadership Divine is.

5. I'm the Magian Elder's bondman, Who from ignorance redeemed me;
Whatsoever doth our elder Very holiness, in fine, is.

6. Prayer and proudness for the zealot! Drunkenness for me and meekness!
Of us twain, o God, I wonder Whether favoured in Thine eyne is?

7. For this thought last night I slept not That a sage spoke thus; "If Hafiz
"Leave not drunkenness in season, Certes, reason for repine is."

[761] i. e. that of sobriety and lawfulness.

CXCI

1. I fear me lest our tears Veil-renders for our woe be, [762]
Our pain the talking-stock Of all men, high and low, be.

2. Stones in the stead (they say) Of patience turn to rubies:
In liver's blood alone Can they transfigured so be. [763]

3. In strait amaze am I For th' arrogance of rivals;
Honoured, o Lord, I pray, Let not the rascal foe be!

4. Seeing the stubborn pride That in thy cypress-head is,
How in this girdlestead Shall my short hand e'ermo be? [764]

5. From every nook I launch The shafts of supplication,
So one effective may, Of all that leave the bow, be.

6. That court imperial, Whereto as moon thou servest,
Its door-dust lovers' heads, That still its thresholds strow, be!

7. By thy love's alchemy My cheek's grown gold; [765] yea, truly,
Gold, by thy grace's spell, Become the clods below be.

8. Full many traits of grace Behove, not beauty only,
In who accepted will Of those that see and know be.

9. I'll to the winehouse go, Weeping and craving succour;
For there for me from grief Deliv'rance shall, I trow, be.

10. Soul, to the charmer tell Our tale; but on such fashion
That it not borne abroad Of all the winds that blow be.

11. Be patient, o my heart; Nurse not chagrin; for evening
Shall morning grow at last And night with dawn aglow be.

12. If sorrow on thee fall One day, be not strait-hearted;
Nay, give God thanks, lest heaped Upon thee woe on woe be.

13. When, Hafiz, in thy hand The muskpod of her tress is,
Be dumb, lest of the East The tale borne high and low be.

14. Lo, with my mother's milk, The love of thee hath entered
My head and heart and there Shall, till from me life go, be.

15. From out the tomb, his head, Thy foot to kiss, shall Hafiz
Uplift, if trod of thee The weeds, that o'er him grow, be.

[762] i. e. shall reveal our love.
[763] Patience bringeth everything to pass; but it is a painful remedy, bitter as aloes
(*szebr*, syn. "patience") and attended, like the ripening of rabies, with much effusion
of the blood of the liver. See previous note as to the maturation of rubies.
[764] How shall I, powerless as I am, ("short-handedness" id. for "weakness, poverty")
hope to attain to thine enjoyment?
[765] i. e. Yellow, pallid with suffering and wandesire.

CXCII

1. Parting's day and night of sev'rance From the Friend, at last, is ended;
And my need, through favouring planets, Since the lot I cast, is ended.

2. All the weariful vexation, That from Winter came and Autumn,
In the footsteps of the breezes Of the Spring is past, is ended.

3. To Hope's morning, self-secluded In the curtain of the future,
Say, "Come forth, for lo! the business Of the night aghast is ended."

4. God be thanked that, with the coming Of the cap-peak of the rose-bud,
Might of thorn and overweening Of December's blast is ended.

5. All the heart's grief and amazement Of the darksome nights of winter,
With the shadow of the loveling's Ringlets overcast, is ended.

6. Though my case's first embroilment From that tress of hers proceeded,
Yet the tangle of my troubles By her face as fast is ended.

7. To the winehouse-door henceforward Will I go with harp and tabret,
Now that, by her grace, the story Of chagrin, at last, is ended.

8. I'm no longer a believer In the perfidy of Fortune,
Since, in union with the Loved One, Parting's tale at last is ended. [766]

9. Skinker, kindness hast thou shown us, (Be thy goblet full of liquor!)
Our cropsickness, by thy manage, From the head out-cast, is ended.

10. Hafiz in consideration And esteem though no one holdeth,
God be thanked that this affliction, Without limit vast, is ended!

[766] This couplet is a variant of No. 7 and has the same rhyme-word; one of the two is,

in all probability, spurious.

CXCIII

1. Though the saying to the preacher Of this city light no whit is,
While he useth fraud and semblance, Musulman the wight no whit is.

2. Learn thou toping and do kindness: That a beast no liquor drinketh
And a man is not, a merit, In the sage's sight, no whit is.

3. God's Great Name its own end worketh: Heart, content thee; for the demon,
Maugre practice and dissembling, Solomon of might no whit is. [767]

4. Essence pure to that behoveth Which receptive of God's grace is;
Every stone or clod one seëth Pearl or coral bright no whit is.

5. Love I practise; and my hope is That this noble use, like other
Merits, reason of rejection Or of Fate's despite no whit is. [768]

6. Yesternight quoth she, "To-morrow Thy heart's wish I will vouchsafe thee."
Grant it God that she repentant Of her promise plight no whit is!

7. Gentle nature and fair fashions 'Tis my prayer that God vouchsafe thee;
Else assured 'gainst fresh vexation At thy hands our spright no whit is.

8. Hafiz mine, what while it lacketh Loftiness of soul, the atom
Seeker of the sun's resplendence And the fount of light no whit is. [769]

[767] i. e. religious observances and professions are of no avail, unless practised with sincerity and whole heartedness. "God's Great Name" is the secret name of God, known only to the initiate, which gives the knower power over all things; it doth its own work, regardless of the pretentions and frauds of mortals.
[768] Merit of any kind is for the folk a cause of rejection and incurreth the spite of Fortune, that fosters the base and worthless.
[769] An exhortation to the despairing lover to pluck up a spirit and aspire. "She is a woman; therefore, to be won".

CXCIV

1. Quoth I, "I am sad for thy sake;" And "Thy sadness," quoth she, "to head cometh." [770]
Quoth I, "Be my moon;" and "Ay well, If the thing to pass thus," she said, "cometh."

2. Quoth I, "That thy cheek is a moon;" And she, "Ay, and one of a fortnight."
Quoth I, "Will it shine upon me?" "To pass if it thus," she said, "cometh." [771]

3. "Fidelity's usance," quoth I, "I counsel thee learn of thy lovers."
"This fashion from moon-favoured ones But seldom," she answered. "cometh."

4. Quoth I, "On thine image I'll shut The pathway of sight;"but "Mine image,"
Rejoined she, "a night-walker is And by ways sight-unvisited cometh."

5. "The wastril," quoth I, "of the world The scent of thy tresses hath made me."
And she, "An thou know'st, to thy guide, The fragrance my ringlets shed cometh."

6. "How goodly and pleasant," quoth I, "The breezes that blow from Love's garden!"
"How blessed a zephyr," quoth she, "From the charmer's abiding-stead cometh!"

7. Quoth I, "We are slain for desire Of thy ruby lip's honey." She answered,
"Serve well and in time the reward, Thy service hath merited, cometh."

8. "O when will thy pitiful heart," I questioned, "incline to relenting?"
Quoth she, "Speak to no one of this, Till the season of kindlihead cometh."

9. Quoth I, "How to end come the days Of delight!" And she answered, "Peace, Hafiz!
"For anon to an end, on like wise, This anguish and drearihead cometh." [772]

[770] i. e. to end. We may also read, with Soudi, "May it come to end and we be so
    delivered from thine importunity!"
[771] Rhyme word of line I repeated.
[772] i. e. neither gladness nor grief hath any abiding here below.

CXCV

1. He, in whom desire of traffic With thy down, my sweet, shall be,
Whilst he liveth, in this circle Ever fast his feet shall be.

2. From the grave-mould, tulip-fashion, When I rise, Love's scars, for thee
Worn, the secret of my bosom's Innermost retreat shall be. [773]

3. Where art thou, o pearl unvalued, For whose image this mine eye
Is and ever like an ocean, Where all waters meet, shall be?

4. Be the shadow of thy tresses Ever lengthened o'er my head,
So thereby my heart distracted Eased of passion's heat shall be!

5. From my every eyelash water Ever running is: then come,
When in thee desire for pleasance And the streamside seat shall be.

6. Like my heart, come forth a moment From the veil and enter in;
'Tis not certain when another Time for us as meet shall be.

7. Out of pride, thine eye from Hafiz Thou avertest; verily,
Still the blue narcissus' [774] fashion Heavy-head conceit [775] shall be.

[773] Similitude of tulip continued, with allusion to the black marks in the cup, to which

the scars of the lover's heart are likened.

[774] *Nergis-i-shehla*, the dark-blue narcissus, unknown, I believe, to European botany; here of course, a figure for an eye of that colour.

[775] "Heavy-headedness" Pers. id. for "arrogance, conceit". The allusion is, of course, to the pensile habit of the narcissus.

CXCVI

1. When the light of the sun of wine The East of the bowl forth cometh,
O many a tulip the garth Of the cupbearer's jole forth cometh! [776]

2. The breeze on the head of the rose The curl of the hyacinth breaketh,
When midward the meads the scent Of that tress and that mole forth cometh.

3. Hope not that a crumb from the round Of the heavens' inverted platter, [777]
Unbought with an hundred woes, For thee, o my soul, forth cometh.

4. The anguish of sev'rance's night No history is of whose import,
For treatises hundred-fold, One particle sole forth cometh.

5. If thou, 'neath the stress of the Flood, Like Noah, have patience, the deluge
Subsideth and syne for thy wish Its thousand years' goal forth cometh.

6. One cannot attain of oneself To the pearl of desire; 'twere idle
To think that this business, without Heav'n's help and control, forth cometh,

7. O'er Hafiz's tomb if the waft Of thy pleasantness pass, from his ashes,
Incontinent, thousand-voiced, The sound of his dole forth cometh.

[776] i. e. the skinker's cheek becometh flushed and ruddy.
[777] Sky commonly likened to an inverted tray, platter or basin.

CXCVII

1. Why is it my cypress unto the meads, Now Spring is here, inclineth not?
That she to the rose and the jessamine Of the new-born year inclineth not?

2. Since unto the China [778] of that her tress My vagrant heart departed,
From that far clime to its native land The rogue to recur inclineth not.

3. My heart, with the hope of thine union dazed, No longer the mate of the soul is;
My soul, of its wish for thy stead, to serve, At the body's spur, inclineth not.

4. To the bow of her brows I offer up My humble supplications;
But strained and strait are its horns; and so To me its ear inclineth not.

5. To me, of her browlock yesterday Complaining, quoth she, jesting,
"This crookbacked blackamoor unto me Myself its ear inclineth not." [779]

6. Now by the breeze in many a curl The tress of the violet's broken,
What heart, like mine, to call to mind Yon pact-breaker inclineth not? [780]

7. Though my silver-shanked skinker nought but dregs Should skink us, who his body
All mouth, like the goblet of wine, to make, For love of her, inclineth not?

8. The breeze is a brayer of ambergris: From thy pure skirt how is it
The earth of the violet-bed to turn To musk and myrrh inclineth not?

9. I marvel how, for the scent of thy skirt, The East wind, as thou passest,
The dust of thy passage-way to turn To musk and myrrh inclineth not. [781]

10. The water of this my cheek [782] spill not; For never pearls of Aden [783]
The boons of the clouds make, if mine eye Still to concur inclineth not.

11. Slain of thy glances Hafiz is, Who hearkened not to counsel;
Nay, worthy of death is whosoe'er Advice to hear inclineth not.

[778] China. (*Chin*) mentioned only p. g.; because the Persian word *chin* means also curl, twist, plait.
[779] Rhyme-word of No. 4 here repeated.
[780] When Spring cometh, all hearts call to mind the Beloved, who is a covenant-breaker. I suspect *bunefsheh* here (as in other similar passages) to mean "Iris" rather than "Violet".
[781] Nos. 8 and 9 have the same rhyme-word and one is a variant of the other.
[782] "The water of my cheek", i. e. my honour, repute.
[783] The Orientals believe pearls to be formed by drops of rain fallen into the oyster. Aden, though not now celebrated for its pearls, appears to have been a noted pearling-station in Hafiz's time.

CXCVIII

1. In her face's time no lover Inclination for the mead hath;
Foot-bound is he like the cypress, Like the tulip, heart a-bleed hath.

2. This our heart on no wise boweth To the bow of any's eyebrow;
For the heart of the recluses Of the world no manner need hath.

3. Irketh me the violet's boasting Of its likeness to her tresses;
See what guile that good-for-nothing Blackmoor in its heart a-seed hath!

4. Dark the night and wild the waste is: Whither can I win, excepting
Lamp in hand the Loved One's visage, [784] Me upon my way to lead, hath?

5. With the candle of the morning, Well to weep it me behoveth;
For we burn and she, our idol, Of our case no manner heed hath.

6. Walk the meadows and the rose's Throne consider; note the tulip;
Like the Sultan's cup-companion, Goblet still in hand the weed hath.

7. Like the January rain-clouds, Needs must I beweep this meadow:
In the bulbul's nest of joyance, See, the filthy crow its breed hath.

8. By thy face's light, thy tress-tip All night long the heart waylayeth;
What a bold-faced thief, that nightly In its hand a lamp, [784] indeed, hath!

9. Lo, the anguished heart of Hafiz Longing for Love's lore possesseth;
So no mind it to the garden Or to pleasance in the mead hath. [785]

[784] The Beloved's face likened to a lamp.
[785] In this Ode, the rhyme-word 1. 1 is repeated in Couplets 2 and 5 and that of
Couplet 4 in Couplet 8.

CLCIX

1. Drinking and mirth in secret, Things without base [786] are they:
Cast we our lot with the topers, Come of it come what may!

2. Care's knot from the heart-strings loosen Nor reck of the course of the sphere;
For never geometer's science A knot such as this loosed aye. [787]

3. Ne'er marvel at fortune's changes; For tales by the million, such
As these, could the sphere of heaven Recall, if it chose to say.

4. The wine-pot with rev'rence handle; For know 'twas the dust of the skulls
Of Jem and Kobád and Behman, Whereof they fashioned its clay.

5. Where Kei and Kawóus have vaded, Who knoweth? And who can tell
How Jemshid his throne passed under The storm-blast of decay?

6. The lip of Shirín regretting, I see it, from out the blood
Of th' eyes of Ferhád, the tulip Yet blossometh to day.

7. Come let us with wine dead drunken And ruined awhile become!
Mayhap in this place of ruins [788] A treasure find we may. [789]

8. Meseemeth the tulip knoweth The faithlessness of Fate;
For never from hand, whilst living, The wine-cup doth she lay.

9. The breeze of the earth of Musélla And water of Ruknabád
Me never as yet have suffered To travel far away.

10. My soul what befell for sorrow Of love for the fair befell;
Yet ne'er may Time's eye of evil Smite on *her* soul, I pray!

11. The goblet, like Hafiz, take not, Except to the ghittern's wail;
For lo! the glad heart to music's Silk cordlet bound have They. [790]

[786] *Sic*; i. e. drinking and merrymaking in secret is a foolish and unsatisfactory business.
[787] i. e. no geometer (the term here includes astrologer) ever availed to solve the problem of the course of Fortune.
[788] The world.
[789] Treasures being commonly found in ruins.
[790] i e. The Fates, that rule all earthly things, have made gladness of heart dependent on music. Lutes and harps are partly strung with silk.

CC

1. Who of Fortune's grace held worthy At Creation's date, indeed, is,
For Eternity his wish's Cup his spirit's mate, indeed, is.

2. Quoth I, when to make renouncement Of winebibbing I was minded,
"If this plant bear fruit, repentance Early it or late, indeed, is."

3. Granted e'en I cast the prayer-rug, Like the iris, [791] o'er my shoulder,
Unmohammedan the patchcoat Wine-dyed, anygate, indeed [792] is.

4. If the winecup's lamp be lacking, Sit I cannot in seclusion;
Light behoving to the pious Anchorite's estate, indeed, is.

5. With the glow of wine and candle [793] Be our solitude enlightened:
Abstinence in rose-time folly For the profligate, indeed, is.

6. Doltishness it were the winecup From the Loved One's hand to take not,
When with friends we sit in Springtime And of love debate, indeed, is.

7. Strive for loftiness of spirit: "Let the goblet be unjewelled!"
Say. "The grapejuice, for the toper, Rubies-pomegranáte, indeed, is." [794]

8. Good repute an thou desirest, Heart, consort not with the worthless;
Folly, o my soul, the wicked It to tolerate, indeed, is.

9. Though disordered seem our fashion, Hold it not in scorn, for envied
Beggarhood in this our region [795] Of the Sultanate, indeed, is.

10. Yesterday quoth one, "In secret Hafiz drinketh wine". O zealot,
"What is secret undeserving For reproach to rate, indeed, is". [796]

[791] Iris (the common blue flag) likened to a pietist with his prayer-rug over his shoulder.
[792] i. e. even if we set up as pietists, the wine-stains on our clothes would betray us as

180

no true Muslims.

[793] "Candle" here (Soudi) = bright face of Beloved.

[794] The ruby wine standeth us in stead of jewels. *Yacout-i-rummani,* ruby-pomegranate, a kind of ruby so called from its resembling, in colour, the pulp of the pomegranate.

[795] i. e. in the lover's country.

[796] i. e. A fault that is kept hidden is not blameworthy; a true Oriental sentiment.

THE POEMS OF SHEMSEDDIN MOHAMMED HAFIZ OF SHIRAZ

NOW FIRST COMPLETELY DONE INTO
ENGLISH VERSE FROM THE PERSIAN, IN
ACCORDANCE WITH THE ORIGINAL FORMS,
WITH A BIOGRAPHICAL AND CRITICAL
INTRODUCTION, BY JOHN PAYNE, AUTHOR
OF "THE MASQUE OF SHADOWS AND OTHER
POEMS," ETC., AND TRANSLATOR OF "THE
POEMS OF FRANCOIS VILLON," "THE BOOK
OF THE THOUSAND NIGHTS AND ONE
NIGHT", "THE DECAMERON OF BOCCACCIO,"
"THE NOVELS OF BANDELLO" AND "THE
QUATRAINS OF OMAR KHEYYAM." IN THREE
VOLUMES. VOLUME THE SECOND.

ODES
(continued)

CCI

1. Except wine from our mind the thought Of the heart's care shall carry,
The fear of Fortune's shifts the base From our affair shall carry. [797]

2. Except in drunkenness's sea Reason let down the anchor,
Our life o'er this abyss of woes What bark is there shall carry?

3. Alack, that heaven, traitor-wise, With every mortal juggleth!
The vict'ry off from yonder knave There's none soe'er shall carry.

4. My sick soul turneth to the meads; Belike the blight of sorrow
Therefrom the East Wind, with its soft And languorous air, shall carry.

5. The way in darkness is: but where's A Khizr, who shall guide us? [798]
God grant the fire of sev'rance off Our water [799] ne'er shall carry!

6. I am Love's leach: drink wine; for this Electuary easance
Shall bring and from the soul the thought Of love-despair shall carry.

7. Hafiz consumeth and his case None to the Loved One telleth;
Haply, the breeze, 'fore God, [800] his tale Unto the fair shall carry.

[797] i. e. will ruin our lives.
[798] Allusion to the legendary expedition of Alexander and Khizr into the Regio
Tenebrarum, in quest of the water of life.
[799] "Water", i. e. water [of-the-face], honour, repute.
[800] i. e. for the sake of God, for pity's sake.

CCII

1. Yon meddler, at me who for love And toping outcry maketh,
The mysteries of the Unseen E'en bold to deny maketh. [801]

2. Regard thou the myst'ries of Love's Perfection and not sin's blemish:
The meritless man his sole aim Defects to descry maketh.

3. The cupbearer's glances the path Of Islam waylay on such fashion [802]
That none, save he be a Suhéib, [803] O' the grape-juice red fie maketh.

4. There breatheth abroad in the land The scent of the Houris of Heaven,
When she of our winehouse's dust The scent of her ply [804] maketh.

5. Th' approof of the noble's the key Of the treasure of happiness; marry,
There's none who this certitude bold To doubt or belie maketh.

6. The shepherd of Wadi Eimén [805] Attaineth his wish, who his business
With heart and soul Jethro to serve, Till years have gone by, maketh. [806]

7. When Hafiz to tell of the time Of youth and of elderhood's season
Beginneth, his tale tears of blood To drop from each eye maketh.

[801] i. e. those who rail at lovers and topers are infidels, who disbelieve in foreordinance
   etc.
[802] i. e. are subversive of religion.
[803] "Suheib"; see note to Ode LIV, 4.
[804] Sachets of scent are commonly worn in the plaits or folds of the dress, especially in
   the collar-ply.
[805] Moses.
[806] i. e. The lover, who would attain to his desire of the Loved One, must first
   accomplish the rites and services of loverhood.

CCIII

1. Unto us the bird of Fortune Yet its way belike shall make,
And with us (the Friend returning) Union stay, belike, shall make.

2. Though mine eyes avail no longer Pearls and gems to furnish, blood
Shall they drink and shift for strewage To purvey, belike, shall make. [807]

3. None to her our case dare utter But an if the East Wind's self
Bold our story to her hearing To convey, belike, shall make.

4. Flown have I the glance's falcon At a pheasant, [808] so of her,
(It to me the lure recalling), It a prey, belike, shall make.

5. Yestereven, "Will her ruby Lip my med'cine be?" quoth I.
Quoth the Viewless Voice, "Thy sickness Whole it, yea, belike, shall make." [809]

6. Void of lovers is the city; Yet, Love's service to fulfil,
One, somewhence, himself an off'ring To its sway, belike, shall make.

7. Where's the gen'rous, of the banquet Of whose mirth the sorrow-struck
Deep shall drink and with cropsickness Thus away, belike, shall make?

8. Faith or news of thine attainment Or the rival's death; please God,
One of these to have fulfilment Fortune's play, belike, shall make!

9. If from out her doorway, Hafiz, Thou remove not, yet by thee
Passage, from some privy corner, She one day, belike, shall make.

[807] i. e. if, for much weeping, my eyes have no tears left, they shall weep my heart's
blood instead, as a strewage of honour and thankoffering at the feet of the returning
Beloved.
[808] Beloved likened to pheasant.
[809] Ironical?

CCIV

1. The rose is come and best in Spring abideth
That in thy hand, save wine, no thing abideth.

2. Seize thou the hour; drink wine amid the roses,
For but a week their blossoming abideth.

3. Use, use the time of pleasance, for not always
A pearl in every oysterling abideth.

4. Rare way of love, where he his head uplifteth,
With whom no head, for love-liking, abideth! [810]

5. Leave books, an thou wilt be our fellow student,
For Love's lore not in book-learning abideth.

6. Give ear and set thy heart on one whose beauty
In need of no bedizening abideth.

7. Come to our winehouse, elder, and a nectar
Quaff, such as not in Kauther's spring abideth.

8. Thou, who fill'st gold with rubies, [811] oh largesse him
With whom no gold, poor scatterling, abideth!

9. Grant me, o Lord, a draught without crop-sickness,
Wherein no headache for a sting abideth.

10. 'Fore God, I have a silver-bodied idol; [812]
In Terah's [813] joss-house no such thing abideth.

11. With all my heart, I'm Shah Uwéis's [814] bondman,
Of slaves unmindful though the King abideth. [815]

12. The sun,—by his world-bright'ning cap I swear it,—
Than he less crown-embellishing abideth!

13. Those only carp and jibe at Hafiz' verses
In whom no grace of love-liking abideth.

[810] The more a lover abaseth himself, the more is he exalted. "To lose the head' either
    to die or to go mad.
[811] i.e. who drinkest wine out of cups of gold. Addressed to the King.
[812] i.e. Fair one.
[813] "Terah", Abraham's father, whom Muslims fable to have been a maker of idols for
    sale and high in favour with Nimrod.
[814] Gheyatheddin, surnamed Uweis, one of the Ilkhani Sultans of Baghdad, A. D.
    1356—74.
[815] The King had apparently neglected the poet.

CCV

1. Companions, the comrade, the night time Who watched with you, bear ye in mind;
The rights and the obligations Of service true bear ye in mind.

2. The sighing and wailing of lovers, In season of joyance with wine,
When the song of the harp and the bell-staff Ye hearken to, bear ye in mind.

3. What time to the waist of your wishes The hand of your hope ye set,
The time when we communed together And friendship's due bear ye in mind.

4. When the sheen of the winecup reflected Is seen in the cupbearer's cheek,
Midst singing and dancing, the lovers, Though past from view, bear ye in mind.

5. Though the cud of chagrin for their sorrow Ye chew not, who cleave to their faith,
The faithless behaviour of Fortune With old and new bear ye in mind.

6. How swift and fleet-footed soever The steed of your fortune may be,
With the whip-end the waymates, that after Your course ensue, bear ye in mind. [816]

7. For mercy's sake, ye that in honour's High places dwell, Hafiz and how
His head, save the dust of your threshold, No rest-place knew, bear ye in mind

[816] Soudi remarks that it is customary to restrain headstrong horses by touching them softly on the head with the whip-point. This seems wrong; the meaning of the couplet appears to be, "Remember not to urge the steed of your fortune over swiftly, lest your less favoured waymates be left behind".

CCVI

1. Joyful news, o heart! A Jesus-Breathed one, see, there cometh!
By her fragrant scent, that only Lovesome she there cometh.

2. Separation's grief no longer Mourn; for I an omen
Cast last night; and lo! a helper, At thy plea, there cometh.

3. In the fire of Wadi Eimen I rejoice not only;
Moses, eke, in quest of embers, Like to me, there cometh. [817]

4. None there is that hath not business In thy quarter; hither,
By the highway of his wishes, Every he there cometh.

5. No one knoweth where the Loved One's Camp-place is; the tinkle
Of a camel-bell, sure only Can one be, there cometh.

6. Give a draught; [818] for to the winehouse Of the gen'rous-hearted,
With intent of asking, every Debauchee there cometh.

7. If the Friend her woe-sick lover Think to visit, "Hasten,
"Whilst a breath yet from his bosom" (Bid her ye) "there cometh."

8. Of the bulbul of this garden [819] Ask ye; for a moaning
From a cage unto my hearing Momently there cometh.

9. Hafiz' heart the Friend would ravish: Lo, a royal falcon
Alter a poor fly pursuing, Comrades, see, there cometh!

[817] See previous notes.
[818] An appeal to the Beloved for favour.
[819] i. e. The forlorn lover.

CCVII

1. The good news is come that Spring's At hand, with its verdure fine:
An if the allowance come, We'll spend it in roses and wine.

2. Upriseth the birds' song: where Is the wine-jack? The nightingale
Waileth: who teareth the veil From the face of the eglantine?

3. The patchcoat, red as the rose, I'll burn; for the vintner old
Will purchase it not at the price Of a draught of the juice of the vine.

4. A rose from the moonlike cheek Of the cupbearer cull to day;
For, see, round the garden's face There sprouteth the violet's line. [820]

5. Thy foot in Love's land set not, Except with a guide of the road;
For lost is the man without guide Who fareth the way of this shrine.

6. What savour shall he, who ne'er The peach of a loveling's chin
Hath tasted, find in the fruits Of Paradise the divine?

7. The cupbearer's languorous looks Have ravished my heart from my hand,
That so unto others to speak Or hearken no power is mine.

8. Yea, many the marvels are, O friend, of the way of love!
The lion, in this wild waste, Is scared by the wild fawn's eyne.

9. Of anguish complain thou not; For know that, in questing's way,
Those only to easance win Who suffer without repine.

10. Ho, succour, 'fore God, thou guide Of the way to the sanctuary!
For lo! to Love's desert bound There is not nor yet confine.

11. Come, drink thou of wine and give To Hafiz the cup of gold;
Their sins to the Soufis hath Remitted the king benign. [821]

12. No rose from the garth of thy grace Hath Hafiz culled: 't would seem
No breeze of humanity O'erbloweth that mead of thine.

13. Spring fleeteth: come, succour me, O justice-dispensing One!
The season's at end and yet Hath Hafiz not tasted wine. [822]

[820] i. e. the dark down.
[821] i. e. semble, hath repealed the laws against winebibbing.
[822] Apparently, the allowance, mentioned in Couplet 1, was in arrear, as was and is
frequently the case with Oriental court-pensions etc.

CCVIII

1. The wineseller's sins, If he duly the winebibbers' need doth,
God pardoneth, yea, And sorrow from him and his seed doth.

2. Give, skinker, the wine In the measure of right, lest the beggar
Feel envy; for *that* [823] A worldful of misery breed doth.

3. Strike, minstrel, the lute! Without term appointed, none dieth;
And whoso this saw Denieth default 'gainst the Creed doth.

4. O sage, whether ease Or trouble betide thee, ascribe it
To none but to God, Who only whatever's decreed doth.

5. In a workshop, [824] wherein No way is for reason and learning,
What is it weak wit, Presuming the riddle to read, doth?

6. Yet, sure, from these woes Shall come the glad news of assurance,
If the pilgrim the due Of good faith to the compact agreed doth.

7. For us, who are racked With Love's pangs and the woes of cropsickness,
Her lip or sheer wine New health to our hearts all a-bleed doth.

8. In lust after wine, Life's gone and with love Hafiz burneth;
Where's one Jesus-breathed, That raising-again, in our need, doth?

[823] i. e. Envy.
[824] i. e. the world, where reason and learning have no *raison d'être*.

CCIX

1. Of the current coin, I wonder, Can it be assay they take,
So that all the cloister-keepers In transgression's way they take?

2. This my deeming is that lovers Should all business leave and hold
On some loveling's curling browlocks Should, for present stay, they take.

3. Well and wisely do the topers To the skinker's tress-tip cling,
So, if treach'rous Fate forsake them, Something stable may they take.

4. Since no shame the raven thinketh On the rose to tread, 'tis fit
For the bulbuls that, for shelter, To the thorn-set spray they take. [825]

5. Vaunt thee not of continence's Strength of arm before the fair;
In this tribe, with one sole horseman, Strongholds, wellaway! they take.

6. How sharp-set, alack! for bloodshed Be these children of the Turks!
With the arrows of the eyelash, At each glance, a prey they take.

7. Sweet the dance is to sweet singing And the wail of flutes; the hand,
More by token, when, in dancing, Of some lovesome may they take.

8. Nothing, Hafiz, of the wretched Reck the people of the time:
Better 'twere if, from amongst them, To a corner (say) they take. [826]

[825] Since the base and vulgar occupy all the stations of honour and worship, folk merit
must needs resign themselves to humiliation and abjection.
[826] i. e. to retirement.

CCX

1. The wine-cup in my hand, Methought, in slumber's feigning, was:
Interpreting ensued And "Fortune fair" th' explaining was.

2. Affliction forty years And grief I bore, till latterly
I found that in wine's hand Of two years old th' assaining was.

3. That musk-pod of desire, Which I of Fortune sought, within
The plait of yonder fair One's tress, grisamber-raining, was.

4. Cropsickness for chagrin O'ercame me in the dawntide-hour;
But Fortune kind became And "wine in cup remaining was.

5. My heart's blood I devour: But what availeth murmuring?
Our portion thus decreed, By Heaven's foreordaining, was.

6. Wailing and seeking aid, Unto the winehouse I repair;
For there my solace still For sighing and complaining was.

7. Love whoso never sowed, Nor culled a rose from loveliness,
The tulip's guardian still Against the wind's constraining was. [827]

8. I passed the rose-bed by, What while that, in the morning tide,
The bird of dawn engaged In wailing and complaining was. [828]

9. There saw we Hafiz' verse In the King's praise, whereof more worth
Than tractates hundredfold Each couplet heart-entraining was;

10. (That king, in onset swift, To whom, upon the battle-day,
The least of the gazelles The sun [829] in Leo reigning was;)

11. The rose upon her scroll Had written Hafiz' canticles,
Whose every trait more worth Than all books' else containing was.

12. The garden-breezes fire Into the bulbul's bosom cast,
For yonder hidden brand, The tulip's heart that staining was.

[827] i. e. He who liveth without love liveth in vain, expendeth his life in futilities, as he
who would fain protect the tulip against the blast.
[828] Rhyme word of Couplet 6 here repeated.
[829] "Gazelles" here mentioned p. g. with "sun", one name of which, in Arabic, is
ghezaleh, gazelle.

CCXI

1. Not each 'tis that kindleth [830] her face, Heart-charmership's way who knoweth;
Not each, mirror-maker that is, Iskender's assay who knoweth; [831]

2. Not each 'tis that setteth aslant The cap-peak [832] and sitteth austerely
The fashion of sovereignship And th' usance of sway who knoweth.

3. There's many a subtlety fine, Yea, finer than hair, in this fashion:
Of many the noddle that shave, Caléndership, pray, who knoweth?

4. Faith-keeping and troth-plight performed, Indeed, it were well if thou learnedst:
There's no one on whom thou mayst look But tyrant to play who knoweth.

5. The pivot of vision for me, My fair, in thy mole is established;
The jeweller [833] is it the worth Of unions [834] to weigh who knoweth.

6. Serve not, as the beggarly do, On compact of hire and requital:
The Friend 'tis her servants their pains And service to pay who knoweth.

7. I'm drowned in the tears of mine eyes And where is the shift shall avail me?
Not every man 'tis in the sea To swim, well-a-way! who knoweth.

8. The slave of his spirit am I, That safety-surrendering toper,
The alchemist's puissance to wield, In beggar's array, who knoweth.

9. My heart, the distraught, have I staked And lost at Love's table, unwitting
A daughter of Adam there was, The spells of a fay who knoweth.

10. That fair the world taketh by storm, For beauty of face and of fashions
The queen of the lovelings, to fare In justice's way who knoweth.

11. Of Hafiz' heart-ravishing strains None ignorant is, who of nature
Some pleasantness hath and the speech Of the court of the day [835] who knoweth.

[830] i. e. maketh bright, adorneth.
[831] i. e. not every mirror-maker can make a world-showing mirror, such as that of
Alexander.

190

[832] A sign of pride.
[833] Eye likened to jeweller, because it rains pearls of tears and rubies of blood.
[834] "Union", a large single pearl.
[835] "*Deri*", court-speech, may here mean simply "Persian".

CCXII

1. There's none to our Friend for good faith And fashions fair ever attaineth.
To thee of this saw God forfend Denial there ever attaineth!

2. To the worth of our Friend, the sincere, The faithful, no trustiest comrade
Or mate, by old fellowship's dues And rights I swear, ever attaineth.

3. Let those who of loveliness boast Their beauty display! To our Loved One
For beauty of fashions and form, None anywhere ever attaineth. [836]

4. Yea, coins by the thousand they bring To the mart of Creation: but none
Our mint-master's standard of proof, Beyond compare, ever attaineth.

5. The Pen of Creation fair shapes, By thousands, produceth: but no one,
In heart-soothing beauty and charm, To her, our fair, ever attaineth.

6. O heart, sorrow not for the thrusts Of the envious: but trust thou in God;
For no evil to souls, that rely On Heaven's care, ever attaineth.

7. Alack, for that Life's caravan Still hurrieth past on such wise
That no whit of its passage's dust Our country's air ever attaineth.

8. Live we on such fashion, the dust Of the road though we be for abjection,
That nought, by our fault, of heart's dust [837] To whomsoe'er ever attaineth.

9. With longing is Hafiz consumed And I fear me, no word of his case
To the ear of yon monarch august And debonair ever attaineth.

[836] Rhyme-word of 1. 1 here repeated in original
[837] "Heart's dust", an idiomatic phrase for "vexation".

CCXIII

1. Yet once more the East wind's breathings Musk-scattering will go;
Once more the old world rejoicing In youth and Spring will go.

2 The Redbud will give the jasmine The red cornelian cup;
The daffodils' eyes at the windflowers Look-levelling will go.

3. The grief that the bulbuls suffer, For sorrow of severance,
To the heart of the rose's pavilion, Wail-uttering, will go.

4. An if from the mosque to the tavern I go, rebuke me not;
For long was the exhortation And time's a thing will go.

5. O heart, if thou leave till to-morrow The use of to-day's delight,
Who warrant to thee for the Present's Continuing will go?

6. Set not in Shebán [838] the winecup Away from thy hand; for this
Is a sun which from sight, till the crescent The Festival bring, will go.

7. The time of the rose is precious; Its company reckon gain;
By *this* road it came to the garden; By *that* on the wing will go.

8. This, this is the friends' assembly: Come, minstrel; chant songs and odes!
How long "On this wise it gone hath And thus," wilt thou sing," 'twill go?" [839]

9. Lo, into the Land of the Living, For *thy* sake, Hafiz came:
Come bid him adieu, for shortly He wayfaring will go.

[838] "Shebán", the month immediately preceding the Feast of Ramazan.
[839] i. e. how long Wilt thou prate of the Past and question of the Future, instead of
    enjoying the Present?

CCXIV

1. If, one day, of us remembrance That thy musky reed do make,
Richer its account in heaven Slaves two hundred freed do make. [840]

2. Lo, her highness Selma's [841] courier, (Benediction on his head!)
What were it if he with greetings Glad our hearts ableed do make?

3. Lord, the heart of that sweet sovran, [842] Of thy grace, do thou incline,
So she by Ferhád [843] her passage, Pitying his need, do make!

4. My foundation have thy love-looks Rooted up: now let us see
What foundation these wiseacres, Th' old one to succeed, do make.

5. Thy pure essence independent Of our praise is: what increase
Is it to God-given beauty Tirers' skill and heed do make?

6. Do but prove how many a treasure [844] Will They give thee of desire,
If a ruin [844] such as I am Whole thy grace, indeed, do make.

7. Better than the pious practice Of an hundred years for kings
Is one hour when they with justice Happy those that plead do make.

8. Here in Shiraz Hafiz winneth Not his wish. Fair fall the day
When our pilgrimage Baghdad-ward We, it is decreed, do make!

[840] i. e. if thou write us a letter, the good work will be reckoned to thee in heaven as if thou hadst enfranchised two hundred slaves.
[841] "Selma"; a name given to the Beloved in old Arab poetry.
[842] i. e. the Beloved. *Lit. Shirin Khusrau,* of course p. g. with Ferhád.
[843] The lover, himself.
[844] Treasures being found in ruined places.

CCXV

1. Whoso the tale of thy scent, By th' East wind up-brought, heareth,
The sweet, the familiar speech Of Loved Ones in thought heareth.

2. This were unmeet, indeed, For my faith-fulfilling heart,
If from its bosom friend It words that are naught heareth.

3. Monarch of beauty, cast An eye on the beggar's case!
Mine ear many tales how kings With beggars have wrought heareth.

4. Not for the first time to-day We drink to the clang of the harp:
Since ages untold, this sound Yon ceiling star-fraught heareth.

5. Not for the first time the cup To-day 'neath the patchcoat we drain:
The vintner full often the tale Of the devotees' drought heareth.

6. Since wayfarers wise unto none God's mysteries utter, from whom
The wineseller these,—with amaze To deem I'm distraught,—heareth!

7. Cast out from her street if I be, What wonder? Who ever of one,
From Fortune's rosegardens that scent Of lealty caught, heareth?

8. Lord, where is one worthy of trust, In whom this my heart may confide,
Who what it hath spoken and heard And suffered and sought heareth?

9. Come, skinker; for Love, with loud voice, Proclaimeth that "Whoso our tale
"Recounteth from none but ourselves The knowledge dear-bought heareth."

10. I sweeten, with musk-scented wine, My soul, which hypocrisy's tale
In the scent of the patch-coated folk, From cloister wind-brought, heareth.

11. The essence of right is the rede Of the sages: o happy the man
With the ear of acceptance who still Their counsel in aught heareth!

12. The North wind each evening doth tell The story of me and my heart;
The East wind each dawntide what's said 'Twixt me and my thought heareth.

13. Nay, Hafiz, thine office alone Is the offering of prayers for her weal:
For this be thou nowise concerned If she heareth or nought heareth. [845]

[845] The Persian word, which forms the *redif* or rere-word (invariable ending) of this Ode means at once "heareth", "smelleth" and "perceiveth".

CCXVI

1. Heart-sick ones, in whom desire is, But ability is not,
If thou [846] harass, this the usance Of humanity is not.

2. We from thee have no injustice Known; and what is unapproved
Of the Elders of the pathway Holden good of thee is not.

3. One are idol-house and Káabeh, Where no purity there is;
Empty of all good that house is, Where sincerity is not.

4. Till thy witching eye's enchantment Aid the working of the spell,
From the burning of Love's candle Kindled light in me is not.

5. Blinded be the eye whose water Unconsumed is of love's fire!
May that heart be sorrow-darkened, Where Love's light of glee is not!

6. From the Huma of good auspice And its shadow fortune seek;
With the crow and kite since Fortune's King-feather to see is not. [847]

7. Magnanimity in taverns If I seek for, blame me not;
Quoth our elder, "In the cloister Magnanimity is not."

8. Strive for knowledge and good breeding, Hafiz; for with kings and queens [848]
Whoso lacketh wit and breeding Fit to company is not.

[846] Addressed to the Beloved.
[847] i. e. The crow and kite are not winged for soaring, as is the Huma; as to which latter see previous note. The meaning is, "Consort with the noble, not with the mean and base."
[848] i. e. such as the Beloved.

CCXVII

1. The Huma of fairest fortune Into our snare befalleth,
If by our dwelling, haply, Thee it to fare befalleth.

2. Like to the rising bubbles, I throw up my cap for joyance,
If it our cup to mirror Thy visage fair befalleth.

3. Some night when the moon of our wishes Upon the horizon riseth,
A ray of her radiance haply Our roof-tree there befalleth.

4. Since even the wind's admitted Not to thy presence-chamber,
The chance of our salutation How, when or where befalleth?

5. Methought, when my soul I rendered Unto thy lip for ransom,
"A drop of its honeyed water, Sure, to our share befalleth!"

6. "Ne'er think," quoth her tress's phantom, [849] "To buy with thy soul thy wishes:
"Of this kind of game [850] abundance O'ermuch in our snare befalleth." [851]

7. Turn not from this door, despairing: An omen cast; [852] peradventure
It may be the die of good fortune Thy name, unaware, befalleth. [853]

8. Each time of the dust of thy doorway That Hafiz a mention maketh,
A waft from the soul's rose-garden Our palate fore'er befalleth.

[849] i.e. the image of her tress seen in dreams.
[850] i. e. Souls of lovers.
[851] Rhyme-word of line 1 here repeated.
[852] i. e. consult the *Sortes Coranicae* etc.
[853] Maybe a happy omen will reward thy pains and cheer thy heart with an augury of
success near at hand.

CCXVIII

1. Yestermorn relief from sorrow, In the dawntide white, They gave me
And Life's water, in the darkest Deep [854] of parting's night, They gave me.

2. Yea, beside myself they made me With the radiance of her being:
From the beaker of her beauty Wine of very light They gave me.

3. Oh how blessed was that dawntide And that Night of Power how joyous,
When this patent of exemption New from Fortune's spite They gave me!

4. Lo, a voice from heav'n foretold me Of this fortune fair, what season
Patience to endure oppression With a constant spright They gave me.

5. From the mirror of her beauty's Praise mine eye shall never wander,
News therein since of the coming Of herself to sight They gave me.

6. If I hold my wish accomplished And heart-glad I am, what wonder?
Worthy was I and these favours, As an alms-of-right, They gave me.

7. All this honey and this sugar, From my pen that flow, reward is;
For my patience past, this sugar-Cane, wherewith I write, They gave me.

8. That same day I knew that victory I should win yet, when, with patience
And devotion 'gainst oppression To endure, the might They gave me.

9. Mine own courage and the prayёrs Of the dawn-risers, deliv'rance
From the bond of Fate's affliction And the Days' despite they gave me.

10. Sugar of thy thanks strew, Hafiz, In thankoff'ring for that yonder
Lovely fair, so sweet of fashions, To my heart's delight They gave me.

11. "That same time when in the fetters Of thy tress I fell," quoth Hafiz,
"Quittance from the bond of anguish And affliction's blight They gave me."

[854] Allusion to the Regio Tenebrarum, in which springs the Fountain of Life.

CCXIX

1. Still the pearl of mystery's storehouse In the screen, as 'twas, is;
With that seal and mark Love's casket Still beseen, as 'twas, is.

2. Lovers are a trusty people, Well who keep Love's secret;
Yea, the lover's eye still raining Pearls of sheen, as 'twas, is.

3. Ask the East wind how the fragrance Of thy tress our soul-mate
All night long till dawn, in seasons That have been as 'twas, is.

4. Seeker after gems and rubies None there is; and natheless
Still the sun in mine and quarry Busy seen, as 'twas, is. [855]

5. Lo, the colour of our heart's blood, Which to hide thou usest,
In thy lip of ruby patent Still, I ween, as 'twas, is.

6. To the victim of thy glances Come in visitation;
Since the wretch's heart expectant Still, my queen, as 'twas, is.

7. "Thy black tress," quoth I, "will never More be highway robbing."
Years have passed and still its usance And demean as 'twas, is.

8. Hafiz, tell once more the story Of thine eye's blood-water;
In this fountain still the well-spring Flowing, e'en as 'twas, is.

[855] The commentators do not explain this passage; but the meaning appears to be
follows; "No one seeketh or valueth worth and learning nowadays, although they a
still as plentiful as ever they were".

CCXX

1. Plant friendship's tree, for heart's desire To thee its fruitfulness shall bear;
And pluck hate's sapling up; for it Vexations numberless shall bear.

2. An if the tavern's guest thou be, Fair fashions with the topers use;
Or with cropsickness, headache, soul, For thee this drunkenness shall bear.

3. The nights of fellowship with friends Count thou for gain; for, after us,
Full many a night and many a day The Sphere's revolving stress shall bear.

4. The heart of Leila's [856] cameleer, That hath the cradled moon [857] in keep,
Incline, so, Lord, he by Mejnóun [858] His load of loveliness shall bear.

5 Heart, seek Life's Spring, for yet, each year, This meadow [859] roses hundred fold,
Both red and white, and nightingales By thousands, none the less, shall bear. [860]

6. 'Fore God, since with thy tress my heart A covenant hath made, command
Thy ruby lip, so it therefrom [861] The burden of durésse shall bear.

7.O heart, thou'rt helpless grown, because An hundred loads thou bear'st of grief;
Go, drink one draught of wine, which straight Away thy sluggishness shall bear.

8. Gray-headed Hafiz craveth God So in this garth [862] he by a stream
Once more shall sit and in his arms A cypress [863] to caress shall bear.

[856] "Leila", i. e. the Beloved.
[857] "Cradled moon", i. e. the Beloved.
[858] "Mejnoun", i. e. the lover, himself.
[859] "This meadow", i. e. the world.
[860] i. e. Carpe diem.
[861] "Therefrom", i. e. from my heart.
[862] "This garth", i. e. the world.
[863] "Cypress", i. e. a slender mistress.

CCXXI

1. At my ogling, [864] in amazement All the tribe of lackwits goeth:
Deem they what they may, my inward Such is as my outward showeth.

2. Men of wit the centre-point are Of the compasses of being:
But, that head-awhirl the wisest In this circle are [865], Love knoweth.

3. Out on lying love-professions And complaints of the Beloved!
Such a lover light deserving Severance himself avoweth.

4. God my covenant of service With the sweet-lipped ones established;
Each of us a slave is, homage To this lordly folk that oweth.

5. Drunk at once to be and sober There is no one that availeth,
Saving those on whom instruction In this art thine eye bestoweth.

6. Not the only place mine eyeball Of reflection for her cheek is;
Sun and moon, about her turning, Each, the mirror holding, goeth.

7. After this, no Magian youngling Will in pawn the Soufi's patchcoat
Take for liquor, if the vintner With our thought acquainted groweth. [866]

8. Wellaway if they receive not, As a pledge, the woollen patchcoat!
Poor we are and longing in us After wine and minstrel gloweth.

9. If the wind thy perfume carry To the pleasance-place of spirits, [867]
In its path the pearls of being, Soul and wit, there's none but stroweth.

10. Every purblind bat availeth Not unto the sun's attainment;
for amazement from that mirror E'en for folk of insight floweth.

11. If the pietists conceive not Hafiz' winebibbing, what wonder?
Evil spirits shun the mortal That by heart the Koran knoweth. [868]

[864] "Ogling", met. for amorousness, wantonness.
[865] Metaphor of compasses continued.
[866] i. e. if he come to know our purpose to leave the patchcoat in his hands
   unredeemed.
[867] i. e. the angelic world.
[868] As before explained, *Hafiz* means "one who knows the Koran by heart".

CCXXII

1. Yesternight the angels knocking At the winehouse-door I spied;
Adam's clay in cups they moulded, Kneading it on every side.

2. With dust-sitting me [869] the dwellers Of the realms behind the veil,
Pure ones of the world angelic, Wine intoxicating plied.

3. Heav'n could not endure the fardel Of the deposite of love
And the lot on me, poor madman, Cast the burden to abide.

4. God be thanked for reconcilement Her and me between, for which
Houris, dancing, God with beakers Of thankoff'ring magnified!

5. How should we, with hundred harvests Of temptation tried, not stray,
From the path since wakeful Adam With one wheatcorn They awried?

6. Marry, hold excused the wrangles Of the two-and-seventy sects; [870]
For that, when the Truth they saw not, They the door of fiction tried.

7. That no fire is for the candle, In the gleam whereof it laughs;
Fire *that* is, unto the harvest Of the moth which is applied. [871]

8. The recluses' hearts a-bleeding By Love's subtlety [872] are set,
Like that mole wherewith the Loved One's Cheek the Fates have beautified,

9. None the face-veil hath, like Hafiz, From the cheek of thought withdrawn,
Since the comb unto the tress-tip First they set of Speech's bride. [873]

[869] "Dust-sitting me", i. e. me, the frenzied, abject lover; allusion to the idiots who
   couch on the dust-heaps.
[870] "The two-and-seventy sects" of Islam.
[871] "Candle", the Beloved. "Harvest of the moth", existence of the lover. "I have heard
   That love of Gods is like the Eternal Fire, That burns but what it feeds upon; itself,
   Changeless and vivid, freezes in the flame."—Anchiscs.
[872] Syn. "point". Word used p. g. with "mole" in new line.
[873] i. e. "since poets first practised the art of adorned speech".

CCXXIII

1. Friendship in no one I see: To friends of old date what hath happened?
How, marry, did amity end? To comrade and mate what hath happened?

2. Life's water is troubled become : Where's Khizr, with foot of good auspice?
The rose is grown pallid: to Spring And its breezes, of late, what hath happened?

3. None telleth of comrade or friend: The canons of friendship who keepeth?
To those, at their worth who the dues Of fellowship rate, what hath happened?

4. The ball of God's favouring grace They've cast in the midst; but none ent'reth
The lists: to the horsemen, who wont The prize to debate, what hath happened? [874]

5. The roses by thousands have bloomed; No bird-song ariseth to greet them.
Alack, to the nightingale's note and the Thousand Tales' [875] prate what hath happened?

6. Sweet music makes Venus [876] no more: It may be she burned hath her ghittern.
None joyeth in drunkenness more: To topers elate what hath happened?

7. The birthplace of kings and the earth Of the gen'rous aforetime the land was:
Is kingliness come to an end? To gen'rous and great what hath happened?

8. From the mines of munificence years It is since there issued a ruby;
The travail of sun-heat and winds And rains [877] to frustrate what hath happened?

9. None knoweth the myst'ries Divine: Peace, Hafiz! Of whom wilt thou question,
To the round of the whirligig wheel Of Fortune and Fate what hath happened? [878]

[874] Metaphor taken from the game of mall.
[875] "The Thousand Tales", a kind of nightingale or mocking-bird.
[876] The minstrel of the sky.
[877] The Orientals believe rubies to be produced in the mine by the joint influence of
 sun, wind and rain.
[878] i. e. it is useless to question mortals of this mystery, which is known to God alone.

CCXXIV

1. Strike up a moving measure, So for it sigh one may;
Sing thou a strain, whereunto Drink pottle-high one may.

2. If on the Loved One's threshold One win to lay the head,
The voice for exultation Lift to the sky one may.

3. This world and *that* the seërs Stake for a glance. In love,
The coin of life cast only On the first die one may. [879]

4. 'Tis not the cloister holdeth The mysteries of love;
The Magian wine-cup only With Magians ply one may.

5. Adventure with assurance Of fortune: what knowst thou?
Occasion's ball strike haply, Or e'er it hie, one may. [880]

6. The things of the King's palace Befit the dervish not:
Ours the old gown, that kindle (It is so dry) one may!

7. Love, wine and youth the sum are Of wish: when clear th' intent
Is, strike the ball of utt'rance, Nor strike awry, one may. [880]

8. Small wonder if thy glances My peace steal! Caravans
By hundreds stop, with robbers Like that thine eye, one may.

9. With shamefastness I'm straitened: Skinker, thy succour lend,
So on her mouth, wine-boldened, A kiss apply one may.

10. If the Friend cast her shadow On mine eye's stream, the dust
With running water sprinkle, As she goes by, one may.

11. With reason, wit and knowledge, Justice to language can
One render; these all gotten, The ball strike high one may. [880]

12. To thee our bowed shape abject May seem; but from this bow,
Into the eyes of foemen, Arrows let fly one may. [881]

13. Lured by this hope, that fortune A door of union ope
With her, with head on threshold, For ages lie one may.

14. O Hafiz, by the Koran, Dissembling leave and fraud!
Haply, the ball of fortune With true men ply one may.

[879] In vain is the quest of love, which is not initiated with the surrender of life an soul
on the part of the lover. The true lover must carry his life in his hand.
[880] Metaphor taken from the game of mall.
[881] Meaning, as usual, that the prayers of the lover and the recluse are effectual for
good and ill.

CCXXV

1. Once again from myself hath wine ravished me: yea,
Once again over me hath it gotten the sway.

2. Now blessings galore on red wine, from my face
Which the yellow of pallor hath carried away!

3. The hand ever live that first gathered the grape
And the foot that first pressed it ne'er stumble nor stray!

4. Foreordinance lovership wrote on my head:
Fate's forewritten script is indelible aye.

5. Nay, prate not of wisdom; for, like the mean Kurd,
Aristotle must give up the ghost on death's day. [882]

6. Go, pietist, carp not at us for default
In our due; for God's due is no trifle to pay.

7. I counsel thee live in the world on such wise
That, when thou art dead, "He's not dead," they may say. [883]

8. With the Cup of Infinity drunken are all
Their thirst with sheer wine who, like Hafiz, allay.

[882] i. e. The wisest man must die no less than the most abject churl. The Kurds are the
Boers of the East.
[883] i. e. that thy memory may live after thee.

CCXXVI

1. Dainty verse from woeful heart How forthcoming may there be?
From this book one trait we cite: What though more to say there be?

2. From thy ruby lip the ring Of assurance if I get,
Hundred realms like Solomon's Will beneath my sway there be. [884]

3. Nought it skilleth, heart, to grieve For the enviers' girds: for good
May, perchance, for thee therein, If the thing thou weigh, there be.

4. Nought their paintings do I prize Who this image-making reed
Apprehend not, [885] though the famed Limners of Cathay there be.

5. Cup of wine, heart's blood, on each One or other They [886] bestow;
In the circle of the Fates, Dealings on this way there be.

6. That the rose the light-o'-love Of the mart and rosewater
Cloistered be, decrees forewrit, Still from Aye to Aye, there be.

7. Never more from Hafiz' thought Will debauchery depart;
That which in the Prime there was, Will till the Last Day there be.

[884] Alluding to the old custom of kings to give to one, whom they desired to pardon
and assure against enemies, a ring in token of immunity; also to the seal-ring of
Solomon, to which the Beloved's mouth is, as usual, likened.
[885] i. e. I value not painting without imagination. "The image-making reed" is of
course the poet's pen.
[886] "They", i. e. The Fates.

CCXXVII

1. Yon friend, by whom our dwelling A fay's abiding-place was,
In whom, like Peris, nothing, From head to foot, of base was;

2. That sage of me belovéd, That moon in whom united
Good breeding, ay, and insight With every lovesome grace was;

3. The baleful planets tore her From me: how could I hinder?
The author of the evil The moon's revolving race was.

4. "Here," quoth my heart, "I'll sojourn, In hope of her." Poor dullard!
It knew not that its Loved One Departing hence apace was.

5. The veil from my heart's secret Not only hath been rended:
Since Time first was, its usance Still veil to rend from face was.

6. Sweet was the water's margent With rose and green. Woe worth it
That yonder current treasure [887] Here but in fleeting case was!

7. Sweet was the time and goodly We spent with her: all elsewhat
But ignorance and folly, Unworthy of the chase, was.

8. For jealousy the bulbul Himself slew that the rosebud,
At dawn, herself unveiling, In the East Wind's embrace, was. [888]

9. Hold her excused for going, O heart; for thou'rt a beggar
And she in beauty's kingdom Heir to the highest place was. [889]

10. Each treasure of fair fortune, That God hath given Hafiz,
Still to the evening portion And dawntide-prayer to trace was. [890]

[887] *Genj-i-rewan*, the name of one of the eight fabulous treasures of Khusrau Perwiz; an allusion is also intended (p. g.) to "running water". The "treasure" is of course the dead friend.
[888] i.e. blossomed out to the breath of the East wind.
[889] i. e. she was too good for thee and for the world.
[890] i. e. is to be attributed to his habits of prayer to God; the usual precautionary pietistic tag.

CCXXVIII

1. Chance of the mouth of the Friend E'er a sign giveth me not;
News of that mystery hid [891] Fate of mine giveth me not.

2. I die of desire and behind The screen is no way; or if way
There offer, the warder accéss To the shrine giveth me not.

3. To purchase a kiss from her lip, My life, without stint, would I give;
But *this* from me taketh and *that* She, in fine, giveth me not.

4. The East wind caresseth her tress: How niggard is Fortune, behold,
That power, like the wind, in her locks Hand to twine giveth me not!

5. Howe'er, like the compasses, still On the edge of the circle I go,
Ill chance the mid-point to attain,—That waist of thine,—giveth me not.

6. Of patience is sugar at last Begotten; but leisure and peace
For patience the treason of Time And Fate malign giveth me not.

7. Quoth I,"I will slumber and dream Of the charms of the Friend." But alack!
From sighing and wailing surcease My own repine giveth me not.

[891] Beloved's mouth styled "a hidden mystery" by reason of its extreme smallness.

CCXXIX

1. Lo, at dawning wakeful Fortune To my bed hath come;
"Up from slumber! For that sovran Sweet," [892] she said, "hath come.

2. "Drain a cup and blithe with liquor, Fare to look on her;
"How thy fair one, see, with gracious, Swaying tread, hath come!

3. "Give the glad-news-gift, o hermit, musk-pod opener! [893]
"For from Tartary the muskdeer, [894] Desert-bred, hath come."

4. To the cheek of heart-consumed ones Tears have brought new sheen; [895]
Yea, to lovers lamentation In good stead hath come.

5. Skinker, wine! For friend and foeman Grieve not; for the one,
To our heart's desire, the other Being fled, hath come. [896]

6. Once again the heart's bird longeth For a bow-browed one:
Be thou on thy guard, o pigeon, For the gled hath come. [897]

7. Since Time's perfidy the Spring-cloud Seëth, it to rain
Tears on hyacinths and roses, White and red, hath come.

8. Bulbul-told of Hafiz' verses, The East wind, to view
These sweet basils, [898] that grisamber Round them shed, hath come.

[892] Lit. "sweet Khusrau", Khusrau-i-Shirin, p. g. in allusion to the well known story.
[893]This curious epithet means that the recluse (i. e. the poet himself) scatters about him
the perfume of good deeds and sweet verse; the simile turns upon the fact, noted by
Soudi, that people use to open musk-pods in a darkened room with closed doors and
windows, in order better to judge of the quality of the perfume.
[894] "Muskdeer", i. e. The Beloved.
[895] i. e. honour, repute, glory.
[896] i.e. The Foe hath fled and the Friend is come.
[897] "Pigeon", the lover's heart. "Gled", the Beloved.
[898] i. e. the poet's fragrant verses; so called in allusion to "the sweet-basil hand", a kind
of writing, whose flourishes resemble the leaves of the plant in question.

CCXXX

1. When, in prayer, thy curving eyebrow To my memory doth come,
Forth the prayer-niche into clamour, For my ecstasy, doth come. [899]

2. Look henceforward not for patience, Sense nor fortitude from me;
All to empty air that patience, Which thou saw'st in me, doth come.

3. Clarified's the wine and drunken Are the songsters of the sward:
Lover-tide it is, to blossom When Love's mystery doth come.

4. From the world create the perfume Of well-being do I scent;
Joy the rose brought and the East wind Into jubilee doth come.

5. Bride of skill, of Fortune's rigours Moan no longer nor complain;
Peck the bride-chamber of beauty; For the bridegroom, see, doth come.

6. Yonder blooming heart-beguilers [900] All have bound on ornaments,
Save our charmer: in God-given Beauty only she doth come.

7. Lo, the trees are burden-bearing, That on flowers and fruit depend:
Happy cypress, from the burden Of chagrin that free doth come! [901]

8. Minstrel, come; a dulcet ditty Chant of Hafiz' uttering;
Till I say, "To me rememb'rance Of the time of glee doth come."

[899] i. e. When I am engaged in prayer and the thought of the Beloved's eyebrow
occurreth to me, I involuntarily break forth into ecstatic clamour, which is echoed by
the prayer-niche; latter mentioned p. g. with eyebrow.
[900] i. e. the flowers.
[901] A figurative warning against attachment to and dependence on the things of the
world.

CCXXXI

1. Away, companions, with the knots Of the Friend's tress make ye! [902]
Goodly's the night; so, long withal [903] Its goodliness make ye!

2. The privy court of ease is this, Where friends assembled are;
Chant *W'an yekád* [904] and close the door Against accéss make ye!

3. Great, great, indeed, the diff'rence is 'Twixt lover and belov'd:
When the Friend useth coyness, use Of humbleness make ye!

4. Rebeck and harp proclaim aloud, "Open the ear of sense
"Unto the message of the folk Of inwardness make ye!"

5. O'er whosoe'er in this world-house With love's unvivified,
Prayer for the dead, (to be alive Though he profess,) make ye!

6. The first monition of the Sheikh Of the assembly was,
"Yourselves secure from comrades mean And meritless make ye!"

7. By the Friend's life I swear that grief Shall never rend your veil,
So but the Maker's grace your trust, In your distress, make ye.

8. If Hafiz seek a boon of you, Consignment of the wight
To the Friend's heart-consoling lip, For his largesse, make ye.

[902] i. e. unknot it and spread it out to its full length.
[903] i. e., with her long tress.
[904] "*W'an yekád*", opening words of a passage of the Koran (LXVIII, 52) used as a
charm against the evil eye.

CCXXXII

1. The love of a youngling maid In my head grown white hath fallen;
The secret that in my heart I hid Into light hath fallen.

2. The bird of my heart took wing And followed the path of vision;
But see in whose snare, o eye, The wretch, in its flight, hath fallen!

3. In my liver, the musk-pod like, How much heart's blood (woe worth it!)
For love of that black-eyed fawn, That musk-deer bright, hath fallen!

4. From passage along the dust Of thy street each musk-pod cometh,
That into the hand of the breeze Of ended night hath fallen. [905]

5. Since first the world-conquering sword Thine eyelash drew on creation,
Dead, each upon each, how many A heart-live wight [906] hath fallen!

6. O who was it reared this wine, So Paradisal of perfume
That, senseless, the vintner drunk, For its scent, outright hath fallen?

7. The flint, though its life it give, Becometh never the ruby:
Its portion in abjectness, By Fate's unright, hath fallen.

8. Long use in this house of chagrin Hath taught me that whosoever
With topers hath fallen out, Himself, in ill plight hath fallen;

9. Still seared is his heart at the last With a brand from that fire heart-consuming, [907]
Which e'en on the wet and the dry, On bloom and on blight, hath fallen.

10. Alas for that speech-weighing bird! [908] Waylaid of the highwayman Fancy
It was and in jeopardy's snare, Discernment despite, hath fallen.

11. Poor Hafiz, for whom is the tress Of the loveling become as a bridle,
A passing strange mate on his head Is this that alight hath fallen! [909]

[905] i.e. the dawn-breeze derives its fragrance from its passage over the dust of thy
   street.
[906] i. e. lover.
[907] i. e. the fire of love, that enkindleth all alike.
[908] The poet's heart.
[909] "The strange mate" is the untimely passion that has overcome him in his old age.

CCXXXIII

1. From the garden of thy beauty If a fruit cull I, what is it?
By thy lamp if I to lighten What's before me try, what is it?

2. If, O Lord, I sit a moment, All consumed with passion's fire,
In the shelter of the shadow Of that cypress high, what is it?

3. O Jem's seal-ring of good auspice, Blest of working, if for once
Thy reflection on the ruby Of my signet lie, [910] what is it?

4. Forth the house my reason gone is; And if thus the wine abide, [911]
To my faith what will, I wonder, Happen by and by? What is it?

5. Though the love of kings and judges 'Tis the city zealots seek,
For a fair one's love and favour If I choose to sigh, what is it?

6. In pursuit of wine and wanton, Have I spent my precious life:
What from this and that betide me Will, I wonder? Ay, what is it?

7. That I am a lover knoweth E'en the Vizier and saith nought;
And forsooth, if Hafiz also Know that such am I, what is it?

[910] i. e. if the Beloved's mouth be pressed to mine.
[911] i. e. if the rest of wine be as intoxicating as that which I have already drunken.

CCXXXIV

1. Burn, heart; for this thine ardency Full many a thing still doeth;
With many a woe away midnight's Prayer-offering still doeth.

2. The Peri-faced Friend's chidings still Endure thou, like a lover;
For with one glance for wrongs untold Amends the king still doeth.

3. The veil They draw, th'angelic world From this of ours that parteth,
For whoso service to the cup World-mirroring still doeth.

4. Messiah-breathed and pitiful's Love's leach; but what physician
Tending, an if in thee he see No suffering, still doeth?

5. Thy case unto thy Lord commit And be thou of good courage;
For mercy, though the foe do none, God's sheltering wing still doeth.

6. Of drowsy Fortune tired am I; Is there belike no waker [912]
Who supplication for my sake In the dawn-spring still doeth?

7. Hafiz consumeth nor a waft Of the Friend's tress hath gotten.
Mayhap the East wind him the grace This boon to bring still doeth.

[912] i. e. no offerer-up of prayer by night.

CCXXXV

1. The wine-seller old to gladden, The Easterly breeze hath come;
The season of mirth and music, Of joyance and ease hath come.

2. The air is the breath of Jesus; Musk-shedding the earth is grown;
The birds are become in clamour And green on the trees hath come.

3. The wind of the Spring hath heated Th'oven of the tulip [913] so
That the bud is a-sweat and to ferment The rose in the leas hath come.

4. "Nay, hearken to me and study For pleasance." Mine ear unto,
This word from an unseen speaker, What season night flees, hath come.

5. Meknoweth not what the free lily Hath heard from the bird of the dawn,
That, for all her ten tongues, she to silence With every of these hath come.

6. What room for the uninitiate Is in the friends' retreat?
Quick, cover the cup, for the patchcoat (Beware, debauchees!) hath come.

7. Nay, put off the apprehension Of parting and rest content;
For, since that the Div departed, The angel of ease hath come.

8. I give thee the goodly tidings That gone from our neighbourhood
The pietist is and the vintner (Bring wine without lees!) hath come.

9. Lo! Hafiz the cell for the winehouse Hath left; from austerity's craze
And dissembling's debauch to his senses The man, so God please, hath come.

[913] Tulip likened, for its redness and shape, to the ordinary Eastern oven, which is merely a large jar of clay, sunk in the ground, in which, after it has been heated to redness by means of burning wood, bread is baked, the dough-cakes being stuck to the sides.

CCXXXVI

1. Come March-clouds are and the blowing Breezes of the new-born year;
Wine-gold I desire and minstrel Who shall say, "Behold, 'tis here!"

2. Goodly show the fair; but shamefast Am I for my empty purse.
How much longer must I suffer This shamefacedness, o sphere?

3. Dearth of grace there is: the water Of one's face [914] one must not sell:
Wine and roses with the patchcoat's Price must buy the patchcoateer.

4. Yet, belike, some way shall Fortune Open up unto our need;
For I yesternight was praying And the true dawn did appear. [915]

5. With an hundred thousand laughters Lip-lit, comes the garden rose,
As it were it smelt the fragrance Of a generous one anear.

6. In the topers' world, if rended Be a skirt, what matters it?
Nay, the wede of reputation Eke in twain behoveth shear.

7. Who such quaint conceits hath spoken Of thy ruby lip as I?
Who the like of what I've suffered from thy tress-tip e'er did hear?

8. Save the Sultan's justice question Of the love-opprest ones' case,
It behoveth the recluses Sever hope [916] of ease and cheer.

9. Who at Hafiz' heart, I know not, Shot the deadly shaft; but this
Know I, that his blooming verses Drip with many a bloody tear.

[914] i. e. one's honour.
[915] Considered a good omen.
[916] Persian id. for "renounce hope"

CCXXXVII

1. If the Soufi drink with measure, Sweet to him its zest still be!
Else the thought thereof forgotten Of the wight were best still be.

2. And that one who on his fellows Can a single draught bestow,
May the loveling of his wishes To his bosom prest still be!

3. Quoth our elder, "Nought of error Can Creation's pen betide."
May the insight of that pure one, [917] Error-cov'ring, blest still be!

4. To the enemies' suggestion Hearkened erst the Turkman king:
Siyawésh's blood, the guiltless, Of his shame attest still be! [918]

5. This mine eye a mirror-holder Of her mole and down is grown:
May my lip of the kiss-snatchers From her neck and breast still be!

6. Though, for pride, to me, the dervish, Not a word it speak, my soul,
For her mute sweet mouth's pistachio, [919] Sacrifice profest still be!

7. To her drunken eye's narcissus, Man-subduing, blandishing,
Lovers' blood, in beakers drunken, Lawful at her hest still be!

8. World-renowned become is Hafiz For his servitude to thee:
Of thy tress's ring of service May his ear possest still be!

[917] Soudi makes an outrageously long and insipid comment on this couplet, with intent
    to show that "the pure one" (i. e. the Elder of line 1) is Sheikh Senaan before
    mentioned; but I myself see no reason to doubt that the Sheikh of the Magians, i. e.
    the wine-seller, is the person referred to.
[918] Siyawesh, son of Keikawous, King of Iran, being wronged by his father, took
    refuge with Efrasiyab, King of Touran, who received him into favour and married
    him to his daughter, by whom he had a son called Keikhusrau (Cyrus), but,
    afterward, being moved by his jealous ministers to suspicion of his son-in-law, put
    him to death. Keikhusrau, coming to man's estate, overcame Efrasiyab and cutting
    off his head, reigned in his stead. According to Soudi, Hafiz alludes to this story of
    the Shahnameh by way of similitude, because Sultan Mensour, one of the Muzefferi
    princes of Fars, (ob. A. D. 1393), on the instigation of his viziers and chief officers,
    put to death, without cause, his son Esed (Lion), who was a great friend of the poet.
[919] Beloved's mouth commonly likened to pistachio-nut, on account of its shape and
    sweetness.

CCXXXVIII

1. O Lord, in the street of the winehouse What clamour at day there was!
What bustle of cresset and candle, Of skinker and may there was!

2. Love's tale, that is independent Of letter or sound, retold
To the wail of the pipe and the tabor, With din and affray, there was.

3. Discourse in that circle of frenzy, Beyond the debate of the schools
And the give-and-take prate of the college, Its yea and its nay, there was.

4. My heart for the cupbearer's glances Was grateful; but cause somedele
Of complaint for unfavouring Fortune In me, sooth to say, there was.

5. I reckoned and in that wanton Ensorcelling eye of hers,
Methought, of Samíri-like [920] wizards A thousand at play there was.

6. "A kiss of thy lip advance me," Quoth I; and she, laughing, said,
"Nay, when was a time such traffic Betwixten us tway there was?"

7. A-gate is a favouring aspect For me from the stars; for, last night,
'Twixt the moon and the cheek of my fair one Conjunction of ray there was.

8. Alack, in her mouth, which containeth The med'cine of Hafiz's pain,
That, in season of bounty, such straitness Of crop, wellaway! there was! [921]

[920] Samiri, the before mentioned rival of Moses in the black art.
[921] i. e. such lack of capacity (hence, by implication, such niggardliness); alluding to
the smallness of her mouth, which would not suffer her to be liberal of her favours.
The word "crop", (bird's maw), here used p. g. with "mouth".

CCXXXIX

1. Chance to me, at dawn, of drinking Beakers twain of wine hath fallen;
From the skinker's lip the liquor, Trickling down, on mine hath fallen.

2. To the Bride of Youth [922] returning I, for drunkenness, desired;
But 'twixt her and me divorcement Sans recall, in fine, hath fallen.

3. From that tipsy eye a corner Fain would I have sought; [923] but, 'las!
Lack on me of strength to sever From her eyebrows' shrine hath fallen.

4. Claim the good-news-gift, dream-teller; For, in morning's sugar-sleep,
Yesternight, to me for housemate, Lo, the sun ashine hath fallen!

5. In the stages of the Pathway, Wheresoever we have fared,
'Twixt salvation and loveliking Severance condign hath fallen.

6. Cup on cup, o skinker, pour me; For the lover save he play,
In hypocrisy each farer Of the Path Divine hath fallen.

7. What time there of Hafiz written Was this wild and troubled verse,
Sure the song-bird of his fancy Into passion's twine hath fallen.

[922] i. e. Youth simply.
[923] i. e. I was minded to seek shelter in seclusion from the tyranny of her eye.

CCXL

1. If that blessed bird of heaven Through my door come back again,
Youth will certes, in eld's season, As of yore, come back again.

2. Fortune's lightnings, [924] which departed From my vision, will, I hope,
Guided by my tears, that rainlike Stream and pour, come back again.

3. She, whose foot-dust was the crownal Of my head, a king were I,
If unto my brows that head-gear, Once they wore, come back again. [925]

4. What avail me my soul's jewels, In the Loved One's way if I
Strew them not, what time her foot-steps To our shore come back again?

5. In her traces will I follow; Yea, and tidings of me, friends,
Shall ye hear, if I in person Nevermore come back again.

6. 'Tis the sweet morn-sleep and harp-clang Hinder her; for, otherwise,
When she heard my dawntide sighing, She would sure come back again.

7. From the roof the drum of fortune Newly gotten will I beat,
If my late-lost moon, a-travel Gone before, come back again.

8. For her cheek I long, that royal Moon: o Hafiz, still in prayer
Fervent be, so she in safety Through thy door come back again. [926]

[924] Fortune's favours likened to lightning, on account of their brief duration.
[925] Rhyme-word of 1, 2, here repeated.
[926] Rhyme-word of 1. 1 here repeated.

CCXLI

1. There gleamed out a star and straightway The gathering's moon's become;
Our umbrageful heart's companion And house-fellow boon's become.

2. My fair one, who went not to college Nor ever a line hath writ,
With a glance, problem-teacher to schoolmen An hundred eftsoon's become

3. Love's palace and pleasance-pavilion Now first well established is
Its architect since that my fair one's Bright brow's demilune's become.

4. Thine amorous looks to thy lovers A wine of such puissance pour
That knowledge all senseless fallen And reason aswoon's become.

5. Make clean, for God's sake, Beloved, Thy lip from the ooze of wine;
For prompted to sins by thousands My heart, the poltroon, 's become. [927]

6. The Friend in the seat of honour Hath stablished me now of the inn;
Yea, see how the chief of the session The city buffoon's become.

7. The lovers' sick heart, for her fragrance, The sacrifice still of her cheek's
Wild rose and her eye's narcissus, East-wind like at noon, 's become.

8. O friends, from the way of the winehouse, I counsel you, turn your rein;
For lo! by this way went Hafiz And bankrupt, poor loon, 's become.

9. He dreamt of the water of Khizr And beaker of Keikhusráu
And so of the Cavalier Sultan [928] The cupfellow boon's become. [929]

10. As precious as gold are my verses: By th' alchemy of the approof
Of the great on this fashion transmuted Their copper jejune's become.

[927] i. e. by thy wine-dropping lip.
[928] *Aboulfewaris*; "Father of Cavaliers", eke-name of Shah Shejaa.
[929] The Sultan's wine likened to the water of life and his cup to that of Jem, from
   whom it (the magic cup) descended to Keikhusrau.

CCXLII

1. Where's one who loyalty with me, Of generous intent, shall practise?
Who somewhat, whiles, of kindliness With me, the indigent, shall practise?

2. First to my heart, with harp and reed, News shall he bring of the Beloved;
Then, with a cup of wine, the wight Our friendship to cement shall practise.

3. The charmer who hath rent my soul Nor will my heart's desire accomplish,
Behoveth not despair of her; Maybe, she yet relent shall practise.

4. Quoth I to her, "My whole lifelong, In that thy browlock I've been tangled:"
And she, "'Tis my behest that it With thee entanglement shall practise."

5. The crabbed wool-wearer [930] ne'er knew Love's scent: of its intoxication
Bespeak him thou, of continence So he relinquishment shall practise.

6. A loveling such as she uneath For beggars such as I to win is;
What Sultan with the market-sot His privy merriment shall practise?

7. Small matter 'tis if from those locks, That twist and turn, unright I suffer:
No heed of bond or fetter he, On night-walking who's bent, shall practise. [931]

8. The hosts of grief are countless grown: I crave of Fortune aid; it may be
That Fekhreddín Abdússeméd [932] For me some solacement shall practise. [933]

9. Hafiz, attempt thou not her eye, Fulfilled with witch'ries; else her browlocks,
Night-coloured, store of knavish tricks, For thine ensorcelment, shall practise.

[930] "Wool-wearer", i. e. Soufi.
[931] The lover's thought, that wanders in the night-black mazes of the Beloved's hair,
   likened to the night-prowling thief, who recks not of bonds and fetters.
[932] Name of some patron of Hafiz.
[933] An appeal for largesse.

CCXLIII

1. If my heart of the musk-scented grapejuice Incline me to drink, 'tis meet;
For from fast and hypocrisy cometh Not goodness's fragrance sweet.

2. Albeit the whole creation Forbid me from love, yet that,
Forsooth, will I do which the Master [934] Commandeth, what ever be't.

3. Despair not of grace and of favour; For ever the generous soul
Forgiveth the lover's errors And pitieth his defeat.

4. In the ring of the prayers and praisers Abideth the heart, in hope
That the Friend may be moved to open A ring of her tress's pleat. [935]

5. O thou that hast God-given beauty And Fortune's bridal bower,
What needment hast thou of tirers, To busk thee and make thee neat?

6. Fair, fair is the sward, heart-luring The air and the wine unblent;
There's nought but the glad heart wanting, To render our mirth complete.

7. Fair, fair is the world-bride (Fortune); But have thou a care; for know,
In nobody's springes setteth This cloistered one [936] her feet.

8. This world-mead shall never empty Of cypress and tulip bide;
For ever another cometh, As one away doth fleet.

9. The heart of our beggarly nature Ne'er question; but look therein;
For th' image of all things truly This mirror doth repeat. [937]

10. "Nay, where were the harm, o mooncheek," Quoth I to her, coaxingly,
"A heartbroken one if thou solace With somewhat of sugar to eat?" [938]

11. "O Hafiz", she answered, laughing, "That ever a kiss of thine
"The cheek of the moon should sully, For God's sake, hold it not feat!"

[934] According to Soudi, "Master" = Beloved; but "Love" itself is the move probable
meaning.
[935] i. e. and solace her lovers with its scent. Note paronomasia between "ring" (of
dancing or howling dervishes) and "tress-ring".
[936] i. e., maid kept guarded from sight, as in a harem.
[937] As Hafiz often says, "The lover's heart is the true world-showing cup of Jem and
mirror of Alexander".
[938] i. e. Vouchsafe me a kiss.

CCXLIV

1. Whosoever from thy quarter, Weary of abiding, goeth,
His affair, in fine, to nothing Other than deriding goeth.

2. By the light of guidance, pilgrim, Seek the way unto the Friend;
For the goal he reacheth never Who astray, self-priding, goeth.

3. Take thine ease of wine and loveling At life's end; for pity 'tis
If, like youth, old age's season, All in vain betiding, goeth.

4. Guide of heart-astray gone lovers, Help, 'fore God, a little help!
For the stranger, who the pathway Knoweth not, by guiding goeth.

5. Drunkenness and sober living By their issue are to judge;
None can tell in what case any Hence, by Fate's providing, goeth.

6. Still the caravan in pleasance Sitteth and in glory fareth
That, for guidance and protection In God's grace confiding, goeth.

7. Quaff a cup from wisdom's fountain, Hafiz: ignorance's script,
May be, from the bosom's tablet At its hest subsiding, goeth.

CCXLV

1. The East wind, at the break of day, A waft from the Friend's tress hath broughten
And my distracted heart anew Withal in strife and stress hath broughten.

2. From my heart's garden had I torn That sapling pine; [939] for every rose-bush,
That sprang from the concern of her, For bloom but wretchedness hath broughten.

3. My bleeding heart I caused take flight, Fearing th'assault of Love; but it
Dripped blood along the way and Love Thus on its heels to press hath broughten.

4. The splendour of the moon [940] saw From out her palace roof-top shining,
Whereat its face unto the wall The sun for shamefastness hath broughten.

5. With minstrel's song and cupbearer Forth went I, in and out of season; [941]
Since news the messenger uneath, For the road's heaviness, hath broughten.

6 That which the Friend bestoweth all By way of bounty is and favour;
Whether the rosary it be Or girdle [942] her largesse hath broughten.

7. Her eyebrow's fold may God assoil! For though forlorn indeed it made me,
It to the sick the joyful news Of health by its caress hath broughten.

8. Fair fall that season when my heart From out the tangle of her tresses
A work produced, [943] which it for good The foeman to confess hath broughten!

9. For envy of her fragrant locks, Unto the breezes of the desert
The East each musk-pod gave, which it From Tart'ry's wilderness hath broughten.

10. I marvelled yesternight to see Hafiz with cup and flask, but chid not;
Since he them Soufi-wise (to wit, Concealed within his dress,) hath broughten.

[939] i. e. the beloved.
[940] i. e. Her face.
[941] i. e. to meet her.
[942] i. e. Whether it be Islam or infidelity.
[943] According to Soudi, the work in question, which even the adversary was
    constrained to approve, was the extrication of the lover's heart from the beloved's
    tresses.

CCXLVI

1. Who sweetheart kind and fair and mind Unracked of care and pain doth hold,
Fortune to friend and happiness To comrade boon the swain doth hold.

2. The doorway of Love's sanctuary Far loftier than Reason is;
He only may that threshold kiss In hand who heart and brain doth hold. [944]

3. Her strait sweet mouth is as it were The signet-ring of Solomon,
The graving on whose ruby seal The world for its domain doth hold.

4. Red ruby lip and musk-black down, Since that as well as this is hers,
My soul my charmer's ransom be, Whose loveliness these twain doth hold!

5. Whilst on the surface of the earth Thou art, count ableness for gain; [945]
For Time beneath the earth dead folk And powerless amain doth hold.

6. O affluent, with contumely Look not upon the weak and wan;
For oft the wayside beggarman Chief room in honour's fane doth hold.

7. The poor man's prayers calamity From soul and body still avert:
Who by his harvest profiteth, That gleaners in disdain doth hold?

8. Speak thou, o East wind, of my love To yonder sovran of the fair,
Who Jems and Keis, as her least slaves, By hundreds, in her chain doth hold;

9. And if "I want no bankrupt swain", She say, "like Hafiz," answer thou,
"There's many a Sultan beggarmen To comrades boon full fain doth hold."

[944] i. e. who is ready to stake life and soul for love.

[945] i. e. Carpe diem: addressed to the Beloved.

CCXLVII

1. Long 'tis since message my fair Anywise sendeth,
Letter, to lighten our care, Anywise sendeth.

2. Letters an hundred I wrote; But never that proud one
Messenger, greeting to bear, Anywise sendeth.

3. Never a fawn-footed one, With gait like the partridge,
To wild beast-like me, wit a-scare, Anywise sendeth.

4. She knoweth my heart's bird would fain From hand go and yet
Of that handwriting chain-like no snare [946] Anywise sendeth.

5. Alack, that that skinker sweet-lipped No cup of the grapejuice,
Though well of my sickness aware, Anywise sendeth!

6. Of merits and stages achieved However I boast me,
She news from no station soe'er Anywise sendeth. [947]

7. Peace, Hafiz! No room for appeal There is, if no message
To bondmen the queen of the fair Anywise sendeth.

[946] Sic; p. g.
[947] Note paronomasia between "stages" (i. e. of the Path, the journey towards perfection in the mystic sense.) and "station", (i. e. halting-place on an ordinary journey).

CCXLVIII

1. Thou whose mouth the tale of sugar Laugheth unto scorn,
One sweet smile vouchsafe a lover Wistful and forlorn.

2. O pistachio, where, sweet smiling, Breatheth my Belov'd,
What art thou? For God's sake, laugh not Thus thyself to scorn!

3. E'en the Touba-tree for stature Cannot vie with thee;
Be the subject (lest o'er lofty Wax the talk) forborne!

4. An with petulance thou use us, Scoffing at our pain,
We are none that mate with mortals Self-conceit upborne.

5. How shall he the perturbation Of my case conceive
Anydele, whose heart was never Of Love's springes torn?

6. Bind thy heart not on the lovelings' Constancy, with blood
An thou wilt not have thine eyelids Streaming night and morn.

7. Brisk Love's mart is [948]: where's that lamp-cheek [949], On whose face's fire
Soul and heart I may, like rue-seed, Scatter, all love-lorn?

8. Since thou wilt not lack the glances, Hafiz, of the Turks,
In Khujénd or Khuwarézm Shouldst thou have been born.

[948] i. e. the lover's desire waxeth hot.
[949] i. e. the Beloved.

CCXLIX

1. My hand from the quest I will not Withhold till my need forth cometh; [950]
My love till I win or my spirit The body's wede forth cometh.

2. We cannot new friends, like the faithless, Each breath take: we and the dust
Of her quarter are one till spirit, From body freed, forth cometh.

3. My life's at the lip [951] and regretful My heart is, for that from the flesh
My soul, of her lip ungotten The true lover's meed, forth cometh.

4. The soul upon me is straitened For hopeless desire of her mouth;
Thereof the desire of the beggar On what wise, indeed, forth cometh?

5. My tomb, when I'm sped, do thou open And note through the shroud how the smoke
From the fires, on my burning vitals Forever that feed, forth cometh.

6. Arise, in the meads since because of Thy shape and thy standing-up,
The cypress fruit-bearing waxeth, To height the low weed forth cometh. [952]

7. In hope that a rose like thy visage It may in the garden find,
The zephyr is come and each moment, To circuit the mead, forth cometh.

8. Display thou thy face, whilst a people Astonied abide; and speak,
Whilst wailing from man and woman, That hearken thy rede, forth cometh.

9. Each bend of thy tress hath angles An hundred: from such a coil,
Lo, how shall it chance that scatheless My heart all a-bleed forth cometh?

10. Yea, still with approof of Hafiz They speak in the lover-tribe,
Whenever his name in banquets, With ghittern and reed, forth cometh.

[950] "Forth cometh" here = becometh accomplished.
[951] i. e. is ready to depart.
[952] i. e. such is the desire and emulation aroused by thine appearance that the barren

cypress beareth fruit and the mean shrubs grow high. The latter hemistich of line 2 is obscure and is ill explained by the commentators. "*Narwen ber ayed*"; lit. "the pomegranate(syn. elm, wild cherry and another tree for which we have no name) cometh forth or up, riseth to height", but the meaning appears to be as given in the text, i. e. "the plants are excited by love of thee to transcend the bounds of Nature".

CCL

1. If thy face to the moon likened, Yea, and to Perwín [953] they've made,
Estimation by conjecture Of a thing unseen they've made.

2. But a scantling of the story Of our sense-bewild'ring love
Are the tales Ferhád concerning And his love Shirín they've made.

3. Wine, o skinker! For no striving Is against Foreordinance;
Unsusceptible of change is What, for weal or teen, They've [954] made.

4. Eyelash long and witching glances Ne'er such havoc made as that
Swarthy mole and musky tresses, With their sable sheen, they've made.

5. Look with scorn not on the topers' Earthern tankards, for themselves
Servants to the cup that showeth All the worldly scene [955] they've made.

6. How shall one, Who's strange to wisdom, Take the daughter of the vine
To his heart, whose dowry reason's Cash, since Time hath been, They've [954] made?

7. Abject wretches, without portion In the dregs of bounty's cup,
What a practice of oppression, Lo, of lovers mean They've [954] made!

8. Of the chase and jess unworthy Is the wing of crow and kite;
This the portion of the merlin And the peregrine They've [954] made.

9. Life-renewing scent for lovers Still the charmer's street-dust hath;
Therewithal the spirit's palate Ever sweet and clean they've made.

10. Much, in truth, wherever hearkened It hath been, of Hafiz' verse
(Which is nothing but the praises Of thy charms, my queen,) they've made.

[953] *Perwin*; i. e. the Pleiades.
[954] i. e. The Fates.
[955] i. e. the wine-cup, which makes the toper lord of the world of dreams.

CCLI

1. Thy fair form on goodly fashion, O Beloved mine, They've [956] stablished;
In the very soul of sweetness, Sure, that lip of thine They've stablished.

2. Passing fair and heart-alluring Are thy cheek and tender down,
'Tis as if grisamber hedges Round the eglantine They've stablished.

3. For the coming of thine image In full state, with blood-red tears
Decorations in the city Of the lovers' eyne they've stablished.

4. Musk-diffusing is the business Of thy tress; but nowadays,
The repute in China's musk-pods, Fearing Fate malign, they've stablished. [957]

5. Can that be a face, I wonder, And a fillet round it bound?
Or the Pleïads' necklace is it Round the moon ashine They've stablished?

6. All that of Ferhád they fable And Shirín but figures are
That aforetime of my passion And her face divine They've stablished.

7. Thou alone the truth and essence Of Love's myst'ry, Hafiz, speak'st:
All the rest is but conjecture, That on vain opine they've stablished.

[956] i. e. The Fates.
[957] i. e. as a precautionary measure against the evil eye.

CCLII

1. Fragrance of the musk of Tart'ry On the East wind, lo! there cometh.
What's this breeze, from which your fragrance, Loves of long ago, there cometh?

2. Breaths of Tartar musk are wafted From the bosom of the zephyr:
Nay, a caravan from China, By this scent, I trow, there cometh.

3. Ne'er from her my heart I'll sunder, Till the soul my body quitteth:
From my utterance the fragrance Of faith-keeping, know, there cometh.

4. Make not, heart, the breast a target For the darts of grief for her;
Shut the eye, for by the eye 'tis That the stroke of woe there cometh.

5. By love-liking for thine eyebrow Still solicited am I;
'Tis a king to whom remembrance Of the beggar low there cometh.

6. Oft, for that thy foot still sinketh In the mire my tears have made,
On mine eye-man, [958] in thy presence, Shame himself to show there cometh.

7. Hafiz, spare thou not the wine-cup; For the rose into the garden
Back again, with all its hundred Petals full ablow, there cometh.

[958] The Persians call the iris the "man of the eye".

CCLIII

1. Days of union with the friends gone by, remembered,
Still remembered be their season, ay, remembered!

2. For grief's bitter is my palate grown like poison:
Be the winebibbers' carousal-cry remembered!

3. Though the loved ones no remembrance of me cherish,
Be they thousandfold of me, forby, remembered!

4. Though in severance's bonds to-day I'm tangled,
Be their kindness past, until I die, remembered!

5. Be the Zíndehroud [959] of garden-haunters ever,
Though an hundred rivers flood mine eye, remembered!

6. Though I lack of salve for sorrow, be the solace,
That those care-dispellers did apply, remembered!

7. Though to-day in none faith bideth, be the faithful
And the loved ones of the days gone by remembered!

8. Hafiz' secret, now they're gone, untold abideth;
Be those secret-keepers still, say I, remembered!

[959] "Zindehroud", a stream flowing through Ispahan: its banks were covered with
pleasure-gardens, in which Hafiz was wont to carouse with the friends of whom he
speaks, on the occasion of his visits to the city.

CCLIV

1. Minstrel Love with voice and ghittern Wondrous skill possesseth:
All he soundeth its especial Fashion still possesseth.

2. Be the world of lovers' plaining Never void, for virtue
Joy-imparting that its cadence Sweet and shrill possesseth.

3. Though nor gold he hath nor puissance, Our dreg-draining elder [960]
None the less a Lord gift-giving, Cov'ring ill, [961] possesseth.

4. Dear my heart hold; for enamoured Since this sugar-craving
Fly of thee is, it the Huma's Pomp at will possesseth.

5. 'Twere but justice if a monarch Of his neighbour question,
Who for shadefellow a beggar, will or nill, possesseth.

6. Tears of blood I showed the leaches. "Love", quoth they, "thine ill is
"And a remedy heart-fretting, Cure or kill, possesseth." [962]

7. From the glance oppression learn not; For in Love's religion,
Every action its requital, Good or ill, possesseth.

8. Rightly said the Magian youngling, "Drink thou to his welfare
"Who a soul as pure as water In the rill possesseth!" [963]

9. King, the Fátiheh reciteth Hafiz; Yea, and craving
For thy blessing him, low sitting On thy sill, possesseth.

[960] i. e. the wine-seller.
[961] i. e. Fault-concealing.
[962] i. e. patience is the only remedy for love.
[963] i. e. let thy cup-companion be pure of soul; drink not, with churls and worldlings.

CCLV

1. There's no fair one in the city That my heart away shall carry;
Fate's my friend, if it elsewhither Me and my array shall carry.

2. Where's a merry, winsome comrade, To whose gen'rous ear the lover
Heart-afire his thoughts and wishes All, without affray, shall carry?

3. Heedless, gardener, [964] I see thee Of the coming of the autumn,
When thy rose from thee the scathing Windblast of decay shall carry.

4. Time the highwayman ne'er sleepeth; Trust him not; for off, to-morrow,
He what he, belike, forgotten Hath to take to-day shall carry.

5. In my fancy all these puppets Move I, so some man of insight
Yet abroad the name and mention, Haply, of the play shall carry.

6. What my heart of wit and learning Hath in forty years ingathered,
Yonder languorous narcissus [965] Off, I fear, to prey shall carry.

7. Sorcery, be sure, availeth Not with miracle to match it;
What Samiri over Moses' Hand of white the sway shall carry? [966]

8. Though the lurking-place of bowmen [967] Is Love's highway, whoso fareth
Well and wisely off the vantage From the foe in fray shall carry.

9. Still the way the crystal goblet On strait-heartedness forecloseth;
Set it not from hand; for sorrow's Flood it from thy way shall carry.

10. Hafiz, if the fair one's tipsy Eye thy life seek, clear the dwelling [968]
Of all else and leave it empty, So this [969] that [970] away shall carry.

[964] "Gardener", addressed to the Beloved.
[965] i. e. Her eye.
[966] See previous note.
[967] "Bowmen"; i. e. the eyebrows of the fair.
[968] i. e. the heart.
[969] "This"; i. e., the Beloved's eye.
[970] "That", i. e., the lover's life.

CCLVI

1. The world with the new moon decketh The Festival's eyebrow-bend;
The moon of the Feast behoveth Behold in the brow of the Friend.

2. Lo, like to the back of the crescent, My stature is bowed become,
Since the Loved One the bow of her eyebrow With henna afresh hath penned.

3. Nay, cover thou not thy visage Nor reck of the gaze of the folk;
For the down on thy cheek reciteth And breatheth its "God forfend!" [971]

4. It is as a waft of thy fragrance Hath passed o'er the meads at dawn,
That the rose, for thy scent, like the morning, Her raiment in twain doth rend.

5. Or ever were harp and ghittern, Or ever were rose and wine,
The clay of my life with grapejuice And rosewater Fate did blend.

6. O come, that to thee I may utter The sorrow and stress of my heart;
For, without thee, my fair, I neither Can speak nor to speech attend.

7. Though life be the price of thy favours, I, I am the purchaser;
The sage the good gear still buyeth, How dear it soe'er they vend.

8. Far be it from thee, Beloved, My tears to provoke, for lo!
Without thee, like wind, to roll in The dust of thy way they wend.

9. What time in the night of thy tresses The moon of thy cheek I see,
Thy face to my night the likeness Of luminous day doth lend.

10. My soul's at the lip for longing And never a wish achieved!
My hope's at an end and my questing Is not yet come to an end.

11. For longing after thy visage Hath Hafiz these verses writ:
O read them aright and after, For pearls, to thine ear append. [972]

[971] i. e., the down (likened to writing) perpetually reciteth a prayer or charm to guard
thee against the evil eye; so be not afraid of exposing thyself thereto, by unveiling
thy face to the folk.
[972] "To string pearls" is a common Persian figure for verse-composition.

CCLVII

1. Cell-sitter Hafiz yestr'even The winehouse's guest's become;
He's cast off the Compact [973] and after The winecup in quest's become.

2. The loveling of youth's sweet season Came back unto him in dreams;
Again he in eld a lover And passion-opprest's become.

3. There passed him a Magian loveling, Waylayer of heart and faith,
And after that Friend pursuing, He strange to the rest's become. [974]

4. There burnt up the bulbul's harvest The fire of the rose's cheek;
The face of the laughing candle The moth-lover's pest's become.

5. Thank God that our weeping of morning And evening hath not been lost!
Each drop of the tears we've showered A pearl of the best's become

6. The Soufi distraught, who winecup And wine-pitcher yesterday broke,
Last night, with one wine-draught, sober And reason-possest's become

7. The skinker's narcissus [975] cast hath A spell upon us, whereby
Our prayer-ring a vain assemblage Of babblers confest's become.

8. The dwelling of Hafiz grown is The banqueting place of the King;
His soul is the Friend's and the charmer's The heart in his breast's become.

[973] i. e. of abstention.
[974] i. e. he hath forgotten all else.
[975] i. e. Eye.

CCLVIII

1. Lo, thine image from the tablet Of my heart and soul ne'er goeth;
Yonder graceful-moving cypress From my mem'ry's scroll ne'er goeth.

2. From the brain of me distracted The concept of that thy tress, 'Spite the cruelty of heaven And misfortune's dole, ne'er goeth.

3. In Creation's Prime, conjunction With thy tress-tip swore my heart;
Till Creation's End, obedient, It from that control ne'er goeth.

4. Whatsoever (save grief's burden For thy sake) within the heart
Of me wretched is departeth: But that burden sole ne'er goeth.

5. On such wise in heart and spirit Hath the love of thee ta'en root
That, though life itself departeth, Love of thee from soul ne'er goeth. [976]

6. If my heart go after fair ones, 'Tis excused: it hath the pain:
Do what may it, if it after That which maketh whole ne'er goeth?

7. Whoso would not heart-bewildered, Like to Hafiz' self, become
Heart to lovelings giveth never, After tress and mole ne'er goeth.

[976] Rhyme-word of 1, 1, repeated

CCLIX

1. Of thy love the young shoot Of amazement there cometh;
Of thine union the fruit Of amazement there cometh.

2. How many an one, plunged in the ocean of union,
To the nethermost root Of amazement there cometh!

3. Enjoyment abideth not, neither enjoyer,
Whereas the repute Of amazement there cometh.

4. From what side soever whereunto I hearken,
The clamour and bruit Of amazement there cometh.

5. Nay, show me one heart, whereupon, in her pathway,
No mole [977], at the suit Of amazement, there cometh.

6. With awfulness crushed is the man, in whose vision
The light undilute Of amazement there cometh.

7. To leafage, for love, in the being of Hafiz,
The plant, head to foot, Of amazement there cometh.

[977] *Sic*; but meaning "scar, brand".

CCLX

1. Here the fair, with cheek enkindled, Yesternight hath been;
What new heart of her grief-stricken, Burned outright hath been?

2. Lo, the use of city-troubling, Lover-slaughtering
Is a wede, which on her body Of her dight hath been!

3. Lovers' souls as rue she holdeth For her face's fire
And her cheek of very purpose Set a-light hath been.

4. So her tress, that Giaour [978] may better Stop the way on Faith,
Of that stone-heart lit the face's Cresset bright hath been.

5. Store of blood the heart had garnered, Which the eye hath spent:
Who hath squandered? And advantaged, God, what wight hath been? [979]

6. For the world sell not the Loved One; For their profit, who
For base coin of yore sold Joseph [980], Passing slight hath been.

7. Though, "I'll slay thee without mercy," Quoth she, yet I see,
Favour still for me in secret In her sight hath been.

8. "Hafiz, go," said she; "the patchcoat Burn;" And well said. Strange
'Tis by whom she taught to fathom Heart and spright hath been!

[978] Pronounced Jozor, in one syllable. Poets commonly call the Beloved's tress and eye
infidels, because they oppress the Faithful.
[979] i. e. one squandered and another profited thereby.
[980] Koran, XII, 20.

CCLXI

1. By thy sword thy wretched lover's Slaughter foreassigned is not;
Else in thy bewitching glances Shortcoming to find is not. [981]

2. Lord, I wonder of what essence Is the mirror of thy charms
That to move it in my sighing Power of any kind is not.

3. Madman that I am, thy tresses Since I loosed have, aught for me
Fitter than the fetters, madmen Wherewithal they bind, is not.

4. Aught more graceful than thy stature Groweth not in beauty's mead;
Fairer than thy face's limning Pictured of the mind is not.

5. Otherwhat my nightly practice Than the cricket's wailing note,—
So once more I may thy tress-tip Reach, like the East wind,—is not.

6. In amazement, at the winehouse Door I lifted up my head,
For that elder in the cloister Unto thee inclined is not. [982]

7. So from thee, o fire of sev'rance, Have I suffered, candle-like,
That resource, save self-destruction, Left for me behind is not.

8. Hafiz' suff'ring, in thine absence, As a "Verse of torment" is;
Need whereto of exposition, Sure, for all mankind is not. [983]

[981] i. e. if thou hast not slain me, it is not the fault of thy glances; they have done their
best; but it was not ordained that I should perish by thy hand.
[982] i. e. I betook myself to the tavern, in my amaze at finding none in the cloister who
appreciated thee.
[983] A "Verse of Torment", i. e. one of the numerous verses of the Koran, in which
transgressors are menaced with pains and penalties. Such verses are commonly plain
and need no explanation.

CCLXII

1. My heart of thy lip desire fore'er hath:
What wish of thy lip my heart, o rare! hath!

2. The draught of desire and the wine of love
My soul in the heart's cup all soe'er hath.

3. The madman, who's bound with the tress of the Friend,
His rest-place still in calamity's snare hath.

4. So hearts she may capture at will, she o'er
The roses the violet's net [of hair] [984] hath.

5. Lo, how were it seemly that I should ask
What name or repute our witching fair hath?

6. Nay, how shall one sit with the Friend in peace,
Of gentle or simple who thought or care hath?

7. O happy, thrice happy the mortal who
The Friend to comrade all-when and where hath!

8. How goodly, Hafiz, a gathering-tide
That perfect pleasance's gear and ware hath!

[984] i. e. she spreadeth the snare of the dark down over the roses of her cheek.

CCLXIII

1. Credit for worth and uprightness None doth to me assign;
For none of the tavern toper Would on such wise opine.

2. This coat of patches and tatters An if I wear, it is
That none misdoubteth how under The patchcoat I carry wine.

3. Of theory, Scribe, and practice Conceit not thyself, for lo!
None saveth his soul from the Maker's Foreordinance Divine.

4. Nay, be not the dupe of colour And fragrance; [985] but drain the cup;
For nothing but wine will carry Care's rust from this soul of thine.

5. Albeit, o heart, thy watchman The eye be, have a care
Lest haply thy ready money The watch to the foe consign. [986]

6. Apply thee to strait endeavour, O heart, an thou look for wage;
For those who no service render No hire shall receive, in fine.

7. Nay, prate not in presence, Hafiz, Of those who are skilled in speech;
One bringeth not pearls and jewels For gifts to the sea and the mine.

[985] i.e. outward show, the veil of Maya.
[986] i. e. lest Love enter in by thine eye and thou be delivered by it to the enemy (i. e.
the Beloved), body and soul.

CCLXIV

1. Quoth the wine-seller old (Fair fall The name of him!) yesterday,
"Drink wine and the heart's chagrin From the memory do away!"

2. Quoth I, "To the wind my name Wine giveth and my repute."
Quoth he, "As I bid thee, do, And happen thereof what may!

3. "Since all the world's capital, loss And profit, from hand must go,
"Rejoice not over the gain Nor grieve for the losing aye.

4. "In a world where Solomon's throne To the wind went, wind in hand
"Thou hast, [987] if thou set thy heart On aught which must needs decay.

5. "Honey from bee-stings free Nor rose without thorn there is:
"What help for it? On this wise Is fashioned the world's array.

6. "Fill, fill up the bowl with wine And list, with the ear of sense,
"To the talk of the cup, as the tale It telleth of Jem and Kei.

7. "If, Hafiz, thou grudge to list To the counselling of the wise,
"With "Long be thy life! Farewell!" [988] We'll make an end of our say!"

[987] i.e., nothing; thou art empty-handed, wastest thy pains.
[988] i. e. "Go give thee up".

CCLXV

1. Him, unto whom the goblet Of wine clear red They give,
Place in the Holiest Holy's Withinmost stead They give.

2 Rail not at toss-pots, Soufi; For, from Creation's Prime,
Love's secret to the toper, In tavern bred, They give.

3. Wine, boy, rose-hued, musk-scented, Bring, 'spite the folk of sense;
Since still annoy to wastril And fuddlehead they give.

4. Of life's delight no profit Hath he, to whom to-day
Promise of some to-morrow, In heav'n foresaid, they give.

5. Hafiz forswears the gardens Of Heaven, so to him
In thine enjoyment's precinct A covert spread They give. [989]

[989] "They", in I, II and V, = The Fates.

CCLXVI

1. To quittance, for spiteful Fortune, My need arriveth not;
To solace my heart, for dolour Ableed, arriveth not.

2. Although in the dust of her quarter I grovel it, like the dog,
My face-water [990] floweth ever, But feed arriveth not.

3. A morsel of bone or sinew, For gnawing, to me, except
With thousands of wounds my palate Be flead, arriveth not. [991]

4. By the Friends' heart, I'm weary Of life; but where's the help
For the helpless, what while the period Decreed arriveth not?

5. See, Jacob's two eyes for longing Are waxen white [992] and yet
From Egypt to Canaan tidings, Indeed, arriveth not. [993]

6. Full sore is my heart beladen With love for thee. Alack
That that which I seek to-me-ward With speed arriveth not!

7. Excepting an hundred thousand Of thorns from the soil do spring,
A single sweet rose from rosebush To mead arriveth not. [994]

8. Of all Time's wrongs to the worthy, This one annoy's enough
That hand unto soul, to cancel Life's seed, arriveth not.

9. The worthless uplift to Saturn [995] Their heads; but aught, save sighs,
Of folk of desert to the heaven Of meed arriveth not.

10. Be patient, Hafiz; for whoso His soul surrend'reth not
To loved one (Thus ordaineth Love's creed) arriveth not.

[990] "Face-Water" here may mean either "honour and repute" or "sweat".
[991] Simile of dog continued.
[992] i. e. blind.
[993] Allusion to history of Patriarch Jacob and Joseph.
[994] For one pleasure, an hundred thousand pains.
[995] i. e. to the seventh heaven. Fortune favours the mean.

CCLXVII

1. O happy, thrice happy the time when the Friend shall return,
To the grief-stricken's wish, sorrow's darkness to rend, shall return!

2. The eyeball's pied horse 'fore her image august do I lead, [996]
So haply that queen by the way she did wend shall return.

3. The heart of the prey, on her shafts await, throbs with the thought
That she yet to the chase, with her bow on the bend, shall return.

4. At the end of her path my abode have I made, like the dust,
In the hope she by that the same highway (God send!) shall return.

5. Except in the crook of her mall my head go, what's to do?
What gain to me, else if the thing [997] I expend, shall return?

6. A heart with the tip of her tress that a compact hath made,
Deem not that repose to that wretch prison-penned shall return.

7. The waves of my tears will not beat, like the sea, on the shore,
If to these my embraces the waist of the Friend shall return.

8. What cruelties have not from winter the nightingales borne,
Of the hope that the season of Spring in the end shall return!

9. In the Graver of Destiny [998] Hafiz's hope is; to wit
That that cypress-shaped fair to the arms I extend shall return.

[996] i. e. I keep mine eye fixed upon the road by which she will return. Black and white
    eye likened to piebald horse. Led horses, in as great a number as possible, form an
    especial feature of the pomp of an Eastern monarch.

[997] i. e. my head, syn. life.

[998] i. e. God, as having, in the Prime, engraved the decrees of the destinies of mankind on the Preserved Tablet, a record laid up in heaven.

CCLXVIII

1. At the soul-adventurers' [999] mart-head [1000] Proclamation lo! they make,
"Hearken, dwellers of the Loved One's Quarter! hearken, for God's sake!

2. "Some days is it since the daughter Of the vine from us hath strayed:
"Us, the lusts that she might follow Of her soul, did she forsake.

3. "She a coronet of bubbles And a robe of rubies hath:
"Wit and lore she reaveth: sleep not Safe from her, but watch and wake!

4. "Whoso giveth me that bitter One, my soul shall guerdon him:
"If in hell she hide her, thither, In her quest, yourselves betake!

5. "She's a wake-night, bitter, shrewish, Rosy, fuddleheaded maid;
"If ye find her, prithee bring her Straight to Hafiz' house, the rake!" [1001]

[999] "Soul-adventurers"; *lit.* "soul-players", i. e. soul-and-life venturing lovers.

[1000] Brockhaus omits the *izafet* after *bazar*, which omission spoils both metre and sense. Soudi gives the reading followed in the text.

[1001] This Ode (says Soudi) appears to have been written at a time of prohibition of wine.

CCLXIX

1. The violet spake to the rose last night And a goodly sign hath given;
"A fair one's curl to the world," quoth she, "This crook of mine hath given." [1002]

2. My heart is the storehouse of mysteries; But Fate hath locked the portal
And into a heart-stealer's hand, alack! The key of the shrine hath given.

3. I come to thy door on cripple-wise; For unto me prescription
The leach of those favours (mummy-like That heal) of thine hath given. [1003]

4. By me as she passed, poor broken wretch, "'Las," quoth she to the watcher,
"My lover slain! Lo, what a soul He up, in fine, hath given!"

5. Sound be his body and glad his heart And goodly still his humour
Who unto the weak, in fellowship, The hand benign hath given!

6. Go, monisher! medicine thyself! When was there mortal ever,
Whom anydele annoy or hurt Sweetheart or wine hath given?

7. The treasure of Hafiz' heart to men Enough of mystery's jewels,
Thanks to thy love, to stock the world With gems Divine, hath given.

[1002] i. e. "hath caused the world torment". The word *tab*, here used (p. g.) for "curl",
means also "heat, splendour, torment, twist".

[1003] Beloved's favours likened, as an all-heal, to the well-known mediaeval panacea,
mummy-powder, which (says Soudi) was specially sovereign in cases of paralysis
and broken limbs; hence "cripple-wise" in 1. 1. The "leach" is apparently Love.

CCLXX

1. This my love for thee no whim is, That, from mem'ry flown, shall go;
Nor my passion such as hither, Thither, fancy-blown, shall go.

2. Thine affection in my bosom, In my heart the love of thee,
With my mother's milk did enter And with life alone shall go.

3. Love's chagrin is an affliction, Which howe'er thou seek to salve,
Still from worse to worse increasing, Ever sharper grown, shall go.

4. First of lovers in the city, Whose lament for love and dole
Nightly to the sky ascendeth, Still to heav'n my moan shall go.

5. If my tears' full tide I suffer Flow into the Zíndehroud, [1004]
All to ruin, overflooded, Fars's plain corn-sown shall go.

6. Yesterday, amidst her tresses, Yonder fair one's cheek I saw,
As it were the moon enshrouded In a cloudy zone shall go.

7. "Shall I make," quoth I, "beginning With a kiss?" "Nay, wait," she said,
"Till the moon have passed the Scorpion [1005] And with face full shown shall go."

8. Hafiz, if to the well-being Of her ruby lip thou drink,
Have a care thereof lest tidings To the carping foen shall go.

[1004] Zindehroud", the river of Ispahan before mentioned.
[1005] i. e. "till my face be clear of the tress". Beloved's tress likened to the sign of the
Scorpion. Soudi says that it is considered unlucky to undertake any business when
the moon is in Scorpio.

CCLXXI

1. If God upon every mortal Should visit every sin,
The world were a waste of wailing And Time were all chagrin.

2. The Lord whiles pardoneth mountains, Whiles fescues punisheth;
Alike in the sight of the Maker Are mount and fescuekin. [1006]

3. Man of world-wide transgression, Knowest thou not that the moon
In heaven eclipse doth suffer For malison of sin? [1007]

4. Pure is thy skirt, [1008] o Soufi; But plain thy sins shall be
To morrow, when justice-seekers [1009] Cling to thy gaberdine.

5. Of shame for my sins and sorrow All night with floods of tears
I'll weep, till my place of kneeling With green to sprout begin.

6. At leave-taking time, such torrents I'll weep that my tears the way
Shall stop on the Friend, whatever The land that she fareth in.

7. When, Hafiz, the Sultan [1010] willeth The death of a man, what wight,
How bold though he be and puissant, To hinder his hand may win?

[1006] Small matters and great are alike in God's sight.
[1007] Rhyme-word of I, I, repeated.
[1008] i. e. thou hast a good repute, contrivest to make a good show before men.
[1009] i. e. those who have cause to complain of unright at thy hands.
[1010] i. e. the Beloved.

CCLXXII

1. The secret of the love of thee In this our brain still turneth.
Behold, how many a thing in this Our head insane still turneth!

2. If in thy tress-tip's mallet-crook A man his heart adventure,
Certes, ball-wise, from head to foot Awhirl, the swain still turneth.

3. Though that heart-charmer cruelly And falsely with us dealeth,
Natheless, our heart, to hope and faith True, in her train still turneth.

4. For heav'n's oppression and the rage Of Time, the shirt of patience
Upon my body to a vest, Rended in twain, still turneth.

5. My wretched body, lean and weak, Is as the new moon's crescent,
Which, for a pointing-stock to men, In heaven's plain still turneth.

6. This many a day, sans help and hope, The bulbul of our nature
For sev'rance from that rose-garden, Her cheek, in vain still turneth.

7. How often shall I bid thee, heart, Ensue not lust and passion:
For this an air [1011] is that to sin And very bane still turneth.

8. For love of thee, o tulip-cheek And cypress-shape, how many
An one, like us, with heart distraught And whirling brain, still turneth!

9. Hafiz' sick heart at thy street-end, East-Wind-like, is a dweller
And there, in hope of solacement, To ease its pain, still turneth.

[1011] *Hewa*, syn. "desire, passion"; hence used p. g.

CCLXXIII

1. Every moment I bemoan me Of the hand of separation:
Woe's me if the wind my wailing Weak convey not to thy station!

2. Since, for sev'rance, such my case is As God render thine ill-wisher's,
What's to do for me but weeping, Crying out and lamentation?

3. How should I not suffer sorrow Day and night? In what, since ever
From the sight of thee I'm distant, Should my heart feel jubilation?

4. Ah, how many a bloody fountain, From mine eye, my heart hath opened,
Since thou'rt far from me heart-stricken, Far from sight and salutation!

5. From the root of every eyelash Trickle blood-drops by the hundred,
When my heart complaining maketh Of the pains of separation. [1012]

6. Drowned in thought of thee is Hafiz Night and day; but of the bondman
Woebegone thou reckest nothing, Heedest not his desolation.

[1012] Rhyme-word of 1.1 repeated.

CCLXXIV

1. If union with thee vouchsafed To me of the sky shall be,
From Fortune for me what left, Whereafter to sigh, shall be?

2. What wonder if lovers throng And clamour it at thy door?
For, where is the sugar-cane, There also the fly shall be.

3. What need of a scimitar is, The lover to slay? For souls,
Like mine, half-alive, enough A glance of the eye shall be.

4. One breath in this world and that If I draw with the Friend, that breath
Enough of the goods for me Of the earth and the sky shall be.

5. Too short since for this my wish The hand of my fortune is,
What ableness mine to win Thy cypress [1013] anigh shall be?

6. Nay, where shall escape be found Of thy shipwreckéd one, for whom,
Before and behind, Love's flood Of woes piled high shall be?

7. A thousand times I with her Was private; yet, when again
She seëth me, "Who is this?" Lo, still her reply shall be.

8. Right goodly is rose-coloured wine And company eke of the Friend:
Poor Hafiz, heart-lorn, in desire Of these, till he die, shall be.

[1013] "Cypress", i. e. the Beloved's shape.

CCLXXV

1. Longing for the wind of Springtime Did me to the open plain take,
Where thy fragrance, breeze up-broughten, Did repose from us again take.

2. Wheresoe'er a heart to find was, It astray thine eye hath carried;
Not alone did it my weary Heart, all sick with love and pain, take.

3. Tears like silver came and carried Off perforce my face's lustre; [1014]
Gold for gold gave they, who, coming, This my merchandise would fain take. [1015]

4. Lo, my tears into the highway [1016] That thy stony heart have broughten;
For the torrent can the boulder To the margent of the main take.

5. Sorrow's hosts last night the squadron Of my patience bore from station;
Longing for thy sight my joyance Captive did, as in a chain, take.

6. Yon bow-eyebrowed Turk waylaid us With her glance; the hyacinthine
Tress of that straight-statured cypress Did our gear of heart and brain take.

7. Yesterday itself wine vaunted Of thy lip's life-giving virtue;
Wherefore did thy lip its lustre, For that arrogance profane, take.

8. Name the bulbul not to Hafiz For sweet speech: before the parrot,
Nightingale or Thousand-Voices [1017] Who into account would deign take?

[1014] i. e. my honour, repute; i. e. they revealed the secret of my love and so shamed me
    before the folk.
[1015] "To give gold for gold" is an idiomatic phrase for "to give money for money's
    worth". Here the meaning is, "My tears gave gold (i. e. rendered my face yellow as
    gold) in return for the merchandise, (i. e. my repute) which they took away".

[1016] i. e. (according to Soudi) into the path of pity and kindness.

[1017] "Thousand-Voices", another name for the Thousand-Tales, the Persian mocking bird.

CCLXXVI

1. At dawntide, when the Orient's king [1018] His standards on the hill-tops pight,
My Friend upon the hopers' [1019] door Did with the hand of mercy smite.

2. When to the morning manifest It was how 'tis with Fortune's love,
It rose and laughed a goodly laugh At the conceit of men of might.

3. My fair one from her tresses loosed The knots and bound them on the hearts
Of lovers, when she rose to dance In the assembly yesternight.

4. My hands of righteousness I washed With my heart's blood that moment when
The sober unto drunkenness Her eye wine-measuring did cite.

5. What iron heart taught her this use Of roguery, that, when she first
Appeared, the way she stopped on those Who watch and wake till morning white?

6. My wretched heart a warrior-queen Desired and made for her forthright;
God guard it! On the very midst Of all the horsemen it did light. [1020]

7. For her cheek's lustre, how much blood We quaffed, how many lives we gave!
Yet, her end gained, she turned upon The soul-surrend'rers with despite.

8. How should a wool-clad patchcoateer, Like me, into his springes bring
That hair-mailed fair, whose eyelashes Outwar the champions in the fight?

9. My gaze intent upon the King's Felicity and fortune is:
Grant thou the wish of Hafiz' heart, Who cast for thee this omen bright!

10. Mensour the Conqueror [1021], King of Kings, The Champion of the Folk and Faith,
Whose boundless liberalities To scorn the Spring-clouds laugh outright:

11. Since the fair hour when by his hand The winecup honoured was, the time,
Unto the topers' health and weal, The goblet plieth of delight.

12. From his gold-dropping scimitar The sun of victory flashed that day
When, like the star-consuming sun, Alone on thousands he did smite.

13. Continuance of his life and sway Ask of God's favour, heart; for heav'n,
By the duration of the days, Hath struck the coinage of his might. [1022]

[1018] The sun.
[1019] "Hopers"; i. e. lovers in hope of her coming.
[1020] i. e. on the main battle, where the King (here the Beloved) would be stationed, in

the midst of his guards.

[1021] i. e. Heaven hath framed his fortune to last for ever. (N. B. by the irony of Fate, the poor wretch, who is thus hyperbolically praised and who was the last Muzefferi Sultan of Fars, was in 1393 put to death by Timour Leng (Tamerlane), only five years after his accession to the throne).

[1022] "Mensour" may here mean, not the name of the king, but merely "victorious", as an epithet of "flag".

CCLXXVII

1. Up, for the conquering flag Of Mensour [1023] the King is come!
Glad tidings to sun and moon Of victory, sing, is come!

2. Fair fortune from victory's cheek Hath drawn back the veil; the full
Of justice for those who plain Of wrong-suffering is come!

3. The firmament plieth its course In joy, now the moon is here;
The world to its heart's desire Hath won, since the king is come.

4. Assured are the caravans Of knowledge and heart from thieves
That lurk by the way, now he From travel-faring is come.

5. Forth from the womb of the pit And up to the height of the moon,—
His jealous brothers despite,—Now Egypt's dearling [1024] is come.

6. To the Soufi, Antichrist-like, The infidel, say, "Consume,
"For the Mehdi, [1025] that sheltereth The Faith 'neath his wing, is come."

7. Tell, Wind of the East, for love's cark, On my head, from the smoke of sighs
And the fire of the burning heart, How many a thing is come. [1026]

8. For lack of thy face, o king, To this captive of severance
What cometh of wont to straw, On fire that they fling, is come. [1027]

9. Go, sleep not; for Hafiz' self To the presence-chamber of grace,
By the middle-night chant and the dawn's Prayer-offering is come. [1028]

[1023] "Mensour" may here mean, not the name of the king, but merely "victorious", as an epithet of "flag".
[1024] i.e. Joseph, to whom the king is likened.
[1025] The Mohammedan Messiah, the Divinely appointed "Guide", who is to come in the latter days and convert the whole world to Islam. The King is here likened to him.
[1026] i. e. Tell what I have suffered for longing in the King's absence.
[1027] i. e. I have been consumed.
[1028] i. e. it behoveth whoso would attain to his desire to wake the night in supplication and prayer.

CCLXXVIII

1. O justice-doer, thy bosom-friend And cup-companion the Sphere still be!
Drowned, like the tulip, thy black-heart foe In blood, for sorrow and fear, still be!

2. The topmost turret of thy renown, For very muchness of altitude,
For thought to travel, the pilgrimage Of many and many a year still be!

3. Thine ebon tress, with its many a coil,'s The eye and lamp of the world. May souls
Cast in the crook of its curling chain By zephyr of Fortune dear still be!

4. O moon of the heaven of equity, The eye and the lamp of the world thou art:
God grant that thy beaker brimmed with wine Of bliss unmingled and clear still be!

5. Since Venus in heaven above the song Of thy praises hath taken up, may those
Who envy and hate thee, hearing this, The housemates of sigh and tear still be!

6. The ninefold trays of the firmament [1029] And loaves of silver and gold, [1030] that shine
Aloft in the sky, thy lightest part Of majesty's table-gear still be!

7. The maid of my virgin fantasy Is consecrate to the praise of thee:
Committed unto thy bounty's hand The dow'r of this bride sans peer still be! [1031]

8. Thy Hafiz in this ghazél to thee Avouchment maketh of servitude:
And witness to this indenture mine Thy servant-cherishing cheer still be! [1032]

[1029] i. e. the nine stages of heaven.
[1030] i. e. the moon and sun, likened to the round Oriental bread-cake.
[1031] A broad hint at largesse. The constant recurrence of this kind of appeal calls to mind the popular Anglo-Indian parody of the Early Victorian sentimentality, "What are the wild waves saying?" "What is the black man saying, Sister, the whole daylong?... Brother, he is not praying, He is not doing so. The only thing he's saying Is, "*Sah'b, mera bukhshish do*" (Sir, give me backshish or largesse).
[1032] Addressed to the reigning king.

CCLXXIX

1. At dawn, when the wind of the East The scent of the soul's delight taketh,
The mead, for the soft of the air, At Paradise self to slight taketh;

2. The thousandfold wafts of the rose Weave veils o'er the sward of the meadow;
Th'horizon the rose-garden's hue, For the glow of the morning-light, taketh;

3. The clang of the harp on such wise To the cup of the morning inviteth
That the way to the Magians' door The cloister-bound anchorite taketh;

4. The King of the Sphere, [1033] with the sword Of the dawn and the mace of th'
   horizon,
The world, when, his face before, he His buckler of gold hath dight, taketh;

5. Aloft in yon high-vaulted dome Cerulean, the golden-winged falcon, [1033]
The sky's tiercel-royal, its nest And place, in the crow's despite, taketh;

6. To the banqueting-hall of the sward Go; sweet 'tis to see how the tulip
The Redbud and eglantine's cup To mimic with red and white taketh.

7. How cometh to pass that the rose Her cheek in the meadows displayeth?
What fire such effect on the soul Of the bird of the end of night taketh?

8. What radiance is it the lamp Of the morning still kindleth to splendour?
What cresset is that from whose blaze The candle of heaven [1033] light taketh?

9. Excepting in Hafiz's head The thought be of kingship, how is it
That he, with the sword of the tongue, The world-all, to left and right, taketh?

10. Behold the East wind, how it still, Like the whoremonging toper, each moment
The lip of the rose and the tress Of the basil, in middle flight, taketh!

11. Of oneness of essence and form Still varying, see, from each rosebud,
That bloweth, ensamples and proofs An hundred the sage's sight taketh. [1034]

12. I'm still in conjecture, whose breath This blessed breath is, by whose auspice
This darksome dust-heap of the world New fire in the dawning white taketh.

13. Why is it yon circle-shaped sphere Me still, like the point of the compass,
Amidward an hundredfold ring Of sorrow and care and fright taketh?

14. My innermost heart unto none I open; for me it is better;
For Fortune is jealous and out Of season to sudden spite taketh.

15. Whoe'er, like the candle, himself In secret-divulging engageth,
The point of Fate's scissors his tongue, The candle-wick like at night, taketh.

16. That moon-visaged skinker of mine, Where is she, the maid, who, of kindness,
In hand the full winecup for me, Half-drunk with her charms' delight, taketh?

17. Who bringeth me news of the Friend And after, a cup full of wine,
To the cheek of the lovesome Belov'd And her gladness a health to plight, taketh?

18. The minstrel, the usance of song Who plieth in this our assembly,
The mode of Irác whiles and whiles Ispahán on the lute to smite taketh.

19. The Sheen of the Face of God's grace, Sheikh Abou Ishác [1035], he, the King,
In whose footsteps auspicious the land The rose-garden's beauty bright taketh;

20. Forsooth, an Iskender he is, In whose courts whoso dwelleth, like Khizr,
Life etern, from the grace of the dust Of his doorway, the benedight, taketh.

21. Whenever he fareth aloft To the heaven of lordship, the Sultan
His stead, at the first of his strides, At once on the Polestar's height taketh.

22. The lamp and the eye of the clan Of Mehmóud, [1036] from the flash of whose falchion,
When bared in the battle-field, fire Ten-tongued on the foe in flight taketh;

23. A billow of blood to the moon Upmounteth, when he the sword draweth;
Heav'n's Arrow [1037] he reacheth, what time In hand he his bow of might taketh.

24. The bride of the Orient [1038] doth well, For shame of his luminous wisdom,
That, leaving the East, she her way To Morocco (The West) at night taketh.

25. So great is thy glory and grace, That whoso thy bondman becometh
For rank high-uplifted, a hold On the Gemini's belt of light taketh

26. From Mercury's sphere unto thee Come "Well may he fare!" 's by the thousand,
When the fashion and form of the hest Of "Be and it was" thy spright taketh. [1039]

27. The Lancebearer [1040] still with the spear ,Thy haters and enviers smiteth:
His weapon in hand, night and morn, Forsooth, to this end, the Knight taketh.

28. The sky, when it seëth thy steed Its graces, bride-fashion, displaying,
The Straw-stealers' crown [1041] for its feet A litter o'er mean and slight taketh.

29. The somewhat of stress aforetime Thou hast suffered shall bring thee fair fortune;
For Jupiter's [1042] ordinance still Its governance by this rite taketh.

30. In proving thee after this wise, [1043] The purpose of Fortune is but
That of discipline's pureness serene The ímpress thy heart contrite taketh.

31. Nay, but for this cause is the rank Of the Book of all Books [1044] all-surpassing
That Time of its worth the assay To the utmost extreme of might taketh. [1045]

32. The champion in wisdom and wit Is he who, on every occasion,
Considereth firstly and then The way which he deemeth right taketh.

33. Assured from the bitter of grief And affliction is every man's palate
In mouth who the sugar of praise Of thee both by day and night taketh.

34. He only hath profit of life Who, in every betidement soever,
Himself first bethinketh and then The way which he deemeth right taketh. [1046]

35. No cause when he seëth for war, His hand to the winecup he setteth;
When season of action it is, The life-reaving sword the wight taketh.

36. Avert not thy visage, in stress, From hope of the long-hidden favours
Of Fortune; for still the hard bone The marrow full sweet for site taketh. [1047]

37. Nay, sugar by length of durésse Perfection of sweetness acquireth;
Which first its abode in the strait Of the cane and the ass-pack tight taketh.

38. E'en there, where from left and from right The flood of vicissitude cometh,
So needs to the side of the way Who fain would be safe his flight taketh,

39. What mattereth it, be the case What it may, to the firm-stablished mountain,
Though the storm-swollen torrent, with waves Like oceans, the heaven's height taketh?

40. Though proudly thine enemy go And hold his head high in vainglory,
Be thou of good cheer; for conceit The rein of the losel's spright taketh. [1048]

41. Yea, slander and ill though he speak 'Gainst the due of this household of fortune,
In substance and children and wife, Requital at last the wight taketh.

42. Long, long be the term of thy life! Thy fortune a God-given boon is,
Which both upon men and on Jinn Effect, for the soul's delight, taketh.

43. The Chief of the Kings of the Word [1049] Is Hafiz; and so he the horse-course
Of speech, with the Dhóulficar [1050] sword Of poesy, day and night, taketh.

[1033] i. e. the sun.
[1034] The pure Vedantic doctrine of the Undifferenced Self in Nature.
[1035] The last viceroy of Shiraz (A. D. 1336—53) for the Ilkhani Sultans of Baghdad.
[1036] i. e. of the family of Mehmoud Shah, his father and predecessor in the viceroyalty.
[1037] i. e. to the planet Mercury, figured by the Orientals as an archer.
[1038] i. e. The sun, which is feminine in Persian, as in German, Arabic etc.
[1039] i. e. when thou exercisest command over the world in the spirit of the Divine government. "Be-and-it-was" = the Deity, Who is fabled to have said, in the Prime, to the world of created things, "Be!" And it was, by the mere might of His word. The Gnostics would have rendered the phrase by the single word *Logos*.
[1040] "The Lancebearer", or Knight, is the Arab name for Arcturus; because before it is *η*, Boötis, which they style *Er Rumh*, the Lance.
[1041] "The Straw-stealers' crown", i. e. the summit of the Galaxy, which the Persians liken to the track of folk who are carrying off straw and have dropped it here and there; hence the mention of "horse's litter", p. g.
[1042] Jupiter is the patron of theologians and savants and the scribe of heaven.
[1043] i. e. by the difficulties and privations suffered by thee, before coming to the

throne.

[1044] "The Book of Books", i. e. the Koran
[1045] i. e. that it hath resisted all the trials of Time.
[1046] A variant of 32, of which it repeats the rhyme-word.
[1047] i. e. fair fortune abideth hidden in foul, even as the sweet marrow in the hard bone.
[1048] i. e. And will carry him into calamity.
[1049] i. e. the Sovereign of Speechcraft, the Prince of Poets.
[1050] *Dhoulficar*, ("vertebrated", i. e. scalloped like the spine,) the legendary sword of the Khalif Ali.

CCLXXX

1. My body for chagrin No moment's rest doth know;
For dolour without end, My heart doth wasting go.

2. When mists of grief for her From heart to head ascend,
The dew of sorrow's rains Down from the eye doth flow.

3. My two eyes cannot brook To see my yellow cheek;
Wherefore with heart's blood [1051] o'er They daub it high and low;

4. Lest, if my face be seen Of those who wish me ill,
My cheek unto their gaze Should saffron-coloured show.

5. Ill fate to me, where'er Calamity there is,
Adorns it as a bride, To lure me to my woe.

6. Time ravished hath from me All that which once was mine,
Except the love of her, Which bideth evermo'.

7. How should mine eyes not weep? How should my soul not wail?
How should not patience less And sorrow greater grow?

8. What while Heav'n saw me glad, It measured all my joys;
But, now it giveth griefs, It meteth them not so.

9. Since that my bosom friend Is grown averse from me,
Alack! how should I look For pity from the foe?

10. If I bemoan me not, They say, "He needeth nought;"
And "Thistles," if I do, "He chews;" [1052] they say, heigho!

11. Yet these things irk me not; For God Most High no door
Shutteth, excepting He Another open throw. [1053]

[1051] i. e. bloody tears
[1052] i. e. "He talks idly, he is an ass".

[1053] i. e. "I rely on the Divine compassion to open to me a door of solace".

CCLXXXI [1054]

1. "Wrong," quoth I, "is this thou doöst; Ill-advised the thing, to wit, is."
"What is to be done?" she answered. "On this wise foreordered it is."

2. "Many a trait of evil-doing Folk," quoth I, "'Gainst thee have written."
"All from *that* is which," she answered, "On the forehead's tablet writ is." [1055]

3. Quoth I, "'Twas the ill companion That unto this pass hath brought thee."
"Nay," quoth she, "My own ill fortune My companion every whit is."

4. "Why, o moon, hast thou," I asked her, "Thus thy love from me dissevered?"
And she answered, "Know that Heaven Wroth with me for love unfit is."

5. "Many a cup of mirth and joyance, Heretofore," quoth I, "thou'st drunken."
"In the lattermost," she answered, "Healing for the heart and wit is."

6. "Thou who'rt very life," I questioned, "Why again art thou departing?"
"Nay, how should I do?" she answered. "Life like this fore'er aflit is."

7. "For departing hence so quickly, Sure," quoth I, "there's no occasion."
But "Belike," quoth she, "for going Cause and season apposite is."

8. "Wherefore art thou thus from Hafiz Minded to remove?" I asked her.
"Evermore," said she, "my purpose Thee and thine, indeed, to quit is." [1056]

[1054] A dialogue between lover and beloved.
[1055] The Easterns, as before remarked, believe that the sutures of the skull form a
mystic charactery recording the destiny of the mortal in question. The meaning of the
line is, "I am not to blame for what I do; it is all foreordained to me by destiny."
[1056] According to Soudi, this insipid and obscure poem (which, by the way, is left
practically untouched by the commentators) is, with the exception of c. 8, the
composition of Hafiz's contemporary Jelaleddin Mohammed Selman Saweji, ob. A.
D. 1366.

CCLXXXII

1. Ho, parrot, [1057] thou Love's mysteries That utt'rest still,
God grant that sugar never lack Unto thy bill!

2. Green be thy head and glad thy heart For evermore!
Since well the Friend's down limned for us Is by thy skill.

3. Friends with hard sayings thou bespeak'st. For heaven's sake,
Unravel thou this maze, that all May read who will!

4. Upon our faces, drowsed with sleep, O Fortune wake,
Somewhat of rose water from out The goblet spill!

5. What tune was this the minstrel smote Upon the strings,
That drunk and sober, one and all, Dance to its trill?

6. What is this opiate, in cup The skinker cast?
For head nor turban's left to those Her wine that swill.

7. Nought of Life's water did the Fates Iskender grant:
Not to be got is this by gold Or might or skill.

8. The current coin though Reason be Of things create,
With Love the alchymist, forsooth, It weigheth nil.

9. Come, then, and hearken to the case Of folk of pain;
A tale that's scant of words, but much Of meaning still.

10. A Chinese idol [1058] of our faith's The foe become;
Safe guard my heart and faith, O Lord, Against her ill!

11. Intoxication's secrets tell The sober not;
Nor of the soul the pictures ask Of wall and sill. [1059]

12. By the good auspice of the King's Victorious flag,
The standard of the poet-host Is Hafiz' quill.

13. The part of God towards the slaves Performeth he; [1060]
Guard him, o Lord, I supplicate, From every ill. [1061]

[1057] "Parrot" = poet, i. e. Hafiz himself.
[1058] "A Chinese idol", i. e. a fair one as beautiful as a Chinese picture.
[1059] i. e. To treat with the pietist of the mysteries of Love and toping is to question the
     soulless paintings upon wall and door anent the soul
[1060] i. e. the King aforesaid.
[1061] Rhyme-word of 10 repeated.

CCLXXXIII

1. If life last me and the tavern I once more attain another
Season, thing save toper-service Ne'er to do I'll deign another.

2. Fair befall that day of gladness When I go with eyes a-weeping,
Once more on the tavern-threshold Casting tearful rain another!

3. In this folk's no understanding; Grant me, Lord, the means to carry
This my jewel to another Buyer less ungain, another! [1062]

4. Though the Friend depart and leave me, Ancient friendship's dues ignoring,
God forbid that I should follow In another's train, another!

5. If the course of heav'n's revolving Azure sphere to me be gracious,
Her my hand shall in another Compass-round [1063] regain, another.

6. Fain my soul is to salvation, If her wanton eye and cutpurse
Tress would suffer me another Time to break the chain, another.

7. See, with drum and pipe the minstrels Every tide our hoarded secret
Publish at another market-Head and yet again another!

8. Still for anguish I bemoan me; Since that Fortune, every moment,
At my wounded bosom launcheth Yet another pain, another.

9. Yet, quoth I, "In this affliction Not alone immerged is Hafiz;
"Gone astray is many another In this desert plain, [1064] another."

[1062] The poet complains of lack of appreciation among his own folk and begs God to
aid him in finding a better market for his wares.
[1063] i. e., in another round of the sphere, another space of time.
[1064] i. e. desert of Love.

CCLXXXIV

1. Yet to Canaan the lost Joseph Will return once mo'. Repine not,
Sorrow's cell shall yet with roses, Like a garden, blow. Repine not.

2. Care-worn heart, thy case shall better Yet become; fret not thyself;
For yon giddy-pate of Fortune Yet aright shall grow. Repine not.

3. If Life's Spring once more betide thee, On the sward-throne, o'er thy head,
Bird night-warbling, yet the rose's Canopy thou'lt throw. Repine not.

4. Nay, despair not, since thou knowest Not the Unseen's mysteries;
Many a spring [1065] behind the Veil is Working to and fro. Repine not.

5. If the wheel of heaven turn not For a season to our wishes,
Not for ever on one fashion Will the matter go. Repine not.

6. When, for longing after Mecca, In the desert foot thou settest,
Though the thorns of hindrance bring thee Many an irk and woe, repine not.

7. Though the torrent of perdition Raze existence's foundation,
Since thy pilot's Noah, reck not Of the Deluge; no, repine not.

8. Passing parlous though the stages And the goal be not apparent,
There's no road to which an ending Is not, high or low. Repine not.

9. All our case, for separation From the Loved One and for noyance
Of the rival, God, the Changer Of the case, doth know. Repine not.

10. Hafiz, in the nook of poortith And the darkling nights' seclusion,
Whilst thy practice Koran-reading Is and praying, oh, repine not!

[1065] *Lit.* "sports", in the sense of the French "jeux", workings or operative parts of
machinery.

CCLXXXV

1. Show thy face and self's existence From my memory tear away;
Bid the wind the heart-consumed one's Every harvest bear away.

2. Heart and eye since we have given To the deluge of chagrin,
"Life's foundation," say, "come carry, Torrent of despair, away!"

3. So the Magian Elder's favour Stable be, the rest is nought;
Bid all others from their mem'ries Do our name fore'er away.

4. Who shall scent her tress like virgin Ambergris? Wan wishful heart,
Do from out thy thought this idle Fancy of her hair away!

5. Yesternight quoth she, "I'll slay thee With mine ebon eyelashes."
Lord, from out her thought the purpose Of oppression wear away!

6. Bid the heart outvie the flaming Of the Fire-Temple of Fars;
Bid the eye the face's water [1066] Of the Tigris scare away.[1067]

7. In this Way no place thou reachest Without striving; nay, thou must
With obedience to the master, An the wage thou'dst share, away.

8. Promise me thy sight a moment, Sweet, upon my dying day,
And straight bear me to the graveyard, Free from pain and care, away!

9. Hafiz, have a care; bethink thee Of the Loved One's tender case;
With this crying and lamenting From her threshold fare away.

[1066] i. e. honour, lustre.
[1067] i. e. Bid the eye become such a torrent of tears that the Tigris in comparison shall
show but as a rill.

CCLXXXVI

1. Fragrance, East Wind, from the pathway Which the fair doth wend, bring thou;
Bear heart's grief away and joyful Tidings of the Friend bring thou.

2. Bring a soul-dilating saying From the mouth of the Belov'd;
Ay, a letter of glad tidings From the World Unkenned bring thou.

3. Somedele dust, despite the watchers, From the Loved One's passage-way,
For the solace of the lover's Eye, still blood a-spend, bring thou.

4. Artlessness and rawness profit Nought to life-adventurers;
News of what yon roguish charmer Doth with us intend bring thou.

5. So my palate I may pérfume By the favour of thy wafts,
Look some scantling of the fragrance Of her breath, God send, bring thou.

6. Way-dust, by thy faith I charge thee, Of the dear-belovéd one,
So that no annoy from others Thereupon attend, [1068] bring thou.

7. Long my heart hath not, o skinker, Seen the face of its desire;
Yonder cup, that mirror-service To the soul doth lend, bring thou.

8. In thankoffering for gladness, News, o songster of the sward,
Of the rosebed to the captives, In the cages penned, bring thou.

9. Bitter is my soul for patience, [1069] Used without the Friend; a sign
From her lip with sugar raining, This my case to mend, bring thou.

10. What availeth Hafiz' patchcoat? Dye it, dye it deep with wine!
And then homeward him, dead-drunken, From the market-end bring thou.

[1068] i. e. in secret.
[1069] "Patience", *szebr*, syn. "aloes". Word used p. g.

CCLXXXVII

1. From her stead a waft of fragrance, Eastland breeze, bring thou to me.
Sick am I for grief; a somewhat Of heart's ease bring thou to me.

2. To our barren heart th'elixir Of desire apply; to wit,
What of dust from the Friend's doorway Thou mayst seize bring thou to me.

3. In the ambush-place of vision, With my heart at war am I;
Bow (her brows) and shafts (her glances), Prithee, these bring thou to me.

4. Old in exile, grief and sev'rance Am I grown; the cup of wine,
By the hand of Youth the lusty, Ere life flees, bring thou to me.

5. Cause the railers of this liquor Beakers two or three to taste
And the cup, except they drain it To the lees, bring thou to me.

6. Leave not, skinker, till to-morrow This day's pleasance or a writ
Of immunity [1070] from Heaven's Chanceries bring thou to me.

7. Forth the veil last night, for envy, Came my heart, when Hafiz said,
"From her stead a waft of fragrance, Eastland breeze, bring thou to me." [1071]

[1070] "A writ of immunity", i. e., an assurance of immunity from Time's oppression and
the calamities of vicissitude.
[1071] Line 1 repeated.

CCLXXXVIII

1. Thou, by whose bright face bloometh The tulip-bed of life,
Come, for, without thy cheek-rose, The Spring's forshed of life.

2. They reck not of the ocean Of nothingness, for whom
The compass of thy mouth [1072] is The pivot-head of life.

3. Small marvel if the teardrops Rain from mine eyes; for, in
The grief of thee, like lightning, The time hath sped of life.

4. I, without life, alive am; And this no wonder is.
When were the days of sev'rance Strung on the thread of life? [1073]

5. On every side's an ambush Of Fate's vicissitudes;
Whence with drawn rein must slowly The horseman tread of life.

6. This day or twain, when Fortune Vouchsafeth us her [1074] sight,
Enjoy, for none may fathom The secret dread of life.

7. How long the wine of dawn tide And dulcet morning-sleep?
Awake! Beware! for surely The flower is fled of life.

8. By us she passed nor cast us An eyeglance yesterday:
Poor heart, that nought hath gotten By all it's led of life!

9. Sing, Hafiz; for this writing, Thy pen on the world's page
Graveth, shall bide for memory, When thou art dead, of life.

[1072] Beloved's mouth likened, for minuteness, to the compass-point in the centre of a
circle.

[1073] i. e. Reckoned as part of life.
[1074] "Her", i. e. the Beloved's.

CCLXXXIX

1. Come is the festal season, With friends and roses late:
See, in the King's face, skinker, The moon; [1075] and wine bring straight.

2. Hope of the rose's season Had I renounced; but, lo!
A miracle the topers' Fast-keeping did create. [1076]

3. Set on the world thy heart not; Nay, but the winebibbers
Ask of the beaker's bounty And of Jemshíd's estate. [1076]

4. Save the soul's coin, I've nothing In hand. Where, where is wine,
That to the skinker's glances Withal I may oblate?

5. What if the foredawn meal-tide [1077] Be past? The dawn-cup's left.
Let seekers of the Loved One With wine the fast abate.

6. I fear the toper's patchcoat And the Sheikh's rosary
Will, on the Day of Rising, Go rein by rein for weight. [1078]

7. Goodly the Sultan's sway is And he a bounteous king.
O Lord our God, preserve him From the ill eye of Fate!

8. Drink wine to the slave's verses; For to these royal pearls
New charm thy jewelled goblet Will e'en communicate. [1079]

9. Since that thy bounteous nature A blemish-screener is,
Forgive our heart a coinage That's under current rate. [1080]

10. Since, Hafiz, gone the Fast is And on the go the rose,
Drink wine, for the occasion Eftsoon will be a-gate.

[1075] i. e. See the moon, whose appearance is the signal for the end of the Fast, in the
beloved's face; there is no need to look in heaven for it.
[1076] i. e., the rose-season has, by a miracle, been prolonged till the Festival time.
[1077] "Foredawn meal-tide". It is the custom, during Ramazan, to eat a substantial meal
just before dawn, the better to enable the faster to endure the fatigues of the Fast,
which must be strictly observed from dawn-peep till dusk.
[1078] i. e. will be of equal value in the sight of God.
[1079] Addressed to the Sultan.
[1080] The punning allusion to the heart as "base coin" has been before explained.
Bibeksh means both "pardon" and "give". The poet, therefore, expects the royal
pardon to take the form of largesse.

CCXC

1. O East, by the Loved One's dwelling To fare deny thou not
And news to the wretched lover From there deny thou not.

2. In thanks that thou thus hast blossomed, O rose, to thy heart's desire,
To the bird of the morning union's Sweet air deny thou not.

3. Henceforth, since the fount of sweetness Thy lip of ruby is,
The parrot [1081] thy speech's sugar To share deny thou not.

4. The love of thee was my housemate, Whilst yet thou a new moon [1082] wast,
And now thou'rt at full, thy favour, O fair, deny thou not.

5. The world and all that is in it A trifling matter is;
To people of wit this trifle Fore'er deny thou not.

6. The poet thy glory beareth To th' utterest ends of th' earth;
To him, for the road, provision Of fare deny thou not.

7. If thou wouldst be well remembered, Lo, this is the word for thee;
In payment of speech, gold, silver, Sans spare, deny thou not. [1083]

8. Hafiz, the case grows better; The dust of grief departs:
Her path with thy tears to water, In prayer, deny thou not.

[1081] "Parrot", i. e. poet, himself.
[1082] i. e., yet a youngling maid.
[1083] i. e. Be lavish to poets, in payment of their praises.

CCXCI

1. Show thy face and to thy lovers, "Leave of living," say, "take!"
"Fire of moth, before the candle," Bid, "the soul for prey take." [1084]

2. Note our thirsting lip and water Of thy grace deny not;
Hither come and up thy victim's Head from off the clay take.

3. Leave the dervish not! If silver His nor gold, for silver
Hold his tears, for gold his visage, Yellow with dismay, take.

4. Tune the harp and play; if play-wood [1085] Lack, my heart for burn-wood [1086]
Take, my love for fire and bosom For the censing-tray take.

5. Doff the cowl and join the dancers' Ring or else to cloister
Go and on thy back the patchcoat; one or t'other way take.

6. Wool from head draw off [1087] and vinejuice Sheer draw in; spend silver
And for gold to heart a goodly Silver-bosomed may take. [1088]

7. So the Friend to me be friendly, Let both worlds be hostile;
So Fate back me, all earth's surface Let the foes' array take.

8. Turn not yet to go, Beloved; Bide with us a moment;
Joyance by the stream ensuing, Come, the goblet gay take.

9. Take thee gone from me and yellow, For heart's fire, my visage,
Dry my lip and wet my bosom With my tears that day take. [1089]

10. Hafiz, make the banquet ready And unto the preacher,
"View our feast and of the pulpit Leave for ever," say, "take."

[1084] i. e., bid the fire of thy beauty consume the moth (the lover) before the candle of thy face.
[1085] "Play-wood", i. e. a musical instrument, such as harp, lute etc.
[1086] "Burn-wood" i. e. aloes-wood, used as incense. The gist of this conceit lies in the triple meaning of the Arabic word *oud*, which signifies at once "wood", "lute" and "aloes-wood".
[1087] i. e. "put off the Soufi gown", which is made in one piece and is put on and off, like the South American poncho, by the opening for the head.
[1088] i. e. Spend thy money like a man and buy thee a sweetheart.
[1089] i. e. Thou mayst take it for granted that all these things will befall me, as a necessary consequence of separation from thee.

CCXCII

1. Still from the cypress branches The patient bulbuls cry,
"Far from the rose's visage, Far be the evil eye!"

2. Rose, as a least thankoff'ring That beauty's queen thou art,
Forbear the lovelorn bulbuls With pride to mortify.

3. Complaint anent thine absence I make not; for, indeed,
Who's never absent giveth Scant pleasure, being nigh.

4. Let zealots hope for Houris And palaces: the inn
Our palace is, the Loved One Our Houri black of eye.

5. Drink to the harp, unfearing; And if one bid thee drink
No wine, "The Great Forgiver", Say thou, "is God Most High!" [1090]

6. If other folk in pleasance And mirth delight, for us,
The very source of gladness Is for the fair to sigh. [1091]

7. Why for chagrin of sev'rance, O Hafiz, mak'st thou moan?
The seeds of light and union In night and sev'rance lie.

[1090] i. e., therefore I will disobey Him and drink wine, so as to give Him the opportunity of exercising His attribute of forgivingness, which would otherwise be unused. It will be remembered that Kheyyam (v. Quatrain 81) has a like conceit upon the subject.
[1091] "All other pleasures are not worth Love's pains".

CCXCIII

1. 'Tis Hallowe'en [1092] and shut the book of parting;
Therein be peace until the dawn's upstarting! [1093]

2. O heart, in loverhood be steadfast-footed;
For in this Way all work's reward-imparting.

3. I will not turn from toping with repentance,
Though thou me plague with severance and thwarting.

4. Gone though my heart is, my love's face I see not;
Out on this cruelty, 'neath which I'm smarting!

5. Come forth, bright morn of hearts, by God His mercy!
For passing dark I see the night of parting.

6. Wilt thou be faithful, practise patience, Hafiz;
For loss and profit are in every marting.

[1092] i. e. the Night of Power (Foreordinance), before explained; but the name of the holy night is here profanely bestowed by the poet on some occasion of union with his mistress.
[1093] Koran, XCVII, 5.

CCXCIV

1. An admonition I make thee: Give ear nor except thereto.
Nay, all that the kind adviser Shall tell thee accept for true.

2. Thine easance of lovelings' faces Enjoy thou, whilst yet thou mayst;
For th' old world's perfidy ambushed Still lieth for life perdue.

3. The goods of both worlds to lovers Are but as a barleycorn;
For *these* [1094] are of little value And *those* [1095] are o'er dear to woo. [1096]

4. Nought else but a pleasant comrade And ghittern in tune I crave;
My pain so to tell, the wailing Of treble and bass unto.

5. If but with my wish accordant Were that which is foreordained,
Nor wine would I drink henceforward Nor aught that is sin would do.

6. The cup with intent of repentance I've put by an hundred times;
But the cupbearer never a moment The spell of her glance withdrew.

7. God wot, this for me sufficeth Of commerce with old and young;
A loveling of fourteen summers And wine that hath lived for two.

8. Since They, [1097] without our accordance, Foreordered our earthly lot,
If somewhat in us blameworthy Show, make not withal ado.

9. Come, into my cup like the tulip Pour, cupbearer, wine of musk,
So haply the mole of the Loved One Go not from my spirit's view.

10. O heart, said I not to thee rightly. "Beware of her ebon tress?"
For see how They [1097] even the breezes In chains in this ring enmew.

11. The goblet, with pearls and rubies Thick-jewelled, bring and say,
"Look, look on this Asefi bounty [1098] And die!" to the envious crew.

12. Drink wine, man, and strive for union With her whom thou lovest. List
To that which to thee the angels Cry from yon dome of blue.

13. Our runaway heart who holdeth? Proclaim ye the madman 'scaped
From prison, that they may take him And clap him in chains anew.

14. Since sweeter are Hafiz' verses Than even Zehír's [1099] sweet verse,
What room for Selmán's discoursements And verses of Sheikh Khwajóu? [1100]

15. Nay, in this banquet, Hafiz, Name not repentance; lest
The bow-eyebrowed cupbearer smite thee With glances through and through.

[1094] "These", i. e. the goods of this world.
[1095] "Those", i. e. the goods of the next world.
[1096] i. e., the goods of the next world are only to be bought at too high a price; e. g.,
the renunciation of wine and toping. Soudi takes a different view of this couplet and
makes "these" cover the goods of *both* worlds, whilst "those" he renders by "the
goods of Love"; but his explanation seems unnecessarily far-fetched.
[1097] "They", i. e. the Fates.
[1098] "This Asefi bounty", i. e. this jewelled goblet, the gift of the Asef of the time, the
Grand Vizier.
[1099] Zehireddin Feryabi, a renowned Tebrizi poet of the 12th century.
[1100] "Khwajou", i. e. Khwajeh Kirmani, a celebrated Kirmanian poet and
contemporary of Hafiz. "Selman" has before been noticed. According to Soudi,
Zehireddin Feryabi was, in his (Soudi's) time, considered the sweetest of Persian
poets after Hafiz and Jami. He is now little read.

CCXCV

1. How long, o heart, wilt shed my blood? Before the eye take shame at last
And sleep thou, too, o eye, and so Fulfil the heart its aim at last. [1101]

2. Was't I indeed, that from my love's Fore-arm did kisses cull, o Lord?
Behold, now, how the foredawn prayer Effectual became at last. [1102]

3. My wish of *this* world and the next To me did the Provider [1103] grant;
The harp's speech to mine ear and eke To hand the Friend's tress came at last.

4. How long, wind-like, wilt thou an ear Snatch from the harvest of the mean? [1104]
Pluck up a heart; provide thyself; Sow seed in thine own name at last.

5. Though well I wot thy house will ne'er Be China's Picture-stead [1105], withal,
With thy musk-mixing pencil's point, Some picture do thou frame at last.

6. If in the night-watch realm, o heart, Thou shun not stress, [1106] the breath of dawn
Good news shall bring thee from the land Of thy beloved dame at last.

7. A moon-like fair the knee doth bend And wine like rubies proffereth:
Say'st thou, "I'm penitent?" [1107] Before The skinker have thou shame at last. [1108]

[1101] When the eye sleepeth, the heart is at rest; and when the eye waketh, the heart is troubled and sheddeth the lover's blood through the eye.
[1102] i. e. in bringing me to my desire of union with the Loved One. The Muslim belief in the peculiar efficacy of the foredawn prayer has before been noticed.
[1103] "The Provider", God.
[1104] i. e. be dependent upon mean folk for crumbs of kindness.
[1105] i. e. the celebrated picture-gallery so called (and composed entirely of his own compositions) of the mystical painter Mani, the Persian Blake, who was the founder of the Manichæan sect and suffered martyrdom under Shahpour in the third century of our era.
[1106] i. e. if thou be assiduous in night-waking and supplication.
[1107] i. e. "I repent of winebibbing and will drink no more".
[1108] "At last", syn. "at least".

CCXCVI

1. Skinker, youth's capital [1109] here come bring;
Cups one or two of wine sheer come bring.

2. The cure for love's malady,—wine, to wit,—
The old and the young man's cheer, come bring.

3. The sun and the moon are wine and cup:
The sun in the mid moon's sphere come bring.

4. Since reason is stubborn, the rope of wine,
To halter this restive steer, come bring.

5. Cast somewhat of water on this my fire;
Yon fire-like water anear come bring.

6. If gone be the rose, say, "Go in peace!"
Pure wine as rosewater clear come bring.

7. If past be the nightingale's song, what then?
The wine-flask's gurgle to ear come bring.

8. Toping may wrong be or right; but wine,—
Right or wrong be it, ne'er fear,—come bring.

9. For time that is past fret not; the song
Of ghittern and viol (dost hear?) come bring.

10. Since her [1110] but in sleep we may enjoy,
The draught that is sleeping-gear come bring.

11. Though drunken I be, three cups or four,
That I may be fuddled sheer, come bring.

12. A double pottle to Hafiz fill;
Be't sin, be't merit, wine here come bring.

[1109] syn. origin, source; i. e. wine.
[1110] i. e. The Beloved.

CCXCVII

1. Cypress of lofty stature, goodly of gait,
Rosy-cheeked robber, lying for hearts in wait;

2. Since thou our heart hast ravished by roguery,
Prithee, for God's sake, keep it inviolate!

3. Since thy two eyes of glamour I first beheld,
Ease from my heart and patience departed straight.

4. When thou thy tress's spikenard shakest abroad,
Civet and musk thenceforward folk nothing rate.

5. Falseness no longer practise, o fair; for faith
Strive, if indeed thou wouldest live fortunate.

6. Solace thou me thy lover whiles with a kiss,
So thou wouldst have enjoyment of life elate.

7. Dazéd is wretched Hafiz: to be thy slave
Still, without gold or silver, [1111] it is his fate.

[1111] i. e. gratis and voluntarily.

CCXCVIII

1. I, unto whom Thou gavest To look on the Loved One's face,
How shall I thank Thee, Thy servants That fosterest of Thy grace?

2. Say to affliction's beggar, "Wipe not the dust from thy cheek;
"Th' elixir of life to the lover's The dust of the praying-place." [1112]

3. For one or two tears thou strewest In Fortune's highway, eye,
Full many's the look of kindness That thou on her cheek shalt trace.

4. Excepting the swain ablution With blood of the liver make,
His prayer, by the diet of the mufti Of Love, is void and base.

5. O heart, for the stress of the pathway, Turn not thy bridle-rein;
The wayfarer true ne'er counteth The ups and downs of the chase.

6. What profit shall I of the zephyr, The talebearer, get, since e'en
The cypress upright in the garden No confidant is for love's case?

7. In hand, in this dwelling of idle Illusion, [1113] take nought but the cup;
In this playhouse of puppets, [1113] no venture, Except it be love, embrace.

8. Albeit thy beauty's needless And heedless of others' love,
I'm none of the faint-heart lovers, Who tire of the quest apace.

9. Nay, how shall I tell thee the burning That I in my vitals feel?
Go, question my tears of the story: I'm none of the blabbing race.

10. The smile and the glance of beauty Love's goal is; else no need
Had Mehmoud of Ghezni's fortune Of Ayaz's tress and face. [1114]

11. God wotteth, where Hafiz voiceth His story of love in song,
The ditties of Venus take not In heaven the foremost place.

[1112] Self-abasement is the lover's "Open Sesame".
[1113] i. e. The world.
[1114] Mehmoud of Ghezni and his favourite Ayaz have before been noticed.

CCXCIX

1. A thousand thanks that I see thee Again, to my full intent,
In truth and purity's fashion Become to my heart's consent!

2. The wayfarers true of the Pathway The track of calamity tread;
The Son of the Road [1115] unrecking Is of ascent and descent.

3. One's grief for the Friend 'tis better To hide from the watcher's eye;
No holders of secrets the breasts are Of folk malevolent.

4. In thanks for this grace that our session Is lit by the face of the Friend,
If noyance betide, like the candle, Consume and be content.

5. With half-a-kiss buy thee a blessing From one of the men of heart,
The spite of thy foes from body And soul which shall prevent.

6. The grief that my soul o'ercometh, O Asef, [1116] of care for thee,
A twelvemonth might scarce suffice me To tell, to its full extent.

7. The strains of the dulcet ditties Of Hafiz of Shiraz forth
To Araby and Chaldaea Their murmur of love have sent.

[1115] i e. the true pilgrim of Love's way, the real lover.
[1116] i. e. The Grand Vizier. The grief felt by the poet was for his absence.

CCC

1. O fair fall the night when thou earnest With many an amorous air!
Coquettish disdain thou usedst And humbly I must it bear.

2. Nay, how shall its secret hidden Abide for my heart, which hath,
Rose-bud-like, the East wind taken For confidant of its care?

3. From loftiest fortune my hope is Thy shape in mine arms to clip;
And what from long life I ask is The scent of thy fragrant hair.

4. What troubles for men did the Tirer Of Fate Forewrit, what time
It blackened thy bold narcissus [1117] With coquetry's kohl, prepare! [1118]

5. How oft, of long nights, for yearning, I knocked at the door of the heart,
So haply the day of attainment To thee I might bring anear! [1119]

6. What reck I of thine oppression And what of the spies' despite?
The bondmen of love grudge never For sorrow, how long soe'er. [1120]

7. With news of the rose's coming, Heart's easance the East wind gave:
A thousand blessings of Heaven On such a tale-bearer!

8. The dust of our heart's affliction The eye of the foe doth blind:
Thy cheek in the dust, o Hafiz, Come, lay and consume and bear!

[1117] eye.
[1118] Rhyme-word of 1. 1 repeated.
[1119] Rhyme-word of 3 repeated
[1120] Rhyme-word of 3 and 5 repeated.

CCCI

1. No less must the lovers suffer, Who press in the tavern's way,
Than pilgrims to Mecca bounden, Astoniment and affray.

2. My self, for thy separation, Had seeled up its eye from the world;
The hope of thy sight restored me My soul, that was gone astray.

3. Henceforth from the Loved One's presence I'll go to no door; for, since
The Káabeh I've found, I've turned me From idol-worship away.

4. A night such as this till morning From Fortune I ask, therein
The tale of my case to open To thee that begin I may.

5. Though Fate with desire consume thee For yonder pavilioned moon, [1121]
Yet, like to the candle, Hafiz, Stand fast and constant aye.

[1121] i. e. "moon in halo", fig. for "veiled or cloistered beloved".

CCCII

1. The bride of the rose is come Again to the Feast of Spring;
Where is the bulbul sweet-tongued? Say, "Lift up thy voice and sing!"

2. Plain not of severance, heart; For rose in this world and thorn
Are coupled and up and down And gladness and sorrowing.

3. Bent double, bow-like, with grief Am I; yet no word I breathe
Of leaving the brow-browed fair, Whose eye-glances arrows fling.

4. Abroad by thy browlock blazed My heart's distraction's grown;
No wonder of musk it is If it be tale-bearing. [1122]

5. From Time Unbegun and not Now only, I, heart-distraught,
My face on thy threshold laid, With burning and wearying.

6. All one in the way of Love To Hafiz are hard and eath;
What differeth hill from vale, Indeed, to the bird on the wing?

[1122] Beloved's browlock likened to musk, for colour and scent. Musk is, of course, the
most penetrating and self-assertive of all perfumes.

CCCIII

1. Come, so may strength return To my heart contrite again;
Come, so my body dead Win life and might again.

2. Come, for thy loss hath shut Mine eye on such wise that nought
But the door of thine union oped Will bring it to light again.

3. My heart, that is whelmed in blood By th' Ethiop hosts of grief,
Shall be by the Roumi troop [1123] Of thy cheek made bright again.

4. The mirror of this my heart, Whatever I hold thereto,
Nought else than thine imaged charms Gives back to the sight again.

5. By th'adage, "Big is the night [With changes]," afar from thee,
I count the stars, wond'ring what Will come of the night again.

6. Come; till, in the hope of the rose Of thine enjoyment, sing
The loveworthy nightingale Of Hafiz's spright again.

[1123] *Roum*, i. e. Asia Minor, Anatolia, the inhabitants of which (*Roumis*) were, in
comparison with the Arabs and Persians, fair-complexioned and white-skinned; here
used as a synonym for "whiteness", as opposed to *Zeng*, (Ethiopia, syn. "rust"), as a
type of blackness. "The signs of royal merit in a bride are, face of Roum, tress of
Sham (Syria) and buttocks and breasts of Berber, (Barbary)", Khusrau of Dehli,
Derya-i-Ibrar. The latter part of this couplet, however, represents rather the Indian
than the Persian and Arab idea of female beauty, "les petits seins rondelets", round
virginal "pomegranate" breasts being far more acceptable to the refined taste of the
compatriots of Mohammed and Hafiz than the over-voluminous charms of the North
African women.

CCCIV

1. O cypress fresh of beauty, That far'st with gracious gait,
An hundred needs in lovers Thy charms each breath create.

2. Fair fall thee beauty's vesture! For, in Creation's Prime,
Cut to thy cypress-stature Was grace's wede of Fate.

3. Be whosoe'er desireth Thy locks' grisamber scent,
Like aloes in the censer, Content to burn and wait!

4. The standard of my passion, For all the enviers' girds,
Though, gold-like, in the forceps [1124] They clip me, ne'er shall bate.

5. Heart-burning from the candle The moth hath; but my heart,
Without thy face's candle, Indeed, is melted straight.

6. The heart, that once hath compassed The Káabeh of thy street,
For love of thy high places, Forgetteth Mecca's state.

7. What boots each breath ablution With eyeblood, when, without
The prayer-niche of thine eyebrows, Unlawful prayer I rate?

8. The Soufi, who, without thee, Had wine renounced, last night
His compact broke, when open He saw the winehouse gate.

9. Like must at jar-head, [1125] Hafiz, When yesternight he heard
The secret from the cup-lip, Went dancing, all elate.

[1124] "Forceps", i. e. instrument for trying goodness of coin.
[1125] i. e. as new wine (must) ferments and works in the jar, beating at the lid.

CCCV

1. Though my wish of thy lip's honey Not vouchsafed have They [1126] to me yet,
For thy ruby goblet hoping, "Dreg-drainer!" folk say to me yet.

2. Heart and faith of yore forsook me For desire of those thy tresses;
What (I wonder) end befalleth, In this traffic's way, to me yet?

3. One draught of that fire-hued water, (For that I, among the cooked ones
Of the love of her, still raw am,) Skinker, give, I pray, to me yet. [1127]

4. To thy hair one night, in error, "Thou", quoth I, "art musk of Tart'ry."
Smiting swords since then my body's Hairs are, well-a-way! to me yet. [1128]

5. To the Loved One's lip, unwitting, Came my name once: since that season,
The soul's fragrance still, for lovers, Round that name doth play to me yet.

6. In my cell thy face's radiance Saw the sun and like the shadow,
Every breath, on door and roof-tree Cometh since its ray to me yet.

7. In the Prime thy red lip's skinker From a cup a draught did give us
Such that drunkenness betideth From that wine to-day to me yet.

8. Ye that say, "Thy soul surrender, So that thine may be heart's easance;"
To her grief my soul I rendered: Ease not giv'n have They [1129] to me yet.

9. Since thy ruby lip's sweet story Put hath Hafiz into writing,
From the reed [1130] life's water welleth, Without let or stay, to me yet.

[1126] "They;" i. e. the Fates.
[1127] i. e. I am raw (immature) in Love; cook me (and make me mature) with the fire of
wine.
[1128] i. e. because I lightlied her hair by likening it to (the far inferior) Tartar musk, the
hair on my body (moved by esprit-de-corps) tormenteth me by way of punishment.
[1129] "They;" i. e. the Fates.
[1130] i. e. pen.

CCCVI

1. The case of the heart a-bleed who shall speak again?
From heaven the blood of the jar who shall seek again? [1131]

2. The tipsy narcissus in all wine-worshippers' eyes
Be shamed, into bloom if it venture to break again! [1132]

3. Save the cask-dwelling Stoic of wine, [1133] the mystic speech
Of philosophy's secrets who shall speak again? [1134]

4. Let whoso cup-passer-around, like the tulip, is
For this tyranny wash in blood his cheek again! [1135]

5. O many's the word in the veil [1136] that the harp doth speak!
Its tress [1137] come cut, that it may not shriek again.

6. My heart, if the tulip-hued cup it scent once more,
Would ope, like the rose-bud, unto its reek again.

7. By his head, so he may, will Hafiz compass round
The Holy House of the wine-cask eke again! [1138]

[1131] i. e. "Who shall demand justice for the blood shed by the topers' hearts, on the
occasion of the prohibition of wine, and for the wine poured out and wasted by the
Mohtesib's officers, in pursuance of the edicts?" This ghazel was written at a time of
persecution of winebibbers.
[1132] i. e. if it do not refuse to blossom, in sympathy with oppressed topers.
[1133] Wine likened to Diogenes.
[1134] i. e. wine is a sage, who teacheth the secrets of philosophy.
[1135] i. e. weep tears of blood.
[1136] i. e. in secret or in ambiguous language. *Perdeh*, veil; syn. "musical mode etc.";
word used p. g.
[1137] "Tress" i. e. strings.
[1138] "Wine-cask" audaciously likened to the Kaabeh.

CCCVII

1. Up and in the golden goblet Water of delight [1139] cast thou;
Ere the goblet of the costard [1140] Turn to dust outright, cast thou!

2. Lo, the Valley of the Silent In the end is our abode:
Noise of mirth, what while life lasteth, Up to heaven's height cast thou!

3. From the cheek of the Beloved Far be sin-polluted eyes!
Glance thereon but from the mirror [1141] Pure and clean and bright cast thou!

4. By thy verdant head, I charge thee, Cypress, when I'm dust become,
Shade therefrom upon mine ashes, Putting by despite, cast thou. [1142]

5. This our heart, that by the serpent Of thy tress-tip hath been stung,
In the house of balm and healing, By thy lip's sweet might, cast thou!

6. Well thou wottest, the possession Of this world abideth not.
In its harvests, with the liver Of the cup, [1143] a light cast thou.

7. With my tears I make ablution; For the folk say of the Path,
"First be pure and on that Pure One [1144] Then, indeed, the sight cast thou!"

8. Lord, yon bigot, who in lovers Findeth but default, the smoke
Of his sighing on the mirror Of his wit and spright cast Thou! [1145]

9. Rose-like, for her fragrance, Hafiz, Make a tunic of thy wede [1146]
And that tunic in the pathway Of yon cypress slight [1147] cast thou!

[1139] i. e. wine.
[1140] i. e. the skull or brain-pan, called by the Persians "the cup of the head".
[1141] "Mirror" here = heart.
[1142] Appeal to beloved to visit his grave.
[1143] "Liver of the cup", i. e. wine.
[1144] "Pure One", originally said of God, but here applied to the Beloved.
[1145] i. e. darken his heart and soul with affliction.
[1146] i. e. rend it down the front.
[1147] "Cypress," i. e. beloved.

CCCVIII

1. My heart of a gipsy-like charmer, A trickstress, is captive made,
A troth-breaking, mischief-making And murderous-fashioned jade.

2. A thousandfold wedes of abstention And patchcoats of piety
Be ransom for moonfaced younglings, In tunics torn arrayed!

3. Come, call for the cup and sprinkle With rose-water Adam's clay,
Of thanks that in beauty's ball-game The angels thou hast outplayed.

4. Lo! Weary and poor, to thy doorway I'm come: show somewhat of ruth;
For, saving the love of thee, nothing I bring in my hand displayed.

5. The bondman am I of those speeches Which quicken the flame, not those
Whereby, as it were cold water, The quickest of fire's allayed.

6. Come drink; for the winehouse Speaker Unseen unto me last night,
"Abide in contentment's station And Destiny flee not," said.

7. Exult thou not thus in thy puissance; For it upon record is
That thousands of secret chances By Heaven's command are swayed. [1148]

8. Bind, bind in my shroud the winecup, That so, on the Judgment Morn,
The fears of the Day of Outcry [1149] With wine may be awayed.

9. Beloved between and lover, Hafiz, no barrier is:
Thyself art thine own obstruction: Up and no more be stayed! [1150]

[1148] i. e. Heaven hath a thousand fashions of abasing the mighty and exalting the
    lowly.
[1149] i. e. The Day of Resurrection.
[1150] i. e. sever thyself from self and thou wilt find no further obstacle in the way of
    union.

CCCIX

1. Cupbearer, come: our boat [1151] On th'ocean of wine cast thou:
In the bosoms of old and young, Come, clamour and pine cast thou.

2. Me into wine's boat cast, Skinker; for they have said,
"Do thou good works and on Water, in fine, cast thou." [1152]

3. I, on deluded wise, Strayed from the tavern-street:
Me in the path of right, Skinker benign, cast thou.

4. Bring me a beaker a-brim With rose-coloured, musk-scented wine
And sparks into rosewater's heart Of envy malign cast thou.

5. Ruined and drunk though I be, Show thou me somewhat of grace;
A glance on this heart, distraught And ruined, of mine cast thou.

6. If there behove thee the sun Ashine in the midst of the night,
The veil from the rosy face Of the maid of the vine cast thou.

7. Let them not me commit To the clay on the day of my death;
But tavernward bear me and there In the barrel of wine cast thou.

8. Since, Hafiz, for Fortune's despite, Thy soul to extremity's come,
At the Div of afflictions and woes Those star-shafts of thine [1153] cast thou.

[1151] i. e. boat-shaped cup; cf. the (Roman) *scaphium* of Plautus etc.
[1152] A well-known proverbial saying, given by Soudi as, "Do good and cast it in the
water"; (i. e. reck not what cometh of it, whether it is appreciated or not;) "if the fish
(*balic*) know it not, the Creator (*khalic*) knoweth it".
[1153] i. e. "thy verses" or perhaps "the arrows of thy sighs and prayers". The allusion is
to the Muslim legend of the shooting-stars, which are fabled to be fiery shafts
launched by the angels at the Divs (demons), who draw near by stealth to heaven, to
hearken to their talk.

CCCX

1. If, o East wind, o'er the Ares' [1154] Plain to pass to thee befall,
Kiss that valley's earth and musky Look thou make thy breath withal.

2. Selma's stead (to whom an hundred Greetings be each breath from us!)
Full thou'lt find of bells a-clamour and of camel-drivers' bawl.

3. Kiss for me the Loved One's litter And thus humbly to her say,
"For thy sev'rance I consumed am; Come, o dear one, to my call!"

4. I, who styled the warners' counsel Erst the chirp of the rebeck, [1155]
Now have proved enough of chast'ning From estrangement's heavy maul.

5. Pleasance and night-waking practise, Unafraid, for, in Love's land,
Hand and glove are nightly prowlers With the watchmen, one and all.

6. Lovership no thing of sport is: Heart, needs must thou stake thy life;
Else it with the mall of passion Booteth not to smite Love's ball.

7. Fain the heart its life doth render To the Loved One's drunken eye,
Though to no one else the sober Give themselves beyond recall.

8. In the sugarcane plantation Live the parrots at their ease,
Whilst the wretched fly for longing Smites its head against the wall.

9. If there come the name of Hafiz To the pen-nib of the Friend,
This is all the boon he craveth From the Sultan's presence-hall.

[1154] "Ares", according to Soudi, the river of Ispahan, *not* the Araxes.
[1155] i. e. idle prate, empty sound, vox et præterea nihil.

CCCXI

1. Tell me, o soul, who bade thee Thus of our case ask not,
Stranger to play, of loved ones Tidings or trace ask not?

2. Never a whit of knowledge Had of the dervish-world
Whoso "The dervish" bade thee "Of his own race ask not."

3. True to thy generous nature, Pardon a fault undone [1156]
And of the past and happened, Eke, of thy grace, ask not.

4. Wilt thou Love's burning clearly Know, of the candle ask,
And of the wind, that bloweth, Place unto place, ask not.

5. Yea, of the cloister patchcoats Seek not the coin of quest;
And of the Grand Elixir Mendicants base ask not.

6. We of Sikender never Nor of Darius read;
Us save of Trothplight's story And of Love's case [1157] ask not.

7. Lo, in Leach Reason's volume Chapter is none of Love;
Heart, learn to bear and balsam, Pain to efface, ask not.

8. Come is the rose's season; Hafiz, the present time
Use and of How and Wherefore, Now, for a space, ask not.

[1156] i. e. a fault which has been falsely ascribed to us by slanderers.
[1157] Syn., "Of the tale of Mihr and Wefa", which, according to Soudi, is the name of a
    well-known love-story.

CCCXII

1. Of her ebon tress such reason Have I to complain that ask not;
For from me't hath peace and puissance On such manner ta'en that ask not.

2. Heart and soul let none surrender, In the hope of faithfulness;
For on such wise, for so doing, To repent I'm fain that ask not.

3. For one draught, [1158] whereon ensuing Was no hurt to any one,
From the know-noughts such annoyance Needs must I sustain that ask not.

4. Go from us in peace, o zealot; For this ruby wine from hand
Heart and faith on such a fashion Beareth off amain that ask not.

5. Peace and safety in seclusion Were my wish; but yonder rogue,
Her narcissus-eye, such witch'ry Wrought with heart and brain that ask not.

6. In Love's pathway are contentions, Clamours that dissolve the soul,
Each one bawling, now "*This* look not At" and now again "*That* ask not."

7. Heaven's ball (quoth I) I'll question Of the present case; and it,
"Neath the mall of Fate I suffer Durance such and pain that ask not." [1159]

8. "Whom to spite, hast thou," I asked her, "Plaited thus thy tress?" And "Hafiz,
"Long the tale is: by the Koran," Answered she, "refrain; *that* ask not."

[1158] i. e. for my wine-drinking.
[1159] i. e. "Heaven itself is subject to necessity", truth affirmed by all religious systems,
except the Semitic, to whose Anthropomorphism it would be fatal.

CCCXIII

1. Suffered for love such woe Have I, that ask not;
Drunk parting's poison so Have I, that ask not.

2. Travelled have I the world And now a charmer
Chosen, so sweet of show Have I, that ask not.

3. After the dust of that Her door for longing,
Eyes on such wise aflow Have I, that ask not.

4. With this mine ear, from out Her mouth, yest'reven,
Such sweet words hearkened, lo! Have I, that ask not.

5. At me why bite the hp, As saying, "Speak not?"
A ruby bitten, know, Have I, that ask not.

6. Without thee, in my cell Of beggary suffered
Vexations such, heigho! Have I, that ask not.

7. An exile in the way Of Love, like Hafiz,
Reached such a stage, I trow, Have I, that ask not.

CCCXIV

1. Heart, for thy running-footman Let favouring fate suffice!
The breeze of Shiraz' gardens For travel-mate suffice!

2. Leave not the Loved One's dwelling, Dervish; but let for thee
Travel of thought and corner Of cloister strait suffice!

3. For thine excuse with people Of travel, let the love
Of wonted home and trothplight Of ancient date suffice!

4. Sit at the tavern bench-head And tipple wine: for thee,
This much of the world's profit In wealth and state suffice!

5. And if from the heart's corner A grief in ambush lie,
Let thee, for sure asylum, The tavern-gate suffice!

6. Seek not superfluous riches; Make light thy need on thee;
A flask of wine like rubies And moon-faced mate suffice!

7. Heav'n giveth to the dullard The reins of wish; thou'rt one
Of lore and sense: to damn thee These sins with Fate suffice. [1160]

8. Lean not on others' bounties; For in both worlds the King's
Good graces and acceptance With God Most Great suffice. [1161]

9. None other pious practice, Hafiz, behoveth thee:
The prayers of dawn and midnight, Early and late, suffice. [1162]

[1160] Soudi quotes the Turkish proverb, "Heaven still giveth wealth to the cur and
    power to the ass".
[1161] i. e., Let the King's favour suffice thee for this world and God's grace for the next.
[1162] The inner meaning of this couplet is that the winebibbing lover, who, of his
    employ, is necessarily a watcher of the night and passes his time in tears and
    supplications, is altogether dispensed from pious practices of any kind.

CCCXV

1. Out of all this world's rose-garden Us a rose-cheeked fair sufficeth;
Of this mead, the shade of yonder Swaying cypress rare sufficeth.

2. Far be converse with the people Of hypocrisy from me!
Of the heavy [1163] ones, the heavy [1164] Pottle us to bear sufficeth.

3. Paradise and its pavilions Give They in return for works:
But the winehouse for us topers, Beggars poor and bare, sufficeth.

4. On the brooklet's margent seated, View the passing by of life;
Us this token of the fleeting Of this world of care sufficeth.

5. Note the coin of the world's market And the miseries thereof;
If not *you*, this loss and profit *Us*, when we compare, sufficeth.

6. Since with us the Friend abideth, More what needeth that we seek?
For our happiness the converse Of yon soul's mate there sufficeth.

7. From thy door, 'fore God, I prithee, Send us not to Paradise;
For thy street-end, o Beloved, Us of What- and- Where [1165] sufficeth.

8. In our heads none other wish is Than of union with thee;
Us of this world and the other's Goods this one affair sufficeth.

9. Of the course of Fortune, Hafiz, To complain unjust it were;
Subtle spright and flowing verses, This unto our share sufficeth.

[1163] "Heavy", *syn.* "tedious, fashious". "Heavy ones" = "bores".
[1164] "Heavy", *syn.* "full", the cup, when full, being, of course, heavy.
[1165] i. e. the world of heated things.

CCCXVI

1. Art thou a friend well-willing? True to the given plight be;
Fellow of bath and closet, Rosegarth and day and night be.

2. Into the breeze's clutches Give not thy wildered tresses;
Unto the hearts of lovers, "Wildered," say not, "outright be!"

3. If with the prophet Khizr Thou wouldst be fellow-sitter,
Still, as thou wert Life's water, Hid from Sikender's sight be. [1166]

4. Not for each bird that flieth Is it Love's psalms to warble.
Come; of this songful bulbul [1167] Rose the new-blown and bright be.

5. Ours be the path of service, Ay, and the bondman's usance;
And to thyself, 'fore heaven, Lotted the Sultan's right be!

6. Sword on the Holy Places' Game look thou draw no longer [1168]
And of the hurt repentant, Done to our heart and spright, be.

7. Thou'rt the assembly's candle: One-tongued be and one-hearted;
Look on the moth's endeavour And smiling as the light be.

8. In love-looks the perfection Of heart-charming and grace is;
Thou of the age's rare ones, In th'usance of insight, be.

9. Peace, Hafiz, nor complaining Make of the Friend's oppression:
Who bade thee love-distracted For yonder fair-faced wight be?

[1166] i. e. shun the commerce of the people of the world and company only with lovers
and topers, with the servants of the ideal.
[1167] The lover, the poet himself.
[1168] Allusion to the prohibition of hunting and the like in the territories of Mecca and
Medina. By "the game of the Holy Places" lovers are here meant.

CCCXVII

1. Thou whose every part is charming, Every whit of thee is fair;
Made my heart by that cornelian [1169] Sugar-sweet of thee is fair.

2. As a newly opened rosebud Is thy being delicate;
Like the cypress of heav'n's meadows, Head to feet of thee is fair.

3. Sweet thy coquetry and coyness, Lovesome are thy down and mole;
Goodly eye and brow and stature, Fine and feat, of thee is fair.

4. Filled with images the rosegarth Of my fancy is by thee;
Made my heart's scent by that jasmine Tress's pleat of thee is fair.

5. 'Neath thine eyes I'll die; for, maugre All the languishment they cause,
Made my pain by that bright visage (When I see't) of thee is fair.

6. In Love's Way, wherein no 'scaping From Woe's torrent is, my thought,
With the viewing of that stature, Straight and fleet, of thee, is fair.

7. Yea, the way of heart-lorn Hafiz, Though on each side perils are
In quest's desert, with the loving, How so be't, of thee is fair.

[1169] i.e. lip.

CCCXVIII

1. All the bulbul's thought his lover How the rose may be is;
But *her* sole concern to baffle Lovers at her gree is.

2. Every thing is not heart-charming, That the lover slayeth;
Whoso tendereth his servant, Lord and master he is.

3. 'Tis no wonder,—if the potsherd Prime it in the market,—
That in blood the ruby's bosom Whelmed, as with a sea, is. [1170]

4. Only from the rose's favour Learned the bulbul singing;
Hence his throat with all this music Filled and warbling glee is.

5. God preserve that gone-a-travel Fair, with whom an hundred
Caravans of hearts go faring, Wheresoever she is!

6. Have a care, o thou that passest Through the Loved One's alley;
Of its wall a-pieces broken Else the head of thee is.

7. Though the practice of salvation Fair, o heart, befall thee,
Love forsake not, for its quarter Dear and sweet to see is.

8. Leave the spirit's lusts and longings And for thee, ne'er doubt it,
To the precinct of her presence Plain the path and free is.

9. Since the Soufi, when wine-merry Only, wried his skull-cap,
With two goblets more, his turban Fallen to his knee is. [1171]

10. Hafiz' heart, that to thy presence Now is grown accustomed,
Vex thou not, for it the reading Of thy grace and gree is.

[1170] i. e. it is no wonder if folk of worth and learning are strait-hearted, when they see
the public ear monopolized by log-rollers and intriguers.
[1171] The Oriental turban is composed of (1) the skull-cap, fitting closely to the
(shaven) head and (2) the turban-cloth, which is wound round the cap in many folds,
according to the wearer's taste. The meaning is, "If the Soufi's skull-cap be
disordered, when he has only drunk enough to make him merry with wine [of the
love of the Beloved], two or three goblets more would undo his turban-cloth and
make it hang down to his knees".

CCCXIX

1. Come back and soul's ally Unto my bosom strait be;
Unto this blighted heart A confidant and mate be.

2. Of yonder wine they sell In Love-liking its tavern,
Give us two cups or three, Though Ramazan-tide may't be.

3. O wise wayfaring sage, Since thou hast burned the patchcoat,
An effort make and chief Of topers small and great be. [1172]

4. Unto that friend, who said, "My heart for thee is looking,"
Say thou, "Behold, I come In peace: upon the wait be."

5. My heart's ableed for love Of that life-giving ruby: [1173]
O casket thou of Love, In this same seal and state be! [1174]

6. Lest on her heart grief's dust Sit, in my letter's traces,
O torrent of my tears, Aflow without abate be!

7. Bid Hafiz, if he seek The cup world-showing, ever
In noble Asefs [1175] sight, That Jem-like potentate, be. [1176]

[1172] i. e, it needs but an effort to raise thee to this position.
[1173] The Beloved's lip.
[1174] i. e. be constant to thy troth.
[1175] i. e. the Grand Vizier.
[1176] i. e. be assiduous in devotion to him. Instead of the version of 1. 2 above given, we may read, with equal probability, "Be in the sight (syn. favour) of the Asef (Vizier) of the one (King) of Jem-like place or power." But, as Soudi would say, "God (alone) is most (i. e. all-) knowing!"

CCCXX

1. In tulip-tide take the cup And no hypocrite be thou!
In the hope of the rose, a mate Of the East Wind a-flit be thou!

2. An if, like Jemshíd, thou'dst attain To the mystery of the Unseen,
Come and the mate of the cup World-showing, to wit, be thou.

3. I bid thee not all the year Wine-worshipping use; nine months
Abstain thou from wine and three A drinker of it be thou.

4. If th' elder of Love's highway Should charge thee to drink of wine,
Go, drink, and in God a-trust, Thy sins to remit, be thou.

5. Though, bud-like, the things of the world In straitness for aye consist,
Knot-opening, like to the wind Of Spring, if thou've wit, be thou. [1177]

6. To no one for faith look thou. My rede an thou hearken not,
A-seek for Philosopher's Stone And Phoenix 'tis fit thou be. [1178]

7. Hafiz, ensue not the ways And the laws of the folk of the world;
Of those, with the winebibbers pure Forever that sit, be thou.

[1177] i. e. as the Spring breeze looses the knots of the rosebud and brings it into bloom,
so do thou loose the knots of care and affliction from thy heart.
[1178] i. e., if thou look to any one for fidelity, thou wastest thy life in the pursuit of the
impossible and the non-existent, even as they who seek chimaeras, such as the
Phœnix and the Philosopher's Stone.

CCCXXI

1. To the gard'ner, if the five-days Commerce of the rose behoveth,
Bulbul's patience 'gainst estrangement's Thorn and winter's snows behoveth.

2. In her tresses' bond complain not, Heart, of wilderment; endurance
To the wise bird, when it falleth In the snare of woes, behoveth.

3. For that man be love forbidden Unto whom the jasmine-visage
And the jacinth-curl, by tresses And by cheeks like those, behoveth!

4. What to do with worldly prudence Hath the world-surrendering toper?
'Tis to state affairs reflection, Ay, and counsel close behoveth.

5. Trust in piety and knowledge Heresy in Love is; merits
Though the pilgrim have an hundred, Faith to him, God knows, behoveth.

6. Scorn and pride from that her drunken Eye this frenzied heart must suffer,
Since the curl of yonder browlock Unto its repose behoveth.

7. How long, skinker, wilt thou tarry With the circling of the wine-cup?
Nay, continuance, when 'twixt lovers Round the goblet goes, behoveth.

8. What is Hafiz, that he drinketh Not without the ghittern's warble?
What to him, the wretched lover, Of such pomps and shows behoveth?

CCCXXII

1. Hail to Shiraz and its station past compare!
God preserve it from cessation! Is my prayer.

2. O'er our Rúknabád an hundred "God preserve it's!"
For its dulcet waters life eternal bear.

3. Lo, betwixten Jaaferábad and Musélla,
All the breezes still grisamber-shedding fare.

4. Come to Shiraz and the Holy Spirit's blessing
Ask from men of pure perfection dwelling there.

5. Egypt's suckets, lest to scorn of Shiraz' sweet ones
He be laughed, herein to mention who shall dare?

6. Say, how fares that lovely tipsy-headed wanton?
Tidings what hast thou of her, o Eastland air?

7. Wake me not, for Heaven's sake! For in this slumber
I've sweet commerce with the image of my fair.

8. Heart, my blood to yonder loveling, if she shed it,
Make thou lawful, as her mother's milk it were.

9. Why, o Hafiz, separation since thou fearest,
Didst thou not give thanks for union had whilere?

CCCXXIII

1. Easance and strength and sense from me ravished clean
Of a stony-hearted, silver-eared fair have been;

2. An agile, Peri-like, humoursome, tricksy maid,
A subtle, moon-favoured, open-vest wearing quean.

3. For the heat of the fire of the frenzy of love for her,
I'm still, like the cauldron, a-boil with dole and teen.

4. If her, like the tunic, I had in my embrace,
Shift-like, I were tranquil ever of mind and mien.

5. At her oppression I carp not, for, thorns without,
The rose none findeth nor stingless is honey seen.

6. Albeit my very bones should rotten be,
The love of my love in my soul would still be green.

7. My heart and my faith, my heart and my faith, her breast
And shoulder, her breast and shoulder, have ravished clean.

8. Thine only balsam, o Hafiz, thy sole remeid
Her honey lip is, Her lip of ruby sheen.

CCCXXIV

1. My heart is run wild and I, also, Poor wretch, am witless sheer:
What manner of thing betided Hath to yon scared wild deer? [1179]

2. Like to the leaves of the willow, I tremble and quake for my faith;
For it, at a bow-browed wanton's, An infidel's hand, I fear.

3. Myself for the maw of the ocean I fancy. [1180] Away! What things
There be in the head of this droplet, So full of idle gear!

4. I praise me that saucy, wanton, Health-murdering lash of hers,
A-top of whose thorn [1181] Life's water For lovers welleth clear.

5. The sleeves of the leaches trickle, When for approof they lay
The hand on my wounded bosom, With many a bloody tear.

6. Weeping and head down hanging, I go in the tavern-street,
Because to me shame betideth Of that which I've garnered here. [1182]

7. Nor Khizr [1183] for aye abideth Nor yet Sikender's realm:
So fret not thy heart, o dervish, For the world's worthless gear.

8. A bondman thou art; of loved ones Make not complaint, o friend!
Love's law complaint forbiddeth Of worse or better cheer.

9. The hand of no beggar winneth, Hafiz, to that her waist;
Go, get thee in hand a treasure, That Korah's shall out-peer. [1184]

[1179] i. e. my heart.
[1180] i. e. My tears flow in such torrents that I imagine myself therefore to be the very maw of the ocean.
[1181] Eyelash likened to thorn.
[1182] i. e. of my wasted life and the little I have made of it.
[1183] Though he is supposed to be immortal. The meaning is; how long soever a man may live, yet he must die at last.
[1184] i. e. The Beloved's favours are not to be had for nothing; so "put money in thy purse".

CCCXXV

1. Yestereven, one keen-witted, Myst'ry-knowing, said to me,
"Hid one may not hold the secret Of the wine-seller from thee."

2. "Lightly," said he, "bear life's burdens; For the fashion of the world
"Is that hard on the hard-striving Presseth it and heavily."

3. Then a goblet such he gave me That its brightness in the skies
Venus brought to dance and smiting Hand on ghittern, "Drink!" cried she.

4. Lend, my son, thine ear to counsel; For the world's sake sorrow not;
Pearls of price, God wot, my rede is: Keep it in thy memory.

5. Like the cup, with heart a-bleeding, Ever show a laughing lip,
Nor, the harp like, into clamour Break, if smitten thou shouldst be.

6. Till adépt thou be, no inkling Of Love's myst'ry shalt thou hear;
Ears profane are no receivers For the angels' melody.

7. In Love's sanctuary one must not Breathe a word of "Say-and-hear;" [1185]
Lovers all must there be only Ears to hear and eyes to see.

8. At the feast of men of insight Out of place is idle prate;
Either speak of what thou knowest, Man of sense, or silent be.

9. Skinker, wine! For Hafiz' toping Hath the Vizier of the King
Blemish-hiding, sin-remitting, Covered up with his decree.

[1185] i. e. there is no room for "argle-bargling" there.

CCCXXVI

1. In the days of the error-hiding, Transgression-pardoning king,
Took Muftis to cup- and Hafiz To flagon-emptying.

2. The Soufi from cloister-corner Sat at the wine-jar's foot,
Since high on the Mohtesib's shoulder He saw the pitcher swing.

3. At dawntide the wine-selling elder I questioned anent the case
Of Elder and Cadi, touching Their Jew-fashion wine-bibbing. [1186]

4. "Nay, bridle thy tongue," he answered; "Drink wine and the veil respect;
"For even to thee, initiate, Behoveth not tell this thing."

5. Spring is at hand and money Lacketh for wine; perpend,
Skinker; [1187] my heart's blood boileth For sorrow and wearying.

6. Accept my excuse and cover The fault with clemency's skirt;
The blame is with youth and poortith And love and the new-born Spring.

7. How long, like the candle, comrade, Wilt practise length of tongue?
Peace! Peace! For the moth of longing [1188] Already's on the wing.

8. O sovran of sense and seeming, Whose like no eye hath seen
Nor ear of his equal heard hath, Still mayst thou live, o King,

9. Till that thy youthful fortune The patchcoat blue, in fine,
From heaven, that rag-clad elder, Shall take, inheriting!

10. A voice, last night, from the Viewless Unto my heart's ear said,
"Hafiz, drink wine and chew not The cud of sorrowing!"

[1186] The Jews, says Soudi, though they drink much, never become intoxicated and
keep their winebibbing hidden; because in their religion wine is not forbidden, as in
Islam, but only drinking to excess. "Jew-fashion drinking" here, therefore, means
drinking in private.
[1187] i. e. Cast about for a means of raising the wind.
[1188] "The moth of longing", syn. "the desired mandate", i. e. the warrant for payment
of Hafiz's allowance from the Sultan, which seems to have been, as usual, in arrear.
A broad hint to the Sultan.

CCCXXVII

1. At dawn from the Unseen Speaker Came the glad news to mine ear;
"The time it of Shah Shejáa is! Drink, then, and make good cheer!"

2. Past, past are the days when the people Of vision withdrew apart,
Mouths full of a thousand sayings And silent the lips for fear.

3. To the sound of the harp we will utter Those words, for the hiding whereof
The breast, like a boiling cauldron, Was ever in ferment sheer.

4. The wine, that in secret drunken, For fear of the Censor, was,
We'll quaff to the topers' clamour, In face of the comrades dear.

5. Aback, from the street of the winehouse, They carried him yesterday,
His Worship th' Imám, the prayer-rug A-shoulder that bore whileare!

6. Good guidance, o heart, I give thee, To fare in salvation's way;
In lewdness, indeed, nor glory Nor vaunt thou thyself austere.

7. The mind of the king the focus Of manifestation is; [1189]
Make pure thine intent, whenever Thou drawest his presence near.

8. Be nought but the praise of his glory The exercise of thy heart;
For th'angels their revelations Make to his privy ear.

9. The secrets of state expedience Kings only know: thou'rt nought
But a beggarly dervish, Hafiz: Prate not, but watch and hear.

[1189] i. e. men's purposes lie open to his piercing sight; he searcheth all hearts.

CCCXXVIII

1. That bitter wine I crave, whose might Man's wit and will oppresses,
So of the world I may awhile Be quit and its distresses.

2. Bring wine, for none on earth assured Against the heavens' malice,
For Mars their bully's pranks and eke Venus their harperess, is.

3. The board of this base-fostering age No honey hath of easance:
Wash from thy sense's palate, heart, Its salt and bitter messes.

4. Leave Behram's lasso and Jem's cup Take up; [1190] for I this desert,
The world, have traversed and to find Nor Behram nor his ass is. [1191]

5. To look with favour on the poor No blemish is to greatness;
Nay, Solomon the Great gave ear Unto the ant's addresses.

6. Come, and the mystery of Time I'll show thee in wine's mirror;
But tell it not to blinded hearts And Nature's crookednesses.

7. Wine ruby-red from emerald cup I drink; for this the virtue
To blind the viper of the age (The pietist) possesses. [1192]

8. The bow of the Beloved's brow Still aims its shafts at Hafiz;
But at his forearm void of strength It smiles, while it oppresses.

[1190] i. e. (according to Soudi) "Forswear the pursuit of the goods of the world and drink wine".

[1191] Allusion to the story of Behram Gour (Behram V of the Sasanian dynasty, A. D. 420—438), who owed his ekename to his passion for the chase of the wild ass (*Gour*) and who, at last, following a *Gour* into a marshy and cavernous district, was lost in a morass (Soudi, "a cavern") and never again heard of, although his mother caused his armbearer and varlet perish under the question, saying, "What have you done with my son?" *Gour* (wild ass) signifies also "tomb"; and we may therefore read, "Nor Behram nor his *tomb* is to be found". The meaning is, "Behram and all his pomp and all that he strove after are vanished as if they had never been"; a warning of the vanity and instability of worldly goods and endeavours. It should be noted that the lasso was in ancient Persia (as in modern South and Central America) the favourite weapon of the hunter of large game, such as the deer, wild ass etc.

[1192] The emerald is supposed by the Orientals to possess the virtue of blinding (some say, killing) snakes. See anecdote on this subject quoted in my "Quatrains of Omar Kheyyam", p. 82, note.

CCCXXIX

1. Roses come cull and to thorns, Soufi, that patchcoat of thine give;
Up, for delectable wine, Abstinence bitter as brine give!

2. Dervishes' fashion and prate Cast at the foot of the ghittern;
Chaplet and coif unto wine, Ay, and to drinkers of wine give.

3. Noyous austerity, nought Valued of loveling and skinker,
Unto the zephyrs of Spring, Full in the meadows ashine, give.

4. Wait for me ruby wine lay; Quittance, o sovran of lovers,
The pit of the lovely one's chin, For shedding this heart's blood of mine, give.

5. O Lord, in the time of the rose Forgive the default of the servant
And pardon for that which hath passed, By the riverside cypress's sign, give.

6. O thou that hast founden thy way To the watering-place of thy wishes,
A drop from that ocean to me, Dust-like in the dust of repine, give. [1193]

7. As off'ring of thanks that thine eye Ne'er looked on the face of a fair one,
Us sots to the pardon of God And eke to the favour Divine give. [1194]

8. When, skinker, the Vizier our lord The draught of the morning-tide quaffeth,
Entreat him to Hafiz, anights That waketh, the cup of gold fine give.

[1193] i. e. abject as the dust.
[1194] i. e. consign, commend. This couplet appears to be addressed to some pietist, as who should say, "Thou hast never fallen, because thou hast never been tempted"; ("Je résiste à tout, sauf a la tentation", said gentle and sweet-natured Gounod;) "ergo, be indulgent to such as I and leave us to the Divine compassion".

CCCXXX

1. Fair are rill-bank and willowfoot And songful spright and friend, full fair;
A charmer sweet to mate, a maid Rose-cheeked, our cup to tend, full fair!

2. O Fortune-favoured one, that hast All these and know'st the worth of time,
Hail, for the Fates, indeed, to thee A portion fair extend, full fair!

3. Bid whoso hath a charmer's love At heart cast rue upon the fire,
For from the evil eye he hath A matter to defend full fair.

4. Jewels of virgin thought I bind On this my nature's bride; may be
The cast of Fortune's dice to me An idol fair shall send, full fair.

5. The nights of union enjoy And take thy share of heart's content;
Heart-kindling for the moonlight is, Ay, and the streamlet's bend full fair.

6. In her eyes' cup the skinker hath A wine, God wot, that to the wit
Gives drunkenness delectable And to the very end full fair. [1195]

7. In folly, Hafiz, hath life passed: With us unto the winehouse come,
So blithesome fair ones there to thee A business may commend full fair. [1196]

[1195] i. e. without headache or the other unpleasant consequences of ordinary
winebibbing.
[1196] i. e. that of wine-drinking.

CCCXXXI

1. All compáct of grace and beauty Is my loved one's moonlike face;
Love and faith, o Lord, vouchsafe her; For of these she hath no trace.

2. My heart-ravisher a child is; But she will some day in sport
Slay me abject and the canon Hold her guiltless of the case. [1197]

3. Best it were from her that straitly I my heart should guard; for she
Good and bad not yet hath proven, Knoweth worthy not from base.

4. I a fourteen-year-old idol Have, a fair one, slim and sweet,
Whose the full moon ring-in-ear is, Slave and bondman of her grace.

5. From her lip like sugar cometh Yet the scent of mother's milk,
Though upon her black eye's glances Followeth the blood apace.

6. Whither is our heart, I wonder, After yonder new-blown rose
Gone a-stray? We have not on it Looked this many a long day's space.

7. If my lovely one continue Hearts to shatter on this wise,
Soon the Sultan will impress her For his guard in war and chase.

8. In thanksgiving would I render To that peerless pearl my life,
If the shell [1198] of Hafiz' eyeball Should become its biding-place.

[1197] Children not being responsible in law.
[1198] i. e. socket; word used p. g. with "pearl".

CCCXXXII

1. Our fortune in this city We've proven many a year;
Behoveth from this whirlpool To carry off our gear.

2. I kindle, for much gnawing Of hands and heaving sighs,
My body, rended piecemeal, Like roses fallen sere.

3. Last night to me how sweetly A bulbul sang, what while
The rose, upon its branches, Made wide to hark its ear,

4. Saying, "O heart, be merry; For that strait-natured [1199] Friend
"Herself must oft sit sorry, Because of Fortune drear."

5. If thou wilt have pass o'er thee The world-all's hard and soft,
Leave thou thy soft [1200] troth-keeping And thy hard words arear.

6. Though Chance's stormy billows Against high heaven beat,
With not one drop of water The sage doth wet his gear. [1201]

7. O Hafiz, if enjoyment For ever were vouchsafed,
Jemshíd his throne had never Abandoned for the bier.

[1199] i. e. churlish, ill-conditioned.
[1200] i. e. "lax"; word used p. g.
[1201] i. e. "he suffereth not vicissitudes to affect him", being "confit en mépris des choses fortuites", as says Rabelais of Pantagruel. Rhyme-word of I repeated 4 and 6.

CCCXXXIII

1. From the nook of the tavern last night a voice said,
"Sins pardon They; [1202] drink, then, and be not a-dread.

2. "God's grace still a-work is: still Gabriel brings
"Glad tidings of mercy for quick and for dead.

3. "More great than our sin His forgiveness is." Peace!
What sayst thou? A riddle uneath to be read! [1203]

4. "To the winehouse go bear thy raw wit, so its blood
"Into ferment be brought by the wine ruby-red. [1204]

5. "Though union for striving They [1205] give not, o heart,
"The path, as thou mayst, of endeavour still tread."

6. Mine ear and the ring of her forelock are one;
The dust of the wine-seller's door and my head.

7. Small sin in the sight of the fault-hiding King
Is Hafiz's toping, when all hath been said.

[1202] "They", the Fates.
[1203] Hafiz's objection to the dictum of the unseen speaker.
[1204] The latter's rejoinder. "When thy blood is warmed with wine, thou wilt better understand my speech".
[1205] "They", the Fates.

CCCXXXIV

1. Lord, that new-blown rose and smiling, Which to me Thou didst commit,
From its envious fellows' glances To thy safeguard I remit.

2. Though an hundred stages distant From Faith's stead she's wandered, far
Be the moon's revolving chances From her body and her wit!

3. If to Selma's camping-quarter, O East wind, thou chance to come,
Bear to her from me, I prithee, Salutation fair and fit.

4. Gently open thou the muskpod Of her jetty tress: but soft!
For of lovers' hearts the prison 'Tis: so never touzle it.

5. Say, "My heart the right of faith hath O'er thy down and mole: it safe
"Keep in that grisamber browlock, Where in bondage it doth sit."

6. In a stage, where to the memory Of her lip they quaff, full base
Is the sot with whom self-knowledge Yet abideth anywhit. [1206]

7. Wealth one may not win nor honour From the winehouse-door; needs must
Whoso of this water [1207] drinketh To the waves his gear commit.

8. Unto him who fashery feareth Be the grief of love forbid!
At her gree, our heads her footstool Or our lips with hers be knit!

9. Hafiz' verses all the chiefest Couplet are of Wisdom's Ode:
Blessings on his speech so gracious And his heart-alluring wit!

[1206] In communion with the Beloved, it behoveth the true lover cast off all consciousness of self.
[1207] Wine styled "water", p. g. with "waves".

CCCXXXV

1. Whenas the East wind waveth Her ambergris-shedding tress,
New life unto all it bringeth Who languish in durésse.

2. Oh, where is a like-souled comrade, That I may show him what
My heart, in the days of her absence, Doth suffer of distress?

3. The courier of morn a letter Faith-promising bore to the Friend:
Our eye-blood its superscription Did for a seal impress.

4. Time erst of the rose-leaves fashioned The counterpart of thy cheek,
But, seeing thee, straight in the rosebud Hid it for shamefastness.

5. Lo, thou art asleep, nor limit To Love apparent is.
Now blessed be God from this pathway, Whose length is limitless! [1208]

6. It is as the Kaabeh's [1209] beauty To pilgrims itself excused
That true lovers' souls in its desert Are lost without redress.

7. News of our heart's lost Joseph, Out of the pit of her chin,
Who bringeth this shattered dweller In th' house of heaviness?

8. Into the hand of the Vizier, That so of its fraud and guile
Maybe he shall do me justice, I give the tip of her tress.

9. At dawn, on the marge of the meadows, I heard from the nightingale
A ditty of sweet-voiced Hafiz, The bard of allegresse.

[1208] To be without end and limit appertained absolutely to God alone, the endlessness of other things being only relative; hence says the poet, "Be no derogation to the attributes of God implied by this saying of the endlessness of Love's pathway!"— Soudi.
[1209] "Kaabeh", here = the Beloved's quarter.

CCCXXXVI

1. I am drunken with loveliking For yon tavern-friend of mine:
At my wounded heart her glances Launch the arrows of repine.

2. When the cross (to wit, the pleatings) Of thy tress thou openest,
Many a Muslim is perverted By that infidel of thine.

3. Unto thee I clave and severed Have from all but thee the heart;
He who is thy mate to stranger Nor to kinsman doth incline.

4. Nay, vouchsafe a glance of kindness Unto me, the heart-bereft;
For, without thy helping favour, Prospers none of my design.

5. If thy ruby lip strew somewhat On my wounded heart of salt,
O thou queen of beauty's kingdom, Where would be the harm, in fine?

6. Lo, behind me and before me, Ambush set thy tipsy eye
And the harvest of my patience To the winds it did consign.

7. From thy mouth, that honey-casket, Lay a salve on Hafiz' heart,
All a-bleeding with the glances, Lance-and-sting like, of thine eyne.

CCCXXXVII

1. Whenas thy ruby cup [1210] I quaff, Where doth my wit remain?
Me, when thy tipsy eye I see, Who is there shall restrain?

2. I am thy bondman and of me Unneeding if thou be,
Unto the tavern wine-seller To sell me prithee deign.

3. In hopes that in the winehouse I May come a tankard by,
I go and on my back to bear The tapster's jug am fain.

4. The water-bearer of the street Of topers, for desire
Of that thy lip, the vintner's sill Doth ply with tearful rain.

5. Say not to me, "Draw in thy breath; Forbear and silent be!"
Nay, in the meads, one cannot bid The bird from song refrain.

6. If in thy trace I would ensue, Where's patience, ay, and calm?
And if thy tale I'd tell, to bear Who hath the heart and brain?

7. To the cold-hearted give old wine, For wine a sharp fire is;
But they who're ripe of wit are still A-boil with love and pain.

8. When they the robe of honour gave Of Sultan Love to me,
"Hafiz", they bade me, "don it, man, And tell it not again."

[1210] i. e. lip.

CCCXXXVIII

1. From the lasso of thy tress-tip Is deliverance for none;
Wretched swains thou slay'st nor fearest Punishment for what thou'st done.

2. In the wilds of self-effacement Save the heart-burnt lover fare,
In the spirit's holy places He is no accepted one.

3. From Rustém [1211] thine eyelash-arrow Beareth off the victory;
From Weccás [1212] thine eyebrow's bowman Hath the prize of arch'ry won.

4. Candle-wise, in all sincereness, In the midst my soul I set;
Strewage made I of my body In the road thy feet did run.

5. What while thou, for longing, moth-like, Burnest not in love and truth,
Verily, for thee deliv'rance From the grief of love is none.

6. Into our moth-heart thou castest Fire, albeit we, moth-like,
In desire of thee still dancing, Death and danger did not shun.

7. Lo, thy love's alchymic virtue Our base-metal earthy self
Hath to purest gold transmuted, Bright and shining as the sun.

8. Marry, what should know the vulgar Of the worth of pearls of price?
Hafiz, waste thy peerless jewels Not on every mother's son.

[1211] "Rustem", the well-known legendary hero of the Shahnameh, the Persian Hercules.
[1212] Saad ibn Abi Weccas, a champion archer and one of the Companions of the Prophet, who is recorded to have said to him, during a battle, being moved to admiration of his prowess, "Shoot, o Saad, my father and mother be thy sacrifice!"

CCCXXXIX

1. Ne'er of thy watcher this heart of mine is quit;
Tale-teller tale-teller cherisheth not, to wit. [1213]

2. The Mohtesib broke the pitcher and I his head:
"Tooth for a tooth and eye for an eye!" 'tis writ.

3. Like Jesus the wine-cup is, since live again
The dead by its special virtue maketh it.

4. Play a tune, minstrel, such that, on Venus-wise,
Shall Jupiter dance to its sound in the sphere star-lit.

5. Hafiz to heart, from the page of the Loved One's cheek,
The chapters of "Praise" and of "Constancy" [1214] doth commit.

[1213] Two of a trade never agree.
[1214] Chapters 1 and 112 of the Koran.

CCCXLI

1. Come, so the spirit's fragrance That I may retrace from that cheek;
Come, that I may discover My lost heart's place from that cheek.

2. Ask thou the explanation Of that which they tell in books
Of the charms of the heavenly Houris, Their beauty and grace, from that cheek.

3. The form of the haughty cypress Is left in the dust by that shape;
The rose of the rose-garth shrinketh, In sheer amaze, from that cheek.

4. The jessamine shamed abideth By reason of those her limbs;
The heart of the Redbud goeth In bloody case from that cheek.

5. The musk-pod of China taketh Its fragrant scent from that curl;
The odours of Paradise gaineth Rosewater base from that cheek.

6. The sun of the sky for envy's Asweat of the sun of thy face;
The moon up aloft's grown meagre And pallid of face from thy cheek.

7. The water of life distilleth From Hafiz' heart-charming verse,
As souls, into sweat resolved, Do trickle apace from that cheek.

CCCXLII

1. Since the cheek of our Friend the new-sprung down Hath compassed about with its
rounded line,
The moon of the skies her face mistakes For another moon on the earth ashine.

2. For wish of her lip, the which, God wot, Is goodlier far than the water of life,
A fountain of tears, like the Tigris stream, Is welling still from my weeping eyne.

3. Anon, for desire of her, I give My heart and spirit, as dust they were;
Whiles, duck-like, [1215] the fire of the love of her I quench with water of tears and
wine.

4. An if for a bounden slave of hers My sovran lady will me accept,
The writ to her thrall that bindeth me With benediction I'll seal and sign.

5. Hafiz, the water of life itself Is all confounded before thy verse;
For no one ever, for love of her, Hath made such ditties as these of thine.

[1215] *Bett*, duck, *syn.* flagon; word used p. g.

CCCXLIII

1. Thy lovely cheek, God guard it From th' evil eye! prays Hafiz;
For wrought it hath to-us-ward All manner good, says Hafiz.

2. Come; 'tis the time of concord And faith-keeping and friendship:
That which hath past between us From mem'ry's book raze, Hafiz.

3. What though my lip have drunken Thy heart's blood? Take to bloodwit
A kiss, which all thou'st suffered (And more than all) pays, Hafiz.

4. Nay, who art thou to cherish The hope of her enjoyment?
Upon her skirts no beggar, God wot, the hand lays, Hafiz.

5. To mole and tress of lovelings The heart again bind never,
If, by good luck, thou scapest This snare of Love's maze, Hafiz.

6. Come, sing a dainty ditty, lovesome and fresh and tender;
For joy-bringing and fatal To grief are thy lays, Hafiz.

7. Thou'st donned the juggling patchcoat; Begone from me, o zealot!
Thou'st drunk the dregs of sorrow; Come, reap thou the praise, Hafiz!

8. With heart and soul, at day-break, Make moaning, like the topers,
And offer at that moment A prayer for my days, Hafiz. [1216]

[1216] Couplets 2, 3, 6, 7 and 8 appear to be put in the mouth of the Beloved.

CCCXLIV

1. By the glory and might and power Of Shah Shejaá I swear,
I never had strife with man For wealth and worldly ware.

2. A glance at thy lovers deign, In thanks that I the slave
Obedient am and thou The king obeyed allwhere.

3. We thirst for a draught of the cup Of thy bounty; but hardihood
We use not nor break thy head With over-importunate prayer.

4. The house-wine [1217] sufficeth me: No wine of the Magians bring.
The wine-fellow's come: o friend Repentance, adieu fore'er!

5. 'Fore heaven, my patchcoat scour And launder amain with wine;
For I from this gear scent not The fragrance of good and fair.

6. Nay, see, to the wail of the harp How those go dancing now,
Who wont not to sanction e'en The hearing of song whilere.

7. From the dust of the presence-place Of Shah Shejáa's renown
May Hafiz's face and brow Of God be severed ne'er!

[1217] "House-wine", generally wine smuggled into the house, for fear of the law; but here apparently "the wine of the Beloved's enjoyment", which dispenses the lover from the need of other means of intoxication. Cf. Ben Jonson's "Drink to me only with thine eyes... Leave a kiss within the cup And I'll not ask for wine."

CCCXLV

1. By the world-illumining splendour Of Shah Shejáa his reign,
I never had strife with any For rank or wealth or gain.

2. Bring wine; for whenas his cresset Enkindleth the sun on high,
Down, e'en on the hut of the dervish, His radiant favours rain.

3. A flask and a lovesome cupmate Suffice me of this world's goods;
For all things, save these, are causes Of headache and stress and pain.

4. Go, wiseacre, this thy pity Change for a cup of wine;
For I am the slave commanded, Not the king sovereign.

5. Love from the mosque to the tavern Sent me: the wine-mate's come.
Wherefore, o friend Repentance, Farewell yet once again!

6. Of merit the age recks nothing: And other than this I've nought:
Lo, whither shall I go traffic With ware that all disdain?

7. Of Hafiz's pious fashions And whirligig prate I'm sick:
Come, tune up the harp and sing me A song! For to dance I'm fain.

CCCXLVI

1. When at dawn the Orient's candle Casteth radiance far and nigh
From the innermost recesses Of the palace of the sky,

2. From th' horizon's pouch the mirror Heaven draweth and therein
The world's face on many a fashion Showeth forth unto the eye.

3. In the coigns of the pavilion Of the Sovereign of the Spheres,
Venus, hark! the organ tuneth, With intent to sing thereby.

4. Hark, the cup in laughter breaketh, "'Where is he forbiddeth wine?"
And the harp to clamour cometh, Saying, "Who shall Love deny?"

5. Note the usances of Fortune And the cup of pleasance take;
For the goodliest of fashions Every wise this is, say I.

6. Snare and fraud is all the browlock Of the strumpet of the world;
Men of understanding never Wrangle for that flimsy lie.

7. If thou wish the world's well-being, Seek of God the King's long life;
For he is a generous being, 'Vantager of low and high.

8. Soul of all the world, with knowledge Practice joining, Shah Shejáa,
Incarnation of God's favour, Very splendour of Hope's eye;

9. At his door, on servant-fashion, Hafiz, bide; for he's a king
God-obeying and obeyed is Of the world-all, far and nigh.

CCCXLVII

1. I for constancy renowned am Of the fair, the candle like;
Night-watch in the topers' quarter Keeping e'er, the candle like.

2. Day and night no slumber cometh To mine eyes grief-worshipping;
For thy sev'rance sick, sore weeping Still I fare, the candle like.

3. Severed with the shears of sorrow For thy sake's my patience' thread;
Yet love's fire for thee I, natheless, Smiling bear, the candle like.

4. In this night of separation Me a script of union send;
Else the world shall I enkindle For despair, the candle like.

5. If my tears' rose-coloured courser Had not run so fast, not thus
To the world my hidden secret Blazoned were, the candle like.

6. In the midst of fire and water, This my wan and wasted heart
For thy love's at once tear-raining And a-flare, the candle like.

7. Soft as wax is grown the mountain Of my patience in grief's hand,
Since I in Love's fire and water Waste and wear, the candle like.

8. Very night, without thy beauty World-adorning, is my day;
For sheer love of thee, I'm wasting Into air, the candle like.

9. For one night, my head to heaven With thine union exalt;
Let thy face my cell enlighten, Haughty fair, the candle like.

10. But a breath of life is left me, Like the morn, without thy sight:
Show thy face and life I'll render, Then and there, the candle like.

11. Fast Love's fire for thee on Hafiz Hold hath taken: how, alack!
Quench heart's burning with eyes' water Shall I e'er, the candle like?

CCCXLVIII

1. In quest of the garden of roses At dawn-tide in hope I went
My brain, like the lovelorn bulbul, To solace somedele with the scent;

2. And there in the midst of the greensward Mine eyes on a red rose lit,
That shone as a lamp in the darkness, Such light to the meads she lent.

3. So proudly in youth and beauty She queened it, that all repose
From the bird of the thousand voices She ravished and heart's content.

4. The eyes of the wild narcissus Ran over with wistful tears;
And hundreds of scars of passion The heart of the tulip rent.

5. The lily at her, in chiding, The tongue stretched out, like a sword;
Th'anemone, blab-like, opened Her mouth in astoniment.

6. Anon in her hand the flagon, Like lovers of wine; anon,
Like skinkers that fill for topers, The cup on her palm she hent.

7. Easance, mirth, youth, o Hafiz, Enjoy, while they last, like the rose.
The messenger only bound is To carry the message sent.

CCCXLIX

1. So but of fortune backed I be, Hand on the Loved One's skirt I'll lay:
An if I win it, what delight! Yea, and what honour, if she slay!

2. Vantage of pity hath from none Gotten this hopeful heart of mine,
Albe my speech my tale of woes Unto all quarters doth convey.

3. Idols with hearts of stone how long Shall I with love and fondness tend?
Children unnatural, of the sire, Fondly that reared them, think not they. [1218]

4. Door of deliverance none for me Is there from that thine eyebrow's curve:
'Las! in pursuit of that crook'd conceit Dear life hath perished and passed away.

5. How shall the brow of the Friend, indeed, Hand-holding [1219] be to me, poor wretch?
None with this bow in the clout of hope The arrow of wish hath shotten aye.

6. With pious purpose am I become A corner-sitter; but lo! 'tis strange
That from all quarters the Magian youth With drum and dulcimer me waylay

7. Dolts are the zealots; no droning psalms Chant, but a wanton ditty sing.
The Mohtesib drunk with dissembling is: Give wine, then, skinker, without affray.

8. See how the city Soufi eats The doubtful morsel! Well-foddered beast!
Long be his crupper and may he wax In better beastlihood night and day!

9. Hafiz, if thou thy feet address To fare in the path of the folk of Love,
The blessing of him, who o'er Nejéf Waketh and watcheth, [1220] guide thy way!

[1218] Lovelings likened to spoilt children and lovers to fathers who have fostered and
cherished them.
[1219] i. e. Succourable.
[1220] i. e. Ali, who is buried at Nejef, near Cufa, and is dubbed by Jami, in his
Anecdotes of the Imams, the "Watchman of Nejef". The English reader maybe
reminded that Ali, next to Mohammed himself, is the great saint of the schismatic
(*Shiah*) Persians.

CCCL

1. A sojourn of peace and safety, Sheer wine and a loving friend,
Now glory to God for favour, If Fortune to thee these send!

2. The world and its need and its fashions Are nothing in nothing all;
Nay, thousands of times this saying For truth have I proved and kenned.

3. Go, find thee a place of safety And reckon time's plunder gain;
For highwaymen lie in ambush For all in Life's way that wend.

4. Alas and alack that I knew not Till now that the one belov'd,
The Loved One, the sole elixir Of happiness is in the end!

5. Come drink; for the lip of the loveling To leave and the laugh of the cup
A whim is, to which no credence Doth understanding lend.

6. One whit of that charm of beauty, That hides in thy dimpled chin,
The deepest of thoughts avail not Its depths to apprehend.

7. O where is a man of mettle, That he may guide us to good?
For we on no wise may light on The way to the house of the Friend.

8. Albeit thy waist hair-slender Be never for such as I,
That subtle conceit [1221] doth solace Withal to my soul commend.

9. What wonder an if my tear-drops Cornelian-colour be?
The seal [1222] of mine eye in redness Cornelian doth transcend.

10. Quoth she to me, laughing, "Hafiz, The slave of thy will am I."
Alack, how she still befooleth And flouteth at me, perpend!

[1221] i. e. the thought of thine impalpable waist.
[1222] i. e. pupil.

CCCLI

1. The tongue of the pen refuseth To set forth the bale of sev'rance;
Else had I to thee expounded, Beloved, the tale of sev'rance.

2. The mate of the troop of thine image I am and the horseman of patience;
The comrade of fire of estrangement And fellow all-hail of sev'rance.

3. Alas for the days of my lifetime, That come to an end in the hope are
Of union, nor come to an end are The days of the vale of sev'rance!

4. My head, that for glory aforetime I struck on the roof of the heavens,
I've laid, by the true ones I swear, At the door of the jail of sev'rance!

5. Oh how shall I open my pinions, To fly in the ether of union,
Since shed hath the bird of my bosom Its plumes on the gale of sev'rance?

6. Nay, how shall I make pretention To union with thee, since the puppet
Of Fortune become is my heart And my body the bail of sev'rance?

7. Roast meat, for the ardour of longing, Become is my heart; and afar
From the Loved One, the blood of the liver I drink from the pail of sev'rance.

8. What help for me, now, on the ocean Of grief, in a whirlpool is fallen
The bark of my patience, because Of the stress of the sail of sev'rance?

9. Not much did it lack but the bark Of my hope had been foundered and sunk
Of the billows of longing for thee On the sea without pale of sev'rance.

10. The firmament, whenas it noted My head in Love's carcanet taken,
The neck of my patience constrained With the halter of bale of sev'rance.

11. Estrangement and sev'rance, I wonder, Who was it that into the world brought?
The day of estrangement be darkened And may the house fail of sev'rance!

12. If, Hafiz, Love's way to the end With the foot of desire thou hadst followed,
In hand none had given estrangement The rein of avail of sev'rance.

CCCLII

1. May none, like me, be shattered of the woes of separation,
Whose life hath all been wasted in the throes of separation!

2. An exiled, lovelorn beggar, enamoured and bewildered,
I've borne the spite of Fortune and the blows of separation.

3. If ever separation in my hand should fall, I'd slay it
And pay with tears what bloodwit Fate chose of separation.

4. What do, where go, I know not! To whom my heart's case utter?
My dues who is't shall render and those of separation?

5. With sev'rance from thy presence I'll separation harrow,
Till heart's blood from the eyelids o'erflows of separation.

6. What kin have I with severance and grief? 'Twould seem my mother
Had borne me for the sufferance, that grows of separation.

7. Hence, day and night, like Hafiz, with the bulbuls of the morning,
Of passion's brand I plain me and the woes of separation.

CCCLIII

1. Thou, upon whose lip the salt-right Hath my wounded heart, [1223] with me
Look thou keep the pact of friendship; For I go; and God with thee,

2. Thou pure soul, for whose well-being, In the spiritual world,
Prayer the sum is and the purport Of the angels' psalmody!

3 If thou doubt of my sincereness, Put me to the proof. By nought
Like the touchstone, folk the fineness Of pure gold avail to see.

4. Thou didst say, "I will be drunken And will give thee kisses twain."
Past the limit is; but neither Two nor one beheld have we.

5. Ope thy smiling mouth's pistachio And thy speech's sugar strew:
Let the folk no longer doubtful Of thy mouth's existence be. [1224]

6. Not the man am I oppression From the firmament to bear;
Topsy-turvy will I set it, If it turn not to my gree.

7. Since thou lettest not the Loved One To her Hafiz, at the least,
Farther from her side betake thee, Watcher, paces two or three.

[1223] i. e. thy lip having strewn salt on my wounded heart, the latter can claim the rights

arising from the eating of [bread and] salt in company; see previous note.
[1224] i. e. thy mouth is so small that folk doubt its existence till thou openest it to speak.

CCCLIV

1. If wine thou drink, with somewhat Thereof earth's thirst allay:
What harm in sin, whose doing Another profit may?

2. Whatso thou hast, go eat it Nor grieve; for ruthless Time
The falchion of destruction Still plieth without stay.

3. By thy foot's dust, o cypress Full fondly cherished mine,
When I am dead, remove not Thy foot from off my clay!

4. In all sects, men and angels, Dwellers in heav'n and hell,
Strait-handedness and meanness Are treason to the Way. [1225]

5. The Architect of Heaven So made this six-square [1226] house
That no way is of 'scaping The pitfall of decay.

6. The grape-vine's daughter's [1227] malice Waylayeth sore the wit:
Yet may the vine-garth flourish Until the Judgment Day!

7. Thou'st left the world, o Hafiz, To fare the tavern-path:
The prayers of all true lovers Tend on thy pure heart aye!

[1225] Way [of Love].
[1226] The Persians reckon six sides to every thing, i. e. right, left, front, back, above and
below.
[1227] "The grape-vine's daughter", i. e. wine.

CCCLV

1. Albeit a thousand foemen To work my ruin try,
If thou be my friend, Beloved, No whit of foes reck I.

2. 'Tis nought but the hope of thine union That holdeth me still on life;
And else, in the fear of thy sev'rance, An hundred deaths I die.

3. Except from the breath of the breezes Each moment thy scent I smell,
Each breath, like the rose, for sorrow, My wede I rend in twy.

4. Do these my two eyes from thine image E'er sever in sleep? Away! [1228]
Or patient, from thee when parted, My heart is it? God deny!

5. A wound at thy hand is better Than healing from other folk
And poison from thee than balsams, Which other hands apply.

6. For me, to be slain of thy sword-stroke Were everlasting life,
By token my soul delighteth Thy buffets to aby.

7. Nay, turn not away! If thou smite me With sabre, my head a shield
I'll make nor aside from thy halter My hands will I awry.

8. How, marry, shall every vision Conceive thee as thou art?
For after his measure of vision Each only may descry.

9. When Hafiz the face of abjection Laid in the dust of thy door,
Then first did he wax exalted Of worth in the general eye.

[1228] Energetic formula of denial = our "God forbid!"

CCCLVI

1. So but it were vouchsafed me To win unto thy street,
My case, by union's blessing, Were stablished firm of feet.

2. Repose from me hath ravished That hyacinthine tress;
Sleep from mine eyes have stolen Those two narcissi [1229] sweet.

3. The jewel of thy loving Hath polished clean away
The rust of worldly trouble, That erst my heart did eat. [1230]

4. Whenas the sword of sorrow For thee had struck me dead,
Then first, ill fortune shattered, I won to life complete.

5. How have I sinned against thee, O heart and soul, from thee
That my sincere devotion Acceptance doth not meet?

6. Since at thy door, I, helpless, Without or means or might,
Have neither road of ingress Nor pathway of retreat,

7. How shall I do? Go whither? How live? What shift devise?
I, that am sick of Fortune's Oppression and deceit.

8. A place than my heart waster Found not the grief of thee,
When in my straitened bosom It first took up its seat. [1231]

9. Hafiz, love's pain with patience Suffer and silent be;
Nor blazon forth its secrets Unto the indiscreet.

[1229] "Narcissi", i. e. eyes.
[1230] Heart likened as usual to a (metal) mirror.
[1231] The grief of love likened to a treasure deposited in a ruined place.

CCCLVII

1. Of repentance from wine in the rosetide, I'faith, I grow ashamed.
Because of unrighteous dealing May none be so ashamed!

2. My righteousness nought but a snare is In Love's highway; and thus
Of loveling and wine and skinker I'm not, I trow, ashamed.

3. We were, of the blood that trickled But yesternight from our eyes,
In sight of the shapes, in slumber That come and go, ashamed.

Thou'rt fairer of face than the sun is; And God be thanked that I
Am not of thy cheek, in presence Of his full glow, ashamed!

5. God send, of her generous nature, She question not of sin!
For of question I'm tired and of answer I'm long ago ashamed.

6. My cheek since I turned from thy threshold, A lifetime it is; and cause,
Before it, by Allah's favour, I have not to show ashamed.

7. Why laugheth the wine, in the winecup, The laugh of despite, except
It be at thy lip of ruby, Or will it or no, ashamed?

8. Well, well may the tipsy narcissus Hang downward its head; for needs,
At the glance of thine eye reproachful, Behoveth it grow ashamed.

9. The pearls of great price for this reason Their heads in the mussel hide
That they're at the pearls, in my verses That glitter arow, ashamed.

10. Its face with the veil of the darkness The water of Khizr bound,
Because 'twas at Hafiz's ditties, Like water a-flow, ashamed.

CCCLVIII

1. Thou, whose cheek is like the gardens of the skies,
Thou, whose lip is as the springs of Paradise,

2. Round thy mouth the tender younglings of the down,
Like to ants that swarm round Sélsebil, [1232] arise.

3. Do with *me*, Lord, as with Abraham Thou didst;
Quench the fire, that in my soul is, on like guise. [1233]

4. Lo, no strength I have remaining in me, friend;
For that fair she is and lovesome past apprize.

5. Short our hand is and the date is on the palm;
Lame our foot and far as heaven the emprise.

6. Hundreds, such as I, of slain ones, in each nook
Fall'n and perished, hath the arrow of thine eyes.

7. To the World-King fall endurance, might and ease
And whatever else he willeth on this wise!

8. In the grip of love and longing for the fair,
Hafiz, ant-like at the elephant's foot, lies.

[1232] "Selsebil", a stream of Paradise.
[1233] Alluding to the legend of Abraham, who was cast into rescued by God, who
changed the fire into a rose-garden.

CCCLIX

1. Love is guide enough to farers in Love's road;
Tears the means I made of finding her abode.

2. How shall *she* regard the billows of our tears,
She, whose bark o'er bloody oceans ever rode?

3. This my ill-repute free-willing is not: He [1234]
Caused me stray in Love, the pathway me who showed.

4. Or the fire of fair ones' faces shun or pass
Uncomplaining o'er the flames, on Abram's mode. [1235]

5. Either look to miss thy purpose, or thy foot,
Save with one to guide thee, set not in this road.

6. Long I've pondered o'er this couplet, that whilere
Sang a máhout, by the Nile-bank as he strode;

7. "Have in mind the máhout's fashions or the way
"After elephants to India leave untrode."

8. On thy face draw not the lover's line of blue
Or upon the wede of virtue cast the woad. [1236]

9. Unto heav'n, sans wine and minstrel, bid me not;
Wine, not nectar, my delight is; *paid*, not *owed*.

10. Hast thou aught of meaning, Hafiz? Bring it forth:
Else no more than idle prate is this thine ode. [1237]

[1234] i. e. God.
[1235] See note to last Ode.
[1236] i. e. Be one thing or the other, lover or pietist; but not both at once.
[1237] This Ode appears to be a variant of the last.

CCCLX

1. Good-news-bringer be, O breeze of the Northland air!
Come, say that the time Of union draweth near!

2. God safeguard thee! Come; For welcome thou art to me,
O courier that com'st From the camping-place of the fair!

3. With Selma how is't And the dwellers in Dhou Selém? [1238]
How fareth the Friend And where are the Loved Ones, where?

4. The banqueting place Abideth uncheered and void
Of pottles brimful And winebibbers debonair.

5. Lo, ruined and razed The house is that flourished erst!
Its case wilt thou know? Go ask of the ruins bare.

6. Now fall'n is the night Of estrangement, how wild and high
The prowlers-by-night Of fancy will revel there!

7. Unending the tale Of love is; the tongue of speech
Is lamed, if it seek To meddle with this affair.

8. Our wanton-eyed Turk [1239] Bestoweth on none a look:
Out, out on this pride And harshness and haughty air!

9. In beauty complete Thy wishes thou hast outpassed:
May God from the eye Of jealousy guard thee e'er!

10. Nay, patience and love, Hafiz, how long wilt thou use?
Bemoan thee; for sweet Is the sound of the lover's prayer.

[1238] "Dhou Selem", a name for the Beloved's abiding-place, taken from the opening
lines of the Arabic poem *El Burdeh*, written by Sherefeddin el Busiri, an Egyptian
poet of the 13th century, in honour of Mohammed and in imitation of the ancient Pre-
Islamitic poems, such as the Muallecat etc.
[1239] i. e. his mistress.

CCCLXI

1. Thou, that hast ta'en my heart with those Thy lovesome parts and graces,
Of none thou reck'st and all the world Enamoured of thy face is.

2. Whiles from my heart the sigh and whiles, O soul, I draw thine arrow:
How shall I tell thee what I draw From out my heart's dark places?

3. The praises of thy ruby lip How utter to the watchers?
The coloured meaning [1240] wasted on The ignorant and base is.

4. Since greater than the day before Thy beauty daily groweth,
Thy cheek to even with the moon Inapt unto the case is.

5. My heart thou stolest and my soul I gave thee: since sore woeful
We are, what need of dun? More grief Why launch upon our traces?

6. When in Love's sanctuary the foot, O Hafiz, once thou settest,
Seize on her skirt and wash thy hands Of all but her embraces.

[1240] i. e. "figurative expression"; note paronomasia with "ruby lip".

CCCLXII

1. Lo, by thy bright eye's magic, O happy-favoured fair,
And by thy down, that auspice Of fortune writ in hair;

2. By thy red ruby's honey, For me the Fount of Life;
By thy sweet scent and colour, O Spring of beauty rare;

3. By thy path's dust, that formeth The canopy of hope;
By thy foot's earth, that driveth Fresh water to despair;

4. By thy distracting graces, Thy dainty partridge-gait;
By thy gazelle-like glances And thy coquettish air;

5. Yea, by thy goodly fashions And by the morning breeze,
Thy tress-scent and the odours The Northland zephyrs bear;

6. By those cornelian tear-drops, That are our eye-ring's seal,
And by thy speech's portal Of pearls beyond compare;

7. By thy cheek-page, that's waxen The rose-mead of the wit,
And by that garth of vision, [1241] Where fancy hath its lair;

8. So thou but look on Hafiz With favour, he'll not grudge
His life. To speak of substance And good what need is there? [1242]

[1241] i. e. the eye.

[1242] i. e. it goes without saying that still less will he grudge his substance, in such a case.

CCCLXIII

1. Lord of the world-all, Help of Religion, accomplished King,
Yéhya Muzéfferi, [1243] sovereign justice-administ'ring!

2. On the world's face the soul's window thou op'st and the door of the heart,
Thou whose protection sheltereth Islam under its wing.

3. Reason and judgment still it behoveth magnify thee;
For that thy bounty embraceth every created thing.

4. On the moon's face, [1244] on the Day of Creation, out of Thy [1245] pen
Fell a black drop, to all questions solution destined to bring. [1246]

5. When the sun saw that black mole, he complaining made in his heart,
"Would that I were but yon fortunate blackmoor!" still murmuring.

6. King, for the noise of thy banquets, the heavens carol and dance;
Still may thy halls with the burden of joyance echo and ring!

7. Drink and carouse and th' universe lavish at will; for thy foes
All are grown ta'en by the neck with thy lasso, slain of thy sling.

8. Heav'n's revolution converted to justice through thee's become;
Live blithe, for the wicked ones miss of their purpose, whilst thou art king.

9. Since the provision-allotter's the door of the king of the world,
Idle concern for thy life to the breezes, Hafiz, come fling!

[1243] "Yehya Muzefferi", Nusret-ed-din Yehya, the last but one of the Muzefferi Sultans of Fars.
[1244] i. e the moon-face of the king.
[1245] "Thy" app. = God's.
[1246] Soudi gives a very far-fetched explanation of this couplet; but his reading is inconsistent with the following couplet, which suggests the necessary explanation. "The black drop" is of course the mole on the king's face, which is so charming that it solves all questions for (i. e. does away all chagrin from) those who view it.

CCCLXIV

1. The fragrance of love I've scented, The lightning of union [1247] see;
Come, breath of the Northland zephyr; I die for the scent of thee.

2. Guide of the Loved One's camels, Stand and unload; for lo!
Patience, for love and longing, Hath all forsaken me.

3. Forbear, o my heart, complaining Of separation's night,
In thanks that the day of union Hath from the screen won free.

4. Since that the Friend excusement Desireth and accord,
One of the watcher's noyance Can unregardful be.

5. Come, for with sevenfold tissues, The eye's rose-coloured wede,
The workshop and place of thine image Hung and adorned have we. [1248]

6. My grief-straitened heart holds nothing, Excepting the thought of thy mouth;
May never one follow after A vain conceit, [1249] like me!

7. Shall I with the true beloved For aught be vexed? Nay, none
Can with his own 'soul angered Be; and my soul is she.

8. Slain of thy love is Hafiz The exile; yet do thou
Visit our dust, [1250] and lawful Our blood shall be to thee. [1251]

[1247] The lightning of union is a figure borrowed from the old Arabic poems, in which
the severed lover often represents himself as catching, in the darkness of the night, a
glimpse of the hills of Nejd or some other upland abode of the Beloved, by the aid of
the flashes of the lightning; hence an omen of union.
[1248] i. e. I have adorned mine eye with the seven membranes thereof, rose-hued with
bloody tears, in honour of thy coming.
[1249] The pursuit of her mouth is a vain conceit, because of its minuteness.
[1250] i. e. in the grave.
[1251] i. e. our death shall be forgiven thee.

CCCLXV

1. At every word I utter In praise of those her graces,
Quoth all who hear, "His milk-flow From God most High to trace is." [1252]

2. "When wilt thou have compassion On my sad soul?" "I asked her.
Quoth she, "What time our union Unbarred by time and space is." [1253]

3. Erst loveliking and toping Seemed easy of achievement;
But now my soul outwearied And wasted in the chase is.

4. On what a goodly fashion [1254] Helláj upon the gibbet
Said, "Question not the Mufti Anent this manner cases!" [1255]

5. My heart a friend I've given, A dainty saucy fair one,
A loveling full of favour, In whom no whit of base is.

6. Erst, like thine eye, the straitest Was I of corner-sitters;
But, like thy brows, to topers [1256] Inclining now my face is.

7. Floods by the hundred thousand, For tears, I've borne like Noah's;
Yet from my bosom's tablet thine image nought effaces.

8. Woe's me, the charmer gives me No áccess to her presence,
Though go-betweens I summon Of many kinds and races!

9. O Friend, the hand of Hafiz A charm against the Eye is
Would at thy neck [1257] I saw it, Whereas its proper place is!

[1252] An odd Arabic phrase, signifying "Divinely is he gifted!" The "milk-flow" figure
indicates the great antiquity of the phrase, as originating with the herd-keeping Arabs
of the desert, who would, in the first place, have spoken thus of some she-camel with
an exceptional yield of milk.
[1253] i. e. in the next world.
[1254] i. e. Mensour Hellaj; see note to Ode 123.
[1255] i. e., "Ask not the theologian about Love"
[1256] The "topers" here are the Beloved's "tipsy" eyes, over which her brows bend or
incline.
[1257] i. e. hung there as an amulet against the Evil Eye. Our word "amulet" is derived
from the Arabic *himalet*, something suspended.

CCCLXVI

1. If it be granted me of Fate With yonder charmer to foregather,
Wine from joy's cup I'll drink, the rose From union's garden will I gather.

2. The bitter, Soufi-madd'ning wine Will undermine my life's foundation;
Thy lip to mine, cupbearer, set And take my life with kisses rather.

3. Methinks, I shall go mad for love Of thee; for all night long, till morning,
I commerce with the moon and see Peris on sleep in heaven's weather.

4. Thy lip to drunkards sugar gives, And thine eye wine unto the drinkers;
But I, divorced from all delight, Forbidden am to share with either.

5. Straight, on the night of death, from couch To Houris' palace shall I wing it,
So by my pillow then thou be A lamp to light my spirit thither.

6. Bethink thee of thy servant old And of his case have recollection;
Since of thy bounty's overflow's Each grain of dust the wind brings hither.

7. Not every one acceptance finds, Of all who ply the craft of versing;
The pheasant rare 'tis I that take; For swift my falcon is of feather.

8. An thou believe it not, go ask The painter of Cathay; for Máni [1258]
Himself the pictures envieth That of my pen are put together.

9. "Good morrow!" Hark, the bulbul cries. "Where art thou, skinker? Up! Be stirring!
"For still there clamoureth in my head The ghittern's yestereven blether.

10. "From me (not Hafiz) hearken ye The mysteries of Love and toping;
"For every night with stars and moon, O'er cup and goblet, I foregather."

11. Truth and good faith are not the wont Of all: the servant of the Vizier
Jelál-ed-dín am I, the time's Aséf and eke the people's father.

[1258] *Mani*; see previous note.

CCCLXVII

1. Let us fare the highway of the winehouse To and fro;
All men for a draught's sake need this doorway Less or mo'!

2. When the First Day's breath in Love and toping First we drew,
In no other path, was it conditioned, Should we go.

3. In a world where Jem's throne-royal goeth To the wind,
Never quaff the cup of sorrow; better Wine than woe.

4. So belike we may upon her girdle Clap the hand,
In heart's blood are we, like ripening rubies, Seated low.

5. On us madmen waste not counsel, preacher! Where the dust
Of the Friend's street is, no glance on Heaven We bestow.

6. Whilst the Soufis in the dance's rapture Feign themselves,
We, with sleight of hand no less, the tankard Set aflow.

7. By thy dregs the dust the ruby's value Doth acquire;
Less than dust before thy sight, poor wretches, Do *we* show. [1259]

8. Since the precious life will soon forsake us, This at least
Grant us, but to look upon thy visage, Ere we go.

9. Since to union's pinnacle, o Hafiz, Is no way,
In this threshold's dust let's end life's weary Tale of woe.

[1259] Thou dost not even vouchsafe us wretched lovers what thou givest the dust, i. e. the dregs of thy cup.

CCCLXVIII

1. Oh, is it not time that the Loved Ones, indeed, should relent,
That the covenant-breakers should turn them to faith and repent?

2. Do they never hear tidings of him who abideth forlorn,
The fire of chagrin in his breast, since they left him and went?

3. O would that my people but knew what hath happened to him,
The distraught for their love! They would pity his case and consent.

4. The Spring-season come is and green once again are the hills:
Yet hear I no warbling: what aileth the songstresses gent?

5. My tears what the bosom concealeth relate and expound:
Nay, hark to the dumb how it speaketh! Oh wonderment!

6. 'Tis the time when the East wind fulfilleth the lover's desire;
But sev'rance our case from the pleasance of Spring doth prevent.

7. A draught of your favour, o sons of our uncle, vouchsafe!
For still by their dealings we measure the excellent.

8. O thou that o'erpassest all Sultans in puissance, have ruth
And God shall requite thee; for goodness is increment. [1260]

9. Each one of my comrades hath substance and wishes fulfilled:
But nought hath poor Hafiz save poortith and debt and lament.

[1260] Sic; i.e. the practice of goodness bringeth increase to the doer; virtue is its own reward.

CCCLXIX

1. At dawntide, intent on repentance, "For guidance," quoth I, "I'll sue:"
But Spring, the repentance-breaker, There cometh, and what shall I do?

2. The truth if I needs must utter, I cannot endure that friends
And comrades should quaff the vinejuice And I from afar should view.

3. Nay, look ye on me as a madman And medicine ye my brain
If I, in the time of the tulip, The banquet of mirth eschew.

4. A loveling in Sultan-fashion I seat on the throne of the rose, [1261]
With bracelets of jacinth and jasmine Her neck and her wrists endue.

5. What time from the Friend's face bloometh The rose of desire for me,
With "Give to the stones their noddles!" My enemies I beshrew.

6. In sooth, I'm the tavern-beggar; But, when I am drunk, behold,
How over the stars I lord it And scoff at the heavens blue!

7. Nay, I, who am no abstainer From that which the Law forbids,
Why, why should I blame the toper And rail at the jovial crew?

8. Yea, laughing-lipped still, like the rosebud, To drink to the king's array
The winecup I take and for longing My raiment I rend in two.

9. An if but a kiss vouchsafe me The ruby lip of the Friend,
I wax young again for joyance And live me my life anew.

10 Aweary of wine that's drunken In private is Hafiz grown;
With ghittern and pipe his secret I'll publish the world unto.

[1261] i. e. the sward.

CCCLXX

1. Come, comrade, come, that roses strew And wine in bowl that cast we may;
Heav'n's roof that rend and up anew At will the whole that cast we may!

2. If sorrow raise a host to shed The blood of lovers, then and there
I and the skinker hasten, down The base of dole that cast we may;

3. That we rose-water in the cup Of Redbud-coloured wine may pour
And in the censer of the breeze, Sugar for toll that cast we may.

4. Since, minstrel, here's a goodly lute, A sweet song sing, that we our hands
May clap and dancing, so from side To side the poll that cast we may.

5. Unto that sovran of the fair The dust of our existence waft,
East wind, a glance upon her face, Our vision's goal, that cast we may.

6. One man of reason boasteth him; Another weaveth whirling words; [1262]
Come, these disputes before the Judge Of form and soul that cast we may.

7. If heav'n on earth thou'dst have, with us Unto the tavern come to day,
Thee into Kauther-pool, [1263] by means Of jar and bowl, that cast we may.

8. Sweet speech nor eloquence they prize In Shiraz town: come Hafiz, come,
Ourselves upon some other land, 'Twixt pole and pole, that cast we may.

[1262] Allusion to the sham ecstatic ravings of the Soufis.
[1263] The heavenly pool of that name, filled with nectar.

CCCLXXI

1. Many a time and oft I've said it And once more I say,
That, of mine own self, I, heart-lorn, Travel not this way. [1264]

2. Parrot-wise, before the mirror [1265] Do the Fates me hold;
What the master of Creation Bade me say, I say.

3. Whether thorn I be or rosebud, There a Gardener is
Up aloft: as me He reareth, So I grow alway.

4. Me, heart-lorn, astonied, blame not, Friends': a gem [1266] I have
And seek one, into whose keeping I commit it may.

5. On the particoloured patchcoat Though a slur be wine,
Chide not, for withal dissembling's Hue I wash away.

6. Lovers' tears and lovers' laughter Other cause than thine
Have: I sing at night [1267] and mourning Make at break of day. [1268]

7. "Smell not thou the dust" quoth Hafiz "Of the winehouse door."
Chide not; for therein the musk-pods Scent I of Cathay. [1269]

[1264] i. e. that of love and toping.
[1265]The Persians teach parrots to talk by placing their cages before a mirror, behind
    which the teacher, being hidden, says what he wishes the birds to repeat. They,
    hearing a voice and seeing their reflection in the mirror, think to hear other parrots
    speak and imitating them, soon learn to talk.—*Soudi.*
[1266] i. e. my heart.
[1267] i. e. When I foregather with the Beloved.
[1268] i. e. When I am parted from her.
[1269] i. e. To the toper the dust of the tavern-door is sweeter of scent than musk.

CCCLXXII

1. Thy lashes black a thousand rents, Sweet, in this faith have frayed of mine;
Come, let me cull a thousand pains From thy sick eye, fair maid of mine.

2. Thou, my heart's fellow, from whose thought Thy friends have faded, may there ne'er
That moment be for me, when thou Shalt from this memory fade of mine!

3. Old and unstable is the world: Out on this lover-murderer!
For weary me its fraud and guile Of this sweet life have made of mine.

4. *This* world and *that* the sacrifice Of cupbearer and loveling be!
For, that the world's Love's parasite, Is to these eyes displayed of mine. [1270]

5. If in my place the Loved One choose Another, she the mistress is;
But deadly sin it were if life For me that Friend outweighed of mine.

6. Rose-like, for absence, drowned in sweat [1271] Am I become: O wind of night,
Bring me a heat-allaying waft From yonder fair's tress-braid of mine!

7. The tale of passion, in this book That is set down, is Hafiz' all:
Certes, I had it from himself; For versing is no trade of mine.

[1270] i. e. all Creation is dependent and consequent upon Love, the Will-to-Be.
[1271] The sweat of the rose is dew or rosewater.

CCCLXXIII

1. Save only that faith and reason I've lost, belovéd one,
I prithee, come say, what profit From love of thee I've won.

2. Though grief to the wind hath given The harvest of my life,
By the dust of thy foot, I've never The pact of love fordone!

3. Though abject I was as the sun-mote, By Love's fair auspice, see,
For wish of thy cheek I've raised me Up even to the sun.

4. Bring wine, for 'tis now a lifetime That, for salvation's sake,
I sit in the nook of safety [1272] And ease and pleasance shun.

5. If thou be sober, preacher, Cast not thy speech in the dust;
For drunken I am and hearken Admonishment from none.

6. How shall I, for shame, my forehead Uplift before the Friend,
Since service I cannot proffer That's worthy such an one? [1273]

7. Though Hafiz consume, that soother Of hearts saith ne'er, "A salve
"I'll send him, since I his bosom Have wounded and undone."

[1272] "The nook of safety" is a pietistic phrase for ascetic reclusion. word of first line
repeated.
[1273] Rhyme-word of first line repeated.

CCCLXXIV

1. Cupbearer, come! Lo, of desire for thy service I die,
Prayer for thy weal Making and yearning thy bonds to aby.

2. Prithee, in thanks That upon thee Fortune's cup is outpoured,
Show me the way, Darkness of doubt and amazement to fly.

3. Though, on all sides, I in sin's ocean am plunged, since acquaint
Grown I with Love Am, of the people of mercy am I.

4. Me for ill-fame, Scribe, and for toping blame not! On my head
This the Diván Wrote of Foreordinance fated on high. [1274]

5. Wine! For to me Lover and toper by birth-right to be
Heritage-wise Came: it was neither to will nor to buy.

6. I, who in life Willed not to stir from the land of my birth,
Now, for thy sight's Sake, after travel and strangerhood sigh.

7. Far in the flesh I'm from that hold of fair fortune, thy door;
Heart but and soul, Still of the dwellers thy presence anigh.

8. Mountain and sea Are in the way of me wounded and weak:
Khizr august, Strength to my feet, of thy favour, supply. [1275]

9. Wind of the East, If thou a breath of her musk-scented locks
Utter, the wrath 'Ware of my jealousy wreaked on the spy!

10. Th'arrow of gaze, Aimed at thine eyebrow, have I to wit's ear
Drawn and await Stand on occasion at thee to let fly.

11. Hafiz intent (So but a respite to him Time vouchsafe)
In this conceit Is to surrender his soul in thine eye.

[1274] "The Divan of Foreordinance", i. e. the Chancery of Foreordained Fate.
[1275] As has before been noted, Khizr is believed by the Muslims to render aid to
strayed way-farers.

CCCLXXV

1. Glad tidings! Behold, salvation On Dhou Selém [1276] hath lit.
To God, the Bestower of blessings, Be praises infinite!

2. Where is the bringer of tidings Of victory, that I
My soul, like gold and silver, May scatter at his feet?

3. The covenant-breaker ever Becometh in evil case:
Yea, sacred are trothplights holden Of men of sense and wit.

4. How wonder-goodly a picture, The flight of his foe to th' House
Of Nought, at the King's back-coming, The pen of Fate hath writ!

5. The foe from Hope's cloud sought somewhat Of mercy; but no; except
The tears of his eye, no moisture It yielded anywhit.

6. He fell in the Nile of sorrow And scoffingly quoth the Sphere
To him, "Marry, now thou repentest, When profitless is it." [1276]

7. Skinker, the rose's season It is and the time of mirth;
Come, troll thou the cup and of sorrow For less or more go quit.

8. Hark from the cup how many A groom yon old, aye new
Wed bride, [1277] like Jem, hath slaughtered, And Keikobád, to wit.

9. "Seek not, o heart, Jem's empire: Call for the cup of wine!"
This was the song of the bulbul That in Jem's gardens lit.

10. Hafiz his place of biding Hath in the tavern-nook,
As lions couch in the thicket And birds in the orchard sit.

[1276] Couplets 1—6 (says Soudi) allude to the reconquest by Shah Shejaa of Shiraz
from the Turcomans, who had expelled him thence.
[1277] i. e. Fortune, the world.

CCCLXXVI

1. Lacking thee, o swaying cypress, Lo! with rose and mead what do I?
Lily cheeks and spikenard tresses, What with these, indeed, what do I?

2. Pity 'tis that for the railing Of the foes, thy face I saw not!
Brass is not my face, like mirrors, [1278] That I should not heed. What do I?

3. Go, admonisher, and cavil Not at those who drain the winecup;
For to them of Fate Foreordered Was this wont decreed. What do I?

4. When the jealous levin leapeth From the ambush of the Viewless,
Lest my harvest burn, some succour Unto me concede. What do I?

5. Since the Turkman king it pleaseth In the pit of woes to cast me,
But an if Tehémten's favour Help me in my need, what do I? [1279]

6. How make head against the darkness Of the night of Wadi Eimen? [1280]
Nay, if Sina's fire afford not Light, my steps to lead, what do I?

7. Topmost Paradise, o Hafiz, Is my patrimonial dwelling:
In this ruined world's encampment, Full of waste and weed, what do I?

[1278] The mirrors referred to in Persian poetry are of course those of polished metal, used before the invention of looking-glass.
[1279] Allusion to the story told in the Shahnameh of how Rustem's sister's son Bizhen loved the daughter of Efrasiyab, King of Touran, who, discovering their amours, took Bizhen and hung him in chains, head downward, in a pit, with a great rock over the mouth; but a waymate of the captive bore news of his case to his uncle Rustem, who went and delivered him. *Tehemten*, a sobriquet of Rustem, here = "Beloved" and *Efrasiyab* = "spy, rival, watcher".
[1280] The valley whence Moses, being benighted, saw the fire of Sinai. See note to Ode LXII, 2.

CCCLXXVII

1. Though her sword slay me, ne'er my hand shall break it;
Yea, if she shoot me, as a boon I take it.

2. Bid our bow-browed one launch at us the arrow,
So we may die her victims: say, I spake it.

3. If the world's noyance bear me from my basis,
If the cup take my hand [1281] not, who shall take it? [1282]

4. Shine forth, Hope's morning sun; for lo! a captive
Still in the night of severance I wake it.

5. Help thou mine eld, o Elder of the tavern!
Come thou and young again with one draught make it.

6. Head at thy foot I've laid and by thy ringlets
Swore I last night that thence I ne'er would take it. [1283]

7. Burn this thy patchcoat of devotion, Hafiz,
Lest my fire catch thereon and none should slake [1284] it.

[1281] i. e. succour me.
[1282] Rhyme-word of Couplet 1, 2, repeated.

[1283] Rhyme-word of 1 and 3 repeated.
[1284] Rhyme-word of 1, 3 and 5 repeated in original.

CCCLXXVIII

1. The moon thou, and I am the candle That fades when the dawn grows red:
But smile thou and see me surrender My soul, like the taper dead.

2. The brand of desire for thy tresses So deep in my heart is impressed,
My grave that, when life I've departed, 'Twill turn to a violet-bed.

3. The door of mine eye on thy threshold I opened, in hope that a glance
On me thou wouldst cast; but thou castest Me out from thy sight instead.

4. Lo, how shall I thank you, o armies Of sorrow (whom God requite!)
That ye, when all else forsook me, Yet ne'er from my bosom fled?

5. The slave of the man [1285] of my eyeball I am; for, black-heart [1286] though he be,
He tear-drops by thousands, whenever I count my heart's pains, doth shed.

6. Our idol to every vision Displayeth herself; but none
Those amorous graces espieth, Whereon but mine eyes are fed.

7. If over the dust of Hafiz The Friend like the wind should pass,
My shroud I shall rend for longing, At heart of that narrow stead.

[1285] i. e. the iris.
[1286] Alluding, of course, to the black pupil. The Persians, as before mentioned, call the
pupil (and sometimes, as here, the iris) of the eye "the man of the eye". The Romans
had a like fancy, as appears from the word *pupilla*, which means a little girl, doll or
puppet; and the student of Elizabethan literature will at once call to mind the phrase,
"Look babies in her eyes", which is of such frequent occurrence in Beaumont and
Fletcher, Massinger etc.; whence it is evident that, strained as the conceit may
appear, it is common to many races.

CCCLXXIX

1. Since that thy blessed shadow On my existence fell,
Prosperity's my servant And grace my manciple.

2. Long years it is since fortune Departed from my side;
But, with thine union's blessing, Back came it to my cell.

3. No man should ever see me Awake in this thy time,
Did in my dreams thine image Fore'er depictured dwell.

4. My life I pass in grieving For thee; but never deem
That without thee a moment I live, the truth to tell.

5. No leach the med'cine knoweth For my disease; for I'm,
Without the Friend, heart-broken And *with* her, passing well.

6. Although thou say, "Thy chattels Bring not to this my street,"
Nought, by thy soul, I swear it, Therefrom shall me expel!

7. I'm the least servant, Hafiz, Of him who rules the land;
For such a King and Vizier All fealties compel.

CCCLXXX

1. Orion, in the dawning, His baldric down doth lay,
As who, "The King's liege-servant I swear to be!" should say.

2. Come, skinker, for by Fortune's Consenting aid, a boon,
Which I of God entreated, Is granted me to-day.

3. Give wine, for, of my joyance In the King's sight, the lusts
Of youth once more revisit My head, for all 'tis gray.

4. Waylay me not with praises Of Khizr's fount; for I
A quaffer am of nectar From the King's cup of sway.

5. Though, Sire, the throne of learning To the ninth heav'n I rear,
I'm still thy portal's bondman, The beggar of thy way.

6. Dreg-drainer of thy banquet This many a year I've been:
How shall my wonted nature From this its well-head stray?

7. Nay, if thou lend not credit Unto thy slave, I'll cite
Kemál the Isfeháni, [1287] In proof of what I say:

8. "If I, my heart up-tearing, My love from thee withdraw,
"Whom shall I cast this love on, Whither this heart convey?"

9. Love of the king conditioned To me was in the Prime
And I in this condition Shall travel life's highway.

10. The name "Mensóur Muzéffer" 's My amulet and I,
By this name's blessing, conquer My foemen in the fray.

11. Since Heav'n itself the Pleïads In the King's name hath strung,
Shall I not in his praises The pearls of verse array?

12. Since I, on falcon fashion, Have fed from the King's hand,
How shall I now address me To pigeons for a prey?

13. How were thy shadow lessened, O lion-conquering king,
If I therein might rest me, In freedom from affray?

14. I've neither wing nor feather: And yet 'tis strange that, save
To reach the Simurgh's [1288] dwelling, In head I've nothing aye.

15. My verse heart-realms an hundred, Thanks to thy praise, hath won;
My tongue thy sword resembleth, Which nothing can gainsay.

16. If, like the wind of morning, I by a rose-bed passed,
'Twas not for love of cypress Or wish of pinetree; nay,

17. 'Twas that thy scent I traced there And to thy face's thought, [1289]
The cupbearer of joyance Gave me a cup or tway.

18. With one or two grapes drunken 'Tis not thy servant's wont
To be: I'm one year-stricken, In winehouses grown gray.

19. With heaven many a quarrel I have and with the stars;
Be the King's justice ever My helper and my stay!

20. Thank God that, from this doorhead, The Peacock of the Throne [1290]
My pinions' rustle heareth And my resounding lay! [1291]

21. The lion's whelp [1292] attempted The capture of my heart;
But, be I fat or meagre, I am the lion's [1293] prey.

22. If my employ be ever Other than praise of thee,
My name be from the bede-roll Of lovers done away!

23. O thou, whose face's lovers More than the sun-motes are,
How shall I reach thine union, I that am less than they?

24. Show me who 'tis denieth The beauty of thy cheek,
His eye with jealous lancet That extirpate I may.

25. Since upon me the shadow Fell of the kingship's sun,
I'm quit of care, henceforward, Anent the sun of day.

26. My aim in this is nowise To make the market brisk;
I never purchased favours Nor praises sold for pay.

27. Hafiz a hearty lover Is of the Prophet's house:
My lord the King is witness, Forsooth, to this I say. [1294]

[1287] i. e. Kemaleddin Ismaïl, a renowned poet of Ispahan, who was murdered by the
Mogul Tartars on the occasion of their invasion of Ispahan in the year 1237 of our
era.

[1288] "The Simurgh", (i. e. "thirty birds", so called from its combining the characteristics of many birds,) a fabulous bird of supernatural attributes and wisdom, which is fabled to inhabit the inaccessible summits of the Caucasus. The word is here used as a simile for "King".

[1289] The Persians say "to drink to any one's thought or memory", where we say "to his health".

[1290] The Angel Gabriel is "the Peacock of the Throne".

[1291] i. e. the fame of my songs attains the ninth heaven.

[1292] i. e. King Mensour's son, who sought to win Hafiz to his own party.

[1293] "Lion", i. e. the King himself.

[1294] Mensour apparently claimed to be descended from Mohammed; a claim, by the by, well next as common in the East as that of all Irishmen to descent from Brian Boroihme or some other of the innumerable petty *Righthean* who elbowed each other out of the sunshine in every alley in the heroic days.

CCCLXXXI

1. Intent upon turning homeward, Why not on the fare shall I be?
Why not, in the Loved One's quarter, The dust of her stair shall I be?

2. Since strangerhood's grief and suff'rance No longer can I endure,
I'll get me to mine own city, Mine own king where shall I be.

3. Once more of the fane of union Shall I of the adepts be;
The servant of mine own master, Once more, again there shall I be.

4. Unknown since the issue of life is, 'Tis better that thus, at least,
On the day of the Term, [1295] in the presence Of her, my own fair, shall I be. [1296]

5. My usance was ever toping And loverhood: strive I will
Henceforth so once more concerned with My proper affair shall I be.

6. Whatever from drowsy fortune And stress without end I bear,
The keeper of mine own secrets Henceforward, I swear, shall I be.

7. Excepting God's grace and favour Way-showĕr to me become,
Ashamed of myself and my dealings, O Hafiz, fore'er shall I be.

[1295] i. e. when I come to die.

[1296] One of the ghazels written by Hafiz on the occasion of his profitless journey to Yezd. See previous note.

CCCLXXXII

1. Why seek'st thou righteousness from us? To topers "Hither! Ho!" we say.
What while thy drowsed narcissus is, Unto salvation "Go!" we say.

2. Come, open me the winehouse door; For by the cloister nought I've gained:
Believe or no, the saying's true; And as we've spoken, so we say.

3. By thine eye, cupbearer, dead-drunk And ruined sheer are we become;
Yet, if it come but from the Friend, "A thousand welcomes, woe!" we say.

4. Quoth I, "Thy shape the box-tree is;" And much confusion us this bore.
Why made we this compare and why This falsehood did (heigho!) we say?

5. An thou forgive us not, thou wilt In fine repent: our purpose bear
In mind and how this saying did, Thinking our zeal to show, we say.

6. My liver, musk-pod-like, all blood's Become; nor less did I deserve;
For that in error to her tress "Cathay!" [1297] did, whiles ago, we say.

7. Hafiz, thou'rt fire become: and yet It taketh not upon the Friend;
As well the rose's faithlessness Might to the winds that blow we say!

[1297] As being the home of musk. The Beloved appears to have been very naturally
offended at the perpetual recurrence of the two threadbare similes mentioned in this
and the fourth couplet.

CCCLXXXIII

1. Since that this boast I uttered, 'Tis forty years, in fine;
"I am the least of servers At the old Magian's shrine."

2. Yea, never, thanks be rendered To the old vintner's grace,
My cup hath fallen empty Of clear and shining wine.

3. What time true topers prospered And Love in worship was,
The tavern's place of honour, God wot, was ever mine.

4. Though stained indeed's the patchcoat, Yet pure of skirt am I;
Nor ill, for that a toper I am, of me opine.

5. I am the king's hand-falcon: How did They bear from me
The memory of my nest-place Beyond the heavens nine?

6. 'Tis pity that a bulbul Like me, so sweet of tongue,
In silence, like the lily, In such a mead should pine.

7. A parlous losel-fost'rer Is Shiraz clime. O where's
A mate, with whom, tent-striking, To leave this earth malign?

8. Under the patchcoat, Hafiz, How long wilt hide the cup?
Unto the Vizier's banquet I'll show this use of thine;

9. To Touranshah [1298] the blessed, Who heapeth gifts on me,
Whose boons, as with a collar, The neck of me confine.

[1298] The Grand Vizier of two of the Ilkhani Sultans of Baghdad, Hassan Buzurg and
    his son Uweis; he was himself an Ilkhani (says Soudi) and a member of the reigning
    (Jelayir) house.

CCCLXXXIV

1. God in the rose-time keep me From e'er renouncing wine!
How should I do this folly, Who boast of wit, in fine?

2. Come, minstrel! To the service Of harp and lute and reed
The sum of all devotion And love let us consign!

3. Sick of the mosque-school's clamour My heart is; now, awhile
The service of the Loved One I'll do and eke of wine. [1299]

4. When was good faith in Fortune? The winecup bring, that I
Of Jem and Kei may tell thee And of Kawóus's line.

5. Of the Black Book [1300] I reck not; For, on the Rising Day,
I shall roll up [1301] an hundred Such books by grace Divine.

6. Where is the day's vauntcourier, [1302] To yonder happy fair
That I may make complaining Of parting's night of pine?

7. Since in the Prime They mingled My clay with wine, o foe,
Say, why should I abandon The daughter of the vine?

8. This borrowed life, the Loved One To Hafiz did commit,
When once her face I look on, I will to her resign.

[1299] Rhyme-word of line I repeated.
[1300] "Black Book", i. e. the scroll in which a man's sins are recorded.
[1301] i. e. close, make an end of. The Oriental "book" is, of course, a scroll.
[1302] i. e. the East Wind.

CCCLXXXV

1. The veil of the face of the Soul is The dust of my body base;
O happy, thrice happy the moment The veil when I cast from this face!

2. A cage such as this is unworthy Of such a sweet singer as I;
I'll get me to Rizwan's rose-garths; [1303] For I am a bird of that race.

3. I know not why I came hither Nor where I had been before:
Alack and alas that unknowing I am of my proper case!

4. O how shall my spirit compass The plains of the Spirit-world,
When cabined I am and bounden In bonds of the body base? [1304]

5. I, in the halls of the Houris Whose true habitation is,
Why in the street of the winehouse Is my abiding-place?

6. Nay, marvel not if from my heart's blood There cometh the scent of musk;
For I'm like the Tartary musk-deer, [1305] That men for their muskpods chase.

7. The fringe of my gold-wrought raiment Regard not; for candle-like,
Thereunder are hidden burnings, That fill all my bosom's space.

8. O come; the existence of Hafiz Take up from before his feet,
That none, whilst thou art, of my being May hearken or see a trace. [1306]

[1303] i. e. Paradise, of which Rizwan is the porter.
[1304] Rhyme-word of 1, 1, repeated.
[1305] By whose extravasated blood the Persians believe musk to be formed.
[1306] i. e. that my being may be absorbed in thine. To the Beloved.

CCCLXXXVI

1. If I on the dust of the sole Of the foot of the fair one light,
A line of dust-script withal On the tablet of vision I'll write. [1307]

2. And if unto me there should come Her warrant in quest of my life,
My soul, as the candle doth, Surrender will I forthright.

3. If she the base coin of my heart Stamp not with the standard of proof,
I'll tell down apace, in her way, Current coin [1308] from the mint of the sight.

4. Nay, shake not the skirt thus from me, The dust-like; for when I am dead,
My dust will refuse to be borne From thy door by the wind in its flight.

5. Of wistfulness for thine embrace, In longing I'm drowned; but I hope
In the waves of my tears, that me yet They will bear to the shore of delight.

6. Thy black tresses twain gave a bond For consoling of lovers forlorn;
And natheless from me my repose And endurance they've ravished outright.

7. Thy face from faith-keeping to me Avert not; beware of the hour
When, of grief for thy sake, I uplift The hand for the prayer of the night.

8. A wind-waft of perfume, o breeze, From that wine of delight to me bring,
So its fragrance for me may allay Cropsickness' annoy and despite.

9. For ever engaged with the praise Of the tip of thy tress is my speech;
Hence breathing of Tartary musk Is all that I say and endite.

10. Since, Hafiz, her ruby-red lip The very dear soul is to me,
That moment's a lifetime for me, When I to the lip bring my spright. [1309]

[1307] i. e. I will impress the image of thy down (poetically likened to "dust-script", a
very minute hand) on my eye.
[1308] i. e. running tears.
[1309] i. e. when I kiss her lip; *syn.* when I give up the ghost.

CCCLXXXVII

1. This, for such as these the present Times, I see expedient
That my chattels to the winehouse I should bear and sit content.

2. Mine be neither friend nor comrade Save the gugglet and the book,
So I may not see the knav'ries Of this world maleficent.

3. Cup in hand I take and hold me From the hypocrites aloof;
One pure heart alone I've chosen Of the world-folk to frequent.

4. Of much vaunting me for righteous In the patchcoat stained, before
Skinker's cheek and wine rose-coloured, Now with shame do I repent.

5. Midst the folk, my head in freedom, Like the cypress, I shall rear,
So my skirt I may ingather From the world's bedragglement.

6. On my heart oppression's dust is: Suffer not, o Lord Most High,
That my sun-like mirror troubled Be of noyance and lament.

7. For my straitened breast o'er heavy Is its burden of chagrin;
My sad heart is all unequal To this load of languishment.

8. Whether I the tavern toper Or the city Hafiz [1310] be,
I'm such stuff as this thou seëst, Ay, and worse than my ostent.

9. I'm the servant of the Asef Of the age: [1311] fret not my heart,
For he'd do me, did I ask it, Justice of the firmament.

[1310] *Hafiz* means "guardian", as well as "he who knows the Koran by heart".
[1311] The Grand Vizier.

CCCLXXXVIII

1. Come, the cassock of the Soufi To the winehouse straight bear we;
To the rag-market the patchcoat Of ecstatic prate bear we.

2. Let us stop our ears and rid us Of the preacher's rigmaroles;
Lackwit-like, how long the noyance Of his vain debate bear we?

3. So that all the closet-dwellers May the cup of daybreak take,
Come, the ghittern of the morning To the vintner's gate bear we.

4. To the devotees of toping, Way-gift wise, the gown of wool
And the prayer-carpet of babble In the mystic state [1312] bear we; [1313]

5. And the zealot, in our pathway If he plant the thorn of blame,
From the rosegarth to the prison Of the reprobate bear we.

6. Shame be ours of this our patchcoat Wine-polluted, if in mind,
With this excellence and virtue [1314] Miracles to rate, bear we!

7. But an if the heart Time's value Know and do some work of worth,
From the harvest of the ages Nought but shame full great bear we.

8. From yon terraced roof of heaven Trouble raineth: up! our gear
To the tavern-nook, for shelter From the spite of fate, bear we!

9. How long shall we in Love's desert Go astray? The way let's ask,
So our steps in the direction Of the things of weight bear we. [1315]

10. Lo! that pact we swore in Eimen [1316] With thee, saying, Moses-like,
"Show thyself," unto the tryst-place, All inviolate, bear we. [1317]

11. From the Empyrean's turrets, Lo, thy glory's drum we beat;
Thy love's ensigns to the rooftree Of the heavens eight bear we.

12. Yea, thy quarter's dust to-morrow, In the Resurrection plain,
As a mark of worth and worship, All upon the pate bear we.

13. Hafiz; spill thy face's water [1318] Not at every losel's door;
Needs to Him who needs acquitteth [1319] Better 'tis that straight bear we.

[1312] i. e. the attributes of the Soufi.

[1313] i. e. that they may pledge them for wine.

[1314] i. e. of toperhood and lovership.

[1315] i. e. so we may know and follow after those things which are of real importance, not after the factitious goods of the world and the idle dreams of the pietists.

[1316] i. e. Wadi Eimen.

[1317] Allusion to the first interview (more than once referred to in previous Odes) of Moses with God in Sinai.

[1318] *Syn.* honour, repute,

[1319] i.e. God.

CCCLXXXIX

1. From the doorway of the winehouse Solace for our pain seek we;
In the Friend's path sitting, wishes Somewhat to attain seek we.

2. For the Sanctuary of Union Road-provision have we none:
At the tavern-door, by begging, Próvant to obtain seek we.

3. Though our bloodstained tears be running, For despatch to her we love,
One of unpolluted nature, Pure and free from stain, seek we.

4. Be our hearts debarred the sweetness Of the brand of grief for thee
If in love of thee, for justice Of affliction's bane seek we!

5. On the tablet of the vision We thy mole may not set down,
But if ink, from out the pupil Of the eyeball ta'en, seek we.

6. Soul and life my heart had bidden For a kiss of thy sweet lip;
But it answered, sweetly smiling, "Greater than these twain seek we."

7. As an amulet of pérfume For our passion-stricken heart,
Somewhat of the fragrant blackness Of thy writing fain seek we.

8. Since the grief of thee unfound is Save in joyous hearts, in hope
Thus the grief of thee to compass, Joyous hearts to gain seek we.

9. How long, Hafiz, at the portals Of the mosque-school wilt thou sit?
Up and from the tavern-doorway Solace for our pain seek we! [1320]

[1320] Line 1 repeated.

CCCXC

1. When the thought of thy face overpasseth The rosegarden red of the eye,
My heart, for the purpose of gazing, To the window is led of the eye.

2. O come, for all manner of rubies And pearls of great price, [1321] in thy way
To strew, from the heart's provant-chamber, We've haled to the stead of the eye.

3. No pleasaunce that's meet for thy session, No couching-place worthy of thee,
I see in the world, save this corner, Ordained for thy bed, of the eye.

4. My heart, the First Day that I looked on Thy cheek in Eternity's Prime,
"If harm anywhit," said, "betide me, My blood on the head of the eye!"

5. My tears, overflowing at daybreak, Were purposed to ruin my life,
If the blood of my liver to seize on The skirt had not sped of the eye. [1322]

6. In hope of the news of thy coming, Last night, in the way of the wind,
Till daybreak, the luminous cresset I planted and fed of the eye.

7. On a man's expectation and striving Have pity, the blood of whose heart,
On his cheek flowing down, from the window All nightly is shed of the eye.

8. For charity's sake, I conjure thee, Launch not at poor Hafiz's breast
That heart-thrilling, man-overthrower, That crossbow-bolt dread of the eye!

[1321] i. e. tears.
[1322] Soudi explains this line thus curiously; "If the blood of my liver had not congealed
   in my eye and so stopped the flow of tears."

CCCXCI

1. Glad that day will be when, parting, From this waste abode go I,
Heart's ease seeking, in the pathway That my love hath trode, go I.

2. Though I know the stranger findeth Not, without a guide, the way,
By the scents her tangled tresses On the breeze have sowed go I.

3 Spite sick heart and strengthless body, Like the East wind, swift and straight,
With the longing for that waving Cypress for a goad, go I.

4. Passing weary of the prison Of Sikender [1323] is my heart;
Unto Solomon his kingdom, [1324] Binding on my load, go I.

5. Since the light ones here reck nothing Of the heavy-laden's case,
Help, ye pious! so that thither, Eath and unforslowed, go I.

6. On the head though it behove me In the path to fare, with eye
Tear-o'erfilled and heart sore wounded, On the reed-pen's mode go I.

7. This I've vowed that, from this sorrow If one day I do me free,
To the winehouse door, rejoicing, Chanting song and ode, go I;

8. Yea, for love of her, sun-mote like Dancing, to the fountain-head, [1325]
Whence the river of the radiance Of the sun hath flowed, go I.

9. But if, Hafiz-like, I win not Forth this desert, with the star
Of the Asef of the epoch, Waymate in the road go I. [1326]

[1323] Ispahan (according to Soudi)
[1324] i. e. Shiraz.
[1325] The gist of this curious figure lies in the fact that the pen travels over the paper on
    its head, i. e. what we call its point.
[1326] i. e. I rely upon the Grand Vizier to help me out of my troubles.

CCCXCII

1. In the Magians' stead the very Light of God (o rare!) I see;
Mark this light and note this wonder, What it is and where I see.

2. Who's the dreg-drainer, I wonder, Of this tavern, Lord, whose door
Cynosure of mortal wishes, Niche of all men's prayer, I see?

3. All I vaunt of rank and worship, Lover, toper, amorist,
From the favour of your teaching, Spirits debonair, [1327] I see.

4. O Commander of the Pilgrims, Boast thee not of grace Divine;
An the House [1328] *thou* see, its master, Him that dwelleth there, *I* see.

5. None from China's muskpods ever Nor from Tartar musk hath seen
What, each dawntide, from the waftings That the East winds bear I see.

6. In the circle of existence, Save the point of Unity,
Nought there is: of how and wherefore, Yea, this question bare I see. [1329]

7. Muskpod-opening from the tresses Of the fair [1330] I fain would do.
Far the thought be! Nay, my error [1331] Passing all compare I see.

8. Burning heart and brimming eyelids, Night-lamenting, dawntide-sighs,
These all, from thy sweet sight parted, Fallen to my share I see.

9. Momently my thought waylaid is By the phantom of thy face:
Unto whom the visions utter In this veil fore'er I see?

10. For whoremongering, at Hafiz Carp not, friend; for him, indeed,
Of *your* lovers eke, not only Of the wanton fair, I see. [1332]

[1327] "Spirits debonair", i. e. his correspondents of the Invisible World, from whom, as
Socrates from his Demon, he professed to learn all his art and lore.
[1328] i. e., *thou* seest the Holy House (the Kaabeh) at Mecca; *I* see the Lord thereof, i. e.
God.
[1329] An unmistakable avouchment of the Vedantic doctrine of the Unity of Being, i. e.
the Undifferenced Self. By "bare of how and wherefore" he means "not open to
doubt or debate".
[1330] i. e. unravelling and caressing the locks of the Beloved.
[1331] *Khita, syn.* "Cathay", word used p. g. with musk, which comes from Cathay.
[1332] A naïve attempt to conciliate the caviler.

CCCXCIII

1. "Friends, 'tis best that, in the rosetime, After ease and pleasance strain we."
This, the Magian Elder's saying, In our heart and mind retain we!

2. Bounty faileth and mirth's season Fleeteth by; there's nothing for it
But, for wine the prayer-rug selling, That withal the patchcoat stain we.

3. 'Tis a goodly air, joy-giving: Send us, Lord, a dainty loveling,
So the cup of wine rose-coloured, In her face's honour, drain we.

4. Waylayer of men of merit Is the organist of heaven: [1333]
Ask not, then, of this affliction Wherefore clamour and complain we.

5. All aglow with bloom the rose is, Nor a drop of wine we've cast on't:
Hence afire with disappointment And with longing's heat remain we.

6. Far the evil eye! For drunken Are we without wine and minstrel:
From the tulip's cup of ruby Fancy's wine to tipple feign we! [1334]

7. Strange this case is! Of whom other, Hafiz, can be said that "Bulbuls
"Are we; yet in this the season Of the rose from song abstain we?" [1335]

[1333] i. e. Fortune, which is the avowed enemy of men of merit.
[1334] i. e. let us console ourselves with the *Trunkenheit ohne Wein* of poetry and
imagination.
[1335] This Ode embodies the usual complaint of want of means to buy wine in Spring-
time.

CCCXCIV

1. Last night, with the torrent of tears, The passage of sleep I waylaid;
On water, in mind of thy down, A charactery I pourtrayed. [1336]

2. The patchcoat I cast on the fire And having the prayer-niche in view,
A cup to the mem'ry I quaffed Of the cheek of that loveliest maid.

3. The face of the fair shone out, Methought, in my sight, unveiled,
And I, from afar, a kiss On the cheek of the moonlight laid.

4. Mine eye on the cupbearer's face And ear on the chant of the harp
Intent, this, with eye and with ear, An auspice of good I made.

5. In the workplace, to wit, of mine eye The sleepless, still picturing
The form of that face of thine, The limner, till dawn, I played.

6. The wine-cup, at sound of this song, The cupbearer proffered me;
I chanted this ode and my thirst With wine unmingled I stayed.

7. Each birdlet of fancy, away That flew from the bough of delight,
Still back to the harbour of mirth I beat with thy tresses-strap's aid. [1337]

8. For Hafiz full fair was the time; And thence, for friends' life and estate,
Good omen I augured of wish Accomplished and longing allayed.

[1336] i. e. I limned thine image with the pencil of fancy on my wet eye.
[1337] i. e. "I beat the tabret with the strap of thy tresses and so lured the birds of my
imagination back to melodious plaining". The Arabs and Persians beat drums and
tambourines with a strap, instead of a drumstick. See my "Book of the Thousand
Nights and One Night", "The Story of Hassan of Bassora and the King's Daughter of
the Jinn," VII, 133, for an instance of this.

CCCXCV

1. "From my heart", quoth I, "the passion Of her cheek away I'll do!"
"Where's the chain", quoth she, "this madman To secure, as is his due?"

2. To her shape quoth I, "O cypress!" And in wrath away she turned.
What's to do, o friends? My fair one Taketh umbrage at the true!

3. If an unweighed speech I uttered, Prithee, hold me, sweet, excused;
With some token of thy favour, Set my mind at ease anew.

4. Pale for shame, before that dainty One, without my fault, am I:
Skinker, wine! That I may render To my cheek the rose's hue.

5. Breeze from Leila's stead, 'fore heaven, How long with my tears the camp
Shall I flood, and with my sighing All the house in ruins strew?

6. When I once the boundless treasures Of the Loved One's charms have won,
Beggars like myself, an hundred, I'll with Korah's wealth endue.

7. O thou moon of happy auspice, Hafiz bear in mind, the slave,
So to God for that thy beauty, Waxing daily, I may sue.

CCCXCVI

1. Eyes an ocean making, patience To the wilderness I'll cast
And my heart, for love and longing, In the sea of stress I'll cast.

2. From my sinful, straitened bosom Such a sigh I'll heave, that sheer
Into Adam's sin the firebrand Of forgetfulness I'll cast.

3. Heaven's shafts enough I've suffered: Wine but give me; and a knot
On Orion's quiver-baldrick, In my drunkenness, I'll cast; [1338]

4. Yea, upon this travelling litter [1339] I the goblet's dregs will spill;
Up to yon blue dome the gurgle Of the harp, no less, I'll cast.

5. In the heart-possessor's dwelling Is the source of heart's content:
Thereinto myself, if fortune My endeavour bless, I'll cast.

6. O my moon, sun-crowned, the laces Of thy tunic loose, and then
At thy feet my head love-stricken, Like thy trailing tress, I'll cast.

7. Since, o Hafiz, fault and folly Is reliance on the Days,
Never more upon the morrow This to-day's liesse I'll cast.

[1338] i. e. I will bind up the quiver of Orion, so that Mercury, the archer of heaven,
    whose arrows he keeps, may no longer launch his shafts (which are calamities) at me
    and others.
[1339] i. e. The revolving sphere.

CCCXCVII

1. Yesternight thy languorous glances Of my life and soul beraught me;
But thy ruby lip with kisses, Of its favour, new life brought me.

2. No to-day's growth my love-liking For that musky down of thine is;
Long time with the wine of passion Hath its crescent-cup [1340] distraught me.

3. Well my constancy this showeth That, in spite of thine oppression,
From thy quest I rested never, Albe weariness besought me.

4. Righteousness nor yet amendment Hope from me, the tavern-haunter;
For unto the topers' service, Ere I was, The Fates forethought me.

5. In Love's way an hundred perils, On Death's thither side, are: say not,
"Once Life ended, I'm delivered From the woes which Love hath wrought me."

6. With the arrows of the envious What concern have I henceforward,
Since with yonder bow-browed loveling Union, indeed, I've bought me?

7. Well, forsooth, I've earned thy kisses, Since, for all thy scorn and rigour,
Love and faith I've never broken, Never did but what they taught me.

8. Wellaway! A warrior fair one Stole my heart and then forsook me.
Woe is me, except the Sultan's Favour by the hand had caught me!

9. Hafiz' fame to heav'n uplifted Was for wisdom; but the chewing
Of the bitter cud of sorrow For thy box-tree [1341] low hath brought me.

[1340] Curving down enclosing the cheeks in a double crescent likened to new-moon
    shaped cup, filled with the wine of passion.
[1341] "Box-tree", i. e. shape.

CCCXCVIII

1. From the Friend my dole is, My delight no less;
Be my head her ransom And my spright no less!

2. "Better charm than beauty Is," if any say,
This [1342] the Friend and *that* [1343] hath (Tell the wight), no less.

3. Of her face's splendour Both worlds are one ray:
This by day I tell thee And by night, no less. [1344]

4. Friends, behind the curtain Now this thing we say;
But it shall be blazoned Forth outright, no less.

5. Her intoxicated Eye my blood doth shed,
And her tangled tress-tip Black and bright, no less.

6. For us no reliance Is on this world's course
Nor on yon revolving Sphere of light, no less.

7. Be that fair remembered, Who, to shed our blood
Meaning, broke Love's compact And her plight, no less!

8. As the nights of union's Gladness pass away,
So the days of sev'rance Take to flight, no less.

9. Often her mole's image Doth mine eyeblood shed, [1345]
Privily and also In men's sight, no less.

10. Nothing of the Cadi Lovers reck (Bring wine!);
Nay, they hold the firman Royal light, no less.

11. Hafiz for a lover Knows the Mohtesib
And the Vizier-Royal, Asef hight, no less.

[1342] "*This*", i. e. charm.
[1343] "*That*", i. e. beauty.
[1344] i. e. both by night, when I am drunk, and by day, when I am sober.
[1345] i. e. the thought of it makes me shed tears of blood.

CCCLCIX

1. In my bosom's pleasance-chamber Hid an idol fair I hold,
For whose cheek and tress the horse-shoe On the fire of care I hold. [1346]

2. Lover, winebibber and rakehell; From that Houri, Peri-faced,
All these titles of distinction, Loudly I declare, I hold.

3. What an if this wise thou hold me Helpless, lacking ease and power?
Still thy tresses all dishevelled With the dawn-tide prayer I hold;

4. And if in the toper's dwelling It should please thee set thy foot,
Sugared verse and wine unmingled At thy service there I hold.

5. If the Loved One's down so tender Thus to me display itself,
This my cheek with bloody water [1347] Painted will (I swear) I hold.

6. Bring the arrows of thy glances And the mail-coat of the tress;
For contention with my wounded Stricken heart fore'er I hold.

7. Hafiz, since the grief and gladness Of the world alike depart,
Better 'tis my heart that tranquil, Quit of joy and care, I hold. [1348]

[1346] Alluding to a love-charm, which is worked by writing certain names upon a
horseshoe and secretly casting it into the fire, to the accompaniment of a prescribed
magical formula; whereupon the heart of the Beloved becomes inclined to the lover.
[1347] i. e. tears of blood.
[1348] Rhyme-word of line 1 repeated.

CCCC

1. Vouchsafed is the sight of the fair To me and her kiss and embrace, too;
To Fortune I render my thanks And Time, for the granted grace, too.

2. Peace, pietist, go! For this luck If t truly intended for me is,
My hand shall the goblet uprear And the tress of the loveling enlace, too.

3. Come, no one henceforth let us blame For toping and draining of goblets;
For goodly the wine is and sweet The lovely one's lip and her face, too.

4. I give thee glad tidings, o heart! The Mohtesib ruleth no longer;
Full, full is the world-all of wine And lovelings that quaff it apace, too.

5. Yea, past is the time when await The Evil Eye watched us from ambush;
Gone, gone are the foes from the midst And tears o'er the bosom a-race, too.

6. 'Tis foolishness into the hand Of trouble the mind to surrender;
Nay, call for a booklet of songs And a flagon of wine set in place, too.

7. Come, strew on the dustlings [1349] of love The dregs of her goblet of ruby,
So rubied their dust may become And raining with musk be their trace, too.

8. Since all things create, o my fair, Put live in the hope of thy favour,
O sun, then, withhold not from us Somedele of the shade of thy grace, too!

9. Since born of thy beauty's o'erflow The sheen of the tulip and rose is,
Rain, favouring cloud, upon us, Thy lovers, the abject and base, too.

10. Though captive the wise thou hast ta'en, I rede thee fear God and his justice,
The Vizier august of Jemshíd, The monarch of Khúsrewi race, too;

11. The Asef hight Búrhan el Múlk W'ed Dín, by the hand of whose statecraft
A mine is Time waxen of wealth And an ocean of riches is Space, too;

12. The man, to whose luminous wit The heavens, at dawntide, in homage,
Do render the soul and the stars Themselves in his presence efface, too.

13. The ball of the universe off Is borne by the mall of thy justice,
And so is yon blue-vaulted dome, That ceileth the heavens' high-place too.

14. Thy purpose, so light of rein-hand, It is unto motion that urgeth
Yon high-vaulted, firm-centred sphere, Yon firmament stable of base, too.

15. What while, by the course of the sphere And the Days' revolution, the Autumns
And Springtides alternate and years And months years and months ever chase, too,

16. Unfurnished with chieftains and lords Be never the halls of thy glory,
With cupbearers, cypress of shape, And lovelings rose-coloured of face, too!

17. Poor Hafiz, in spite of the pearls Which he in thy praises hath lavished,
Confounded withal is before Thy presence and shamefast of case, too. [1350]

[1349] "The dustlings of Love", i. e. lovers abject as the dust.
[1350] i. e. great as have been his praises of thee, they are yet unequal to thy merit.

CCCCI

1. In the quarter of the winehouse Service many a year I practise;
Yea, the use of folk of fortune In the beggar's gear I practise.

2. Our admonisher perceiveth Not the scent of truth; I say it
In his presence; for backbiting Ne'er (so God me hear!) I practise.

3. So that in the snare of union I may take a strutting pheasant, [1351]
Expectation, in my ambush, Till the prey draw near, I practise.

4. Like the East wind, rising, falling, In her street I go and suing
To the basils and the roses, For support and cheer, I practise.

5. Pathway-snare the charmer's tress is And her glance misfortune's arrow:
Think, o heart, how oft this warning In thy heedless ear I practise.

6. Since thy quarter's dust, o idol, Our annoy may bide no longer,
Henceforth, light'ning of its burden Will, by absence sheer, I practise.

7. Hide Thou from the eye ill-seeing, O Thou Bounteous Blemish-Hider, [1352]
What of licence in the corner Of seclusion here I practise!

8. God forbid that I be heedless Of the Resurrection-Reck'ning!
Nay, I'll cast the lot to-morrow; [1353] But to-day good cheer I'll practise.

9. Still "Amen" the Faithful Spirit [1354] From the Throne's right hand exclaimeth,
Orisons when for the monarch, Faith and country dear, I practise.

10. Prayer for leave to kiss the threshold Of thy majesty, o Sultan,—
So myself to glory's summit Thus I may uprear,—I practise.

11. In one company I'm Hafiz And dreg-drainer in another:
See, with what a saucy boldness On the folk austere I practise!

[1351] Beloved likened to pheasant.
[1352] i. e. God.
[1353] i. e. I will consult the Sortes Coranicae for Divine direction, with a view to repentance.
[1354] The Archangel Gabriel.

CCCCII

1. My soul, for poortith's load, in sorry case is;
I am ashamed before the lovelings' faces.

2. Except some chain-haired maid on me take pity,
I shall go mad without the fair's embraces.

3. Of the Sphere's motions ask mine eye; for nightly
I count the stars, till daybreak them effaces.

4. I kiss the goblet's lip; for by its magic
The secret known to me of Time and Space is.

5. Much thanks to heav'n I render that no puissance
In this mine arm to vex the human race is.

6. If for the wine-seller I pray, what matter?
I do but pay the debit of his graces. [1355]

7. Thou wilt not raise me from the dust of sorrow,
Although mine eyes rain pearls in teardrops' places.

8. Me for blood-drinking in this desert blame not;
My teacher for the musk-deer of the chase is. [1356]

9. Crack-brained as Hafiz is, upon the favour
Of yonder gen'rous one his hopes he bases.

[1355] i. e. it is but in requital of his favours to me.
[1356] Musk (as before stated) is believed by the Persians to be the extravasated blood of
the musk-deer. The meaning of the line is; "It was from the musk-deer that I learned
to turn my suffering to good account, so that my verse, arising from my anguish, as
musk from that of the musk-deer, is, like the latter, sought and valued of the whole
world."

CCCCIII

1. If again my footsteps Fortune To the Magians' temple bore,
Prayer-rug would I pledge and patchcoat Straight, to pay the tavern-score.

2. If the knocker of repentance, Zealot-like, to day I ply,
Sure, the taverner to-morrow Will not open me the door;

3. And if aught of freedom, moth-like, Be vouchsafed to me of wing,
Round that candle-cheek I'll flutter, As I fluttered heretofore.

4. If my heart with an embracement, Harp-like, thou wilt not content,
With thy lips caress me, pipe-like, For a moment, if no more.

5. With the Houris to foregather Never wished I; for 'twere sin
That with others he should commerce Who at heart thine image wore.

6. Since for me no bosom-friend is, Save the sword of grief for thee,
Unto none the case I utter Of my heart that's drowned in gore.

7. Had my wet-skirt eye not public Made the secret of my love,
In my heart it had abidden, Hidden in its inmost core.

8. From this cage of clay, a dweller Of the air, [1357] bird-like, I'm grown;
So belike that royal falcon [1358] Make of me a prize of war.

9. If a head on Hafiz' body Were for every hair thereof,
All and sev'ral, like thy tresses, Would I cast thy feet before.

[1357] *Hewa, syn.*, love, desire. Word used p. g.
[1358] i. e. the Beloved.

CCCCIV

1. Give thy tress not to the breezes, Lest thou give unto the gale me;
And disdain's foundation lay not, From foundation lest thou hale me.

2. Light thy cheek and independent Make thy lovers of the rose-leaf;
Rear thy shape aloft, that yearning For the cypress may not ail me.

3. Be not noted in the city, Lest thou drive me to the mountain;
Shirin's coquetry display not, Lest Ferhád's fate thou entail me.

4. Drink not wine with other lovers, Lest myself I drink my heart's blood;
Nor of all the folk be mindful, Lest of thee remembrance fail me.

5. Twist thy hair not into ringlets, Lest thou cast me into fetters;
Render not thy visage lustrous, Lest thou render to the gale me. [1359]

6. Be familiar not with strangers, Lest beside myself thou make me;
Neither fret thyself for others, Lest with joylessness thou quail me.

7. Be not each assembly's candle: Otherwise thou wilt consume me;
Turn thy face not from thy servant, Lest to heaven I bewail me.

8. Nay, on me, poor wretch, have pity, Lest unto great Asef's doorway
Pierce the voice of my complaining; Let my cry for help avail me!

9. Heaven like, no more on Hafiz Do oppression, lest thou slay him:
Nay, be kind, so favouring fortune For the past may countervail me.

[1359] Second hemistich and rhyme-word of first line here repeated.

CCCCV

1. This my love for thee, my fair one, On what wise shall I assain?
Yea, how long shall I of sorrow For thy sake all night complain?

2. Long ago past hope of healing Is my frenzied heart become:
Peradventure, of thy tress-tip I may fashion it a chain.

3. Scope where shall I find and leisure, So the full perplexity,
Which I suffer for thy tress-tip, Once for all I may explain?

4. What I suffered in the season Of estrangement from thy sight,
'Twere impossible one letter Should the whole of it contain.

5. On my soul to look whenever I'm desirous, in mine eye
Still to conjure up the image Of thy lovely cheek I'm fain. [1360]

6. If I knew that thine enjoyment Should thereby to me betide,
Heart and faith would I surrender, Ay, and count the loss a gain.

7. Get thee gone from us, o preacher; Leave this idle prate of thine:
None am I who unto leasing Ear will any longer deign.

8. Of deliverance from lewdness, Hope, o Hafiz, is there none:
Since 'twas thus of Fate foreordered, Care and counsel are in vain.

[1360] i. e. because my soul cleaveth ever to the Beloved's cheek.

CCCCVI

1. If ever it be vouchsafed me The hand in thy tress to twine,
O many's the head that, ball-like, I'll smite with that mall of thine! [1361]

2. Thy tress unto me long life is; And yet of that same long life
No end of a hair, woe worth it! I hold in this hand of mine.

3. Vouchsafe me a writ of easance, O candle, that, candle-like,
In fire of the heart, before thee, To-night, I may melt and dwine.

4. That moment when, like the flagon, I give up the ghost with a laugh,
May prayers for my soul's well-being Be said of thy drunken eyne!

5. The prayer of a man polluted Like me is no proper prayer;
And hence in the winehouse, melting And burning, fore'er I pine.

6. In tavern and mosque if thine image Beseek me, of thy brows
A viol in one I fashion, In t'other a praying-shrine.

7. And if for a night thou lighten Our cell with thy radiant cheek,
All over the world, like morning, My head shall arise and shine.

8. Yea, worthy of praise the issue Of quest in the path of Love,
Albe for desire of the Loved One The life one must needs resign.

9. To whom the heart's grief shall I utter, O Hafiz? In this our time
There's no one my secret worthy To share but the cup of wine.

[1361] i. e. How many other lovers I shall madden with jealousy!

CCCCVII

1. From the usance of the topers Many a year I never strayed
Till desire I put in prison, As the understanding bade.

2. Of myself the way I found not To the Anca's [1362] dwelling-place;
Nay, this journey with the guiding Bird of Solomon [1363] I made.

3. In my hand nor thine the usance Is of drunk- or sober-ness;
This I do the Lord Eternal Bade me do, and I obeyed.

4. Heaven yet I hope to merit By the grace of God Most High;
Though door-keeping in the winehouse Long I practised to my trade.

5 That in my old age by Joseph's Company I'm comforted,
Is the recompense of patience, In the cell of grief displayed. [1364]

6. On my wounded heart some shadow Cast, o treasure of desire!
Since that house, indeed, in ruins, For the love of thee, I've laid.

7. I, repenting, said, "The skinker's Lip I will not kiss," and now
Bite my lip, because I hearkened Unto what the foolish said.

8. From the contrary of usance Seek thy heart's desire; for I
Ease and heart's content have gotten From her tangled tress's braid.[1365]

9. If I hold the seat of honour In the Chancery of Song,
Marvel not, for long the servant Of the President [1366] I've played.

10. Morning-rising dost thou practise, Hafiz-like? Salvation seek'st?
What I've made, all by the blessing Of the Koran have I made.

11. Never Hafiz, [1367] 'neath the prayer-arch Of the heavens, such a life
Led of ease and cheer as I have By the blessed Koran's aid.

[1362] "Anca", a fabulous bird, something in the nature of our Phoenix: it dwells in the
    Caucasus and is supposed by some to be identical with the Simurgh. The secondary
    meaning, in this case, is "the Beloved".
[1363] "The Bird of Solomon" is the hoopoe, which acted as love-messenger between
    Solomon and the Queen of Sheba. Some experienced friend, as well versed in love-
    matters as was the hoopoe in question, is here meant.
[1364] Beloved likened to Joseph and Hafiz to the Patriarch Jacob.
[1365] Which is a synonym for wilderment, perturbation.
[1366] i. e. the Grand Vizier, who was Sahib-i-Diwan, i. e. President of the Council or
    Chancery (not *Chancellery*, as grotesquely phrased by modern newspapers) of
    Ministers, just as Hafiz was Sahib-i-Diwan, taking Diwan in its other sense of a
    collection of poems. Note paronomasia.
[1367] "Hafiz" here has its theological sense of "one who knows the Koran by heart".

CCCCVIII

1. Hilarious my heart is with wine And still I proclaim it on high,
"In quest of the zephyr of life, Myself to the bowl I apply."

2. No pietist's crabbedness sits On the face of the seller of wine;
And so for no patchcoat but that Of the jolly dreg-drainers I sigh.

3. The winehouse's door if the Sheikh Of the Magians shut in my face,
What door shall I knock at, on whom For succour and solace rely?

4. Reproach thou me not for that wild I grow in this meadow: as Fate
And Fortune Foreordered me reared, I grew, without questioning why.

5. 'Twixt cloister and winehouse, indeed, No difference look that thou see
Nay, God is my witness, with Him, Wherever He dwelleth, am I.

6. The dust of the highway of quest Th' elixir of happiness is;
That blissful grisamber-breathed dust, Its servant I'll live and I'll die.

7. For love of a tall-statured fair's Befuddled narcissus, alack!
The cup, like the tulip, in hand, I languish the rivulet by.

8. A fable I'm grown for amaze; The brows of the Loved One my heart
Have caught in the curve of their mall, And so at her mercy I lie.

9. Bring wine, that, as Hafiz prescribes, I may with the life-giving tide
Of the flagon, hypocrisy's dust Wash off from the heart and the eye.

CCCCIX

1. Come, Soufi, off for ever Fraud's patchcoat pied draw we!
The line of "cancel" over The writ of pride draw we!

2. The convent's alms and off rings, Come, let us spend on wine!
Dissembling's cassock thorow The tavern-tide [1368] draw we!

3. Leap we the convent barriers And from the rival's halls
Wine plunder and from cloister, Come, forth the bride draw we!

4. Fate's secret, screened and hidden In the Invisible,
Its cheek from, drunkard-fashion, The veil aside draw we!

5. Come, let us do; confusion We else shall reap what day
To the next world our chattels, With death to guide, draw we.

6. If Paradise to morrow They grudge us, boys from this
And girls from t'other heaven, With us to bide, draw we! [1369]

7. One glance from that her eyebrow, And with that moon-like mall
Of hers, the sphere-ball hither, Its course awried, draw we!

8. Beyond our proper limit Are vauntings such as these:
The feet without our blanket, O Hafiz, why draw we? [1370]

[1368] i. e. Wash it in wine.
[1369] If they deny us Paradise at the Resurrection, we will make a Paradise for ourselves
with the Beloved's face and wine and lure the boys and girls of heaven to keep us
company.
[1370] A proverbial saying, equivalent to "Ne sutor ultra crepidam".

CCCCX

1. A lifetime 'tis that in Love's quest Each day I hither, thither fare,
That still to those of good repute I lift imploring hands in prayer.

2. So that my day I may not pass Without my love-enkindling moon,
Snares in the way I've set and clapped A bird (my heart) within the snare.

3. So haply tidings I may gain Of yonder cypress-straight one's shade,
Love's clamour, on all sides, I launch At every goodly-gaited fair.

4. I know that those blood-raining sighs I heave at eventide and dawn
Affliction to an end will bring And fruit of happy case will bear.

5. Where's Gulchihréh and where Auréng? Mihr's usance where and where Wefá's? [1371]
I only now can claim to be A lover perfect as they were.

6. Though well I know yon Ease-of-Hearts [1372] Vouchsafeth not the heart's desire,
I still go cherishing the thought Of union that shall last fore'er.

7. Though absent from myself I am And wine (like Hafiz) have forsworn,
Yet, in the angels' banquet-halls, I quaff a goblet here and there. [1373]

[1371] Auréng and Gulchihréh, Mihr and Wefa, renowned lovers of Eastern romance.
    Mihr and *Wefa* mean (etym.) "Love" and "Faith". Note word-play.
[1372] i. e. The Beloved.
[1373] i. e. Though I do not drink with Tom, Dick and Harry, I quaff a cup now and then
    with certain choice spirits of my own fashion.

CCCCXI

1. The Festival day to-day is And I've for to-day forecast
To barter for wine and winecup The sum of the four weeks' fast.

2. 'Tis many a day that severed From winecup and wine I am;
And sore is the shame't hath wrought me Among the toper caste.

3. No more will I sit secluded, Though zealot and pietist
Of convent and cell and cloister The chain to my foot make fast.

4. Sage counsel the city preacher Me giveth; but this I know,
That counsel no more from any I'll hearken, as in the past.

5. Where's he who the ghost gave up in The dust of the tavern-door,
That I, too, may die before him, My head at his feet downcast?

6. The winecup I drain, with the prayer-mat Of piety shouldered: alack
If conscious of this my imposture The folk should become at last!

7. "O Hafiz", the folk say, "hearken The elder!" But more to me
Than hundreds of elders wine is That years in the jar hath past.

CCCCXII

1. Youth, loveliking and dalliance And wine of ruby hue;
Fast friends in private gathered, Companions fit and few;

2. Minstrel sweet-voiced and singer And skinker sugar-lipped;
Comrades right kind and lovesome And cup-companions true;

3. Lovelings, for very sweetness, The envy of Life's fount;
Charmers, for grace and beauty That make the full moon rue;

4. A banquet-place heart-taking As topmost Paradise,
In roses bow'red, such roses As feed on heaven's dew;

5. The general guests well-willing And nobly bred the chiefs;
The hosts adept and comrades The topers' wish unto;

6. Wine brisk and bright and bitter, Delectable and light;
Its zest the loveling's ruby And talk of liquor new;

7. The fair one's tress snare-spreading, To take withal the heart;
The skinker's glance sword-drawing, The reason to undo;

8. A world-enlight'ning teacher Of bounty like Kiwám;
A wit like sweet-tongued Hafiz Amid the jovial crew;

9. Whoso this joyance shunneth, To him be life forbid!
This converse who escheweth May heart's content eschew! [1374]

[1374] This Ode was apparently composed in praise of the festive assembly of the poet's
   patron, the Grand Vizier Hajji Kiwameddin Hassan.

CCCCXIII

1. In thy footsteps' dust our faces Many a time and tide we've laid;
Yea, aside the thought our secret From the folk to hide we've laid.

2. All the age-long reputation Of our forbears of good name
In the cup's and moonfaced skinker's Way, forswearing pride, we've laid.

3. Vault and porch of mosque and mosque-school, talk and prate of learned lore,
In the way of mirth and joyance And of rose-cheeked bride we've laid.

4. Our weak hearts we have not burdened With the load of worldly care;
Nay, aside the heavy fardel, With one hairlet tied, we've laid.

5. Not with troops the realm of safety Have we taken; nor the base
Of Love's kingdom, by our only Might, unfortified, we've laid.

6. To those witching two narcissi [1375] Have we rendered up the soul
And the heart in yonder blackmoor Hyacinths [1376] to bide we've laid.

7. See the Loved One's eye, what magic It dispenseth, that once more,
Hope's foundation on an eyeglance, On a smile espied, we've laid!

8. In hope's corner, on her eyebrow, Lo! the eye of quest (like those
Who bewatch the new moon's coming In the Fasting-tide) we've laid.

9. Like the violet, withouten Her narcissus-eye's caress,
On the knee the head of passion, Dazed and heavy-eyed, we've laid.

10. Hafiz, seek for present pleasure; For the cash of wit and sense,
In the love of that Beloved, Curly-locked, aside we've laid.

[1375] i. e. eye.
[1376] i. e. tresses.

CCCCXIV

1. Enamoured am I of a fair one, A youngling new a-blow;
I've sought it with prayer from heaven, The gladness of this woe.

2. Whoremonger, amorist, toper, I tell thee outright, I am;
So thou, that with all these merits Endowed I am, mayst know.

3. Now shame of my sin-soiled cassock Is over me come, whereon
I, patch upon patch, devices An hundred still did sew.

4. Yea, well mayst thou burn, o candle, In passion for her! For see,
Upstanding in that same business, Loin-girt, am I e'enso.

5. The profit of my endeavour, In this my bewilderment,
I've lost: as in heart and spirit I dwindle, in grief I grow.

6. So haply that new-blown charmer May me to her bosom draw,
To the tavern, with robe (like Hafiz) All open in front [1377] I go.

[1377] The robe open in front is the sign of the debauchee and the frenzied lover.

CCCCXV

1. For the cark of the time, whereunto Bound or confine I see not,
Med'cine or salve or solace, Save Red-bud wine, I see not.

2. Ne'er of the Sheikh of the Magians Will I forswear the converse;
Since that, in this, advantage Or profit mine I see not.

3. A draught in this sore cropsickness Of Love to me none giveth;
Alack, in the world-all, mortal Of heart benign I see not!

4. Come, by the sun of the winecup The altitude of life take;
For truly the time's ascendant Fast in this line [1378] I see not.

5. Enamourment's still the token Of sages: keep thy counsel;
For lo! in the city's teachers And sheikhs this sign I see not.

6. Question me not of her middle, Whereto my heart I've bounden;
Since mine own self,—much less, then, Her waist hair-fine,—I see not. [1379]

7. Pity that I so blinded Am with my tears that plainly
Her face with these double mirrors, My weeping eyne, I see not!

8. Since that thy shape, Beloved, The stream of mine eyes departed,
Aught there save running water, For [1380] cypress and pine, I see not.

9. I to this bark [1381] of Hafiz Forever cleave; for, saving
In *this* sea [1382], pearls heart-luring Of speech divine I see not.

[1378] i. e. that of fair fortune, security for winebibbers.
[1379] i. e. I am not conscious of my own existence, much less of her invisibly small
waist.
[1380] "For," i. e. in place of.
[1381] *Syn.* "book".
[1382] *Syn.* "Diwan" (collection of poems.) Note word-play.

CCCCXVI

1. Openly the words I utter, And heart-glad am I of it;
I'm Love's slave and of the burden Of this world and that I'm quit.

2. I'm a bird of heaven's rosemeads; Who shall tell how thence I fell,
How in this our nether snare-place Of vicissitudes I lit?

3. I an angel was and topmost Paradise my dwelling-place:
To this ruin-peopled cloister Adam's sin did me remit.

4. Touba's shade and Kauther's margent, Houri's heart-seducing charms,
In the longing for thy street-end, From my memory did flit.

5. No astrologer the planet Of my fortune apprehends:
Why, o Lord, of earthly mother To be born was I forewrit?

6. Since a bondman in Love's winehouse, Ring in ear, I'm grown, each breath
Some chagrin anew accosteth Me with "Hail, fellow! Well hit!"

7. My heart's blood the apple drinketh Of the eye; and meet it is.
Why unto the folk's heart's darling, Why, my heart did I commit?

8. Nothing's writ on my heart's tablet Save the Elif [1383] of her shape:
What's to do? No other letter Me my master taught than it.

9. Clear of tears the face of Hafiz Make thou with thy tress's tip,
Lest their torrent sap and ruin The foundations of my wit.

[1383] "Elif, first letter of Arabic alphabet, a straight perpendicular stroke, to which the
Beloved's erect and slender shape is likened.

CCCCXVII

1. From the Elder of the Magians This pronouncement do I hold;
"Wine unlawful is, when shared not With the Friend." The saying's old.

2. Needs this cassock of dissembling Must I doff, for to the wise
Torment sore it is to cómmerce With the base and grief untold.

3. So maybe the Friend's lip scatter Of its goblet's dregs on me,
At the winehouse-door abiding, Years I've suffered heat and cold.

4. If belike my ancient service Have her memory escaped,
O remind her, breeze of dawning, Of the covenant of old! [1384]

5. If, though after years an hundred, On my dust thy scent should breathe,
Up my bones would rise to greet it, Dancing, from the graveyard mould.

6. With an hundred hopes to lure us, Erst the charmer snared our heart;
Surely, covenants forgotten Are not of the generous-souled.

7. To the rosebud say, "Straithearted Be not for thy straitened case:
"Morning's breath and zephyr-waftings Yet shall help thee to unfold."

8. Heart, take thought for thy well-being By another door than this;
Lovers' pain by leaches' tending Never yet hath been consoled.

9. Seek to gain the pearl of wisdom, So with thee thou mayst it bear; [1385]
Others' portion since the treasure Is of silver and of gold.

10. Puissant are the snares of Satan; Nor may mortal ever hope
Over him to win the vantage, If its succour heav'n withhold.

11. An thou lack of gold and silver, Hafiz, grieve not: grateful be;
Grace of speech, sound wit, what better Wares were ever bought or sold?

[1384] Rhyme-word of line 1 repeated.
[1385] i. e. to the next world.

CCCCXVIII

1. Though to the service of the King we bound are,
Kings of the realm of morning-tide we crowned are.

2. Treasure in sleeve and empty purse, world-showing
Cup we, at once, and way-dust of the ground, are.

3. Sober in practice and illusion-drunken,
We're seas of Unity [1386] and yet sin-drowned are.

4. We, whenas strumpet Fortune looketh kindly,
The mirror of her cheek like the moon's round are.

5. Each night, about the crown our prayers still watching
Of yonder king, for fortune high-renowned, are.

6. Bid him our blessing reckon gain; for sleeping
What while he is, we waking him around are.

7. Shah Mensour knoweth that to wheresoever
Our faces set in resolution found are,

8. In bloody shrouds we cause the foemen welter
And by our blessing friends with victory crowned are.

9. On us no stain of fraud is; we one-coloured, [1387]
Red lion like, black asp and sandy mound, are.

10. Bid them, O King, his dues to Hafiz render [1388];
Avouched hast thou and we to witness bound are.

[1386] i. e. Orthodoxy.
[1387] i. e. sincere.
[1388] Apparently an appeal for payment of a sum of money which had been accorded to
    the poet by the King, withheld by the court officials.

CCCCXIX

1. Me unto oppression, dust-like, For a trampling-stock, she gave;
Yet her dust I kiss and pardon Of her trampling foot I crave.

2. None am I that for oppression Rail at thee. Nay, God forbid!
I am but thy faithful servant And thy weal-desiring slave.

3. To the crook-end of thy ringlet I my long hope bounden have;
God forbid that it the shortness Of my hand of quest outbrave!

4. Dust-mote that I am, right goodly In thy street's the time for me;
Yet I fear lest thence some wind-waft Bear me with a sudden wave.

5. I'm a Soufi of Heav'n's cloister; But the Fates have presently
My abiding-place appointed In the Magians' convent-cave. [1389]

6. In the dawn the tavern-elder Brought me the world-showing cup
And impartment of thy beauty In that mirror to me gave.

7. Up! With me, the wayside sitter, To the winehouse come and see
What a man of worth and worship Held am I in that conclave.

8. Drunk thou passest and of Hafiz Tak'st no thought; but woe to thee
To thy beauty's skirt if ever These my sighs fire-kindling clave!

9. Well it came to me at dawntide That the monarch of the East [1390]
Said, "I am, for all my kingship, Touranshah the Vizier's slave."

[1389] i. e. the wine-cellar.
[1390] i. e. the sun.

CCCCXX

1. Though in ferment, like the wine-jar, For the heart a-fire, am I,
Seal on lip, on blood I batten And in silence I aby.

2. On her lip to set the fancy Is to aim at one's own life;
See me, madman, how this matter With my soul I seek to buy!

3. How from heart's grief shall I sever, Since each breath the blackmoor tress
Of some fair the ring of bondage In the ear of me doth tie?

4. Not of fervour of religion This my patchcoat-wearing is:
On this veil for hiding secret Faults an hundred I rely.

5. I, whose only wish to drink is Of pure wine, what shall I do,
To the Magian Elder's bidding But the ear of wit apply?

6. God forbid that I confide not In mine own devotion! Nay,
Such my trust is that the winecup Still, from time to time, I ply.

7. 'Spite the enemy, my hope is That, upon the Reckoning Day,
His forgiveness will not suffer On my back sin's burden lie.

8. For two grains of wheat my father [1391] Sold the meads of Paradise;
And except for *one* [1392] I sold it, No true son of his were I.

9. If the minstrel play the measure Hight of Love and sing thereto
Hafiz' verse, from wit and feeling Ravished shall I be thereby.

[1391] Adam. As before mentioned, the Muslim legends substitute a grain (or grains) of
    wheat for the apple of Jewish mythology.
[1392] "*One*", i. e. the beloved's mole, likened to a grain of wheat.

CCCCXXI

1. If the enemies' reproaches In myself I meditate,
'Twas not I that set the fashion Of wine-bibbing, anygate.

2. Since, for topers new, repentance All in vain is, how should I,
Whose ill-name the whole world's fable Is, amendment contemplate?

3. "King of madcaps" call me, witless, An thou wilt, for I indeed
Overpass, in lack of judgment, All creation, small and great.

4. With my heart's blood on the forehead Limn a mole, so all may know
That for thee, the unbeliever, I'm a sacrifice to Fate.

5. Take me upon trust, 'fore heaven, And pass on, lest thou perceive
That no dervish in this patchcoat Hideth, but a reprobate.

6. These my blood-bedropping verses To the Friend, o wind, recite,
Who my spirit's vein hath punctured [1393] With her lashes black and straight.

7. Draw thy skirt in, lest the droppings Of my bleeding heart it touch;
For th'effect will thee bespatter, If my wound thou irritate.

8. Toper if I be or Elder, What with folk have I to do?
I'm the keeper of my secret, Bide my time and go my gait.

[1393] This odd expression is equivalent to "hath wounded my soul".

CCCCXXII [1394]

1. Lo! from this dwelling of exile Homeward if e'er I shall go,
With forethought and care, elsewhither Whenever I fare, I shall go.

2. Yea, if from this travel safely I win to my native land,
By way of the wine-house only, I vow and declare, I shall go!

3. To tell what I've learned and suffered By travel and wayfaring,
To the door of the tavern ghittern And goblet to bear, I shall go.

4. Though friends in Love's way hereafter My blood with oppression drink,
No true man am I, if complaining To strangers elsewhere I shall go.

5. Henceforward my hand for ever Shall cleave to the tress of the Friend:
If after my mad heart's fancies, I wonder, fore'er I shall go?

6. If ever again her eyebrow Prayer-niche like I see, I'll make
Prostration in thanks and after To off'ring of prayer I shall go.

7. O joyful the time when, like Hafiz, By means of the Vizier's grace, [1395]
Hilarious with wine, from tavern To house, with the fair, I shall go!

[1394] This Ode refers to his unprofitable expedition, before mentioned, to Yezd.
[1395] i. e. the means of merry-making being provided by the Vizier's bounty.

CCCCXXIII

1. Though my case, indeed, is tangled Grown by those her tresses two,
Hope I have that, by her bounty, Yet the knot I shall undo.

2. Not to mirth ascribe the redness Of my face; nay, from my cheek
'Tis the heart's blood is reflected, As the wine the flagon through.

3. Sure, the minstrel's tune is minded Me beside myself to make;
For, alack! to me forbidden Áccess is that screen [1396] into!

4. So that nought that fane may enter, Save the thought of her alone,
Nightly o'er my heart's high places Watch I till the day grow blue.

5. Fall'n asleep, by her enchantments, Is my fortune's eye: alack!
Where's a breeze of heaven's favour, That shall wake it me anew?

6. Lo! I am that poet-wizard, Who, by speech's sorcery,
From the reed-pen's bill, around me Sugar still and honey strew.

7. With an hundred hopes I entered In this desert; o thou guide
Of my strayed heart, never leave me In this waste without a clue!

8. Since myself I cannot see her, In her wind-swift passing by,
How shall I entreat another That for me to her he sue?

9. Yesternight, "All face is Hafiz And hypocrisy," quoth she.
Nay, thy doorway's dust excepted, Say, with whom have I to do? [1397]

[1396] "Screen", i. e. the sanctuary of Love. The word *perdeh* means both "tune" and
    "screen" and is, of course, used p. g.
[1397] i. e. how can I be double-dealing ("face" here = "double-facedness"), since I have
    no dealings but with thy doorway's dust?

CCCCXXIV

1. A lover of fair faces And heart-alluring hair,
I'm drunk with wine unmingled And glances debonair.

2. Sayst thou, "The myst'ry tell me, The Compact of the Prime?" [1398]
When I two cups have drunken, I'll tell thee then and there.

3. From burning and enduring In Love there's no escape;
Me, like the candle standing, Think not with fire to scare.

4. A man am I of heaven, That, in this exile here
Below, a love-lorn captive Am of the moonfaced fair.

5. The Houris with their ringlets Shall sweep my couch, if Fate
Vouchsafe me aid, my chattels Towards the Friend to bear.

6. Shiraz is beauty's quarry And mine of ruby lips;
But here, poor bankrupt pedlar, I languish in despair.

7. For all that in this city Of languor-drunken eyes
I see, though wine I drink not, I fuddled am, I swear.

8. The town of lovelings' glances Is full on all six sides:
I've nothing; else a buyer Of all the six I were.

9. The bride of Hafiz' genius Would fain herself display;
But I've (alack!) no mirror Wherewith to make her yare.

10. Hafiz for heat consumeth Of barren thought-taking:
Where is the skinker, water [1398] To cast upon the flare?

[1398] i. e. the covenant, before mentioned, made between God and the souls in without beginning.

CCCCXXV

1. Hands we lift anights to heaven, So a prayer that we may make,
So the sorrow of thy sev'rance Shift to bear that we may make.

2. Sped my sick heart is: friends, help me! To its bed-head bring the leach,
So provision for assaining Its affair that we may make.

3. She, without my fault, who smote me With the sword of wrath and went,
Bring her back, so peace, 'fore heaven, With the fair that we may make.

4. Heart, from topers' hearts some succour Seek; or hard Love's case will be:
God forfend mistake in seeking Succour there that we may make.

5. 'Gainst the lusts, whereby our bosom Is an idol-temple grown,
Sighs let's launch for shafts; make ready, War thereon that we may make!

6. Withered is the root of joyance: To the winehouse where's the way,
Growth and blossom in that water [1399] And that air that we may make?

7. No effect for good the shadow Of the mean bird hath: arise,
To the bléssed Huma's shadow Our repair that we may make?

[1399] i. e. wine.

CCCCXXVI

1. Hoping friendliness From the friends abode we;
But, in this conceit, Lack of judgment showed we.

2. When will friendship's tree Fruit vouchsafe, I wonder?
For the nonce we go; But a seed first sowed we.

3. Many a thing there happed; Yet complaint we made not
Nor observance' bound Ever overstrode we.

4. Idle talk and prate Are not dervish-usance;
Else to thee a grudge For things happened owed we.

5. War and wiles of war Still thine eyes intended:
But, unwotting this, Peace their purpose trowed we.

6. Beauty's rosebush waxed Not of self heart-charming;
Breath of blessing first On thy charms bestowed we. [1400]

7. Quoth she, "Of free-will Thou thy heart didst give me:
"With tax-gatherers, else, None to love us goad we."

[1400] i. e. The charms of the Beloved are in great part owing to the fostering influence
of the love of her lovers.

CCCCXXVII

1. Welcome, bearer of glad tidings! Welcome bird of happy trace!
Glad thy coming! Where's the Loved One? Which the way unto her place?

2. Heaven's blessing guide her travel, So the enemy the snare
And the Loved One find her wishes, By the Fore-eternal grace!

3. There's no bound to my complaining Of my suff'rance from the Friend;
If a thing beginning lacketh, There's no ending to the case.

4. Go, admonisher! The patchcoat Is for us unlawful grown,
Since the charmer's tress the girdle [1401] Bade us on our body lace.

5. Thou my spirit's bird, that warbled From the Sidreh-top [1402] whilere,
With thy mole to bait, inveigled Hast into this world-lure base.

6. Over-prideful is the cypress: Walk and put her shape to shame!
Over-arrogant the rose is: Come, confound her with thy face!

7. Unto this mine eye blood-raining, Marry, how should sleep befit?
From his eyes, whom suff'rance slayeth, Pain and anguish slumber chase.

8. "Ruth on me heart-lorn thou tak'st not," Said I; "This is my complaint:
"Time will come when thou'lt repent thee; And the days draw on apace."

9. Meet it is if inclination To thine eyebrows Hafiz have:
In the corner of the prayer-niche [1403] Make the eloquent their place.

[1401] "Girdle", emblem of infidelity (i. e. non-Musulmanhood) and hence of toping.
[1402] "Sidreh", the Lote-tree of Heaven, the perch of the Archangel Gabriel.
[1403] Beloved's eyebrow likened to prayer-niche.

CCCCXXVIII

1. Care-nothing sots, who've given The heart from hand, are we;
Cup-intimates and ádepts Of Passion's band are we.

2. Since with the Loved One's eyebrow We've solved our need, the butt
For many a bow of censure, By envy spanned, are we.

3. 'Twas but last night, o rose-bud, Thou puttest on the brand
Of the dawn-draught [1404]; but tulips Born with the brand are we.

4. If vexed with our renouncement The Magian Elder be,
"Strain wine, for in excusement," Tell him, "a-stand are we." [1405]

5. To thee we look for furth'rance: Guide of the way, a glance!
So we may own that baffled And failure-banned are we.

6. Heed not our tulip-usance Of cup-holding; but see
Our bleeding hearts, how branded Of our own hand are we.

7. "What's all this play of fancy?" Sayst thou? Quoth Hafiz' verse,
"Read us aright and easy To understand are we."

[1404] Redness of new-blown rose likened to brand (i. e. stain) of wine.
[1405] i. e. we are already afoot, with intent to return to the tavern and make our excuses
for our absence.

CCCCXXIX

1. Shoot not my heart with glances; for I die,
Of mine own choice, before thy languorous eye.

2. Since passing rich thou art in loveliness,
Give me an alms; for mean and poor am I.

3. I am a bird, whose warblings night and morn
Are wafted from the roof-tree of the sky.

4. Fill up the cup; for in Love's realm, though old,
I'm young in luck o'er all men, far and nigh.

5. My bosom's space so full is of the Friend
That from my heart the thought of self must fly.

6. Except the score of minstrel and of wine,
Be nothing set to mine account on high!

7. In that dread hour, [1406] when none of other asks,
The vintner's bounties I shall magnify.

8. How long with heaven's apples, honey, milk
Wilt lure me, zealot, as a child were I?

9. A compact with the wine-seller I've made,
Nought but the cup in sorrow's hour to ply.

10. Fair fall the hour when I, for drunkenness,
Vizier and king in my content defy!

11. Abounding treasures in my breast I have,
Though abject in the adversary's eye.

12. The heart from Hafiz I withdrew [1407] what time
I took the skinker for my heart's ally.

[1406] i. e. in the hour of Judgment.
[1407] i. e. I ceased to reck of myself.

CCCCXXX

1. Winecup and love and loveling I'll nevermore forsake;
Renouncements have I many Made and no more will make.

2. The Friend's street-dust I value Above the Houris' halls,
Above the meads of heaven And Kauther's nectar-lake.

3. Their lesson men of insight Teach with a hint: a trope
I've said nor will repeat it, Let whoso may mistake.

4. The Sheikh to me, in anger, Said, "Go! Leave love." No need
Is there for strife, my brother: With love I will not break.

5. This is my whole devoutness, That I the city fair
Nor from the pulpit ogle Nor play the pious rake. [1408]

6. What while the head I lift not Up in the tavern's midst,
I'm never unto knowledge Of mine own self awake.

7. "Wine is forbidden; drink not;" The preacher, chiding, said:
Quoth I, "I never hearkened To every ass that spake.

8. "The Magian Elder telleth A reasonable tale;
"Excuse me, of *thy* fables If I no heed do take."

9. The Magian Elder's threshold Is fortune's dwelling-place,
Hafiz: I'll ne'er the kissing Of this door's dust forsake.

[1408] As do the hypocrites.

CCCCXXXI

1. We've cast off, for love of the winehouse, The usance of dawntide prayer;
The produce and gain of devotion We've laid in the path of the fair.

2. This caut'ry, wherewith we have branded, For passion, our frenzied hearts,
The harvest of hundreds of sages With pity hath set a-flare.

3. The Lord of Eternity gave us The treasure of love and grief,
When first to this wasted desert Our faces we set whilere.

4. There cannot a worse dissembler Than we in the patchcoat be,
Who've stablished in toper-usance The basis of our affair.

5. No longer our hearts we'll open Henceforward to wantons' love;
We've set on this house's portal The seal of her lip fore'er.

6. That kiss, that the prideful zealot Would have on his hand impressed,
The lip of the brimming wine-cup Henceforward alone shall bear.

7. Now heaven be thanked that the teacher, We lauded for sage and staid,
Like us, without heart befallen And faith is, for love-despair!

8. Nay, how shall this storm-tossed vessel Elsewhither itself betake,
Since spirit and heart we've set on That pearl without peer and rare?

9. Content with a semblant (like Hafiz) Of thee until now we've been:
How beggarly poor of spirit And abject, o Lord, we were!

CCCCXXXII

1. I've limned with thy face's likeness The tablet of mine eyne;
For ne'er have I seen or hearkened A fair with a shape like thine.

2. Mine, mine was the hope of lordship: And so thy bonds I sought:
The kingship I wished and therefore To serve thee did incline.

3. Although in thy quest the North Wind's Reinfellow still I am,
Ne'er yet have I overtaken The dust of thy waving pine. [1409]

4. In the night of thy tress I dream not Of hope in the day of life;
All thought of the heart's desirement, In time of thy mouth, resign.

5. The fault of thy neck heart-luring It was and thine eye of black
That I from the folk to the desert Have fled like the deer and kine.

6. What tears have I shed for longing, Because of thy honey-fount!
What cheats from thy lip I've purchased, That ruby seller of wine!

7. What arrows of looks thou launchedst At this my wounded heart!
What burdens of woe I've suffered At that street-end of thine!

8. Bring, bring of the dust of her quarter, Breeze of the morning, bring!
The scent of the lovers' heart's blood I breathe in that earth divine.

9. Late, over my head, like the rosebud, A breeze from her quarter passed
And lo! at its fragrance opened This weariful heart of mine.

10. I swear by the dust of thy footsteps, O sun of Hafiz's sight,
That, lacking thy cheek, no lustre I see from the lamp of the eyne!

[1409] "Waving pine", i. e. the Beloved's shape.

CCCCXXXIII

1. To this doorway not for worship Or array, indeed, we've come;
Here, for shelter 'gainst ill fortune And affray, indeed, we've come.

2. From the bounds of non-existence, Farers of the stage of Love,
Even to the realms of Being, All this way, indeed, we've come.

3. Thy fresh down we spied and leaving Straight the meads of heav'n, the quest
Of that herb-of-grace of passion To essay, indeed, we've come.

4. Though at our command are treasures Such as Gabriel doth guard,
At her threshold, beggar-fashion, Us to lay, indeed, we've come.

5. Where's the anchor of thy mercy, Ark of Grace? For, drowned in sin,
To the ocean of God's bounty, Wellaway! indeed, we've come.

6. Gone the water of our face [1410] is: Rain on us, fault-washing cloud!
For, black-booked, [1411] unto our actions' Reckoning Day, indeed, we've come.

7. "Doff this woollen patchcoat, Hafiz; For behind the caravan,
"It with fire of sighs to kindle," [Lovers say,] "indeed, we've come." [1412]

[1410] i. e. our honour, repute.
[1411] i. e. with a terrible record of sin.
[1412] i. e. we lovers purpose to consume the caravan of hypocrisy with our fire-raining
    sighs; so do thou leave it, lest thou be consumed with it.

CCCCXXXIV

1. Ill we speak not nor inclining Practise to despite, not we;
Make not blue our wede [1413] nor blacken Face of any wight, not we.

2. Ill the dervish or the puissant 'Tis to blame for less or more;
The essential is, we do not Aught ourselves unright, not we.

3. In content the world we traverse, In the sight of wayfarers;
Of black horse and gilded saddle Reck we not a mite, not we.

4. Ne'er the charact'ry of error In the book of lore we write;
Nor Truth's secrets with the juggler's Gear do we unite, not we.

5. If the pietist forbid us From the winecup, better 'tis
That we honour not the lurdane With our liquor bright, not we.

6. If the king with rev'rence drink not Of the topers' dregs, his case
We'll not render bright and shining By our blessing's might, not we.

7. Heav'n the bark of men of merit Wrecketh: better 'tis we trust
Not to this inverted ocean, Hung in yonder height, not we.

8. If an envier aught of evil Utter and a friend be vexed,
Say, "Content thee; for we hearken Not the witless wight, not we."

9. If the adversary, Hafiz, Falsehood speak, we'll heed him not;
But, if truth he utter, never 'Gainst the truth we'll fight, not we.

[1413] i. e. as do the Soufis.

THE POEMS OF SHEMSEDDIN MOHAMMED HAFIZ OF SHIRAZ

NOW FIRST COMPLETELY DONE INTO
ENGLISH VERSE FROM THE PERSIAN, IN
ACCORDANCE WITH THE ORIGINAL FORMS,
WITH A BIOGRAPHICAL AND CRITICAL
INTRODUCTION, BY JOHN PAYNE, AUTHOR
OF "THE MASQUE OF SHADOWS AND OTHER
POEMS," ETC., AND TRANSLATOR OF "THE
POEMS OF FRANCOIS VILLON," "THE BOOK
OF THE THOUSAND NIGHTS AND ONE
NIGHT," "THE DECAMERON OF BOCCACCIO,"
"THE NOVELS OF BANDELLO" AND "THE
QUATRAINS OF OMAR KHEYYAM." IN THREE
VOLUMES. VOLUME THE THIRD.

ODES
(continued)

CCCCXXXV

1. I have a compact with the Friend, Whilst soul in body still I have,
That aye in honour, as my soul, Her quarter's lovers will I have.

2. With yonder moon of far Cathay The closet of my soul is bright;
Radiance of heart and eye from her, That candle of Chigíl, [1414] I have.

3. Since, to my heart's desire, a place Of shelter with the Friend I've won,
Let whoso will of me missay; No heed of their ill-will I have.

4. A friend host-quelling, thanks to God, Although an hundred thousand fair
In ambush 'gainst this heart of mine Should tilt with all their skill, I have.

5. Thine eyes to-night, o watcher, shut, 'Fore God; for many a privy word
To barter with her silent lip, Before the dawn grow chill, I have.

6. Since in the rosemead of her grace Proudly I walk, extoll'd be God!
No wish for rose or eglantine, Tulip or daffodil I have.

7. Harkye, o elder sage, forbid Me not the winehouse; for a heart,
That no renouncement's covenant Could ever yet fulfil, I have.

8. None hath a comrade like my fair, Indeed, to keep him company;
Delightsome wine and lovely maid, To boot, the cup to fill, I have.

9. A cypress in my house I hold, Beneath the shadow of whose shape,
No need of box-tree of the mead Or cypress by the rill I have.

10. Thanks to her ruby signet's grace, I vaunt myself a Solomon:
Since mine the Most High Name become Is, no concern of ill I have.

11. After long abstinence, renowned For toping's Hafiz: what care I?
Since in this world Emín-ed-Dín [1415] For friend and fautor still I have.

[1414] "Chigil", a district in Chinese Tartary, celebrated for the beauty of its women.
[1415] Keeper of the seals to Sultan Uweis.

CCCCXXXVI

1. Who am I that I should happen To thy fragrant memory?
Kindness dost thou, thou whose door-dust Of my head the crownal be!

2. Who this kindness to thy servants Taught thee, o heart-charmer? Say;
For this fashion in thy watchers Never, certes, might I see.

3. Let, o holy bird, thy blessing Be our road-guide; for, indeed,
Long the pathway to the goal is And new travellers are we.

4. Prithee, breezes of the dawning, Bear my service to the Friend,
Saying, "At the dawn-prayer season Be we not forgot of thee!"

5. Glad the day when from this hostel I shall bind my burdens on, [1416]
When, at thy street-end, the comrades Question what is come of me!

6. Guide me to thy privy chamber, Wine with thee that I may drink
And henceforward from the burden Of the world's chagrin be free.

7. Lofty is the poet's office And world-conquering. Hafiz, speak,
So thy mouth be filled with jewels By the Sovran of the Sea. [1417]

8. If thou seek the pearl of union, Of thine eye a sea of tears,
Harkye, must thou make, o Hafiz, And therein a diver be.

[1416] i. e. depart this world.
[1417] i. e. (says Soudi), the King of Hurmouz, (*hod.* Ormuz, an island in the Persian
Gulf,) who, though personally unknown to Hafiz, was one of his patrons and had
bestowed largesse on him. (See post, Ode DLXXVII, 3, 4.) This Ode appears to have
been composed in answer to an unexpected letter or message from him.

CCCCXXXVII

1. On me thou lookest and my dole Incontinent mak'st wax amain;
On thee I look and unto thee I every moment wax more fain.

2. After my weal thou askest not: I know not what thy purpose is:
But for my healing striv'st thou not: Belike thou knowest not my pain.

3. That thou shouldst cast me in the dust Is not the way of equity;
Nay, pass and ask of me, that I Thy pathway's dust may be again.

4. Till in the dust I lie, thy skirt I will not loose, and even then,
If o'er my clay thou chance to pass, My dust shall cleave unto thy train.

5. My breath for love and grief is spent: How long wilt bubble us with breath? [1418]
On me thy rancour still thou wreak'st Nor unto me dost respite deign.

6. My heart, one night, back from thy tress I in the darkness sought; thy cheek
I saw and from thy ruby lip A cup of bliss once more did drain.

7. I drew thee to my bosom straight And all a-tangle grew thy locks;
Lip to thy lip I set and made A sacrifice of heart and brain.

8. When, in the quest of mead and plain, Thou without us departedst hence,
My blood-red tears, for jealousy, Adown my yellow cheeks did rain.

9. Be thou to Hafiz only kind And let the enemy go hang!
When favouring to me thou art, His idle rancour I disdain.

[1418] i. e. with empty words, promises.

CCCCXXXVIII

1. I am no half-hearted toper Wine and wanton that foregoes;
Ask the Mohtesib if ever I such foolish fashions chose.

2. I who at repentance-makers Railed for years have, I were mad,
If of wine I should repent me In the season of the rose.

3. Love's the pearl and I the diver And the winehouse is the sea;
Lo, I've plunged my head thereunder: Where I bring it up, who knows?

4. Store of tears of pearls and rubies I who hold, what need have I
Of the high-starred sun's resplendence, I with treasures such as those?

5. I, who, in a beggar's seeming, Am a king, upon the course
Of yon sphere, the losel-fost'rer, How should I my hopes repose?

6. Each narcissus drunk, each tulip Cup in hand is; I alone
Branded am for lewdness: Justice Who shall do me of my woes?

7. "In the rosetime be abstemious," Bidst thou me? Nay, first I'll go
Speak thereof with bowl and sweetheart, Counsel take with friends, not foes.

8. If it please the Friend that lovers In the fire of grief should burn,
He's a renegade a single Look on Kauther's fount who throws?

9. Pure and barren like the willow If I should become, my head
How should I uphold hereafter In the presence of the rose?

10. When the East the rosebud washeth With the dews of Heaven's grace,
Call me crookback, if a single Page I look at, verse or prose.

11. Though berayed I am with poortith, Shame upon my spirit be
If my skirt I wet with water, Such as from the Sun-fount flows! [1419]

12. Small reliance on the compact Of the heavens is to place;
To the flagon will I pledge me; With the winecup will I close.

13. Stay a moment, o my wanton City-troubler, [1420] till thy way
With the raining pearls and rubies Of my weeping eye o'erflows!

14. Though the usances of toping Ill my case beseem, therein
Since I've fall'n, henceforth why suffer Other thought to interpose?

15. Yesternight quoth they, "Her ruby Spendeth sugar;" but their speech,
Till within my mouth I taste it, How shall I for true suppose?

16. For a prayer-niche I the angle Of thy brows from fortune seek,
So therein upon Love's lesson, Morn and even, I may gloze.

17. How shall I, who have already Present Paradise in hand,
Trust in the to-morrow's blisses That the pietist foreshows?

18. Marvel not if I, Shah Mensour's Servant being, vaunt myself
Higher than the sun that yonder In the Orient heaven glows.

19. Yesternight thy lip of ruby Unto Hafiz gave fair words;
But I'm not the man to credit Idle fables such as those.

20. Hafiz, "I with God take refuge," Say, and think of otherwhat:
Nay, what madness is abstention In the season of the rose!

[1419] i. e. I will not lay myself under obligation for bounty to the rich and great.
[1420] To the Beloved.

CCCCXXXIX

1. Where's the tidings of thy coming, So that life I may forswear?
Heaven's bird I am and soaring, Will I leave this worldly snare.

2. By my love of thee I swear it, If thou call me but thy slave,
I will never crave the lordship Of the world of What-and-Where.

3. From the rain-cloud of Thy guidance, Lord, vouchsafe Thou me a shower,
Ere from off the scene of being, Like the dust, away I fare.

4. Lacking wine and minstrel, sit not On my grave; so from the dead
I may haply rise up, dancing, To thy fragrance, o my fair!

5. Old am I; yet to thy bosom If thou clasp me but anights,
In the dawn, from thine embracements I shall rise up young fore'er.

6. Up and show thy shape, o idol Of the sweet harmonious gait,
So desire of world and being, Hafiz like, I may forswear.

CCCCXL

1. At the hour when the exiles offer The prayer of evening,
With tears, on the strangers' fashion, My song of woes I sing.

2. So sore do I weep for mem'ry Of friends and fatherland
That forth of the world I've driven The use of travelling.

3. I am of the Loved One's country, Not of the strangers' lands:
Back to my friends, Protector, Prithee do Thou me bring!

4. Guide of the way, 'fore heaven, Aid me, so once again
Abroad in the street of the tavern My standard I may fling.

5. How of my eld shall reason Reckon aright, since now
Again with a youngling beauty I go a-wantoning?

6. Save only the East and the North wind, There's none conceiveth me;
For, saving the wind, no helpmate I have in anything.

7. The air of the Loved One's land is The water of life for me:
A waft from the dust of Shiraz Hither, o East wind, wing!

8. My tears have my hidden blemish Published to all. Of whom
Complaint shall I make? The traitor's My proper fosterling.

9. I've heard of the harp of Venus, That thus in the dawn it spake,
"The pupil am I of Hafiz, The sweet-voiced poet-king."

CCCCXLI

1. Though weak and broken-hearted, Grown old and gray am I,
When of thy face I mind me, Yet young and gay am I.

2. Thanks be to God, whatever Of Him I sought I had;
Possessed of all my wishes, Without gainsay, am I.

3. Ee'n as my friends could wish me, Winecup in .hand, upon
The throne of bliss abiding, In Luck's highway am I.

4. Good luck to thee, young rosebush! For that the nightingale
Become of the world's garden, Beneath thy spray, am I.

5. Erst of the world no knowledge I had; but, schooled of grief
For thee, become the expert Thou seest to-day, am I.

6. Since upon me there lighted Thine eyes' calamity,
Assured 'gainst Fortune's mischief And Time's affray am I.

7. Open the door of vision Is to my heart become,
Since on the Magians' threshold A dweller aye am I.

8. My fate unto the winehouse Consigned me for all time;
Howe'er to this inclining Or t'other way am I.

9. Not old by years and seasons I am: the faithless Friend,
Like life, hath passed me over And hence grown gray am I.

10. Last night God's grace bespoke me; Said, "Hafiz, fret no more;
"Thy warrant for forgiveness, Betide what may, am I."

CCCCXLII [1421]

1. What is all this perturbation In the Sphere I see?
In all quarters nought but trouble, Strife and fear I see.

2. Daughters all at war with mothers And contention are;
Sons to fathers all ill-wishers, Far and near, I see.

3. All a rosewater-and-sugar Sherbet is for fools;
But his liver's blood the sage's Only cheer I see.

4. Back all galled with pack and pannel Is the Arab steed;
On the ass-necks all the golden Collar-gear I see.

5. List to Hafiz' counsel, Khwajeh: [1422] Go and goodness do;
For than gems this counsel better And more dear I see.

[1421] Composed (according to Soudi) on the occasion of the invasion of Fars by
Timour.
[1422] "Khwajeh", common address to men of learning and gentlemen, answering to our
"Sir".

CCCCXLIII [1423]

1. On the marges of the meadows Come again's the rose's queen;
Be its coming to the cypress Blessèd and the jessamine!

2. Glad this session of a monarch In his proper place, since each
In his proper room henceforward Will be seated, high and mean.

3. To Jem's seal-ring the glad tidings Of the happy issue give,
How the hand of Satan shortened By the Most High Name hath been.

4. May this mansion, from whose doorway, Every breath, the Yemen breeze
Wafts the fragrance of God's mercy, Flourish evermore, serene! [1424]

5. Still the majesty and puissance Of the son of old Peshéng [1425]
Live in story; still folk fable Of his conquering falchion keen.

6. Lo, the blue mall-steed of heaven Tame beneath thy saddle's grown!
Strike a ball, o royal horseman, Since thou'rt come upon the green!

7. Irrigation for the kingdom Is the water [1426] of thy sword;
Do thou plant the tree of justice And uproot ill-willers clean.

8. Hence no wonder, for the fragrance Of thine excellence, it were
If the barren sands of Irej [1427] Should produce the musk of Chin. [1428]

9. For a goodly revelation The recluses look to thee;
Set thy cap apeak for joyance; Show thy cheek without the screen.

10. Counsel late I took with Reason; "Hafiz, drink!" quoth it. Give wine,
Skinker! for to the consulted Still hath heed behoving been.

11. Speak, o East wind, to the skinker Of the banquet of the king,
So that he a draught vouchsafe us From that goblet gold-beseen. [1429]

[1423] Said to have been composed on the occasion of Shah Mensour's victorious return to Shiraz, after defeating and expelling the usurping Turcomans.

[1424] The poet likens Shah Mensour, who was a man of learning, to Sheikh Uweis el Kerani. See note to Ode LXVI, 4, as to "Yemen breeze".

[1425] i. e. Efrasiyab, king of Touran.

[1426] *Syn.* lustre.

[1427] "Irej", a desert plain in Laristan.

[1428] China.

[1429] A hint at largesse

CCCCXLIV

1. Light of mine eye, a counsel I have; give ear to me:
Since full thy cup of bliss is, Drink and let drink with thee.

2. The old speak by experience; And this to thee I say;
Son, hearken to my counsel, So old thou too mayst be.

3. Love's hand upon the sober No chain doth lay: an thou
The loveling's tress wilt handle, Forswear sobriety.

4. Chaplet and patchcoat give not The joys of drunkenness;
For help in this transaction, Unto the vintner flee.

5. Substance and life are nothing, With friends compared: the Friend
With souls an hundred ransom, Who heark'neth to thy plea.

6. Since Ahriman's [1430] suggestions Are many in Love's way,
Look, to the angel's message Alone the ear lend ye.

7. Kernel and leaf are rotted And means of mirth are none;
O drum, lament! And clamour, O harp and psaltery!

8. O skinker (never empty Thy cup be of sheer wine!)
Cast thou an eye of favour On goblet-draining me!

9. When in thy gold-wrought tunic Thou passest, warm with wine,
One kiss on wool-clad Hafiz Bestow thou in thy glee.

[1430] i. e. Satan.

CCCCXLV

1. Yon slender, cypress-statured, Coquettish, tricksy fair of mine
The tale in short hath sundered Of this long patch coat-wear of mine.

2. Eld, piety and learning Despite, thou sawest, o my heart,
What wrack with me hath wroughten This wanton eye unware of mine!

3. Because of the eyes' water, I'm seated on the fire of shame;
For it in every quarter This secret hath laid bare of mine.

4. "Beneath dissembling's cassock," Quoth I, "I'll hide the trace of love:"
But tears, the tell-tale playing, That screen in sunder tare of mine.

5. That tipsy fair rememb'reth Her not of friends; but thou for good
Be still remembered, skinker, That solacest this care of mine!

6. I my religion's ruin Fear; for the prayer-niche of thy brows
The peace of mind off-beareth, That's needful for this prayer of mine.

7. Myself o'er, like the candle, I laugh and weep: I wonder what
With thee my meek consuming Will do, o stone-heart fair of mine?

8. Thine image still on water Of tears I limn: how long before
Reality replaceth this phantom of the air of mine?

9. When will, o Lord, I wonder, That East Wind blow, by means whereof,
The fragrance of her favour Will order this affair of mine?

10. Since from thy prayers, o zealot, No gain to thee ensuing is,
Better this nightly toping And heat and yearning share of mine!

11. Hafiz for woe consumeth: His case, o breezes of the East,
To yonder king, friend-fost'ring And foe-destroying, bear of mine!

CCCCXLVI

1. My grief howsoever I tell to the leaches,
Impuissant to solace The exiled one each is.

2. O Lord, be the rival's desire unaccomplished!
Alack, in the seal of Love's casket a breach is!

3. Be ever ashamed in the nightingale's presence
That rose which each moment within a thorn's reach is! [1431]

4. Let lovers' eyes look on the face of the Loved Ones
Once more, of thy grace, Lord, a lover beseeches!

5. Our secret of suff'rance we've told to the Loved One;
For pain it behoveth not hide from the leaches. [1432]

6. O thou that art bounteous to all, at thy table
How long shall we be of the portionless wretches?

7. He had not become the world's madman, if hearkened
Had Hafiz the sages' admonishing speeches.

[1431] i. e. the fair one who bestoweth her favours on the base.
[1432] Rhyme-word of line 1 repeated.

CCCCXLVII

1. O thou whose moon-bright cheek's The fresh Spring's face of beauty,
Whose mole's the centre-point And pivot-place of beauty;

2. Hid in whose languorous eye's The amulet of magic,
In whose unresting tress The rest we trace of beauty;

3. No cypress like thy shape By grace's river springeth;
No moon like thee e'er lit The zodiac-space of beauty.

4. Thy loveliness the age Of charmership hath gladdened,
And blessed are the days Grown, by thy grace, of beauty.

5. For thy tress-snare and bait Of mole, in all the world is
No heart-bird but's become The prey of chase of beauty.

6. The violets [1433] around Thy lip are fresh; for water
Of life they drink at that The fount and base of beauty.

7. Nurse Nature tenderly, With all her heart and spirit,
Hath ever fostered thee In the embrace of beauty.

8. Hafiz hath hope renounced Of looking on thine equal;
There's none except thyself Left of the race of beauty.

[1433] The dark down likened to violets.

CCCCXLVIII

1. Spring and the rose repentance Have slain and raised up glee;
Grief's root, with the rose's gladness, Pluck from the heart of thee.

2. The zephyr is come and the rosebud Is grown beside herself;
Nay, see how, for love and longing, The shirt on her rent hath she. [1434]

3. The usance of truth and frankness From pure-hearted water learn
And seek from the meadow-cypress Upright to become and free.

4. The new-bedecked bride of the rosebud, With that her goodly smile,
Doth heart and religion ravish From all in the world that be.

5. The wail of the frenzied bulbul And moan of the Thousand Tales,
Because of the rose's beauty, Are heard from the cypress-tree.

6. Nay, see, for the East wind's ravage, The elf-locks about the rose;
The curl on the face of the jasmine [1435] Of hyacinth-ringlets see!

7. The tale of Time's case, o Hafiz, Go seek from the cup of wine,
Ensuing the minstrel's dictate And Elder expert's decree.

[1434] i. e. she hath broken out into bloom.
[1435] i. e. the Beloved's face.—*Soudi*

CCCCXLIX

1. Rose-like, my wede, whene'er I smell thy scent,
I rend in twain for love and languishment.

2. The rose, sure, saw thy body in the meads,
That, drunkard-like, her raiment she hath rent.

3. Life from the grief of thee uneath I saved;
But thou bor'st off my heart incontinent.

4. At the Foes' bidding, from the Friend thou'st turned;
With foes 'gainst friends behoveth not consent.

5. Cause not the sigh heart-burning from my breast
Forth of the window, smoke-like, find a vent.

6. Thy body in thy wede's like wine in cup,
Thy heart in breast like steel in silver pent.

7. O candle, cloud-like, from thine eyes rain tears;
Thy burning heart's to all grown evident.

8. Break not my heart nor cast it under foot;
For in thy tress-tip hath it pitched its tent.

9. Since Hafiz to thy tress hath bound his heart,
Use not its good [1436] with this disparagement.

[1436] i. e. thy tress's property, my heart.

CCCCL

1. When myself I make her way-dust, She her skirt shakes quite from me,
And if "Turn thy heart" I bid her, Turns away her sight from me.

2. Unto all creation, rose-like, She her rose-hued cheek displays,
And if "Cover it" I bid her, Covers it forthright from me.

3. If I, candle-like, before her Die, she laugheth like the morn;
If I'm vexed, her heart so tender Turneth in despite from me.

4. To mine eye quoth I, "At least, now, Look for once thy fill on her."
"Nay, a stream of blood," it answered, "Wouldst thou have take flight from me?"

5. Marry, she my blood desireth, I her lip: shall I my wish
Win of her or will she, ruthless, Take revenge's right from me?

6. Comrades, for her mouth I'm willing Life and soul to give: behold,
Her consent how she withholdeth, For a thing so slight, [1437] from me!

7. Though in bitterness, Ferhád-like, Up the ghost I give, forsooth,
Many a sweet [1438] and piteous story Will abide, poor wight, from me.

8. Hafiz, make an end! Love's lesson On this fashion an thou read,
Love in every nook and corner Parables will cite from me.

[1437] i. e. a thing so minute as her mouth.
[1438] *Shirin*, p. g. with Ferhad.

CCCCLI

1. For heaven's sake, with patchcoat-wearers sit not;
Thy cheek, from hapless topers cover it not.

2. There's many a stain of fraud upon the patch coat:
Fair fall the topers' wede, Where stains have lit not!

3. Thou'rt dainty-natured and for thee the fash'ries
Of yonder crew of patchcoateers befit not.

4. Ne'er saw I aught of pain in yonder Soufis: [1439]
Long live the dreg-drainers, Whom Love's pains quit not

5. See how the flagon bleeds and the lyre clamours
At yonder hypocrites, who wine admit not!

6. Since thou hast made me drunken, sit not sober;
Poison for nectar to my lips commit not.

7. The wine's a-work with wish for thee: to open
Wine-coloured lips and tipsy eyes omit not.

8. Hafiz a heart hath like a seething cauldron; Look that its fire consume thee every whit
not.

[1439] i. e. they are feeling-less hypocrites.—*Soudi.*

CCCCLII

1. Than the thought of wine and winecup Sweeter and more fair, what shall be?
Would I knew, for end and issue Of the whole affair, what shall be?

2 Fret thou not the heart with sorrow, Till the days of ease forsake thee:
Heart and life once gone and wasted, Left thee, save despair, what shall be?

3. Wine, not sorrow, quaff nor hearken To the imitators' [1440] counsel;
To the babble of the vulgar Given heed soe'er what shall be?

4. To the bird without endurance, "Eat thy grief," [1441] say; for upon it,
Trow, the mercy of the fowler, Him who set the snare, what shall be?

5. Better were thy whole endeavour To thy heart's desire directed:
Of the undesired, in th'issue, Well art thou aware what shall be. [1442]

6. Yesternight, the Magian Elder A dark saying quoted, graven
On the cup, to wit, "The issue, Look thou have a care, what shall be." [1443]

7. From the Path I've drawn, with tabret Harp and song, the heart of Hafiz:
What, I wonder, my requital, Here or otherwhere, what shall be?

[1440] i. e. the *servum pecus*, who cannot think for themselves, but follow after others, sheep-like.
[1441] i. e. *Scoticé*, "Dree thy weird".
[1442] i. e. Endeavour after thy desire; for what thou desirest not (such as death and calamity) will, as well thou wottest, come anyhow.
[1443] i. e. Aspice finem.

CCCCLIII

1. Know'st thou what happiness is? The face of the Friend to see,
The beggar's estate in her street To choose before royalty.

2. The hope it is easy, forsooth, To sever from being and life;
But oh! from the friend of the soul None severeth easily.

3. Strait-hearted, like roses in bud, I'll go to the garden, and there
My garment of goodly repute I'll rend, like the rose on the lea.

4. Anon, to the rose, like the breeze, Hid secrets I'll tell; and anon,
In loveliking's mysteries rare The bulbuls shall lesson me.

5. Nay, let not the season from hand Of kissing the lip of the Friend,
Lest weary of biting the hand And the lip, [1444] in the issue, thou be.

6. Gain reckon the converse of friends; For, once from this two-gated house
We're parted, with comrades no more For ever foregather can we.

7. 'Twould seem as if Hafiz's thought The mind of Shah Mensour had 'scaped:
The case of the dervish recall, O Lord, to his memory! [1445]

[1444] i. e. in token of regret and repentance for the missed opportunity.
[1445] A hint at largesse.

CCCCLIV

1. Come in at our door and illumine Our darkling cell with thy light
And perfume, to boot, with thy fragrance The banqueting-place of the spright.

2. To eyebrow and eye of the Loved One I've given my heart and my soul:
Come, come, on the arch and the window [1446] We'll gaze it our fill to-night.

3. To Paradise, breeze of the Gardens Of Heav'n, of our banquet's dust
Go bear and withal for a perfume The censers of Eden dight.

4. The light of thy lovely aspect's The veil of the eye of the wit:
Arise and the sun's pavilion Illume with thy beauty bright.

5. The stars of the night of sev'rance No radiance shed: come forth
To the roof of thy house and kindle The lamp of thy moon-face white.

6. Since under the hand of thy beauty The brides of the meadows [1447] are,
Well, well mayst thou mock at the jasmine And scoff at the pinetree's height.

7. Cupbearer, pride and o'erweening Make much superfluous prate;
Nay, give not from hand thine office, But fill up the bowl forthright. [1448]

8. No business of ours to hope for The cash of thine union is:
A draft on that lip of sugar Come draw me, to pay at sight.

9. The lip of the cup kiss, skinker, And syne to the topers pass
And so with this subtlety perfume The palate of sense and spright.

10. An if the scribe lesson thee, saying, "Go, play not the amorist!"
The man with a cup of the grapejuice To moisten his brain invite.

11. By right of those goodly graces And parts that in thee do meet,
Uplift thou the head, like the candle, In all the companions' sight.

12. I'm weary of cowl and patchcoat: One Soufi-destroying glance
Come give me and Love's Calénder [1449] Make me and acolyte.

13. After the practice of pleasure And love of the moon-faced fair,
By heart, next, the verse of Hafiz Behoveth thee get and cite.

[1446] Eye likened to (round) window set in semi-circular arch (the eyebrow).
[1447] i. e. The flowers.
[1448] He bids the cupbearer leave conceit and prate and attend to her business.
[1449] i. e. Devotee

CCCCLV

1. Quaff the red wine and the face Of the moon-browed fair behold:
Their beauty, despite the cant Of the shavelings [1450] there, behold.

2. Under the patchcoat pied Nooses they [1450] hide: the length
Of hand of yon canting crew, Short sleevelets that wear, [1450] behold.

3. These (Lovers) the head bow not To the harvest of either world:
The pride of this starveling folk, These mendicants bare, behold.

4. The Friend from her brow the frown Undoth not, whate'er they do:
The lovelings' disdain and the stress Of the lovers' despair behold.

5. Of none nowadays I hear That keepeth the pact of love;
The falseness of mates and friends To oaths that they swear behold.

6. By being the captive of Love, I'm freed from the bonds of the world;
The foreseeing mind of folk, For the issues that care, behold.

7. Love's burnisher borne hath the rust From Hafiz's mirror-like heart;
Their brightness of heart, in Love's way Who faithfully fare, behold.

[1450] i. e. the members of the religious orders, such as Calenders, Dervishes, Soufis etc.

CCCCLVI

1. Hear from me a trait heart-luring, "Yonder moon-cheek's mole regard;
"In the chain of that her ringlet Bounden, wit and soul regard."

2. Lo, my heart I chid, "Wild-beast like," [1451] Saying, "Be not;" but quoth it,
"Yonder fawn's [1452] eye, that half-drunken Wanton rantipole regard."

3. In the circlet of her tresses Is the East Wind's pleasance-place;
Lovers' hearts by hundreds bounden To each hairlet's scroll regard.

4. Marry, they the sun who worship Nothing of our charmer know;
Prithee, not the sun's face, censor, But her cheek for goal regard.

5. Her heart-stealing tress the halter Layeth on the East Wind's neck;
How this blackamoor [1453] wayfaring Lovers doth cajole, regard.

6. She, in quest of whom I've wandered From myself, the like of her
None hath seen nor will, though wander He from pole to pole, regard.

7. If upon her eyebrows' prayer-niche Hafiz rub his face, 'tis right:
Nay, her eyebrow, an thou blame him For his lover's dole, regard.

8. Heav'n, thy countenance avert not from the wish of Shah Mensóur;
His sword's sharpness and the puissance Of his arm and soul regard.

[1451] i. e. be not mad nor wander in the deserts, like a wild animal.
[1452] Beloved styled "fawn" p. g. with "wild-beast like".
[1453] i. e. the black tress.

CCCCLVII

1. That princess of box-tree shaped ones, She, the sweet-lipped charmers' queen
Who the hearts of all the champions Pierceth with her eyelash keen,

2. Drunken, passed and on me, dervish, Cast a glance and said, "O thou
"Eye and lamp of all sweet-spoken Ones that are or aye have been,

3. "Void how long of gold and silver Will thy purse be? Be my slave
"And from all the silver-bodied Fruit of love and union glean.

4. "Less thou art not than the sun-mote. Courage! unto love apply,
"So thou mayest, mote-like dancing, Reach the inmost sun's demesne.

5. "On the world have no reliance; Nay, if wine thou have in cup,
"Drink unto the Venus-browed ones, With the breasts of silver sheen."

6. Quoth our measure-draining elder, (Fair befall his pious soul!)
"Commerce not with compact-breakers, An thou look to sit serene."

7. To the East wind, in the dawning, Quoth I, in the tulip-mead,
"Whose are all these martyrs standing, Bloody-shrouded, in the green?" [1454]

8. "Talk of ruby wine," it answered, "Hafiz, and of silver chins;
"Knowledge of this myst'ry given Nor to thee nor me hath been.

9. "To the skirt of the Beloved Cleave and sunder from the foe:
"Be God's liegeman and in safety Pass from Satan the unclean."

[1454] Red tulips likened to martyrs in bloody shrouds.

CCCCLVIII

1. Hide with the musky spikenard The rose-leaf; that's to say,
Cover thy cheek and ruthless, The world in ruins lay.

2. Sweat from thy face come scatter And fill with rosewater
The meads, as full the vials Are of our eyes to-day.

3. Thy drunken drows'd narcissi Open with languorous grace
And cause the field narcissus For envy swoon away.

4. The season of the roses, Like life, is swift of flight:
The rose-hued wine come circle, Skinker; make no delay.

5. The vi'lets smell and handle The tresses of the fair;
Look on the tulip's colour; Drink wine, friend, and be gay.

6. Thine eyes ope, like the bubbles, Upon the goblet's face
And this our life's endurance By that of bubbles weigh.

7. O fair, since lover-slaying Thy native usance is,
Drain thou with foes the goblet And chide with us alway.

8. Lo, Hafiz seeketh union By dint of prayer. O Lord,
Hear Thou the broken-hearted And answer when they pray.

CCCCLIX

1. Skinker, 'tis morning! Quick, fill up the goblet with wine!
The sphere's revolution Ne'er resteth; so haste thee, soul mine.

2. Or ever all ruined Becometh this perishing world,
Come, make thou us drunk with The rose-coloured juice of the vine!

3. The wine-sun uprising Hath made from the East of the bowl;
If life and its pleasance Thou seekest, come, slumber resign!

4. The day when the heavens Make gugglets and cups of our clay,
The bowl of our noddle Brim thou with this liquor divine.

5. No folk of austereness And cant and renouncement are we;
Nay, speak thou with us, an Thou wilt, of the cup of sheer wine.

6. Wine-worshipping, Hafiz, The way of true righteousness is.
Arise, to devotion Address thou the face of design!

CCCCLX

1. When to a sick one's bed thou com'st, Say thou a prayer above his head;
Open thy lips, for very life Their ruby giveth to the dead.

2. Bid her, who came to visit us And said the Fátiheh and went,
Tarry a moment, so my soul May on her track of me be sped.

3. Leach of the sick, upon my tongue Look, for my bosom's fume and smoke,
From the oppression of my heart, Lay thereupon a load of lead.

4. Though hotter than the sun my bones Hath fever made and gone away,
Yet from my bones the fire of love, Unlike the fever, ne'er hath fled.

5. E'en as thy mole my heart's case is; Still on the fire [1455] doth it abide;
Hence is my body, like thine eye, Languid and sick for drearihead.

6. Feel thou my pulse, if happily Token or sign of life it give,
And with the water of the eyes Quench thou my heat, of fever bred.

7. He, who the vial unto me Whilere for pleasance wont to give,
Why with my vial, every tide, Presently leachward doth he tread? [1456]

8. A draught of the water, lo! of life Hafiz, thy verse hath given me;
Leave the physician; come, recite This my prescription aforesaid.

[1455] Beloved's glowing cheek likened to fire.
[1456] i. e. why is the skinker constantly occupied in carrying my water to the physician
　　　for inspection, instead of plying me with wine as of yore?

CCCCLXI

1. Tis I am the city byword For wantoning; I am he
Who hath not his eye polluted With rancour and jealousy.

2. We practise fair faith and suffer Reproach and are content;
To vex and be vexed, in our canon, Is infidelity.

3. I asked of the Tavern-Elder The way of deliverance;
He called for the cup and answered, "Concealment of mystery."

4. What is it we crave in viewing The pleasance-place of the world?
It is with the iris [1457] roses To cull from that cheek of thee.

5. By worship of wine, on water The image of self I cast;
So shattered mayhap the image Of worship of self may be.

6. My trust in thy tress-tip's mercy I place; for, except therefrom
Attraction betide, what profit In striving is there for me?

7. The down of the Friend may lesson Thee love for the lovesome cheek;
The face of the fair 'tis pleasant To compass about at gree. [1458]

8. The rein from this congregation [1459] We'll turn to the winehouse-ward;
The preachment of those who practise Alone do we hearken, we.

9. Nay, kiss but the lip of the Loved One, Hafiz, and that of the cup;
The hand of austerity-sellers [1460] To kiss is impiety.

[1457] " Iris" of the eye.
[1458] As doth the down.
[1459] i. e. that of the hypocritical pietists.
[1460] "Marchands d'austérité", those who make a boast and traffic of devotion and claim
　　　to have their hands kissed as saints.

CCCCLXII

1. To the toper crew some favour Prithee show, more worth than this is;
By the winehouse door some manner Passage go, more worth than this is.

2. Well and good are all these favours That thy lip on us doth lavish;
But to us behoveth somewhat That heigho! more worth than this is.

3. Say to her whose thought the tangles From the world's need all resolveth,
"On this point a look, 'fore heaven, Deign to throw, more worth than this is."

4. How I can my heart but render Unto yonder precious youngling?
Mother Time a child hath never Borne, I trow, more worth than this is.

5. Quoth th' admonisher, "What merit, Say, hath love, save only sorrow?"
"Doctor sage," quoth I, "a merit Dost thou know more worth than this is?"

6. When the skinker's lip I bid thee Kiss and take the winecup, hearken,
Soul, for nought that any speaketh, High or low, more worth than this is.

7. Hafiz' reed [1461] a sweet-fruit plant is: Pluck and feed withal thy spirit,
For in this world's garden never Fruit did grow more worth than this is.

[1461] i. e. pen.

CCCCLXIII

1. Consumed am I for sev'rance: From cruelty thy face turn thou:
From us estrangement-stricken, O Lord, this sore misgrace turn Thou.

2. The moon in heav'n paradeth On the blue stallion of the Sphere;
Unto thy dapple courser, Her vaunting to abase, turn thou.

3. Men's wit and faith to ravish, Strut, fuddled, forth with cap a-peak,
And on thy breast the tunic Withinside out, for grace, turn thou.

4. Shake out thy curls, the spikenard To spite; East Wind like, round the meads,
With censer fragrance breathing About thine every trace, turn thou.

5. Light of the topers' eyesight, In expectation sore am I:
With wailing harp and beaker, About the banquet-place turn thou.

6. When on her cheek Time writeth A goodly line, to wit, the down,
Lord, from our Friend the writing Of ill and sorry case turn Thou.

7. This that thou suff'rest, Hafiz, From fair-faced maids was all forewrit:
An thou repine, Heav'n's canons And Fate's foreordered pace turn thou.

CCCCLXIV

1. With a languishing look, the whole fabric Of sorcery shatter thou;
With an ogle, the bright reputation Of Sámiri [1462] shatter thou.

2. To the winds give the heads and the turbans Of all the world's peoples; to wit,
Thy cap-corner, after the usance Of coquetry, shatter thou. [1463]

3. The usance of pride and oppression Bid, bid thou thy tress renounce;
And say to thy glance, "The army Of cruelty shatter thou."

4. Come forth and from all the creation The ball bear of beauty away;
Give Houris their meed and the splendour Of Faërie shatter thou.

5. Yea, let the gazelle of thy glances The lion enthrall of the sun;
With thine eyebrows the bow of the archer Of Múshteri [1464] shatter thou.

6. When pérfume-exhaling the spikenards Become for the breath of the breeze,
With the tip of thine ambergris tresses Their empery shatter thou.

7. Herself when the nightingale boasteth, O Hafiz, of eloquence,
With dulcet court-speech, her pretensions To vie with thee shatter thou.

[1462] The Samaritan rival, before mentioned, of Moses in thaumaturgy.
[1463] "To shatter the cap-corner" is (id.) to set it apeak.
[1464] Here = the zodiacal sign Sagittarius.—Soudi.

CCCCLXV

1. The bird of my heart is a holy bird; The Empyréan's its native nest;
Sick of the body's cage it is, Weary of life and world-opprest.

2. When from the dustheap of this our world The bird of the spirit taketh wing,
The topmost court of the heavens nine It maketh again its place of rest.

3. Yea, when the bird of the heart doth soar, Its roost is the Lote-tree of Paradise;
The perch of our royal falcon is The Empyréan's pinnacle-crest.

4. Lo, if our Huma its wings unfold And spread its pinions above the world,
The shadow of full felicity On all folk falleth from East to West.

5. No place for it in the two worlds is, Save only above the firmament;
Its body is from the mine [of souls], [1465] Its soul from the heaven of God's behest.

6. In the highest world of the worlds above It hath its manifestation-stead;
As for its pasturing-place, it is The rosemeads of Paradise the blest.

7. Of Unity since thou vauntest thee, Hafiz, distraught for ecstasy,
Let on the tablet of men and Jinn The pen of Unity be imprest! [1466]

[1465] Soudi.
[1466] i. e. since Thou vauntest thee of being one with the Beloved, do thou cancel from
thy mind the thought of men and Jinn and of whatsoever is not the Beloved.

CCCCLXVI

1. Yonder musk-deer, [1467] of Thy favour, Lord, unto Khutén [1468] bring back;
Yonder cypress to the meadow, Where it stood erewhen, bring back.

2. Prithee, this my faded fortune With a favouring breeze revive;
Gone my soul [1467] is: to the body That its denizen bring back.

3. Since by Thy behest, their stations Do the sun and moon attain,
Unto me, too, my Beloved, Her, my moon of men, bring back.

4. In the quest of that Yemáni Ruby, blood our eye's become;
Lord, that shining constellation, Prithee, to Yemén bring back.

5. This our word was to the Loved One, "Life without thee crave we not:"
Prithee, messenger, this saying To her mind and ken bring back.

6. Prithee, go, o happy-footed Blessed bird; [1469] unto the thought
Of the Anca [1467] this the utt'rance Of the kite and wren [1470] bring back.

7. Her, her dwelling who aforetime Had in Hafiz' eye, o Lord,
To his heart's desire, from exile Hither home again bring back. [1471]

[1467] i. e. the Beloved.
[1468] i. e. her own country, Khuten (in Chinese Tartary) being the home of the musk-
deer.
[1469] To the messenger.
[1470] "Kite and wren", abject lovers.
[1471] The poet's mistress had gone on a journey and he in this ode offers up prayers for
her safe return.

CCCCLXVII

1. In Bedékshan if the ruby From the rocky slate forth cometh,
So the water of the Rukna, [1472] Sugarlike, the "Strait" [1473] forth cometh.

2. Here, within the town of Shiraz, Look thou where thou wilt, a charmer,
Lovesome, tricksy and coquettish, From each house's gate forth cometh.

3. From the mansions of the Cadi, Of the Mohtesib, the Mufti
And the Elder, wine rose-coloured, Unsophisticate, forth cometh.

4. In the pulpit, at the season Of his feigned ecstatic transport,
Bang [1474] from out the very preacher's Loosened turban-plait forth cometh.

5. In the gardens, by the minstrel's Voice and harping stirred, the warble
Of the nightingales, both early Morn and even late, forth cometh.

6. In a city such as this is, Hafiz from his house, for sev'rance
From the Friend and grief of absence, Thus disconsolate forth cometh.

[1472] "Rukna" or Ruknabad, the well-known stream near Shiraz.
[1473] *Teng*, name of place of issue of the Ruknabad; syn. sugar-mould, bale, load, hence
the similitude.
[1474] "Bang", the well known narcotic preparation of Indian hemp.

CCCCLXVIII

1. King, the robes of kingship truly Fit that shape and height of thine,
Crown and seal-ring have adornment From that lofty spright of thine.

2. From the royal cap, each moment Is the sun of victory
Into rising up attracted By that cheek moon-bright of thine.

3. Though the sun of heav'n the lantern And the eye is of the world,
From the dust his sheen he draweth That those feet excite of thine.

4. There the Bird of Fortune showeth, Where its Huma-shade doth cast
Yonder canopy, whose summit Doth the heavens smite, of thine.

5. Spite a thousand contradictions In philosophy and law,
Never point did 'scape the scanning Of that sapient sight of thine.

6. Life's true water still distilleth, From its beak of eloquence,
Yonder sugar-chewing parrot (Else the reed-pen hight) of thine.

7. What Sikender sought and Fortune Gave him not was but a draught
Of fresh water from that goblet Of the soul's delight of thine.

8. No one needeth his requirement In thy presence to expound;
For none's secret hid abideth From that eye of light of thine.

9. Hafiz, in old age, o monarch, Youngling-fashion doth, in hope
Of that clemency life-giving, Pardoning unright, of thine.

CCCCLXIX

1. Thou whose way-dust is the bloodwit Of the musk of Chin,
In the shadow of whose cap-rim Reared the sun hath been;

2. Overproud is the narcissus: With thy graceful gait,
(Be the soul thy black eye's ransom!) Come confound the quean

3. Drink my blood; for never angel Aught 'gainst one so fair
In his heart of hearts could find it To record for sin.

4. Thou'rt the cause of the folk's easance And the world's repose:
Hence thy couching-place the nook is Of men's hearts and e'en.

5. All night long I wake and wailing, Chide with every star
In the heavens, of my yearning For thy moon-cheek's sheen.

6. Comrades all from comrades parted Are; but parted we
From thy threshold, Fortune's refuge, Never will be seen.

7. Hafiz, of God's grace despair not: Sure, in fine, the fire
Of thy sighing will the harvest Kindle of chagrin.

CCCCLXX

1. O thou, of whose bright beauty The sun's the mirrorer,
Unto whose mole the musk-pod Itself is thurifer;

2. In vain with tears mine eye-stead I wash; in this waste nook
There's nought to tempt thine image To light and settle here.

3. This sable point, [1475] the centre Of light that is become,
Is but thy mole reflected In vision's theatre.

4. Where's tidings of the coming Of thine enjoyment's Feast,
That, reconciled with Fortune, I may wish joy to her? [1476]

5. From thy new-moon-like eyebrow Where is a favouring glance,
That we may make the heavens Our bondmen, ring in ear?

6. Thou art, o sun of beauty, In all delight and ease:
Until the Resurrection Thy setting God defer!

7. In that her tress's tangle, Poor heart, how farest thou?
Thy case to be sore troubled The East Wind doth aver.

8. Than this thy form a picture More lovesome never limned
The Scribe [1477] who drew thine eyebrow's Musk-tinctured character.

9. The rose-scent riseth: enter By reconcilement's door,
O thou, whose cheek fair-omened's Our Springtide of the year!

10. Whether of mine oppressions, My need and thine ill-will,
Unto the Vizier's hearing, Alack! shall I prefer?

11. The head of many a champion Is, Hafiz, in this springe: [1478]
Thy thought from vain emprises, Beyond thy reach, deter.

[1475] "Sable point", i. e. pupil of eye.
[1476] As people do to one another on the appearance of the new moon of Shewwal,
  indicating the end of the Fast of Ramazan.
[1477] "Scribe", i. e. the Creator.
[1478] "Springe"; i. e. of the love of her.

CCCCLXXI

1. By the life of the Winehouse Elder And due of his grace, I swear,
That, saving the thought of his service, No wish in my head I wear.

2. Though Paradise no abode be For sinners like us, bring wine;
I trust to the mercy of Heaven The issue of my affair.

3. Bright, bright be the lamp of the levin, That flashed from yon cloud and set
To the harvest of our existence The fire of the love of the fair!

4. Bring wine, for the angels brought me, Last night, from the Spirit-world,
Glad news, that His mercy raineth On all men everywhere.

5. If thou on the sill of the tavern A head spy, with the foot
Spurn thou it not; for no one Of His intent is ware: [1479]

6. Neither the eye of contemning Cast upon drunken me;
For piety nor transgression Without His will was e'er.

7. My heart to repentance tendeth Nor abstinence; but, for the sake
Of the glory and name of the Vizier, I'll strive my best to forbear.

8. O heart, of the limitless favour Despair thou not of the Friend, [1480]
For lo! in His boundless bounties All things created share.

9. In pawn for the grape-juice ever Is Hafiz's gaberdine;
'Twould seem of the dust of the tavern As if his moulding were.

[1479] i. e. none knoweth whether toping is or not sin in God's sight.
[1480] By "the Friend" God appears, for once, to be meant.

CCCCLXXII

1. Those browlocks of thine, musk-scattering, Cause curl for envy the violet;
That smile heart-luring of thine in twain Rendeth the rosebud's coverlet.

2. Thou, o my rose of the dulcet breath, Prithee, consume not thy nightingale: [1481]
For heav'n all nightly, for thee, anights, With supplication he doth beset.

3. Note but the puissance of love for thee: See, of his pride and glorying,
How this thy mendicant maketh mock E'en of the Sultan's coronet.

4. I who was wont whilom to wax Tired of the very angels' speech,
Now, for thy sake, the whole world's prate, See, I endure without regret.

5. Love of thy cheek on my head is writ; The dust of thy door's my Paradise,
My ease thy pleasure: the love of thee, Indeed, did Nature in me beget.

6. Though ill the patchcoat and piety Sit with the winecup, these fashions both
At once I practise, so only thou With thine approval do me abet.

7. The patchcoat pied of the beggar of Love Hath treasures hid in the sleeve of it;
To lordship, yea, and to Sultanhood Eftsoon attaineth thine anchoret.

8. The place of honour of this mine eye The couching-stead of thine image is;
The place of orison 'tis, and ne'er, Without thy presence, the seat be set!

9. Scarce hath my passion-beladen head The dust of thy palace-door become
Ere, that same moment, love's mysteries And wine's bemusement it doth forget.

10. A goodly meadow thy cheek is; more By token Hafiz the silver-tongued
The bird of thy praise became, what while In their Spring season thy charms were yet.
    [1482]

[1481] "Nightingale", i. e. lover.
[1482] cf. "Ronsard m'a celebrée du temps que j'étais belle".

CCCCLXXIII

1. The down of the Beloved, Before whose cheek the moon doth pale,
Is e'en a fair enclosure; But way of issue thence doth fail.

2. The eyebrow of the Loved One The peak of Fortune's prayer-niche is;
Upon it rub thy forehead And unto her thy need bewail.

3. O toper of Jem's conclave, Keep pure thine inward; for the cup
World-showing is a mirror, Hail to it for a mirror, hail!

4. The cloister-dwellers' dealings Have made me a wine-worshipper;
See how their smoke hath rendered My book of record black with bale!

5. Say to the Fiend of Sorrow, "Go, do thy worst; for refuge I
"Have taken with the vintner, Where proof I am 'gainst thine assail."

6. The lamp of wine, o skinker, Set in the pathway of the sun;
Bid him withal enkindle The cresset of the morning gale.

7. Somewhat of liquor sprinkle Upon the daybook of our deeds;
Belike therefrom the record Of sin to blot it may avail.

8. This thought the city-beggar Nurseth,—that one day will the king
Mayhap of him be mindful,—Out on it for an idle tale!

9. Hafiz, who all in order Hath for the lovers' banquet set,
God grant these pleasance-places May never of his presence fail!

CCCCLXXIV

1. The rosebush of pleasance blossomed is: Where is the rose-cheeked skinker, where?
The wind of the Springtide breatheth soft; Where is the vinejuice sooth and rare?

2. Each new-blown rosebud a rose-cheeked maid Bringeth to mind; but where, alack!
Where is the counsel-heark'ning ear, Where is the eye attent and ware?

3. Lo, in the banquet-halls of life Lacketh the perfume of desire:
Breath of the fragrant break of morn, Where is the musk of the Loved One's hair?

4. Wind of the East, I cannot brook The rose's vaunting of loveliness:
My hands in my own heart's blood I wash: For God's sake, tell me, where is the fair?

5. The candle of dawn, on idle wise, Boasteth itself of thy cheek's rose-hue:
Long is the tongue of the foe become: Where are the scissors, it to pare?

6. "Belike," she said, "thou desirest not A kiss of my ruby lip?" "Indeed,
"I die," quoth I, "of that wish; but where For me is the power and the will to dare?"

7. Albe in speechcraft the treasurer Of wisdom's treasury Hafiz is,
Yet who, for the cark of the evil time, His words would waste on the empty air?

CCCCLXXV

1. I have an eye, that all a-bleed Is for a bow, that brow of hers;
Her eyes with trouble fill the world, And evenso that brow of hers.

2. I am the slave of that Turk's eye, Whose face, when flushed with drunken sleep,
Is a fair rose-bed and a bower, Whence musk doth flow, that brow of hers.

3. New-moon-like lean am I become For fear that, with her musky scroll [1483]
In view, no moon from heaven's height Will dare to show that brow of hers.

4. She, Kafir-heart, she donneth not The tress's face-veil and I fear
Lest, with its heart-alluring curve, My prayer-niche grow that brow of hers. [1484]

5. Her forehead, to the hermits' mind, A wonder-goodly rosebed is,
About whose swarded margents to Doth wind and fro that brow of hers.

6. Still be the bow of beauty bent For her intoxicated eye,
Which launcheth arrows at the moon From out its bow, [1485] that brow of hers!

7. Heedless the spies are and to us From eyes and forehead, every breath,
Come thousand tokens; whilst between Doth usher go that brow of hers.

8. In face of beauty such as hers, None saith, "The Houris eyes like this
"Can boast" or "Peris eyebrows such As that can show, that brow others."

9. A wary bird though Hafiz is In loveliking, yet prey of him
That loveling's eye hath made with shafts Launched from its bow, that brow of hers.
     [1486]

[1483] Eyebrow-curve likened to scroll of ornamental writing.
[1484] i. e. Lest her eyebrow seduce me from Islam to Kafirdom, i. e. infidelity,
[1485] Rhyme-word of 1. 1 repeated.
[1486] Ditto.

CCCCLXXVI

1. News of the absent Friend, Courier of lovers true, say thou;
Unto the bulbul the case Of the rose, that is lost to view, say thou.

2. Fear not; initiates Of Love's high places, in sooth, are we:
Speech of familiar friends Friends and familiars to say thou.

3. Letters to me, poor wretch, From yonder worshipful one recite;
Th' utt'rance of yonder queen To me, the beggar, anew say thou.

4. When from her browlock's snare Hearts in dust strewed she, what our heart's
Exile for love befell, Since that we bade it adieu, say thou.

5. If by her blesséd door Once more vouchsafed thee it be to pass,
After the prayer for her weal And payment of service due, say thou;

6. "Lo, in the way of Love, 'Twixt poor and puissant no diff'rence is:
"Prithee, o beauty's queen, A word to beggars or two say thou!"

7. Unto who saith "The dust Of the Friend's door collyrium is",
"This that thou sayest plain Is in our eye to view," say thou.

8. Unto yon Soufi churl, Who from the tavern would us forbid,
"Prithee, this speech before Yonder our Elder renew", [1487] say thou.

9. Cupbearer, yonder wine, That in the jar the Soufi's heart
Ravisheth, when shall it gleam And glitter the goblet through? Say thou.

10. Whenas a tangled maze Made she her musky tresses twain,
Wind of the East, oh what Thought she with us to do? Say thou.

11. The bird of the meads last night Wept for my wailing; and thou, East Wind,
Know'st what betided hath. Prithee, what made him rue? Say thou.

12. Speech of the folk of wit Spirit-consoling is. O breeze,
Them of the mystery ask And to us syne the clue say thou.

13. Base though we be, in wrath Prithee rebuke us not: their sins,
After kings' clement wise, Unto the beggar-crew say thou.

14. Hafiz, if They admit Thee to her feast, 'fore God, drink wine,
Yea, and "Hypocrisy I from this day eschew," say thou.

[1487] i. e. thou wilt see how he will refute thee.

CCCCLXXVII

1. When heav'n's cornfield and the sickle Of the crescent moon I spied,
Of mine own seed-sowing minded Was I and the reaping-tide.

2. "Fortune mine," quoth I, "thou sleepest And the sun in heaven is up."
"Maugre this," it answered, "hopeful Of Prevenient Grace [1488] abide."

3. If detached and pure, like Jesus, To the heav'ns above thou go,
By thy lamp with rays an hundred Will the sun be glorified.

4. In the stars, those nightly prowlers, Trust not; for these tricksters stole
Kei-Khusráu's imperial girdle And Kawóus's crown of pride.

5. Bid the heav'ns boast not of grandeur; For the harvest of the moon
At a wheatcorn and the Pleïads, In Love's mart, at two are cried.

6. Though the ear the gold and ruby Earring dear and counsel light
Holdeth, fleet is beauty's season: Cast my warning not aside.

7. Far the ill eye from thy mole be! For on beauty's board a pawn
Urgeth it, which doth the vict'ry Over sun and moon decide.

8. Sure deception and dissembling's Fire Faith's harvest will consume;
Hafiz, put this woollen patchcoat Off and go, ere worse betide.

[1488] Allusion to Koranic saying, "Verily My mercy preventeth (forestalleth) My
anger".

CCCCLXXVIII

1. "On the new-risen moon Wentest thou forth," quoth she, "to gaze.
"Go; of the moon of my brow Shame on thee be and eke amaze!

2. "Life-long that heart of thine Hath of our tress the captive been:
"Heedless be not to give Unto thy friends their due of praise."

3. Vaunt not thyself of wit Unto the Loved One's blackmoor tress;
Thousands of pods thereof [1489] There at a wheatcorn they appraise.

4. Love and faith-keeping's seeds, In this old field [the world, to wit),
Then at the first become Patent, when come are the gathering-days.

5. Cupbearer, ho! bring wine! So I may tell thee a mystery,
Both of the new moon's course And of the ancient planet's ways.

6 Lo, for a sign, the moon Yonder in heav'n, at each month's end,
Siyamek's crown and eke Zhau's helmet-cap aloft doth raise. [1490]

7. The door of the Magian sage, Hafiz, fidelity's stronghold is;
The lesson of Love to him Recite and hearken to what he says.

[1489] i. e. of wit.
[1490] i. e. At the month-end the moon, being full, resembles the round tiara of Siyamek (son of the Peshdadi king Keyoumerth) and then, changing to new, assumes the form of the horned helmet-cap of Zhau (a brother of Rustem or, by other accounts, the penultimate king of the first or Peshdadian dynasty of Persia). These figures, fading and reappearing with the changes of the moon, form an emblem of the instability of human grandeur.

CCCCLXXVIII

1. Minstrel, thy dulcet song ensue, Ever afresh and still anew:
Wine, heart-expanding, seek and woo, Ever afresh and still anew.

2. Ever in private with a fair, Decked like an idol, sit apart:
Sip from her lips their honey-dew, Ever afresh and still anew.

3. Where is my skinker, silver-limbed? Ho, there! to me the wine come bring!
Fill to me quick a cup or two, Ever afresh and still anew.

4. When of Life's fruits wilt thou enjoy, An if thou quaff the grapejuice not?
Wine her remembrance quaff unto, Ever afresh and still anew.

5. See how my heart-alluring fair Doth for my sake all charms display,
Beauty and scent and goodly hue, Ever afresh and still anew.

6. When at the end of that Peri's street, Wind of the East, thou passest by,
Prithee to her for Hafiz sue, Ever afresh and still anew. [1491]

[1491] This Ode is only found in the Indian bazaar texts of Hafiz and is manifestly spurious. I have, however, translated it, as, though showing no sign of Hafiz's hand, it is not without prettiness and forms the text to which the charming Indian air "*Taza be-taza*" is commonly sung.

CCCCLXXIX

1. Thou that with the longsome tress's Trailing chain art come,
Luck attend thee, that for tending The insane [1492] art come.

2. Deign to change thy wonted usance; Doff despite awhile;
Since thou presently to visit Those in pain art come.

3. I'm the ransom of thy stature, Who, for peace or war
Here, in every case, displayer Of disdain, [1493] art come.

4. In that ruby lip thou blendest Fire and water: far
Be the Eye! for thou a master In chicane art come.

5. On thy gentle heart be blessing, Since thou e'en to pray
For his soul, who of thy glances Lieth slain, art come!

6. Nought thou reck'st of my abstention, [1494] Since, my heart to steal,
Drunk and touzled, to my closet Thou profane art come.

7. "Once again wine-stained thy patchcoat, Hafiz, is," quoth she;
"Back, 'twould seem, from Soufi usance Thou again art come."

[1492] "The insane", i. e. frenzied lovers, whom she binds with her tress-chain.
[1493] Sic. i. e. one who showeth disdain.
[1494] i. e. of the fact that I have made profession of ascetic austerity and have secluded
myself from the world for the practice thereof.

CCCCLXXX

1. Unto the Friend a letter With my heart's blood I wrote,
Saying, "The Last Day's terrors I feel, when thou'rt remote."

2. An hundred signs of sev'rance I have in these mine eyes:
My tears it is not only My suff'rance that denote.

3. Howe'er I strove, no profit From her was ever mine;
Whoso the Tried re-trieth, Repentance is his lot.

4. Late of the Loved One's fashions A leach I asked, and he,
"Her neighbourhood is torment, Her absence antidote."

5. The East wind lifted sudden The face-veil from my moon;
'Twas as the forenoon sunshine The clouds in sunder smote.

6. Quoth I, "If round thy quarter I turn, I'm blamed;" and she,
"Love without blame," made answer, "Yet never did I note."

7. Thy love since Hafiz seeketh, Grant him a draught; so he,
With that thy bounty's savour, May soothe his thirsting throat.

CCCCLXXXI

1. Remove thou not from me, For still mine eye-light been hast thou,
My spirit soothed and made My frighted heart serene hast thou.

2. No hurt from envious eyes Upon thee fall; for that the height
Of excellence attained In beauty and in sheen hast thou!

3. The hand of suppliance Lovers withdraw not from thy skirt;
The shirt of their content In sunder rended clean hast thou.

4. Be thou not strait of heart; For Union's day thou yet shalt see,
Since tasted many a night Estrangement's poison keen hast thou.

5. O Mufti of the time, Forbid me not from loving her!
Yet thee excused I hold, Her face since never seen hast thou.

6. Hafiz, not undeserved Is this the Friend's reproach to thee:
Beyond thy blanket's bound The foot outstretched, I ween, hast thou. [1495]

[1495] i. e. thou hast overweened, overstepped the bounds of propriety.

CCCCLXXXII

1. Thou, at whose face's lustre The lamp of vision's lighted,
Thy tipsy eye's coequal The world's eye never sighted:

2. A loveling such as thou art, All grace from top to bottom,
The world hath ne'er beholden Nor God to make delighted.

3. Intent on lover-slaughter Thy brow and drunken eye are;
Whiles *this* the bow hath bended, Whiles *that* an ambush pighted.

4. Till when, like fowl half-slaughtered, Of that thy crossbow wounded,
Shall my heart's pigeon flutter, With dust and gore bedighted?

5. Unto my head, each moment, My bosom's smoke ascendeth:
How long shall I, like aloes, Upon the fire be sited?

6. Of that her mouth, if docile To me be skittish Fortune,
The wish I will accomplish Of this my heart affrighted.

7. If to thy cheek thine eyebrow Incline not, why above it
Is't ever bent, as aping The shape of me grief-blighted?

8. If on my lip thou layest Thy lip, I life eternal
Shall gain, although my spirit Upon the lip be lighted. [1496]

9. O thou my two eyes' lustre, How long, as on thy tresses, [1497]
Upon my heart wilt trample, Bewildered and despited,

10. At parting's thorn-foot fallen Astonied, its endeavour
With no rose from the rosebed Of thine enjoyment 'quited?

11. This verse our stock in trade is; So be it to thy liking,
Of thee the pearls of Hafiz Be in a book endited.

12. Lo, if my hand thou take not, I'll plain me to the Vizier
How hearts thine eye hath ravished From lovers sorry-plighted.

[1496] i. e. although I be ready to give up the ghost.
[1497] Her long tress, trailing on the ground, figured as liable to be trodden on by her
    feet.

CCCCLXXXIII

1. Sweet are the scented breezes, Heart-soothing, soft and low,
That, for thy love awaking, At early morning blow.

2. Bird of auspicious aspect, Be thou our guide, whose eyes,
Her doorway's dust desiring, Are all with tears aflow.

3. In thought of my meagre body, That drowned in heart's blood is,
They look at the new moon, cleaving The marge of the evenglow.

4. When I from the world, Beloved, For love of thy face, depart,
From out of my grave red roses, In lieu of grass, shall grow.

5. Alas that I breathe without thee! Shame on me! What excuse,
Excepting belike thou pardon, Were for my sin to show?

6. The breath of the dawn from thy lovers This usance of love hath learnt,
The vest of the dark in sunder To rend from top to toe. [1498]

7. Nay, let not thy tender bosom Wax weary of my complaint;
For Hafiz hath but this moment Begun his tale of woe.

[1498] i. e. as frenzied lovers rend their garments.

CCCCLXXXIV

1. The door of the Magians' palace Was swept and sprinkled new;
The host, on the threshold seated, Bade old and young thereto.

2. The winebibbers all in his service Girded and ready stood;
The tent of his crown [1499] was pighted Above the heavens blue.

3. The lustre of cup and flagon The light of the moon obscured;
The cheeks of the Magian younglings The sunshine veiled from view.

4. The amorous grace of the skinkers White roses and sugar shamed;
The noise of their dulcet clamour The viols and lutes outcrew.

5. Bride Fortune, in that bride-chamber, With many an amorous air,
Did indigo [1500] bray and her tresses Eke with sheer musk endue.

6. The angel of mercy, taking The cup of delight in hand,
In Peris' and Houris' faces Its dregs for rosewater threw:

7. I made him my salutation And laughing, to me quoth he,
"O cropsick poor wretch, wine-smitten, Did any the like e'er do

8. "Of that which, for lack of judgment And spirit thou dost? Who e'er
"His tent from the place of the treasure, To pitch in the waste, withdrew?

9. "Enjoyment of wakeful Fortune, I fear me, They'll grant thee not:
"In sleep-stricken Fortune's bosom Thou liest and sleepest, too."

10. The heav'ns are the led-horse-holders Of Shah Nusrét-ed-dín: [1501]
Behold how their hands the angels Have clapped on his stirrups two.

11. Yea, wisdom, th' inspired of heaven, For honour and glory's sake,
Full often, to kiss his threshold, Hath stooped from the vault of blue.

12. Come to the winehouse, Hafiz, that I a thousand troops
Of those whose prayers are answered May tender to thy view.

[1499] i. e. the canopy of state spread over his head, as over that of a king.
[1500] "Indigo"; i. e. for the penciling of the eyebrows.
[1501] i. e. Sultan Yehya, before mentioned.

CCCCLXXXV

1. To the tavern yestereven I betook me, sleep-polluted,
Wet the patchcoat's skirt and prayer-rug With the grape-juice deep polluted.

2. Forth there came a Magian youngling Of the wineseller's and mocking,
Unto me quoth he, "Awaken, Wayfarer, thou sleep-polluted! [1502]

3. "Washing must thou do and scouring, Ere thou get thee to the tavern,
"So that this our ruined cloister May not be by thee polluted.

4. "Pass in purity the season Of old age and never suffer
"Hoariness's robe of honour With youth's wede to be polluted.

5. "How much longer, of thy yearning For the sweet-lipped fair, the jewel
"Of thy soul with liquid ruby, Marry, wilt thou keep polluted?

6. "The familiars of Love's pathway Drowned, indeed, in this vast ocean [1503]
"May become, but with the water Never of the sea polluted.

7. "Pure be thou and clean and issue Forth the pit of earthly nature;
"Ease nor pleasure giveth water With Earth's rubbish-heap polluted."

8. "O thou World's Delight," I answered, "In the rose it is no blemish
"If it in the Spring-tide season With sheer wine we see polluted."

9. "Hafiz," said he, "quips and quillets Sell not friends." "Nay, these thy favours
"Are with overmuch of chiding," Answered I, "for me polluted." [1504]

[1502] Rhyme-word of 1. 1 repeated.
[1503] Of Love.
[1504] The gist of the young Magian's reproaches is not that Hafiz is a toper and a lover,
but that he has committed the (in a lover) unpardonable offence of letting his
condition become known to the profane vulgar.

CCCCLXXXVI

1 She went, behind her trailing Her skirts of gold-embroidered lawn,
An hundred moons, [1505] for envy Of her, their collars having thrawn.

2. For heat of wine, the sweat-drops Showed on the circuit of her cheek,
Like drops of dew, that trickle Upon the rose-leaf in the dawn.

3. That sweet and fluent utt'rance, Tall, slender shape and lovesome face;
Heart-luring eyes and eyelids, For languor half together drawn;

4. That soul-dilating ruby, Her lip, of grace's water born;
That smile, the spirit-troubling, That still from out her visage shone;

5. Her shape, that swaying cypress, Nurtured in every daintiness,
That goodly gait and gentle, Wherewith she moved in mead and lawn;

6. How shall I do, companions, With this distracted heart of mine,
Since from our snare departed And fled is yonder black-eyed fawn?

7. Look thou the folk of vision Vex not, if in thy power it be;
Because faith-keeping's usance Is from this world of ours withdrawn.

8. How long shall I thy chiding Endure? From, that heart-luring eye,
Prithee, one day, Beloved, A glance thy lover cast upon.

9. An if thy noble nature With Hafiz anywise be vexed,
Relent thou, for repented Have we; let bygones be bygone.

10. Unto the Vizier's service Many the thanks that I shall give,
If but the fruit of union Into our hand befall anon. [1506]

[1505] i. e. fair ones.
[1506] Regarding the achievement of union as due to the blessing attendant upon the
    Vizier's service. The usual complimentary tag.

CCCCLXXXVII

1. At dawn, when, dazed with yesternight's potation,
With wine and harp and bells I took my station,

2. Reason, with wine for way-provénd, I started
Off for the city of intoxication.

3. The vintner's girl gave me a glance that made me
Assured from faithless Fortune's machination.

4. Quoth she to me, the cupbearer bow-eyebrowed,
"O target for the shafts of reprobation,

5. "Thou shall not clasp that middle, like the girdle,
"Whilst self thou seest amiddleward creation.

6. "Nay, for another bird go set thy springes;
"The Anca's nest's beyond thine usurpation."

7. She's all, mate, minstrel, skinker; clay and water [1507]
In love are figures of hallucination.

8. Give me the ark of wine, so I may haply
Win forth this boundless sea of tribulation.

9. Who shall have vantage of a queen of beauty,
That's busy ever with self-adoration?

10. This life of ours is an enigma, Hafiz,
Whereof 'twere vain to seek interpretation.

[1507] i. e, the body, the forms of being, the world-illusion.

CCCCLXXXVIII

1. Grown is the very candle A moth to the lamp of thy face;
Because of thy mole, I'm heedless Grown of my proper case.

2. Reason itself, that bindeth The madmen of loveliking,
Because of thy tress's fragrance, Is grown of the madmen's race.

3. As good-tidings-gift to the zephyr, The candle hath given its soul,
For that unto it the mandate It brought from the lamp of thy face.

4. What harm, for the scent of thy tresses, If life should go to the wind?
A thousand sweet souls, to ransom The Loved One, I'd give apace.

5. Excepting the mole, [1508] that rideth The fire of her lovely cheek,
Whoever good grain in censer Saw casten in rue-seed's place?

6. To earth, with amazement smitten And maddened with jealous pain,
I fell yesternight, when my fair one I saw in the foe's embrace.

7. What shifts have I used without profit? To her but a laughing stock
Are grown whatsoever devices I practise to gain her grace.

8. An oath have I sworn that never, So long as her lip exists,
To aught but the tale of the winecup My tongue will I abase.

9. Nay, prate to me not of mosque-school And cloister; for now once more
There's nought but the wish of the winehouse In Hafiz's head to trace.

[1508] Mole likened to grain.

CCCCLXXXIX

1. That heart-desired ruby's my constant delight;
All goeth, thank God, to our wishes aright.

2. Proud Fortune, the Friend straitly press to thy breast;
Now the cup of gold quaff, now her ruby lip bite!

3. Us ignorant elders and gone-astray sheikhs
As bywords for toping and wantonness cite.

4. From the pietist's prate we repentance have made
And for devotee-deeds we God's pardon invite.

5. Soul, how shall I tell thee of sev'rance's pain?
Hundred tears and one eye, Hundred sighs and one spright!

6. May Kafirs [1509] such anguish be spared as the pine
Hath felt for thy shape and the moon for thy sight! [1510]

7. Than patience for lovers nought goodlier is:
Yea, patience from God do thou seek with thy might!

8. The girdle and patchcoat [1511] are one in the Path;
This usance, o Soufi, cast off and this rite!

9. My life for a while with her face hath been sweet:
An hundred "God guard us from parting's despite!"

10. My head I'll not raise from her door nor my face
From her service I'll turn To the left nor the right!

11. Desire for her cheek hath made Hafiz forget
The reading of dawn and the prayer of the night. [1512]

[1509] "Kafirs", i. e. infidels.
[1510] i. e. for jealousy.
[1511] i. e. Infidelity and Islam
[1512] i. e. devotional exercises.

CCCCXC

1. Though swords in the street of that moon-face should rain,
Our head there we'd lay; be it God's to ordain!

2. We also the canons of piety know;
But fortune is froward and striving in vain.

3. We reck not of Preacher or Elder, not we:
Or give us the winecup or silent remain!

4. Repentance and me in one breath to conjoin!
Ask pardon of God, pardon ask, [1513] scatterbrain!

5. No ray of thy sunlight, o mirror-faced fair,
(Beshrew thy hard heart!) unto us dost thou deign.

6. O bitter is patience and fleeting is life!
Would I knew when and where I shall meet her again!

7. If union, o Hafiz, thou seekest, the cup
Of blood both in season and out must thou drain.

[1513] Repetition here as in original.

CCCCXCI

1. Feast-tide and time of roses It is: wine, skinker, bring!
Who ever saw the goblet Set without wine in Spring?

2. My heart with this abstention And piety's opprest:
Skinker, bring wine and solve it Of this its wearying.

3. The Soufi, who at lovers Railed yesternight, to day
To all the winds, befuddled, I saw devoutness fling.

4. This day or two of blooming, The rose enjoy. If thou
A lover be, to joyance With smooth-cheeked skinkers cling.

5. The rose will soon be going: Why sit ye heedless, friends,
Uncheered by cup and comrade And sound of pipe and string?

6. Upon the wine-cup fallen, The skinker's mirrored cheek
At dawn-tide showeth sweeter Than whatsoever thing.

7. When in the prince's banquet The minstrels music make,
Behoveth songs and ditties Of Hafiz' fashion sing.

CCCCXCII

1. Since in the tavern-precinct My portion God hath made,
What fault in me, o zealot, 's To find, when all is said?

2. Since thus to me foreordered It was, to my account
Why at the Resurrection Should this for sin be laid?

3. Say to the two-faced Soufi, the patch-gowned hypocrite,
The short-sleeved rogue, that plieth The thieves' long-fingered trade,

4. "Thou puttest on the patchcoat For simulation's sake,
"So from the Path the faithful By fraud may be astrayed."

5. I am the spirit's servant Of topers frank and free,
Who *this* world and the other Set not at one grass-blade.

6. Accomplished of the tavern Since my desire's become,
My heart is grown aweary Of cell and colonnade.

7. Play not the beggar, Hafiz, at every beggar's door.
By none but men of substance Thy need shall be allayed. [1514]

[1514] Soudi.

CCCCXCIII

1. Suddenly the screen of pudour Overthrown hast thou! Why is it?
Forth the house, intoxicated, Marry, flown hast thou! Why is it?

2. Tresses to the East Wind given, Ear unto the rival's prate;
Thus with every churl hail-fellow Well-met grown hast thou! Why is it?

3. Thou, that wast the queen of fair ones, Art the beggar's gazing-stock
Grown: the worth of this thy station Nowise known hast thou! Why is it?

4. Gav'st thou not whilere thy tress-tip, Of thy grace, into my hand?
Yet again to earth me wretched Stricken prone hast thou! Why is it?

5. 'Twas thy tongue and zone the secret Of thy mouth and middle told:
Sword yet drawn on me by means of Tongue and zone hast thou. Why is it?

6. Each a lucky cast ensueth With the dice of love for thee:
With us all, in fine, played falsely, Heart of stone, hast thou! Why is it?

7. Hafiz, in thy straitened bosom When the Friend alit, forborne
All thereout to cast, excepting Her alone, hast thou! Why is it?

CCCCXCIV

1. Union with her Than life fore'er is better:
Lord, give me *that*; For that, I swear, is better.

2. Me with the sword She smote and I complained not;
Friends' secrets not With foes to share is better.

3. Heart, be thou still The beggar of her quarter;
Than bliss etern Her yoke to bear is better.

4. Prate not to me Of heaven; for her chin's apple,
Zealot, than all The gardens there is better.

5. God wot, to die A bondman in her doorway
Than all the crowns Of earth to wear is better.

6. That rose's dust, Our cypress' foot hath trampled,
Than Redbud-blood, Beyond compare, is better.

7. Ask ye, for heaven's sake, Of my physician
What time this sick one like to fare is better. [1515]

8. From old men's counsel, youth, the head avert not;
For old men's wit Than fortune fair is better.

9. Quoth she one night, "None ever saw a jewel
"Which than mine eardrop anywhere is better."

10. "Speech in the Friend's mouth is a pearl," I answered;
"But Hafiz' verse Than jewels rare is better."

[1515] i. e. ask the Beloved when she means to heal my sick heart with her favours.

CCCCXCV

1. Why is it to her street That, heart, thy way thou makest not?
The means of union hast And yet assay thou makest not.

2. The mall of wish in hand Thou hast; yet ball thou strikest not:
With falcon such as this In hand, a prey thou makest not.

3. The blood, that in thy heart Still billoweth, the colouring
Of yonder fair one's face Why is it, pray, thou makest not?

4. Not musky is thy breath, East wind-like; for that, it unlike,
The dust of the Friend's street Thy passage-way thou makest not.

5. I fear me, from this mead No roses shalt thou win, since shift
To bear the thorns, that guard Its rosebeds gay, thou makest not.

6. Pleasant's the cup and full; But in the dust the wine thou cast'st
And of tomorrow's dole Account to day thou makest not.

7. In thy soul's sleeve thou hast Musk-pods an hundred; sacrifice
To a friend's locks thereof Yet, sooth to say, thou makest not.

8. Hafiz, how cometh it That thine obeisance at that court
Of hers, where all the world Their homage pay, thou makest not? [1516]

[1516] The poet rebukes himself for want of spirit and neglect to seize the occasion of
    winning the Beloved's favour.

CCCCXCVI

1 Richer far, o heart, what season Drunk with rose-hued wine thou art,
Than Caróun [1517] of old, albeit Gold nor gems be thine, thou art.

2. There, whereas the seats of honour To the beggars They appoint,
More than all in rank and worship, Marry, I opine, thou art.

3. In the parlous way that leadeth Unto Leila's camping-place,
This is the first step's condition, That Mejnóun, [1518] heart mine, thou art.

4. Thus Love's centre-point I've taught thee: Look that thou forget it not,
Else thou'lt find, without the circle, Outcast from Love's shrine, thou art.

5. Gone's the caravan, whilst sleptest Thou: in front the desert lies.
What wilt do? Of whom ask guidance? Know'st thou where, in fine, thou art?

6. Quaff a cup and at the heavens Cast the dregs thereof, howe'er
Bleeding-hearted for affliction Of the Days malign thou art.

7. Seekest thou the drown of kingship? First, approve thy worth innate,
Though of Feridóun's descendance And of Jemshid's line thou art.

8. Hafiz, plain thee not of poortith; For, with this thy gift of song,
Witless must thou be if sunken Still in dull repine thou art.

[1517] "Caroun", Koranic form of *Korah*.
[1518] "Mejnoun" means "mad".

CCCCXCVII

1. Hail to Ahmed, [1519] son of Sultan Sheikh Uwéis the Ilkhanide!
For the justice of his kingship, God the Lord be magnified!

2. Khan and son of Khans, descended, Sháhinsháh, from Shahinshahs,
Unto whom were well the title, "Soul of all the world," applied!

3. Those who knew thee and who knew not To thy fortune credit gave,
"Welcome, o thou well-deserving Of such heavenly favour!" cried.

4. If the moon come forth without thee, It in twain they break: the heir
Of the Prophet and the wonder Art thou of the Glorified. [1520]

5. King and beggar thy fair fortune Dazzleth: far the evil eye
Be from thee, for soul and loveling Art thou of the world-all wide.

6. Curl thy forelock, Turkman fashion; [1521] For thy horoscopes predict
Bounty Khacan-like, [1522] with vigour As of Chenghiz Khan allied.

7. Though we're far from thee, the goblet Yet we empty to thy health;
Distance is not in that travel Where the spirit is the guide.

8. From the soil of Fars there bloometh Ne'er a rose of ease for me:
Oh how sweet the Baghdad wine is And how fair the Tigris tide! [1523]

9. To the lover's head, that is not The Beloved's threshold dust,
How shall freedom from affliction And astoniment betide?

10. Dust from the Beloved's doorway Bring, oh bring me, breeze of dawn,
So that therewithal may Hafiz' Spirit's eye be clarified!

[1519] Sultan Ahmed, (A. D. 1382—1410) last Ilkhani king of Baghdad.
[1520] A name of God.
[1521] In token of pride.
[1522] "Khacan", title of the Emperors of Chinese Tartary.
[1523] Sultan Ahmed's residence was at Baghdad.

CCCCXCVIII

1. Help me, o queen of the fair! For sore is my soul's distress.
'Tis time that thou earnest back To lighten my loneliness.

2. Estrangement and wan-desire Have worn me away on such wise
That patience in me to endure Still waneth and waxeth less.

3. My solace upon the couch Of sorrow's the grief of thee;
Thy thought is my bosom-friend In solitude's wilderness.

4. We are the compasses' point In the circle of destiny;
Grace what thou deemest and what Thou sayest we law confess.

5. Thought nor opinion of self Is in the winebibbers' world;
Heresy here conceit Is and self-willedness.

6. This subtlety, how, to wit, Yon all-present fair to none
Displayeth her countenance, To whom is it meet t' express?

7. Last night, to the wind of the East I made my complaint of her locks.
"Thou dotest," it said. "Forswear This fancy of foolishness.

8. "Here, in her fetters there dance Hundred of winds of the East;
"Look lest thou measure the wind, Heart, in the quest of her tress."

9. Up! With thy box-tree-like shape, Skinker, the meads come grace:
The rose of the garden, without Thy visage, is colourless.

10. The rose of this rose-garth of thine Fresh will not forever abide: [1524]
Come, come to the aid of the weak In the days of thine ableness.

11. Because of yon circle of blue, [1525] My heart all a-bleed is; give wine,
That I in this goblet of glass May put off my load of durésse.

12. Gone, Hafiz, is sev'rance's night And come is the fragrance of morn
Fair fall thee, o lover distraught! Fair fall thee of joy and liésse!

[1524] i. e. thy beauty will not endure for ever.
[1525] i. e. heaven, Fortune.

CCCCXCIX

1. The scent of the sanctuary [1526] myrtles Cometh and waxeth my heat.
Who is it will travel thither, Su-áad [1527] for me to greet?

2. To hear of the Loved One's tidings Is gladness and health and peace:
My life will I give to purchase The dust of the Loved One's street.

3. Nay, come to the exiles' quarter Anights and see from our eyes
The tears, like the ruddy vinejuice In Syrian flagons, fleet.

4. If e'er after heav'n I hanker And fail of my faith to thee,
May never my sleep be pleasant, May never my dreams be sweet!

5. When warbleth the bird of good omen Of Dhou el Arák, [1528] no more
Their croon of regret for thy gardens My turtle-doves repeat.

6. The days of the Loved One's absence Will come to an end ere long:
Already I spy the striking Of tents from the hill-retreat.

7. O happy the time when in safety Thou enterest in at my door
And thee I with "Blest thy coming And blest thine alighting!" meet!

8. Yea, hopeful, by happy fortune, To see thee eftsoon am I,
Thou still to command rejoicing And I to serve at thy feet.

9. Because of reward for goodness, Accept thou of me to slave,
Though nought for the entertainment Of princes I have that's feat.

10. In absence from thee, all meagre I'm grown, like the waning moon,
Though never thy moon-like visage At full have I seen, my sweet.

11. Thy verse is a string, o Hafiz, Of pearls of the purest sheen;
The verse of Nizámi [1529] passing In sweetness and fair conceit.

[1526] i. e. the Beloved's encampment.
[1527] i. e. the Beloved. Name taken from opening of Kab ibn Zuheir's "Mantle" poem.
[1528] The place of the Beloved's abode in pre-Islamitic poetry.
[1529] "Nizami", a famous Persian poet of the 12th century, best known by his
Sikendernameh, a metrical history of Alexander the Great.

D

1. If from the pit of that chin, Heart, in despite thou comest forth,
Go where thou wilt, therefrom, Quickly, contrite, thou comest forth.

2. Nay, thou deservest not Heav'n with a draught should succour thee,
If from that fount of life, Thirsty of plight, thou comest forth.

3. 'Ware! For if ear thou lend To the suggestions of thy lusts,
Harkye, from Paradise, Adam-like, spright, thou comest forth.

4. Dawn-like, will I the ghost Render, of longing for thy face;
Maybe that, like the sun After the night, thou comest forth.

5. Like the East wind, the breath Of my desire on thee I'll send,
Till, as the rose from bud, Smiling, to light thou comest forth.

6. Come to the brink's my soul, In the dark night of lack of thee:
Time, like the shining moon, 'Tis that to sight thou comest forth.

7. In thy door's dust I've laid Rivers two hundred from mine eyes;
Maybe that, cypress-like, Stately and slight, thou comest forth.

8. Heart, in the house how long Wilt thou abide of blame and grief?
Time, by the Sultan's luck, 'Tis that forthright thou comest forth!

9. Hafiz, grieve not; for back Yet will that moon-faced Joseph come!
Yet, from the den of dole, Back to delight, thou comest forth!

DI

1. If yonder musk-downed fair to us A letter had but writ,
The Sphere our being's manuscript To roll had not seen fit. [1530]

2. Albeit severance the fruit Of union bringeth forth,
Would the World's Husbandman had not E'er sown the seed of it. [1531]

3. Thy pen no love in thee espied For us; it else had penned
An answer, may its sugared tongue Be ne'er in sunder slit!

4 Had not Creation's Architect Thine image stamped on Love,
With Adam's clay the particles Of Love He had not knit.

5. Talk not to me of heav'n to come, Zealot; for, with a friend
Like to the Houris, in a house Like Paradise I sit.

6. Wine-flask and cornfield-marge and maid Sweet-lipped for Irem's meads
And Sheddad's pomp [1532] sell not, o heart (For heaven to come, to wit).

7. Thy [1533] knowledge and mine ignorance Are one in Heaven's eyes;
Where there's no sight, [1534] what difference 'Twixt fit is and unfit?

8. Not only I the josshouse make The Káabeh of the heart:
The world with synagogue and church Is covered, every whit.

9. On Love's stone bench one looketh not For dalliance and ease:
Where the gold [1535] pillow faileth us, A brick shall serve for it.

10. How long, o understanding heart, Wilt care for this base world?
Pity the fair should love the foul, Virtue its opposite!

11. The soiling of the patchcoat is [1536] The ruin of the world.
Where is the wayfarer heart-whole, Pure and uncounterfeit?

12. Why from his hand did Hafiz let Thy tress-tip go? Alack,
'Twas thus ordained: what could he do But yield to Fate forewrit?

[1530] i. e. to close the book of our life.
[1531] "It", i. e. severance.
[1532] For a detailed account of the Garden of Irem (here = Paradise to come) and its founder, Sheddad, see my "Book of the Thousand Nights and One Night", Vol. III, 334, "The City of Irem".
[1533] "Thy", i. e. the pietist's.
[1534] i. e. since Fortune is blind.
[1535] Sic; but "gold-embroidered" is, of course, meant.
[1536] i. e. the hypocrisy and fraudulent practices of the Soufis, Calenders and other dervish orders, whose distinctive garb was the oft-mentioned "patchcoat".

DII

1. Thou, that lovers with rejection Meet to mortify dost hold,
Thou, that still thyself removed From thy lovers' eye dost hold,

2. With a draught of limpid water Succour thou the thirsty one
Of Love's waste, if hope of succour Thou from God most High dost hold.

3. Thou the heart from me hast ravished, Soul, and I forgave it thee;
But in better keeping hold it Than thou me that sigh dost hold.

4. That our goblet [1537] other topers Share with us, will we endure,
Since thou lawful and befitting This that we aby dost hold.

5. Fly, the Símurgh's court no play-ground Is for thee: [1538] thine own fair fame
Thou but losest and us others In annoy thereby dost hold.

6. Hafiz, by thine own shortcoming From this door shut out art thou:
Then of what is't thou complainest? Wherefore this outcry dost hold?

7. Folk for service done advancement Seek from kings: thou, having done
Nothing, Hafiz, expectation Of requital why dost hold?

[1537] "Goblet" = Beloved's good graces.
[1538] "Fly" here = rival. "Simurgh" = Beloved.

DIII

1. Thou that art still with conceit upblown,
If love be not thine, thee excused we own.

2. Harkye, frequent not the love-distraught,
Thou that for goodness of wit art known. [1539]

3. Not in *thy* head is Love's drunkenness:
Thou'rt drunk with the wine of the grape. Begone!

4. By sighs grief-laden and yellow face
To lovers' sickness is witness shown.

5. Unbrightened by winecup and Houris' lip,
The gardens of Heaven were dull and lone.

6. Behoveth thee strive for that moon-cheek's love,
Though far as the sun in heav'n thou'rt known.

7. Hafiz, leave caring for name and fame;
Come, call for the winecup; thou'rt cropsick grown!

[1539] Ironical; addressed to the typical "argle-bargling" pietist.

DIV

1. Thou, that in the tavern-quarter An abiding-stead possessest,
Thou'rt Time's King, if thou a goblet Of the grape-juice red possessest.

2. Thou, thy night and day that passest With the Loved One's cheek and tresses,
Hail, for thou a morn and even Full of goodlihead possessest!

3. Thou that union in seclusion Choosest with thy love, the moment
Prize, when thou thy heart's intendment, Quit of doubt and dread, possessest.

4. Lovers heart-afire, o East wind, In thy pathway stand, awaiting
If thou news of yonder Loved One, Hence a-travel sped, possessest.

5. Say, [1540] "Though constant in faith-keeping Art thou not, at least I'm thankful
"That thou constancy in purpose Lovers' blood to shed possessest." [1541]

6. Thy fresh mole a seed of easance Is and life; but ah, woe worth it!
What a snare thou, on the margent Of its meadow spread, possessest!

7. Lo, I scent the spirit's fragrance From the goblet's lip that laugheth:
Smell, if thou a sense of smelling, Khwájeh, [1542] in thy head possessest.

8. If, to day, of thee a stranger Seek a name, nay, where's the wonder?
Since thou only in the city Name, of live and dead, possessest.

9. Many a dawn-prayer will be watching O'er thy soul, who slaves like Hafiz,
Waking in the midnight-watches, Rising up from bed, possessest.

[1540] i. e., "O East Wind, say to the Beloved".
[1541] i. e., I am thankful, at any rate, that thou art constant in something.
[1542] "Khwajeh", = our "Sir", the ordinary address of men of learning and of officials,
    as primarily such.

DV

1. Thou that on thy cheek the face-veil Castest of the musky hair,
Well thou dost to cast a shadow On the sun's resplendent glare!

2. Since, with this first sketch [1543] thou castest On the water of our sight
Dazed we are, thy cheek's full radiance How, I wonder, shall we bear?

3. Beauty's ball from all the fair ones Of the world thou bear'st: be blithe;
Cyrus' [1544] cup seek, for thou conquered Hast Efrásiyáb fore'er.

4. In our ruined heart the treasure Of the love of thee thou'st laid;
Cast the shadow of thy mercy On this corner waste and bare.

5. Every one the lover playeth With the candle of thy cheek;
But the moth [1545] alone amazement And destruction findeth there.

6. Ruined though I be and drunken, My devotion ne'er reject;
Thou, with promise of requital, Urgedst me to this affair.

7. When thy cheek thou dost a moment In the bride-chamber unveil,
Lo, the Houris and the Peris Hide their faces for despair.

8. Sleep from lovers' eyes thou stealest And suspicion, on account
Of thine image, still thou castest On the prowlers of the air. [1546]

9. With thy tipsy eye's beguilement And thy red wine-coloured lip,
The seclusion-haunter Hafiz Hast thou cast into wine's snare;

10. Yea, his heart to take, thou castest On his neck thy tress's chain,
Like the noose of kings that hold it In their hand to slay or spare.

11. Thou, Nusrét-ed-dín Shah Yéhya, Who the kingdom's enemies
Into ruin's water castest With thy flashing sabre's flare;

12. Lord of glory like Darius, Who, to magnify the sun,
Causest him to vail his crownal In the dust beneath thy chair;

13. Wine from out the cup world-showing Drink; for, seated on Jem's throne,
From the loveling of thy wishes Thou the bridal veils dost tear.

14. Of thy flashing sword, that maketh Lions thirsty-lipped for fear
And in water champions casteth, Let thine enemies beware!

[1543] i. e. thy beauty, obscured by the veil.
[1544] "Cyrus", the Kei-Khusrau of the Persians, (though some writers identify the latter
    with Cambyses I,) captured and put to death the redoubtable Efrasiyab, thus ending
    the long war between Iran and Touran. "Cyrus' cup" here = "Jem's cup", i. e. the
    world-showing wine-cup.
[1545] i. e. the lover, himself.
[1546] i. e. the dreams.

DVI

1. Thou, upon whose radiant cheek Bright the lights of kingship shine,
In whose thought concealed abide Hundred mysteries divine;

2. Thou, whose blesséd pen doth ope, For the people of the Faith,
Hundred water-springs of life From each drop of ink of thine;

3. Thine the Realm is and the Ring; Whatsoe'er thou wilt, command:
Not on Ahriman, forsooth, Do the Great Name's splendours shine.

4. Whosoe'er displayeth doubt Of the might of Solomon,
At his knowledge and his wit Bird and fish to laugh combine.

5. Though the kite upon his head Whiles the cap of state may set,
Kingship's usances are known Only to the Anca's line.

6. Swords like thine, to which the skies, Of their bounty, lustre give,
Without armies win the world, With no aid but the Divine.

7. Amulets for friends thy pen Writeth, life to life that add,
And for foemen spells that cause Life in them to fail and dwine.

8. Thou whose being's elements Are of honour's alchemy
And whose fortune certified Is from ruin and decline,

9. Straw-coloured, for jealousy, Lo! the red-cheeked rubies grow,
If the radiance of thy sword Fall on quarry and on mine.

10. Witness is the Mohtesib Unto this thy slave's complaint:
Lo, a life-time 'tis, o king, Since my cup was full of wine!

11. Sure thy heart will pity take On the lover's wretchedness,
If thou of the wind of dawn Question of this case of mine.

12. Water from the tavern-fount, Skinker, bring; the cloister-pride
From our patchcoats let us wash With the life-blood of the vine.

13. Since the use of governance Was in Adam's family,
None like thee this art hath known In its essence fair and fine.

14. Heav'n oppression hath forsworn, With angelic-natured thee;
Thou'rt the world's resort; yet I 'Neath the world's oppression pine.

15. Here, on Adam, hight the Pure, Where trangression's levin fell,
How were claim to sinlessness Meet for one of Adam's line?

16. Since the king, from time to time, Hafiz, mentioneth thy name,
Fate accuse not, but, contrite, To thy lot thyself resign.

17. O thou giver of good gifts, Refuge of created things,
Be thou gracious to a wretch, Overcome of fate malign! [1547]

[1547] A complaint of the royal neglect and an appeal for largesse.

DVII

1. Sweet, the talk of heaven's nothing But a story of thy street;
They who prate of Houris' beauty Legends of thy face repeat.

2. Jesu's breath [1548] the least of virtues Is of that thy ruby lip;
But a trope is Khizr's water For thy mouth, so honey-sweet.

3. All my heart's a tale of anguish, Every whit; and every trait
Of thy qualities a token Coming from the Mercy-seat.

4. If thou hadst not to the roses Of thy fragrance made a gift,
How should they become the censers Of the halls where angels meet?

5. With desire for the Friend's way-dust We consume; bear thou in mind
That as yet, o East wind, nothing Hast thou done to ease our heat.

6. If hell-fire reflect the image Of thy cheek, I'll not complain:
Come, o cupbearer; for toping If I go to hell, so be't.

7 Filled the whole created world is With the smell of my roast heart,
And the burning of my vitals Into every thing doth eat.

8. Life in vain, o heart, and knowledge Hast thou spent; an hundred means
Of attainment thou possessedst And hast gotten but defeat.

9. Knowest thou what Hafiz' purpose In this tale of anguish is?
'Tis a glance from thee and favour From the Sultan to entreat.

[1548] i. e. the power of reviving the dead, like Jesus.

DVIII

1. In pledge for the juice of the grape This patchcoat of mine were best;
This book [1549] without meaning drowned In the blood of the vine were best.

2. Now life I have wasted, drunk, In the nook of the inn, to lie,—
The more I consider thereof, The more I opine,—were best.

3. Since care for the things of the world Is foreign to dervishhood,
The breast full of fire and the eyes To have full of brine were best.

4. I will not divulge to the folk The case of the pietist;
This office, indeed, to the lute And harp to assign were best.

5. Since thus without reason or rhyme, Head or tail, are the fashions of Fate,
The love of the skinker at heart And in hand to have wine were best.

6. My heart from a charmer like thee I will not uproot: if I must
Bear torment, from yonder tress-curl To suffer of thine were best.

7. Since, Hafiz, grey-headed thou'rt grown, I rede thee the tavern eschew:
Gallanting and toping, i'faith, To youth to resign were best.

[1549] "This book", i. e. the Koran?

DIX

1. Thou that neither heed nor mercy In our slaughter practisest,
Us thou recklessly consumest, Capital and interest.

2. Deadly poison at disposal Have affliction-stricken ones:
Have a care, for it is parlous Tristful lovers to molest.

3. Since thou'rt able our affliction With one look to do away,
'Tis unrighteous thus all solace To refuse to our unrest.

4. Since, in hope of thine attainment, We have made our eyes a sea,
Why by the sea-shore, for pleasance, Is't thou never wanderest?

5. All the tales of thine oppression Are the fictions of ill-will:
Such unrighteousness hath never Harboured in thy gentle breast.

6. If, o pietist, our Loved One Should to thee her charms display,
Otherwhat than wine and wanton Thou of God wouldst not request.

7. Hafiz, unto that her eyebrow, Prayer-niche-like, prostration make;
For no heart-whole supplication, Saving here, thou profferest.

DX

1. Knowledge, o witless one, seek; Else cast of one side shalt thou be.
Thou that no wayfarer art, How, then, a guide shalt thou be?

2. Harkye, o son, in Truth's school, At foot of the Master of Love,
Study, that Elder in turn So in due tide shalt thou be.

3. Eating and sleep from Love's goal Far hold thee; with eating and sleep
What time thou dispensest, arrived Where Love doth abide shalt thou be.

4. If on thy heart and thy soul Fall the light of the love of the Truth,
By Allah I swear that more fair Than the sun in his pride shalt thou be!

5. Thy hands, like the Men of the Path, An thou wash of existence's dross,
The Elixir of Love shalt thou find And gold, three times tried, shalt thou be.

6. When headless and footless thou art In the way of the Master of Might, [1550]
From head unto foot with the light Of God glorified shalt thou be.

7. One moment be plunged in God's sea Nor thenceforth misdoubt thee that wet
In a hair of thy head by the surge Of the Seven Seas' tide shalt thou be.

8. If only God's countenance be The beacon and goal of thy sight,
Thenceforward, ne'er doubt it, possessed Of vision clear-eyed shalt thou be.

9. Though ruined and cast to the winds Thy being's foundation become,
Yet fear not; unshaken thyself, Whatever betide, shalt thou be.

10. If union, Hafiz, thou seek, The dust of the door of the folk
Of vision, needs must, heart and soul To their service applied, shalt thou

[1550] i. e. when once thou hast surrendered thyself without volition (meaning of
"headless and footless", like a ball, which offers no resistance to impulse) to the
guidance of Love.

DXI

1. Tell not the foe the secrets Of Love and compotation,
But let the lack-wit perish In his self-adoration.

2. Though weak thou be and pow'rless, Be gladsome like the zephyr;
For in Love's pathway better Than health is tribulation.

3. Us while thine eye bespeaketh Of drunkenness's myst'ries,
Who can inhabit, sober, The corner of salvation?

4. A lover be: the world-all Will else one day be ended
And thou wilt not have gotten Thy purpose of Creation.

5. On thy love's threshold reck not Of heaven, lest thou stumble
From loftiness's summit Into humiliation.

6. Wine's bitterness a trifle Is to the joys of toping;
The rose doth make requital For all the thorn's vexation.

7. A cup-sipper's the Soufi, A flagon-drainer Hafiz:
flow long, o short-sleeved Soufi, wilt practise usurpation? [1551]

[1551] *Derazdesti*, lit. long-handedness, (word used p. g. with "short-sleeved") meaning
idiomatically, "usurpation, robbery, rapacity".

DXII

1. Heart, be not quit a moment Of love and drunkenness
And so go free from recking Of life and nothingness. [1552]

2. When patchcoateers thou seëst, About thy business go;
For any Kibleh's [1553] better Than sheer self-righteousness. [1554]

3. In the Path's canon rawness [1555] Is token of unfaith;
The usances of toping Are briskness and address.

4. Be thou not self-conceited, And so from self be free:
Who his own wit and wisdom Vaunteth is knowledgeless.

5. These troubles, that betided Have, I foresaw that day
When thou with us no moment Wouldst sit, for frowardness.

6. Help, o my queen, 'fore heaven! Thy tress destroyeth us.
How long shall such a blackmoor Use this long-handedness? [1556]

7. Well said that Magian loveling Last night to me, "If thou
"Serve idols not, with pagans What is thy business?" [1557]

8. Downtrodden of abjection Hafiz, for all his pride,
Became, since in abasement He saw thy trailing tress.

[1552] i. e. of all concern anent the puzzles of Existence and non-Existence.
[1553] "Kibleh"; i. e. goal of prayer.
[1554] "The followers of various religions worship God; but the Soufi worships himself".—*Soudi.*
[1555] "Rawness" i. e. the dulness and sluggishness arising out of innate duncery and ineptness.
[1556] "Long-handedness", i. e. oppression.
[1557] i. e. "if thou be not a lover, what dost thou in the winehouse?"

DXIII

1. Hark to me, so with my counsel Free thyself from care thou [1558] make:
Blood thou drink'st, if search for other Than thy destined share thou make.

2. Marry, clay for gugglet-makers, At the last, wilt thou become;
Wherefore full of wine the tankard Look that then and there thou make.

3. If of those thou be whose wishes Point to Paradise, 'tis meet
Now that merry with the lovesome Peri-visaged fair thou make.

4. Thou uneath canst clap thy cushion On the great man's place, unless
All provision appertaining Unto greatness' wear thou make.

5. How the charact'ry of heaven's Bounty shall thy mind receive,
Save of vain imaginations First the tablet bare thou make?

6. Heaven's favours shall requite thee, O my Khusrau Shirin-lipped,
This Ferhád [1559] if with an eye-glance Lightened of despair thou make.

7. Hafiz, of God-given fortune Ease galore shalt thou enjoy,
To the grace of God commitment If of thine affair thou make.

8. Strive, o East wind, in the service Of the Lord Jeláleddín, [1560]
Full of rose and lily-fragrance Till the whole world's air thou make.

[1558] The Beloved.
[1559] The lover himself.
[1560] "Jelaleddin", Controller of Finances to Sultan Mensour.

DXIV

1. If to the voice of the bulbul And dove thou drink no wine,
Caut'ry's the only med'cine For such a case as thine. [1561]

2. When the rose doffeth the face-veil And the bird praiseth God,
Set not from hand the goblet. Why shouldst thou wail and whine?

3. Since in thy hand life's water Bideth, die not athirst;
Die not, I say; by water For all things live, in fine.

4. Próvant of colour and fragrance Lay up in Spring, for lo!
Highwaymen Autumn and Winter Follow with fell design.

5. Time giveth nought but it taketh Again: from this base churl
Seek not largesse; his bounties Are nought but empty shine.

6. Pomp of domain and kingship, When had it stableness?
Nought but the name abideth Of Kei's and Jemshid's line.

7. Cupbearer, ay, and minstrel, Reed-pipe and tabret, all
To chide at substance-hoarding, As heresy, combine.

8. This on the halls of the Garden Of Refuge [1562] have they writ,
"Whoso the base world's favours Buyeth shall reap repine!"

9. Bounty is dead; I'm silent: Where is the flask? Come pour,
Pour me to Hátim Téyi's [1563] Mem'ry a cup of wine!

10. Fragrance of God ne'er scented Puckfist nor miser: drink,
Hafiz, and practise bounty And be the warrant mine. [1564]

[1561] i. e. Whoso drinketh not in Spring is mad and the remedy for madness is cautery
(moxas applied to the head). "Cautery is the last (extreme) of medicine".—*Traditions
of the Prophet.*
[1562] i. e. Paradise.
[1563] "Hatim Teyi", the Oriental type of liberality.
[1564] i. e. Do this and I war thee salvation

DXV

1. In content awhile and leisure On a moon-faced fair to gaze
Better is than crown and kingship And a life of festal days.

2. Of my proper eye, 'fore heaven, I am jealous for thy cheek;
For oppression to a tender Face like thine's the very gaze. [1565]

3. Gone my heart is and I know not Of the exile what is come;
For life passeth and no tidings Come of it from any ways.

4. My breath faileth me nor sated With thy sight mine eyes have been.
Other than this wish abiding Is not in my heart's amaze.

5. East Wind, ruffle not the tress-tip Of that Peri-visaged maid;
For each hair of hers doth Hafiz At a thousand lives appraise.

[1565] Rhyme-word of line 1 repeated.

DXVI

1. Thy charms and my love-liking Are come to consummation;
Bide blithe; for this thy beauty There will be no cessation.

2. It passeth my conception That anything more lovely
Than this can e'er be pictured Of man's imagination.

3. A year, passed in thy presence, A day is and a moment
A year, when thou art absent, Is in my computation.

4. Life's aim will be accomplished, If but one day of union
With thee we be allotted, In all our life's duration.

5. O soul, thy face's semblant How shall I see in slumber,
Whenas mine eyes of slumber See but a simulation?

6. Have pity, for my body, For love of thy fair aspect,
Grown like the crescent moon is, For sheer extenuation.

7. If union with the Loved One, Hafiz, thou crave, complain not:
For more than this behoveth Endure of separation.

DXVII

1. With courtly speech the bulbul, From off the cypress-spray,
Last night Love's mystic lesson Chanted, that is to say,

2. "Come, for the rose displayeth The fire of Sinaï,
"So from the bush the lesson Of *Oneness* learn ye may." [1566]

3. The song-birds of the garden Make music, that our lord [1567]
Unto their dulcet ditties May tipple and be gay.

4. Sweet is the sleep of safety Upon the beggar's mat:
This easance not the portion Is of the throne of Kei.

5. Jem from the world took only The story of the cup:
Look that thy heart thou set not Upon the world's array.

6. Well said the ancient peasant Unto his son of yore,
"Child, what thou sow'st (and only That) shalt thou reap one day."

7. Thine eye man's house hath darkened [1568] With looks: God keep from thee
Crop-sickness! For thou goest Intoxicated [1569] aye.

8. This topsy-turvy marvel Of graceless fortune hear:
The Loved One us with Jesu's Life-giving breath doth slay.

9. More than his share to Hafiz 'Twould seem the skinker gave,
That fall'n his doctor's turban Is into disarray.

[1566] Rosebush likened to the burning bush, from which God declared His unity to
Moses. Love is here the God whose unity is proclaimed.
[1567] i. e. the Vizier.
[1568] i. e. made it a house of mourning.
[1569] i. e. Drunken with pride.

DXVIII

1. Come; for with us o'erlong Used this despite hast thou;
O'erlong, indeed, ignored Old friendship's right hast thou.

2. Hearken my rede; for sure This pearl is [1570] more of worth
Than all in store of gems And jewels bright hast thou.

3. Unto the succour come Of weary cropsick folk,
If aught, 'fore heav'n, of wine Left from last night hast thou.

4. Yet how to topers show Shouldst thou thy cheek, since that
For mirrors sun and moon In heaven's height hast thou?

5. Go, elder, speak not ill Of topers; have a care
Lest 'gainst the love and laws Of God despite hast thou. [1571]

6. Fear of these burning sighs Hast not of mine? God wot,
A gown of threadbare wool, Easy to light, hast thou.

7. Fairer than this thy verse, Hafiz, I've never seen
Aught, by yon blessed Book, That in thy spright hast thou! [1572]

[1570] i. e. the counsel in question.
[1571] i. e. lest thou missay, in railing at topers, of God's decrees, which have
  foreordained them to be as they are. Rhyme-word of line I here repeated in original.
[1572] i. e. the Koran, which thou hast by heart.

DXIX

1. The brow of a moon-faced maiden I've stablished in this mine eye;
The shape of a fresh-downed loveling Depictured anew have I. [1573]

2. My hope is that yon bow-eyebrow The patent of this my love,
It may be, with its sign-manual, [1574] Will docket and ratify.

3. Distraught is my heart and wasted My eye for expectancy;
The sight of a banquet-adorner [1575] It is, for which I sigh.

4. My heart of the patchcoat's weary; Yea, fire will I set thereto:
Come, see; for a sight worth seeing It is, I certify.

5. In places where lovelings battle And smite with the glance's sword,
What wonder if many a headpiece Fall'n underfoot thou spy?

6. I, in my nightly chamber Her cheek for a moon who have,
How should I have occasion For light from the moon of the sky?

7. To one my heart's rein I, dervish, Have given, who recketh not
Of any for crown or kingship, So prideful she is and high.

8. Union or sev'rance, what matter? Seek the approof of the Friend:
For otherwhat, sure, 'twere wrongful To crave of her, this forby. [1576]

9. Our bier, on the day of parting, [1577] Make ye of cypress-wood,
So we in that tall one's likeness And token [1578] herefrom may hie.

10. The fishes would pearls for rapture, To strew in its way, bring up,
If Hafiz's ship [1579] of verses Should draw to the ocean nigh.

[1573] i. e. I have fallen in love anew.
[1574] Eyebrow-curve likened to scroll or flourish of ornamental writing, with which a
    royal mandate is countersigned and without which it is not executor.
[1575] i. e. a pretty girl.
[1576] i. e. a true lover should be content with whatever the Beloved deemeth fit, whether
    it be union or separation.
[1577] i. e. of death.
[1578] i. e. that of the Beloved, commonly likened to a cypress-tree.
[1579] *Sefineh*, syn. Divan, collection of verses

DXX

1. God wot, if my soul to render My hand but free had been,
My life of my gifts to her servants Least in degree had been.

2. And were not my heart to her browlock Bound by the foot, my soul
Fain forth of this darkling dust-heap [1580] Long since to flee had been.

3. Would heaven she had by my doorway Come in like a flash of light,
That so on my two eyes current Her high decree had been!

4. For cheek, like the sun of the heavens, Unpeered in the world she is:
Oh, would that somedele warm-hearted, Like him, too, she had been!

5. Not even in sleep I see her: Of union, then, what hope?
Since this is denied, would th'other [1581] Vouchsafed to me had been!

6. The cypress herself the servant Would own of the Loved One's shape,
If hers but a tongue like the lily, Y-clept the free, had been.

7. Nay, how should the plaint of Hafiz Have issued forth of the screen, [1582]
Except of the birds of the morning The song-mate he had been?

[1580] The world.
[1581] i. e. the sight of her in dreams.

[1582] i. e. become known.

DXXI

1. Would heaven the heart of the Loved One But lovesome and kind had been!
Like *this* had not been our condition, Like *that* if her mind had been.

2. Had Fortune and Time been minded To honour and cherish me,
My throne in the dust of her threshold Of worship enshrined had been.

3. The price of the dust of her pathway Would manifest be,—forsooth,
I'd pay it,—if life eternal To me but assigned had been.

4. The worth of the scent of her browlock Would I have declared, if mine
A thousandfold lives, for each hairlet Therein that's entwined, had been.

5. Nay, how had it lessened, I wonder, The writ of our heart's content,
With the rescript, "Immune from Time's malice," If it countersigned had been?

6. Would heaven she had, like a tear-drop, Come forth from the veil, upon
Mine eyes so her ordinance current, To loose and to bind, had been!

7. Love's circle for heart-lorn Hafiz Hath blocked up the way of escape;
Else ne'er in the midst of amazement He, point-like, confined had been.

DXXII

1. 'Tis as if thou never sattest On a stream-bank, lover-wise;
Or thou'dst see that all the troubles, Which thou feel'st, from self arise.

2. By the Godhead I conjure thee, Whose elected slave thou art,
That o'er me, thine ancient servant, No one other do thou prize!

3. Unto beggarhood, henceforward Will we cleave; for in Love's stage
For the wayfarer there's nothing Helpful but self-sacrifice.

4. Modesty and breeding made thee Monarch of the moon-faced fair:
Hail to thee, for thou deservest Hundred honours on this guise!

5. If the pledge of faith in safety Off I bear, there's nought to fear;
Loss of heart, whilst faith abideth, Skilleth not in Love's emprise.

6. How can I but bear in patience With thy watchers' tyranny?
No recourse, except abasement, Open to the lover lies.

7. A disinterested counsel Hearken from thy slave sincere,
Thou that still the goal of vision Art unto the great and wise;

8. One like thee, a tender loveling, Innocent and pure of heart,
Better were it that thou sit not With the-reprobates and spies.

9. Woe is me that, for the viewing Of the meadows, thou shouldst walk,
Thou whose brow the wild white roses And whose cheek the red outvies!

10. At thy kindness, rose, I marvel, That thou sittest with the thorn: [1583]
Haply, thou in this th' expedience Of the time dost recognize.

11. Nay, to right and left the bubbling Of my tears thou mayst discern,
If thou but abide a moment Wilt to look upon mine eyes.

12. Hafiz' patience hath the torrent Of his streaming tears off borne:
Apple of mine eye, [1584] for pity Succour him, before he dies!

13. With thy heart-alluring fashions, Thou, o candle of Chigíl,
Worthy art to grace the banquet Of Jeláleddín [1585] the Wise.

[1583] i. e. that thou, beloved, deignest to consort with the unworthy.
[1584] i. e. Beloved.
[1585] The before-mentioned Finance-minister of Sultan Mensour.

DXXIII

1. Well have the heavens helped thee Upon the day of fight!
Marry, with what thankoff'rings Wilt thou their favour 'quite?

2. By kingly pomp and puissance In Love they set no store:
Profession make of service And claim a servant's right.

3. To him, whom God, when fallen, Hath taken by the hand,
Say "Bound art thou to suffer [1586] With those in evil plight."

4. In at my door come, skinker, With news of joy and so
Put from my heart a moment The world's chagrin to flight.

5. The path of rank and lordship Is set with dangers dire;
'Twere best that lightly laden Thou pass that parlous height.

6. The cares of troops and treasure And crown the Sultan hold;
The dervish hath the corner Of ease and peace of spright.

7. Success after the measure Of thought and spirit is;
The King's good purpose aided Is still of heaven's might.

8. One word, on Soufi fashion, An if I may, I'll say,
Light of our eyes,—that better Is peace than strife and spite.

9. Wash from thy cheek not, Hafiz, Content and poortith's dust;
For than the Grand Elixir 'Tis better in our sight. [1587]

[1586] i. e. to feel sympathy, *Mitleid*.
[1587] This ode was apparently addressed to some king, by way of congratulation on victory.

DXXIV

1. Two comrades of understanding, A nook on the marge of a mead,
Two pottles of wine and leisure, Ay, and a book to read;

2. These things for this world and the other I'd not exchange, although
There bark at my heels each moment The whole reviling breed.

3. If any for this world's treasure Contentment's corner sell,
He bartereth Joseph of Egypt For a mean price, indeed. [1588]

4. Come, let us drink and be merry, For this world's space will not
Wax more by thy devoutness Nor less by my misdeed.

5. Behoveth, in time of trouble, One's cares to the cup confide;
For trusting is not in any, In this our time of need.

6. Go, sit in the nook of quiet And gaze on the show; for none
The like of these marvellous troubles In mem'ry hath or heed.

7. My fair in the hands of caitiffs I see. Doth heav'n requite
The service of such a servant As I with such a meed?

8. Strive, o my heart, for patience; For God to Satan's hand
A signet rare and precious As this will ne'er confide. [1589]

9. Vicissitude's wild whirlwind Hath made uneath to see
That ever rose or lily Hath blossomed in this mead.

10. Because of this storm, that's blasted The garths, if hue of rose
Abide or scent of jasmine, A marvel 'tis, indeed.

11. The health of the time is ruined, Hafiz, by this mischance:
Where is a leach's counsel Or sage's healing rede? [1590]

[1588] Allusion to Koranic story of Joseph and his brethren.
[1589] Allusion to familiar story of Solomon's signet-ring.
[1590] Written (says Soudi) during the temporary occupation of Shiraz by the Turcoman hordes.

DXXV

1. Not in all the Magians' convents [1591] Is there one like me distraught;
Patchcoat here in pawn and Koran There for wine to stay my drought.

2. Dust of care the royal mirror Of my heart hath dimmed: to God
Sue I for a sage's friendship, One serene of mind and thought.

3. Streams of tears have I established From mine eye unto my skirt,
So the Fates may in my bosom Plant a cypress straight and haught. [1592]

4. Bring the wine-ark of salvation; For, without the Loved One's cheek,
With a sea is every corner Of mine eyes, for heart's grief, fraught.

5. To the liquor-selling loveling Have I vowed that never more
Wine I'll drink, except the goblet By a charmer's hand be brought.

6. If the candle [1593] tell the secret Of the subtlety of Love,
Well and good 'tis; but in silence Else the moth [1594] to suffer ought.

7. Name ye not to me, the lover, Otherwhat than the Belov'd;
For, excepting of the winecup And of her, I reck of nought.

8. Be not wroth if the narcissus Boast herself of thine eye's charm;
Those who see uneath to follow After sightless ones are wrought.

9. O how goodly was the saying, From a Christian in the dawn,
At the tavern doorway singing To the pipe and drum, I caught;

10. "An like this that Hafiz useth Músulmánship be, alack!
If a morrow follow after This to-day, woe worth the thought!" [1595]

[1591] i. e. winehouse.
[1592] Beloved likened to cypress, which loves running water.
[1593] i. e. the Beloved.
[1594] i. e. the lover.
[1595] i. e. "If Hafiz's fashions be a sample of the way in which Muslims practise (or
rather infringe) the precepts of Islam, there will be a terrible reckoning for them on
the morrow of death, if such a morrow there be". A hypothetical proposition which
reminds one of the famous agnostic prayer, "O God, if there be a God, save my soul,
if I have a soul!" It not unnaturally gave great offence to the orthodox party and
involved Hafiz in an impeachment for heresy, from which he is said to have
extricated himself by the interpolation of Couplet 9, attributing the objectionable
speech to an unnamed Christian.

DXXVI

1. Last night I saw in slumber A moon the heav'ns ascend,
Whose rays the night of sev'rance Sundered and brought to end.

2. Doth this the absent Loved One's Return denote? Pray God
It may her speedy entrance In at my door portend!

3. Blest be her name, my skinker Of auspice fair, whose steps
Unto my door with flagon And cup did ever tend!

4. Well were it if in slumber She'd seen her native land,
That thus remembrance led her To-us-ward of the friend!

5. Would that his foot had happened Upon a stone, who caused
Thee in the way of hardness Of heart thy steps to bend! [1596]

6. Fallen had Khizr's water Unto Sikender's lot,
Did Providence's favour On gold and might depend.

7. If, like a spright unbodied, She'd show herself to me,
In that heart-soother's pathway My life I would expend. [1596]

8. Remembered be that season When news, by roof and door,
The Friend to me and letters The charmer wont to send!

9. How had thy watcher gotten Such power of tyranny,
Did to the Ruler's doorway Anights a victim wend? [1597]

10. What know of love and longing The raw, untravelled ones?
Seek thee a finished champion, An ocean-hearted friend.

11. The merit-fost'ring Sultan Would of another have
Accepted, had another Such verse as Hafiz penned.

[1596] Rhyme-word if l. 1 repeated in original.
[1597] i. e. if oppressed lovers complained to God anights.

DXXVII

1. Many a day it is, Beloved, That thou holdest us await:
Thou entreatest not thy servants After other charmers' gate.

2. Ne'er on me thou op'st a corner Of the eye of thine approof;
Is it thus the folk of insight That thou dost propitiate?

3. Quit is neither rose nor bulbul Of the brand of grief for thee;
Her thou holdest raiment-rending And complaining him her mate.

4. Better 'twere thy wrist to cover, Since, instead of henna-dye,
With the heart's blood of thy lovers Thou thy hand dost decorate.

5. Thou, o heart, that hast experience Of the world, from these young maids
Love and loyalty to trothplight How canst thou anticipate?

6. Clean thy purse of gold and silver Must thou empty at their feet,
If thy longing of these lovelings Silver-bosomed thou wouldst sate.

7. Gone are wit and faith; and natheless I am pow'rless to complain
How thou me, the heart-consumed one, Holdest still in this estate.

8. "Though debauchery and toping All our sins be, in this case,"
Lovers say, "'tis thou that holdest Us thy slaves disconsolate."

9. Thou that from the patchcoat-wearers Seekest the delight of ease,
From know-nothings thou to gather Think'st a secret wonder-great.

10. Of sight's garden the narcissus Since thou art, o eye and lamp,
Wherefore me, the heavy-hearted, With such arrogance dost bait?

11. Since the East Wind to the roses And the bulbuls read the page
Of thy beauty, all astonied Them thou holdest and await.

12. From another world-all's quarry Is the jewel of Jem's cup;
Yet from potter's clay thou lookest It to get, thou addle-pate!

13. Waste thou not the day of safety In contention and reproach,
Hafiz: what hast thou to hope for From this world the runagate?

DXXVIII

1. I went to the garden one morning, That I might pluck a rose,
When, suddenly, full in my hearing, The song of a bulbul rose.

2. With love for a rose afflicted, Like me, was the wretch become
And so to the meadow-breezes Was casting his tale of woes.

3. The grass of that garden often I've compassed about since then
And still on the rose and the bulbul My fancy musing goes.

4. The rose of the thorn the comrade, The bulbul of grief became:
Thus still hath it been and will be For ever with these and those.

5. Since thus on my heart hath fallen The voice of the nightingale,
No patience with me abideth To suffer estrangement's throes.

6. Full many a rose in the garden Hath blossomed of this our world;
But no one, without a thorn-prick, E'er gathered thereof a rose. [1598]

7. Hafiz, no hope of joyance Have from this round of life;
For in it a thousand thorn-spikes And not one rosebud grows.

[1598] Rhyme-word of line 1 repealed in original.

DXXIX

1. By means of that goodly writ On the cheek's rose-red thou drawest,
The cancelling line o'er the page Of rosebush and bed thou drawest.

2. The tears, that were cloistered close In the cell of the eye, from out
The sevenfold screen, the mart Of the face to tread, thou drawest.

3. That sluggard and slow to move, The soft-going wind of the East,
To action, each breath, with the scent Of thy tresses shed, thou drawest.

4. Each breath, with the thought of that lip Wine-hued and that tipsy eye,
My feet from seclusion's cell To the wineseller's stead thou drawest.

5. Saidst thou, "To our saddlestrap Beseemeth thy head to bind."
"So be't, if on thee th' annoy Of this burden," I said, "thou drawest." [1599]

6. What shift for my heart against Thine eye and thy brow's to make?
Alack for this bow that on me, The weakling half-dead, thou drawest!

7. Come back, that the Evil Eye I may with thy cheek repel!
O new-blossomed rose, thy skirt From this thorn 'neath thy tread [1600] thou drawest.

420

8. Hafiz, what else wouldst thou have From the favour of Fortune? Wine
Thou quaff'st and the curls through thy hand Of the heart-charmer's head thou drawest.

[1599] i. e. "if thou choose to load thyself with such a burden, I make no objection".
[1600] i. e. "thou turnest in scorn from thy down-trodden lover".

DXXX

1. Who from the charmer will bring me A courtesy of the quill? [1601]
Where is the East Wind's courier, Can do it, if it will?

2. I make no complaint; but the Loved One's Rain-cloud no drop of dew
On the field of the thirsting-hearted Of favour doth distil.

3. The more I consider, the counsel Of reason, the more I see,
Is but in Love's way as a dewdrop That wrinkles the face of a rill.

4. Come, friend; for, although my patchcoat The dow'r of the tavern is,
No doit of endowment-monies Thou'lt find to my name in the bill. [1601]

5. At one of his sugar-canelets [1602] Why value they not the man
Who maketh an hundred scatt'rings Of sweets from a single quill? [1603]

6. My heart of this drum-under-blanket [1604] Is sick and hypocrisy:
Come, comrades, that I my standard May plant on the tavern-sill.

7. The roadside physician [1605] knoweth Nought of love's pains: dead heart,
Go get thee a Jesus-breathed one, [1606] An thou wilt be healed of thine ill.

8. The babble of How and Wherefore The headache giveth; heart,
The wine-beaker take and hold thee From life a moment still.

9. Come drink, for the time-conceiver [1607] This world and the next will sell
For a cup of the unmixed grapejuice, Ay, and a fair to fill.

10. Endurance of ease and pleasure No usance is of Love;
If thou'dst with us lovers commerce, Grief's poison must thou swill.

11. Hafiz hath nought to offer That's worthy thee, o king;
To pray for thy welfare morning And night is all his skill.

[1601] i. e. I do not, like the hypocritical pietist, live upon the *Wecf* or endowment-funds
    settled by the faithful to pious uses.
[1602] "Sugar-canelets", i. e. the poet's reed-pens.
[1603] Rhyme-word of line I repeated in original.
[1604] "Drum-under-blanket", idiomatic phrase meaning "profligate habits hidden under
    sanctimonious appearance."

[1605] i. e. the ordinary common-sense matter-of-fact person, who has no apprehension
of the things of the spirit, here likened to an itinerant quacksalver.
[1606] i. e. a fair mistress.
[1607] "Time-conceiver"; i. e. one who knows the value of time.

DXXXI

1. The wind-wafts of the new-born year From the Friend's street blow soft and light:
Withal, if aid thou seek therefrom, The heart's quenched lamp thou mayst relight.

2. If, like the rose, thou've gold in store, For God's sake spend it in disport;
For the desire of hoarding gold Caused Korah wander from the right.

3. A wine soul-pure I have and yet Thereat the Soufi cavilleth:
God, may ill fortune to the share Fall of no reasonable wight! [1608]

4. The way to gain the wish in love Is one's own wishes to forswear;
The crown of lordship for thyself By this renouncement dost thou dight.

5. I know not why the cushat thus Complaineth on the river-bank;
Belike she also hath, like me, A grief abiding day and night.

6. Gone is thy dulcet mate, [1609] o wax! [1610] Sit thou alone henceforth; for this
The ordinance of heaven is, Be't good or evil in thy sight.

7. A veiléd word to thee I'll say: Forth of the veil come, rose-bud like;
For but a five days' matter is The story of Prince Springtide's might.

8. Behoveth not that us from mirth The pride of learning should debar;
Come, skinker; for to fools there fall The chiefest portions of delight. [1611]

9. Go; toping practise and drink wine And leave hypocrisy, o heart;
For scarce a better than this way Thou'lt learn, if I conceive aright.

10. Go to the garden, get by heart Love's lesson from the nightingale;
To the assembly come and learn, From Hafiz, ditties to endite.

[1608] A roundabout fashion of imprecating ill-luck upon the unreasonable Soufi.
[1609] The "dulcet mate" of wax is the honey which is extracted from it.
[1610] The "wax" here addressed is that of the candle.
[1611] i. e. Since fools have the best of it in this world, let us be fools awhile.

DXXXII

1. Of Love's wine that to the raw ones Gives maturity,
Though the Ramazan-tide be it, Bring a cup to me.

2. Days have passed since I, poor sinner, In my hand have ta'en
Leg or wrist of silver-bodied Fair like cypress-tree.

3. Howso dear a guest the Fast-tide Be, o heart, its stay
As a boon and its departure As a blessing see.

4. Presently no wise bird flieth To the cloister door;
For in every place of preachment Springes set there be.

5. Since the rule 'tis that each morning Followed is by night,
I complain not of the malice Of the devotee.

6. When my Friend, for her diversion, Walketh in the meads,
Prithee, courier of the morning, [1612] Carry her my plea;

7. "One, sheer wine of ease that quaffeth Night and morning," say,
"Mindful of a mere dreg-drainer, Like myself, is she?"

8. Hafiz, if the age's Asef [1613] Succour not thy heart,
Thy desire, I fear, shall hardly Be fulfilled to thee.

[1612] i. e. the East Wind.
[1613] i. e. the Grand Vizier.

DXXXIII

1. Once, in a certain land, at break of day,
Thus to his mate a wayfarer did say;

2. "Wine, Soufi, first becometh clear when it
"Hath in the flask made forty days of stay."

3. Save to the finger of a Solomon,
What power doth graving on a ring convey?

4. An hundredfold doth God that patchcoat loathe,
Whose sleeve an hundred idols hideth aye.

5. Dark are our hearts: would from th' Invisible
Some hermit's lamp might lighten our dismay!

6. Though bounty's but a name without a trace,
Thy need expound unto a dainty may.

7. O owner of the harvest, if thou take
Ruth on a gleaner, God shall thee repay.

8. Zeal for the faith or solacement of hearts,
Easance or cheer, in none I see to-day.

9. The table of no brow doth loftiness
Of mind or charact'ry of Love bewray.

10. The sage no knowledge of assurance hath,
Hafiz no peace to study or to pray.

11. Show me the winehouse, that I may enquire
My issue from a knower of the way.

12. Though the fair's use be churlishness, what harm
Were it a lover's anguish to allay?

DXXXIV

1. Since in Irác Suléima [1614] made her station,
I long for her with longing past relation.

2. Harkye, o leader of the Loved One's camels,
After thy charge I yearn without cessation.

3. For lack of the Friend's sight my heart a-bleed is:
Oh out upon the days of separation!

4. Cast reason to the Zíndehroud [1615] and tipple
Wine to the young Irákis' acclamation.

5. Minstrel sweet-voiced, sweet-spoken, come; in Persian
Verse, chant thou to Iráki modulation. [1616]

6. The ghittern's sound And cupbearer's hand-clapping
Bring back lost youth to my rememoration.

7. Give me the wine-dregs, so that, drunk and blithesome,
I of life's dregs to friends may make oblation.

8. Come, give me, cupbearer, the heavy pottle,
God fill to thee the goblet of salvation!

9. A moment with well-willers be accordant:
Come, profit by the days of jubilation.

10. Life's Springtide in thy pasturage abideth;
God keep the days of union from mutation!

11. The time of union passed and we unheeding;
And now I'm in the throes of separation.

12. A wonder-goodly bride thou art, vine-daughter!
But whiles thou meritest repudiation.

13. Save a Messiah, free from worldly fetters,
None with the sun may have association. [1617]

14. Eld me forbiddeth from enjoying virgins,
Save in the way of clips and osculation.

15. Scorn not my tears for lack of you: how many
A sea is made by rillets' aggregation!

16. Since union with friends Is not our portion,
Cleave, Hafiz, to the mode of lamentation.

[1614] "Suleima", dim. of "Selma", the poetic appellation of the Beloved.
[1615] "Zindehroud", the river of Ispahan, the capital of (Persian) Irac.
[1616] "Iraki modulation", i. e. plaintive melodies, such as those composed by the famous Hemdani poet and musician of the 13th century, Fekhreddin Ibrahim ibn Shehriyar el Iraki.
[1617] According to Muslim legends, Jesus was called the Free [from worldly bonds] because he was unmarried and possessed nothing but a needle, with which he darned his clothes. When he ascended to heaven, he had the needle about him and this relic of worldly attachment sufficed to arrest his ascent at the fourth heaven, *that of the sun*; otherwise he would have attained, like Mohammed, to the Heaven of the Throne or Ninth Heaven.

DXXXV

1. At break of day I did rehearse The tale of longing to the wind;
The answer came, "Reliant be On heaven's grace and be resigned."

2. The pen no tongue hath to make known Love's mysteries; the words, that tell
The tale of wistfulness, within Expression's bounds are not confined.

3. Thy heart to Leila's tress make fast; By Mejnoun's wit thine actions shape;
For the discourse of reason is Obnoxious to the lover's mind.

4. Joseph of Egypt, whom the throne Forgetful of thy father made,
Harkye, of Jacob ask how sore For love and grief of thee he pined.

5. Giver and solacer of pain, With thy bewitching glance, thou art;
Hearts with thy musky tresses' plait Thou dost at once caress and bind.

6. What hopes upon the world set'st thou? What vantage seek'st thou from its love?
Lo, for this two-faced wanton ne'er Compassion had on humankind.

7. What in this mart of profit is With the contented dervish is:
Lord, be content and dervishhood For portion still to me assigned!

8. Dawn-prayer and night-lament the keys Are of the treasure of desire;
Fare thou this way and union sure With the heart-holder shalt thou find.

9. A Huma high of worth like thee, How shall it covet carrion?
Alas, that shadow of fair fate That on the base thou leav'st behind! [1618]

10. Hafiz, thy heart unto the fair Give not, but bear the perfidies,
The Turks of Samarcand whilere With the Khorasmians used, in mind. [1619]

11. To Hafiz the Shirázi's verse Turn in the mazes of the dance
The Turcomans of Samarcand, Ay, and the black-eyed girls of Ind.

[1618] The legendary bird, the Huma, is supposed to predict fair fortune and high estate
for any one on whom its shadow falls. The meaning is "O Beloved, why dost thou
bless the unworthy with thy favours?" a question which has, from time immemorial,
been asked of womankind and is still as far as ever from an answer.

[1619] Referring to a feud which befell between the Kings of Samarcand and Khorasmia
(Khuwarezm, Khiva,) and to the treachery of the former, who, in true Afrikander
fashion, made proposals for peace and having thus lulled his adversary into security,
swooped suddenly down upon his dominions, pillaged his kingdom and cut off his
head. By "Turks", in the secondary sense, are meant, as usual, the capricious and
lover-oppressing fair ones of the day.

DXXXVI

1. Harkye, skinker, here is cloud-shade; Here are Spring and river-side:
Do, I say not what: let reason, An thou have it, be thy guide. [1620]

2. Single-heartedness's fragrance From this fashion [1621] cometh not;
Wash in wine the Soufi patchcoat, With dissembling double-dyed.

3. Mean the world is; in its bounty Trust not: thou who'st seen the world,
Never look to mean ones, constant In well-doing to abide.

4. Lend thine ear unto the bulbul, How it saith, with plaintive note,
"Seek the rose of Heaven's favour; Tarry not nor turn aside."

5. Counsels twain I give thee; hearken And a hundred treasures gain:
By the door of easance enter; Leave the path of blame untried.

6. Rose nor wild rose ever blossomed From black iron and dull bronze:
An the Loved One's face thou seekest, Mirror fit for it provide. [1622]

7. Ere thou on the winehouse-threshold Dust become, a day or two
In the tavern's privy places From the world's affliction hide.

8. Goodness' root plant and the roses Of God's favour seek, in thanks
That once more to thee it given Is to see the blossom-tide.

9. Sayst thou, "Lo, the scent from Hafiz Cometh of hypocrisy"?
Blessings on thy tongue! For rarely Hath thy wit the truth descried.

[1620] i. e. Reason teaches that this is the time to give wine.
[1621] i. e. that of pietism.
[1622] i. e. Make pure thy heart, (likened, as usual, to a mirror) for its reception. Mirrors
  in Hafiz's days, were, of course, made of polished metal.

DXXXVII

1. The blessing of God, so long as the nights recur,
So long as the lutes respond to the dulcimer,

2. On Wádi-'l-Erák [1623] and its dwellers and on the house
By the bend of the stream, on the sands of the mountain spur!

3. A prayer of prayers for th'exiles I am of the world:
By day and by night I pray for the way-farer.

4. O whithersoever the Loved One fareth, God,
With guarding that never relaxeth, guard Thou her!

5. Nay, grieve not, my soul; For lo, in the chain of her tress,
All ease is the lot of the frenzied prisoner.

6. I die for longing. Oh would that I knew when I
Glad news shall hearken from union's harbinger!

7. Thy love's my solace at every time and tide
And thy remembrance my bosom-comforter.

8. My heart with passion for thee be still afire
Until for judgment I rise from the sepulchre!

9. Nay, how shall I compass the grace of a queen like thee,
I, ill-reputed and reckless reveller?

10. The down hath added an hundred charms to thee.
Thy life continue as many a glorious year!

11. O blessings upon that Limner Omnipotent,
Who compassed the moon with the crescent's character! [1624]

12. Thy life is needful; but else the loss of rank
And wealth's a trifle as light as gossamer.

13. God knoweth what Hafiz wisheth; and that to know
Doth me from asking my wish of Him deter.

[1623] "Wadi-'l-Erak" *poeticé*, abode of Beloved.
[1624] i. e. God, Who hath fringed thy cheek with down.

DXXXVIII

1. A greeting as sweet as love's fragrance I send
To that light of the eye of resplendence, the Friend.

2. A blessing, as 'twere the heart's light of the saints,
That lamp of the cell of the pious attend!

3. No comrade abideth: where, skinker, art thou?
My heart, all a-bleed with affliction, come tend."

4. Wine Soufi-o'erthrowing where is it they sell?
My patience with pious dissembling's at end.

5. My comrades have broken Love's pact on such wise
As if friendship had never existed or friend.

6. Thy face from the street of the Magians turn not,
For a master-key there for all puzzles they vend.

7. The world-bride, though fair to the limit is she,
In faithlessness yet doth all limit transcend.

8. If anydele spirit my wounded heart have,
For solace to stone-hearted churls 'twill not wend.

9. The secret of happiness hearken from me;
Thyself from ill fellowship 'tis to defend.

10. In beggarhood many a kingship I'd rear,
If with me, lustful soul, thou wouldst leave to contend.

11. Cease, Hafiz, of Fortune's durésse to complain:
God's purpose how canst thou, o slave, apprehend?

DXXXIX

1. Unto me the Unseen Speaker Of the inn, at break of day,
"Prithee come, for thou an ancient Of this threshold art," did say.

2. "Quaff, like Jem, a draught, that knowledge Of the World Invisible
"May withal to thee be given By the cup world-showing's ray."

3. At the winehouse-door Calénders [1625] Of debauchery there be,
Who the diadem of kingship Give and take at will away.

4. Brick beneath the head for pillow, Foot upon the Seven Stars,
See the fashion of the puissant And the style of men of sway.

5. Never shall our head dissever From the winehouse-door, whose roof
To the skies its peak upreareth, Though its walls be common clay.

6. Of God's mysteries, o farer Of the Path, if thou be ware,
Look the beggars of this portal That thou honour and obey.

7. If the sultanate of poortith Unto thee, o heart, they give,
Of the least of thy dominions Are the realms of night and day.

8. Save with Khizr for a way-mate, Travel not this road; the land
'Tis of darkness and of danger: In it fear to go astray.

9. Hafiz, of thy wanton wishes Be ashamed: what work, forsooth,
Hast thou done, that of the heavens Thou should ask both worlds to pay?

10. If thou know not how at poortith's Door to knock, the Vizier's seat,
Ay, and Touranshah's assembly, From thy hand-grasp let not aye.

[1625] i. e. devotees.

DXL

1. Brimmed with anguish is my bosom: O for easance of my woe!
Like to die am I for loneness; God, a bosom friend bestow!

2. Who hath any hope of solace From the swift-revolving Sphere?
Skinker, bring a cup, that easance For a moment I may know.

3. Come, that we our hearts may render To that Turk of Samarcand,
In whose tress's scent the breezes Of the Móuliyán [1626] do blow.

4. To a man of wit, "This matter See," quoth I. He laughed and said,
"Wondrous case and parlous matter! World distraught from top to toe!"

5. In the pit I burn of patience For that candle of Chigíl:
Nought of us the Turk king recketh: Where's a Rustem here below? [1627]

6. Ease and safety are affliction In the way of loveliking:
Wounded be his heart who seeketh Aught of salving for Love's woe!

7. World-consuming pilgrims only To the topers' street behove;
There nor softlings neither raw ones, Who Love's grief know not, may go.

8. In this world of ours there cometh To the hand no one true man;
It behoveth make another World and other men e'enso.

9. What availeth Hafiz' weeping 'Gainst the Loved One's scorn of love?
By this deluge, [1628] as a dew-drop All the Seven Seas would show.

[1626] "Mouliyan", a river of Bokhara, from whose banks the Beloved probably came.
    Hafiz here recalls a couplet of the famous Bokharan tenth-century poet Roudeki;
    "The wind of the river of Mouliyan cometh; The scent of the loving friend cometh".
    "Mouliyan" is also the plural of *mouli*, robber, plunderer; the poet thus hinting at his
    mistress's Turk-like character.
[1627] See note to Ode 376, 5.
[1628] i. e. his tears.

DXLI

1. Cupbearer, come; for full Grown is the tulip's cup of wine;
Why should we rave? How long, Mummer-like, juggle and rant and whine?

2. Pride and disdain forbear! Time hath the robes of the Kaiser doffed
Seen and the crowns abased Of many a high imperial line.

3. Up, to thy wits return! Drunk is the bird of the sward. Awake!
The slumber of nothingness Followeth hard on thy heels and mine.

4. Marry, o fresh Spring branch, Gracefully swayest thou to and fro:
Mayest thou suffer ne'er Scaith from the Winter's wind malign!

5. Never reliance was On the Sphere's love or its blandishments.
Woe to the mortal who Sitteth secure from its fell design!

6. E'en as to-morrow [1629] are Houris for us and Kauther-pool,
So, on like wise, to-day Skinker moon-faced and cup of wine.

7. Lo, of our boyhood's days How the East Wind rememb'reth us!
Boy, of that balm of life [1630] Give us, that doth away repine.

8. Never the pomp and sheen Heed of the rose: the hangman wind
Still under foot each leaf Streweth of rose and eglantine.

9. Harkye, the pottle-cup Fill to the health of Hatim Tai; [1631]
Let us the puckfist churl's Book of account to nought consign. [1632]

10. Lo, how that wine, that hue Unto the Redbud gave and grace,
Forth of its [1633] cheek, in sweat, Casteth its [1633] nature light and fine!

11. Come, to the meads the couch Bear; for the cypress up hath stood;
Ghittern and reed abide Girded for service at thy shrine.

12. Viol and harp and pipe, Hark, how the minstrels of wood and lea
Do, with their various song, Into one harmony still entwine!

13. Hafiz, to Rei and Roum, Yea. unto Egypt and Cathay,
Fared hath the fame of this Magic-bewild'ring speech of thine.

[1629] "To-morrow", i. e. in the next world.
[1630] i. e. wine.
[1631] The name of the famous Arabian type of liberality is written variously, Hatim Tai
    or Tei^Hatim-i-Tai, Hatim-Teyi or i-Teyi etc., according to the exigencies of Persian
    metre. The (Arabic) form is Hatim et Tayy or Tayyi.
[1632] i. e. let us close our accounts with the miserly folk of the present day, from whom
    it is so difficult to extract largesse, and have no more to do with them.
[1633] "Its", i. e. the Redbud's.

DXLII

1. A city [1634] full of lovelings; On every side a fair!
Friends, if ye would be doing, The call to love is there.

2. The world's eye never looked on A fresher maid than this:
Nor ever goodlier quarry Fell into any's snare.

3. Who ever saw a body, Like hers, of very soul?
Ne'er be her skirt polluted By dust of earthly care!

4. Why driv'st thou from thy presence A broken one like me?
A kiss or an embracement's The utmost of my prayer.

5. Pure is the wine and goodly The season: quick, enjoy
The time; for who to reckon On next year's Spring can dare?

6. See, in the garden topers Are; rose and tulip like,
Each in his hand a goblet, To a friend's health, doth bear. [1635]

7. Love's knot how shall I loosen? This mystery how solve?
A pain 'tis and a sore one; Ay, and a hard affair.

8. Bond to some wanton's tresses Each hair of Hafiz is:
In such a land untroubled Uneath it is to fare.

[1634] "A city", i. e. Shiraz?
[1635] "Des menuisiers, des ébenistes, Des entrepreneurs en bâtisses, Qu'on dirait d'un' prairie en fleurs, Émaillée de mille couleurs".

DXLIII

1. O Wind of the East, the fragrance Her tresses shed thou hast:
Abide thou with us, for her perfume In token-stead thou hast.

2. My heart, full of jewels of myst'ries Of beauty and love, to thee
I'll trust, if a mind to guard it From danger and dread thou hast.

3. The garment of pride in beauty Beseemeth for thee alone;
For, rose-like, all manner colour And fragrance inbred thou hast.

4. To thee, like the sun, pertaineth Of beauty's sovereignty
To vaunt thee; for moon-faced servants, That follow thy tread, thou hast.

5. Against thine acceptable fashions There's nothing one can object,
Save only that churlish guardians And keepers ill-bred thou hast.

6. Nay, how should the nightingale's ditties Be pleasing to thee, o rose,
When idle-tongued birds to hearken Inclining, misled, thou hast?

7. My head with thy draught is fuddled: I wonder from what jar came
The wine that in yonder tankard, Like rubies blood-red, thou hast?

8. Nay, boast not, o stream-side cypress, Of thine erectness; since cause,
For shame, when my love thou meetest, To lower the head thou hast.

9. I prayed for her weal, and laughing, "Who art thou and what's this prate?
"Ay, marry, and what's the business With me that," she said, "thou hast?"

10. Hafiz, from cloister-corner Seek not Love's jewel: forth
Fare, if a mind the highway Of quest to tread thou hast.

DXLIV

1. The parasites of the existence Of Love are men and Jinn;
Show somewhat of will, if somewhat Of happiness thou wouldst win.

2. If able thou'rt not of vision, For union seek thou not;
For Jem's cup profiteth nothing To those that sightless bin.

3. How long the dawn-draught and slumber Of morning? With midnight prayer
And weeping at dawn, endeavour For pardon of thy sin.

4. From us, with the coin of beauty, The Sultanate come and buy.
I rede thee neglect not this traffic, Lest haply thou reap chagrin.

5. Come, do thine endeavour, Hafiz, Nor lack of a lot in love;
For no one a slave will purchase Who knows not to weave nor spin.

6. Since all that I've heard of knowledge A door on amazement hath,
Henceforth with intoxication And witlessness I'll be twin.

7. What manner of magic puppet, O dainty sorcerer, art,
That absent thou'rt not from vision Nor present, indeed, therein?

8. Since morning and eve the candle Thou art of another's halls,
A thousand true-hearted lovers Are wasting to bone and skin.

9. The prayer of the corner-sitters Averteth calamity:
Why is it no glance thou castest On me, the beggarkin?

10. Oh who to my lord the Vizier This word will bear from me?
"This couplet of mine pray treasure Thy memory within:

11. "Come drink, for, the world and its fashions If thou as I have seen,
"Thou'lt drink of the winecup, certes, And not of the cup chagrin."

12. Be never the cap of lordship Aslant on thy goodly head!
For worthy of crown and sceptre Art thou of Fortune's kin.

13. The highway of Love and questing's A wonder-perilous path:
May heaven's protection bring thee Safe to a sheltering inn!

14. The East wind scattereth perfume, To even thy tress, and the rose,
To vie with thy face, unveileth Her cheek of cramozin.

15. By dint of the resolution Of Hafiz, I hope once more
To commerce anights with Leila, When moonlit nights begin.

DXLV

1. O thou, for whom united With grief we are fore'er,
For love of thee I've wasted My life; and nought I care.

2. No lack-wits know how happy The dogs are of thy street:
Would it to me were given With them to sojourn there!

3. Divulged, o friend, my secret Is by my tears become;
O thou my case that knowest, Have ruth on my despair!

4. O company of lovers Sincere, look not for faith
From those possessed of beauty; For faithless are the fair.

5. Dry-lipped we by the water Of Life have passed: our thirst
Quench with a draught of liquor, O skinker debonair!

6. For love of thee, religion And world I've left; for love
Of thee, the quest of honour And wealth did I forswear.

7. If Hafiz, in thy doorway, Die on thy threshold-dust,
For certain, life eternal Shall fall unto his share.

DXLVI

1. Thou, whose cheek for shame the roses maketh wet;
Thou, whose lip in winecups arrack doth beget; [1636]

2. Rain on tulips is't or rosewater on rose,
Dew on fire or on thy visage is it sweat?

3. From my sight went that bow-browed One, and my heart,
Straying after her, was taken in the net.

4. Go, muézzin! "Come to prayer!" say: bawl thy fill!
From my hand to night her tress I will not let.

5. In the minstrel's hand the ghittern place awhile;
Bid him sing, but first the harp-strings throbbing set.

6. Light the chafing-dish: cast wood upon the fire
And for winter's cold and rigour never fret. [1637]

7. Moan henceforth unto our lord the Prince of Rei
Make, if fortune with oppression thee beset.

8. Thou, because of whose largesse, the fame and name
Of the generous deeds of Hatim men forget;

9. Take his life, who would it render for a draught
Of thy grace, and with a cupful pay the debt.

10. Take the cup in hand, like Hafiz, and for Jem
Nor Kawoús concernment harbour nor regret.

[1636] Arrack ('arec), syn. "sweat", is the sweat of wine, as rosewater that of roses.—
Soudi.
[1637] Shiraz is a very cold place in winter.

DXLVII

1. Skinker, bring wine and headache From me come do away;
The suff'rance, from wine that cometh, Wine only can allay.

2. The lamp of the friends' assembly, Without the blood of the grape
And face of the fair one, shineth But with uncertain ray.

3. Conceit not thyself of the magic Of thy seducing glance;
That self-conceit profiteth nothing I've proved this many a day.

4. With many an admonition Thou biddest us leave to love;
In never a code, professor, This canon down they lay.

5. Alive, by the blessing of love is The soul of the man of heart:
If love thou ignore, excusement Thou hast; [1638] so peace, I pray!

6. For one caress from the Loved One, My halidom I sold;
Alack for devotion wasted And abstinence thrown away!

7. The realm of the heart to gladness Its face again hath set:
The sorrows are past of sev'rance And union is come to stay.

8. Our suff'rance for her, o Hafiz, Behoveth not tell to all:
To him who hath suffered sev'rance And to him only say.

[1638] i. e. thou art excusable, because thou art naturally an ass.

DXLVIII

1. O zephyr, the scent of the fair hast thou;
From-her-ward thy musk-breathing air hast thou.

2. Harkye, long-handedness [1639] practise not!
What, marry, to do with her hair hast thou?

3. What art thou beside her face, o rose?
It musk hath and prickles to wear hast thou.

4. Sweet basil, what art thou beside her down?
It freshness and dust to share hast thou.

5. Narcissus, what art to her eye? With wine
It blithe is and headache fore'er hast thou. [1640]

6. O cypress, with that her lofty shape,
Seen in the meads, what compare hast thou?

7. O reason, what choice in the love of her,
What power to escape from the snare hast thou?

8. Union, o Hafiz, one day thou'lt reach,
If patience to wait and bear hast thou.

[1639] "Long-handedness", i. e. usurpation.
[1640] Allusion to drooping habit of narcissus-flower.

DXLIX

1. Rife is unfaith to day Among the human race;
Of friendship there is not In any man a trace.

2. People of merit now, For indigence, the hand
Of beggary extend To all the mean and base.

3. A man of worth, to day, Exemption from chagrin
No moment doth enjoy, In this our time and place;

4. What while the ignorant In affluence and ease
Abide, for nowadays Their ware is high in grace.

5. Nay, if the poet verse As water utter clear,
Whose brightness from men's hearts The dust of doubt doth chase,

6. For avarice and stint, They give him not a doit,
Though he with Sénayí [1641] Might vie it, face to face.

7. Unto my sense's ear Quoth Reason yesternight,
"Thyself this indigence To bear with patience brace.

8. "Make thou thy stock-in-trade Contentment and consume;
"Since 'gainst this pain and grief Resourceless is thy case.

9. "O Hafiz, come; from me This counsel lay to heart:
"If thou wouldst rise, thyself Needs must thou first abase."

[1641] Sheikh Senayi (or Thenayi), a famous Gheznevi poet of the 12th century.

DL

1. Zealot, begone, With the hope that thou cherishest!
I too, like thee, Have a hope of mine own in my breast.

2. Saving the cup, What hath the tulip in hand?
Cupbearer, come; Bring what thou hast of the rest. [1642]

3. Me of the crew Of the frenzied ones render! Good
Though soberness be, Yet drunkenness ever was best.

4. Abstain thou from me, O Soufi, abstain! For lo,
A vow to abstain From abstinence have I profest.

5. Nay, to the curl Of her ringlets come bind thy heart,
If safety thou seek And freedom from strife and unrest.

6. 'Fore heaven, thy vow Of repentance in rosetime renounce;
The time of the rose, At most, is a twenty days' guest.

7. O comrades and friends, The springtime of life passeth by,
As passeth the wind Of the Spring o'er the flower-meadows' breast.

8. Come, Hafiz; drink Of the radiant ruby-red wine!
Why lettest thou life In heedlessness pass unblest?

[1642] i. e. of last night's wine.

DLI

1. Since all that thy soul desireth, Without impair, hast thou,
Of the case of the hapless weaklings, Like me, what care hast thou?

2. Ask soul and heart ofl the bondman And take them incontinent;
For even o'er those commandment, Who freemen else were, hast thou.

3. I marvel, since never a middle [1643] Thou hast, how every tide
The office of middle-holder [1644] Amidst the fair hast thou.

4. Painting nor patch behoveth The whiteness of thy cheek;
Since black of the musky cheek-down On Redbud there hast thou.

5. Drink wine, that withal light-hearted, My fair, thou still mayst be;
The head more by token heavy With wine whene'er hast thou.

6. Nor cruelty henceforth practise Nor chiding against my heart.
Nay, do what thou mayst; occasion For kindness, I swear, hast thou.

7. The power in thy choice a thousand Arrows of cruelty
To launch at my stricken bosom Or to forbear hast thou.

8. The watchers' annoy with patience Suffer and still be blithe;
For this is a straw, the Loved One If debonair hast thou.

9. If but for a breath to union Thy hand with the Friend attain,
Go; all that the world possesseth, Worth wish and prayer, hast thou.

10. Whene'er of her lip of ruby Thou tellest or hearest tell,
Behovement in mouth sheer sugar Of speech to wear hast thou.

11. When, Hafiz, the rose from this garden Thou bearest off by the skirt,
Of the gardener's weeping and wailing What reason for care hast thou? [1645]

[1643] i. e. since thy waist is so small that it may be said not to exist at all.

[1644] i. e. Mediator, as being the queen of them all.

[1645] i. e. If thou canst win to the enjoyment of the Beloved, thou hast no need to reck of the clamour of rivals and enviers.

DLII

1. When, cypress-tree like, in a rose-mead Thou swayest to and fro,
Each rose, for despite at thy visage, Doth thorn-pricks undergo.

2. Because of thy black-heart tresses All rings in turmoil are;
Because of thine eyes' enchantment, All corners sick men show. [1646]

3. Nay, go not to sleep, like my fortune, O languorous eye of the Friend!
For thee from each side pursueth Some waker's wail of woe.

4. The coin of my soul the strewage Be of thy way, albe
The coin of the soul scant value Hath in thy sight, I trow. [1647]

5. O heart, be not ever busy With thought of the tress of the fair:
Whilst black is thy thought, [1648] how easance From dolour shalt thou know?

6. Gone is my head nor cometh Th' affair to head: my heart
Ta'en is and thou on the captive Dost no regard bestow.

7. Quoth I, "Be the midst of our circle, Point-like". She laughed and said,
"How compasses like, o Hafiz, Art thou, that thou speakest so!" [1649]

[1646] i. e. thy tresses have troubled all the Soufi conclaves ("rings", word used p. g.) and made all the cloister-folk love-sick.

[1647] i. e. Thou cravest something more substantial, hard cash.

[1648] Thought styled black (i. e. gloomy) as being of the *black* tress of the Beloved.

[1649] i. e. In what a whirl (like the compass-leg) thy head must be, that thou makest so ridiculous a proposal!

DLIII

1. Thou, who *soul* at once and *souls* [1650] art, Be my soul thy sacrifice!
Be my head no less thy ransom! Else a-whirl 'tis, like the skies.

2. From the street-end of thy quarter I uneath my head can lift:
Marry, folk do not thus lightly Undertake a hard emprise.

3. Raw ones able for endurance Are not, like the wing-burnt moth: [1651]
Unbeseeming is for softlings This soul-scattering exercise. [1652]

4. To be patient in thine absence Only on compulsion is;
And with thee to sit unfrighted From amazement doth arise.

5. 'Tis thy watchers that have patent Made the secret of my heart:
Not for long a secret matter Bideth hidden from the spies.

6. So that sappy may the sapling Of thy shape abide and fresh,
It behoveth that thou plant it By the river of mine eyes. [1653]

7. In thy tress-crook one day seeing That my heart, quoth I to it,
"How is it with thee, o captive, And how far'st thou, prisoner-wise?"

8. "Nay, how otherwhat," it answered, "Canst thou do than envy me?
"For the pomp and place of Sultans Is not every beggar's prize." [1654]

9. Lo, with us to commerce, Hafiz, Is not of thy competence:
'Tis enough if at our street-end Thou dog-tending exercise. [1655]

[1650] *Jan o janan*; the Persian word (*janan*) for "beloved" is the plural of *jan*, soul.
[1651] i. e. the experienced lover.
[1652] i. e. that of loverhood.
[1653] i. e., it behoveth that thy shape be still present to my sight.
[1654] i. e., to be the captive of the Beloved's charms is to be equal to the greatest kings.
[1655] This last couplet appears to be spoken by the Beloved. It is sufficient honour for
the lover to be allowed to commerce with the dogs of the Beloved's street.

DLIV

1. Since in the realm of beauty To-day thou'rt sovereign,
Thee of thy lip to lovers Their wish beseemeth deign.

2. How long wilt thou with lovers Use coquetry and scorn?
How long on heart-lorn wretches Heap malice and disdain?

3. How long shall we in languor Be, like thine eye? How long,
Thy tress like, in contortion And wilderment remain?

4. Thou wouldst on me have mercy, God wot, if aught thou knewst
Of what from thee I suffer Of cruelty and pain.

5. Much capital behoveth Unto the lover's trade,
To wit, hearts fire-resembling And eyes that rivers rain.

6. I pined in separation; But the East Wind hope's scent
From thine enjoyment's garden Hath brought me once again.

7. Though I, in hope of union, Should at the Rising live,
My head, for shame, I never From earth to lift were fain.

8. If of the wine of union With thee a draught I drink,
What while I live, I'll always From soberness abstain. [1656]

9. Ruler art thou all-puissant And slaves and weak are we:
'Tis thine with scorn to slay us, With favour to assain.

10. Some little show of pity For Hafiz' sorry case!
How long shall he be abject, How long hope on in vain?

[1656] That one draught being sufficient to keep me perpetually intoxicated.

DLV

1. Skinker, for liquor if love be thine,
Harkye, set nothing before but wine!

2. Prayer-rug and patchcoat in tavern sell
And bring me a draught of the juice of the vine.

3. Heart-live an thou be, in the rose-mead of souls
Hark the cry of the topers, "O Live One [1657] Divine!

4. "Ye sick, come to healing! Be *this* world and that
"As nothing, with Love when compared, in your eyne!"

5. The secrets of hearts in Love's path are the theme
Of the chirp of the lute and the flageolet's whine.

6. One pure-hearted beggar than Hatim et Tai's
A thousand's more worth in the way of Love's shrine.

7. The townspeople after her, sovereign-like,
There cometh that Peri-faced idol of mine,

8. Men's eyes all fast fixed on her beauteous face
And moon-cheek, with sweat all for pudour ashine.

9. How long shall my heart thus with sorrow be torn?
Till when shall poor Hafiz in grief for thee pine?

[1657] "Live One" (*Heyy*) one of the 99 names of God. *Ya Heyy* is an exclamation of rejoicing.

DLVI

1. Goodlier than the tavern-quarter E'er a place is not:
May the Fates to me a refuge There in eld allot!

2. That which I desire (Why hidden Should it be from thee?)
Is a wineflask and a fair one In a pleasant grot.

3. My abode the Magians' convent Is: a fragrant stead!
All my thought is of the idols: [1658] Troth, a blessed thought!

4. What hast drunken that thou sayest, In the world like me
Is no madcap? This the speech is Of a silly sot.

5. Practise modesty and breeding: For to every one,
Like the Rajah and the Brahmin, [1659] Talk beseemeth not.

6. How aught else than thee, Beloved, Shall our mind contain?
Saving thee alone, of no one Reck I anywhat.

7. Prithee, pity have on Hafiz' Waste and wounded heart;
For to-day a sure to-morrow Followeth, [1660] God wot.

[1658] i. e. of fair ones.
[1659] Allusion to the Hitopadesa, in which the interlocutors are a king and a Brahmin. "It is not every one who can talk like these". One translator makes the extraordinary comment on this couplet that Brahmin "signifies one who hath connection with those of the cloister." I know no reason for this strange suggestion, which, by the way, comes from a man who is too modest to write the words "breast, bosom" etc. and accordingly substitutes for them, when they occur, the grotesque alternative "chest."
[1660] i. e. there will come a certain Day of Reckoning, when thou (the Beloved) wilt be called to account for thy cruel treatment of thy lovers.

DLVII

1. 'Tis morn and from the clouds Of January droppeth dew;
The dawn-draught come prepare And fill the pottle-cup anew.

2. Drink, drink the goblet's blood; For lawful 'tis its blood to drink;
And ply the topers' craft; For 'tis a worthy work to do.

3. And if to thee at dawn Cropsickness give an aching head,
With wine for thee 'tis best To cleave cropsickness' head in two.

4. Cupbearer, be alert; For grief in ambush is for us;
Minstrel, that way and mode Of song thou farest in pursue.

5. Give wine; for the harp bent Its head unto mine ear and said,
"The present still enjoy: This crookbacked elder's rede ensue." [1661]

6. Wine, Hafiz, I conjure By topers' independence, drink
And list the minstrel's cry "He th' Independent is!" [1662] unto.

[1661] The "crookbacked elder" is, of course, the harp itself. See previous note.
[1662] An exclamation of much the same kind as "O Live One!" before explained. "The
Independent" is one of the 99 names of God.

DLVIII

1. Life in fruitlessness and folly Passeth by and all in vain:
Boy, come, give me quick the winecup, If old age thou wouldst attain.

2. From Et Tour [1663] the lightning flasheth; Ay, for certain saw I it:
Haply, with a brand for kindling I shall turn to thee again. [1664]

3. What delights are in this city, [1665] That the falcons of the Path [1666]
With the poor and abject station Of the fly content remain!

4. Yesternight, among her servants, To her doorway I repaired;
But, "Who art thou, friendless, helpless Stranger?" quoth she, in disdain.

5. So that, incense-like, a moment We her skirt might take, [1667] on fire,
For the sake of a sweet savour, We our hearts to lay were fain.

6. It behoveth whosoever's World-renowned for musky breath, [1668]
Though his heart all blood, musk-pod like, [1669] Be, a cheerful mien maintain.

7. Gone's the caravan and sleeping In the ambush-place art thou:
'Las, that heedless of so many Clam'ring camel-bells thou'st lain!

8. Ope thy wings and from the Touba [1670] Warble: pity that a bird
Such as thou should in the birdcage Of this sorry world be ta'en!

9. Nay, how long shall everywhither Hafiz run for love of thee?
God for him the path that leadeth Unto thee, my wish, make plain!

[1663] "Et Tour", Arabic name of the Sinaitic range. The couplet alludes to the Koranic
story (before set out) of the first appearance of God to Moses.
[1664] A parody of Koran XX, 9, 10. "When he (Moses) saw the fire, he said to his
people, 'Tarry ye [here]; verily I perceive fire. Peradventure I shall bring you
kindling-stuff" (i. e. somewhat of live coals to kindle fire withal). The meaning is an
augury of approaching union with the Beloved.
[1665] "This city", i. e. Shiraz?
[1666] "Falcons of the Path", i. e. men of high worth and learning, poets and servants of
the Ideal.

[1667] An allusion to the Oriental custom of holding the lighted censer, fed with aloes-wood, benzoin-berries or other fumigating stuff, under the skirts, so that the clothes may become impregnated with the perfume.

[1668] To say that one is "renowned for musky breath" is equivalent to describing him as a poet, writer or man of genius etc., generally famed for gifts or accomplishments. The rhyme-word of No. 5 is here repeated and Soudi quaintly remarks that Hafiz must have written this ghazel when he was drunk, or he would not have repeated the rhyme; but he (Hafiz) often does this, when Soudi takes no notice of it.

[1669] "Heart all blood, musk-pod like", an allusion to the popular belief, before noticed, that musk is formed by extravasation of blood in the muskdeer.

[1670] "Touba", i. e. the Lote-tree of Paradise, before noticed.

DLIX

1. The tale of my longing I've written; And tearful was mine eye;
O come, for, without thee, for grieving, Indeed, I'm like to die.

2. "O sojourning places of Selma, Where is your Selma gone?"
To these my two eyes, for longing, How many a time said I!

3. Indeed, 'tis a marvellous matter, Ay, and a parlous case
That I, who am slain, am patient: My slayer it is doth cry.

4. Who is it, to whom pertaineth To cavil at thy pure skirt,
Who'rt pure as the dew that falleth On rose-leaves from on high?

5. The Pen of the Prime, on water And earth when it wrote, the dust
Of thy foot took and added lustre To tulip and rose thereby.

6. The East wind an ambergris-shedder Grown is: o skinker, up!
With the sun of the vine, the fragrant, The limpid, us come ply.

7. Sloth leave and thrive; as the adage Telleth, alertness is
The wayfarer's best provision And wakefulness of eye.

8. No tittle, without thy presence, Abideth of me; forsooth,
The goods of my life I nowise Save from thy face descry.

9. How in the praise of thy beauty Shall Hafiz speak? Indeed,
Thine attributes apprehension, Like those of God, defy.

DLX

1. Unto kings from me, the beggar, Who a message will convey?
"In the vintners' street two thousand Jems for one poor cup sell they."

2. Evil-famed am I and ruined; Yet I hope that, with the aid
Of the powerful, to somewhat Of good name attain I may.

3. Thou that sell'st the Grand Elixir, Cast an eye on our base coin;
Stock-in-trade for we possess not And withal a snare we lay.

4. With the chaplet's grains, o elder, From the path allure us not.
Such a wary bird as I am Is not lightly made a prey.

5. Pietists, begone! for gone is Piety from us: sheer wine
Quaffed have we and care for honour And repute have cast away.

6. At the Friend's ill faith I marvel, Who enquiry deigneth not,
Letter neither greeting sendeth, Never word doth write or say.

7. For thy bondage am I longing: Buy and sell me not again;
For a slave of such good auspice Is not met with every day.

8. Marry, whither shall I carry My complaint? To whom relate
How that lip of thine our life was, But, alack! it had no stay?

9. If mature be yonder fellow [1671] And this wine of ours unripe,
Better than a thousand ripe ones Is a raw one anyway. [1672]

10. Loose the arrow of thine eyelash And the blood of Hafiz shed;
For that no one taketh vengeance, When 'tis such as thou that slay.

[1671] i. e. the pietist.
[1672] i. e., Better a thousand times new wine than the company of such as he.

DLXI

1. "Thou, thou art a second Joseph," Rumour the folk of thee:
But, truly, when I consider, Better art thou than he.

2. Than that which they say far sweeter Thou art by thy sugared smile:
Shirin, [1673] o Chosróës of fair ones, Thou art of the century.

3. One cannot the rosebud liken Unto that mouth of hers:
Was ever a rosebud founden So strait of mouth as she?

4. An if at thy shape dumbfounded The cypress bide, move thou;
Because thou the soaring cypress In going dost outsway.

5. An hundredfold times, "I'll give thee Thy wish of my mouth," saidst thou.
Why art thou all tongue, like the lily, That's called of man "the free"?

6. Saidst thou, "Thy heart's wish I will give thee And take in exchange thy life."
I fear, for my life, thou'lt take it Nor give me the promised fee.

7. The shield of my life with its arrows Thy languorous eye doth pierce:
Who ever a sick one wielding So stiff a bow did see?

8. If any, though but for a moment, Thou banish from out thy sight,
Tear-like, from the eye of creation, Cast out forthright is he.

9. Nay, drive not thy grief-stricken Hafiz Away from before thy face;
For heart he and youth and religion Hath given for love of thee.

[1673] *Shirin*, the name of the favourite of Khusrau Perwiz, signifies, as before remarked,
   "sweet".

DLXII

1. Her lip I kiss and wine I tipple: yea,
Unto life's water have I found the way.

2. When she is by, I cannot others see
And can her secret unto none bewray.

3. The cup her lip doth kiss and drinketh blood;
The roses see her cheek and melt away. [1674]

4. The rose from cell to garden's brought its throne;
Like it, aside abstention's prayer-rug lay.

5. Come, give the cup and think no more of Jem:
Who knoweth when Jem was and when was Kei?

6. Clap hand to harp, o moon-faced minstrel: sweep
The strings, that cry aloud of her I may.

7. Leave not the toper cropsick like her eye;
To her lip's health, o skinker, wine purvey!

8. The soul is loath to leave a frame wherein
Through vein and nerve the grapeblood courseth aye.

9. Whenas "Hou! Hou!" the bird of morning saith,
Set not from hand the cup and cry "Hey! Hey!" [1675]

10. Hafiz, draw in thy tongue awhile and hark
What by the reedpipe's tongue the tongueless say. [1676]

[1674] i. e. dissolve into rose-water.
[1675] "Hey!" a toper's exclamation.
[1676] Be silent and list to the speech of inanimate things.

DLXIII

1. Foxed with the cup of Love Am I: bring wine forthright.
Skinker, fill up the cup: Wine's the assembly's light.

2. Love for her moon-like cheek Ill to conceal it is:
Cupbearer, give us wine! Minstrel, the ghittern smite!

3. Bowed like the ring [1677] my shape Made I, so ne'er again
I from her door may be Driv'n by the watcher's spite.

4. Waiting thy face to see, Hoping and we are one:
Union desiring, still Chase we the dreams of night. [1678]

5. Foxed with thine eye I'm grown: Am I unworth a word?
Sick for thy rubies twain: [1679] Passeth reply my right?

6. Hafiz, why set thy heart Thus on the fair ones' thought?
When was the traveller's thirst Quenched by the mirage sight?

[1677] i. e. the knocker-ring.
[1678] i. e. we waste our lives in the pursuit of vain imaginings.
[1679] i. e. lips.

DLXIV

1. "Cry 'Wine!' and scatter roses: From Time what more seek'st thou?"
Thus spake the rose at daybreak. Bulbul, what say'st thou now?

2. The cushion to the garden Bear, there the rose to smell,
Wine drink and kiss the loveling's And skinker's lips and brow.

3. To whom will bliss, I wonder, Thy laughing rosebud give?
For whom is it thou growest, O lovely red rose bough?

4. Unto the meads the box-tree Sway of thy shape, that so
The cypress heart-allurement May learn, its why and how. [1680]

5. To-day, when full thy market Is of the buyers' throng,
Against thy need, provision Of goodness get thee now.

6. Since beauty's candle standeth In the wind's passage-way,
Thyself with store of merit, Against thy need, endow. [1681]

7. Thou, whose each curl an hundred Musk-pods of China's worth,
Well were it if some fragrance Of kindliness hadst thou!

8. Each bird to the king's rosegarth Comes with a different tale,
The bulbul with song-singing, Hafiz with prayer and vow. [1682]

[1680] Rhyme-word of 1. 1 repeated in original.
[1681] Variant of No. 5; same rhyme-word in original.
[1682] Rhyme-word of 1. 2 repeated in original.

DLXV

1. 'Tis the Springtide: strive that in it Blithe and gay thou be;
For full many a rose shall blossom And in clay thou be.

2. With its covert speech, like counsel Giveth thee the harp:
Counsels profit but if minded To obey thou be.

3. What thou now shouldst drink, I say not, Nor with whom shouldst sit:
This thou knowest, if quick-witted Anyway thou be.

4. In the meads each leaf's the record Of a different case;
Heedless of these all 'twere pity If for aye thou be.

5. Full of terrors though the road be To the Friend, 'tis eath,
If acquainted with the stages Of the way thou be.

6. Worldly cark the cash for nothing Of thy life will take,
If in this unease and sorrow Night and day thou be.

7. If, o Hafiz, lofty fortune Aid to thee vouchsafe,
Of that excellent Beloved Shalt the prey thou be.

DLXVI

1. O breeze of felicity's morning, Go with the sign which thou knowest;
Pass at the time by her quarter, That fair one of mine, which thou knowest.

2. The courier thou art of her secrets: Our eye on the end of the way is;
Of grace, uncommanded, go; hasten On that wise, in fine, which thou knowest.

3. Go, say to her, "Out of my hand-hold My weak soul departeth. 'Fore heaven,
"Bestow on us that, [1683] of yon ruby Soul-soothing of thine, which thou knowest.

4. "These words on such wise that none knoweth I've written: do thou of thy favour,
"In secret from all, on that fashion To read them incline which thou knowest.

5. "How else should I do than to centre My hopes in thy gold-wroughten girdle,
"The subtlety [1684] since, o my fair one, Its foldings entwine which thou knowest.

6. "The thought unto us of thy falchion As water, to him who's athirst, is;
"Thy captive thou'st taken; come slay him On that wise divine which thou knowest."

7. All one in this case of Love's traffic Are Turkish and Arabic, Hafiz;
The moods and the tenses of passion In each tongue decline which thou knowest.

[1683] i. e. a kiss.
[1684] i. e. her tiny waist.

DLXVII

1. Harkye, quaff the vinejuice From the gallon-bowl
And from out thy bosom Pluck the root of dole.

2. Like the cup, still open Keep the heart. How long,
Wilt thou, winejar fashion, Stopper up the soul?

3. When thou hast a pottle Drunk of selflessness,
Nevermore thenceforward Wilt thou Self extol.

4. Like the stone be, under Foot; not, water-like,
Wet of skirt, unstable, Mingling deep and shoal.

5. Heart to wine, man-fashion, Bind and so thyself
Sever from dissembling Piety's control.

6. Up and make an effort, Hafiz-like, that Self
In the Loved One's passage Thou mayst cast for toll.

DLXVIII

1. Count, o count the present gain, In so far as in thee lies:
For the very sum of life, Soul, this moment recognize.

2. Life of us the heav'ns require, In exchange for what they give:
Strive thy share of ease to take From the favour of the skies.

3. Lovers' counsel hear and life Enter by the door of cheer:
All the fleeting world can give Is not worth a brace of sighs.

4. Speak before the pietist Not of toping; hidden pain
It behoveth not expose To the uninitiate's eyes.

5. Gard'ner, when from place I pass, Be it counted sin to thee
Other than the Friend to plant On my rest-place, cypress-wise.

6. Nought the pitcher-breaker [1685] knows That the Soufi's household gear
Still a garnet-coloured stuff, Like red rubies, [1686] doth comprise.

7. Swift thou farest and the blood Of the folk thy lashes shed;
Soul, I fear thou'lt lag behind, Ere the end of the emprise.

8. Scorn not, sugar-lips, the prayers Of the folk that watch by night:
Seals of Solomon [1687] the guard Of the most High Name should prize.

9. I my heart essayed to guard From the arrows of thy looks;
But the bowman of thy brows Overcame it by surprise.

10. Gone my precious Joseph is: Pity, brethren, prithee have;
For my anguish for his loss Jacob's sufferance outvies.

11. Craving after wine will slay The repentant penitent:
That, which doth repentance bring, Do not thou, if thou be wise. [1688]

12. Enter thou one day my door, So for joy I may my hands
Clap and say, "My guest become Very light is from the skies."

13. With some scantling of largesse Troubled Hafiz set at rest,
Thou, whose tangled ringlet's curl Doth all troubles tranquilize.

14. If, o stony hearted fair, Heedless thou of me abide,
Asef, [1689] second of the name, Of my case I will apprize.

[1685] "Pitcher-breaker", i. e. the Mohtesib.
[1686] i. e. wine.
[1687] Beloved's mouth likened to Solomon's seal-ring, on which "the Most High Name",

450

i. e. the all-powerful secret name of God, was engraved.
[1688] i. e., do not renounce wine, or thou wilt repent it.
[1689] "Asef", i. e. the Grand Vizier.

DLXIX

1. Thy lover, o my soul, I am And know that thou, too, knowest it;
For thou at once the things unseen Dost see and readest the unwrit.

2. When before Adam angels bowed, Homage to thee they meant; for in
Thy beauty somewhat that o'erpassed Humanity they did admit.

3. Thy ringlets' curve the gathering-place Is, at this present, of all hearts;
May they from that fell wind that brings Disseverance be ever quit!

4. With Fortune's succour yet I hope That I her girdle may unloose.
Thy frowning brows, o firmament, In heaven's name, for me unknit!

5. Shake out thy tress and so to dance And sport the Soufi rouse and shake
From out his cassock's every patch A thousand idols, there that sit.

6. The fragrance of the fair ones' tress Our eye's lamp-kindler is: o Lord,
Grant that this union of the wind Of wilderment be still unsmit!

7. How can the carper apprehend The case of lover and belov'd?
Blind eyes see nought and hidden still Love's secrets are from lack of wit.

8. Angered with wayfellows to be Is not the usance of the sage;
In mem'ry of the time of ease, To hardships patiently submit.

9. Alack that, like the wind of dawn, The nights of bliss have passed away!
Now that of union thou'rt bereft, O heart, thou know'st the worth of it.

10. Hafiz, the fancy of the ring Of that her tress deludeth thee:
Forbear to ply the knocker-ring Of luck impossible, unfit. [1690]

[1690] i. e. to strive after an unattainable felicity.

DLXX

1. A thousand endeavours, Beloved, I've made that my mate thou shouldst be,
That fulfiller of wish and desire to My heart ever strait thou shouldst be;

2. That a breath to the hovel-of-mourning Of lovers forlorn thou shouldst come.
That consoler anights to my bosom, The disconsolate, thou shouldst be;

3. That my lamp thou shouldst be and my lantern, The light of my night-walking eye,
That the hope-bringing comrade and friend of My hopeless estate thou shouldst be.

4. Shall I this desire see accomplished In dreams of the midnight to me,
That, instead of the fast-flowing tears, in My bosom elate thou shouldst be?

5. That when of thy lip I complain, how Ableed is my heart for its guile,
My confidant, keeper of secrets, Both early and late, thou shouldst be?

6. Nay, what should I reck if the monarchs Of beauty should boast of their slaves,
So but that alone, from among them, The queen of my fate thou shouldst be?

7. A booty too mean for my chasing I'd deem the gazelle [1691] of the sun,
If, a moment, a fawn such as thou art, The prey of my bait thou shouldst be.

8. A portion thou diddest assign us, Three kisses, to wit, of thy lip;
My debtor defaulting, henceforward, Excepting thou pay't, thou shouldst be.

9. In meadows where lovelings in kindness The hand to their lovers extend,
An if thou of me but acceptedst, My fair, anygate, thou shouldst be. [1692]

10. For all I am Hafiz the learned, No barleycorn's weight were I worth,
Except, of thy bounty and favour, My comrade and mate thou shouldst be.

[1691] *Ghezaleh* is one of the Arabic names for the sun; the word is of course, used p. g.
    with "fawn".
[1692] i. e. I would choose thee over all the fair maids of Paradise.

DLXXI

1. O mouth, that art e'en as a casket Of pearls of lustre fine,
How meetly about thee curveth The down's new-moon-like line!

2. Anon the conceit of union With thee deludeth me:
'Tis strange what vagaries playeth This vain conceit of mine!

3. Heart fled is and body wounded, Eyes bleeding, life grown weak:
Yea, many a marvel happeth In love and many a sign!

4. My heart is ableed for her fashions And thought of her drunken eye:
'Twixt Love and myself what aileth, That thus oppressed I pine?

5. Excepting thou change thy fashions, No lover evermore
Will hitherward turn nor sages Unto these parts incline.

6. If, rider, that from my compact Hast severed and my guide,
Thou natives of Nejd [1693] encounter, My case to them decline.

7. My blood, in Love's game, the charmer To shed doth lawful deem;
What sayeth Love's canon, judges? How is it ye opine?

8. Mine eyes never sleep for longing And yearning for those of Nejd: [1693]
My heart is dissolved, for passion, In anguish without fine.

9. God's peace upon Dhát-er-Réml! [1694] For there the Beloved is,
The loveling to flight who putteth Men's wits with her fawn-like eyne!

10. Discreet an thou be and prudent, Four things from thy hand let not;
A quiet nook and a loved one, Assurance and unmixed wine.

11. Give wine,—for, although the fable For sin of the world I'm grown,
Can any despair of the bounty And limitless grace Divine?

12. Wine bring me and me from cloister Deliver, o skinker, so
From door I to door may wander, A beggar without repine.

13. Since, Hafiz, Time's writ in nothing Endureth, of this thy case
Complain not, but, now time serveth, Come drink of the juice of the vine.

14. In the time of our Asef the Second, Untroubled's the cup of the mind:
Come, give us of that which is clearer Than water, o skinker; wine!

15. The realm in his [1695] puissant endeavour And ableness glorieth:
Almighty, vouchsafe that never His glory and might decline!

16. The light of the throne of the kingship, The pride of the folk and the Faith,
Bou Nesr, the son of Bou'l Máali, Might's quarry and majesty's mine!

[1693] *Nejd*, ancient Arab poetic name of the Beloved's abiding-place.
[1694] *Dhat-er-Reml*, ancient Arab poetic name of the Beloved's abiding-place.
[1695] "His", i. e. that of the Grand Vizier Abou Nesr ibn Abou'l Maali (dissyllable)
    named in next couplet.

DLXXII

1. My heart hath Selma in her browlocks ta'en
And every day my soul to me doth plain.

2. For God's sake, pity have on me heart-lorn,
Despite the foe, and union to me deign.

3. O carper, thou shouldst first a loveling's face
Have seen, ere thou my love for her arraign;

4. So had thy heart, like mine, forthright become
A drowned one in the sea of love and pain.

5. Our soul we'd render to thy foot for fine,
If aught unmeet thou saw'st in us again.

6. My heart's grief must thou prove; else wilt thou see
That which to see doth not to thee pertain. [1696]

7. O fair one, in the grief of love for thee,
Our trust is in the Lord of the worlds twain.

8. Lost in thy tresses' night is Hafiz' heart.
God be my guide! All others are in vain.

[1696] i. e. because thou art not qualified to judge of it, without having first felt by experience what manner thing love is.

DLXXIII

1. The mirror of self-abstraction, [1697] soul, The light of the Lord will show to thee:
Enter thou in at our door, if thou A seeker of Love Eternal be.

2. Give wine; for, though on the roll of Hell The name of our sin should be forewrit,
Mohammed's miracle on its fire Will cast the water of clemency,

3. Juggling each moment thou practisest; And this, thou knowest, unlawful is;
For God's Apostle himself hath said, "Ne'er of the gamesters, God wot, were we."

4. If, with this splendour of loveliness, Thou to the meadows thyself betake,
Lily and cypress and roses all Will imitators become of thee.

5. Taken and bound in the snare of lust The bird of thy heart, o Hafiz, is:
Thou, that corruption's bondman art, Of self-abstraction [1697] prate not to me.

[1697] *Mujerredi*, detachment from the things of the world, the quality specially attributed to Jesus by Muslim legends.

DLXXIV [1698]

1. Set thy heart not on the world and on its goods;
For none ever saw fidelity from it.

2. Stingless honey from this hive none ever ate;
From this orchard none e'er culled a date thorn-quit.

3. Whoso kindleth for a few days' space a lamp,
The wind bloweth on it, once 'tis fully lit.

4. His own enemy he fostereth, God wot,
Who his hopes unto the world's hand doth commit.

5. He the monarch world-subduing, warrior prince,
He whose scimitar did ever blood emit;

6. With one onset he who routed whiles a host,
With a shout the foe's main battle whiles who split;

7. Who without a cause imprisoned chiefs and lords,
Who without default the champions' heads off-smit; [1699]

8. He, at whose great name affrighted, in the wilds
Cast the lioness her young ones, hearing it;

9. When, in fine, Irác and Shiraz and Tebríz
He'd subdued and came the term to him forewrit,

10. He, by whom his eye world-seeing brightened was,
In his eye world-seeing thrust the blinding-spit.

[1698] The following forty-two pieces, (Nos. 574 to 615 inclusive) are what the Arabs call *Kitaät* or "Fragments", i.e. portions of Ghazels, which lack one or both of the characteristic couplets of that form, the first and the last; the monarch referred to is not, as Soudi says, Shah Mensour, who survived Hafiz himself and was put to death by Timour in the year (of our era) 1393, but Mohammed Muzeffer, the founder of the Muzefferi dynasty of Fars, who was (A. D. 1359) blinded and dethroned by his son, Shah Shejaa.

[1699] This is said, not as a reproach to the king, but as an illustration of his supreme and irresponsible power.

DLXXV

1. Skinker, wine, that the Elixir Is of life, I prithee bring
And the fount of Life Eternal This mine earthly body make.

2. Eye upon the circling goblet And in hand my life have I:
That until thou give, thou shalt not, By the Vizier's head, *this* take. [1700]

3. Shake thy skirt not, as the roses In the meadows for the wind;
For that at thy feet I'm minded Forth my very soul to shake.

4. To the lute and the theorbo Sing, o minstrel! With the praise
Of that moon-face, who in beauty Hath no peer, the echoes wake.

[1700] i. e. I am ready to give thee my life, but only in exchange for the wine-cup.

DLXXVI

1. In the ear of my understanding An unseen speaker cried
These words from the One, the Only, There is no God but He!'

2. "He whose foreordered portion, Friend, is a low estate
"Winneth by no endeavour To rank and high degree.

3. "One cannot, with all the water Of Kauther and Zemzem, [1701] bleach
"His blanket of luck, black woven That is of Destiny."

[1701] "Zemzem", the holy well at Mecca.

DLXXVII

1. Reckon not on this man's bounty Nor on that, o man of wit:
No one knoweth from what quarter Shall relief for him be wrought.

2. Count on God and on Him only: Know'st thou not that whatsoe'er
With my pen I limn befalleth Otherwise than as I thought?

3. Hurmouz' king, me all unknowing, Me an hundred favours did:
Him of Yezd I saw, his praises Chanted and he gave me nought. [1702]

4. On this wise the use of kings is: Thou, o Hafiz, be not vexed:
God the Giver aid and succour Still vouchsafe them, good and naught!

[1702] The poet's adventure with the king of Yezd has before been noticed.

DLXXVIII

1. Lo, on Heav'n's emerald- [1703] vaulted roof,
The Holy Spirit, [1704] that blessed one,

2. "Lord," in the dawntides crieth still,
"In fortune and majesty never done

3. "Aye on the Khúsrewi throne let bide
"Mensour Muzéffer, Mohammed's son!"

[1703] Meaning "blue"; great confusion exists in the Oriental mind (see my notes to the
    Quatrains of Omar Kheyyam) on the subject of colour-names.
[1704] i. e. the Archangel Gabriel.

DLXXIX

1. In the days of the rule of the Sultan Shah Sheikh Abóu Ishác, [1705]
By means of five wonderful persons The realm of Fars was fair;

2. The first one a king such as he was, Who kingdoms did bestow;
A prince who his own soul cherished And gave to mirth its share; [1706]

3. The second, the teacher of Islam, Sheikh Mejd-ed-dín [1707] that hight;
Than whom a more excellent Cadi The heav'ns remember ne'er;

4. The third one the last of the Vicars Of God, [1708] Emín-ed-dín,
Whose favour closed cases opened, By dint of thought and prayer. [1709]

5. The fourth one, the Prince of the Learned, the Cadi Azd-ed-dín,
By whom, in the name of the Sultan, The "Stations" founded were. [1710]

6. The fifth was the ocean-hearted Hajji Kiwám-ed-dín, [1711]
For bounty and grace and justice The name of "The Good" who bare.

7. They all from the world departed And left not their like behind:
May God (be He honoured and lauded!) Accept of them all soe'er!

[1705] Shah Sheikh Abou Ishac, Viceroy (A. D. 1335—1353) of Shiraz for the Ilkhani
princes of Baghdad.
[1706] i. e. He was a bon vivant, who lived and let live.
[1707] Sheikh Mejdeddin Ismayil, Cadi of Shiraz, ob. A. U. 1355.
[1708] *Abdal* [*ul Hecc*], "Substitutes of the Truth (God)", i. e., seventy men, who are, in
all ages, the especial representatives of God on earth: they are unknown and are
always kept up at the same number. See *Miskat ul Mesabih*, II, 556.
[1709] i. e. he was a man whose prayers were answered and whose counsel and judgment
rescued men from trouble and perplexity.
[1710] The Cadi Azd-ed-din was the author of a treatise on theological jurisprudence,
dedicated to Abou Ishac and called *Mewakif fi ilm ul kelam*, i. e. "Stages (Stations or
Progressive Lessons) in the Science of Speech". He died A. D. 1355.
[1711] The Grand Vizier Hajji Kiwameddin Hassan, Hafiz's often mentioned patron.

CLXXX

1. If at the first the beggar Had been of essence pure, [1712]
His shamefastness pivot-centred In honour's pole had been.

2. Nay, had not the sun the planets Mocked with his greater light,
Unvoid of the wine of pleasance His golden bowl had been;

3. And were not to ruin destined The hostel of the world,
Sure, firmlier builded and faster Established the whole had been.

4. If Time to base coin inclined not, Its manage all in the hand
Of Asef, [1713] the Lord of the Touchstone That trieth the soul, had been.

5. Since but of this one high-hearted And noble the age could boast,
Behoving to him a respite From Time's control had been. [1714]

[1712] i. e. of gentle extraction and breeding, *vir generosus.*
[1713] i. e. The Grand Vizier.
[1714] This poem is probably a fragment of an ode composed in commemoration of the
poet's patron, the Grand Vizier Hajji Kiwameddin Hassan.

DLXXXI

1. O time-knowing cup-companion, The Vizier for me bespeak
In a closet where never the East wind, The tale-bearing knave, may be;

2. Accost him with witty greeting And happily make him laugh
With a sally, that apt to solace The hearts of the grave may be:

3. Then this of his grace and bounty, On delicate fashion, ask;
To wit, if to me permitted The stipend to crave may be. [1715]

[1715] According to Soudi, a hinted request for the payment of the arrears of salary of (?)
the professorship of Koranic exegesis said to have been founded for Hafiz by his
patron the Grand Vizier.

DLXXXII

1. Still question thyself of thy good and thy bad:
Judge other than self dost thou need any what?

2. For whoso obeyeth Him God will provide
And will succour him whence he expecteth it not. [1716]

[1716] Quotation from Koran, LXV, 2.

DLXXXIII

1. A verse of faith and magnanimity
I'll read thee, from the Book of Morals ta'en:

2. If one thine entrails with oppression rend,
Gold give him, like the bounteous mine, again.

3. Less gen'rous than the shadowing tree be not:
Fruit upon those who stone thee, like it, rain.

4. Go, from the oyster learn long-suffering
And give those pearls who cleave thy head in twain.

DLXXXIV

1. Hall and debate of learning, College and portico,
What booteth if heart conceiving And seeing eye be not?

2. A well-spring, indeed, of learning's The house of the Judge of Yezd;
Yet insight therein and vision, I certify, be not. [1717]

[1717] The Cadi of Yezd was probably one of those who followed the example of the
king in slighting Hafiz, on the occasion of his visit before mentioned; hence the poet
says that insight [to discern worth] is lacking in his house.

DLXXXV

1. To him who jalóuseth our Khwájeh [1718] Say, "Ill approve thou not;
"Or Time's revolution requital, Save ill, to thee giveth not.

2. "Contend not; for heaven, for reason Or stress of thought-taking,
"The reins to our hand of lordship And empery giveth not.

3. "Although in his sight the world-all They marshal, Jemshíd therefor
"His jewel, the cup that showeth All things that be, giveth not."

4. Albeit (May God forfend it!) An arrow rain from the sky,
Which passage for us to enter His sanctuary giveth not,

5. I swear by the lofty spirit And grace of our lord Kiwám,
Consent, for his own expedience, Thereunto he giveth not. [1719]

[1718] "Khwajeh", i. e. the Vizier.
[1719] i. e. The Vizier would never, of his own motion and for his own commodity, deny
us access to him. The poet had apparently been denied admission to his patron's
presence, an affront which he seems inclined to ascribe to some subordinate official.

DLXXXVI

1. A bearer of glad news As Rizwan [1720] throned and Houri-like,
With hair like Selsebil, [1721] Is come to me from heaven, Sire.

2. Sweet is its speech and pure, Harmonious and heart-solacing,
Lovesome and virginal, Yet full of subtlety and fire.

3. Quoth I, "To this mean place Why comest thou?" And it, "To be
"Recited at the feast Of the good King is my desire."

4. Now is it weary grown Of mine, the beggar's, company!
It to thy presence call And of its bosom-wish enquire. [1722]

[1720] "Rizwan", the gatekeeper of heaven, who is fabled to sit upon a golden throne, inlaid with jewels. The throne here meant is (says Soudi) the poet's heart, adorned with all manner learning and skill.
[1721] i. e. bright as Selsebil, the Paradisal stream, or rippled like its waters.
[1722] The heavenly visitor in question is a poem, which Hafiz has newly composed and of which he solicits the king's acceptance, hinting at largesse in return.

DLXXXVII

1. In expectation of the Friend, How shall I in this darkling house
Sit, whiles with hand in teeth, whiles head On knee bowed down for sorrowing?

2. Patience forspent is, since the wolf Hath couched him in the lion's lair;
Wit's fled, since in the turtledoves' Abiding place the ravens sing.

3. Come, bird of auspice good, and bear Glad news to us of happiness;
Maybe the days the folk again To that which erst they were will bring. [1723]

[1723] The first couplet and 1.1 of the third of this poem only are the composition of Hafiz. Couplet II is by Aboulala et Tenouchi (or Tanouki) and 1. 2 of Couplet III by one of the poets of the Hemaseh.—*Soudi.*

DLXXXIX

1. Hail, o King! The hosts of heaven Are thy waymates: on and prosper,
If, intent upon world-conquest, Ready thee for war thou makest!

2. From thy height of glory, honour To the humble dost thou render
And thyself, indeed, the servant Of the men of lore thou makest.

3. Notwithstanding the beguilements Of yon azure vault, thy dealings
In accordance with the meaning Of God's Law e'ermore thou makest.

4. Marry, no such profit maketh He who four for three [1724] home bringeth:
Be thy fortune such that seven Still of every four thou [1725] makest! [1726]

[1724] i. e. thirty-three and a third per cent gain, which, says Soudi, was the ordinary home-trade profit.
[1725] i. e. seventy-five per cent gain, which, says Soudi, was the ordinary profit in the Indian trade.
[1726] i. e. May thine enterprises (in foreign conquest) be extraordinarily profitable. Commentators and translators have made a frightful hash of this curious and involved passage.

DXC

1. Thou whose high-descended essence Pure of greed is and despite,
Whose auspicious soul was never By hypocrisy demeaned,

2. With such loftiness as thine is, How can it be right that thou
Honours takest from the angel And bestowest on the fiend? [1727]

[1727] i. e. that thou distinguishest the worthless, at the expense of the worthy.

DXCI

1. No expounding doth this poem's beauty need;
To the splendour of the sun who seeketh guide?

2. Be all blessings on the limner's quill, that gave
Such bright beauty to his meaning's virgin bride!

3. Mortal wit its peer for beauty findeth not
Nor can nature for its grace a match provide.

4. Is it miracle or magic? Did these words
Through the Viewless Voice or Gabriel betide?

5. None a mystery can utter on this wise;
None such pearls hath bored and marshalled side by side. [1728]

[1728] The poet (says Soudi) in this fragment praises some friend's verses, by way of endorsement; i. e. dockets them with a metrical certificate of excellence.

DXCII

1. O thou justice-dealing monarch, Ocean-hand and lion-heart,
Thou that with all manner virtues Meritest thy high estate,

2. The renown and reputation Of the Sultan Shah Mesóud
Overtaken hath and conquered All the world of things create.

3. Like it is that viewless voices Have possessed thee of my case,
How my day, that was so radiant, Dark as night hath waxen late.

4. That which in three years I'd gotten From the Vizier and the King,
All from me, in one fell moment, Snatched the mall-player of Fate.

5. Yesternight in sleep my fancy Pictured to me that I chanced
Privily to pass at daybreak By the Sultan's stable-gate.

6. There, stall-bound and eating barley, Was my mule; her nosebag she
Rattled and to me she muttered, "Dost thou know me?" as she ate.

7. What this dream of mine portendeth Know I not: t' interpret it
Deign, o thou in apprehension Who nor equal hast nor mate. [1729]

[1729] The poet gives the king to understand that his mule has been stolen from him and
    is presently in the royal stables and hints that it should be returned to him.

DXCIII

1. Wellaway, my power of versing, For excess of tribulation,
Taking umbrage at thy servant, At the break of light, departed!

2. Set its mind was upon faring To the Oxus bank and Khiva;
And from Solomon's dominions, [1730] Wailing loud, the wight departed.

3. Yea, it went, save whom there's no one That the soul of speech conceiveth:
It I saw, and from my body After it the spright departed.

4. When I said to it, "O comrade, Bosom friend and old companion!"
Harshly it replied and weeping, Heart-sick, on its flight departed.

5. "Who with me will hold sweet converse, Since," quoth I, "yon sugar-spoken
"Silver-tongued one, in all fashions Versed of speech polite, departed?"

6. Straitly I besought it, saying, "Go not;" but it booted nothing;
For that it, of lack of favour In the Sultan's sight, departed.

7. Sire, recall it of thy bounty! What will come of it, poor outcast
That, for stress of disappointment, Burning with despite, departed? [1731]

[1730] "Solomon's dominions", i. e. Shiraz.
[1731] A figurative complaint of the king's neglect. The poet says in effect, "Unless thou
    give me some encouragement, I must leave the country."

DXCIV

1. They see not and they hear not The malice of the sphere;
For blind is every vision And deaf is every ear.

2. Full many an one, whose pillow's The sun and moon, in fine,
Shall have his place of couching Upon an earthen bier.

3. What doth the mail-coat profit Against the shafts of Fate?
Against Foreordination What booteth shield or spear?

4. What though of steel and iron The fortress-walls thou make,
Death at the portal knocketh, When once the term is here.

5. A door to thee They [1732] open: Enter not in desire;
Fare not in lust a pathway That They to thee make clear.

6. Bethink thee of Time's nature And Fortune's frowardness:
Greed's carpet fold together And rend lust's wearing-gear.

[1732] "They", i. e. the Fates.

DXCV

1. A friend unto me a message Yesterday sent, to wit,
"Thou the outcome of whose quill is To me as the black of the eye,

2. "Now, after two years' absence, Fortune hath brought thee home,
"Forth of the Vizier's mansion Comest thou not: and why?"

3. "Hold me excused, for neither From will nor self-conceit
"This that I do ariseth," To him did I reply.

4. "A writ in his hand of summons, The Cadi's officer
"In ambush beside my passage Doth, like a viper, lie.

5. "If over the Vizier's threshold I venture to set a foot,
"He'll hale me away to prison, Disgraced in every eye.

6. "The court of the Vizier's palace My stronghold is; for there
"If any should even mention The debt-exacting spy,

7. "By aid of the Vizier's servants' Strong arms, the crackbrain's pate,
"Till well-nigh in twain I cleave it, With cuffs and thumps I'll ply.

8. "But where is the need for jesting? Since K and N were joined, [1733]
"Excepting the Vizier's service, No final cause have I.

9. "Still be his portals open Thrown to the heart's desire!
"Still, for pure love, to serve him Girt be the azure sky!" [1734]

[1733] Making the word K[u]n (vowel unwritten), "Be", the formula of creation; i. e. since the First Day.
[1734] When (says Soudi) Hafiz returned from a sojourn of some time abroad (i. e. in Yezd or Ispahan, the only two places which he seems to have visited,) the Vizier Kiwameddin Hassan took him to dwell with him and forbade him from going abroad, because of the great love which was between them. His saying that he went not abroad for fear of his creditors is, perhaps, a hint to the Vizier to pay his debts.

DXCVI

1. My verses' rose-conserve From vi'let-syrup sugar taketh;
And envied, therefore, they Of sugar-candy and Fawn's Heel [1735] be.

2. O bitter be his mouth At sugar thrice refined who carpeth!
Dust on the head of him, Sweet water's worth who cannot feel, be!

3. Who from his mother's womb Is blind, the buyer of a sweetheart,
Endowed with loveliness And grace, how should he any dele be? [1736]

[1735] "Fawn's Heel", a soft white sweetmeat, flavoured with bergamot, something like
the well known "Turkish Delight".
[1736] The poet compares his own verses to a fair woman and his malevolent critics to
men born blind.

DXCVII

1. In swiftness of passage, like the clouds,
O brother, is opportunity.

2. Know thou that life is very dear;
'Twere pity if it should wasted be.

DXCVIII

1. The morning of Friday it was, The sixth of Rebi the First, [1737]
When from my bosom the cheek of that moon-faced one did fail.

2. In the year of the Prophet's Flight Seven hundred and sixty-four,
The grievous catastrophe Descended on me like hail.

3. What booteth complaint and pain And wailing and sorrowing,
Henceforth, that my life hath passed In vain without avail? [1738]

[1737] The third month of the Muslim year.
[1738] Apparently written on death of Hafiz's wife or mistress.

DXCIX [1739]

1. That fruit of Paradise Thou haddest in thy hand
Why sow'dst thou not, [1740] from hand Why let'st thou go, o soul?

2. If they should ask the date Of this event, say, "Read
"From 'Fruit of Paradise' The secret of the whole." [1741]

[1739] Written, according to Soudi, on the death of Hafiz's only son.
[1740] i. e. Why didst thou not marry thy son, so that thou mightest have had
  grandchildren by him?
[1741] This, like the six following poems, is a chronogram, the numerical values of the
  letters in the words *Miweh-i-bihishti* ("Paradisal fruit") forming, when added
  together, the date (A. H. 778, A. D. 1376—7) of death of the person in question.

DC

1. Lo, our brother Khwajeh Aadil, after living
Nine and fifty years of life (His rest-place fair be!)

2. Unto Rizwan's garden [1742] bound, of late departed.
God to him and to his actions debonair be!

3. Say thou still, "He was an equitable comrade"
And thereby of his demise's date [1743] aware be.

[1742] Paradise.
[1743] i. e. A. H. 785 = A.D. 1383—4. Soudi eliminates the letter *ya* from his
  calculation, without assigning any reason, and so makes the date ten years earlier.

DCI

1. When God the Merciful, The One that dieth not, perceived
That save unto good works This king himself applieth not,

2. He of His mercies made His soul the fellow; [1744] so the date [1745]
Of this event became "The Merciful that dieth not."

[1744] i. e. translated him to Himself.
[1745] i. e. A. H. 786. Soudi omits the letter *Elif* (value 1) and so makes the date A. H.
  785.

DCII

1. Touranshah, the age's Asef, He the soul of all the world,
Who in life's seedfield sowed nothing But good works and actions wise,

2. 'Twas Rejéb [1746] the one and twentieth, In the middle of the week,
When he left this murky dusthole For the rosemeads of the skies.

3. His demise, whose inclination Unto equity and truth
Ever was, from "Inclination" Do ye seek "to Paradise." [1747]

[1746] "Rejeb", seventh month of Muslim year.
[1747] The date is A. H. 787.

DCIII

1. Behá-el-hécc-w'ed-dín (Fair be his rest-place!),
Imam and elder of the cortgregation,

2. When he the world departed, of this couplet
Unto the wise and good made recitation:

3. "One can to God win nearness by obedience;
"So, an thou mayest, here take up thy station."

4. The date of his demise, then, from these letters
Read, "By obedience approximation." [1748]

[1748] The date is A. H. 782.

DCIV

1. Méjdeddín, [1749] the King and Sultan Of the Cadis, Ismayíl,
He, whose fluent pen from treating Of the Law did never cease,

2. In the middle of the week 'twas And the eighth day of Rejéb
That he left this house unstable, Void of ordinance and peace.

3. His abiding place th'asylum Of God's mercy know and then
From the letters of "God's mercy" Seek the date of his decease. [1750]

[1749] See ante, DLXXIX, 3.
[1750] The date is A. H. 756 = A. D. 1355.

DCV

1. Aázem Kiwám-ed-dáulet-W'ed-dín, [1751] before whose door whilere
The heavens wont, for kissing The dust thereof, to bend the knee;

2. For all his might and glory, Midmost the month of Dhou'l Kidéh, [1752]
From off the face of being And underneath the earth went he.

3. Since hope of generosity Is dead, the date of his decease
Is written in the letters, "The hope of generosity." [1753]

[1751] Grand Vizier after Hajji Kiwameddin Hassan. Soudi says "before"; but the Hajji
died A. H. 754. See DCX post.
[1752] "Dhou 'l Kideh", eleventh month of Muslim year.
[1753] i. e. A. H. 764—A. D. 1362.

DCVI

1. The Springtide is come and the tulip And rose and eglantine
From earth have arisen; but wherefore Art thou in the earth to-day?

2. I'll go, like the clouds of the Springtime, And weep, as I go, so sore,
So sore on the earth above thee That thou shalt come forth from the clay. [1754]

[1754] Soudi says that this pathetic little piece is an elegy on Hafiz's son.

DCVII

1. Who is it that the Sultan Will tell what camel-cats, [1755]
By the unright of Fortune And Time, have come to light?

2. Upon the Cadi's prayer-rug A winebibber doth sit
And to the seat of lordship Is come a catamite.

3. "The eye and lamp," that toper Saith, "of the world am I;"
And "I'm Feríd and Dára's [1756] Essence," the parasite.

4. O thou the age's Asef, [1757] For God's sake, do thou say
Unto a king, whose fortune Be ever at the height!

5. "The done of all who will it Let not, o King, become
"Doer of what he willeth, In season of thy might!"

[1755] "Camel-cat", a Persian phrase signifying a mixture of good and evil, something
monstruously incongruous, a monstrosity.
[1756] i. e. Feridoun and Darius. The abbreviation *Ferid* is used, because it means also
"unique pearl".

[1757] i. e. Vizier.

DCVIII

1. Eat of this green berry; [1758] easy Of digestion for it is:
Whoso one grain eateth clappeth Thirty birds upon the spit. [1759]

2. This it is the Soufi casteth Into ecstasy; there lurk
Hundred ravishments and hundred Símurghs [1760] in each grain of it. [1761]

[1758] i. e. hashish-pill.
[1759] i. e. it is so sustaining.
[1760] *Simurgh* means "Thirty birds", because this fabulous bird is supposed to unite the
characteristics of thirty (i. e. of an indefinite number of) different kinds of birds.
[1761] In praise of hashish, which, Hafiz hints, the Soufis use to throw themselves into
the state of "ecstasy", which they affect as a sign of "other worldliness".

DCIX

1. Years and blessings ever-during, Ease and offspring, wealth and power
Be thy portion in the kingship, Unperturbed of stress and care!

2. Glad thy years and good thine auspice, Case assured and treasure full!
Firm thy stock, thy race abiding, High thy throne, thy fortune fair! [1762]

[1762] A New-year's wish for some unnamed prince.

DCX

1. He, the chief of turban-wearers, [1763] Vizier of the happy king,
Lamp of the assembly, Hajji Hassan, hight Kiwameddín,

2. Seven hundred four and fifty From the Best of Mortals' Flight, [1764]
When the sun and moon were stationed Gemini and Virgo in,

3. On the sixth of Latter Rébi, [1765] In the middle of the day,
On a Friday, by commandment Of the Lord of men and jinn,

4. His soul's bird, that was the Huma Of the spiritual world,
Unto Paradise departed From this snare-place of chagrin.

[1763] "Turban-wearers", men of learning, i. e. theologians, (Muslim learning being
essentially theological,) and hence ministers and government-officials generally, as
primarily men of learning, all this class being distinguished by a special form and
size of turban.
[1764] i. e. A. H. 754.
[1765] *Rebi-el-Akhir*, fourth month of Muslim year.

DCXI

1. When shall the chance to visit The ancient Mage [1766] be mine,
That I may restore my Fortune's Youth by his rede benign?

2. A harbourer in the winehouse Full many a year I've been;
And still, while I live, my service I'll render at this shrine.

3. Yestr'even with me the flagon The Mohtesib saw and broke:
Henceforward, beneath the patchcoat I'll hide the flask of wine.

[1766] i. e. the old wineseller.

DCXII

1. The sage of my thought of Reason Made question yesternight,
Saying, "O chiefest of favours Of God Compassionate,

2. "Which is the peerless jewel Of verse in the world, whereby
"The pearl of the sea of Umman Is shorn of market-rate?"

3. It answered me, saying "Hearken To me, and not to those
"Who, 'Lo, it is this one's ditty Or that one's poem,' state.

4. "Knowest thou who is for certain The chief of the wise of the day,
"By manner of truth and sincereness And not of idle prate?

5. "Selmán [1767] 'tis, the prince of the learned, The king of the realm of speech,
"The pride of the Faith and the Faithful, The Scribe of the world create!"

[1767] Jelaleddin Mohammed Selman (ob. A.D. 1367), a famous poet of Hafiz's time and
court poet of the Ilkhani princes of Baghdad. He was a native of Sewa or Sawa, near
Teheran.

DCXIII

1. Alas for the robe of youth's days! Ah me,
If it had but endurance's broidery!

2. Alack and regret that from this our stream
The water of being will pass and flee!

3. Behoveth us sever from kith and kin;
For thus (woe worth it!) the heavens decree.

4. Brothers from brothers must sunder all,
Excepting the Ferkedán [1768] they be.

[1768] Two small closely-connected stars near the North Pole.

DCXIV

1. O Wind of the East, an if thou may,
For favour and kindness' sake, convey

2. This message from me to my Friend, to wit;
"He, who for love of thee pineth away,

3. "In secret dieth and for desire,
"'Life without thee is a sin!' doth say."

DCXV

1. A man, with knowledge armed, man absolute is;
And when he hath it not, a very brute is.

2. Sheer folly, soul, is action without knowledge:
In vain for ignorance the Truth's pursuit is.

END OF ODES

QUATRAINS

1. Nought of existence had Have I, save grief;
Nought of Love, good or bad, Have I, save grief:
Ne'er have I had a sympathetic friend;
Nor comforter, when sad, Have I, save grief.

2. Of courage, the plucker-up Of the portal of Kheiber [1] ask;
The secrets of bounteousness Of the master of Kember [1] ask;
If, Hafiz, sincerely athirst For favour Divine thou be,
The fountain and well-spring thereof Of the Skinker of Kauther [1] ask.

[1] All appellations of the Khalif Ali, surnamed "The Lion of the Faith". *Kheiber* was a
Jewish stronghold North-West of Medina, at the assault of which (A. H. 7) Ali is
said to have plucked up one of the fortress-gates and used it as a buckler, in place of
his own, which had been cut to pieces by the opposing champions. *Kember* was the
name of a freedman of his. Ali is fabled by the Muslims to be the divinely-appointed
guardian of the Paradisal fount Kauther and the dispenser of its nectareous contents.

3. A victim if, like me, Thou of Love's snare become,
Ruined with wine and cup Thou shalt fore'er become;
Topers are we, that drink And reck not of the world;
Sit not with us, lest foul Thy name from fair become.

4. Her hyacinth tress I caught, beggar-wise, as she past,
And said, "Help thou me, The stricken of loveliking's blast!"
"Nay, take thou my lip", She answered, "And leave my tress;
"To life that is sweet, Not life that is long, cleave fast."

5. Whenas the bud of the rose A flagon-sup [2] becometh
And the narcissus' hand Holder of the cup becometh,
Fair fall the heart of him, Like to the bursting bubbles,
Who, for the sake of wine, House-breaker-up becometh! [3]

[2] i. e. a winebibber. When the rose breaks into blossom, it is likened by the poets to a
   cup of red wine.
[3] i. e. it behoveth spend one's substance on liquor in the blossom-tide.

6. Of that old wine, matured I' the village, give to me
Quick, that I may renew Withal Life's broidery:
Drunk and unconscious make Me of the world's affairs,
So that Time's secret, friend, I may reveal to thee.

7. O thou, on the dust of whose threshold, night and day,
The sun and the moon, in worship, their foreheads lay,
O set me not, straitened of hand, tongue, heart, upon
Expectancy's fire, whilst thou sitt'st heedless aye!

8. Go, sit with the Friend; The wine of the bowl go seek;
A kiss from that rose-limbed cypress, soul, go seek.
If easance the wounded seek of his wound, say thou,
"Of Ben Hijjám's [4] lancet the cure of thy dole go seek."

[4] "Ben Hijjam"; according to Soudi, the person here referred to was one Omar ibn
   Hijjam, ("son of the barber-surgeon",) a well-known loveling of the day.

9. Whilst heav'n by foreordinance wending shall be,
Success on thy wish still attending shall be:
Each cup that thou quaffest from Túctemóun's hand
The cause of delight never-ending shall be. [5]

[5] Addressed to Shah Shejaa. *Tuctemoun* was the name of his cupbearer, a handsome
   Turcoman youth, who (says Soudi) was both singer and player.

10. World's luck by oppression to win is not worth;
Life's easance the anguish therein is not worth;
Nay, trust me, the world's seven thousand years' joy
This stress of seven-day-long chagrin is not worth.

11. To-night, amidst blood, For lack of thy sight, I shall sleep;
Far, far from the couch Of health and delight I shall sleep.
Believest thou not? Send thine image to visit my dreams,
That thus it may see How without thee to-night I shall sleep.

12. Of wish for thy kiss and embrace I die;
Of thirst for thy dewy lip's grace I die.
Why make the tale long? I'll be brief. Come back!
For of longing to look on thy face I die.

13. Since a night with thee, o soul, Brought have I to dawn,
I'm no man, if e'er I draw Breath, when thou art gone.
Death I fear not after this, Now the draught of life
From the fount of honeydew Of thy lip I've drawn.

14. Till when this sore oppression, This durance dread of thine?
Till when this vain vexation And heart's blood shed of thine?
Lo, in the hands of lovers A blood-stained sword [6] there is:
Thy blood, if it o'ertake thee, Be on that head of thine!

[6] The "blood-stained sword" is prayer.

15. Never divorcéd thy lip Make from the lip of the cup;
Thus thy desire of the world Slake from the lip of the cup.
Bitter and sweet at once Are in the cup of the world:
This [7] from her lip and *that* [8] Take from the lip of the cup.

[7] i. e. the sweet.
[8] i. e. the bitter [wine]

16. Saidst thou, "I am thine: So have thou no more concern;
"Come, be of good heart; To patience make o'er concern."
What heart? Where patience? Nay, that which thou callest heart
Is one drop of blood And many a sore concern.

17. The love of the Friend's cheek To me that mourn reproach not;
Nay, trifles, once for all, To hearts love-lorn reproach not.
Thou, Soufi, since the use Of wayfarers thou knowest,
So much to winebibbers, In spite and scorn, reproach not.

18. Lo, neither the tale of that lamp of Chigíl One can tell
Nor his suffrance whose heart is consumed with Love's ill One can tell:
In this my strait heart sorrows harbour, because there is not
One friend unto whom the heart's anguish at will One can tell.

19. The bait for the fair of the time must be laid With gold;
Their favours and graces must ever be paid With gold.
Behold the narcissus, the crown-holding queen of the world,
How also its head to the earth-ward's down-weighed With gold! [9]

[9] Allusion to the yellow corona of the blossom of some narcissi.

20. A moon, with a shape As the cypress straight and fine,
With mirror in hand, Was busking her face divine.
A kerchief I proffered; And "Thinkest thou thus to win
"My favours?" quoth she. "I'faith, a rare thought of thine!" [10]

[10] i. e. thou art a rare fool to think to buy my favours with such a trifle.

21. O Looser of Knots, Allotter of Heaven and Hell,
O let us not fall To ruin unmendable!
O Lion of God, [11] How long shall this rapine last?
Thy foe-quelling claw Display and the tyrants quell! [12]

[11] i. e. the Khalif Ali, who may be called the patron saint of the Shiah sect.
[12] Appeal to Ali to come and heal the fever of the time. The first two lines are
    addressed to the Deity.

22. Saving thine image, to our sight nought cometh;
Save thy street's passage, to our spright nought cometh:
Though to all else sweet sleep come, to our vision
Thereof, 'fore heaven, day or night, nought cometh!

23. O thou from whose eye deceits galore do rain,
O quarter! For thence the swords of war do rain.
O'er quickly of bosom-friends thou weariest:
Out, out on that heart, whence stones e'ermore do rain!

24. Each friend that faith vaunted's an enemy grown;
Each, pure-faced that was, wet of skirt [13] I see grown:
They say, "Night is big with th' Invisible." Strange!
Since no man she knows, by whom big is she grown?

[13] i. e. sin-polluted, here = false to the covenant.

25. In secret my case, O wind of the West, pray tell her!
With hundreds of tongues, The fire in my breast pray tell her!
Yet not on such wise do thou deal that annoy overtake her;
A word or two speak And midmost the rest, pray tell her. [14]

[14] i. e. do not blurt it out abruptly, but begin by speaking of otherwhat and then
    gradually and discreetly introduce the mention of me and my case.

26. Quoth I, "What's thy lip?" "The water of Life," said she.
"Thy mouth?" She replied, "A sugarcorn rare, perdie!"
Quoth I, "As thou say'st, So Hafiz hath said." And she,
"Nay, prayers the delight Of subtlety-speakers be." [15]

[15] A Persian adage, used when two persons say exactly the same thing and meaning,
    "Les beaux esprits se rencontrent."

27. My moon, whose cheek The sun's renown hath taken,
Whose down the skirt Of Kauther's gown hath taken,
In her chin-dimple's pit all hearts hath prisoned
And the pit-mouth With musky down hath taken. [16]

[16] i. e. covered, scaled up.

28. That musky-moled moon, When she draweth the raiment's screen
From her body unmatched In beauty and grace and sheen,
One may in her breast, For clearness, the heart espy,
Hard stone as it were, Through water pellucid seen.

29. The torrent of Time the plain Hath overflowed of Life
And now hath begun to fill The meted load of Life.
Nay, be on thy guard, o Sheikh; [17] For, harkye! ere it be long,
The porter of death will bear Thy gear from th' abode of Life.

[17] "Sheikh" may here mean either "elder" or simply "old man".

30. Of Fortune behoveth thee never despair,
Yet, willow-like, quake with each change in Time's air.
"No colour there is passing black," dost thou say?
Then, prithee, why white Is become my black hair?

31. Thine eye, of the wizards of Babylon taught,
O Lord, may enchantments ne'er pass from its thought,
That ear, that the ring hath in beauty's ear put, [18]
May its pendants be ever of pearls Hafiz-wrought! [19]

[18] i. e. that hath made beauty its bondslave.
[19] i. e., May it never cease to hearken to Hafiz's verse!

32. (Identical with Omar Kheyyam, Q. 348, q. v.)

33. Shamefastly the rose-bud shrinketh Out of sight from thee
And the drows'd narcissus droopeth, Dazed outright, from thee.
How with thee herself to even Shall the rose avail,
From the moon since light she taketh [20] And it light from thee?

474

[20] Soudi gravely remarks that the rose and all the flowers derive their colour from the
   moon.

34. On faithfulness' wise, First union's wine she gave me:
Then, when I was drunk, The cup of repine she gave me:
And when, with both eyes full of water and heart a-fire,
Her way-dust I was, To the breezes, in fine, she gave me.

35. With men of goodness bad Behoveth not to be;
Div and wild-beast like mad Behoveth not to be;
For care of substance sad Behoveth not to be
And proud of learning had Behoveth not to be. [21]

[21] Nearly identical with Omar Kheyyam, Q. 374.

36. Thou in whose spikenards' [22] shade The jessamine is nourished
And Aden's pearl whose lips" Ruby within is nourished,
E'en as thy lip, thy soul Still nourish with the grapejuice,
For *that* a spirit is, Which in the bin is nourished.

[22] i. e. ringlets.

37. Still must my heart a load aby, another;
A thorn for parting's in mine eye, another.
I strive withal: but Fate to me, "A matter
"This past thy competence is, ay, another."

38. A-férment, like wine, What booteth thee be for chagrin?
There's none that to cope With the armies of grief can win.
Nay, green [23] is thy lip: The winecup withhold not therefrom;
'Tis pleasant of wine To drink on the lip of the green. [24]

[23] i. e. fresh, youthful.
[24] i. e. on the marge of the sward. Note word-play. The fresh down is called "green".

39. The season of youth 'tis and wine the best is;
To be drunk, for all mortals who pine, the best is.
Since the world, end to end, is all ruined and wasted,
In ruin's place ruin, [25] in fine, the best is.

[25] i. e. dead-drunkenness, which the Persians call "ruin".

40. Come back, for my soul on thy beauty await is;
Come back, for, for sev'rance's grief, my heart strait is.
Come back, for, without thee, Beloved, a flood
From th' eyes still a-flowing of me addlepate is.

41. Take wine mirth-rousing And up with the prize and come,
Unknown of the watchers! Contend not; be wise and come.
Nay, list not the rival, Who, "Sit thou and go not," saith.
O fair, pray hearken To me , arise and come!

42. The sev'rance from thee, That on me, wellaway! is come,
Like salt on the wounds Of the heart, thou wouldst say, is come.
I feared that I far From thy sight should one day become;
And now, as thou seest, This same evil day is come.

43. Sweet-lipped ones their trothplight often To Love's goal bring not;
Men of insight, yet, from loving Back the soul bring not.
When the Loved One to thy wishes And thy counsel is,
They thy name upon the lovers' Muster-roll bring not. [26]

[26] i. e. Folk do not regard him as a true lover who hath his own way in love, without
 difficulties or hindrance.

44. Thy tress all this twist and turn And tanglement whence hath it ta'en?
That slumberous eye of thine, Its languishment whence hath it ta'en?
Since none upon thee hath cast So much as a leaf of the rose,
Thy body, from head to foot, Rosewater's scent whence hath it ta'en?

45. The way of thy questing thorns Full many of dole possesseth:
What wayfarer strength enough To compass this goal possesseth?
Nay, knowest thou who the renown'd Of Love is? He who the light
Of the blessing of lovers upon The face of his soul possesseth.

46. From the world-dam's allurements Come sever thy heart, o friend;
Forethink thee; consider Her paramours' ultimate end;
Though, without wit abiding, No mortal for such wilt thou know,
Like Hafiz, content if Thou be on her face to depend. [27]

[27] i. e. if, like Hafiz, thou be content to depend upon the false world's illusions, thou
 wilt become witless and unable to distinguish between the folk of the world and
 those of the spirit.

47. My hand to thy zone I set, for I thought therein
Some matter to find, But found not so much as a pin.
Thereof must it first Appear what the zone doth enclose,
Or e'er it appear What I by the zone's self win. [28]

[28] A play upon the usual conceit of the extreme smallness of the Beloved's waist.

48. Accepted of every heart, Whom high and low acclaim,
Sweet-spoken, harmonious-tongued, The bright full moon of fame,
All throughout Shiraz land Known and illustrious
Song-singing Hafiz is, Hajji Ahméd [29] by name.

[29] "Ahmed" is a form of Hafiz's second name "Mohammed". The prefix "Hajji"
(pilgrim) would seem to denote that the poet had made the pilgrimage to Mecca; but
all the evidence points to the contrary conclusion and it may therefore be assumed
that, if he used the title in question, he must have earned it vicariously, by paying
some one to undertake the pilgrimage in his name.

49. The wings of the bird of joy in flight Do I perceive?
The scent of the rosebed of Love's delight Do I perceive?
Or bore the wind somewhat of speech from the Loved One's ruby lip?
Anygates, wonders with sense and spright Do I perceive.

50. With ghittern and pipe and minstrel And sweetheart gamesome and gay,
A flagon of wine in a corner And liberty from affray,
When warm are our veins and sinews With wine, betide what may,
I'd not be obliged for a farthing To ever a Hatim Tai.

51. More than the candle, when thou'rt unnear, I weep;
Still, flask-like, many a rose-hued tear I weep:
Yea, like the winecup, for straitened heart, am I;
For blood, when the wail of the harp I hear, I weep.

52. A great fault 'tis to magnify oneself
And to set store, o'er all folk, by oneself:
Behoveth learn, from th' apple of the eye,
All to descry and not descry oneself.

53. Identical with Omar Kheyyam, Q. 247, q. v.

54. By Khusrau of Delhi.—*Soudi*.

55. Till the case to the wish of the heart afret become,
Till the king-soul quit of the body's let become,
My hope on God's mercy still I rest, to me
That happiness' door will opened yet become.

56. Thy heart from wrong to friend and foe draw in;
The bright-hued wine, with face aglow, draw in.
Thy bosom open to the man of worth
And from the base thy skirt e'enso draw in.

57. Concordance would Fortune Forewrit would practise!
Or Time's course complaisance some whit would practise!
Since eld from youth's hand-hold the bridle hath ravished,
Surefootedness would, stirrup-like, it would practise! [30]

[30] i. e. Would that old age at least had stability and permanence!

58. Life in quest of a wish lost and lived not have I:
By Time's revolution availed what have I?
To whomso I said, "I'm thy friend," he became
My enemy: 'las, what an ill lot have I!

59. Companions, for mirth and for pleasance when, met, ye embrace
And drinking, recall not the round-running firmament's race,
When the turn comes to me and I'm not to be found in my place,
The last of the wine to the memory drink of my face. [31]

[31] Cf. Omar Kheyyam, CCCCLIX.

60. To-day, in this age compact-breaking, heigho!
What friend but in fine doth an enemy grow?
I've cloven to solitude's skirt, to the end
That the friend see me not to the wish of the foe.

61. O Friend, to the wish of the foe hast thou made me:
Like Spring was I; Autumn-like, lo! hast thou made me.
Erst straight as the arrow I was in thy quiver:
Thy victim, why bent like the bow hast thou made me?

62. So weak am I, so abject and discreet
And such thy headstrong pride and self-conceit,
If thou on fire me seat, I sit; but thou,
Thou sitt'st not, if I thee a-horseback seat.

63. Friend, heedless sit not of the might of the dart of the sigh,
Lest fire on thee take from the fire-kindling smart of the sigh.
Disdain not their tears, at thy street-end that wander anights,
Nor the rising, at dawn, from the sorrowful heart, of the sigh.

64. How long on thy heart Fortune's cark and repine hast thou?
The world leave and all That therein, o soul mine, hast thou.
A rosebush, a friend and a somewhat of liquor seek,
What while that in hand Yet a swallow of wine hast thou.

65. Room for the grief of thee In my heart's core I've made:
The pain of thee the salve Of my heart's sore I've made:
The more upon my heart Thou wreakest cruelty,
Resolve to keep my faith Entire the more I've made.

66. Quoth I, "With that mole thou all sweetness outviest."
"O silly and simple," she answered," thou liest:
"No mole on the mirror there is of our beauty;
"Thy proper eye-apple therein thou espiest."

67. The hue of my tears, like her cheek, rose-red's become;
My eye full of blood, that my heart hath shed, 's become.
My fair, out of coquetry, unto me thus, "Dear friend,
"How is it thine eye in this quandary," said, "'s become?"

68. If strangerhood but for a month a man aby,
Though strong as a hill, there's nought of him left, well nigh.
Though stablished the exile be in a foreign land,
His own when he calls to mind, he heaves a sigh.

69. Since, Lord, the Accomplisher Of wish and need Thou art,
Judge and Apportioner Of each man's meed Thou art,
Why should I tell to Thee The secret of my soul,
Since Knower of the Hid, Both thought and deed, Thou art?

END OF QUATRAINS

COUPLETS

I

1. Halloa there, o thou wild gazelle! Where art thou?
With me acquainted passing well, fair, art thou.

2. Two vagabonds, a lonely, friendless pair,
Wild beasts about us ambushed everywhere:

3. Come, that each other's case we may enquire,
That each may seek the other one's desire:

4. For well I see this waste without a path
No glad and goodly pasture-places hath.

5. Who will the exiles' mate be? Comrades, say.
Who will a friend's part to the friendless play?

6. Khizr of happy foot may yet appear
And his aid guide us unto better cheer.

7. At hand mayhap's the time of grace Divine:
For "Leave me not alone" I got for sign. [1]

[1] i.e., consulting the Sortes Coranicæ, the verse "Leave me not alone" (K. XXI, 89)
     came to my hand, in token that God would not forsake me.

8. Whilom a toper, sitting by the way,
Unto a wayfarer did, jesting, say,

9. "What hast thou, pilgrim, in thy budget there?
"If thou have grain for bait, come, set a snare."

10. He answered him and "Grain I have," said he;
"But the Simúrgh for prey behoveth me."

11. Quoth t'other one, "How findest thou its trace?
"Since we've no token of its nesting-place,

12. "Give not the winecup and the rose from hand;
"But on thy guard 'gainst faithless fortune stand.

13. "Since that straight cypress e'en hath fared away,
"Keep thou a watch upon the cypress-spray." [2]

[2] i. e. (apparently), since thou canst not have the high Beloved, content thyself with a
     lesser one.

14. She went and made my happy nature rue:
Ah, when did comrade thus with comrade do?

15. So ruthlessly estrangement's sword she plied
Thou'dst say no love had ever us allied.

16. How should my off'rings with acceptance meet,
When the rich sun pours treasure at her feet?

17. Well-spring and stream-bank, tears and self-commune,
These are my solacement, without that moon. [3]

[3] i. e., in the Beloved's absence.

18. Departed ones and friends remembering,
Be thou accordant with the clouds of Spring. [4]

[4] i. e. weep as they do.

19. When water runneth, murmuring, thee by,
Add to it of the water of the eye.

20. Scant court'sy that old friend to me displayed:
Musulmans, Musulmans, 'fore heaven, aid!

21. Over my head estrangement's waters pass;
There's no dissembling of my case, alas!

22. Only auspicious Khizr's succour can
This lonely join to *yonder* lonely man.

23. Why strive I thus against my destiny?
Wherefore from Fate Foreordered seek to flee?

24. Henceforth, the way of the Friend's street take I:
Die if I must, 'tis there that I will die.

25. The exiles, who of this my case have wit,
Over my dust will come awhile and sit.

26. Exiles remember exiles from afar;
For, each to each, memorials they are.

27. Help of the helpless, God, art Thou; for me
And for my like, Thou knowest remedy.

28. Like as from night Thou bringest forth bright day,
Bring Thou me gladness forth of this dismay.

29. Much of her sev'rance have I to complain,
The tale whereof this space may not contain.

30. Jewels regard and coloured glass eschew;
Nor any way, that's ill-renowned, ensue.

31. When the reed's quiddity I've written, then
Ask its interpreting from "Fish and Pen." [5]

[5] A strange passage, outrageously muddled by commentators and translators. *Mahi* means at once "Fish" and "quiddity". *Noun* is the letter N and means also "Fish". It is one of the titles of Chapter LXVIII of the Koran, also called that of the Pen, in which Mohammed curses those who dubbed the Koran a tissue of lies and nonsense. Hafiz seems to hint that those who do not appreciate his verses deserve to be included in the same category as the enemies of Mohammed.

32. Comrades, each other's value apprehend
And lay the lore to heart, when once 'tis kenned!

33. I give you this one word of exhortation:
"Ambushed the archer is of separation."

34. The soul with understanding did we knead
And what resulted thence we sowed for seed.

35. Cheer in this mixture doth appear; for this
Marrow of verse and soul and body is.

36. Come; with this pérfume, of hope redolent,
The palate of the soul for ever scent:

37. For from the Houris' vest this musk-pod is,
Not from that deer which shunneth mortal quest.

38. Hark, in this vale, the torrent's speech, that runs,
"One grain the blood of hundred guiltless ones! [6]

[6] i. e., in Love's realm they reck not of innocent blood.

39. "Here unto Gabriel's pinions' they set light,
"So children fire withal may haply dight. [7]

[7] Nor have they any regard to rank or station, learning or genius.

40. "Who is't to speak a word shall here avail?
"What scorn of talk, o Lord, is in this vale! [8]

[8] i. e. The current coin of Love is deeds, not words.

41. "Go, Hafiz; speak no more concerning this:
"Cut short thy prate; for God all-knowing is."

II

THE SKINKER-RIME

1. Give, skinker, that wine which elation doth bring,
Perfection and soul-augmentation doth bring!

2. Give, give; for sore woeful of heart I'm become,
In this and in that [9] without part I'm become.

[9] "In this and in that", i. e. in perfection and soul-augmentation.

3. Come, quick, that elixir of victory pour,
That Noah's life giveth and Korah his store.

4. Give, give, so the Fates may throw back in thy face
The door of long life and of prosperous case.

5. Come, skinker, that shining fire give me, I pray,
That fire Zoroaster sought under the clay:

6. For what's, in the code of the winebibbing sot,
Fire-worshipper? Ay, and world-worshipper what?

7. Come, skinker, that wine, by whose magical mean
Jem's cup itself boasted to see the Unseen,

8. Give, so, by the aid of the bowl, I may be
Like Jem, still aware of the world's mystery.

9.Come, skinker, that goblet of Jem give me thou;
Nay, make no excuses, but give it me now.

10. For, though one have treasures and crown, as Jem says,
"No barley-corn worth is this house of three days."

11. Come, skinker, that cup that like Sélsebíl-tide is,
That cup, that to Paradise still the heart's guide is,

12. Give, give me; for well say theorbo and reed,
"One swallow Kei's crownal in worth doth exceed."

13. Come, skinker, that tipsified virgin, veil-bound,
In ruinous places that's still to be found,

14. Quick, give me; for ill of repute will I be;
Yea, ruined and drunk, branch and root, will I be.

15. That liquor, which sorrows and cares doth up-burn,
Which drunken of lions, brake-burners they turn,

16. Give quick, that, pot-valiant, to heav'n I may go
And the snare of yon plaguy old wolf [10] overthrow.

[10] "The plaguy old wolf" is heaven, Fortune, the system of the Universe.

17. Come, cupbearer, give me that liquor, the which
With the angels' grisamber the Houris enrich;

18. That somewhat, for incense, on fire I may lay
And thus reason's palate may sweeten for aye.

19. That wine, skinker, give, whose reflection, cast up,
Sendeth greetings to Kei and to Jem from the cup;

20. With the voice of the pipe that I, speaking, may say,
"Lo, where is Kawóus and Jemshíd where to-day?"

21. Yea, speak of the course of this old world of yore
And call on the monarchs that were heretofore!

22. Give, skinker, that wine which doth kingship confer,
Whose brightness and pureness all hearts do aver;

23. For, king of the heart, once I throned it on high;
But thence now I'm far; for polluted am I.

24. Give wine, so from blemish it may be that pure
I shall wax and from perilous thought be secure.

25. Give wine and the face of felicity see;
Make me drunk and find treasures of wisdom in me.

26. Since the Garden of Souls [11] is my natural ground,
Then why in the jail of the flesh am I bound?

[11] The Garden of Souls, i. e. Heaven, the Spiritual World.

27. 'Tis I who, the goblet in hand when I hold,
Whatever exists in that mirror behold.

28. Whilst drunk, at the door of devotion I beat
And the language of kings I, the beggar, repeat.

29. When, drunken, his voice Hafiz raises on high,
The ghittern of Venus applauds from the sky.

30. Come, skinker, life's faithlessness fear thou and eke
New life, beggar-fashion, from wine do thou seek;

31. For wine will increase thee in life and in hope;
Each moment a door of th' Unseen to thee ope.

32. Come, skinker, array us a banquet of wine;
For the world keepeth faith with no mortal, in fine.

33. The wine-bubbles us of this matter remind,
How Kéikobád's crown was borne off by the wind.

34. Come, seek the heart's wish from the juice of the vine;
For ne'er knew I easance of soul without wine.

35. Could the body avail to dispense with the soul,
The heart, on like wise, one might wean from the bowl.

36. Come, skinker, the goblet fill up, that I may
The history tell thee of Kisra and Kei.

37. Come, skinker; why heedless art thou of Time's spite?
It thinketh to slay thee by way of unright.

38. Come, cupbearer; frowardness use with us not;
Of clay, not of fire, art thou fashioned, God wot! [12]

[12] i. e. thou art no Efrit of the Jinn (the Jinn being made of fire) that thou shouldst be
    froward, frowardness being a special characteristic of Efrits.

39. With wine brim the goblet; for goodly wine, sure, is,
When it, more by token, unblended and pure is.

40. That wine basil-scented me, skinker, in hold
Come give, for there's left me nor silver nor gold.

41. Come, cupbearer, pour me that ruby-bright wine!
A truce to dissembling and evil design!

42. Of patchcoat and chaplet aweary am I;
Go pledge them for wine, one and both; and good bye!

43. From the Magians' convent remove not afar;
For here, in this nook, the soul's treasuries are.

44. If ever "Go not to the tavern" a wight
Say, what wilt thou answer him? What but "Good night!"

45. Come, skinker, that Redbud-hued goblet give here,
Where heart findeth mirth and where soul findeth cheer.

46. Give, give; that release it may bring me from woe
And to Love's privy banquet the pathway me show.

47. Give, skinker, that wine, which the food of the spright is
And needful as life for the heart-stricken wight is,

48. Withoutside the world that I may my tent pitch
And my canopy over the firmament pitch.

49. Give, skinker, that sun-like, that moon-fashioned cup,
So that over the skies I my throne may set up.

50. Come, skinker, with cups of old wine, each on each
Ensuing, intoxicate me, I beseech.

51. When drunk thou hast made me with unalloyed wine,
I'll sing thee sweet sings of this fuddlement mine.

52. Now, ambergris-scented, that, thanks to thy face,
A Paradise grown is our banqueting-place,

53. The cup take and fear not transgression therein;
For in Paradise-garden wine-drinking's no sin.

54. Since, skinker, wine-drinking I cannot give up,
Come, succour thou me with a finishing cup.

55. For the sphere's revolution life-weary become,
To the Magians' Convent a-running I'm come.

56. Come, skinker, that joy-giving liquor provide,
So the courser of happiness we may bestride,

57. So, Rustem-like, we for the horse-course [13] may start
And gallop therein to the wish of our heart.

[13] "The horse-course" of fancy.

58. Give, skinker, that ruby-like cup, to the spright
That opens the door of the days of delight;

59. That through reason the pen I may draw and unfurled,
The standard of drunkenness give to the world.

60. Our talk upon cups cups succeeding let turn,
Casting water of wine on the fire of concern.

61. To day, with each other the cup let us clink;
If season this be not, nay, *when* shall we drink?

62. For those, who made ready the banquet of mirth
And were all taken up with the pleasures of earth,

63. This nether world's snare-place, this Div-haunted cave
Departing, have carried regret to the grave.

64. Who e'er had the best of yon turquoise-hued dome?
Who ever was blithe in this ten-day-long home?

65. Alas, that youth went to the wind! Happy one,
Thrice happy, who reason and justice hath done! [14]

[14] "With this old saw close up this dust, Thrice blesséd man that dieth just!"—Marston,
Antonio's Revenge.

66. Give, skinker, that goblet, which whenas we drain,
We trample on *this* world and *that* with disdain.

67. Bestir and the heavy (full) pottle me give;
If in public thou mayst not, then privily give;

68. For, for him, with drums elephant-borne whom folk greet,
The drum of departure perforce will they beat. [15]

[15] i. e. even great kings, like those of India before whom they beat drums borne on
elephant-back, must in the end die.

69. When the heralds of morning in heaven appear,
Each moment the voice of the Houris I hear;

70. "O bird dulcet-singing, sweet-voiced," they say, "shake
"Thy pinions and forth of the body's cage break.

71. "On the blue six-ceiled palace's pinnacle sit;
"In the heav'n of the Martyrs [16] thy place is forewrit.

[16] Those who die of love are accounted by the Muslims martyrs and have their abode in
the Seventh Heaven, whose *floor* forms the *ceiling* of the Sixth Heaven; hence the
firmament is called "the six-ceiled palace"; although eight and nine heavens (the

ninth being God's throne) are as often counted.

72. "For, conquering-fortuned one, like Menouchíhr, [17]
"Thou hast heard, in the epoch of old Bouzurjmíhr, [18]

[17] "Menouchihr" ("Paradise-face") the name of a prehistoric King of Persia, the successor of Feridoun.
[18] "Bouzurjmihr" was the Vizier of Noushirwan mentioned in next couplet.

73. "How they wrote on the beaker of Anoushirwán, [19]
"'Or ever our traces thou losest, o man,

[19] "Anoushirwan" (*Noushirwan*), a famous King of Persia (A. D. 531-579) and successful opponent of the Emperor Justinian.

74. "'Give ear to our counsel and learn thou a trait
"'Concerning the courses of Fortune and Fate.

75. "'This earth is the dwelling of sorrows and cares;
"'There's little of joy in this sojourn of snares.'"

76. Yet in this we rejoice, that of sorrow and stress
We're quit of concern, if we nothing possess.

77. Lo, where is Jem's goblet and where is himself?
Where's Solomon? Where are his ring and his pelf?

78. Nay, who of philosophers wotteth, indeed,
When Kéikawóus flourished and when was Jemshíd?

79. For, when they set foot in nonentity's road,
Of them but a name in this hostel abode.

80. Why setst thou thy heart on this house of a day,
Since ne'er thou'lt return, when thou'rt once past away?

81. 'Tis madness upon it to fasten the heart;
To trust in its friendship's the simpleton's part.

82. Thou ne'er in this six-gated mansion [20] shalt light
On a spot to thy wish or a place of delight.

[20] "Six-gated mansion", i. e. the world, the six gates whereof are the six sides, East, West, North, South, Above and Below.

83. Give, skinker, that fire-natured water, whereby
From the fire of vexation delivered am I.

84. Aglow is my heart with chagrin and desire;
Give wine, that I water may cast on the fire.

85. Come, cupbearer, give me that ruby-red dew,
That robbeth cornelians and rubies of hue;

86. Pour quick from that fount of the soul, that doth run
Not with water, God wot, but with liquefied sun.

87. On yon ceiling five-arched [21] of the firmaments nine
One can pitch one's pavilion with one cup of wine;

[21] "The five arches" may be either the Five Senses or the Five "Pillars of the Faith",
    Prayer, Belief in God's Unity, Alms-giving, Pilgrimage and Fasting; but the meaning
    is doubtful.

88. O'er the pillarless roof of the nine-vaulted sky,
If forth of oneself one can fare, one may fly.

89. If thou'rt wise, up, go mad, nor thy face-water spill, [22]
But the door-dust be thou of the winehouse's sill.

[22] i. e., abase not thine own honour by doing aught but toping.

90. Be not in the bonds of this dust-heap [23] entwined,
Lest it suddenly give thee, like dust, to the wind.

[23] "This dust-heap", i. e. the world.

91. Come, cupbearer, give me that Khúsrewi [24] bowl,
That addeth new gladness to heart and to soul.

[24] "Khusrewi", i. e. royal, in allusion to Jem's cup.

92. Our wish of this cup is Infinity's wine
And selflessness thence to attain our design.

93. Youth swiftly as lightning from Yémen hath ceased
And life passeth by, like the wind of the East.

94. This six-gated sojourn I rede thee forsake;
Come, wash thou thy hands of yon nine-headed snake. [25]

[25] "Nine-headed snake", i. e. Heaven.

95. An thou of the wayfarers be, in this Way
Soul and substance for strewage behoveth thee lay.

96. To the Mansion of Permanence [26] gird thee to go;
Up! All, save God only, impermanent know.

[26] "The Mansion of Permanence" is the next world.

97. Give, skinker, that jewel, that life-giving spring;
That balm for the heart of the heart-sore come bring.

98. Since of Time snatched away from Jem's hand the cup is,
What good were a world to him, if it were his?

99. Come, skinker, that frozen-up water [27] come give;
Come, cause this dead heart with the vinejuice relive!

[27] "Frozen-up water", i. e. the crystal cup or glass flask.

100. For each piece of brick on a terrace we tread
Was once an Iskender's or Kéikobad's head.

101. There's nought but kings' blood in yon bason [28] up there;
There's nought in this waste [29] but the dust of the fair.

[28] "Bason", i. e. heaven, poetically likened to an inverted bowl.
[29] "This waste", i. e. the world.

102. Of a frenzied wine-worshipper erst have I heard,
Cup in hand, in the tavern, who uttered this word;

103. "Because of the course of the base-fost'ring skies,
"The gladsomest ever have been the least wise."

104. Give, skinker, that bitter that's eath to digest;
For wine from the Friend's hand is sweetest and best.

105. For Dára, [30] who held all the world in his hand,
Who had not his fellow for sway and command,

[30] "Dara", Darius.

106. By the hand of the Term, Heaven snatched from his place
And it was as if ne'er had he been on earth's face.

107. Come, skinker, from me to the Sultan go bring
This utterance, saying, "O Jem-crested king,

108. "First solace the heart of the wretched and weak
"And the world-showing goblet thereafterward seek!

109. "For the cark of this world, from the which in the end
"No gain is, with wine from oneself one can fend."

110. And this to the grace of the Sultan owe we,
To him, the best fruit of the Khúsrewi tree;

111. The Lord of the Land and the King of the Time,
The Moon of the house of felicity's clime;

112. By whom to the throne might and splendour are lent,
To whom fish and fowl owe repose and content;

113. The light of the eye of the rich and the great
And the helper of others less favoured of Fate;

114. World-holder, Faith-fosterer, Doër of right,
By whom hath Kei's throne become glorious and bright;

115. Nay, what shall I say? How his actions appraise,
Whose annals leave Reason itself in amaze?

116. Since his worth overpasseth whate'er can be said,
In shame and impuissance I hang down my head.

117. My hands in sincereness I lift up in prayer
And to God, the Omnipotent One, I repair,

118. Saying, "Lord, by Thy favours and bounties Divine,
"By Thy names and their mysteries, ninety and nine,

119. "By Thy Word, which existed in Time Unbegun,
"By Thy glorious apostle, that mighty-souled one,

120. "Let the King of the World, by whose grace glorified
"Are kingdom and crown, still victorious abide!

121. "So long as of right and unright earth is full
"And the sky is the pasture of Goat and of Bull, [31]

[31] "Goat and Bull", i. e. Capricorn and Taurus.

122. "The Lord of the World Shah Mensóur be, I pray,
"And far from his heart be the dust of dismay!"

123. O King with Jem's seal-ring, (to God be the praise!)
The champion that art of the Faith and the Days,

124. For victory thou of the world art renowned;
For victor o'er foes hast thou ever been found.

125. Ferídoun art thou in the banqueting place
And valiant as Rustem in battle and chase.

126. The sky hath no pearl that is rare like to thee;
Ferídoun nor Jem hath an heir like to thee;

127. Not only the Franks to thee tribute do bring;
Nay, homage thou hast from the Ethiops' King.

128. Be't Roum, be it Tartary, China or Ind,
All heads 'neath thy signet, like Jem's, are inclined.

129. The least of the blackmoors that serve in thy hall
Is Saturn; the sphere is thy gem-girdled [32] thrall.

[32] The sphere is "gem-girdled" with the Zodiacal belt.

130. Thy tent is a Huma, auspicious of shade,
Whose wings o'er the face of the earth are displayed.

131. Sikender-like, China and Roum to thee bow;
If *he* had the mirror, the *fashion* hast thou. [33]

[33] If he (Alexander the Great) had the world-showing mirror (*ayineh*) thou hast the
    usage (*ayin*) of good governance; note word-play.

132. Long years mayst thou bide undisturbed in his place
And solve with thy wit every difficult case!

133. Since the sea of thy praise hath no shore, I forbear
And sum up thine eulogy henceforth in prayer.

134. From the verse of Nizámi (like whom this old earth
Hath never to one sweet of speech given birth,)

135. These three pregnant couplets I cite, which the wise
For better than pearls without counterpart prize;

136. "Past all that thy fancy to thee can suggest,
"World-conquering be from the East to the West!

137. "Fore'er, by the help of high heav'n, mayst thou be
"Victorious with ever new victory!

138. "Be that wine, which new life to the reason doth bring,
"*My* med'cine and water of life to the King!" [34]

[34] A way of drinking the King's health. "May the draught be medicine for me and the elixir of life for the King!" These three couplets are quoted from the *Sikender-nameh* of Nizami.

III

THE SINGER-RIME

1. Where art thou, singer? With pipe and string
That Khúsrewi song to our memory bring.

2. Come, unto the topers glad tidings of song send
And greeting to comrades departed long send.

3. Come, singer, and tune mirth's instruments;
With chant and carol the tale commence.

4. My foot by grief's burden is nailed to the earth;
Come, beat thou the measure and stir me to mirth.

5. From fret draw ditties and string; let's see
What the doorkeeper saith of the sanctuary. [35]

[35] *Perdeh-dar* (screen-holder, doorkeeper) means also "tune, key, fret-possessor or wielder", i. e. musical instrument: i. e. "See what the ghittern saith of the sanctuary [of Love"].

6. So lift up the voice of minstrelsy
That Venus the harpist shall dance for glee.

7. Singer, accord thou the harp and drum;
With melody call upon friends to come.

8. Sing thou the Soufi to ecstasy;
"Union" [36] with drunkenness let his be.

[36] "Union [with the Beloved]," a cant Soufi term, expressing a certain stage of religious abstraction.

9. To organ, singer, set hand and bear
The thought from my heart of the base world's care.

10. My heart shall find somewhat of ease, may be,
When it from the soil of chagrin is free.

11. Come, then; no more at my wishes carp;
Clap hand to the tabret, if thou've no harp.

12. I've heard that, when wine annoy doth bring,
There's balm in the tabret's clamouring.

13. Where art thou, singer? The rose is blown;
The meadows are full of the bulbul's tone.

14. 'Twere good to the boil that my blood thou bring,
The harp to clamour 'twere good thou bring.

15. Singer, come, tune up the lute anew;
Another fashion of song ensue.

16. My heart, patchcoat-like, with *this* tune rend
And with *that* other my pain amend.

17. What harm to do me a kindly deed
And kindle my heart with the song of the reed,

18. To ease me a moment of evil cheer
And shatter my sorrows' household gear?

19. Where art thou, singer? A song come sing
Of greeting to us the sorrowing!

20. Since quit of us soon the world shall be,
Far better than kingship is beggary.

21. Chant the chant, singer! Take up the lute!
Thou art the help of the destitute.

22. Show me the way to Irác by the rill
And Zíndehroud show from mine eyes I will. [37]

[37] i. e. Strike up the measure called Irac, (though, according to Soudi, Ispahan is here
    meant, because the way to Ispahan from Shiraz is by the side of a stream) and I will
    show thee from my eyes a river of tears, like the Zindehroud, the river of Ispahan.

23. Singer, come hearken to what I say;
This saw, of sages approved, obey;

24. "When th' armies of sorrow against thee come,
"With pipe and harp meet them and lute and drum."

25. My confidant, singer, of secrets, art thou:
With pipe awhile sympathy for us avow.

26. If grief take thy heart, with wine do it to death;
Blow a breath in a pipe; for the world is a breath.

27. Come, singer, set hand to that ghittern of thine;
And cupbearer, brim up the beaker with wine;

28. So a moment together at ease we may sit
And merriment practise and glee and unwit.

29. A verse of mine own, to the sound of the string
And the clang of the harp, prithee, singer, come sing:

30. Myself unto dancing that I may betake,
In transport become and the patchcoat forsake.

31. By drunkenness mystery's pearls can one bore;
To selflessness secrets are hidden no more.

32. I'm woeful, o singer: a two-stringed, nay,
A triple-stringed lute, by God's Oneness, come play!

33. This new mode of song, singer, practise and eke
With the voice of the viol the comrades bespeak.

34. Cause the souls of the great of old time to rejoice;
Perwíz and Barbúd [38] call to mind with thy voice.

[38] "*Barbud*", a famous musician and court-minstrel to Khusrau Perwiz, who is said to
    have invented the lyre, (Greek *barbitos*,) which bears his name.

35. Since Fortune still troubles for us doth intend,
Mine wine be and trouble o' th' eye of the Friend!

36. In this blood-overrun Resurrection Plain,
The blood of the flask and the cup do thou drain.

37. I look with amaze on the course of the sphere;
I know not who next will be borne on the bier.

38. The fraud of the world is a patent affair:
The night is with child; watch for what it will bear.

39. Beware lest thy heart on the world be bestowed;
For none on the bridge-head doth make his abode.

40. This ruinous world's the same halt-place which e'en
Efrásiyab's palace aforetime hath seen.

41. This far-spreading waste is the place where the host
Of Selm and of Tour went astray and were lost. [39]

[39] Selm and Tour, two revolted sons of Feridoun, who slew their younger brother Irej
    and were after defeated and slain by the latter's son Menouchihr, grown to man's
    estate. See the Shahnameh.

42. Where's Píran his host-leader's judgment and where
Is Shéideh the Turkman, his sword that did bear? [40]

[40] Piran Wisa was Efrasiyab's Vizier and General in chief. Sheideh the Turcoman was a
    fourth son of Efrasiyab, so called because his mother was a Turcoman woman.

43. Not only his palaces went to the wind;
But none hath his sepulchre even in mind.

44. Fate giveth the pen to the hand of one wight,
To another the sword on the day of the fight.

45. To *this* man pen-wielding of Fate is decreed,
Sword-wielding to *that* in the day of his need.

IV

1. The dog of honour hath more desert
Than he who the heart of a friend doth hurt.

2. Corroboration [41] this saw doth need,
That so in the heart its sense take seed:

[41] i. e. illustration and explanation.

3. Men are commensals with thee, to wit;
The dog on the threshold, shut out, doth sit. [42]

[42] Soudi here quaintly remarks, "If thou give the dog a bone, he eateth: if not, he taketh
    patience; but, in any case, he leaveth not the threshold".

4. Alack that the dog is true till death,
Whilst men think nothing of breach of faith! [43]

[43] Variant, "Alack that the dog should still keep troth, whilst men think nothing of
    breach of oath!" This quaint little piece is remarkable as a rare example of that
    kindly feeling towards the (so-called) brute creation, the absence of which in
    Oriental literature is so depressing to those whose "partiality for animals" (like that
    of the immortal Mr. Fudge and of the writer of these notes,) "borders upon insanity",
    one of the rare exceptions being that of the Companion (of the Prophet)

Abdurrehman ibn Sekhr, nicknamed Abou Hureireh, "Him of the Kitten", because of his habit of carrying a pet kitten in his bosom. Peace to his gentle memory!

V

1. Wind of the East, my bosom ill at ease is;
My soul is scented with thy fragrant breezes.

2. By the rose-meadow's marge at dawn make passage;
Bear to the rose and cypress this our message;

3. Say, "To her face, of beauty boast, o rose, not;
"Gold-broid'ry for the rush-mat weaver knows not.

4. "Boast thee not, cypress, in her presence, tallest;
"For passing short, before her shape, thou fallest."

5. Come, skinker, wine! for 'tis the vernal season,
Despite the folk of abstinence and reason.

6. Come, Redbud wine, with maids that need no prinking,
What while thou mayst, I rede thee still be drinking.

9. Hark not the counsel of the moral teachers:
What boots their rede and what the prate of preachers?

8. Still sing the bulbuls in the garden-closes,
"Set not the cup from hand in time of roses."

9. Reckon as gain the rose's brief enjoyment;
Be winebibbing in Spring thy sole employment.

10. Heedless be not; for the occasion passeth;
Each breath the time of jubilation passeth.

11. This rede of Hafiz on thy mind imprest be;
The winecup ply and in God's hand the rest be!

VI

1. Whoso cometh to this world's turmoilful room,
Needs, in fine, must he betake him to the tomb.

2. As a bridge this world is on the next world's road,
A waste stage and an unpermanent abode.

3. Set thy heart not on this bridge so full of fear;
But provide thee for the road and stay not here.

4. For this three days' house, so say the men of wit,
Is a ruin, with no treasure hid in it.

5. Sure, the pearl of truth the wise have pierced, who say
Of this world, "It is a caravanserai.

6. "Here beseemeth not residing: pass ye on!
"Nay, this world with none's abiding: pass ye on!"

7. Far from love of wealth and rank I rede thee sit;
Wealth a snake to thee will prove and rank a pit.

8. Nay, supposing thou be Behram Gour the Great:
On the grave-snare wilt thou stumble soon or late.

9. An thou be not blind, the grave consider now:
Nor a moment without work in hand sit thou.

10. For escape is not for any from this stage,
Nor for beggar neither monarch, youth nor age.

11. Thou, thy skirt that trailest proudly o'er our clay,
Hafiz asketh thee a "Fátiheh" [44] to say.

[44] The first chapter of the Koran.

EPODES [1]

[1] "Epodes". This title is here used in the old English sense of "a solemn poem", as fairly
expressing the meaning of the Arabic form, the *Kesideh* (*Ckeszideh*) or Purpose-
poem, i. e. a poem written for a definite purpose, generally (in Persian) panegyrical
and intended to induce the bestowal of largesse on the writer. It differs from the Ode
or Ghazel only in length, the latter being theoretically limited to thirteen couplets,
although it often exceeds that number, whilst the Kesideh is unlimited as to length. It
will be noted that many poems are included among Hafiz's Odes which should
properly be classed with the Kesidehs.

I

1. The light of the conquering Sultan's Fair fortune once again
Hath given the face of the world-all New youth, like Irem's plain. [2]

[2] See former note as to the mythical Garden of Irem.

2. Lord of sunrise and setting He is, in East and West,
He of the fair conjunction, [3] Sovran and suzerain;

498

[3] i. e. happy fortune.

3. Doër of right and justice, Fost'rer of folk and land,
Justice-dispensing ruler And Kei-like sovereign.

4. Chief of the high throne-sitters Of "Be and 'twas" [4] is he:
Kingmaker universal Of all the world's domain.

[4] i. e. Creation.

5. Faith and the world's chief glory, He whose exalted might
Fortune its courser holdeth Ever beneath its rein;

6. Time and the Age's Ruler, Sun of the realm, Shejáa,
Fortune-blest Khan and youthful King of all kings mundane;

7. Moon, by whose radiant aspect Enlightened is the earth;
King, by whose grace and auspice Exalted is the reign;

8. There, where his spirit's falcon Maketh its nesting place,
The bird of thought to follow Aspireth but in vain.

9. Current is his commandment, Wind-like, o'er land and sea;
Soul-like, his love the bodies Of men and Jinn contain.

10. Thy [5] form's the realm of beauty And beauty of the realm,
Thine aspect the world's soul is And the soul's world again.

[5] Note sudden change of person in Couplet 10.

11. Thy throne's the despair of the sieges Of Jem and Kéikobád;
Thy crown of the crowns of Dára [6] And Erdewán's [7] the bane.

[6] "Dára", Darius.
[7] "Erdewan", Artabanus.

12. If in the thought of the heavens The gleam of thy sword should fall,
The Gemini's limbs would sever Asunder and fall in twain.

13. Thou art the sun of the kingdom And whithersoe'er thou go'st,
Felicity, like thy shadow, Followeth fast in thy train.

14. The elements never a jewel Like thee perfected have;
No star, in a hundred ages, Like thee doth Heav'n ordain.

15. The marrow, without thy favour, Would not in the bone take shape;
The spirit, without thine aspect, Were not to the body fain.

16. Of every fashion of knowledge, That is in books unwrit,
Thy pen on its fluent tongue-tip The answer doth retain.

17. Who with thy hand shall even The cloud, since, drop by drop,
Doth *this*, and *that*, by purses, [8] Doth its largesses rain?

[8] A "purse" is 10,000 dirhems, about £ 250.

18. Compared with thy throne of glory, Heav'n as a foot-mat is:
The tale of thy hand's full ocean Of boon's the world's refrain.

19. The sun of the sphere of knowledge, The crown of reason's head,
The light of the eye of learning, The kingdom's soul and brain,

20. Learning and wit in honour And splendour are by thee;
The Faith and the Law in worship And safe thou dost maintain.

21.O monarch high-exalted, Sublime of majesty,
O ruler without equal, August of rank and reign,

22. Sun of the state, in presence Of whose magnificence
Shaígan's fabled treasures [9] Are as an atom vain,

[9] "Shaígan's treasure", the name of a legendary treasure (some say, belonging to
   Khusrau Perwiz) said to have been found in a place called Shaïgan (trisyllable).

23. A thousand such accounted Were of thy bounty's sea
But as the drop, for nothing Which thou to give dost deign.

24. Veiled chastity abideth In thy seraglios;
Fortune with thee its dwelling For ever hath up-ta'en.

25. To furnish thy pavilion, Sun-centre-bossed, the skies
Mountain and cloud for cushion And canopy ordain;

26. And yonder nine-fold satin Of azure, gold-y-wrought, [10]
For awning o'er Thy daïs Of state, do they sustain.

[10] i. e. the star-fretted sky.

27. None, since the Keis, [11] in the kingdom Of Solomon, [12] such store.
Of treasure and arms and armies Hath ever wrought to gain.

[11] "The Keis", i. e. the monarchs of the second or Keyanian dynasty of Persia.
[12] i. e. Fars; constantly so styled by Hafiz.

28. Whilst thou in the rosegarth bidest, Because of thy men of war,
There's clamour in Ethiopia And folk in Hind complain.

500

29. Thy tents in Roum thou pightest; The clamour of thy drums
To Sistan's [13] desert reacheth And Hindostan's champaign.

[13] *Sistan*, the ancient Drangiana.

30. Since that the Yellow Palace [14] Thou buildedst, fearfulness
The Khan's [15] and Kaiser's [16] mansions Of pleasance hath o'erta'en.

[14] "The Yellow Palace" a palace so-called, erected by Shah Shejaa in his gardens at
      Shiraz.
[15] "Khan" of Tartary.
[16] "Kaiser", i. e. the Emperor of Constantinople.

31. From Roum to Egypt, China To Kéirewan, [17] with thee
Who is there can be evened For lordship and domain?

[17] "*Keirewan*", the well-known holy city of Tunis.

32. Next year they to thy doorway The Kaiser's crown shall bring;
Tribute the Khan of China Shall send thee yet again.

33. Thou the Creator thankest And thee His creatures thank;
In fortune thou, and peoples In thee, to joy are fain.

34. Behold, in garth and rosemead Thou farest with thy slaves,
And 'neath thy thigh the courser Of Fortune dost constrain!

35. O thou, the heav'n-inspired one, On whose pure soul new grace
From Heaven's hosts cherubic Doth every moment rain,

36. Thou to whose heart is patent Whate'er th' Omnipotent
Behind the Unseen's curtain Fast hidden doth retain,

37. Unto thy hand the heavens, "What am I?" saying, "Nay,
"E'en as thou wiliest, drive me!" Have giv'n the wish's rein;

38. "If war and strife betide thee, I've furnished thee with arms;
"And if largesse behove thee, I've giv'n thee gold amain.

39. "Where be thy foes? Come, trample And tread them underfoot.
"Where be thy friends? Thy dear ones As mine I'll entertain." [18]

[18] The speech of the heavens is continued in Couplets 38 and 39.

40. My wishes by thy service Ordained and fashioned all
Are, as my name eternal Shall by thy praise remain. [19]

[19] The poet speaks in his own person.

II

1. Of charmerhood to boast thee A light affair is not;
A thousand traits thereunto Behove, I'd have thee wot.

2. Matters of beauty other There be, beside sweet speech;
And Solomon-hood by a seal-ring Alone is not begot.

3. A thousand heart-charming queendoms This one thing even not,
That thou one heart by merit Shouldst conquer to thy lot.

4. What troubles, 'las! thou rearest On my existence! May
Thy steed, so fast thou spurrest, [20] Ne'er weary any what!

[20] "To drive or fare fast" is a trope expressive of arrogance, self-will and conceit.

5. Scorn not to sit with topers; For treasures without price
Are in this destitution Of winebibber and sot.

6. Red wine bring, so an hundred Rare matters I may say
And yet in Musulmanship May make nor breach nor blot.

7. By the dust of the dawn-drinkers' footsteps I swear that, since at the door
On watch, in the street of the winehouse, I've stood with cup and pot,

8. There passed by me never a zealot, An outward worshipper,
But, under his patchcoat hidden, He bore the girdle-knot. [21]

[21] "Girdle-knot", the emblem of infidelity, non-Musulmanhood.

9. In the name of thy heart-binding browlock, Some little favour show,
So God o'er thee watch, that wildered, Like it, thou fallest not.

10. I rede thee, the eye of favour Turn not from Hafiz' case;
Or else to the second Asef The thing I'll tell, God wot;

11. The Vizier, sov'reign-seating, Scribe of the world and age,
By whose glad auspice joyful Is man's and genie's lot;

12. Pillar of Faith and Kingdom, Mohammed, Ali's son,
Thou, from whose face the sun-rays Are of God's glory shot;

13. Gifted art thou of Nature! Well mayst thou claim the world,
By thy just thought and judgment, To govern every what!

14. The order of honour of Fortune Enduring meet for thee
Is, whose high thoughts no mention To this frail world allot.

15. Except for the help of the treasures Of thy munificence,
The world and all that is in it Would fall to waste and rot.

16. Nothing of earthly matter Is in thy body's frame;
Thou'rt of the angels' essence, In human fashion wrought.

17. What measure of magnification Established of man may be,
Whereover in fancy's travel Exalted thou art not?

18. In the holiest place of the holies Of Cherubs of Paradise,
The scratch of thy pen is music, As of the spheres begot.

19. Beseemeth lordship's sweetness To thee, whose bounties cause
The generous ones of story Of all men be forgot.

20. How shall thy past good actions Be numbered? Blest be God
For this, like Him, who joyeth In loosing trouble's knot!

21. How shall I tell the lightnings And thunders of thy wrath?
From these o'erwhelming terrors With God be shelter sought!

22. Now that the bride of the rose in The bridechamber is of the sward,
Excepting the Eastland breezes, A mate for the soul there's not.

23. By means of the East wind's waftings, The blood-red anemones
Their tents, for the rose-queen's session, Have pitched on the green grass-plot.

24. By dint of the wafts of the zephyr, The Spring to this pass is come,
For sweetness, of breath life-giving It boasteth itself, God wot.

25. How sweetly it came to my spirit His voice that a bulbul raised
And said to the rosebud softly At dawn, ere the day grew hot,

26. "Why sittest thou thus strait-hearted? Come forth of the screen; for wine
"Like rubies pomegranate-coloured There is in the drinking pot.

27. "To drink to the rose's beauty Spare not in the blossom-month,
"Next month of the cup of repentance To drink ere it fall to thy lot.

28. "Of roses and wine thy portion Of easance take, in thanks
"That gone is the stain of censure And infidelity's blot." [22]

[22] i. e. the laws against toping have been repealed and wine-bibbing is no longer a sin.

29. Nay, heaven forbid that oppression Faith-fosterers' [23] usance be!
For mercy and grace and blessing God's Law is, every jot.

[23] "Faith-fosterers", i.e. Kings (Defenders of the Faith) and their representatives, such
as the Vizier.

30. What knoweth, indeed, of the myst'ries Of Truth that heedless one
Who drawn of Divine attraction To God become is not?

31. Lo, in the screen of the sepals, See how the rose-in-bud
An arrow of ruby [24] forgeth, At th'eye of thy foe to be shot!

[24] Rosebud likened to arrowhead of ruby.

32. This is the Vizier's pleasaunce; Let none of heavy cheer
Be (save the winecup) [25] skinker, In this auspicious spot!

[25] "Heavy", *syn.* "full", relatively to winecup. This word-play has been before
explained.

33. Thou was it, o breath of hope's morning That earnest, for Love's sake, forth
And unto the nights of estrangement And gloom an ending brought. [26]

[26] Soudi remarks that this couplet refers to the Vizier's return to Shiraz, after an
absence in the provinces.

34. Lo, whiles and again, I've heard it, Thou callest me to mind;
And yet to thy privy session Ne'er hast thou me besought.

35. Ne'er of me speech thou seekest And this sheer cruelty
Must be; [27] for what contending With thee in speech is, what?

[27] i. e. it cannot be jealousy, for, etc.

36. Of all the world's scribes there's no one, Like to thy slave, conceits
Koranic and philosophic That can together knot.

37. A thousand years' endurance My praise to thee will give:
Such precious ware beseemeth To none but thee alone.

38. Long this my speech protracted Have I; but 'tis my hope
That with the skirt of pardon Th' offence thou wilt out-blot.

39. Whilst on the page of the garden, In the sweet-basil hand, [28]
In Spring, a thousand limnings Are of the East wind wrought, [29]

[28] "Sweet-basil hand", an ornamental hand, before explained and here mentioned p. g.
[29] i. e. "So long as Spring returns to the meads, year by year".

40. Still in the garth of the kingdom, For thee, from the bough of hope,
Still may the roses blossom Of life and happy lot!

CINQUAINS

1. O idol, for thy love I suffer so
That of my proper life in doubt I go.
Though impotent I am and worn with woe,
Should Fate on me a thousand lives bestow,
All at thy blessed feet, my fair, I'd strow.

2. When shall it be permitted unto me,
Before a solacer of hearts like thee,
Humbly t' expound a hidden mystery? [30]
Away! A falcon of thy high degree
May not to my poor nest such honour show.

[30] i. e. the mystery of his love and suffering, which he has, as becomes a true lover,
kept secret from the world.

3. Though to thy nature cruelty pertain,
Do thou not ill; for nought by ill's to gain.
If thy heart be not bronze or iron, deign
Over my head, o Friend, to pass again;
Regard me as the dust thy feet below.

4. "When with affliction thou hast struck me dead,
"Thou wilt belike the path of mercy tread
"And on thy heart Faith's writ wilt grave," I said.
But thou no thought of union hadst in head:
Too well my froward fortune do I know.

5. Thou, that hast girded thee the blood to spill
Of Turks and Persians, who have done no ill,
If my abode be mean and dark and chill,
Thee in thy truest servant's domicile,
My radiant eye, to wit, will I bestow.

6. Nought do I seek of thee, but to be true;
For nothing but the rose of faith I sue;
None but thy path of service I ensue.
Thy secrets have I kept from all men's view,
Thy praises chanting nor to friend nor foe.

7. Grant that we never opened troth-plight's door,
That love on love we heaped not heretofore,
That there befell not all we did of yore,
In fine, that friendship thou and I ne'er swore,
Thy bond is broke, but I'm the same e'ermo.

8. Though with the sword thou shear the head from me,
I will not swerve from my fidelity;
Nay, though They [31] rend me limbmeal, of my gree,
I will not break the seal of love for thee,
Save when my bones are scattered high and low.

[31] "They", app. the Fates.

9. Let those, who seek the goal of love, no way,
Save that which leadeth by my tomb, essay;
And when they scent my miserable clay,
If o'er my sepulchre thy name they say,
My soul shall make them answer with "Heigho!"

10. Though troops of fair ones should my faith assail,
Each one in beauty brighter than Suhéil, [32]
None should my love to move from thee prevail;
Mad were I if, in price of Leila's sale,
Persia I took and Araby e'enso.

[32] "Suheil", i. e. Canopus.

11. Of longing for thy sight I'm grown, o fair,
Dark-hearted and disordered like thy hair.
Though I reach not thy street, no night is there
When, for estrangement from thee and despair,
The skies I storm not with my wail of woe.

12. Thou, from whose union welleth gladness' tide,
In everlasting joy mayst thou abide!
At thine own Hafiz wherefore dost thou chide?
Yet, so thou do not drive me from thy side,
I reck not if thou rail at me or no.

THE END

NOTES

I

In making the foregoing translation, I have taken as my standard the text upon which Soudi based his great Turkish commentary, written in the seventeenth century, and which was the result of the collation by him of some dozen selected manuscript copies in his own possession. The Bosnian commentator, living at a time, little more than two centuries after Hafiz's death, when the memory of the great Persian poet was still fresh and the records of his work may be supposed to have been yet comparatively un-garbled, must undoubtedly have enjoyed exceptional facilities for the establishment of an authoritative text of his original and I have therefore confined myself to the reproduction (with certain variants and additions of lines and couplets gleaned from the Boulac and Calcutta Editions) of the 693 poems of various lengths admitted by him into his edition. Of these he positively declares one only (Ode XIV, which I have accordingly omitted) to be undoubtedly spurious; although he, from time to time, expresses doubts, which I have, when, as is not always the case, they seemed to me well founded, cited in my notes, as to the authenticity of sundry other poems and passages. Soudi's text I have minutely collated with that (variorum) of Brockhaus (founded, inter alia, upon the important Calcutta Edition of 1827, from which I have adopted a certain number of variants and additions,) as also with the Boulac Edition of 1840; and I have (except when I saw good cause to do otherwise) followed the vocalization of Brockhaus, a most excellent and painstaking editor, whose failure to complete his great task is much to be regretted. The half-hundred or so additional pieces, which might be culled from the Indian Bazaar Editions, I have omitted, as they must have been already rejected by Soudi and other good judges at a time far more favourable than the present for pronouncing upon their genuineness; and it is, indeed, pretty generally recognized that they are comparatively modern additions, most of them bearing unmistakable signs of spuriousness. One exception I have made in the case of Ode 478a, which, although almost certainly not by Hafiz, is pretty in itself and is notable as the text of the beautiful Indian air, *Taza-be-Taza*. My readings of the many doubtful passages in the poems and the notes appended to my translation are, to a great extent, founded upon Soudi's Commentary, [1] the only one which does not hesitate to grapple frankly and fairly with the innumerable difficulties and obscurities of the text, all other commentators insisting on interpreting Hafiz symbolically, which of course begs the question and is worse than no explanation at all; although I have not scrupled to take my own course, independently of the Turkish commentator, in the various cases when (and they are of frequent occurrence) he altogether omits to deal with the real crux of the passage or when I saw good reason to believe that he was mistaken in the view taken by him. [1] The reader must be reminded that the text of Hafiz is necessarily more or less corrupt and that, at this time of day, it is practically impossible to remedy the defects of the existing editions or to establish anything like an authoritative standard text of the poems.

[1] It may here be mentioned that I have had occasion, as a well-nigh indispensable preliminary to the execution of the present work, to prepare, for my own use, a voluminous digest, in three volumes, of Soudi's Commentary, which I may possibly some day publish for the benefit of Orientalists.

II

The Divan (or Collection of Poems) of Hafiz consists of (1) six hundred and fifteen *Ghazels* or parts of Ghazels or Odes, forming the Divan proper, (2) sixty-nine Quatrains, (3) Six *Methnewiyat* or poems in rhyming couplets, (4) two *Kesidehs* or Epodes and (5) one *Mukhemmes* or poem in cinquains, altogether, in round figures, some twelve thousand lines of various lengths, equivalent to about twenty thousand English decasyllable lines. The *Ghazel*, a form of verse peculiar to Persian prosody, is a variant of the Arab *Kesideh* or Purpose-poem, from which it differs only in length and conduct. It consists of a series of couplets, the two lines of the first of which rhyme with each other and with the second line of each succeeding couplet, and the name of the poet should be introduced in the last or crown-couplet. The Kesideh-form is commonly employed by Persian poets for eulogistic purposes only; its various couplets should have some sort of connection with each other and should refer to or advance the same idea or purpose, the latter being explicitly stated in the concluding couplet. It should not contain less than a dozen couplets and is otherwise practically unlimited as to length; whilst the Ghazel is confined within a range of from five to fifteen couplets, [2] but is unfettered by any rules as to conduct and may vary in expression and purpose) with every couplet, according to the writer's fancy; on which account it has been aptly likened to a bee flitting hither and thither over a blossomed meadow and sucking honey at will from this and the other flower. This peculiarity gives the Ghazel a somewhat incoherent and discursive character in the eyes of the European reader, but is considered by the Persians rather a beauty than a defect. The three other forms need no explanation. Two special features of Hafiz's verse may here be noticed: the first, which is peculiar to Persian poetry, is the prevalence of what may be styled the "throw-back" rhyme, which consists in what is technically called a *redif* or "rereword", i.e. an invariable ending of from one to seven or even more syllables, not, in general, of the nature of a burden or independent refrain, but forming an inseparable part of the rhyming line and immediately succeeding the rhyme-word or syllable, which it thus *throws back* towards, and in some cases beyond, the middle of the line. The other is the excessive use of the figure *enallage* or interchange of case etc., Hafiz constantly speaking of himself at once, in the same couplet or even line, as "I" and "We" (and not seldom in the third person also) and treating persons invoked and mentioned by him in the same loose fashion. It will be seen that I have, in the present work, followed the same system of rhythm and rhyme reproduction as in my version of the Quatrains of Kheyyam, although, from the nature of the task, the difficulties to be overcome in the isometrical rendering of Hafiz have been far greater than those which had to be dealt with in the case of the earlier poet, inexpressible and inappreciable as were the latter, except to the Oriental scholar and the connoisseur of metrical form. According to the strict rules of Persian prosody, in the case of the Ghazel and the Kesideh forms, the same rhyme-word should not recur until after an interval of at least four (and according to some authorities, of five, six or even seven) rhyming lines; but this is a rule which Persian poets and Hafiz, in especial, constantly transgress; and accordingly, whilst allowing myself, on the whole, (notwithstanding the much greater difficulty of rhyming in English,) far less license than my original in the matter of rhyme, I have not thought it necessary to be *plus royaliste que le roi* in this particular; nor have I concerned myself to note every occasion on which an irregular repetition of the rhyme-word occurs in the Persian text, although I have done so in many instances. [3]

[2] It will be remarked that several of the pieces (e. g. Odes CCLXXIX, CCCLXXX, CCCCXXXVIII etc.), included by Soudi (from whose classification I have not thought it necessary to depart) among the Ghazels, are in reality Kesidehs and should strictly be classed with the other examples of that form.

[3] As an example of quantillâ scientiâ homines doceantur by the overwhelmingly numerous class of *savants qui ne savent pas*, it may be noted that Professor Forbes, in his Persian Grammar (1873), gravely informs his readers that "in Persian poetry, the *same word* in the *same sense*" (the italics are his) "may form the rhyme of each hemistich of a couplet; and not unfrequently does the same word, or succession of words, form the rhyme throughout a whole *Ghazal* or Ode"; the learned gentleman having evidently mistaken the *redif*, of which he does not appear to understand the nature, for the rhyme-word!

III

Three professedly complete translations exist of the Divan, two, those of Hammer-Purgstall (1813) and Rosenzweig-Schwannau (1858-64), both in German verse, and one, by Col. H. W. Clarke, (1891) in English prose. Of these the second alone is of practical value to the student of Hafiz; but it is, unfortunately, although, on the whole, the best of its kind and a vast improvement on its predecessor, extremely defective and incomplete. Had the translator (Herr von Rosenzweig) really studied, instead of skimming, the great Commentary of Soudi, on which he professed to base his version, he might have avoided many, if not most, of the errors which disfigure his work. A prose translation was promised by Hermann Brockhaus, the editor of the only really complete and scholarly edition yet published of the Persian text (1863); but this, to the great regret of all students of Hafiz, has never made its appearance. Of the many fragmentary versions which have appeared in England, the only one which seems to me to require special mention is the little book entitled "A Century of Ghazels from the Diwan of Hafiz", published in 1875 and understood to be by the late Mr. Samuel Robinson, a Manchester merchant, who, though manifestly deficient in Persian scholarship and depending, as he admits, mainly upon Rosenzweig, a not very trustworthy guide, has, by sheer force of intuition and sympathy, contrived to inform his prose rendering or paraphrase of a hundred of the Odes with more of the savour and spirit of the original than is to be found in any other translation with which I am acquainted.

IV

A word of explanation is necessary as to the course I have followed in dealing with the Oriental proper names which abound in the Divan. Most of these, when dissyllables, (such as Yehya, Hatim, Khusrau, Kaabeh, Mekkeh (or, as we call it, Mecca,) Hafiz, Rustem, Dara, Jemshid, Behram, Shiraz, Ahmed, Mensour, Sheddad, Leila, Mejnoun, Ferhad, Shirin, Mehmoud, Asef, Khwajeh, Sultan, Simurgh, Anca, Mufti, Rukna, Baghdad, Khacan, Perwiz, etc. etc.) are, according to the rules of Persian prosody, spondees, although liable to become, by accident of position, trochees, as which they are commonly pronounced by Europeans. Accordingly, as spondees have practically no place in English verse, I have, as a general rule, treated Persian dissyllabic names as trochaic, indicating, by the use of accents, when they are to be otherwise pronounced. For familiar names of more than two syllables I have adopted the common European pronunciation, subject to occasional alteration by accentuation; which latter expedient I have used to indicate the form of unfamiliar names such as Efrasiyab, Tehemten, Tuctemoun, Siyamesh, etc. As to certain English words of continual recurrence, I have (in accordance with general custom) treated "Beloved," when used as a noun, as trisyllabic and when used as an adjective, as dissyllabic. [4] The word "blessed" is also to be read as a dissyllable, unless where otherwise indicated; and the word "seeth" as a monosyllable, except when divided by diæresis. Other particularities will, I think, speak for themselves.

[4] In Vol. I, p. 44, line 7, and p. 160, line 7, this word is in error printed "beloved", instead of "beloved" (trisyllable).

ADDITIONAL NOTE TO ODE II, 9 and 10 (Vol. I, p. 3.)

Soudi's statement, reproduced in my note to this passage, that the city of Yezd is only three days' journey distant from Shiraz, appears to require some explanation; and I therefore here give the Bosnian commentator's actual words upon the point, with my own comments.

"The city of Yezd is, *they say*, distant three days' journey from Shiraz "and the stream Ruknabad, which has its source at the latter place, runs to "Yezd, willows being planted on both sides thereof, so that the wayfarer "[between the two places] suffers no inconvenience from the sun."—*Soudi.* "The responsibility", adds the Turkish commentator, as if dubious of the correctness of this statement, "be upon the narrator!" There can be little doubt that Soudi was, on this point, misled by his informant, who seems to have been thinking of another and nearer Yezd, perhaps one of the villages of the same name in the adjoining provinces of Khuzistan and Laristan, both mere hamlets, with no pretention to civic rank; as a rivulet, like the Ruknabad, which is described by modern travellers as being now a mere runnel of limpid water, not more than three feet wide, can never have run two hundred and fifty miles to Yezd in Khorasan or even (one would think) to either of the two nearer ones, and three days seem an impossibly short space of time for the accomplishment of the journey to the further place; although the statement of Soudi's authority is, in this particular, to a certain extent corroborated by a passage in the Zubd-et-Tewarikh (Cream of Chronicles) of Mohammed Kemal ibn Ismail, a seventeenth century history or book of annals written by a courtier of Shah Abbas II, which represents Shah Abbas the Great as having ridden from Yezd to Shiraz (a distance there stated at 89 parasangs or 303 miles) in little more than twenty-eight and a half hours, or at the rate (including stoppages) of over 10½ miles an hour; so that, assuming the correctness of the modern and more moderate estimate of the distance and taking into consideration the peculiar qualities of the Oriental horse, which enable him to accomplish feats of endurance incredible in the case of European animals, it would appear possible, with an allowance of twelve out of the twenty-four hours for rest, to achieve the journey in three days, or at the rate of rather more than 6¾ miles an hour. In this connection, it may be noted that the Persians consider eight parasangs (about 30 miles) a fair day's journey for a *loaded* camel, the common camel (which must not be confounded with the dromedary, a superior variety, specially bred for speed,) being a sluggish and ill-conditioned brute, whose rate of travel is considerably less than half that of an ordinary horse.

NOTE ON SOUFI TERMINOLOGY

The following are some of the symbolical equivalents prescribed by Soufi usance for the interpretation of the various expressions of most frequent occurrence in the works of Hafiz and other Persian poets claimed by the sect as affiliates and fellow-mystics. Thus, according to the Soufis, by the *Way*, so often mentioned in the Divan, is meant the progress of the pietist towards spiritual perfection and identification (*Union*) with the Deity; the Wayfarer is the devotee himself; the *Stations* or stages of the Way are the various degrees of his religious progress; the *Elder of the Magians* or wine-seller is the wayfarer's spiritual head or chief of the sect; the *Minstrel* and the *Cupbearer* are his *Murshids* or religious instructors; the *Winehouse* is the oratory or dervish cell; the *mole* on the Beloved's cheek is the point of indivisible Unity, her *tress* the mystery of the Godhead, her *down* the world of spirits about God's throne, her *waist* or middle the state of the wayfarer, when nothing remains to veil from his sight the Divine glories, her *lip* the unheard, but understood words of God, her *embraces* the rapture of devotion, her *beauty* the perfections of God and her *ringlets* the details of His mysteries; *union* with the Beloved is the ecstasy of oneness with the Deity; *sleep* is meditation, *gales* are illapses of grace and *wafts of perfume* hope (a pun, the Persian word *boui* having both meanings,) of the Divine favour; *debauchees*, *amorists* and *idolaters* axe devotees who have renounced the world and *mirth*, *drunkenness* and *wantonness* religious ardour and abstraction from all terrestrial thoughts.

SULTAN AND KHALIF

The word "Sultan," among Mohammedan peoples, is properly applied to a *temporal* ruler only, who has no pretentions to spiritual authority; whilst the title "Khalif" (*Khelif* or *Khelifeh-ur-Resoul-Illah*, Successor or Vicar of the Apostle of God and hence, by implication, Vicegerent of God Himself) is reserved for the actual head of the Faith, the supreme spiritual and temporal Chief of the Faithful, who must be a descendant of Mohammed himself or of some member of his family and tribe. Hence, Hulagou did not, after overthrowing the Khalifate of Baghdad, claim to succeed to the title of Khalif, which was, in fact, assumed by Ahmed el Mustensir, a son of Ez Zahir, the antepenultimate, and nephew of El Mustasim, the last Khalif of the Abbaside dynasty. Mustensir took refuge in Egypt and was there recognized by the Memlouk Sultan Bibers, who caused him to be proclaimed, in the mosques of Cairo, as spiritual head of Islam, reserving to himself the temporal power. The new Khalif survived only a year; but his successors continued to exercise a semblance of authority at Cairo, as nominal Khalifs or Popes, (much as the present head of the Catholic church at the Vatican,) under the protection of the Memlouk Sultans, until the capture, in 1517, of Cairo and the extinction of the Memlouk power by the Turkish conqueror, Selim the First, who carried El Mutawekkil, the last mock Khalif of Egypt, to Constantinople, where the latter after Selim's death in 1520, resigned his rights as Khalif, for a consideration, into the hands of Selim's son and successor, Suleiman the Magnificent, and being thereupon suffered to retire to Egypt, there died in 1538. Hence the claim of the Ottoman Sultans to the exercise of the Khalifate or spiritual headship of Islam, a claim which has never, I believe, been recognized by the canonical authorities or by Musulmans in general, out of Turkey.